Piet Mondrian (1872-1944)

Art has to be forgotten: Beauty must be realized.

Piet Mondrian, 1938

MONDRIAN

from figuration to abstraction

Thames and Hudson

25 July—31 August, 1987
The Seibu Museum of Art, Tokyo

Organized by
The Tokyo Shimbun
The Seibu Museum of Art, Tokyo
The Haags Gemeentemuseum

5 September—4 October, 1987
The Miyagi Museum of Art

Organized by
The Miyagi Museum of Art
The Kahokushimpo
Tohoku Broadcasting Co.
The Haags Gemeentemuseum

10 October—8 November, 1987
The Museum of Modern Art, Shiga

Organized by
The Museum of Modern Art, Shiga
The Chunichi Shimbun
The Haags Gemeentemuseum

14 November—20 December, 1987
Fukuoka Art Museum

Organized by
Fukuoka Art Museum
The Nishinippon Shimbun
The Haags Gemeentemuseum

With the support of
The Ministry of Foreign Affairs, Japan
The Agency for Cultural Affairs, Japan
Royal Netherlands Embassy in Japan

With the assistance of
KLM Royal Dutch Airlines

20 February—29 May, 1988
Gemeentemuseum, The Hague

Including works from the Sidney Janis Family Collections, New York and acquisitions by The Gemeentemuseum, The Hague, 1980-1988. Separate catalogues published.

Exhibition and catalogue presented with support of
KLM Royal Dutch Airlines and Rabobank Nederland.

The artistic revolution that began in the nineteenth century with the Impressionist and Symbolist movements swelled to an even greater crescendo after the turn of the century with the Fauvist and Cubist movements. Within this atmosphere of dynamically changing ideas of artistic value, bold and determined artists led the way to what would eventually be recognized as one of the great turning points in the history of art—the evolution of abstract art.

Piet Mondrian (1872-1944), born in Amersfoort in the Netherlands, was one of the brilliant pioneers of abstract art who dared to explore previously unknown realms of spatial expression. Of course, his path to "pure abstraction," as we know it today, was not necessary a smooth one. It was only after he digested the results of contemporary art movements and repeated countless trials and explorations that he was able to develop his logical and analytical abstraction of the object. Then, proclaiming his artistic theory as "Neo-Plasticism," he arrived at a style of pure geometric abstraction, which abolished all unnecessary shapes and colors and limited itself to planes of basic colors divided by absolute horizontal and vertical lines. This universal vision, which was based on Mondrian's introspective and deeply penetrating intuition and insight, gave rise to an orderly and balanced beauty, which developed even more dynamically after his move to the United States. Mondrian's art strongly influenced not only painting, but also such fields as architecture, applied art, and design.

The present exhibition features a total of 116 works: oils, watercolors, and drawings selected from the unrivaled Mondrian collection of the Haags Gemeentemuseum in the Netherlands, as well as one of the artist's last works of his New York period from the Sidney Janis Gallery in New York. We feel that this first large-scale showing of the works of Mondrian in Japan succeeds in introducing the full scope of his progression from figurative to abstract art.

We are grateful to the Haags Gemeentemuseum for their tremendous cooperation and valuable advice, as well as the Sidney Janis Gallery, the Solomon R. Guggenheim Museum, New York and Galerie Tokoro, Tokyo for their generosity and great kindness. We would also like to thank all those who have given their valuable support in making this exhibition possible.

The Tokyo Shimbun

general composition:
herbert henkels

assistants:
Frieda Bleyenberg, Petra Heggers, Michel Meenk.
A. Gewald served as communication nerve-centre throughout the preparation of exhibition and catalogue.

Renée Hanegraaf

translations:
Ruth Koenig

photography:
Haags Gemeentemuseum (Th. Strengers, coordinator P. Couvée); Museum of Modern Art (New York): R. Kollaard, J. Zweerts (Den Haag), T. Haartsen (Ouderkerk a/d Amstel), F.H. ter Weeme (Winterswijk), Lieverdink (Winterswijk), Rijksdienst Beeldende Kunst (The Hague), H. Meister (Paris), herbert henkels.

design:
Kiyoshi Asai

production:
Imex Inc.
15-20 Ichibancho, Chiyoda-ku, 102 Tokyo, Japan

publication:
The Tokyo Shimbun ©1987
2-1-4 Uchisaiwaicho, Chiyoda-ku, 100 Tokyo, Japan

This exhibition was composed and realized by The Tokyo Shimbun with the cooperation of The Haags Gemeentemuseum.

Catalogue distribution for Gemeentemuseum:
Erik Wierda Art Books

Published in Great Britain in 1988 by
Thames and Hudson Ltd., London

Printed in Japan

Contents

Foreword

It has frequently been pointed out both at home and abroad that Holland has brought forth three painters whose powerful personalities raised them above the already reputable level of Dutch art: Rembrandt van Rijn, Vincent van Gogh and P.C. Mondrian. There is no doubt that Mondrian is one of this century's greatest figures in the history of western art, although he himself would not have been at all pleased at such a qualification. 'I think the great masters of the past are very beautiful and very great, but you will agree with me that everything—in our times—ought to be depicted in a very different way.' The past meant less than the future to him.

But as time passes and 1944, the year of Mondrian's death in New York, recedes, the fame of his work increases. In his lifetime only a few understood him; only a small group of fellow-artists and collectors laid the basis for his later reputation. Shortly after his death only twelve of his works were in Dutch museums, two of them purchased, ten of them private donations. Subsequently, though, his star rose rapidly; dozens of purchases and hundreds of donations followed. Currently more than two-thirds of his total œuvre in Dutch museums belongs to the Haags Gemeentemuseum. With its almost 250 paintings and drawings, this is the largest Mondrian collection in the world. More than the power of numbers it is the quality of the collection that counts; it displays the trail which Mondrian first pursued and later blazed through occidental art. Around the turn of the century pictorial Europe was evolving from one style to another. Mondrian put these artistic samples to the test thoroughly and persistently, finally dealing modern art a telling blow. To this day the discussion about the meaning of the western avant-garde focusses on his work, keeping it as vital as ever.

The possession of such an exhaustive, excellent collection imposes a heavy responsibility. Mondrian's rising fame creates a growing demand for loans. However, conservation, scholarly examination and exhibitions for a wide public call for careful decisions as to where and under what conditions Mondrian's work may be displayed. With the odd exception, the collection has thus always remained in The Hague. On rare occasions a Mondrian has been sent to, say, the Guggenheim Museum in New York. Another exception occurred at the end of 1986 when twelve works were supplied to the

County Museum of Art in Los Angeles for the important exhibition 'The Spiritual in Art'. It was in fact this exhibition which cleared the way for a major presentation in Japan. After visiting Chicago, 'The Spiritual in Art' will wind up in the Haags Gemeentemuseum in September 1987. This exhibition is so vast that the permanent collection will have to make room for it. This enables the composition of a unique presentation of 115 works for Japan which closely follows Mondrian's development and demonstrates how Neo-Plasticism finally freed him from European painting.

Never before has the Haags Gemeentemuseum sent so many of Mondrian's paintings and drawings abroad. The accompanying catalogue, edited by herbert henkels, provides an insight into several aspects of Mondrian the artist. Copious photographs, letters, personal data and texts are published for the first time. This has been made possible by generous contributions from Michel Seuphor (Paris), the Gard family (Paris) and Anne van der Jagt (Paris). An intensive restoration programme crowns the intention with which our museum has sent the collection to Japan. In months of painstaking labour the restorers A.A. Diependaal, J. Venema, W. van der Noort (paintings), C. Bitter and L. Schrier (drawings), G. Hozee and J. Groen (frames) have made it possible to present Mondrian in all his perfection to the Japanese nation. No trouble has been spared by the museum's photography department (photographer Th. Strengers, coordinator P. Couvée).

The more people make the acquaintance of Mondrian's work, the simpler it becomes to interpret it, as it were. In the Netherlands, for instance, parallels are observed between Neo-Plasticism and the severe lines of the Dutch polders, a horizon met at right angles by canals and waterways, or the vivid splendour of the straight rows of our bulb fields. Visual associations will also be rife in Japan. Whenever I sleep in a ryokan on my first visit to your country, my post-modern western eye seeks analogies between the serenity and equilibrium of traditional Japanese architecture and Mondrian's search for harmony. But despite every arbitrary association, I realize above all how universal the language of Mondrian's art is, free of visible reality. For some time now I have been in an environment where I can arrange a meeting with Mondrian every day. From my own experience I realize how his work sets standards, how demanding it is on the beholder. I hope that many Japanese will not only see his work, but to an even greater extent experience the intensity and power of Mondrian.

Henk Overduin
Director a.i. of the Haags Gemeentemuseum

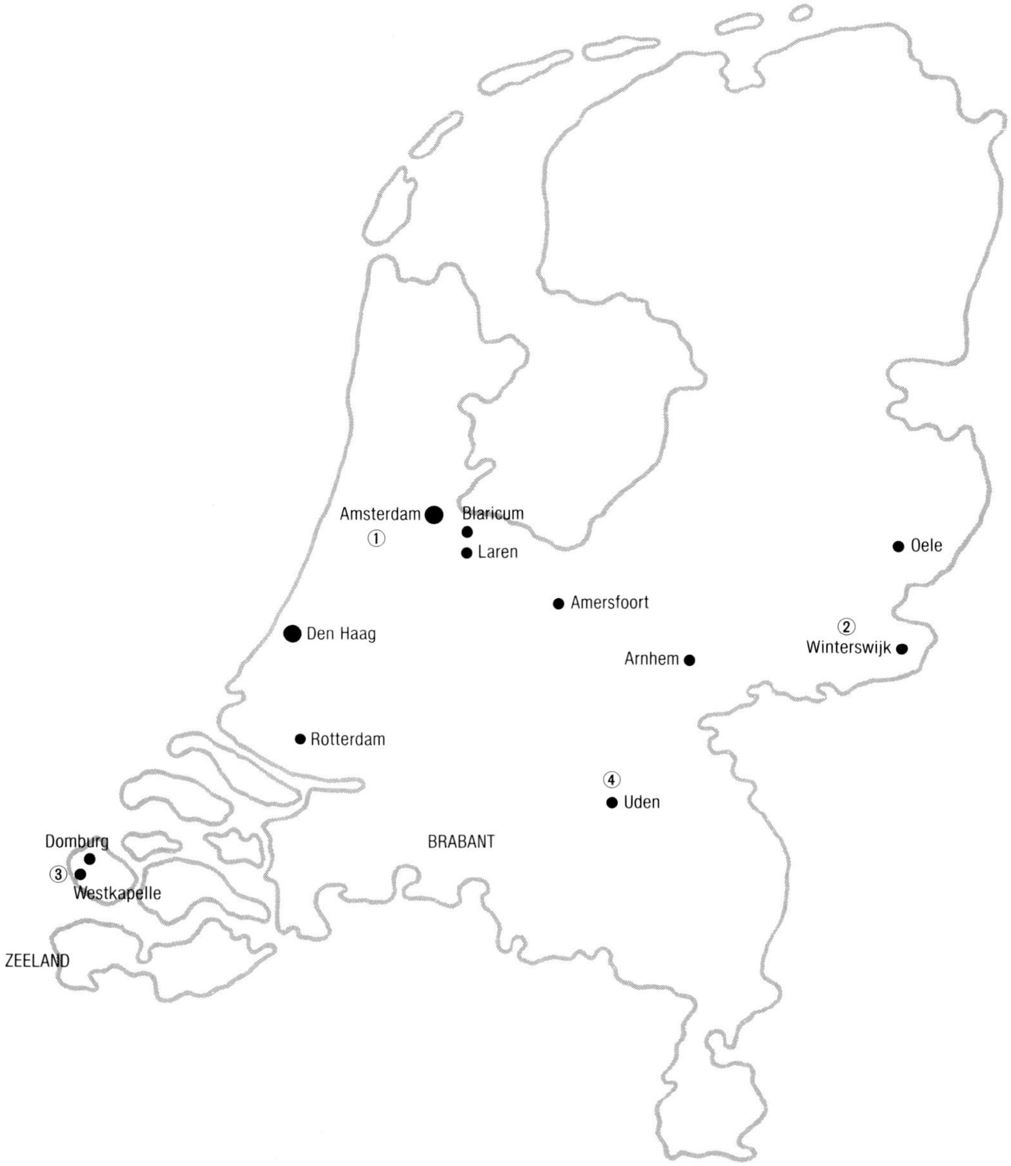
Amsterdam
Blaricum
①
Laren
Oele
Amersfoort
Den Haag
②
Winterswijk
Arnhem
Rotterdam
④
Uden
Domburg
BRABANT
③
Westkapelle
ZEELAND

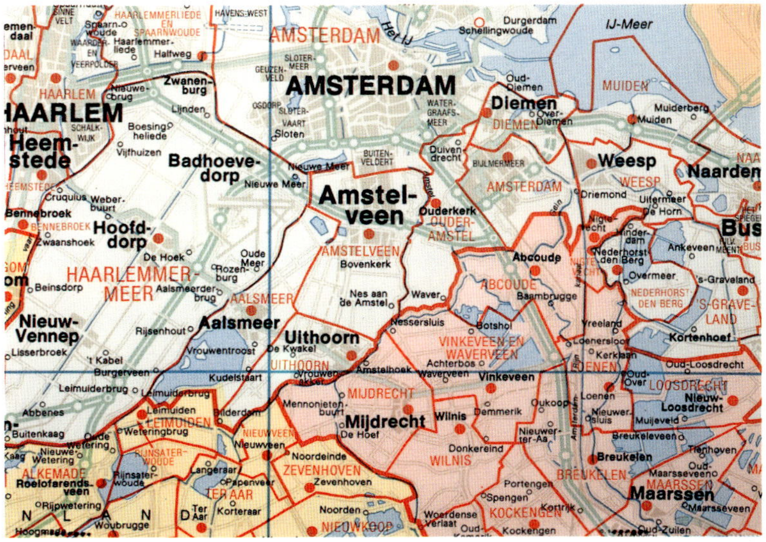
AMSTERDAM
HAARLEM
Heemstede
Badhoevedorp
Amstelveen
Diemen
Weesp
Naarden
Hoofddorp
HAARLEMMERMEER
Aalsmeer
Uithoorn
Nieuw-Vennep
Mijdrecht
Vinkeveen
Breukelen
Maarssen
Abcoude
Ouderkerk
IJ-Meer
①

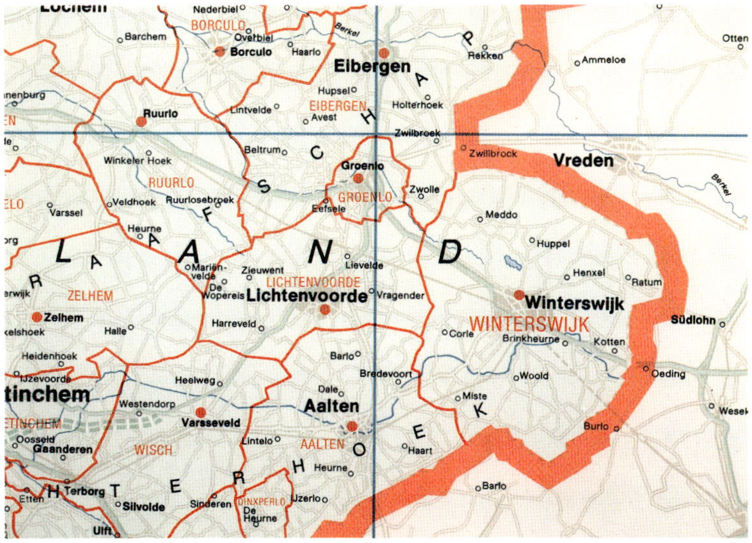
Eibergen
Borculo
Ruurlo
Groenlo
Vreden
Lichtenvoorde
Winterswijk
WINTERSWIJK
Aalten
Zelhem
Varsseveld
Südlohn
Terborg
Silvolde
Sinderen
②

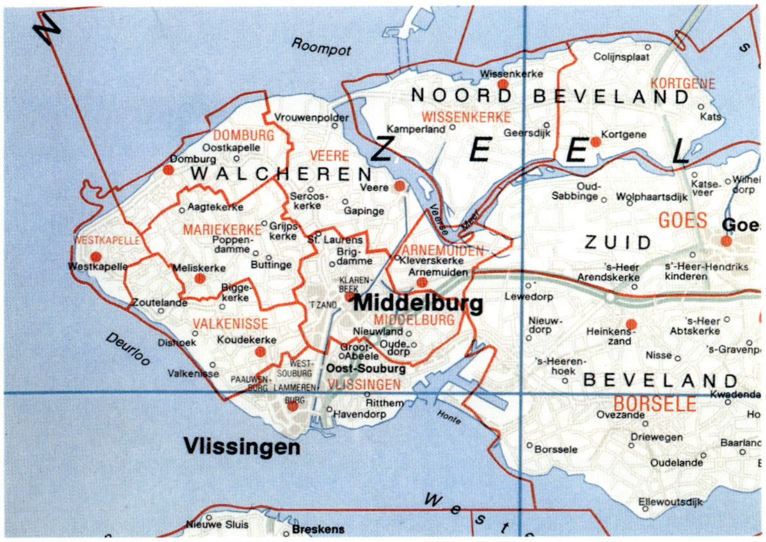
Roompot
NOORD BEVELAND
WALCHEREN
ZEEL
ZUID
BEVELAND
Middelburg
Vlissingen
Domburg
Westkapelle
Veere
Arnemuiden
Oost-Souburg
GOES
BORSELE
Deurloo
Breskens
③

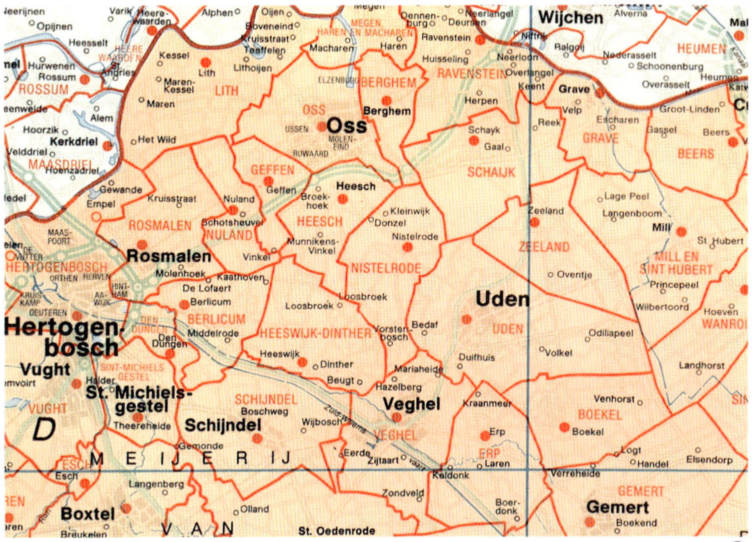
Wijchen
Oss
Rosmalen
Hertogenbosch
Uden
Veghel
Schijndel
St. Michielsgestel
Vught
Boxtel
Gemert
Grave
MEIJERIJ
④

Plastic Art and Pure Plastic Art
(Figurative Art and Non-Figurative Art)

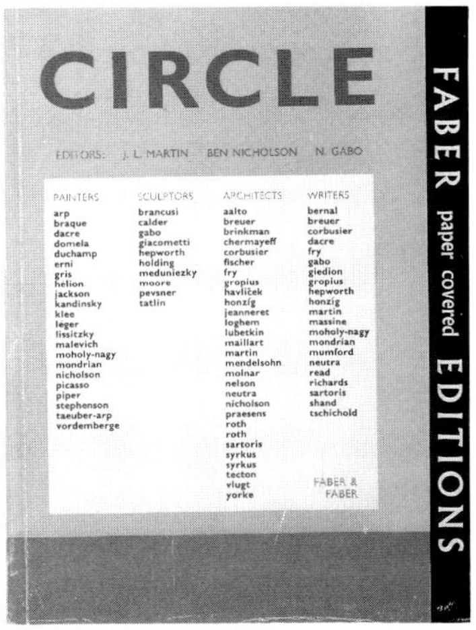

Piet Mondrian

PART I

Although art is fundamentally everywhere and always the same, nevertheless two main human inclinations, diametrically opposed to each other, appear in its many and varied expressions. One aims at the *direct creation of universal beauty,* the other at the *aesthetic expression of oneself,* in other words, of that which one thinks and experiences. The first aims at representing reality objectively, the second subjectively. Thus we see in every work of figurative art the desire, objectively to represent beauty, solely through form and colour, in mutually balanced relations, and, at the same time, an attempt to express that which these forms, colours and relations arouse in us. This latter attempt must of necessity result in an individual expression which veils the pure representation of beauty. Nevertheless, both the two opposing elements (universal—individual) are indispensable if the work is to arouse emotion. Art had to find the right solution. In spite of the dual nature of the creative inclinations, figurative art has produced a harmony through a certain co-ordination between objective and subjective expression. For the spectator, however, who demands a pure representation of beauty, the individual expression is too predominant. For the artist the search for a unified expression through the balance of two opposites has been, and always will be, a continual struggle.

Throughout the history of culture, art has demonstrated that universal beauty does not arise from the particular character of the form, but from the dynamic rhythm of its inherent relationships, or—in a composition—from the mutual relations of forms. Art has shown that it is a question of determining the relations. It has revealed that the forms exist only for the creation of new relationships: that forms create relations and that relations create forms. In this duality of forms and their relations neither takes precedence.

The only problem in art is to achieve a balance between the subjective and the objective. But it is of the utmost importance that this problem should be solved, in the realm of plastic art—technically, as it were—and not in the realm of thought. The work of art must be ‘produced’, ‘constructed’. One must create as objective as possible a representation of forms and relations. Such work can never be empty because the opposition of its constructive elements and its execution arouse emotion.

If some have failed to take into account the inherent character of the form and have forgotten that this—untransformed—predominates, others have overlooked the fact that an individual expression does not become a universal expression through figurative representation, which is based on our conception of feeling, be it classical, romantic, religious, surrealist. Art has shown that universal expression can only be created by a *real equation of the universal and the individual.*

Gradually art is purifying its plastic means and thus bringing out the relationships between them. Thus, in our day two main tendencies appear: the one maintains figuration, the other eliminates it. While the former employs more or less complicated and particular forms, the latter uses simple and neutral forms, or, ultimately, the free line and the pure colour. It is evident that the latter (non-figurative art) can more easily and thoroughly free itself from the domination of the subjective than can the figurative tendency; particular forms and colours (figurative art) are more easily exploited than neutral forms. It is, however, necessary to point out, that the definitions ‘figurative’ and ‘non-figurative’ are only approximate and relative. For every form, even every line, represents a figure, no form is absolutely neutral. Clearly, everything must be relative, but, since we need words to make our concepts understandable, we must keep to these terms.

Among the different forms we may consider those as being neutral which have neither the complexity nor the particularities possessed by the natural forms or abstract forms in general. We may call those neutral which do not evoke individual feelings or ideas. Geometrical forms being so profound an abstraction of form may be regarded as neutral; and on account of their tension and the purity of their outlines they may even be preferred to other neutral forms.

If, as a conception, non-figurative art has been created by the mutual interaction of the human duality,this art has been *realized* by the mutual interaction of *constructive elements and their inherent relations.* This process consists in mutual purification; purified constructive elements set up pure relationships, and these in their turn demand pure constructive elements. Figurative art of today is the outcome of figurative art of the past, and non-figurative art is the outcome of the figurative art of today. Thus the unity of art is maintained.

If non-figurative art is born of figurative art, it is obvious that the two factors of human duality have not only changed, but have also approached one another towards a mutual balance; towards unity. One can rightly speak of an *evolution in plastic art.* It is of the greatest importance to note this fact, for it reveals the true way of art; the only path along which we can advance. Moreover, the evolution of the plastic arts shows that the dualism which has manifested itself in art is only relative and temporal. Both science and art are discovering and making us aware of the fact that *time is a process of intensification,* an evolution from the individual towards the universal, of the subjective towards the objective; towards the essence of things and of ourselves.

A careful observation of art since its origin shows that artistic expression seen from the outside is *not a process of extending but of intensifying one and the same thing,* universal beauty; and that seen from the inside *it is a growth.* Extension results in a continual repetition of nature; it is not human and art cannot follow it. So many of these repetitions which parade as 'art' clearly cannot arouse emotions.

Through intensification one creates successively on more profound planes; extension remains always on the same plane. Intensification, be it noted, is diametrically opposed to extension; they are at right angles to each other as are length and depth. This fact shows clearly the temporal opposition of non-figurative and figurative art.

But if throughout its history art has meant a *continuous and gradual change in the expression of one and the same thing,* the opposition of the two trends—in our time so clear-cut—is actually an unreal one. It is illogical that the two principal tendencies in art, figurative and non-figurative (objective and subjective) should be so hostile. Since art is in essence universal, its expression cannot rest on a subjective view. Our human capacities do not allow of a perfectly objective view, but that does not imply that the plastic expression of art is based on subjective conception. Our subjectivity realizes but does not create the work.

If the two human inclinations already mentioned are apparent in a work of art, they have both collaborated in its realization, but it is evident that the work will clearly show which of the two has predominated. In general, owing to the complexity of forms and the vague expression of relations, the two creative inclinations will appear in the work in a confused manner. Although in general there remains much confusion, today the two inclinations appear more clearly defined as two tendencies: *figurative and non-figurative art.* So-called non-figurative art often also creates a particular representation; figurative art, on the other hand, often neutralizes its forms to a considerable extent. The fact that art which is really non-figurative is rare does not detract from its value; evolution is always the work of pioneers, and their followers are always small in number. This following is not a clique; it is the result of all the existing social forces; it is composed of all those who through innate or acquired capacity are ready to represent the existing degree of human evolution. At a time when so much attention is paid to the collective, to the 'mass', it is necessary to note that evolution, ultimately, is never the expression of the mass. The mass remains behind yet urges the pioneers to creation. For the pioneers, the social contact is indispensable, but not in order that they may know that what they are doing is necessary and useful, nor in order that 'collective approval may help them to persevere and nourish them with living ideas'. This contact is necessary only in an indirect way; it acts especially as an obstacle which increases their determination. The pioneers create through their reaction to external stimuli. They are guided not by the mass but by that which they see and feel. They discover consciously or unconsciously the fundamental laws hidden in reality, and aim at realizing them. In this way they further human development. They know that humanity is not served by making art comprehensible to everybody; to try this is to attempt the impossible. One serves mankind by enlightening it. Those who do not see will rebel, they will try to understand and will end up by 'seeing'. In art the search for a content which is collectively understandable is false; the content will always be individual. Religion, too, has been debased by that search.

Art is not made for anybody and is, at the same time, for everybody. It is a mistake to try to go too fast. The complexity of art is due to the fact that different degrees of its evolution are present at one and the same time. The present carries with it the past and the future. But we need not try to foresee the future; we need only take our place in the development of human culture, a development which has made non-figurative art supreme. It has always been only one struggle, of only one real art; to create universal beauty. This points the way for both present and future. We need only continue and develop what already exists. The essential thing is that *the fixed laws of the plastic arts must be realized.* These have shown themselves clearly in non-figurative art.

Today one is tired of the dogmas of the past, and of truths once accepted but successively jettisoned. One realizes more and more the relativity of everything, and therefore one tends to reject the idea of fixed laws; of a single truth. This is very understandable but does not lead to profound vision. For there are 'made' laws, 'discovered' laws, but also laws—a truth for all time. These are more or less hidden in the reality which surrounds us and do not change. Not only science, but art also, shows us that reality, at first incomprehensible, gradually reveals itself, by the mutual relations that are inherent in things. Pure science and pure art, disinterested and free, can lead the advance in the recognition of the laws which are based on these relationships. A great scholar has recently said that pure science achieves practical results for humanity. Similarly, one can say that pure art, even though it appear abstract, can be of direct utility for life.

Art shows us that there are also constant truths concerning forms. Every form, every line has its own expression. This objective expression can be modified by our subjective view but it is no less true for that. Round is always round and square is always square. Simple though these facts are, they often appear to be forgotten in art. Many try to achieve one and the same end by different means. In plastic art this is an impossibility. In plastic art it is necessary to choose constructive means which are of one piece with that which one wants to express.

Art makes us realize that there are *fixed laws which govern and point to the use of the constructive elements of the composition and of the inherent inter-relationships between them.* These laws may be regarded as subsidiary laws to the *fundamental* law of equivalence which creates *dynamic equilibrium and reveals the true content of reality.*

PART II

We live in a difficult but interesting epoch. After a secular culture, a turning point has arrived; this shows itself in all the branches of human activity. Limiting ourselves here to science and art, we notice that, just as in medicine some have discovered the natural laws relating to physical life, in art some have discovered the artistic laws relating to plastics. In spite of all opposition, these facts have become movements. But confusion still reigns in them. Through science we are becoming more and more conscious of the fact that our physical state depends in great measure on what we eat, on the manner in which our food is arranged and on the physical exercise which we take. Through art we are becoming more and more conscious of the fact that the work depends in large measure on the constructive elements which we use and on the construction which we create. We will gradually realize that we have not hitherto paid sufficient attention to constructive physical elements in their relation to the human body, nor to the constructive plastic elements in their relation to art. That which we eat has deteriorated through a refinement of natural produce. To say this, appears to invoke a return to a primitive natural state and to be in opposition to the exigencies of pure plastic art, which degenerates precisely through figurative trappings. But a return to pure natural nourishment does not mean a return to the state of primitive man; it means on the contrary that cultured man obeys the laws of nature discovered and applied by science.

Similarly in non-figurative art, to recognize and apply natural laws is not evidence of a retrograde step; the pure abstract expression of these laws proves that the exponent of non-figurative art associates himself with the most advanced progress and the most cultured minds, that he is an exponent of denaturalized nature, of civilization.

In life, sometimes the spirit has been over-emphasized at the expense of the body, sometimes one has been preoccupied with the body and neglected the spirit; similarly in art content and form have alternately been over-emphasized or neglected because *their inseparable unity* has not been clearly realized.

To create this unity in art *balance of the one and the other must be created.*

It is an achievement of our time to have approached towards such balance in a field in which disequilibrium still reigns.

Disequilibrium means conflict, disorder. Conflict is also a part of life and of art, but it is not the whole of life or universal beauty. Real life is the *mutual interaction of two oppositions of the same value but of a different aspect and nature.* Its plastic expression is universal beauty.

In spite of world disorder, instinct and intuition are carrying humanity to a real equilibrium, but how much misery has been and is still being caused by primitive animal instinct. How many errors have been and are being committed through vague and confused intuition? Art certainly shows this clearly. But art shows also that in the course of progress, intuition becomes more and more conscious and instinct more and more purified. Art and life illuminate each other more and more; they reveal more and more their laws according to which a real and living balance is created.

Intuition enlightens and so links up with pure thought. They together become an intelligence which is not simply of the brain, which does not calculate, but which feels and thinks. Which is creative both in art and in life. From this intelligence there must arise non-figurative art in which instinct no longer plays a dominating part. Those who do not understand this intelligence regard non-figurative art as a purely intellectual product.

Although all dogma, all preconceived ideas, must be harmful to art, the artist can nevertheless be guided and helped in his intuitive researches by reasoning apart from his work. If such reasoning can be useful to the artist and can accelerate his progress, it is indispensable that such reasoning should accompany the observations of the critics who talk about art and who wish to guide mankind. Such reasoning, however, cannot be individual, which it usually is; it cannot arise out of a body of knowledge outside plastic art. If one is not an artist oneself one must at least know *the laws and culture of plastic art.* If the public is to be well informed and if mankind is to progress it is essential that the confusion which is everywhere present should be removed. For enlightenment, a clear demonstration of the *succession of artistic tendencies is necessary.* Hitherto, a study of the different styles of plastic art in their progressive succession has been difficult since the expression of the essence of art has been veiled. In our time, which is reproached for not having a style of its own, the content of art has become clear and the different tendencies reveal more clearly the progressive succession of artistic expression. Non-figurative art brings to an end the ancient culture of art; at present therefore, one can review and judge more surely *the whole culture of art.* We are not at the turning-point of this culture; *the culture of particular form is approaching its end. The culture of determined relations has begun.*

It is not enough to explain the value of a work of art in itself; it is above all necessary to show *the place which a work occupies on the scale of the evolution of plastic art.* Thus in speaking of art, it is not permissible to say 'this is how I see it' or 'this is my idea'. True art like true life takes a *single road.*

The laws which in the culture of art have become more and more determinate are *the great hidden laws of nature which art establishes in its own fashion.* It is necessary to stress the fact that these laws are more or less hidden behind the superficial aspect of nature. Abstract art is therefore opposed to a natural representation of things. But it *is not opposed to nature* as is generally thought. It is opposed to the raw primitive animal nature of man, but it is one with true human nature. It is opposed to the conventional laws created during the culture of the particular form but it is one with the laws of the culture of pure relationships.

First and foremost there is the fundamental law of *dynamic equilibrium* which is opposed to the static equilibrium necessitated by the particular form.

The important task then of all art is to destroy the static equilibrium by establishing a dynamic one. Non-figurative art demands an attempt of what is a consequence of this task, the *destruction* of particular form and the *construction* of a rhythm of mutual relations, of mutual forms or free lines. We must bear in mind, however, a distinction between these two forms of equilibrium in order to avoid confusion; for when we speak of equilibrium pure and simple we may be for, and at the same time against, a balance in the work of art. It is of the greatest importance to note the destructive-constructive quality of dynamic equilibrium. Then we shall understand that the equilibrium of which we speak in non-figurative art is not without movement of action but is on the contrary a continual movement. We then understand also the significance of the name 'constructive art'.

The fundamental law of dynamic equilibrium gives rise to a number of other laws which relate to the constructive elements and their relations. These laws determine the manner in which dynamic equilibrium is achieved. The relations of *position* and those of *dimension* both have their own laws. Since the relation of the rectangular position is constant, it will be applied whenever the work demands the expression of stability; to destroy this stability there is a law that relations of a changeable dimension-expression must be substituted. The fact that all the relations of position except the rectangular one lack that stability, also creates a law which we must take into account if something is to be established in a determinate manner. Too often right and oblique angles are arbitrarily employed. All art expresses the rectangular relationship even though this may not be in a determinate manner; first by the height and width of the work and its constructive forms, then by the mutual relations of these forms. Through the clarity and simplicity of neutral forms, non-figurative art has made the rectangular relation more and more determinate, until, finally, it has established it through free lines which intersect and appear to form rectangles.

As regards the relations of dimension, they must be varied in order to avoid repetition. Although, as compared with the stable expression of the rectangular relationship, they belong to individual expression, it is precisely they that are most appropriate for the destruction of the static equilibrium of all form. By offering him a freedom of choice the relations of dimension *present the artist with one of the most difficult problems.* And the closer he approaches the ultimate consequence of his art the more difficult is his task.

Since the constructive elements and their mutual relations form an inseparable unity, the laws of the relations govern equally the constructive elements. These, however, have also their own laws. It is obvious that one cannot achieve the same expression through different forms. But it is often forgotten that varied forms or lines *achieve—in form—altogether different degrees in the evolution of plastic art.* Beginning with natural forms and ending with the most abstract forms, *their expression becomes more profound.* Gradually form and line gain in tension. For this reason the straight line is a stronger and more profound expression than the curve.

In pure plastic art the significance of different forms and lines is very important; it is precisely this fact which makes it pure.

In order that art may be really abstract, in other words, that it should not represent relations with the natural aspect of things, the law of the *denaturalization of matter* is of fundamental importance. In painting, the primary colour that is as pure as possible realizes this abstraction of natural colour. But colour is, in the present state of technique, also the best means for denaturalizing matter in the realm of abstract constructions in three dimensions; technical means are as a rule insufficient.

All art has achieved a certain measure of abstraction. This abstraction has become more and more accentuated until in pure plastic art not only a transformation of form but also of matter—be it through technical means or through colour—a more or less neutral expression is attained.

According to our laws, it is a great mistake to believe that one is practising non-figurative art by merely achieving neutral forms or free lines and determinate relations. For in composing these forms one runs the risk of a figurative creation, that is to say one or more particular forms.

Non-figurative art is created by establishing *a dynamic rhythm of determinate mutual relations* which *excludes the formation of any particular form.* We note thus, that to destroy particular form is only to do more consistently what all art has done.

The dynamic rhythm which is essential in all art is also the essential element of a non-figurative work. In figurative art this rhythm is veiled.

Yet we all pay homage to clarity.

The fact that people generally prefer figurative art (which creates and finds its continuation in abstract art) can be explained by the dominating force of the individual inclination in human nature. *From this inclination arises all the opposition to art which is purely abstract.*

In this connection we note first the *naturalistic conception* and the *descriptive or literary orientation*: both a real danger to purely abstract art. From a purely plastic point of view, until non-figurative art, artistic expression has been naturalistic or descriptive. To have emotion aroused by pure plastic expression one must abstract from figuration and so become 'neutral'. But with the exception of some artistic expressions (such as Byzantine art)* there has not been the desire to employ neutral plastic means, which would have been much more logical than to become neutral oneself in contemplating a work of art. Let us note, however, that the spirit of the past was different from the spirit of our own day, and that it is only tradition which has carried the past into our own time. In past times when one lived in contact with nature and when man himself was more natural than he is today, abstraction from figuration in thought was easy; it was done unconsciously. But in our more or less denaturalized period, such abstraction becomes an effort.

However that may be, the fact that figuration is a factor which is unduly taken into account, and whose abstraction in the mind is only relative, proves that today even great artists regard figuration as indispensable. At the same time these artists are already abstracting from figuration to a much greater extent than has been done before. More and more, not only the uselessness of figuration, but also obstacles which it creates, will become obvious. In this search for clarity, non-figurative art develops.

There is, however, one tendency which cannot forego figuration without losing its descriptive character. That is surrealism. Since the predominance of individual thought is opposed to pure plastics it is also opposed to non-figurative art. Born of a literary movement, its descriptive character demands figuration. However purified or deformed it may be, figuration veils pure plastics. There are, it is true, surrealist works whose plastic expression is very strong and of a kind that if the work is observed at a distance, i.e. if the figurative representation is abstracted from, arouse one's emotions by form, colour and their relations alone. But if the purpose was nothing but plastic expression, why then use figurative representation? Clearly, there must have been the intention to express something outside the realm of pure plastics. This of course is often the case even in abstract art. There, too, there is sometimes added to the abstract forms something particular, even without the use of figuration; through the colour or through the execution, a particular idea or sentiment is expressed. There it is generally not the literary inclination but the naturalistic inclination which has been at work. It must be obvious that if one evokes in the spectator the sensation of, say, the sunlight or moonlight, of joy or sadness, or any other determinate sensation, one has not succeeded in establishing universal beauty, one is not purely abstract.

As for surrealism, we must recognize that it deepens feeling and thought, but since this deepening is limited by individualism it cannot reach the foundation, the universal. So long as it remains in the realm of dreams, which are only a re-arrangement of the events of life, it cannot touch true reality. Through a different composition of the events of life, it may remove their ordinary course but it cannot purify them. Even the intention of freeing life from its conventions and from everything which is harmful to the true life can be found in surrealist literature. Non-figurative art is fully in agreement with this intention but it achieves its purpose; it frees its plastic means and its art from all particularity. The names, however, of these tendencies, are only indications of their conceptions; it is the realization which matters. With the exception of non-figurative art, there seems to have been a lack of realization of the fact that it is possible to express oneself profoundly and humanely by plastics alone, that is, by employing a neutral plastic means without the risk of falling into decoration or ornament. Yet all the world knows that even a single line can arouse emotion. But although one sees—and this is the artist's fault—few non-figurative works which live by virtue of their dynamic rhythm and their execution, figurative art is no better in this respect. In general, people have not realized that one can express our very essence through neutral constructive elements; that is to say we can express the essence of art. The essence of art of course is not often sought. As a rule, individualist human nature is so predominant, that the expression of the essence of art through a rhythm of lines, colours and relationships appears insufficient. Recently, even a great artist has declared that 'complete indifference to the subject leads to an incomplete form of art'.

But everybody agrees that art is only a problem of plastics. What good then is a subject? It is to be understood that one would need a subject to expound something named 'Spiritual riches, human sentiments and thoughts'. Obviously, all this is individual and needs particular forms. But at the root of these sentiments and thoughts there is one thought and one sentiment: these do not easily define themselves and have no need of analogous forms in which to express themselves. It is here that neutral plastic means are demanded.

For pure art then, the subject can never be an additional value, it is the line, the colour and their relations which must 'bring into play the whole sensual and intellectual register of the inner life'... not the subject. Both in abstract art and in naturalistic art colour expresses itself 'in accordance with the form by which it is determined', and in all art it is the artist's task to make forms and colours living and capable of arousing emotion. If he makes art into an 'algebraic equation' that is no argument against the art, it only proves that he is not an artist.

If all art has demonstrated that to establish the force, tension and movement of the forms, and the intensity of the colours of reality, it is necessary that these should be purified and transformed; if all art has purified and transformed and is still purifying and transforming these forms of reality and their mutual relations; if all art is thus a continually deepening process: why then stop halfway? If all art aims at expressing universal beauty, why establish an individualist expression? Why then not continue the sublime work of the cubists? That would not be a continuation of the same tendency, but on the contrary, *a complete break-away from it and all that has existed before it.* That would only be going along the same road that we have already travelled.

Since cubist art is still fundamentally naturalistic, the break which pure plastic art has caused consists in becoming abstract instead of naturalistic in essence. While in cubism, from a naturalistic foundation, there sprang forcibly the use of plastic means, still half object half abstract, the abstract basis of pure plastic art must result in the use of purely abstract plastic means.

In removing completely from the work all objects, 'the world is not separated from the spirit', but is on the contrary, *put into a balanced opposition* with the spirit, since the one and the other are purified. This creates a perfect unity between the two opposites. There are, however, many who imagine that they are too fond of life, particular reality, to be able to suppress figuration, and for that reason they still use in their work the object or figurative fragments which indicate its character. Nevertheless, one is well aware of the fact that in art one cannot hope to represent in the image things as they are, nor even as they manifest themselves in all their living brilliance. The impressionists, divisionists, and pointillistes have already recognized that. There are some today who, recognizing the weakness and limitation of the image, attempt to create a work of art through the objects themselves, often by composing them in a more or less transformed manner. This clearly can not lead to an expression of their content nor of their true character. One can more or less remove the conventional appearance of things (surrealism), but they continue nevertheless to show their particular character and to arouse in us individual emotions. To love things in reality is to love them profoundly; it is to see them as a microcosmos in the macrocosmos. *Only in this way can one achieve a universal expression of reality.* Precisely on account of its profound love for things, non-figurative art does not aim at rendering them in their particular appearance.

Precisely by its existence non-figurative art shows that 'art' *continues always on its true road.* It shows that 'art' is *not the expression of the appearance of reality such as we see it, nor of the life which we live,* but that *it is the expression of true reality and true life... indefinable but realizable in plastics.*

Thus we must carefully distinguish between two kinds of reality; one which has an individual and one which has a universal appearance. In art the former is the expression of space determined by particular things or forms, the latter establishes expansion and limitation—the creative factors of space—through neutral forms, free lines and pure colours. While universal reality arises from determinate relations, particular reality shows only veiled relations. The latter must obviously be confused in just that respect in which universal reality is bound to be clear. The one is free, the other is tied to individual life, be it personal or collective. Subjective reality and relatively objective reality: this is the contrast. Pure abstract art aims at creating the latter, figurative art the former.

It is astonishing therefore, that one should reproach pure abstract art with not being 'real', and that one should envisage it as 'arising from particular ideas'.

In spite of the existence of non-figurative art, one is talking about art today as if nothing determinate in relation to the new art existed. Many neglect the real non-figurative art, and looking only at the fumbling attempts and at the empty non-figurative works which today are appearing everywhere, ask themselves whether the time has not arrived 'to integrate form and content' or 'to unify thought and form'. But one should not blame non-figurative art for that which is only due to the ignorance of its very content. If the form is without content, without universal thought, it is the fault of the artist. Ignoring that fact, one imagines that figuration, subject, particular form, could add to the work that which the plastic itself is lacking. As regards the 'content' of the work, we must note that our 'attitude with regard to things, our organized individuality with its impulses, its actions, its reactions when in contact with reality, the lights and shades of our spirit', etc., certainly do modify the non-figurative work, but they do not constitute its content. We repeat, that its content cannot be described, and that it is only through pure plastics and through the execution of the work that it can be made apparent. Through this indeterminable content, the non-figurative work is 'fully human'. Execution and technique play an important part in the aim of establishing a more or less objective vision which the essence of the non-figurative work demands. The less obvious the artist's hand is the more objective will the work be. This fact leads to a preference for a more or less mechanical execution or to the employment of materials produced by industry. Hitherto, of course, these materials have been imperfect from the point of view of art. If these materials and their colours were more perfect and if a technique existed by which the artist could easily cut them up in order to compose his work as he conceives it, an art more real and more objective in relation to life than painting would arise. All these reflections evoke questions which have already been asked many years ago, mainly: is art still necessary and useful for humanity? Is it not even harmful to progress? Certainly the art of the past is superfluous to the new spirit and harmful to its progress: just because of its beauty it holds many people back from the new conception. The new art is, however, still very necessary to life. In a clear manner it establishes the laws according to which a real balance is reached. Moreover, it must create among us a profoundly human and rich beauty realized not only by the best qualities of the new architecture, but also by all that the constructive art in painting and sculpture makes possible.

But although the new art is necessary, the mass is conservative. Hence these cinemas, these radios, these bad pictures which overwhelm the few works which are really of our era.

It is a great pity that those who are concerned with the social life in general do not realize the utility of pure abstract art. Wrongly influenced by the art of the past, the true essence of which escapes them, and of which they only see that which is superfluous, they make no effort to know pure abstract art. Through another conception of the word 'abstract', they have a certain horror of it. They are vehemently oppposed to abstract art because they regard it as something ideal and unreal. In general they use art as propaganda for collective or personal ideas, thus as literature. They are both in favour of the progress of the mass and against the progress of the elite, thus against the logical march of human evolution. Is it really to be believed that the evolution of the mass and that of the elite are incompatible? The elite rises from the mass; is it not therefore its highest expression?

To return to the execution of the work of art, let us note that it must contribute to a revelation of the subjective and objective factors in mutual balance. Guided by intuition, it is possible to attain this end. The execution is of the greatest importance in the work of art; it is through this, in large part, that intuition manifests itself and creates the essence of the work.

It is therefore a mistake to suppose that a non-figurative work comes out of the unconscious, which is a collection of individual and pre-natal memories. We repeat that it comes from pure intuition, which is at the basis of the subjective-objective dualism.

It is, however, wrong to think that the non-figurative artist finds impressions and emotions received from the outside useless, and regards it even as necessary to fight against them. On the contrary, all that the non-figurative artist receives from the outside is not only useful but indispensable, because it arouses in him the desire to create that which he only vaguely feels and which he could *never represent in a true manner without the contact with visible reality and with the life which surrounds him.* It is precisely from this visible reality that he draws the objectivity which he needs in opposition to his personal subjectivity. It is precisely from this visible reality that he draws his means of expression: and, as regards the surrounding life, it is precisely this which has made his art non-figurative.

That which distinguishes him from the figurative artist is the fact that in his creations he frees himself from individual sentiments and from particular impressions which he receives from outside, and that he breaks loose from the domination of the individual inclination within him.

It is therefore equally wrong to think that the non-figurative artist creates through 'the pure intention of his mechanical process', that he makes 'calculated abstractions', and that he wishes to 'suppress sentiment not only in himself but also in the spectator'. It is a mistake to think that he retires completely into his system. That which is regarded as a system is nothing but constant obedience to the laws of pure plastics, to necessity, which art demands from him. It is thus clear that he has not become a mechanic, but that the progress of science, of technique, of machinery, of life as a whole, has only made him into a living machine, capable of realizing in a pure manner the essence of art. In this way, he is in his creation sufficiently neutral, that nothing of himself or outside of him can prevent him from establishing that which is universal. Certainly his art is art for art's sake...for the sake of the art *which is form and content at one and the same time.*

If all real art is 'the sum total of emotions aroused by purely pictorial means' his art is the sum of the emotions aroused by plastic means.

It would be illogical to suppose that non-figurative art will remain stationary, for this art contains *a culture* of the use of new plastic means and their determinate relations. Because the field is new there is all the more to be done. What is certain is that no escape is possible for the non-figurative artist; he *must stay within his field and march towards the consequence of his art.*

This consequence brings us, in a future perhaps remote, towards the end of *art as a thing separated from our surrounding environment, which is the actual plastic reality.* But this end is at the same time a new beginning. Art will not only continue but will realize itself more and more. By the unification of architecture, sculpture and painting, a new plastic reality will be created. Painting and sculpture will not manifest themselves as separate objects, nor as 'mural art' which destroys architecture itself, nor as 'applied' art, but *being purely constructive* will aid the creation of an atmosphere not merely utilitarian or rational but also pure and complete in its beauty.

* As regards these works we must note that, lacking a dynamic rhythm, they remain, in spite of the profound expression of forms, more or less ornamental.

from *Circle*, 1937

At Piet Mondrian's

three interviews with the artist

A visit to Piet Mondrian

(from our correspondent)

Paris, June 1920—Whitsun. A brilliantly sunny day, under a blazing blue sky. Dense Sunday crowds throng the Porte d'Orléans. The cafés spill out onto the pavements. Close by the ancient ramparts (where the poorest of the poor pluck their spring flowers) is where Piet Mondrian lives. A street with picturesquely neglected gardens, a verdant courtyard, a dark staircase—and the painter comes towards me in his overall. What a difference to Kees van Dongen's house. True, both have furnished their own apartments, but at Van Dongen's one is staggered by a drunken riot of colours and cushions through which it takes a while to distinguish in the blue cigarette smoke the graceful lines of a Parisian gesture. Mondrian's, however, is a severe, businesslike room flooded with limpid, cool light, where the painter, deaf to the Whitsuntide jollity around him, grapples with his material in monklike solitude in his quest for his lofty, highly controversial ideal.

On an easel in the middle of the studio is a square canvas, the painter's most recent work. It is divided into rectangular fields painted in the principal colours of bright red, blue, black. It does not represent anything. No regularity can be discerned in the figure. And yet there is a not unpleasing balance about it, the painter says, and having said so, promptly turns the canvas round in order to keep it steady...

While I recover from my initial surprise in a cubic cane chair, the painter discloses the name of his creation: Foxtrot. It has the same modern, rhythmic feeling, the regular steps to and fro. I myself have often danced the foxtrot at Van Dongen's, and am amazed to find the artistic essence of this profane activity in Mondrian's ascetic cell. However, the painter goes on to explain in succinct terms how the foxtrot led to his depiction, or transformation, and how the mundane representation has mysteriously and totally vanished. It is the history of the last half-century of painting.

Formerly, Subject Matter was everything; then it became merely an excuse for the composition; the impressionists spirited it away in a cloak of Light and Air; the cubists rediscovered Form, reducing everything to the simplest geometrical shape; the futurists, finally, assembled different images from different points of view in order to convey Motion, the motor of modern life. Not only the futurists but the cubists, too, still partly cling to representation: the unprincipled Picasso has been known to produce (excellent) classical drawings in his time; in the work of Gleizes, Metzinger, Braque etc., a variety of souvenirs of real life (newspaper cuttings, linoleum patterns) are treated anecdotally; Léger, Hellesen, etc., with their cylindrical cubism, are already further. Mondrian himself has taken the aims of this group (the Section d'Or, with whom he has exhibited in the Netherlands) to the utmost consequence. All such traditional values as natural colour, form, atmosphere, perspective, are completely banished. At last the painting has become an independent entity, like absolute music. The gradual evolution of the painter himself towards the Extreme Left, however, is demonstrated by his studio.

He shows me a large canvas on which lines and planes intersect, painted in shades of delicate pink and soft brown (ideal for a dressing-gown). A step further: paintings with lines. The entire white surface is covered with horizontal and vertical black lines. At first they remind you of Morse code, but you soon start to make out empty and filled-in patches and currents moving in different directions. My feeble intuition still fails wretchedly to guess the titles of pictures like this.

One of them represents Domburg Pier with the sea and a starry sky. On a closer look you can see how distinctly the painter, with geometrical artistry, makes each point express the sum of horizontality and verticality (in rather the same way that iron filings make a magnetic field visible). Another canvas with an upward-surging current in the middle represents a House Under Repair, and a mainly vertical system of lines is supposed to be (as opposed to depicting) a Cathedral.

Above the door is a geometrical motif: a square suspended from one corner, divided into small squares and containing all the diagonals. Bob's your uncle. Child's play. A knitting pattern. But if you look at it for a long time you notice that some (which?) lines are thinner, others thicker, that there is no balance, that your eyes are irresistibly drawn in a certain direction... It is as though some mysterious life pulses through the magic motif.

The paintings with rectangular shapes are the most recent. The formerly scattered horizontal and vertical lines now meet to demarcate rectangles of various size and position, filled in with strongly contrasting colours. At first the painter was sensitive to the purely sensual values of colour, to which a splendid mosaic in pale grey and orange testifies, only to return irrevocably to the stark, schematic primary colours. One by one the painter has abandoned the pictorial means and, resorting to practically nothing, is now attempting to depict a general mood, whether brazenly vivid or more tender in tone.

My host's arguments are evidently watertight, but I am still not convinced. In desperation I clutch at an oriental cushion on the divan, decorated with arabesques: isn't Mondrian's art a geometrical ornament in disguise, like those of the Arabs, who for religious (not artistic!) reasons are forbidden to depict objects? No, Mondrian says, I am not making dead, symmetrical formulae but a moving, living arabesque!

But doesn't this extreme simplification, this abstraction, signify the end of painting, after which nothing more can be done? Mondrian concedes that it means an end, but suggests it may well last for thousands of years.—But what does the painter think about his work—which in itself appears to be unresolved—being framed, enclosed, placed in an interior? After all, the easel painting is passé, isn't it? Mondrian doesn't have to reply to this question: his studio answers for him. The walls of the room with its pleasing stereometrical shape are hung with unpainted or primed canvases, so that each wall is actually a kind of larger-scale painting with rectangular fields. It is seemingly Mondrian's aim, then, to complement the architect by bringing life to the latter's monotonous surfaces. Now, I can imagine brightening up a glass window, a yacht's sail, the wing of an aircraft in this fashion, but isn't it a shame to break up a monumental wall by decorating it with rectangles? No, for he takes the window and door openings into account as far as possible. But doesn't M.'s notion suggest a purely stereometrical space enclosed by ideal planes, like those dreamed of by the great architect Peter Behrens in his second creative period? Perhaps that could be executed in reinforced concrete, but post-and-lintel construction has a far more constructive and material nature: the material can and may not be disguised.

With these wholly undigested ideas I take my leave of the hospitable and so utterly modest painter (quite the opposite of a charlatan). I feel like a schoolboy with a tough algebra sum in his head, or an undefined threat from the Trinity, coming out into the marvellously mild air, shrugging off all cares and plunging back into everyday life. How delightful it is after all that sterilized art to look at banal reality again, at all that shimmering green, that heap of cherries, that ice-cream cart cleverly decorated with that glorious bunch of peonies.

Descending into the maw of the Métro, however, I sense its living beauty too, and Mondrian's laboratory experiments suddenly seem to assume real shape. Rectangular the long tubes, rectangular the trains gliding in and out of them; the very walls, also rectangular, are divided into coloured planes by red and green advertisements, almost in accordance with M.'s recipe. The advertisements are hideous, so hideous, happily, that I have never looked at them, their effect being simply that of coloured surfaces which together form a lively background to the bustling crowds. I have found confirmation of M.'s proposition! But alas, the rectangles disappear. We are now speeding through a round tube, the next station lies round a bend and is topped by a cylindrical roof upon which electric lights cast elliptical lines. All around us the straight line gives way to the circle. My doubts return. Why has Mondrian jettisoned the circle in favour of the straight line? Our almost round planets rotate around spherical cores; most temples, factories and stations have curved roofs; our planet is governed by circular motion, not leverage: wheels and axes revolve. And finally, all the things that exist and move in M.'s box of a room: machines, flowers, women, cigarettes, etc., have a cylindrical, conical or

Later, Mondrian returns to tragedy in modern painting. He regards that element of tragedy, even in the art of a great Dutch comrade, as self-deception. As is sometimes the case with religion in art, it is a euphemism for something wholly individual. Mondrian feels that Cézanne, for example, is much purer. He abhors individuality in art, like Marinetti, who wants to banish the (petty) ego from literature. He is eagerly pressing forward towards the complete, or more grandly, the universal. He regards what he has been doing in recent years as far more essential than his former naturalistic work. He repeats that characteristic, *essential,* several times in this connection, not sure whether it really expresses what he means. He searches and searches, but fails to come up with anything better.

I ask him about the connection between the reaction to external things in—if I may be permitted to call it so—inspiration, and he replies that this perception is absorbed in the inner process. I am aware that this constitutes a danger of total rarefaction; the uninitiated cannot make head or tail of this later work. And he agrees that there is something very sad about that. If he painted 'normally' he would have an easier time of it. He does keep in touch with life; he has to, he enjoys it. I met him at a musical soirée given by mutual acquaintances. He said:—Did you know that I'm interested in music too? Last year I heard the futurist *Bruiteurs.* I'd like to do something like that, and told them so. The instruments would have to be slightly different, though. I like the idea of breaking up the melody. That's what I like about jazz bands. There's still a tune, but it's mixed up with woodwind sounds. I want sounds to stop abruptly. I enjoy dancing at public balls.

Mondrian is not alone in his views on futuristic music. A few Paris papers, including the clever Bidou, have observed its salutary principle. I once met the conductor, Russolini [Luigi Russolo], I think he was called. He seemed perfectly normal. When Mondrian hears 'old-fashioned' music, he wonders whether he is wrong, whether the composers and all the people who swear by them knew what they were doing. No, he adds guilelessly: I am strengthened in my opinion every time.

I now ask him about the report this paper carried about his exhibition in the *Hollandsche Kunstenaarskring,* a review which pleased him, and about the relationship between his paintings and applied art. Yes, that is an essential point; decorative art is all the rage at the moment. He refuses to climb on the bandwagon, though, but sticks to painting pure and simple. He does not regard his work as a design for tiles or stained-glass windows. True, there have been attempts in the Netherlands to combine this type of work with modern architecture—in vain.

True, he has decorated his studio in a style that echoes his art, with squares of coloured cardboard; a black cupboard stands out against them in harmonious contrast. It is all temporary; permanent decoration in this style would be too costly! While on the subject, he shows me some paintings from yet another stage. The painted rectangles are now separate. He gazes particularly fondly at one picture, which arouses in him sensations of innocence and charming, Italian mediaeval art. The visitor recalls what Mondrian told him briefly about the 'secret' doctrine which he has been exploring. The painter is also particularly partial to a picture on the wall. At a first glance it looks like a lattice; the artist discerns a faint pattern in it. He explains another work as follows: a few little lines, you might say, but I see the sea in it, waves rolling towards me under a starry sky. Yet another picture gives him a sensation of space.

Again, he stresses:

—The work must retain an intuitive and aesthetic sensation. A young artist recently reduced art to numbers. That's going too far for me; perhaps it's something for a future, more sophisticated race. My dealer tells me I am too advanced for my time. I think that applies more to the writers who are working in my fashion. I once wrote some of my own impressions for the (now defunct) *Nieuwe Groene.* They were too futuristic. That kind of literature is meant for much later generations. You can break away from musical and pictorial idioms, but not words, although the futurists have tried. The result is totally incomprehensible. You ought to read Papini's collection *De Blinde Loods* (The Blind Pilot); I recognize something of myself in it.

Thus spoke the painter, faltering because of the profound and volatile character of such matters. Is he right...? The question remains unasked: at the level of the work he has just been talking about, it is a moot point. The visitor listens, fascinated by such valiant perseverance, admiring the intellectual and spiritual strength of a man in search of new forms of expression.

I went to see the Mondrians at Léonce Rosenberg's gallery in order to test the theories propounded by the painter.

He specializes in hyper-modern art. As we know, several of his colleagues here have their own genres.

While I was looking round M. Rosenberg's sanctum, an exhibition of art 'from cubism towards a plastic renaissance' was being arranged. Among work by Braque, Gleizes, Gris, Hayden and Herbin, Léger, Metzinger, Ozenfant, Picasso and Valmier, were examples of Mondrian's most recent period. A chance passer-by might smite his forehead, wondering who was out of his mind, himself or the artists. At a second glance he might think *he* was, rather like a man from Mars among earthlings. Despite their different approaches, the painters all speak roughly the same language. As the title of the exhibition implies, they are moving in the same direction. Broadly speaking, they have the same goal.

Their starting points are different and so, therefore, are the distances to their goal, which has one thing in common for all of them: it is vague and constantly receding.

Mondrian stands here alone; none of them achieves such tense abstraction. The difference between him and the rest is all but fundamental in the face of the nuances between the others. This work is so tense that it no longer seems to vibrate. Each picture differs from its neighbour in the size of the squares and the relationships of the colours. These are yellow, blue and rust-red, contrasted with creamy white. No other work displays such simplicity coupled with transparent colour. Does this mean the Mondrian is the most advanced...?

Development usually goes hand-in-hand with complexity. Evolution progresses spirally, rather than in accordance with Mondrian's logical construct. It sometimes returns to its starting point, apparently. Take Léger, for example: he is becoming comprehensible again, giving human and animal shape to his rounded and taut figures, which look as though they are made of wrought iron. In the work of the others, though, the beholder gropes vainly for something to get hold of. No help is forthcoming from the vague likenesses he discovers—newspaper cuttings, violin shapes. The uninitiated enjoys the symphonies of colour, but not in the way the artists intended.

By way of corroboration of the above opinions, finally, I quote a few passages from Mondrian's *Le Néo-Plasticisme* (Léonce Rosenberg, Paris). The beginning, translated from the French, goes like this:

Although art is partly the plastic expression of *our* aesthetic feelings, it does not follow that it is merely 'the aesthetic expression of our subjective perception'. Logic demands that art be the plastic expression of our entire being: hence that it express the plastic appearance of the non-individual so well that the total and annihilating opposite would be for the direct expression of the universal to dwell in us, meaning: the exact appearance of the universal outside us.

The universal, thus understood, is what *is* and remains, more or less unconsciously for us, as opposed to the more or less conscious being—the individual, repeating and renewing itself.

Our entire being is both the one and the other: the conscious and the unconscious, mobile and immobile, born and changing shape through their reciprocal effect.

That effect embodies all the misery and all the bliss of life: misery is caused by the constant division, bliss by the constant birth of change. Immobility surpasses all wretchedness and all happiness: that is equilibrium.

Because we are unchanging, we merge with everything; change destroys our equilibrium, restricts us, separates us from everything outside. Art emerges from this equilibrium, the unconscious, the immobile. It receives its plastic expression from consciousness. The phenomenon of art is hence the plastic expression of the unconscious and the conscious. It displays a common context: this changes, but art is unchangeable.

The writer goes on:

The new spirit destroys form; its aesthetic expression restricts and restores a corresponding phenomenon of the subjective and objective, of the surrounded and the surrounding: a balanced duality of the universal and the individual. This duality creates a purely aesthetic context.

The lack of balance between the individual and the universal creates tragedy and is expressed in tragic plasticity. Everything that exists is dominated by nature: this causes tragedy.

The tragedy of life leads to the creation of art: art, being abstract and the opposite of natural tangibility, heralds the gradual disappearance of tragedy. The more tragedy is reduced, the purer art becomes.

In the vital reality of the abstract, modern man has transcended feelings of nostalgia, joy, ecstasy, grief, horror etc.: through being steadily affected by beauty these are purified and deepened.

In painting, Neo-Impressionism, Pointillism and Divisionism have attempted to abolish the prevailing corporeality in plasticism by abandoning modelling and normal perspective. Not until Cubism, however, was this done systematically.

Truly abstract painting or Neo-Plasticism has shaken this off, being an essentially new plasticism.

The female and the material govern life and society and hamper the male tool of spiritual expression. A Futurist manifesto's proclamation of hate of the female is perfectly valid. The Woman in Man is the direct cause of the domination of tragedy in art. At the same time the new spirit renounces description in art. Now that the impediment of form has been abolished, the new art is purely plastic.

Every art form is currently trying to express its plastic means more directly and to make them as free as possible.

The three primary colours, red, yellow and blue, are still prismatic colours despite the distance between them in the prism, and despite Neo-Plasticism, in which their spectral qualities are not expressed.

The decorative arts do not exist in Neo-Plasticism: furniture, vases, etc., are a result of the simultaneous effect of modern architecture, sculpture and painting, and automatically obey the laws of Neo-Plasticism.

Dances like the tango and foxtrot impart something of the new idea of equilibrium caused by opposites.

Those are some of P. Mondrian's ideas.

Nieuwe Rotterdamsche Courant
Thursday March 23rd, 1922
Evening edition B

At Piet Mondrian's
The crystal-clear studio—an apology for the Charleston

(from our special correspondent)

Paris, September—In a squalid yard behind the clamour of the Gare Montparnasse, a dingy staircase leads to Piet Mondrian's door. What a contrast! No Thousand-and-One Nights here, opening up a treasure-filled cave to the poor camel-driver. Instead of riches, this lonely ascetic offers a dazzling purity, causing everything to be bathed in a pristine glow.

Van Dongen's sophisticated tango palace and Conrad Kikkert's old-style Dutch studio with its smell of paint both pale into insignificance beside this geometrically impeccable room with its dancing colours in which, relieved of all material burdens, one is absorbed into the all-highest. I well remember my chagrin, as a student of mathematics, at the my stuffily conventional lodgings. Here, though, the atmosphere is so snowy, the air so glacially pristine, that one almost automatically starts pondering on the origin and aim of one's existence. The interior evolves continuously. On my last visit the walls were filled with virginal primed canvases which combined to form one huge chequered painting. Now all the walls are rhythmically divided into horizontal and vertical rectangles, the balance magically preserved by the negative colours of white, grey, black, and the positive red, blue, yellow. The large mirror in whose depths one used to drown, has been divided by the magician into small sections which impart their matt sheen to the composition here and there. The brightly coloured cushions on the divan and the rectangular rugs on the floor also preach the principal doctrines of the neo-plastic gospel.*

On the easel is the artist's latest painting: a white square, tilted to stand on one of its corners, in which three or four horizontal and vertical lines cross to chop off little slices of yellow and blue—a patently more austere approach than the familiar red-blue-yellow mosaics.

The artistic conception of the wall, however, seems to render the canvas redundant, superfluous. I therefore ask Mondrian's views about the interrelation.

'There are no absolute differences for me, not like Léger, who makes a distinction between the easel painting as compressed inwardness, and the pleasing outward effect of the decorative wall. Just as my painting is an abstract surrogate for the whole, the abstract plastic wall is part of the profound content of the entire room. Instead of being superficially decorative, the whole wall conveys the impression of an objective, universal mentality, displayed in the strictest of stylistic forms.'

To those who have observed the evolution of his studio, it was obvious that the painter who called his first chequered composition 'Foxtrot', shaking off the last traces of subjectivism, would one day rise to monumental art. Mondrian is indeed occupied in designing interiors. While the German dancer Gret Palucca seeks tranquillity in her absolutely white salon with a single choice Mondrian panel, the artist has applied his principles to the entire plan for Frau Bienert's interior in Dresden. It would nonetheless be wrong to call it spatial art, for the abstract artist persists in seeing architecture as an intersection of planes which, due to the beholder's rapid visual and mental movements, are always seen from the front, thus not affecting the fundamental rectangularity.

Besides decorating walls, Mondrian is currently also painting scenery. The Belgian constructivist Seuphor has written a play entitled '*L'éphémère est éternel*', a 'critique théâtrale en trois actions et deux intermèdes avec chœurs et ballets', to be performed in November at the Théâtre du Donjon in Lyon and perhaps later in Brussels and Rome. Our compatriot has been invited to create a 'colour environment'.

Mondrian's scale model is most attractive. The rectangular stage has three screens which are raised successively to form the setting for the three acts. Not on earth, of course, but in eternity. The three well-balanced non-representational compositions mark off the extremely shallow stage. They demonstrate Mondrian's aversion to depth, which he regards as far too naturalistic. Is he not at the antipodes of present-day three-dimensional theatre?

'And the actors?'

'They are not my concern. They wear modern American dress. As far as I'm concerned they are unnecessary. If I had my way I'd put the actresses behind screens so that the audience wouldn't have to look at them and could just follow the text.'

'Why don't you give the actors geometrically patterned neo-plastic costumes?'

'But they'd still be moving around, whereas the neo-plastic idea is static.'

Aren't Mondrian's views rather like those of the Italian futurist, Prampolini, who banishes actors from the stage and has phonographs and loudspeakers blare out their parts?

Mondrian is wild about jazz and modern dance. I recently ran into him at the Jockey Club. Every time a tango dragged out its melancholy plaint, he would scorn its cloying sentimentality, only brightening up at the taut, steely, horizontally structured music of the jazz negroes. He is an ardent admirer of the Charleston.

'But don't you think it's frightfully physical and basely sensational?'

'Yes, the way Europeans dance it, it often looks hysterical. But negroes like Josephine Baker have an inborn, brilliantly controlled style. All modern dances look feeble against such powerfully maintained concentration of speed. Whatever can they be thinking of to ban this strenuous dance in Holland! After all, the couples keep their distance and dance so energetically that there's no time for any amorous ideas. If they go on forbidding the Charleston I shan't be coming back...'

Mondrian has fanatical supporters and no less violent antagonists.

In 'Vouloir', the highly talented sculptor Vantongerloo has just published a geometrical explanation of Mondrian's tiled tableaux. It is of course quite possible to see the focal points of certain compositions by inscribing and circumscribing the square. A much easier way than using formulae, however, is to cover Mondrian's canvas with a sheet of transparent paper on which all the bisectors of the square are drawn, in order to discover the key to the secret of his creations. It's as easy as winking, and surely a little far-fetched to compare Mondrian's conception with the secret numbers of Cheops' pyramid. If Vantongerloo's demonstration were really watertight and we could express all Mondrian's compositions in numbers, we might be tempted to believe in tricks. Furthermore, the writer completely ignores the colours, whose diminishing and augmenting optical properties interfere with the geometrical effect. It's impossible to express Mondrian's subtle intuition with sums like that.

This dangerous kind of defence is matched by an opponent's naivety.

Van Doesburg, that worthy manager of *De Stijl*, sailed in Mondrian's wake for many years before suddenly realizing that the horizontal and vertical (H.V.) were much too naturalistic, occurring as they do in physical, real and optical nature. Since human laws must always defy nature, the artist abandoned H.V. in favour of the Oblique, the Diagonal. His counter-compositions consist of normal verticals with a rectangular framework tilted at an angle of 45 degrees. If you tilt your head to one side to look at Mondrian's compositions of dots governed by the H.V. system, you see exactly the same effect, but how much more pure and sensitive! The counter-composition seems more like a bad joke played by an inveterate rebel than a new, revolutionary discovery.

And after all that, what is our opinion of Mondrian and Neo-Plasticism?

We sincerely admire the artist who employs the sparsest means to make such finely balanced creations, refusing to be deflected from his ideal by material or mental opposition. In this age of flaunted reputations this modest man who never blows his own trumpet is a splendid exception; is it not strange that almost 'malgré lui' some of his work has penetrated to the antipodes? Mondrian is one of the few Dutchmen with an International Reputation!**

But what about Neo-Plasticism?

This doctrine came at just the right moment, first as a continuation of cubism and when it seemed to be petering out, as an aid to modern architecture which, due to its starkly simplified rectangular concrete character, happened to be a suitable candidate. Our objection to the neo-plastic system, however, is that its foundations are entirely *a priori* and arbitrary. Seen in a certain way, the circle is just as basic as the straight line, and why the restriction to schematic yellow, blue and red? There is absolutely no case for allowing such a tightly dogmatic system to limit the interplay of colours and planes.

For one moment we thought we had discovered an element of natural weakness in Mondrian. In his studio we spied a 'round vase with a...flower'. We were about to point this out in triumph when the painter said apologetically:

'I needed something to symbolize feminine grace and charm. But take a good look: the flower is artificial, and what is more, I whitewashed the leaves in order to banish that impossibly naturalistic green from my interior.'

Is Mondrian, the hermit of the Rue du Départ, explorer of the furthest abstract limits, who only dances in order to experience 'the union of opposites', in danger of becoming the victim of the consequences which he has taken to such inhuman extremes?

* Everything in the studio is calculated to the last millimetre. When Mondrian was given a cylindrical teaset by Vantongerloo, he was in a most awkward position. The items could not possibly be left together. It took *two months* to distribute them evenly around the room, but what would happen if one of them broke?

** The extremely progressive Bauhaus in Weimar has acknowledged his achievements by publishing his most important essays in a fine volume.

De Telegraaf
Sunday September 12th, 1926

Catalogue:

Introduction

herbert henkels

The earliest extant drawings by Piet Mondrian are too few in number to afford a complete view of his technical development and talent at the age of eighteen. And yet drawing had been instilled in him almost in infancy. As soon as it was feasible, his father, early aware of the son's talent, quite naturally recruited his help in perfecting the pictures which Mondrian senior drew for political and religious purposes. Furthermore, ever since the middle of the nineteenth century, all art education had been based on the drawing method of the Frenchman Dupuis. The most important aspect of this method was that it dissuaded students from drawing as much detail as possible in their attempts at a "true-to-nature" rendering of natural objects, encouraging them to concentrate on the object's basic forms instead. Many examples in Dupuis' manual may thus be regarded as mechanistic-geometrical models. This kind of drawing has an identity of its own, and bears scant reference to a model from nature.

When he was about eighteen, Mondrian industriously set about studying for certificates which would qualify him to work as an independent teacher later. The Dupuis method was an excellent basis for his preparations, not least because teachers with these qualifications were entitled to teach technical draughtsmanship at training colleges for aspiring mechanics, bridge-constructors and engineers. Not one of the dozens of drawings which Mondrian must have made during his preparations for the examinations has been preserved.

This exhibition starts in fact with two drawings of an entirely different character. The "Woods with Stream" (cat.no.1) and "Girl Writing" (cat.no.2) clearly show that the young Mondrian had more and different models than those supplied by his father and a drawing method.

In his memoirs of the artist, his younger brother Carel tells of Mondrian's custom of borrowing portfolios of old master reproductions from Braet van Uberfeldt, an old drawing-teacher who lived in Doetinchem, not far from Winterswijk. It is quite likely that Mondrian's drawing talent benefited substantially from copying these reproductions. The "Woods with stream" has the air of an advanced example of a drawing copied from older painters. The drawing harks back to the Dutch landscape painters of about 1820-1830: the minute detail and "true-to-life" rendering of the pattern of the light through the trees evoke the atmosphere of a type of landscape popular at the turn of the century, the Koekkoek family being notable representatives of the genre. The "Girl writing" has a far more personal character. The beholder's viewpoint is roughly in the middle of the drawing, a well-chosen position for showing the folds of the dress in a mesh of hatching and shading, and for demonstrating the artist's skill in modelling the arm and head. A splendid example of the academic linear style which Mondrian was later to perfect at the Rijksakademie in Amsterdam, a style in which his teacher there, A. Allebé, was highly proficient.

The third work in this exhibition, "Hayrick" (cat.no.5) displays a third influence in Mondrian's early work: the work of the Hague School painters. This watercolour appears to have been particularly inspired by Jacob Maris. The painters of the Hague School had created a vogue for certain manners of laying down a composition—the depiction of illusion—which towards the end of the century lapsed into a stereotype pattern of composition and rendering of depth. The "Hayrick" bears a few characteristic traces of this. Two willows—at the left and right—provide a prospect of a hayrick which closes off the space. The two willows are used as the compositional device of the "repoussoir", which creates an impression of depth enhanced by the perspective of the stream with the idyllic ducks. The willow's boughs dominate the top half of the picture and provide a splendid opportunity for drawing minute detail.

A considerable period of time elapsed between these works and the next exhibits: roughly 6-8 years. What happened to Mondrian during this period, and how did he develop into what in 1898 could already be regarded as a mature artistic personality? In the first place Mondrian had attended the Rijksakademie in Amsterdam: little of the work he did there still exists. He also painted a few landscapes—a far cry from the tradition of the Hague School—still lifes, commissioned portraits and illustrations for books with a strongly Protestant air. Notably these illustrations, drawn in about 1894, give some idea of Mondrian's ability to depict the human figure in a variety of poses and to illustrate stories with a strong emotional import. Expressive force—dramatic chiaroscuro—appears to have been one of Mondrian's strong points. Commissions were certainly not uncommon during this period. A striking aspect Mondrian's case was his rigid separation of commissions from his other work. Quite a lot of other painters, once they had achieved success in a particular genre, never managed to find time for their own work.

The semicircular painting "Uw Woord is de Waarheid" (" Thy Word is Truth", 1894), which Mondrian painted at the request of and in collaboration with his father for the Christian school in Winterswijk, displays a certain skill in the painting and the fairly complicated composition. The painting was intended to hang high up on a wall, and Mondrian was obviously able to cope with the perspective distortions resulting from a low viewpoint. We notice strong colour contrasts for the first time: a striking aspect at the turn of the century. In about 1895 Mondrian left the Christian Reform Church milieu in Amsterdam in favour of the more typically artistic circles there.

The strength and identity of a series of works dating from about 1898—the so-called "Winterswijk group" and similar pictures of Amsterdam and the surrounding countryside—are such that they are immediately recognizable as typical "Mondrians".

Two pictures of the Winterswijk countryside— "Women with Child in front of a Farmhouse" (cat.no.10) and "At Work"(cat.no.9)—are an excellent illustration. The two women occupy the middle of the surface and are painted as if in close-up, like small portraits. Without the slightest illusion of depth, the facades of the barns close off the picture plane. This greatly enhances the tension between the almost geometrical division of the farmhouse and the human figures. The vivid orange-brown hue is evidence of Mondrian's intense involvement in the expressive value of composition, colour and brushwork, employed to invest the work with an identity of its own—separate from a naturalistic depiction—revealing signs of the "real" Mondrian as we know him today. There is a direct connection between this work and the watercolour "At Work": the strong purple hue dominating the entire work show that Mondrian was trying to add an extra dimension to the realism of a powerful depiction of nature in a landscape: an almost symbolic, metaphorical landscape of a different kind from what he had seen near Winterswijk. A few pictures of the environs of Amsterdam dating from about the same period, such as "House at Abcoude" (cat.no.7), have a similar character. There is a striking resemblance between the right-hand half of "At Work" and the foreground treatment of this work. The composition is again typically Mondrian-esque: the facade of the house is parallel to the surface of the picture and puts paid to any chance of experiencing an illusion of depth. Concentration is focussed all the more intently on the outlines and windows of the house. Only on the left does the simple compositional device of a canal convey an idea of "distance". The bushes on the left and the colours of the windows bear witness to Mondrian's sophisticated use of pictorial means in order to evoke an atmosphere of monumentalism. His "Landscape with a Canal" of a few years before—its style completely in the tradition of the Hague School—shows how radically he had changed in the intervening few years.

Generally speaking, Mondrian's affinity with the Hague School survived only in his manner of painting: rapid oil sketches. Some fifteen years later he described this in one of his articles for *De Stijl* review. "In the force of the first intuitive emotion, the studies and sketches of the naturalistic painters [i.e. the painters of the Hague School, hh] are often far more powerful and more beautiful than their paintings." (*De Stijl*, III, 1919, no. 2, p.19). But we also encounter in these oil sketches the characteristic traits which clearly show that Mondrian—quite unlike the Hague School—was in search of powerful expression. "Farmhouse with Clothesline"(cat.no.4) and "View of a Village" (cat.no.11) are such sketches: Mondrian sharply contrasts the brown-red earth colours with the white washing which runs across the surface in a compositional counter-rhythm. Due to his childhood in Winterswijk—a region of woodland and meadows—Mondrian was particularly fascinated by water and moored boats (cat.no.12). The earliest pages from his sketchbooks which have been preserved not only display a highly sophisticated drawing style but also—in the reflection of the water—a sophisticated sense of picture construction. It was probably a little later that the same theme was completed in the manner to which we are accustomed in Mondrian's work, in "The Weesperzijde: Evening" (cat.no.18): the heavy, prominent contours and balanced chiaroscuro bestow on what is basically a simple town view the dramatic expression which was later to develop into immense tension.

It is surprisingly difficult to link Mondrian's work with that of his contemporaries during this period. He appears to have concentrated exclusively on the progress of his own work, paying scant attention to prevailing trends. This is highlighted by his abortive efforts to win the "Prix de Rome". Mondrian wanted recognition of his own artistic merits, refusing to cater to current taste, a taste which we now call typically decadent, more akin to the vapid, meaningless, so-called erotic "pompier" art of the prevailing French milieu than to the new impulses which painting received from the work of the Impressionists, Neo-Impressionists and Symbolists.

In terms of style and composition there was little change in Mondrian's works of the first years of this century. They display the same features as the Winterswijk works. "Ditch near the Kalfje" (cat.no.16)—Het Kalfje is a village south of Amsterdam, just outside the city limits—is a textbook example of how Mondrian gave form to his vision of space: the willow runs vertically from the top edge of the picture to the bottom, with a very high horizon. The beholder's attention consequently focusses on the interaction of the planes of the canal and meadow. A similar composition occurs in a few other oil sketches of this period .

The great changes in Mondrian's work seem to have been sparked off by his stay in Brabant in the south Netherlands, far from the artistic circles of Amsterdam. Mondrian's talent for bold compositions based on a structure of lines and planes is demonstrated in "Farm at Nistelrode" (cat.no.20) A preliminary study shows the composition to be based on the relationship of a few large planes (cat.nos.20, 21). On the back of the drawing is one with a similar character, another farmhouse.The finished version of "The White Calf"(cat.no.25) plainly shows Mondrian's distance from the impressionist style of the Hague School painters. He was not playing with patches of light, but composing light and dark "planes" with the aim of achieving the utmost expression. The drawing, too, shows how far removed his intention was from the aims of the Hague School. The entire composition is based on the verticals formed by the willows and the marked horizontals of the wooden fence (cat.no.24). The importance of Mondrian's drawing style in this period is demonstrated by his drawing "Pollard Willows"(cat.no.17). The "Interior in Nistelrode" is further evidence of Mondrian's totally different points of departure. The subject-matter as such is one which some artists painted by the hundred, mainly for the foreign market, not only their theme but to an even greater extent their execution being highly stereotype. This kind of subject-matter was popular among painters because it permitted them to display their skill in depicting light falling through a window. There is none of that in this watercolour: the window does not give the beholder the impression that there is an "outside" at all. On the contrary: all the concentration is focussed on the figure. Even the empty chairs are charged with an emotion far exceeding that of an ordinary realistic depiction of a Brabant peasant interior.

Many of Mondrian's pictures of this period display something "dark" and "heavy" which is otherwise rare in his work. On the one hand we know from very direct sources that this year was extremely important for Mondrian in that he formulated his artistic points of departure then. Many researchers have wondered why so little of this artistic innovation is apparent in the works which he painted there. In my opinion the basis for seeking innovation was due less to any doubt on Mondrian's part as to his artistic expressive resources—he was completely confident about his gifts and talent as an artist—but rather to doubts about the basis and points of departure of the notion of art which he had pursued up to then. I do not believe that his search for a new orientation was confined to that one year in Brabant. What really happened in Brabant was the dawn of a totally new attitude, a continuous search for new possibilities of form, content and expression. It is no coincidence that Mondrian, in his autobiographical articles for *De Stijl* (Dialogue and Trialogue on Neo-Plasticism), took this Brabant period as the starting-point of his subsequent development. Of course this does not mean that a vast change suddenly took place in Mondrian's life and work during this period. We have already seen that his artistic personality started to emerge as early as 1898. From 'Brabant' onwards, it became clear that Mondrian was seeking contact with the latest artistic trends of his day.

1905 was a highly significant year, not only for Mondrian's development but in a wider sense for Dutch art history too. Work by Vincent van Gogh was displayed on a scale never since matched. More than four hundred and twenty pictures were exhibited in the Stedelijk Museum, Amsterdam, a show which did not fail to make its mark on several levels. In the first place Mrs. Kröller-Müller's plans for a modern art collection assumed more concrete shape, culminating ten years later in one of the finest Van Gogh collections; in the second place painters previously influenced by the latest Paris developments received fresh impulses. A second phase of Neo-Impressionism dawned in the Netherlands, and the Fauvist work of the Dutch Parisian expatriate Kees van Dongen prompted constant artistic discussion. If the first phase of Neo-Impressionism in the Netherlands can be characterized—in emulation of the French source of inspiration—as one in which paint was applied to canvas with almost scientific precision in minute specks of paint—"pointillés"—in a fairly stereotype composition, the second phase, which lasted roughly from 1905 to 1911, was characterized by the motoric action of painting with expressive force as the prime aim.

After 'Brabant' Mondrian pursued maximum expression more hotly than ever, but not as an end in itself. A work's expressive, emotional charge—rendered in an extreme use of pictorial means—cannot exist alone, but must be partnered by "content". Nowhere is the problem more apparent than in a group of works known as the "Evening and Night Landscapes". Mondrian spent the period from the autumn of 1906 until at least the summer of 1907 with his young painter-friend Hulshoff Pol at the latter's family farm in the village of Saasveld in the east Netherlands. Not far from Winterswijk, this was a region in which Mondrian and his uncle Frits may well have worked in the past. Titles such as "Evening Landscape" or "Landscape at Sunset" also occur in the work of Hague School painters such as Théophile de Bock and Frits Mondrian himself. These works, however, obviously aimed at effects quite different from Mondrian's. They were concerned with depicting light-effects, whereas Mondrian's intention was again to charge a realistic landscape with meaning, with a "mood" transcending what was depicted. For the first time we observe Mondrian's consistent attempts in a large number of works to form and develop new pictorial means. "Landscape" (cat.no.45), "Farmhouse at Evening" (cat.no.46) and "Landscape" (cat.no.47) plainly show a new aspect: extremely direct brushwork in the turbulent clouds and dramatic lighting. Sometimes, as in "Farm in the Evening" (cat.no.42), the dramatic effect of natural light is enhanced by the contrast from the glinting window. At other times Mondrian was intent on emphasizing the outlines of farmhouses or trees, allowing the details to blur (cat.nos.33, 34). In a fairly "finished" painting like "Summer Night", everything is concentrated on the evocation of an ethereal, immaterial mood without demanding attention for brushwork or violent drama. The status of this work is definitely different from that of the aforementioned "sketches": it was very likely intended for sale. "The Amstel: Haze" occupies an intermediate position: on the one hand it is quite small; on the other hand the balanced composition is executed in fairly restrained brush-strokes. The composition is moreover highly characteristic: the surface is divided horizontally into two sections. There is no longer any question of an illusionistic space: the tension of the surface stretches from the top half to the bottom half of the picture plane. This was a problem which Mondrian was to tackle in a number of later works, such as "Trees on the Gein" (cat.no.52). The focus of the composition, the construction of the picture, is often on the right-hand side of these works, frequently in the form of dominating groups of trees as in "Sheepfold in the Evening" (cat.no.32), in which the combination of detail and a strongly linear character suggests that this was another work intended for sale. In a few drawings we can see that Mondrian examined the possibilities of a more symmetrical construction very carefully (cat.nos.28, 48). The focus is noticeably on the centre of the composition, the edges of the picture plane being less distinct (cat.no.28).

Such drawings—and also the "Landscape with Trees" (cat.no.29)—show signs, albeit extremely tentative ones, that the act of drawing and hence the status of the drawing was beginning to acquire a different and more autonomous meaning. We must be extremely careful, especially with regard to Mondrian's work after 1905, about the status we consciously or unconsciously assign to a work. It is vital to realize that this was a period in which the nineteenth-century tradition of executing a number of preliminary studies in a variety of techniques (pencil or oils) so as to arrive at the final result by way of a number of stages, was abandoned and the distinctions became less clear.

Whereas prior to this it was possible to indicate a work's status in the entire process of creation with a fair degree of certainty, from about 1890 the distinctions started to become very vague. This was mainly due to both art criticism and the art trade. Take the example of the rising demand for pictures with a Hague School character, which prompted artists like Frits Mondriaan to become fairly quickly convinced that it was worth their while to offer oil sketches, quite large amounts of them, for sale. These sketches were no longer made in preparation for a large, finished canvas but had acquired a status of their own. In Mondrian's work this problem remained in evidence until about 1920. On the one hand works previously only classified as studies acquired greater autonomy; on the other hand the artist continued to feel a need to achieve a cohesive, finished painting. In terms of everyday practice this created tension between painting outdoors and finishing and/or revising a work in the studio on the one hand, and purely studio work on the other, the studio being where the actual creative process takes place. It goes without saying that art-historical investigation must take good note of the mutual relationships of works and of the shifts that occur in those relationships, if statements are to made about the genesis of a work, or in a broader context about the problems which preoccupied the artist.

One of the criteria for establishing a work's status is its size. It is striking that after 1905 the dimensions of many pictures increased, some of them even acquiring monumental character. "Pond near Saasveld" (cat.no.36) is one of the best demonstrations of the above problem. It is a very large picture, even according to the standards of the Hague School, whose painters tended not to cut corners in matters of size. The pond at Saasveld is a very secluded spot with an intimate character; it has the form of a figure-8, with dense vegetation on the banks, bordered by clumps of trees. All this distinguishes it from the surrounding, gently sloping countryside. Mondrian blows it up into almost monumental proportions. The groups of high trees on the left continue in a gradually descending line towards the right. In order to prevent the eye wandering off into empty space, Mondrian resolutely cuts off the right-hand side by means of a single tree with a powerfully vertical effect. The whole painting conveys an impression—due to the exceedingly balanced, restrained composition and fairly regular transitions between light and dark—of being painted as a "summary", a compilation of countless studies. A highly striking aspect of the "Large Landscape" (cat.no.50)—surely related to the "Pond at Saasveld"—and "Red Cloud" (cat.no.49) is the quite different use of colour. In previous works—all belonging to the group of "evening and night landscapes"—Mondrian had opted chiefly for moments of transition from day to night which were closer to night, when the moon, either plainly visible or shrouded in clouds, had already attained its full brightness. These last two works still belong to the "evening and night landscapes" but, and this is the essential difference, Mondrian chose a different point in time; not the moment at which night is already established but the time at which it is first apparent that day is over and light acquires a different meaning. No matter how tempting it is to see in these two pictures the first signs of "unnatural" colours, i.e. colours not derived from the observation of nature, such is not the case. Here Mondrian's colours are still directly derived from a very intense observation of nature. He has switched the time of his observation to the moment just before or exactly at sunset, a change he experienced during his stay in Saasveld and the local countryside. Nowhere else in the Netherlands are such special light reflexes of the setting sun to be seen. These two works—and also the "Mill in the Evening" (cat.no.51)—still belong to the "evening and night landscapes", and in fact conclude it. The "evening landscape" theme was however by no means at an end for Mondrian. Quite the contrary!

A number of questions automatically come to mind as to what might have prompted Mondrian's decisions. His decision to paint sunsets—a shift of a few hours compared with his observations of nature as depicted in the night landscapes—resulted in an entirely different palette. The work of other artists which he might have seen at exhibitions in Amsterdam—including that of the Swiss painter Ferdinand Hodler—may have opened his eyes to the new possibilities. It is in any case certain—and this seems to me to be the essence of the changes that took place in his work—that Mondrian's notion of the relationship between man and nature assumed more distinct shape. The interest he had had in esoteric religions since about 1898 now appeared to have developed into the fundament of his ideas and work. Three "Self Portraits" (cat.nos.54, 55, 56) express his ideas. The strong emphasis on the eyes clearly shows that Mondrian was trying to say something about a world which remains hidden: the "innermost" soul is indissolubly linked with the "outside" visible world. The eyes symbolize the tangent of "inside" and "outside". The colours and brushwork in the "Portrait of a Girl" (cat.no.53) and "Zeeland Farmer" (cat.no.63) symbolize the unity of this duality. In the "Portrait of a Girl" (cat.no.15) Mondrian had already combined the portrait—again emphasizing the eyes—with flowers, in this case early spring flowers, symbolizing the budding life of the sitter. In "Art Nouveau"—from posters to furniture and architecture—the combination of females and flowers was a frequent cliché. Mondrian destroyed this cliché, adding an extra dimension to portrait art. Whereas such portraits placed "women", people, in a particular relationship to organic nature, Mondrian's pictures with flowers are striking for their quasi-anthropomorphic character. The composition of the "Sunflowers" (cat.nos.97, 98) is practically identical to that of the "Chrysanthemums" (cat.nos. 99, 100, 102, 103, 104): the beholder's eye is swiftly guided over the surface towards the top left-hand corner. This creates a strong focus on the flower. The rapid brushwork of the "Sunflowers"—just past their prime, but only just beginning to fade—directly expresses the brief moment of flowering and fading. The "Chrysanthemums" impress with their particularly fine drawing, which has much in common with late nineteenth-century Japanese prints. In "Dying Chrysanthemum" (cat.no.101) the anthropomorphic character of Mondrian's "flowers" emerges most distinctly. The "Chrysanthemum" is no longer in full bloom but in an advanced state of decay. It is completely deformed, and it is quite easy to discern a human skull in it. "Tiger Lily" (cat.no.106) and especially "Lily" (cat.no.111) depict the moment of full bloom and radiance. The connection between the symbols of "eyes", "flowers" and a human figure/woman is expressed for the last time in this form in the "Evolution Triptych". From Mondrian's first trip to Domburg on the island of Walcheren in the south Netherlands in the summer of 1908 until his last visit in the summer of 1914, he was especially inspired by tower-structures—lighthouses and spires—, dunes and seascapes. His methods appear fairly traditional; preliminary studies exist of the lighthouse and church (cat.nos.73, 74). Both drawings are minutely detailed graphic notes with immense attention to detail. There is none of that in the painted versions (cat.nos.76, 66, 67, 68, 57): this is Mondrian painting full steam ahead! Sometimes with broad, long strokes, sometimes in extremely fine "pointillés"; sometimes with strongly contrasting colours, sometimes with extremely fine gradations of pink and blue (cat.no.66).

The pronounced verticality of the composition is sometimes reflected in the upright format of the entire canvas (cat.no.75). The "Dunes" and "Seas" (cat.nos.64, 65, 70, 69, 71, 76) are a direct continuation, really. Mondrian situates the contour of the dunes quite high in the picture plane, so that attention is focussed on the dappled sunlight on the sand in the hollows and slopes of the dunes. In contrast to the ostentatious treatment of the "tower" and "facade" subjects, the dunes and seas are almost amorphous. The "seas" are painted at the moment—and there we have the theme again—at which the sun has just set and the light, broken up into several colours, plays on the sky, the sea and the shore. The consequence of this atmospherical depiction of the natural phenomenon for the composition is an almost totally indistinct transition between water/land and sky.

1910 marked a turning-point in the history of Dutch art. The motors of the manifest changes in the ensuing years were a number of artists who had been closely observing recent developments in art in Paris. Together with Jan Sluyters and Cornelis Spoor, Mondrian concluded a period with the Stedelijk Museum exhibition, a retrospective of his work of the previous ten years. He now turned his back on the traditional artistic circles which he had frequented, and joined the "Paris group". Kikkert and Lodewijk Schelfhout—the one long since a commuter between Holland and Paris, the other an established Parisian who worked in the direct circle of Matisse and later in what was known as the "Montparnasse group"—helped to found the "Moderne Kunstkring", or Modern Art Circle whose aim, in emulation of the Paris *Salon d'Automne*, was to organize exhibitions and manifestations devoted exclusively to the latest developments in primarily the Parisian avant-garde. Shortly after the first public appearance of this group in 1911 the Dutch were able to observe the most recent products of Futurism and Expressionism. The group was fairly solid until about 1915, after which it finally split up; the crucible period was over and each went his own way: some following the trail of Expressionism (like J. van Heemskerck), others pursuing more traditional paths (Kikkert, Schelfhout). Mondrian struck out in his own direction.

One is frequently inclined to assess Mondrian's encounter with Cubism as the start of a development which automatically led to his abstract work. From the above it will have become clear that Mondrian's artistic personality is marked by a strong degree of continuity. At no single moment in his development can an important rupture and the start of an entirely new period be designated. The state of ferment in which Mondrian already was, received an extra impulse from the reception of Cézanne's work and of Cubism. It is this very tension between continuity and innovation—a constant interaction with perpetually shifting relationships—that inspired Mondrian to such astounding and totally individual results. One of the loveliest examples is the "tree" or "trees" theme. Trees had already played an important—and often metaphorical—role in his work of about 1898 (the Winterswijk period). The tension between trees/organic nature and buildings/human culture was often significant. Around 1908 the tree theme was given a tremendous metaphorical and expressive boost (cat.nos.60, 59), and in fact occupied a major part of Mondrian's output between 1911 and 1914. Incidentally, the "tree" theme featured prominently in the work of several artists in the so-called "Domburg-Paris" circle, particularly because of its symbolism. One should bear in mind that this symbolic meaning was one of Mondrian's reasons for his frequent and intensive treatment of the theme.

It has already been pointed out that the relationship between drawing and painting, each with its own individual status, is sometimes very traditional, the drawing being one of the many preliminary studies for a painting; during this period that distinct demarcation started to fade. Some drawings (cat.nos.82, 86, 92) grew extremely large, acquiring an individual status through such monumentalism. On the other hand we cannot fail to notice the predominantly "drawing" character of some of the painted trees (cat.nos.87, 88). The composition of these last two versions is markedly vertical: the beholder's eye is swiftly guided to the tree's crown. The character of linear drawing, coupled with an extremely restrained use of colour—reduced to ochres, greys and browns—is typical of early Cubist works (cat.nos.77, 78,79, 81). The dark, almost monochrome palette is characteristic of the work of Picasso and Braque from 1908 to 1911, but also of Le Fauconnier during that same period. Mondrian deliberately exploited it as a means of spreading a markedly linear structure over the entire picture plane. This is particularly evident on comparison of "Still Life with Gingerpot I" (cat.no.80), with its painterly, expressive brush-strokes, and "Still Life with Gingerpot II" (cat.no.81) in which the said aspects of "Gingerpot I" are barely visible, the whole surface being dominated by the strongly linear contours. The same problem is encountered on comparison of the "Grey Tree" (cat.no.84) and the "Flowering Apple Tree" (cat.no.85): the paint is treated in an expressive, motoric fashion in the former, the latter displaying a powerful urge towards simplification of the contours in order to achieve greater expression of the tensions within the actual linear pattern. Mondrian, energetically painting, wiping lines away, or half away, emphasizing others, the result being almost two structural layers—hardly any distance apart. It is fascinating to the beholder to trace these semi-visible lines. One no longer asks: "Is the picture finished or not?", but follows the movements of the lines in a force-field of expression.

Mondrian's acquaintance with the analytical Cubism of Picasso and Braque is not digested in his work in the manner one might expect. There is practically no far-reaching fragmentation of the subject-matter. In the "Oval Composition" (cat.no.91) and the related painting "Composition no.3" (cat.no.90) the pattern of lines is more angular and hence further removed from the subject, especially in the top half of the work. The linear structure pervades the entire surface, however, not one part having a function separate from the rest. The "tree" theme came to an abrupt end in 1913: Mondrian abandoned the subject, never again using it either directly or indirectly as the basis for a picture. One naturally wonders what his reasons were. One of the most important is undoubtedly that if the subject of the "tree"—a long-cherished vehicle for so many meanings— is still used as the starting-point of a composition—as Mondrian obviously did—it can never result in pictorial organization with a contradictory structure. In other words: the structure of a tree is hierarchical, subordinating; the structure of branches cannot be seen in pictorial terms as separate from the rest of the tree or, in other words, the organically developed structure of a tree still basically defines the structure of the surface. Over the next few years Mondrian's themes were marked by two kinds of subject-matter: on the one hand the "seascapes"—a process similar to that of the period from 1908 to 1910, when the almost amorphous dune and seascapes brought about intent concentration on the formal plastic means, and "facades" whose architectural proportions in the detail caused the plastic structure and the structure already inherent in the architecture to move closer together. I must stress most emphatically that in Mondrian's work the tension between plastic structure and seen or experienced reality is always present, both then and later continuing to form the basis of his work.

In "Sea (Starry Sky above the Sea)" (cat.no.95) the point of departure is still plainly recognizable, especially in the lower half of the work; the top half clearly shows the artist's endeavour to achieve a structure emerging more from the organization of the surface. In the "Church at Domburg" (cat.no.94) the artist had less need to act organizationally, since the architecture was organized already! In "Composition no.6" (cat.n.93)—again based on a facade—we see how he builds up the tension between the structure of the architecture and the structure of the surface to a terrific extent. Neither the one—visible reality—nor the other—the intuitively experienced basic structure—predominates. The tension between 'symbol' and 'structure' appears to have reached a climax here.

Certainly from 1911 on, Mondrian gave some thought to the future direction of his art by writing brief statements about the character of the reality he was seeking. The sketchbooks from this period which have been preserved show that drawing—an artistic occupation—and writing were somehow related: the text occasionally runs over a drawing, or the drawing overlaps the text. In about 1915 Mondrian had finished his 'book', as he himself called it. When Theo van Doesburg contacted him about establishing a new avant-garde art review a little later, he had enough copy to fill the next few volumes. From the first issue of *De Stijl* in October 1917 until the last volume, in 1920, Mondrian's articles occupied a major part of the revolutionary magazine. In the first series of instalments Mondrian expounded his theories on Neo-

Plasticism. He then embarked on a series partly intended to popularize this rather 'indigestible fare', and partly intended to report on the latest developments in his painting. The two were so closely linked that he once wrote to Van Doesburg: "Today I looked at my work and was so struck by its lucidity that I wrote another article." (ca. 1919). The organization which preoccupied Mondrian in his latest work was still the toughest task he had ever set himself. His "Composition no.3 with Colour Planes" 1917 (cat.no.112) was one such step towards greater clarity: an investigation of the plastic expression of coloured fields of varying intensity and size, as well as in relation to the so-called 'ground'. The impressive self-portrait (cat.no.96) has a similar composition in the background. It seems as if Mondrian is appealing to the beholder to join him in judging the expressive results of his work. No doubt the verdict was that the compositions were too 'fanciful', i.e. that the artist did not yet have sufficient control of the expression and that there was still too much unclarity in the composition as a whole, for instance the relation of the composition to the edges. In the years that followed a whole series of works were based on a regular grid, usually divided into squares of eight fields or double that number. However, Mondrian abandoned this too, not being interested in symmetrical compositions but in fact with the 'balance of opposites' which is created in the beholder's eye and nowhere else!

Two compositions of 1921 (cat.nos. 113, 114) afford an opportunity to admire Mondrian's complete mastery of balance. In both the small picture—almost an icon—and the majestic composition with red, yellow and blue, the expression of each part is in balance with the whole. The eye only experiences the expression of the individual parts in the context of the expression of all the others; no single part can function separately without forfeiting the clarity of the entire composition. This clarity of the whole and the balance of the parts—without resulting in a static division of the surface—exerted an enormous attraction on countless architects and planners of Mondrian's day. The work of the twenties may be termed lucid and clear, whereas the work of the thirties is regarded as complicated. Practically all the work of the last ten or twelve years of his life have a majestic, monumental character. Surprisingly, Mondrian started giving them titles again. The titles either refer to a dance (Foxtrot A, 1930) or a city or city district (Place de la Concorde, for example). There is no separating Mondrian's work from where he was, both geographically and socially: the artistic circles he frequented and the discussions conducted there had a direct bearing on his work. He himself frequently referred to this on various occasions, the last of which was in 1943: "Where you live, you belong to it, and when you feel a place is the nearest to you, you should become a part of it."

The social developments of the thirties in Europe were not very promising: totalitarian social and intellectual systems were about to destroy all free, democratic expression. The artistic equivalent of Mondrian's ideas about society, which he started to record in an essay called "L'Art et la Vie" that he worked on for several years without publishing it, is encountered in his works in the form of double 'lines'. This is obviously an inadequate description of a picture which is experienced as highly complex at a first glance. The beholder's eye swiftly scans the white/grey and black parts of the canvas, constantly creating and destroying relationships. The expressive intensity of these pictures is enhanced by the frequently single area of colour. The term 'clarification' is still relevant—to a greater extent in fact—when we realize how unpredictable and complicated all expressions of life appeared to be—particularly in the thirties. The "Composition with Blue" of 1937 (cat.no.115) and the related work in Ottawa are full-blooded examples. The plastic rhythm pervades the entire surface in strong cadence. From 1938/39 on, the surface of Mondrian's pictures grew increasingly complex. In the "Composition with Yellow Lines" of 1932 (Haags Gemeentemuseum), he only used coloured lines/bands. From 1938/39 more coloured areas occur. The rhythm of the coloured area/bands climaxed in Mondrian's last finished work: "Broadway Boogie-Woogie" (1943, Museum of Modern Art, New York). The title of this last work conveys that Mondrian's works are the genuine plastic expression of the pulsing vitality of Life.

Catalogue:

Illustrations

The data for the works are arranged in the order of 1) catalogue number, 2) title, 3) year of execution, 4) medium, 5) dimensions (The height precedes the the width), 6) inventory number of the Haags Gemeentemuseum, 7) Blok number, 8) Seuphor number

Abbreviations:
Blok: Cor Blok, *Piet Mondriaan: Een catalogus van zijn werk in Nederlands openbaar bezit*, Amsterdam, 1974
Seuphor, c.c.: Michel Seuphor, *Piet Mondrian, life and work*, Amsterdam, New York, Cologne, 1956

Some catalogue numbers have a quotation. These quotations are selected from an autobiographical essay by Piet Mondrian, 'Dialogue and Trialogue on Neo-Plasticism', published in *De Stijl* 1918-1920.

A: a singer, B: a painter

X: a naturalistic painter, Y: an art-lover,
Z: an abstract-realist painter

Complete text in: Holtzman/James, ed., *Piet Mondrian. The New Art-The New Life*, Boston, 1986

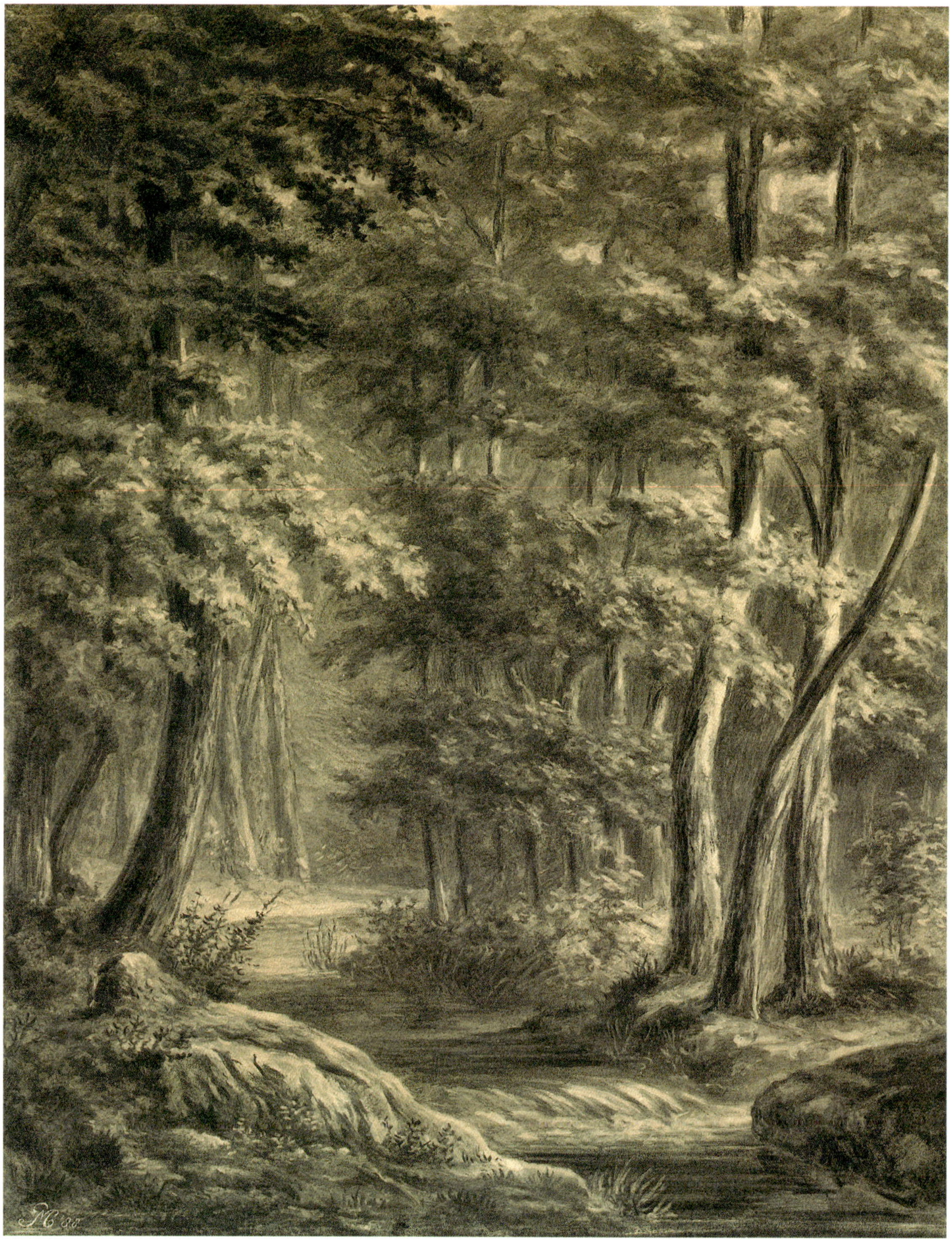

1

Woods with Stream

1888
charcoal/crayon/paper
60.3 × 45.4 cm

inv.no.T54-1971
Blok 1

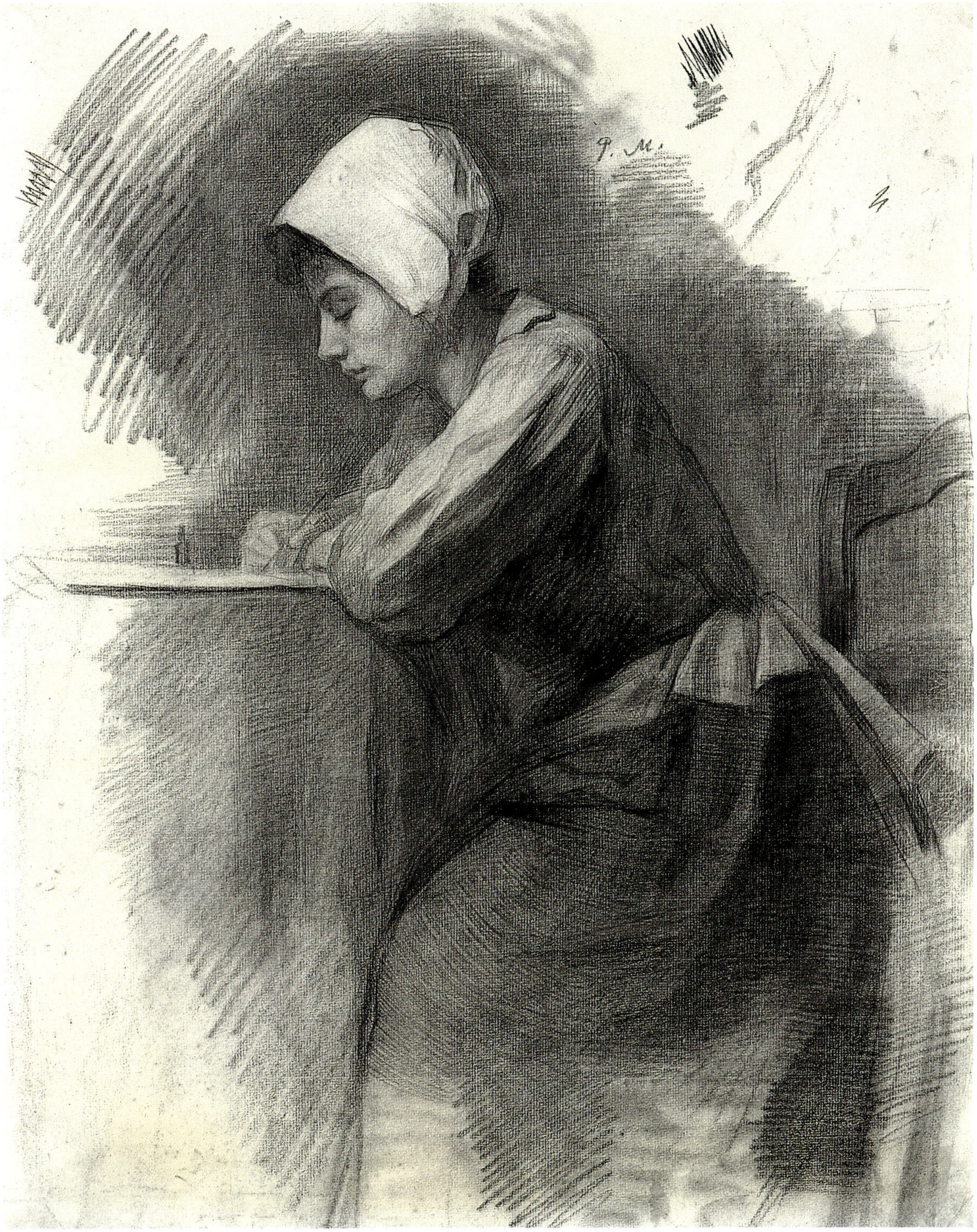

2

Girl Writing

ca.1890
black crayon/paper
57 × 44.5 cm

inv.no.T37-1942
Blok 2
Seuphor 11

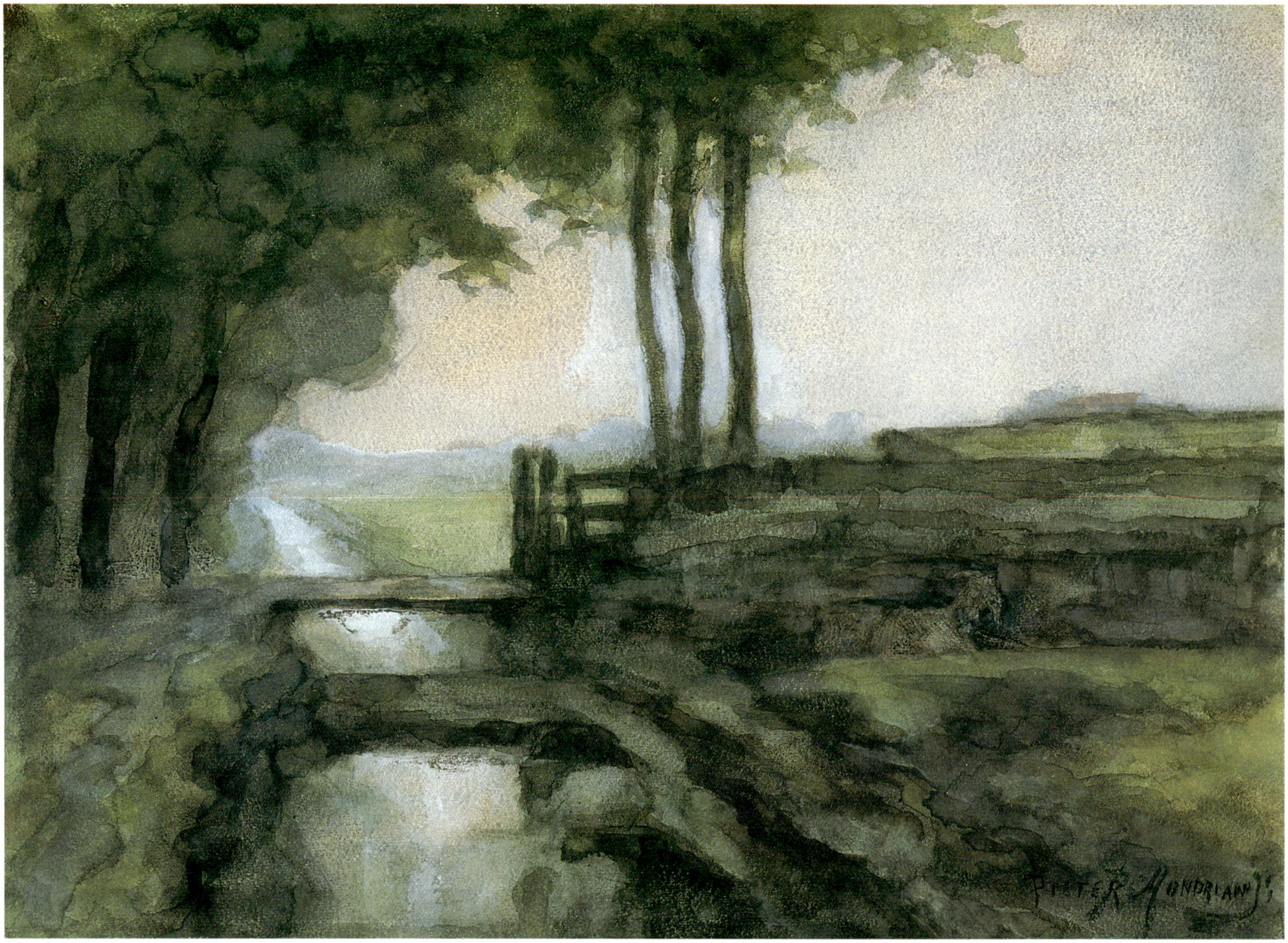

3

Landscape with a Ditch

ca. 1895
watercolour/paper
49 × 66 cm

inv.no. T71-1962
Blok 8

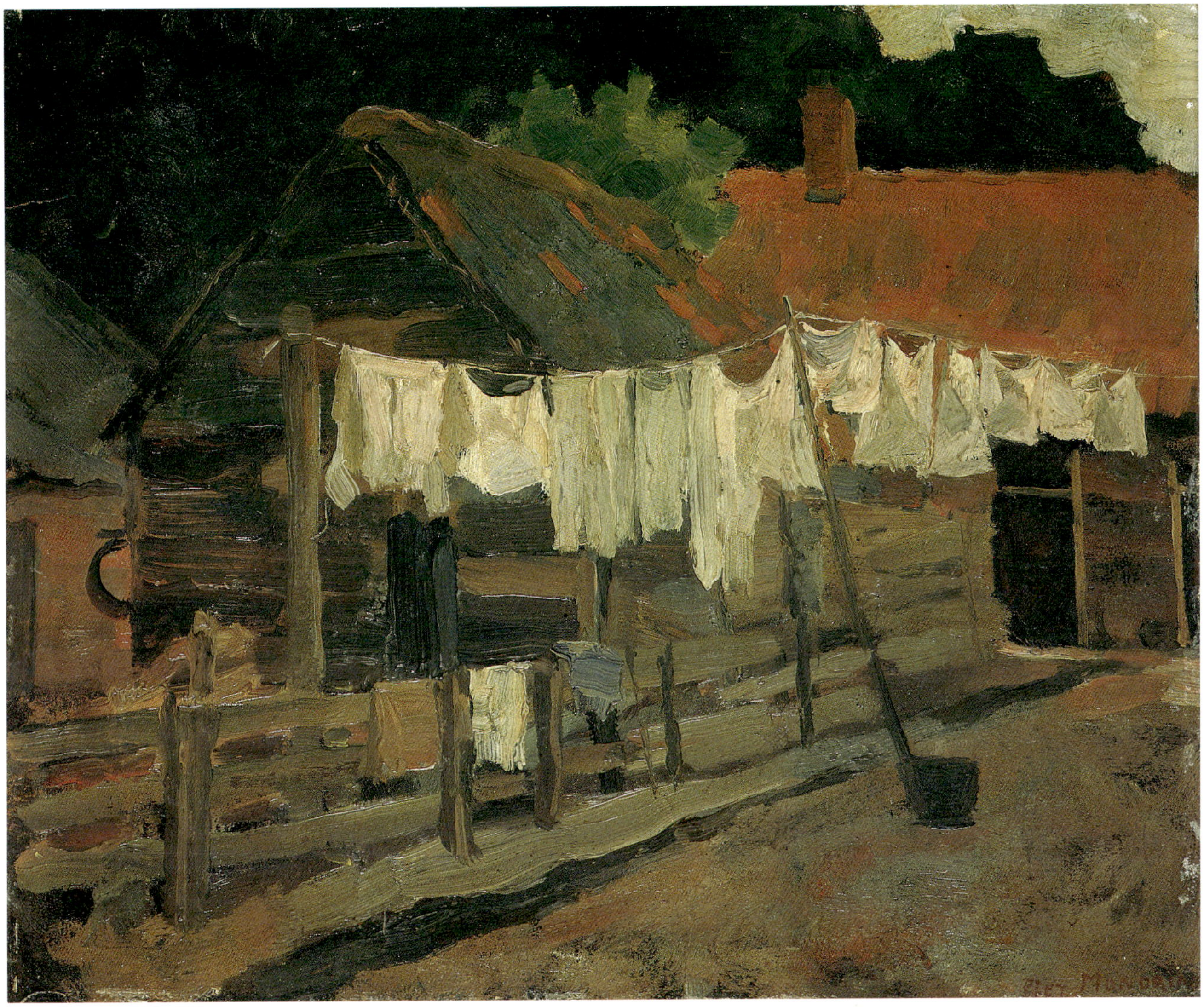

4
Farmhouse with Clothesline

1895
oil/cardboard
31.5 × 37.5 cm

inv.no.27-1960
Blok 11

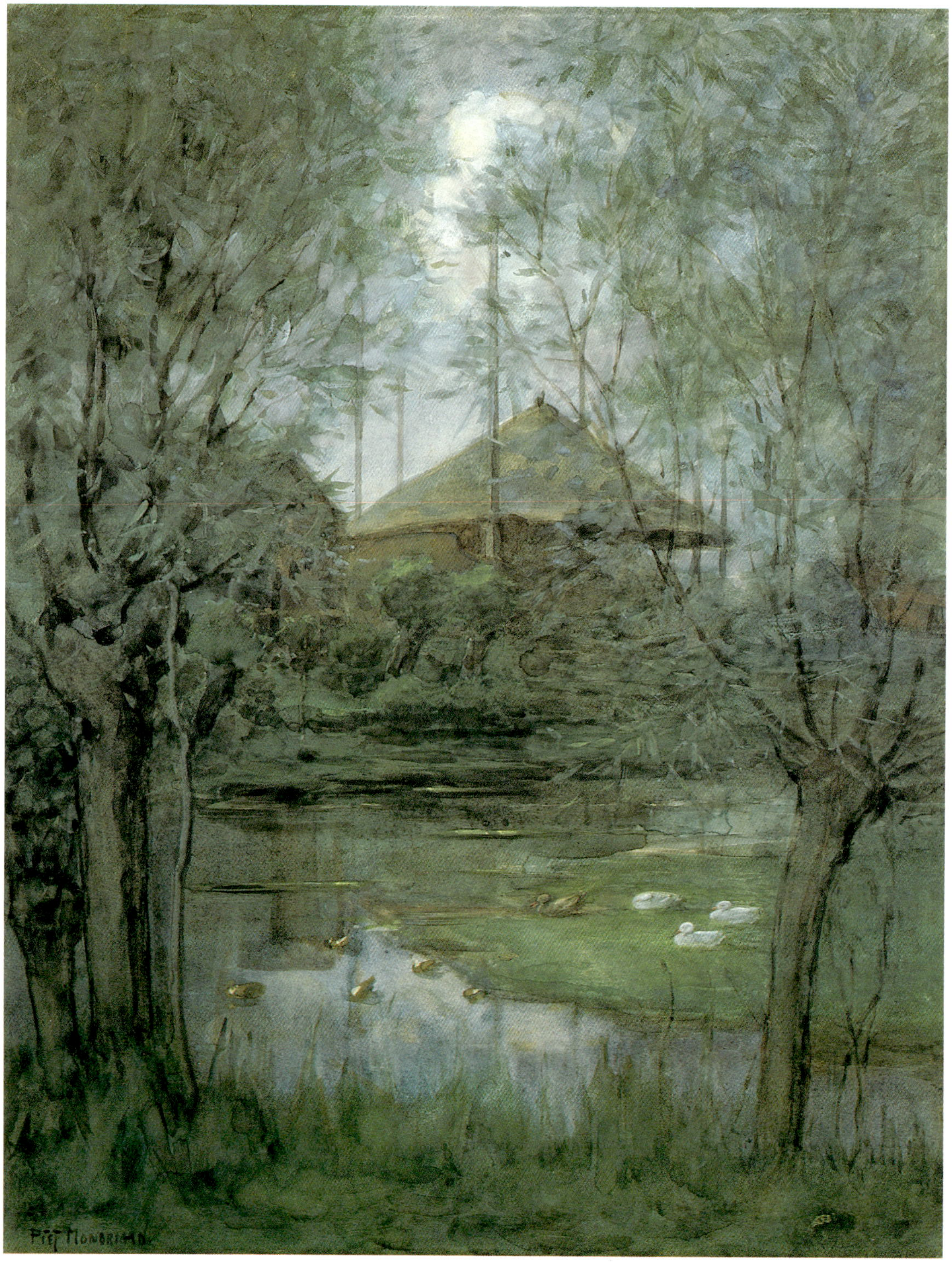

5

Hayrick

1897/98
watercolour/paper
64 × 47 cm

inv.no.T78-1962
Blok 12
Seuphor 9, c.c.36

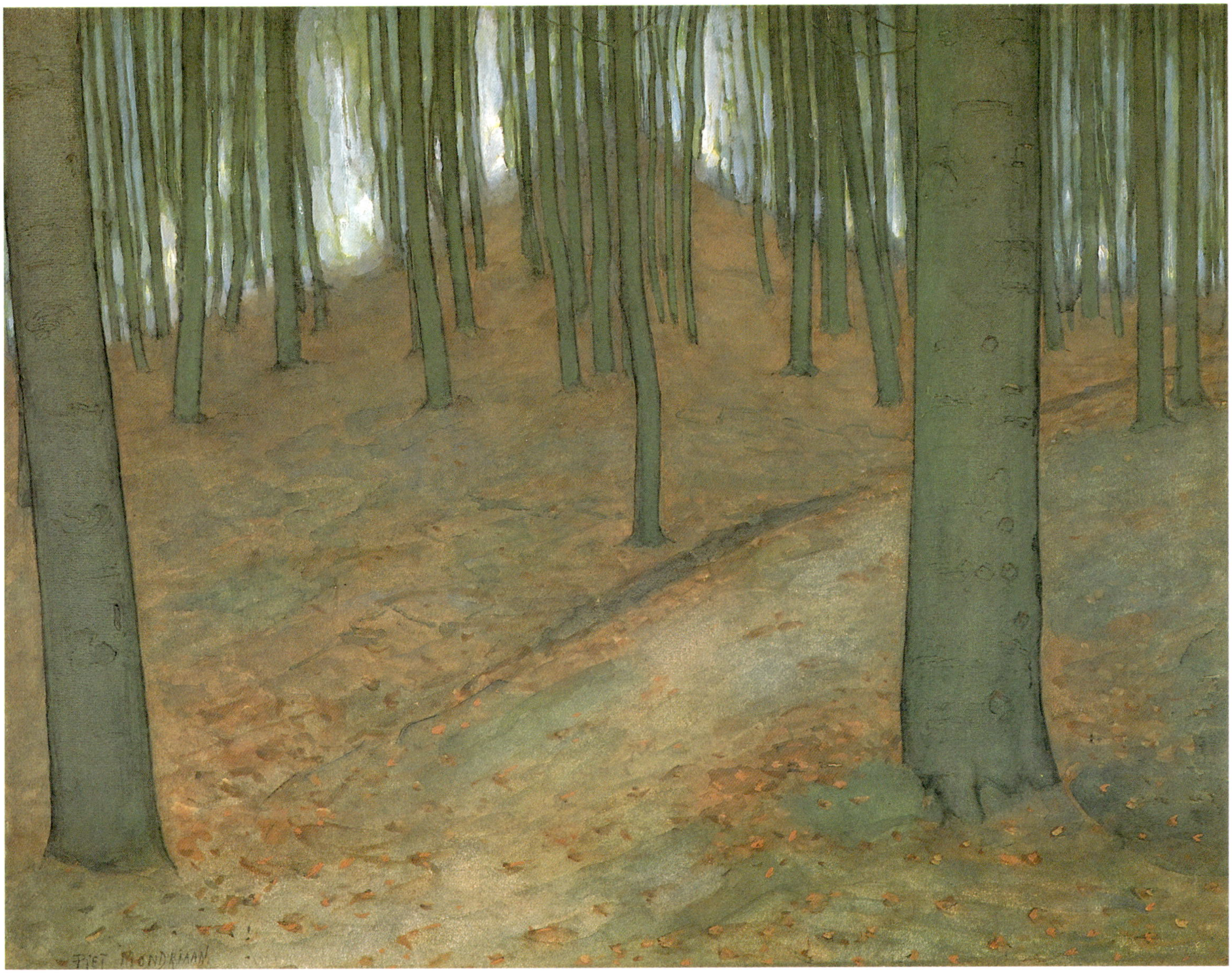

6

Forest

1898/1900
watercolour/gouache/paper
45.3 × 56.7 cm

inv.no.T58-1971
Blok 13
Seuphor 64, c.c.61

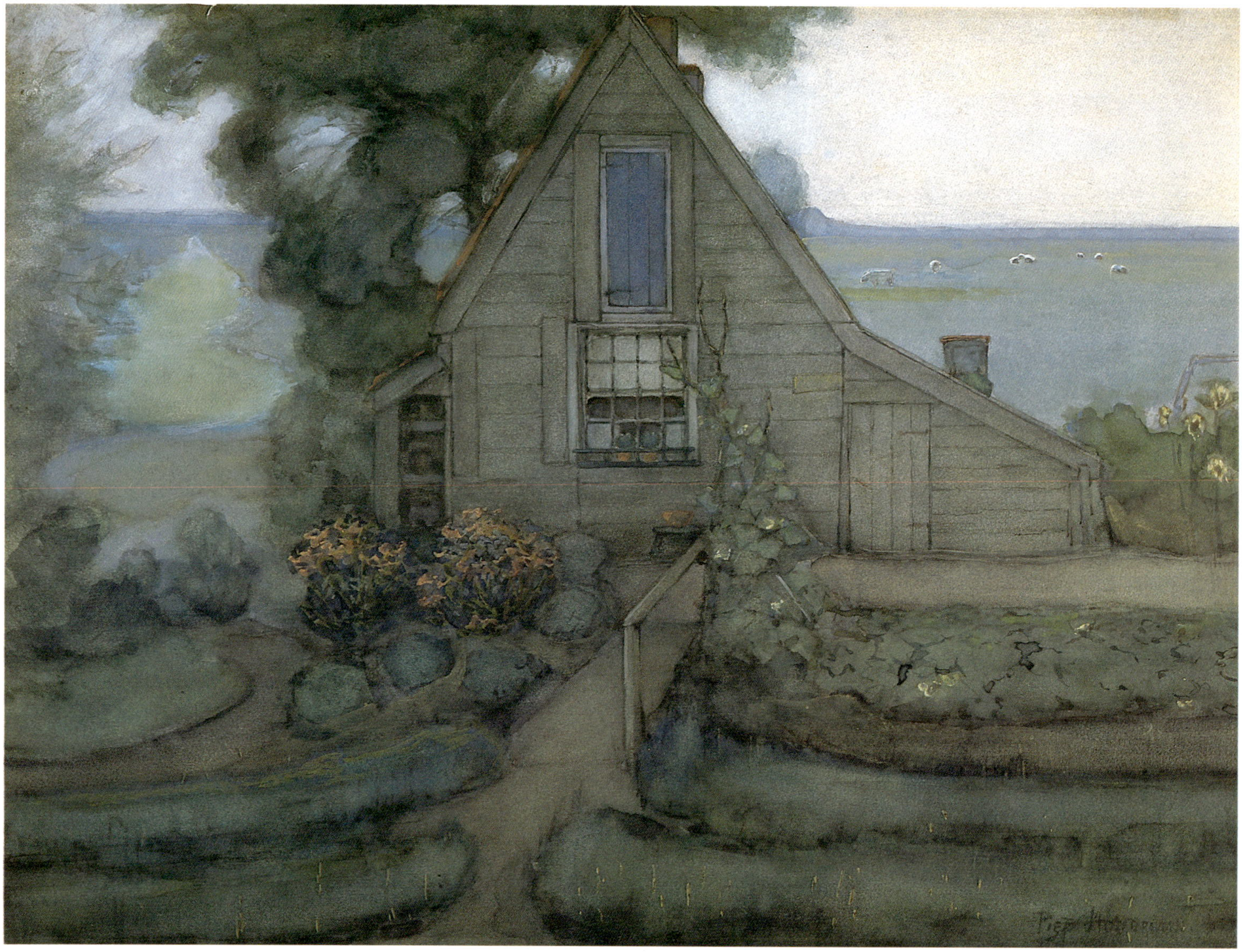

7

House at Abcoude

1898/1900
watercolour/gouache/paper
45.5 × 58.5 cm

inv.no.T55-1971
Blok 14
Seuphor 176, c.c.98

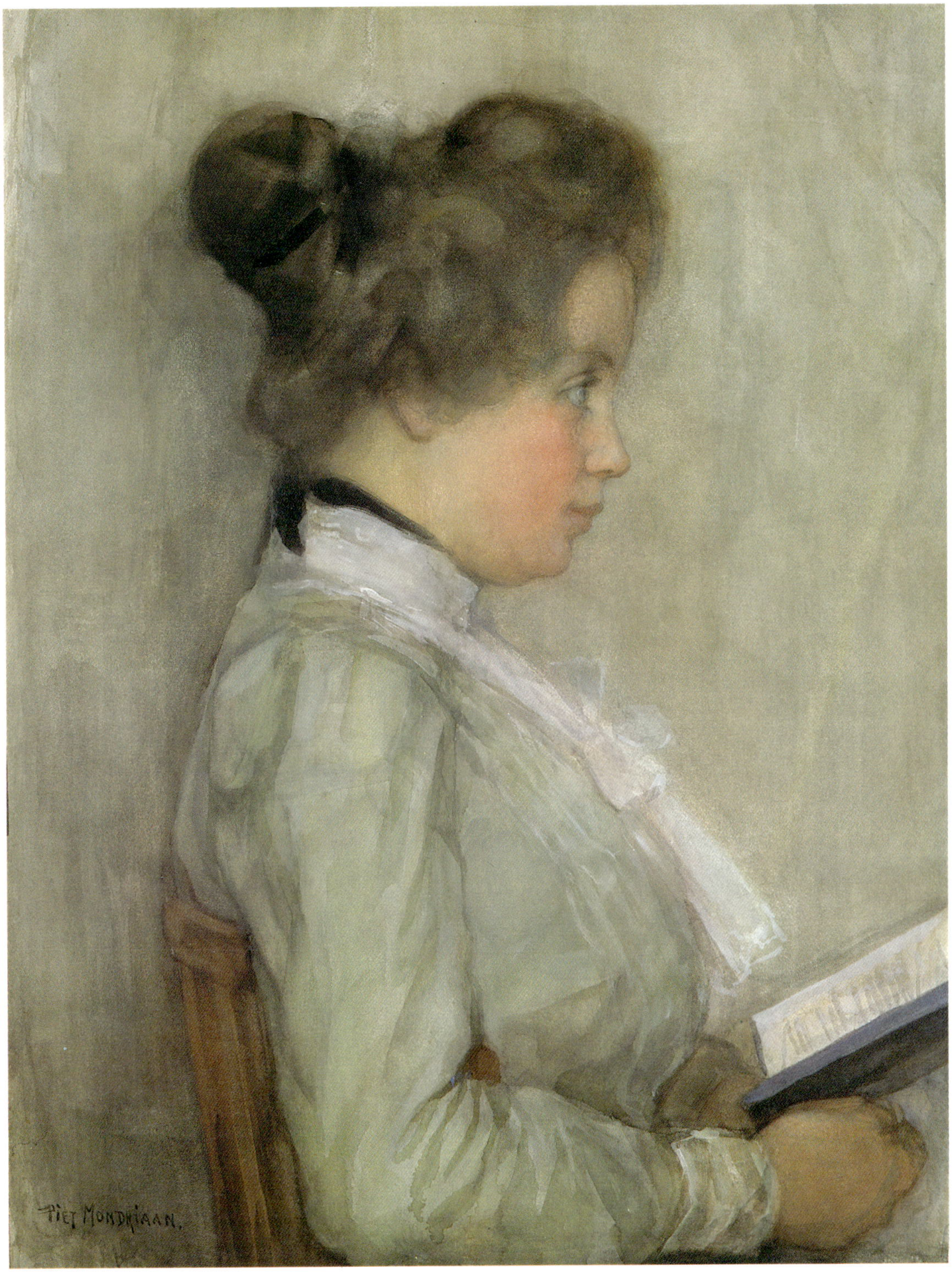

8

Portrait of a Lady

1898/1900
watercolour/paper
89 × 50 cm

inv.no.T108-1971
Blok 17
Seuphor 40, c.c.10

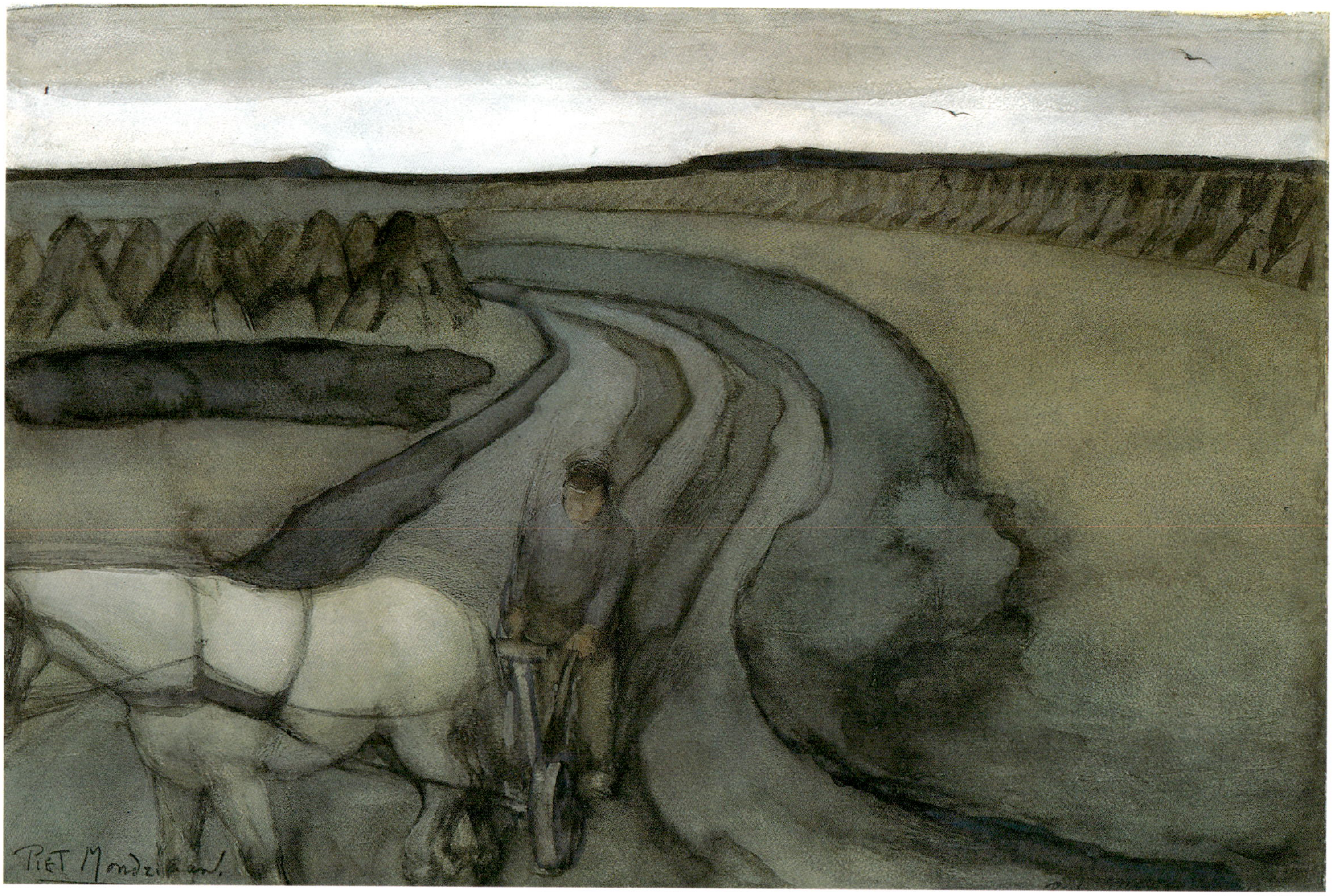

9

At Work

1898
gouache/paper
54.4 × 78.7 cm

inv.no. T66-1986
(acquired 1986)

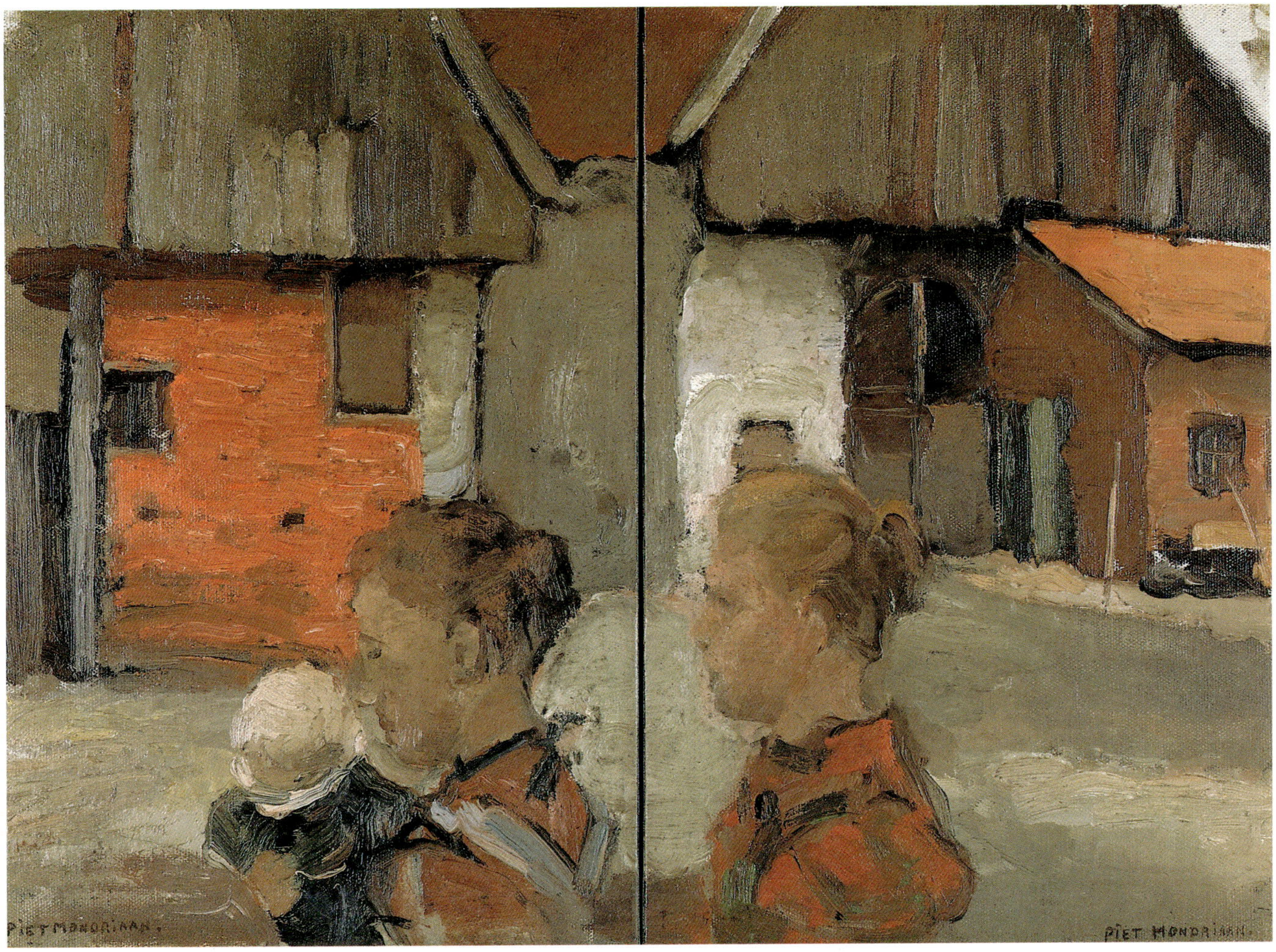

10

Women with Child in front of a Farmhouse

1898/1900
oil/canvas
33.5 × 45 cm

inv.no.116/117-1971
Blok 18
Seuphor 84/83, c.c.93/92

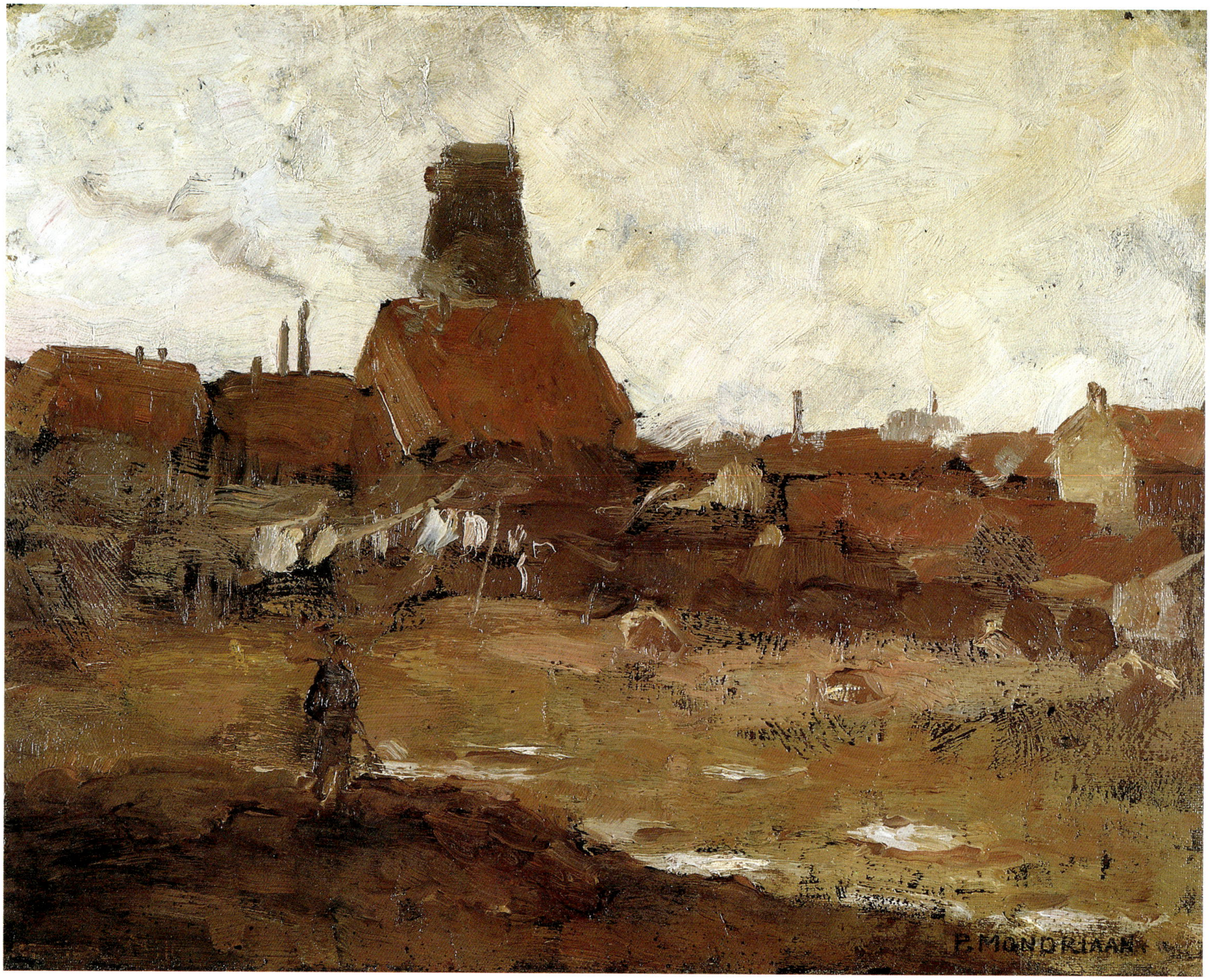

11
View of a Village

ca.1898
oil/canvas
31 × 38.5 cm

inv.no.76-1971
Blok 19
Seuphor 142, c.c.46

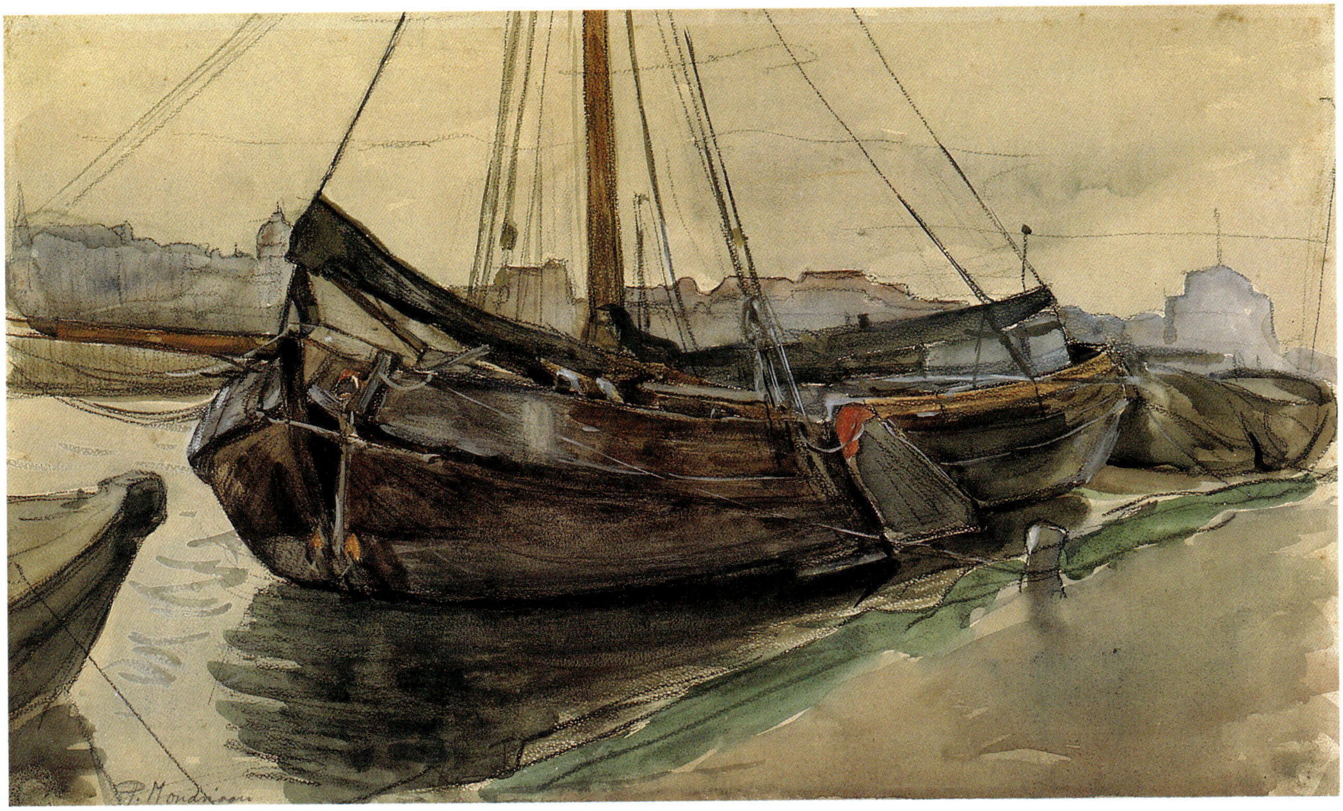

12

Moored Barges

1898/99
watercolour/crayon/paper
33 × 55 cm

inv.no. T60-1971
Blok 26

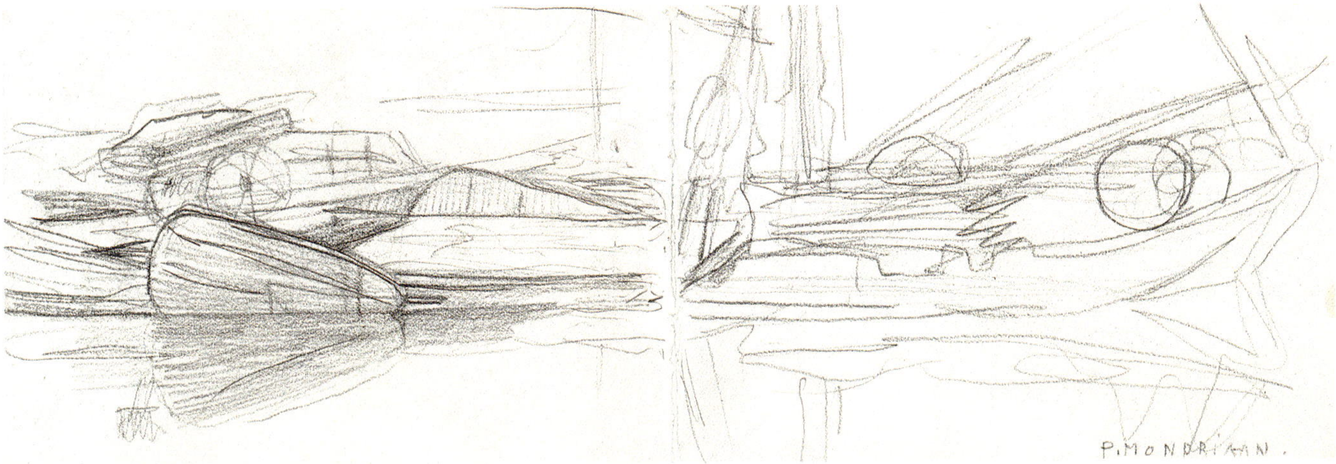

13

Barge

1898/99
pencil/conté/paper
11.3 × 31.9 cm

inv.no. T79-1971
Blok 30

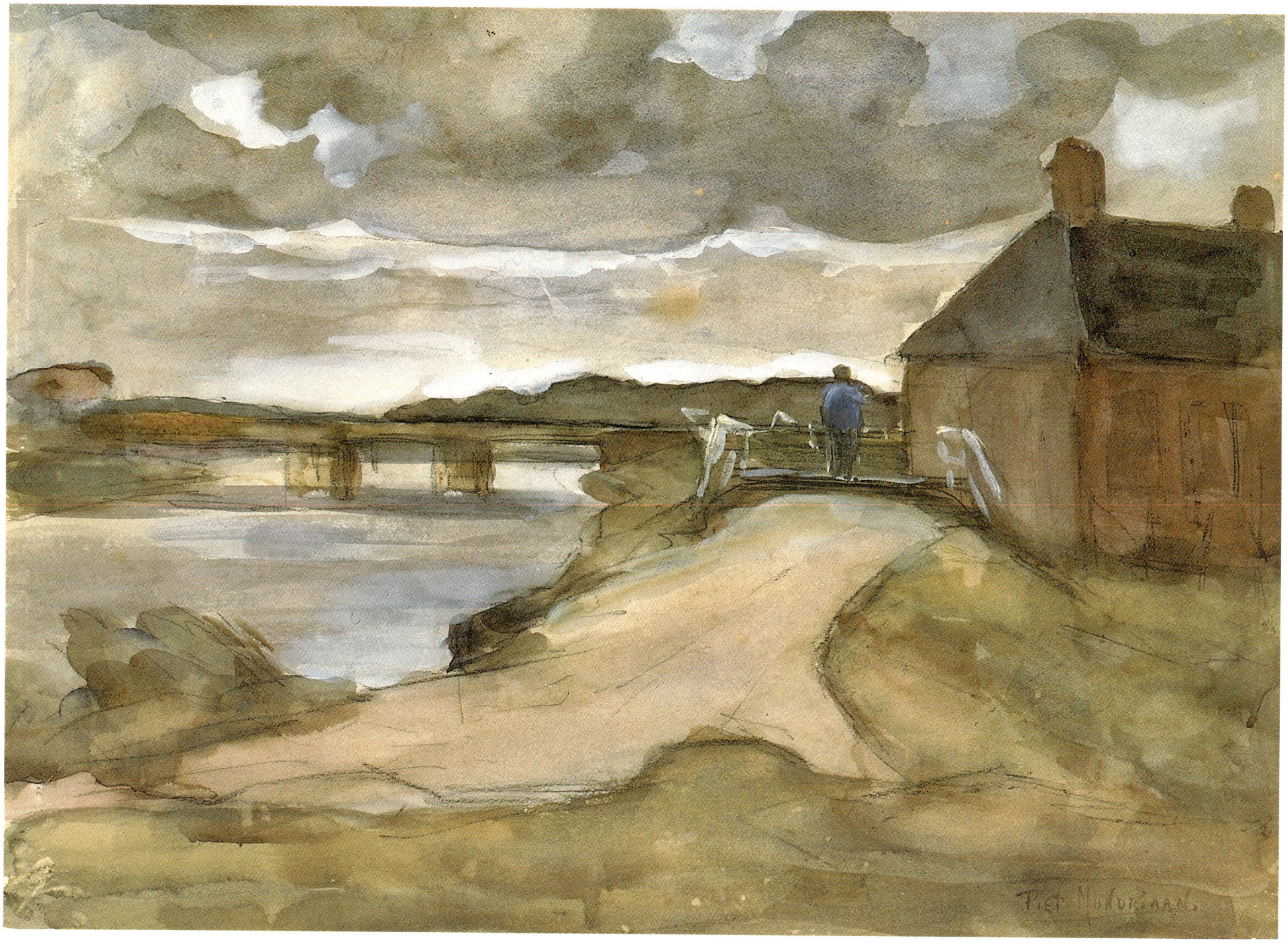

14

Landscape with Bridge and Farmer

ca. 1898/99
watercolour/paper
41 × 56 cm

inv.no.T105-1971
Blok 31
Seuphor 30, c.c.40

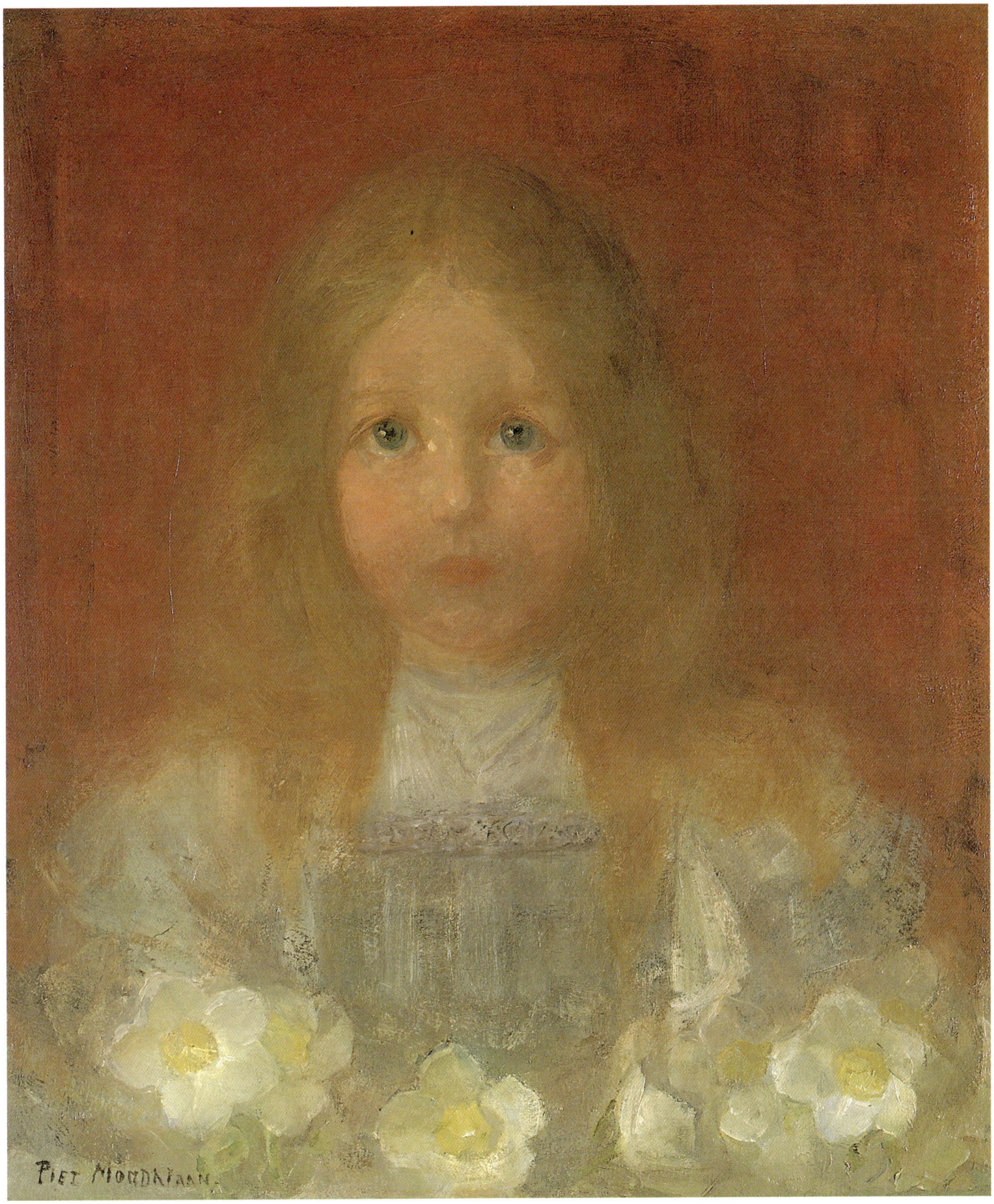

15

Portrait of a Girl with Flowers

1900/01
oil/canvas
53 × 44 cm

inv.no.102-1971
Blok 35
Seuphor 228, c.c.13

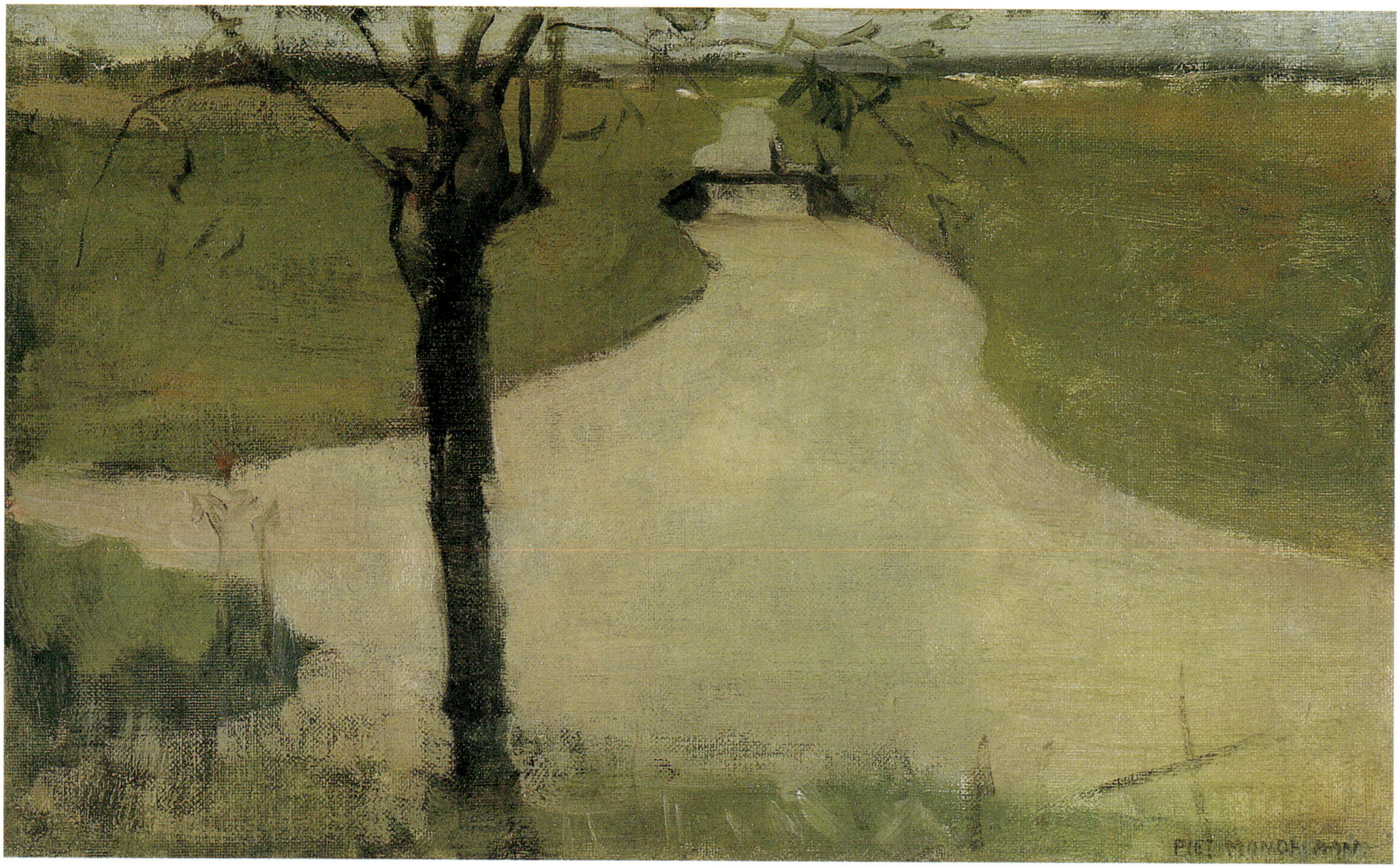

16

Ditch near the Kalfje

1901/02
oil/canvas
23.5 × 37.5 cm

inv.no.25-1956
Blok 41

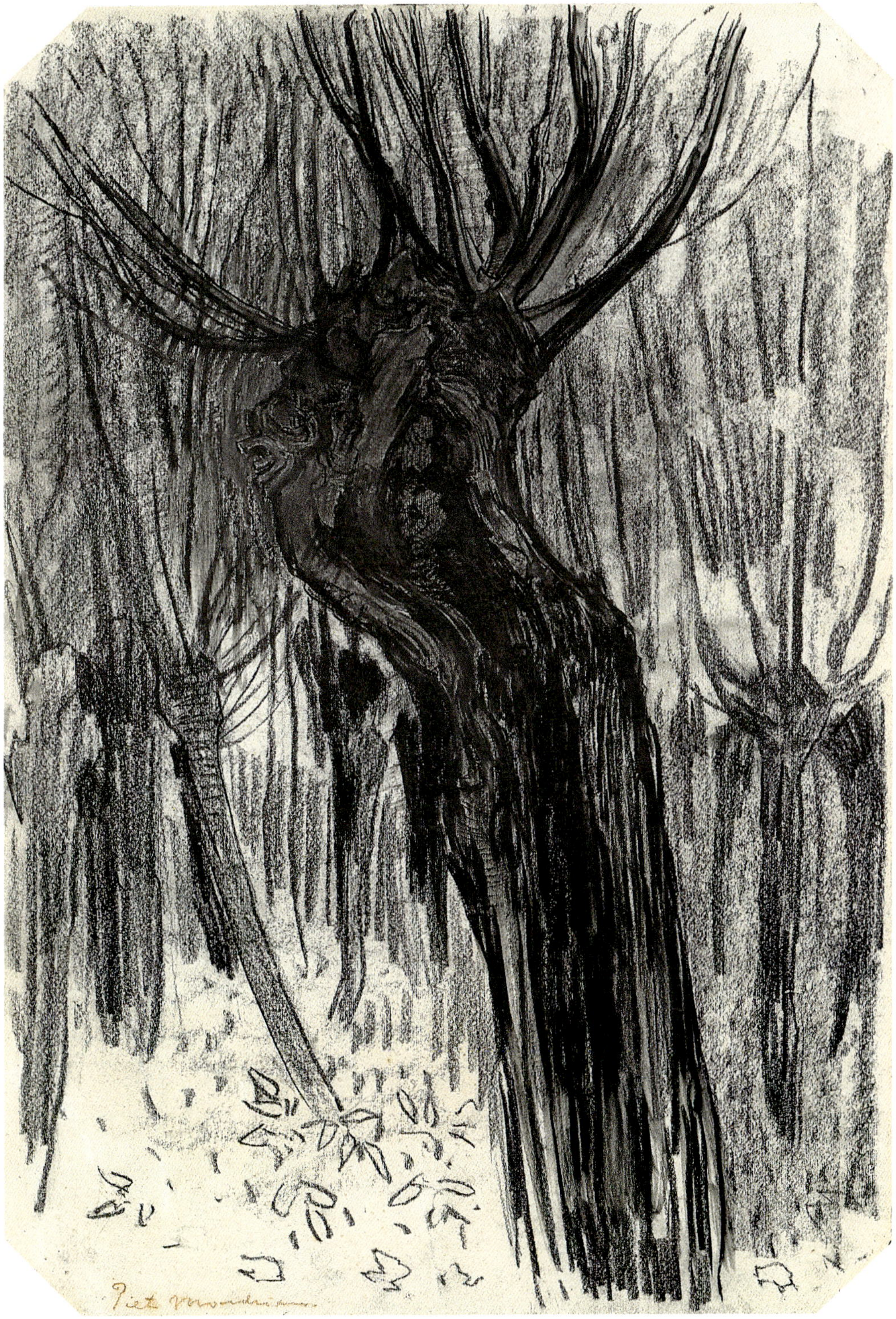

17

Pollard Willows

1902/04
charcoal/crayon/paper
60 × 40 cm

inv.no.T62-1971
Blok 46
Seuphor 54, c.c.78

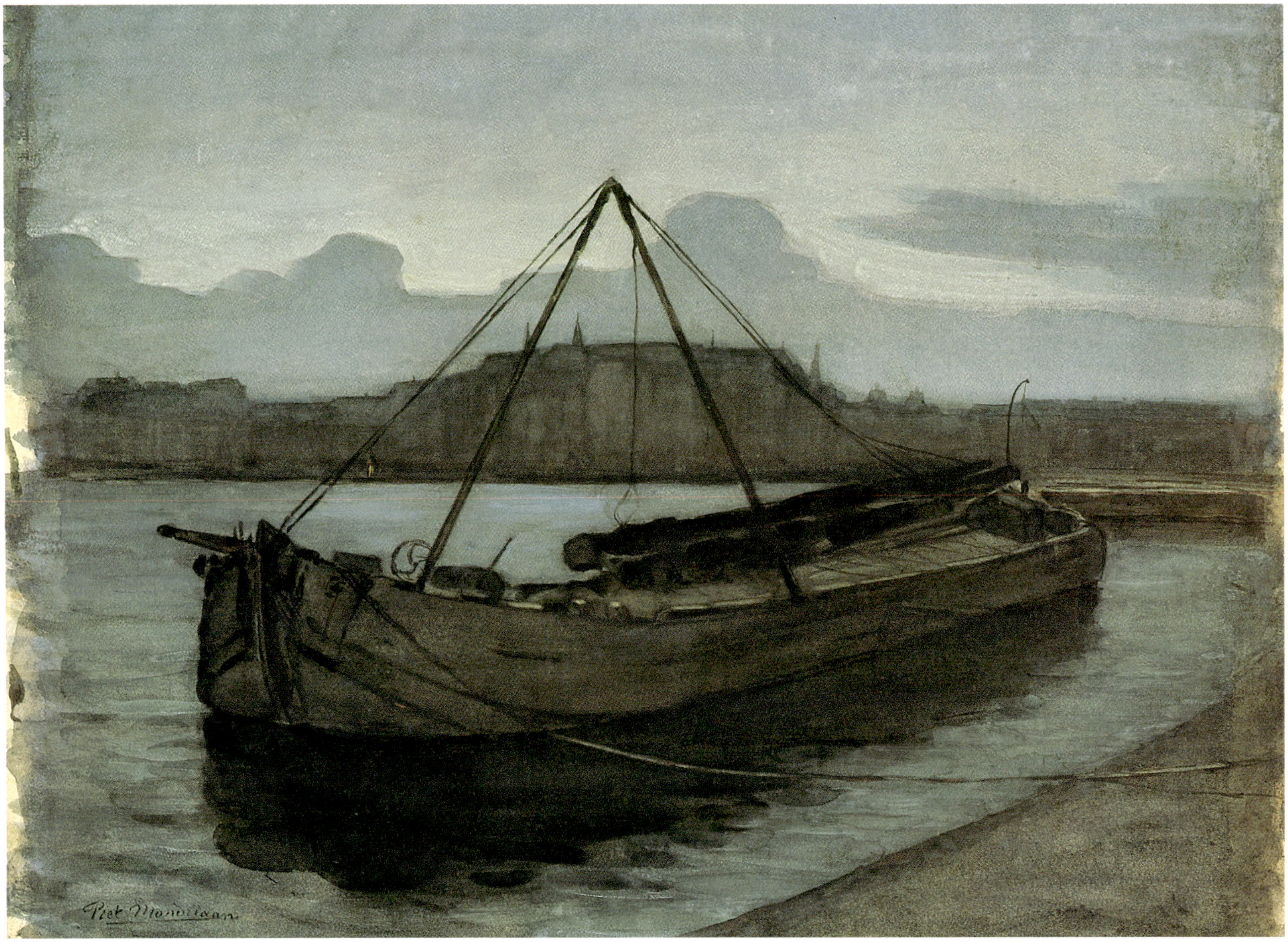

18

The Weesperzijde: Evening

1902/03
watercolour/gouache/crayon/paper
55 × 65.7 cm

inv.no.T50-1971
Blok 56
Seuphor 2, c.c.123

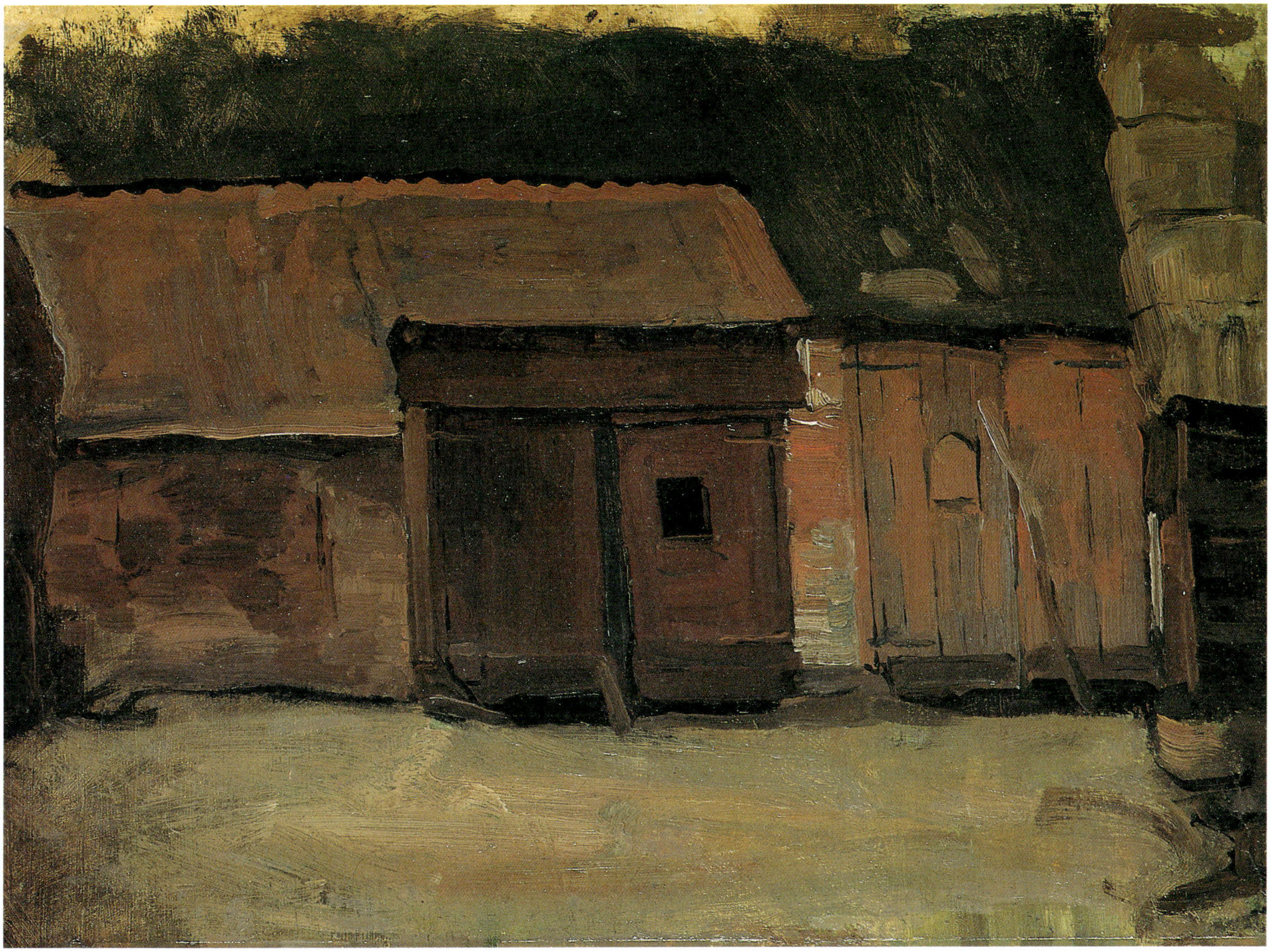

19

Barns at Nistelrode

1904
oil/cardboard/paper
33 × 43 cm

inv.no.29-1956
Blok 61

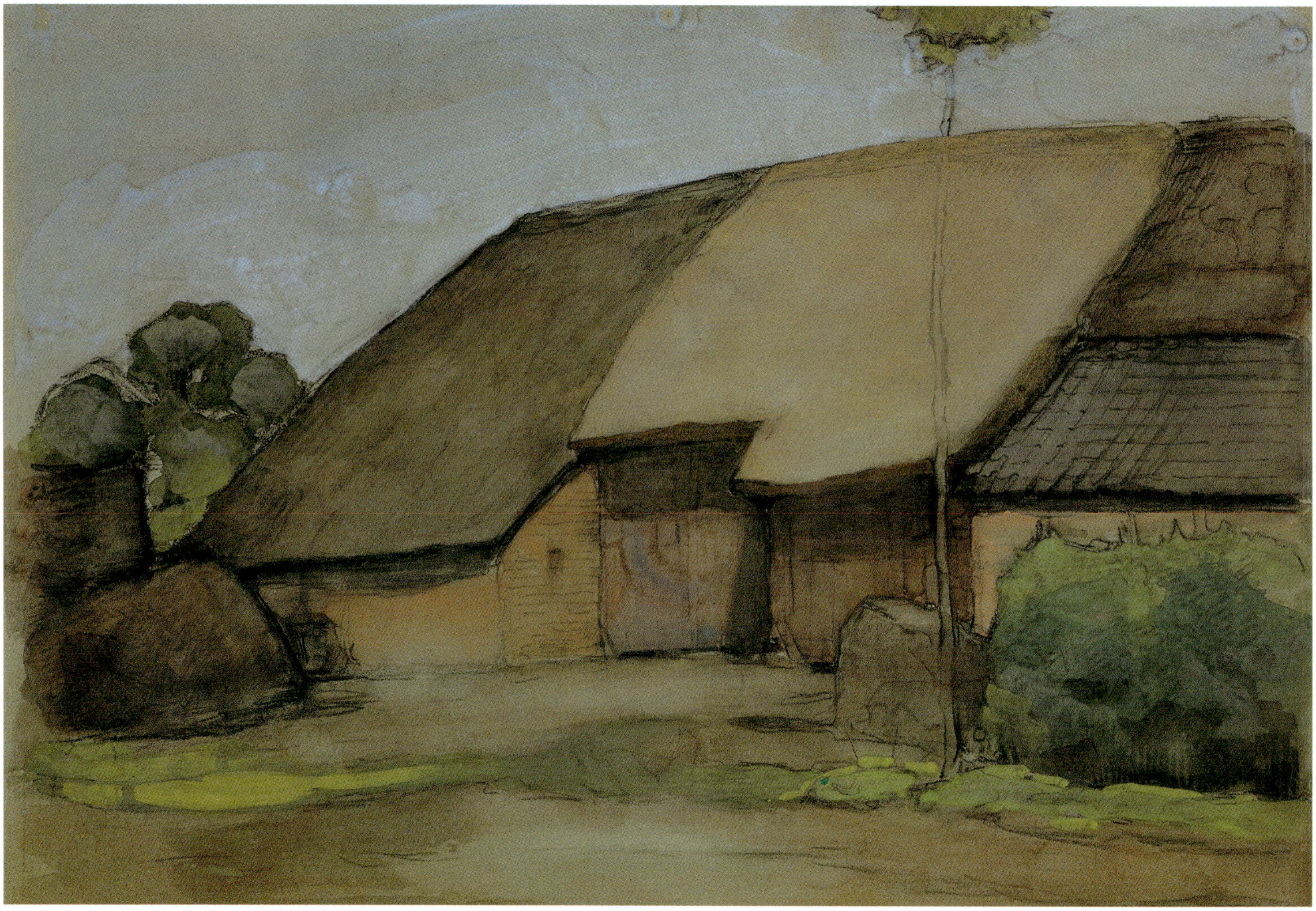

20

Farm at Nistelrode

1904
watercolour/paper
44 × 63 cm

inv.no. T366-1964
Blok 65
Seuphor 75, c.c.94

Z—They form a composition of areas of colour which depict a defined relationship. I have also been struck here however by architectural and decorative arrangement: in the farmhouses of Brabant, for example.

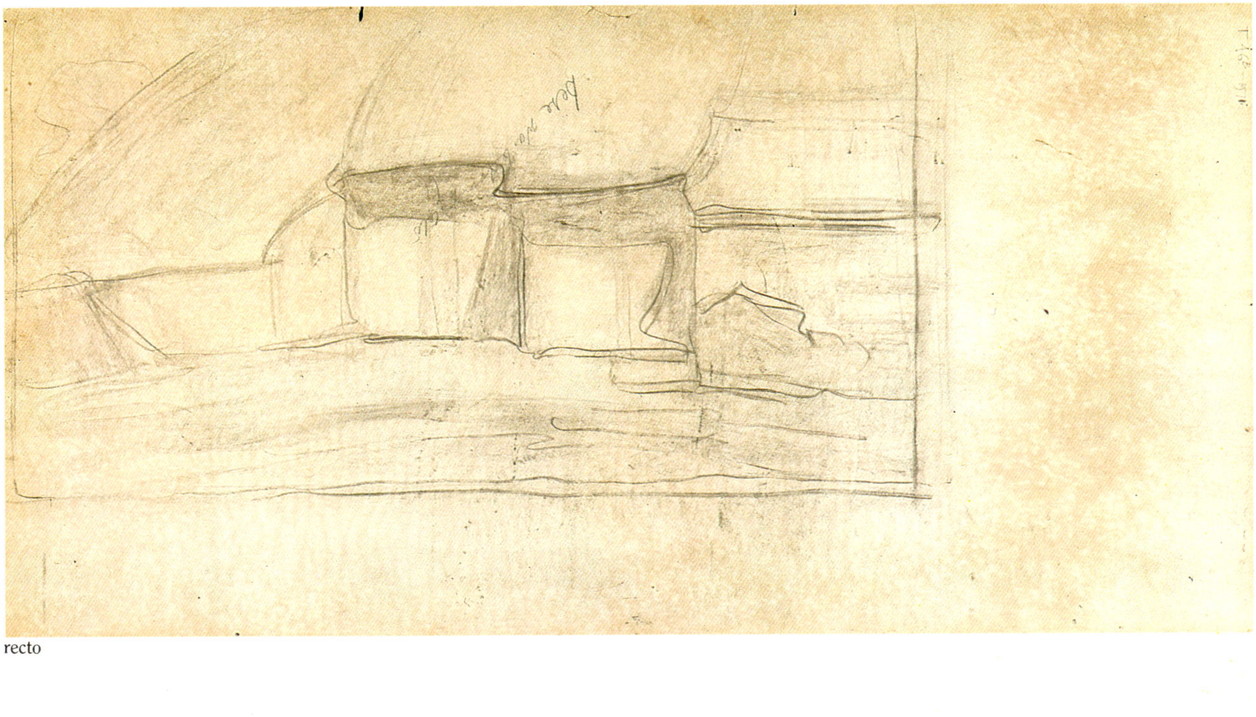

recto

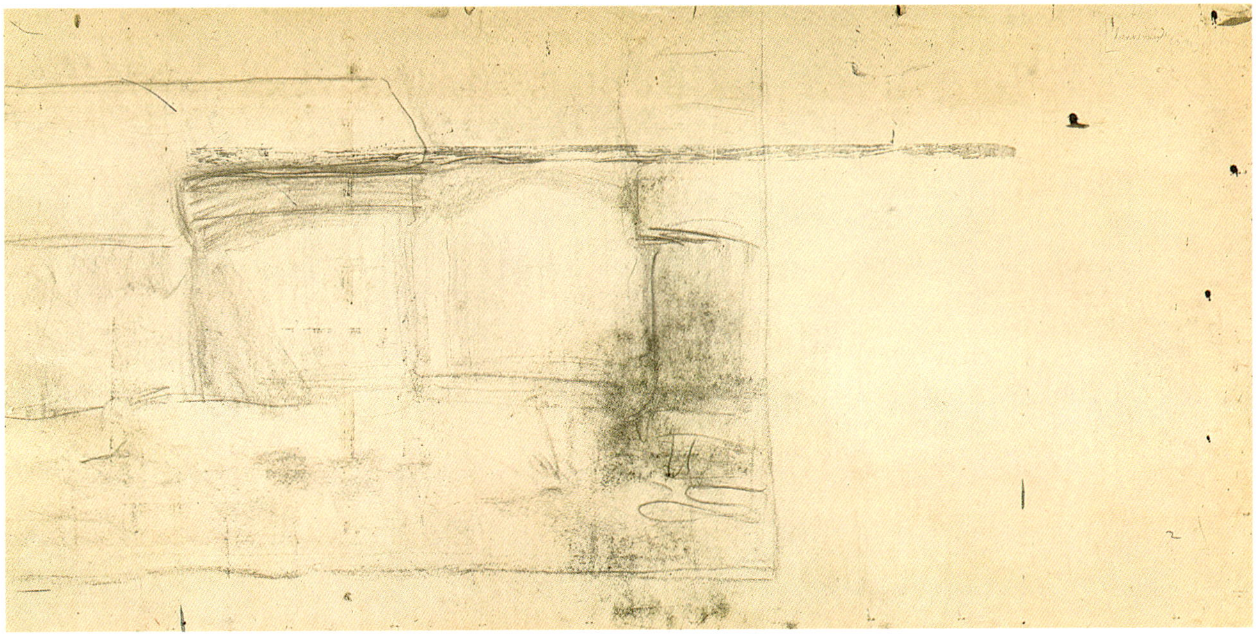

verso

21

Farm at Nistelrode (recto)

Farm at Nistelrode (verso)

1904
pencil/ charcoal/paper
44 × 63 cm
inv.no. T46B-1971

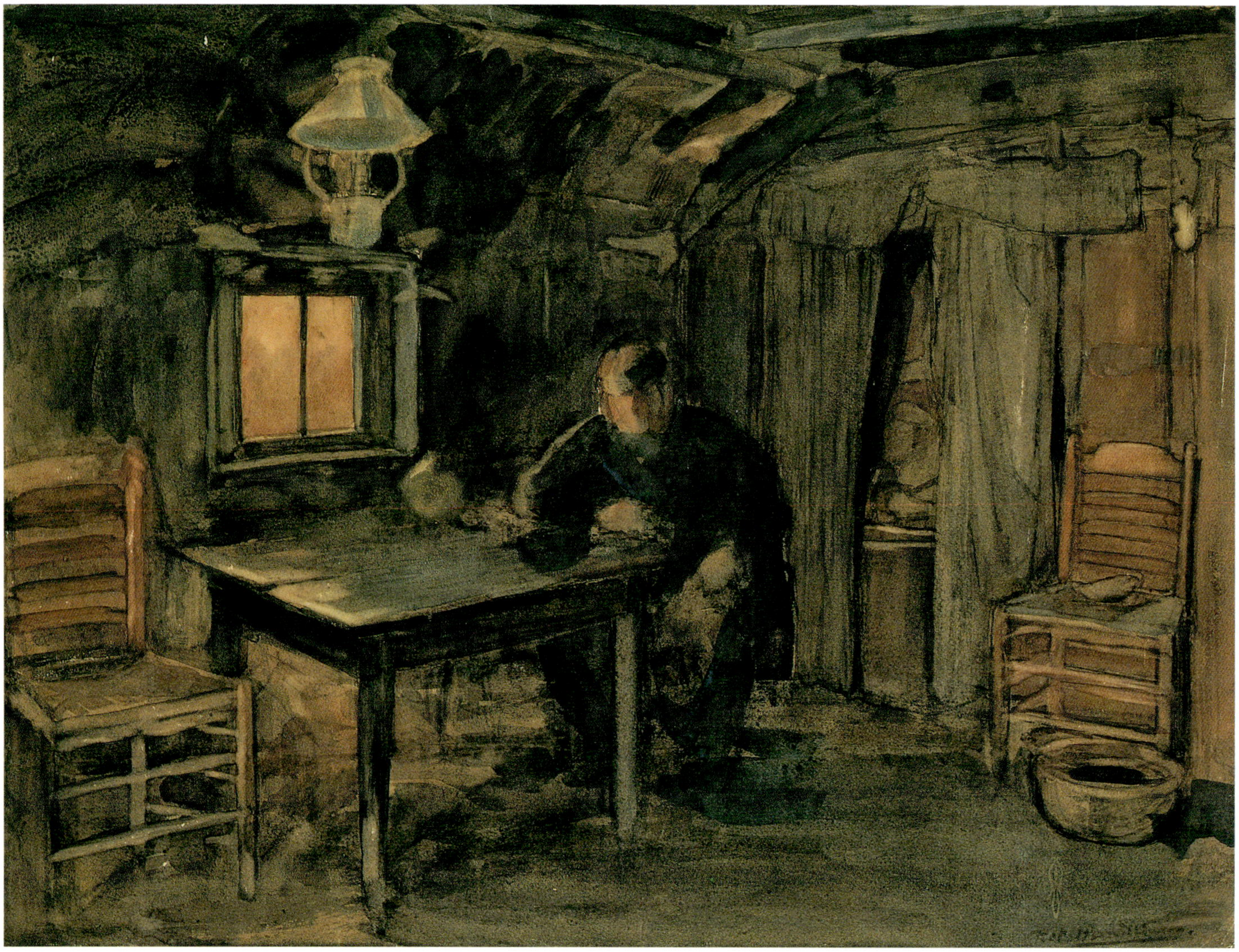

22

Interior at Nistelrode

1904
watercolour/paper
48 × 62 cm

inv.no. T79-1962
Blok 66

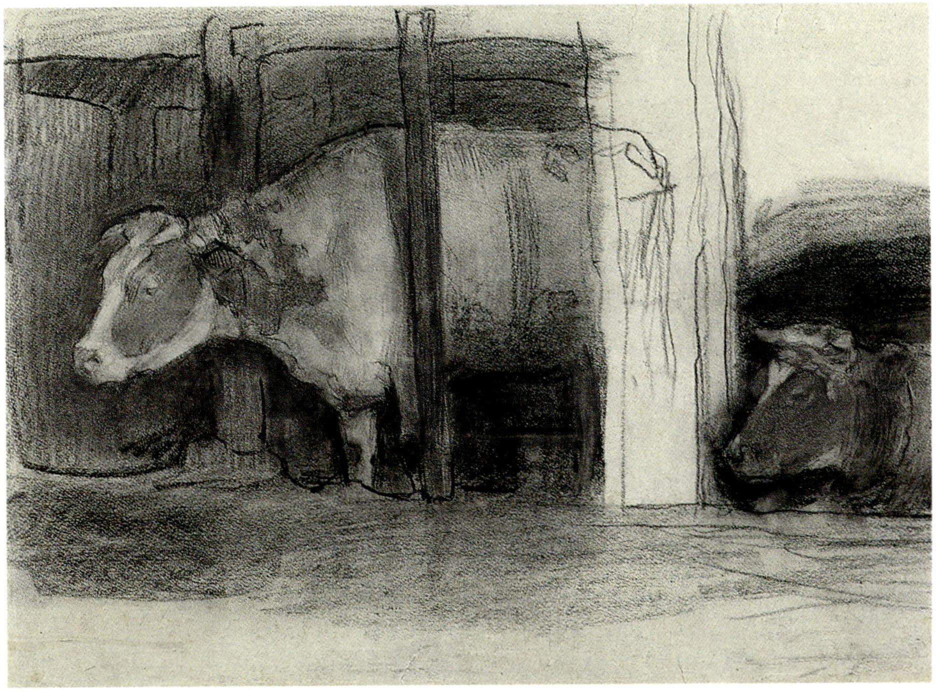

23

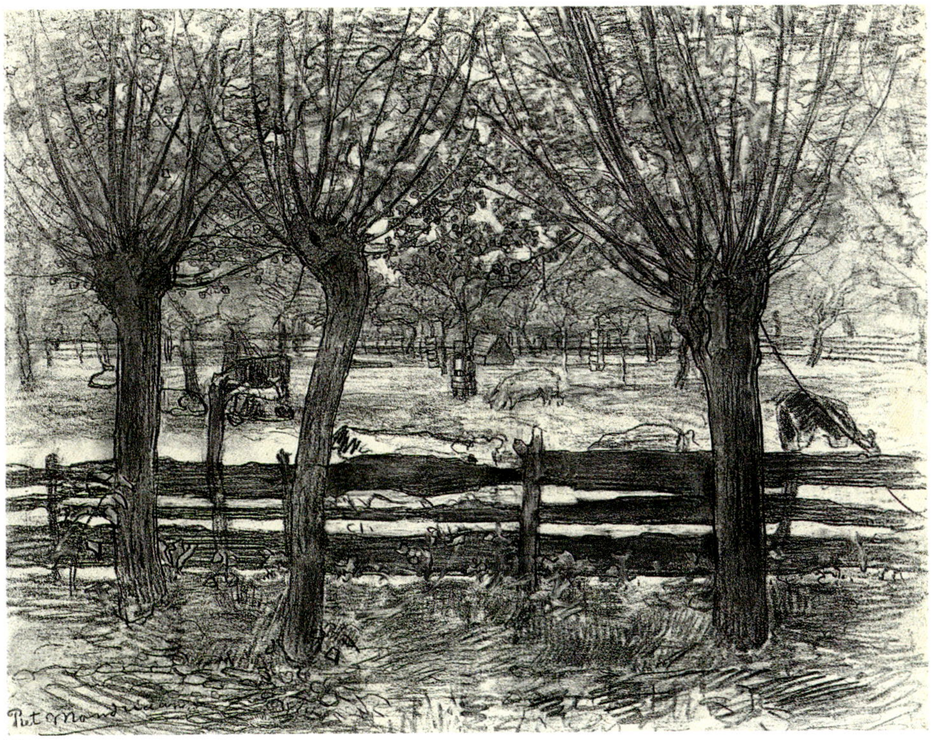

24

23

Cows in a Shed

1904
charcoal/crayon/paper
33 × 45 cm

inv.no.T66-1971
Blok 68

24

Farmyard with Cattle and Willows

1904
crayon/paper
46.5 × 58.2 cm

inv.no.T57-1971
Blok 72
Seuphor 52, c.c.76

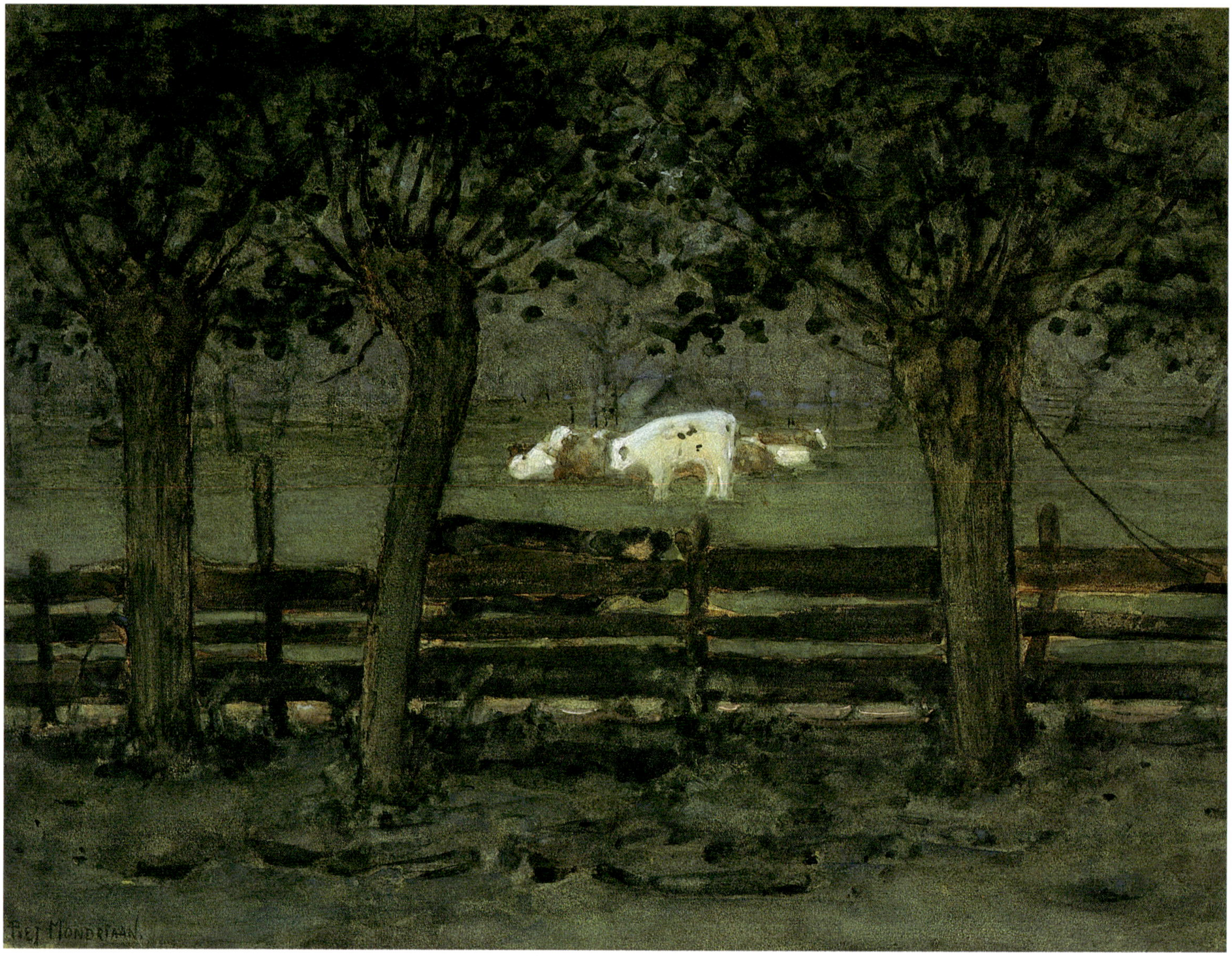

25
The White Calf

1904/05
watercolour/paper
44.5 × 58.5 cm

inv.no.T4-1965
Blok 73
Seuphor 62, c.c.83

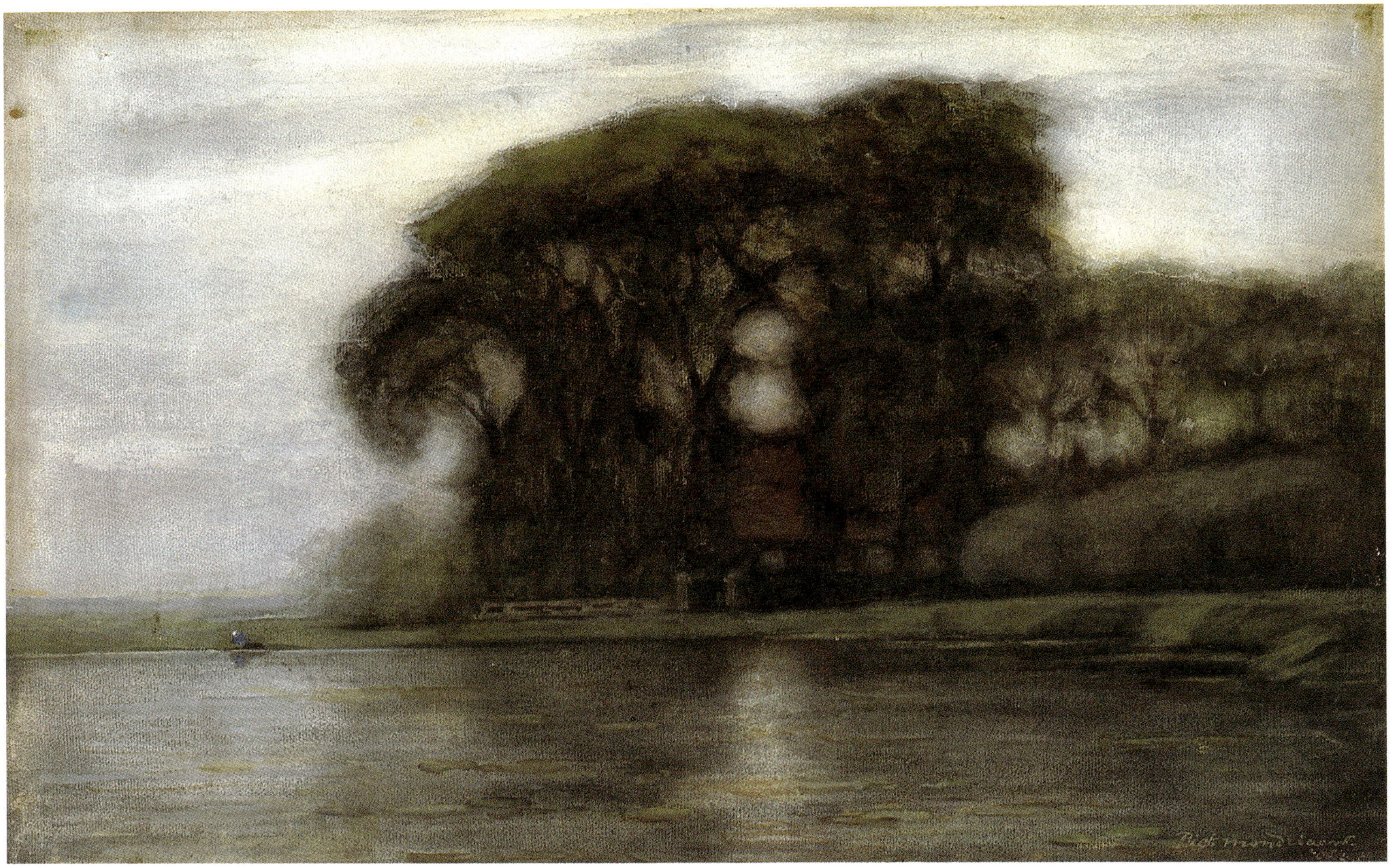

26

Duivendrecht

1905
watercolour/paper
38.4 × 61.2 cm

inv.no. T46-1960
Blok 79

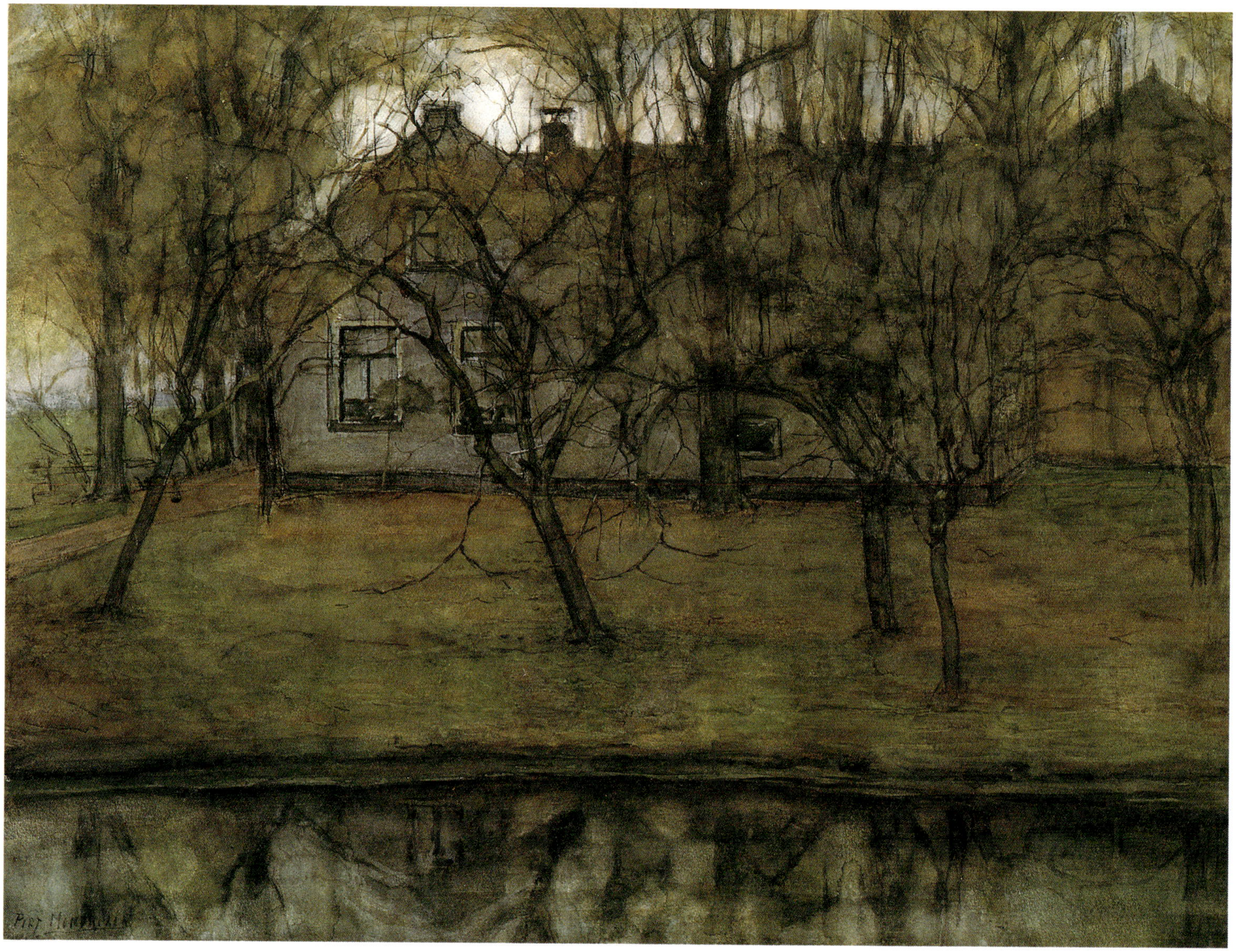

27

Farmstead

1905
watercolour/paper
51 × 65.5 cm

inv.no.T101-1971
Blok 88
Seuphor 223, c.c.122

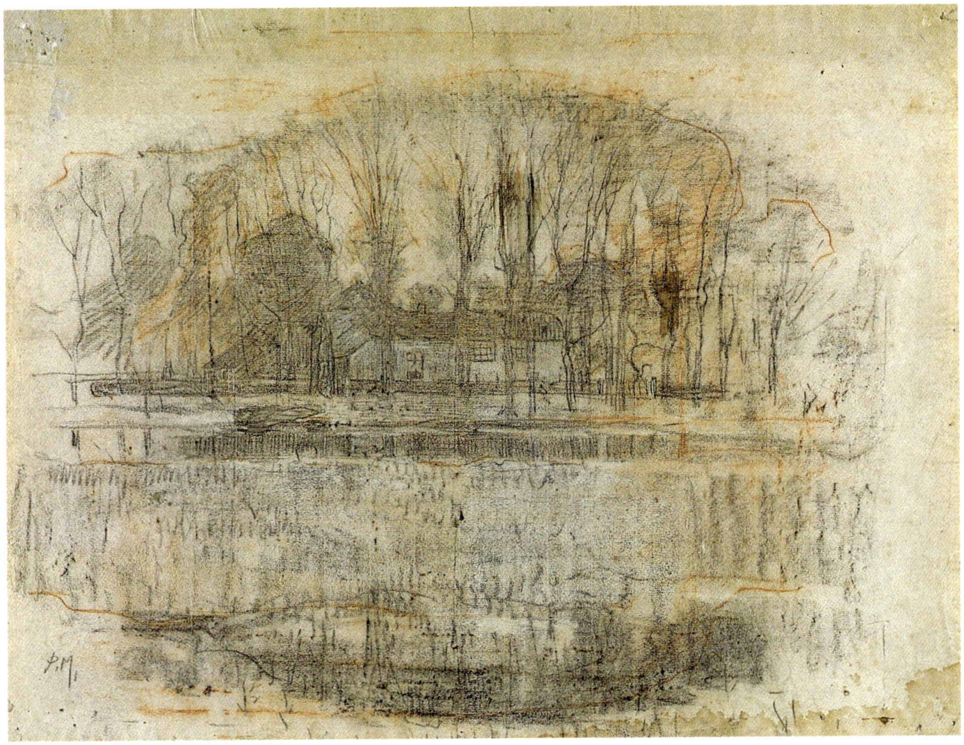

28

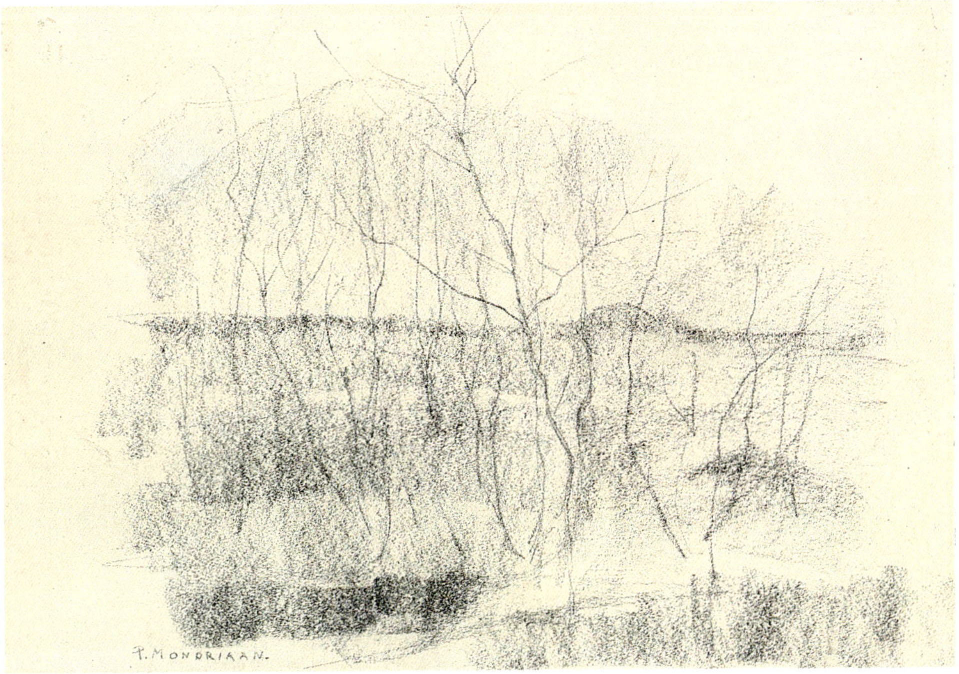

29

28

Farm with Trees and Water

1906
crayon/sanguine/pastel/paper
47.5 × 61.5 cm

inv.no.T74-1971
Blok 93

29

Landscape with Trees

1906
charcoal/paper
33.5 × 47 cm

inv.no.T63-1971
Blok 94

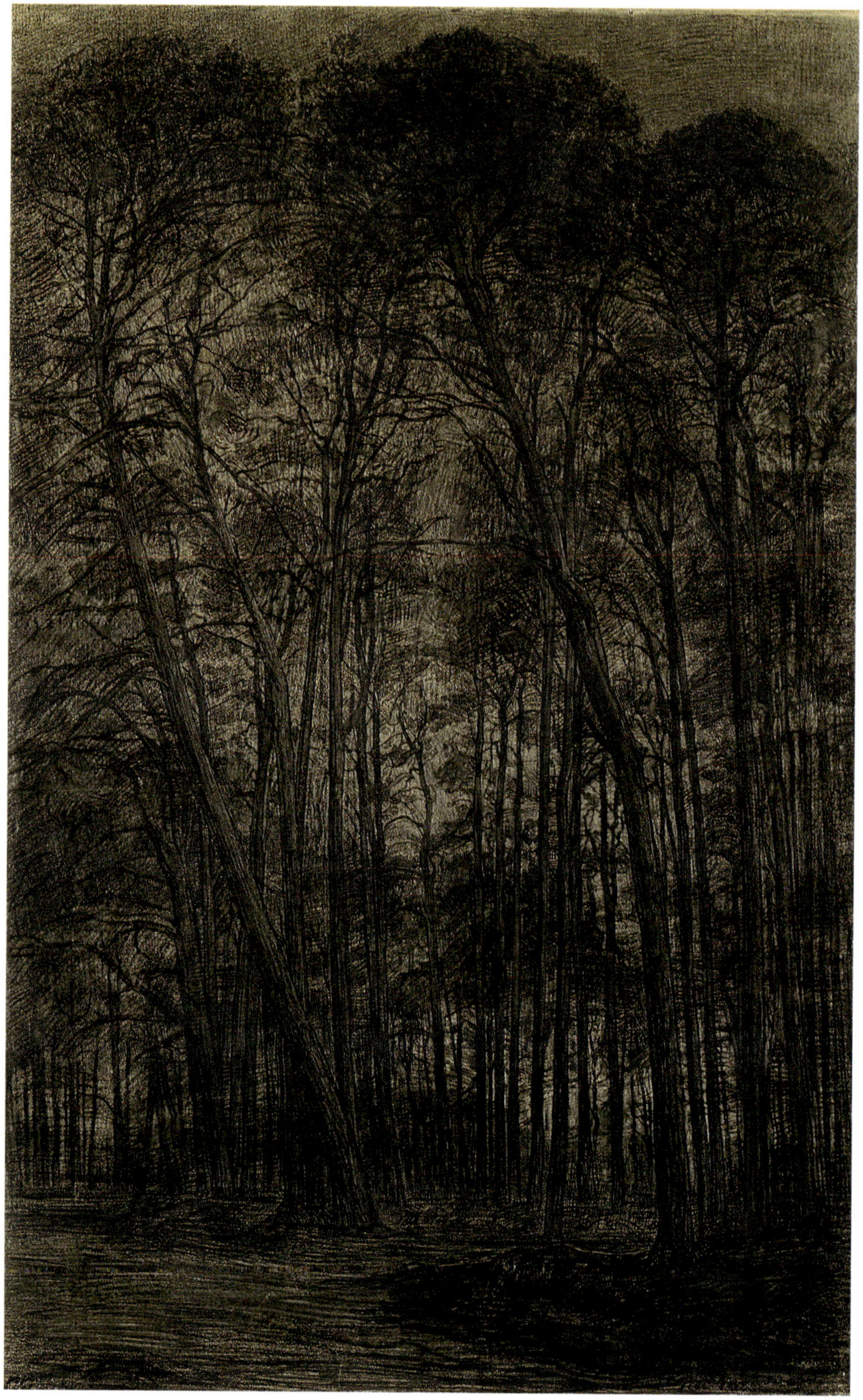

30

Woods at Oele

1906
crayon/paper
111 × 67 cm

inv.no.T102-1971
Blok 98
Seuphor 182, c.c.64

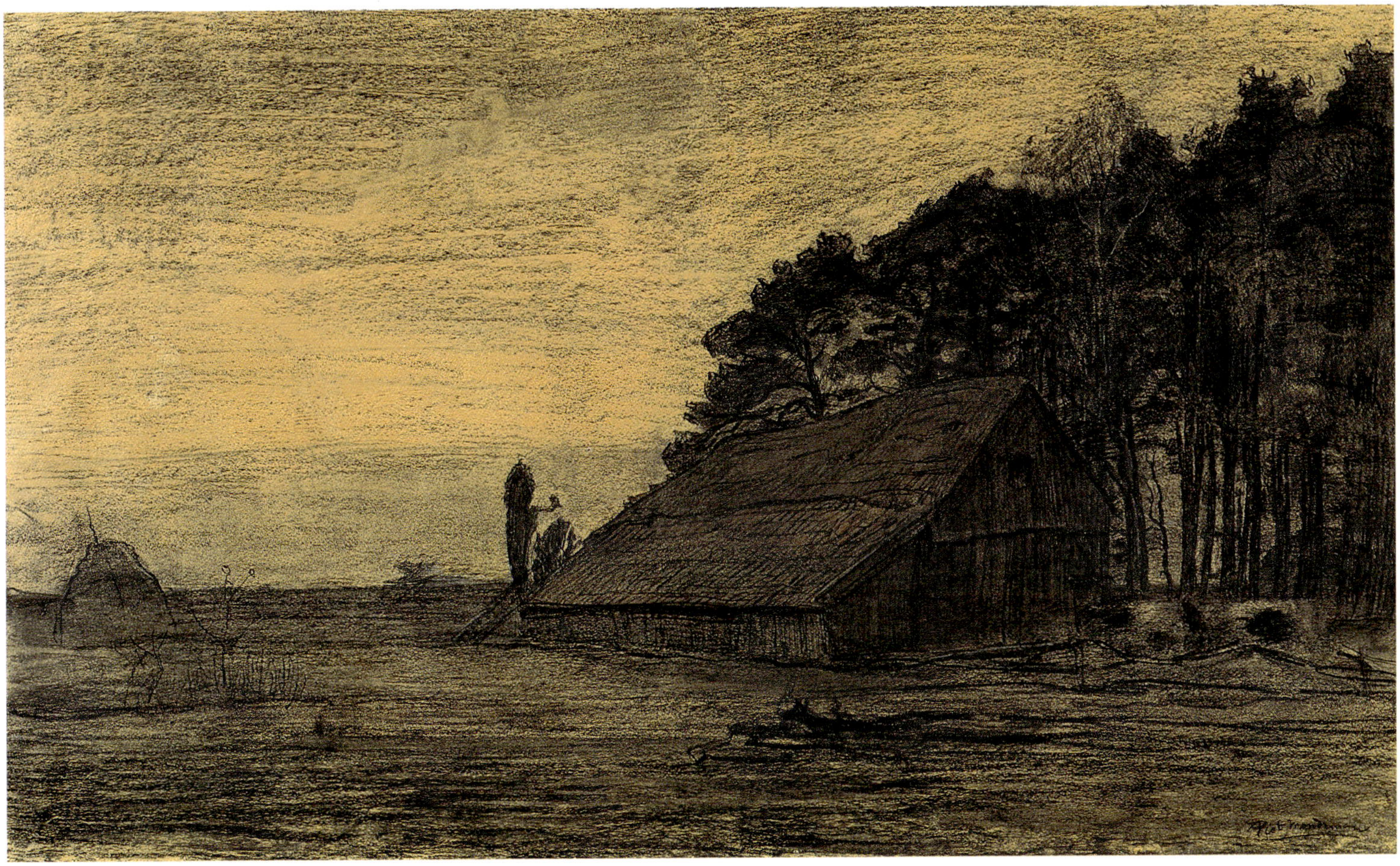

31

Sheepfold

1906
charcoal/crayon/sanguine/gouache/paper
68.5 × 110 cm

inv.no. T47-1971
Blok 99

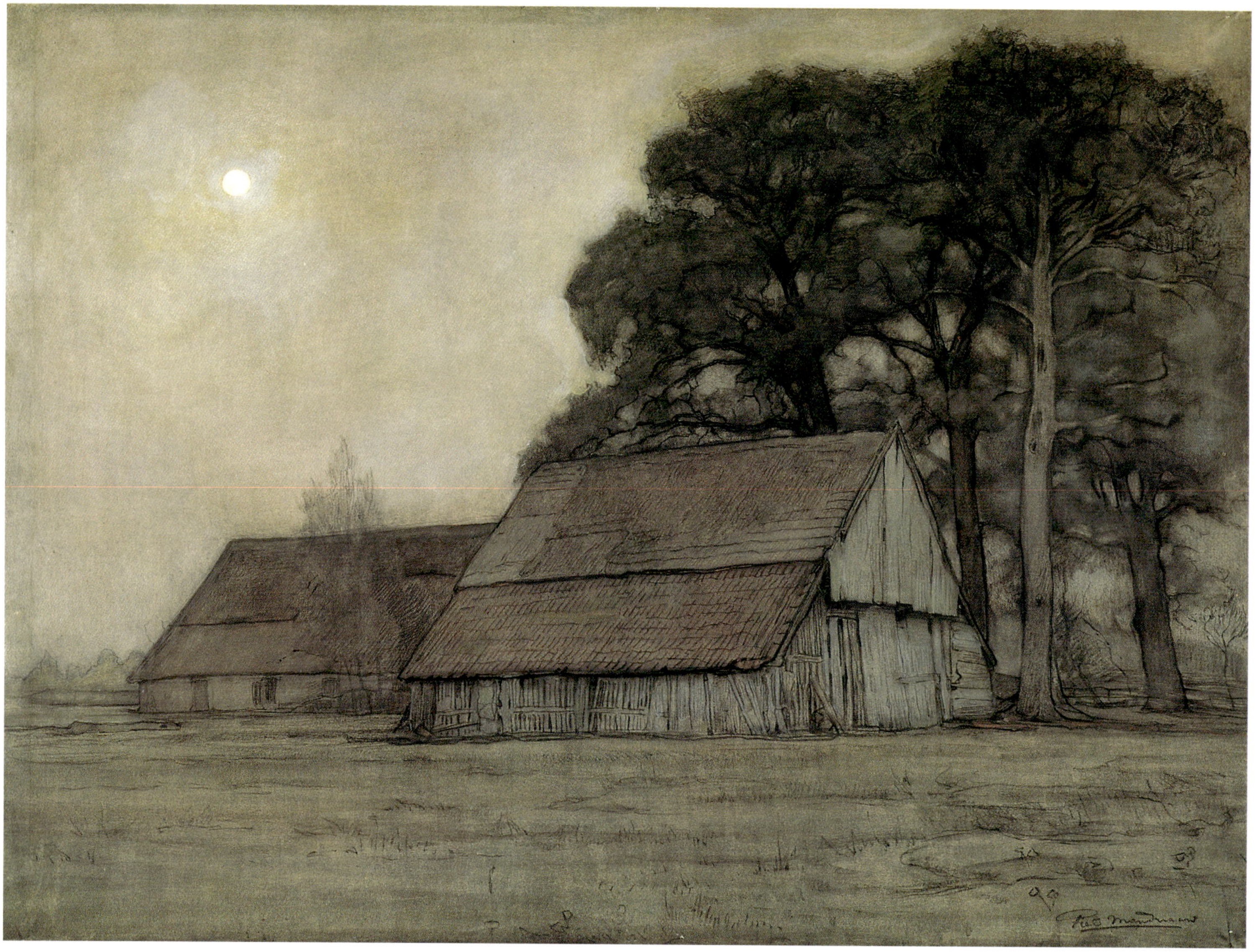

32
Sheepfold in the Evening

1906
charcoal/crayon/watercolour/paper
73.7 × 98.1 cm

inv.no.T51-1971
Blok 100
Seuphor 194, c.c.99

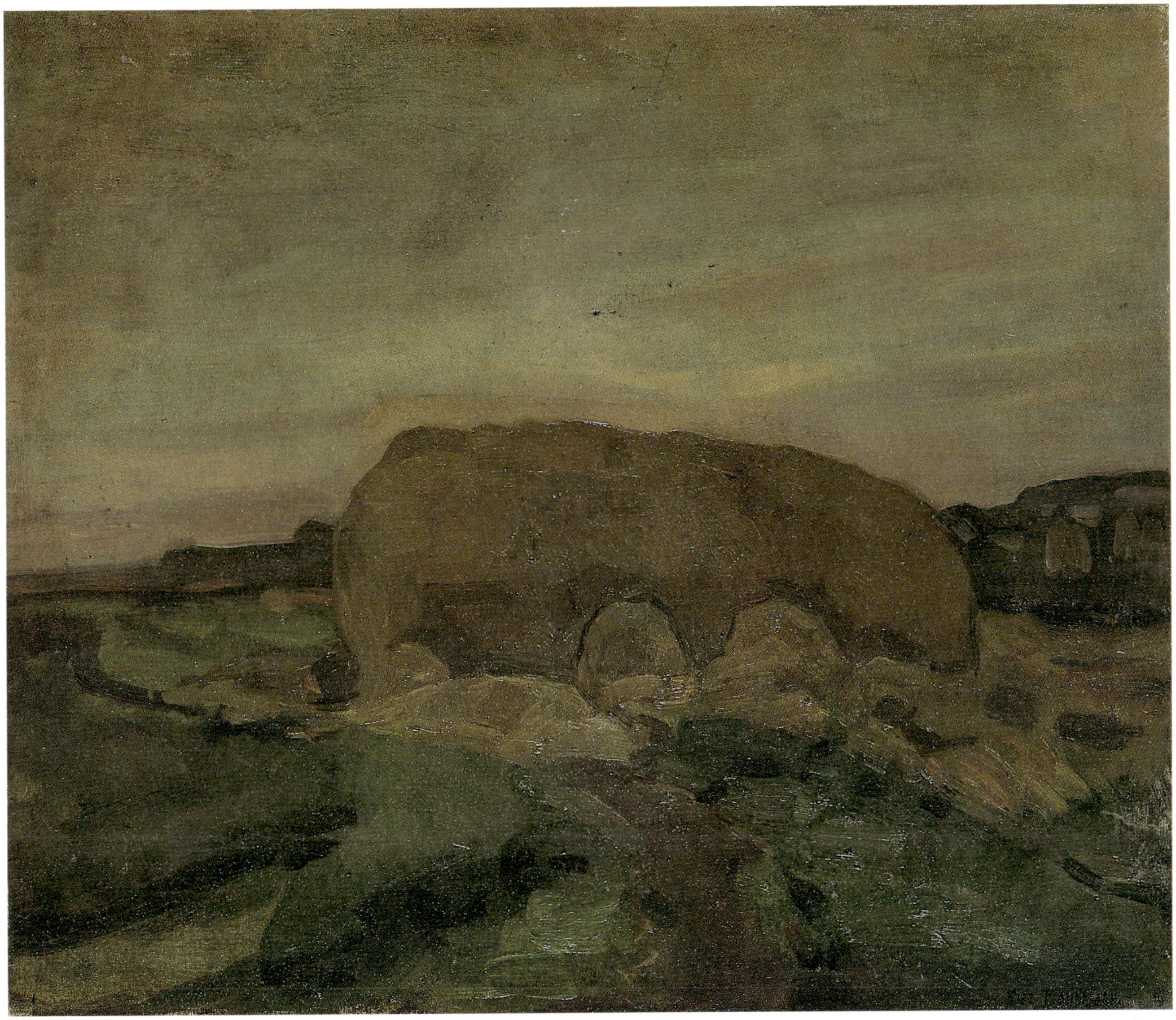

33

Haystack

1906
oil/canvas
66 × 76 cm

inv.no.74-1971
Blok 101

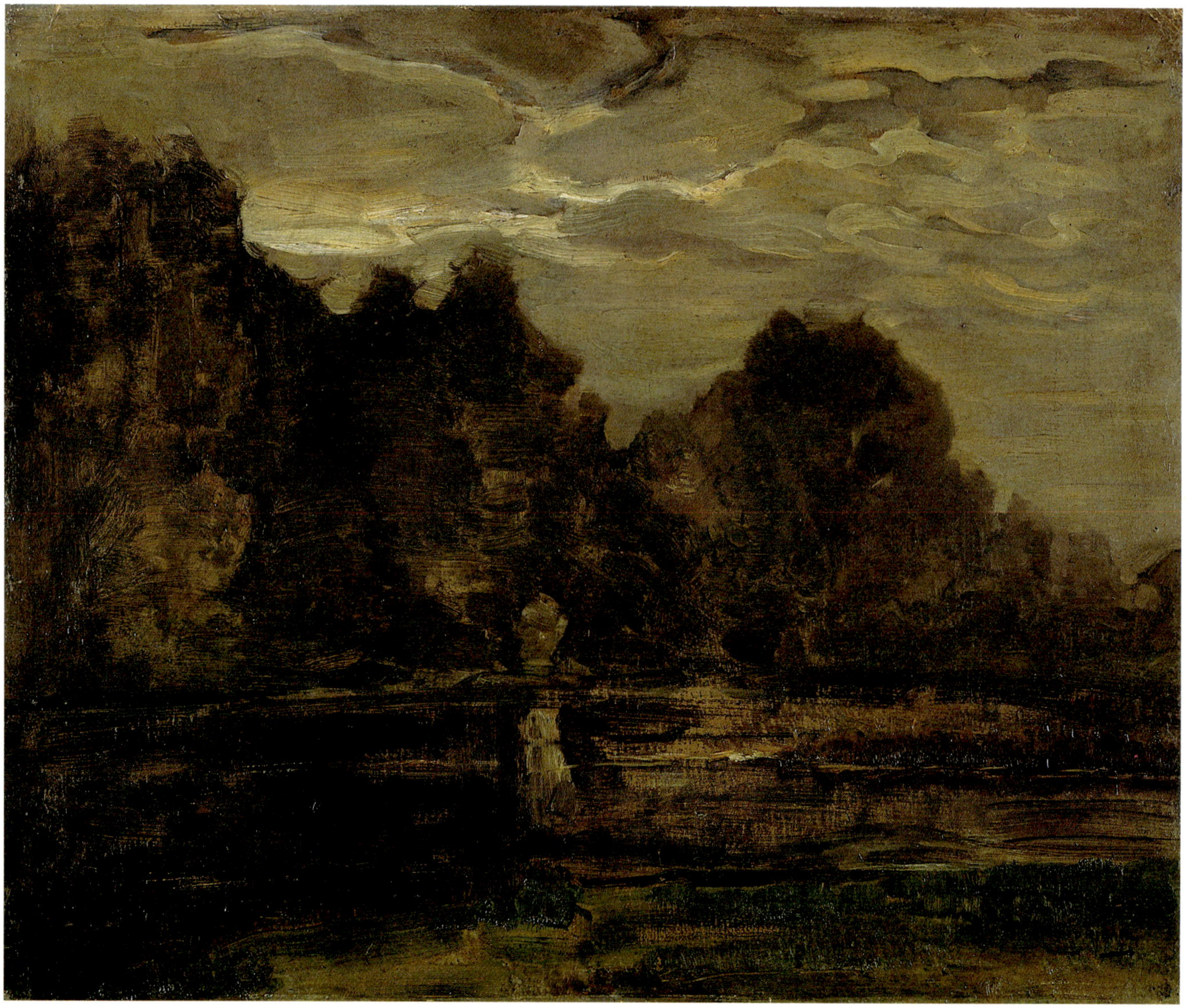

34

Landscape with Trees and Water

1906/07
oil/cardboard
63.5 × 76 cm

inv.no.81-1971
Blok 102

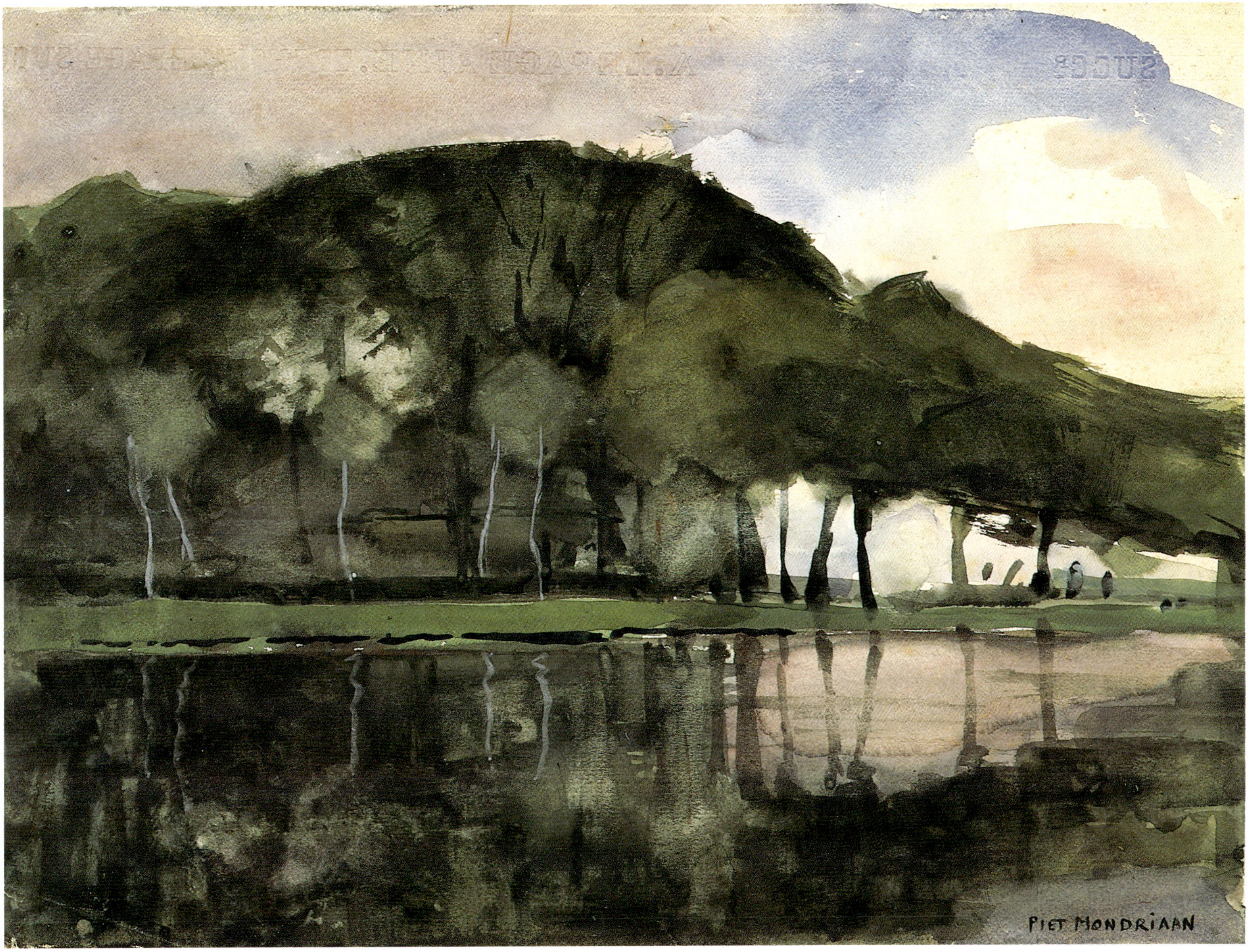

35

Along the Amstel

1903
watercolour/paper
31 × 41 cm

inv.no.T100-1971
Blok 104
Seuphor 99, c.c.73

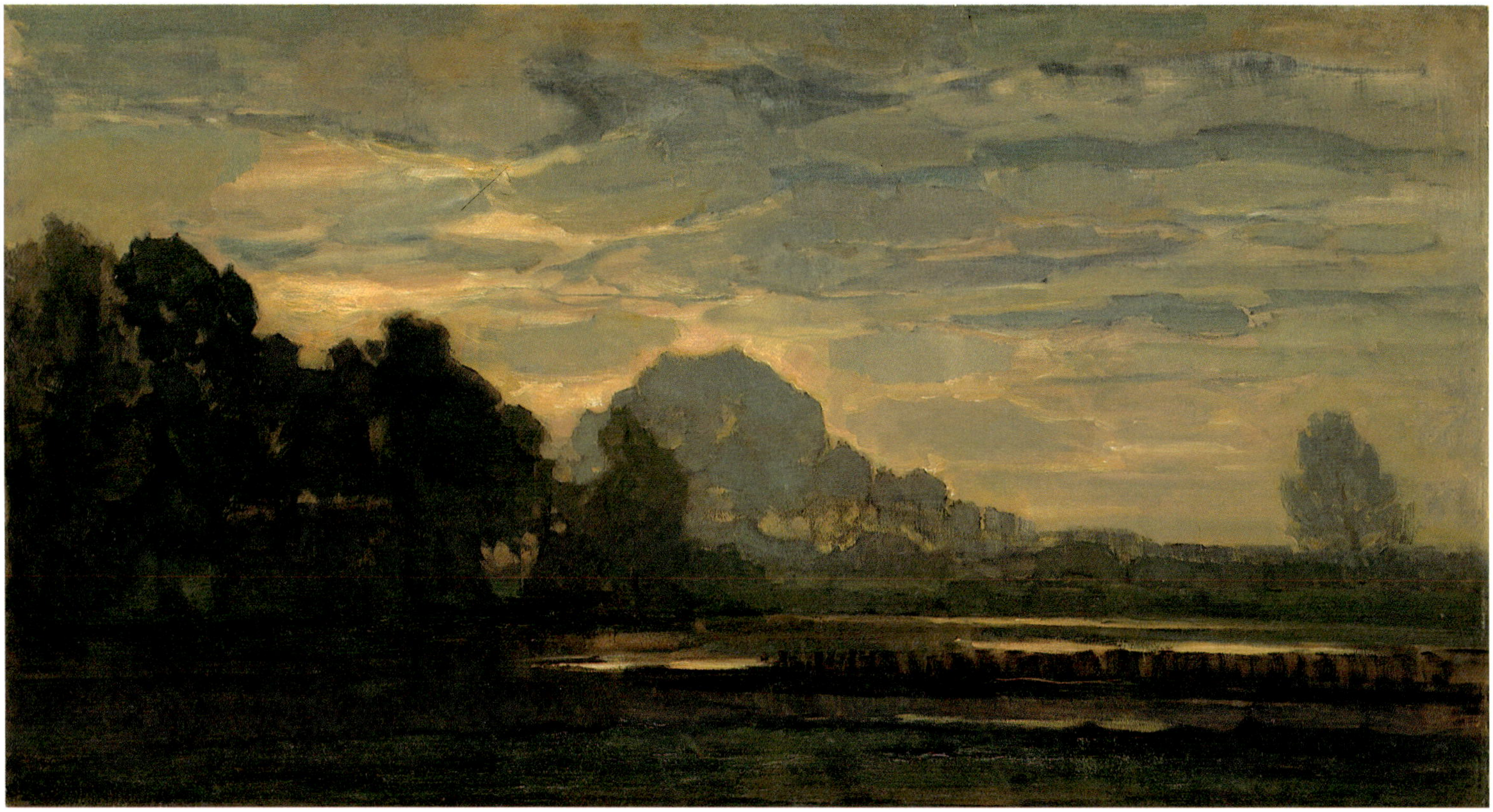

36

Pond near Saasveld

1906/07
oil/canvas
102 × 180.5 cm

inv.no.110-1971
Blok 107
Seuphor 210, c.c.53

Y—How curious!

X—What majesty!

Z—Indeed...both curious and magnificent! These magnificent contours convey the whims of nature most clearly.

Y—I see all kinds of faces and forms in them.

Z—You can clearly see how *relative* phenomena are: everything looks different to us than by daylight.

Y—Perhaps because we can't see the details now...but what makes everything look so *impressive* now?

X—First of all the *merging* of details, as you already noticed. We painters could learn a lesson there. The greatest difficulty in painting is to keep the details subordinate to the whole.

Y—But I don't see any details!

X—You only think you don't: movement, form, colour are everywhere, but it is all *dominated* by the large contour.

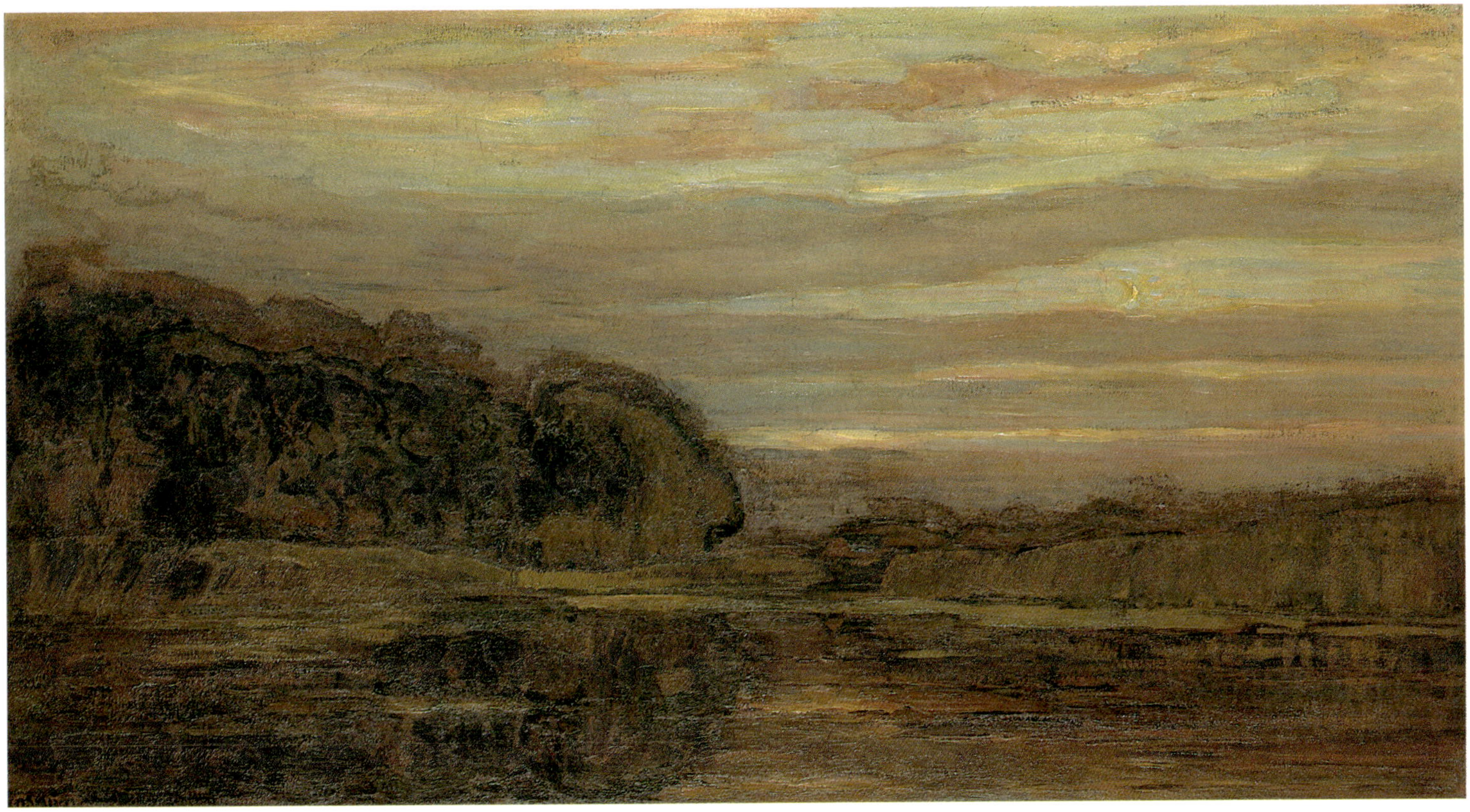

37

Landscape with Trees and Water

1906/07
oil/canvas
76 × 135.5 cm

inv.no.93-1971
Blok 108

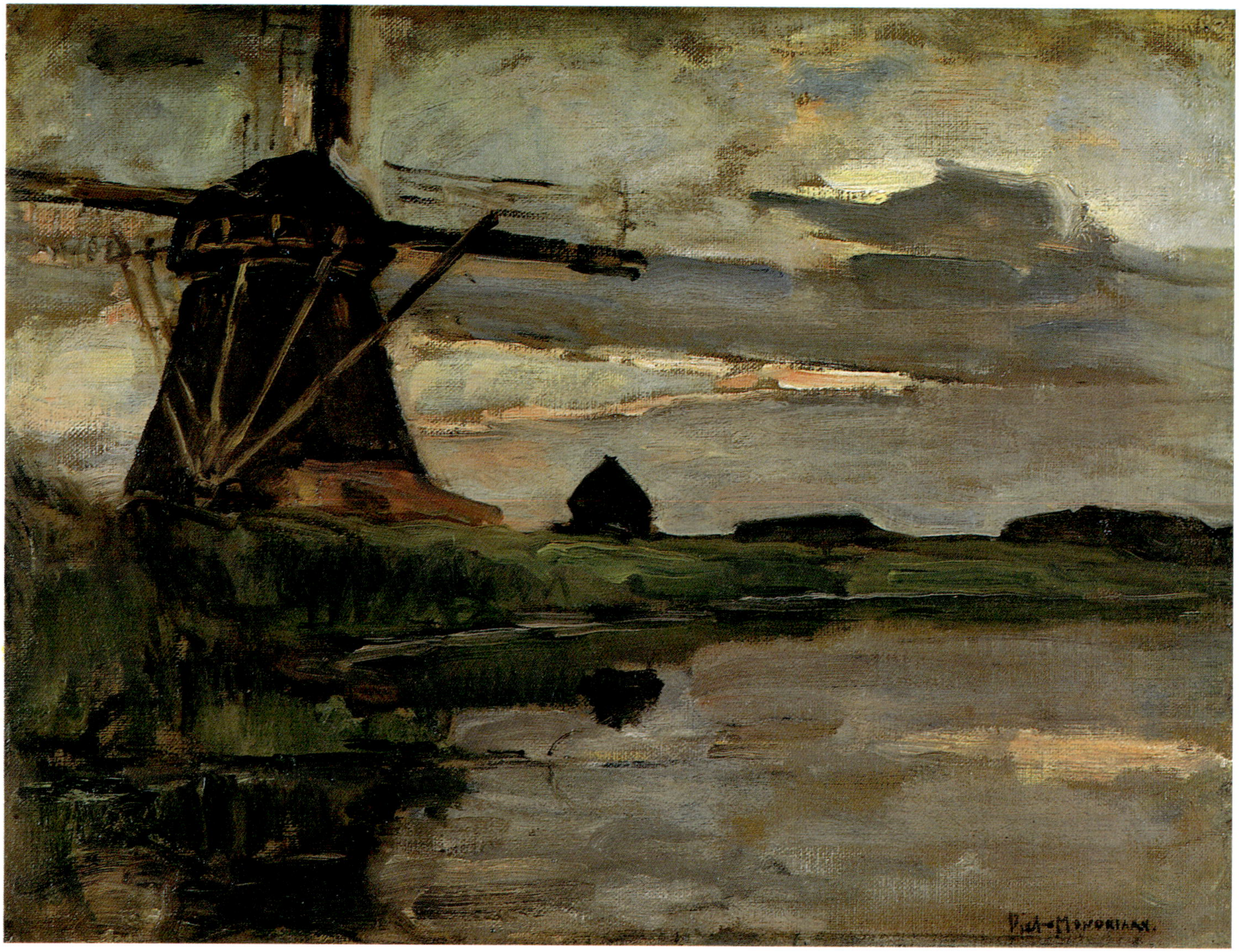

38

Mill on the Gein

1906/07
oil/canvas/paper
34.5 × 44.5 cm

inv.no.39-1967
Blok 110
Seuphor 49, c.c.106

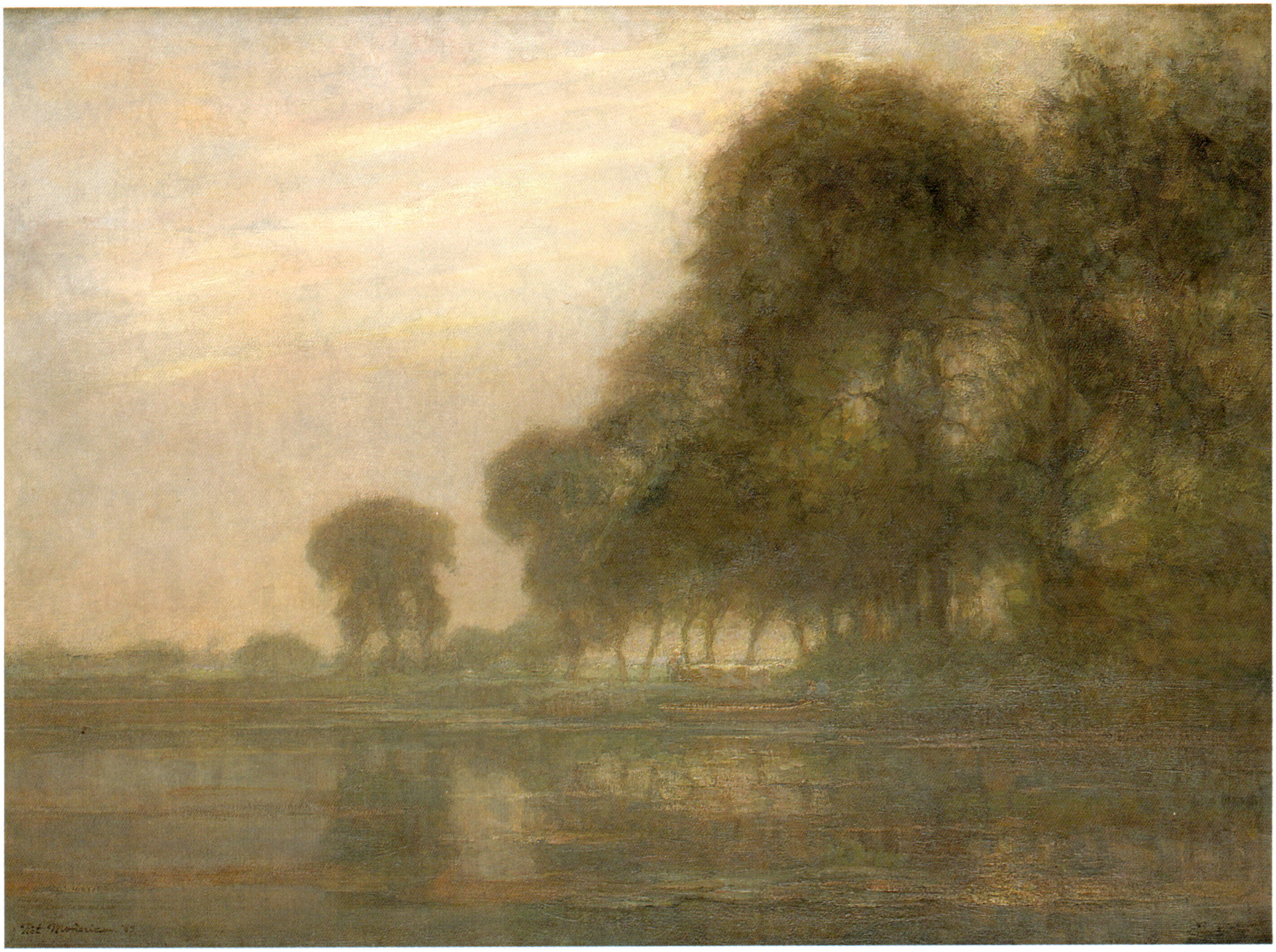

39

Landscape with Trees and Water

1907
oil/canvas
100 × 136 cm

inv.no. 73-1971
Blok 113

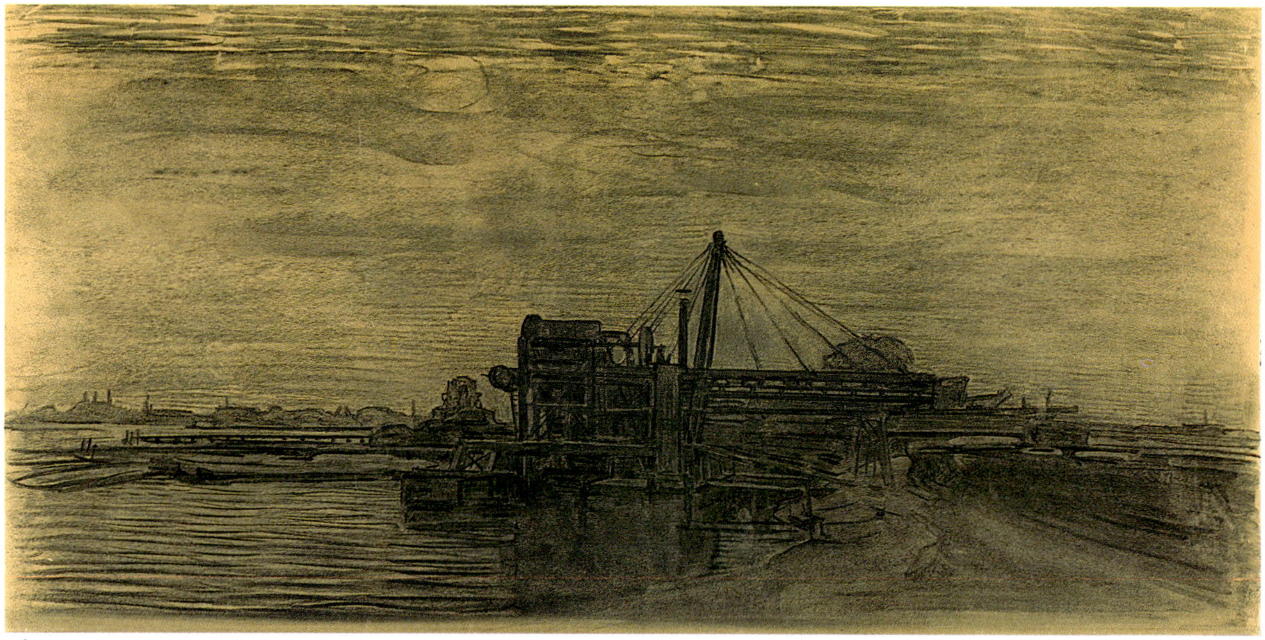
recto

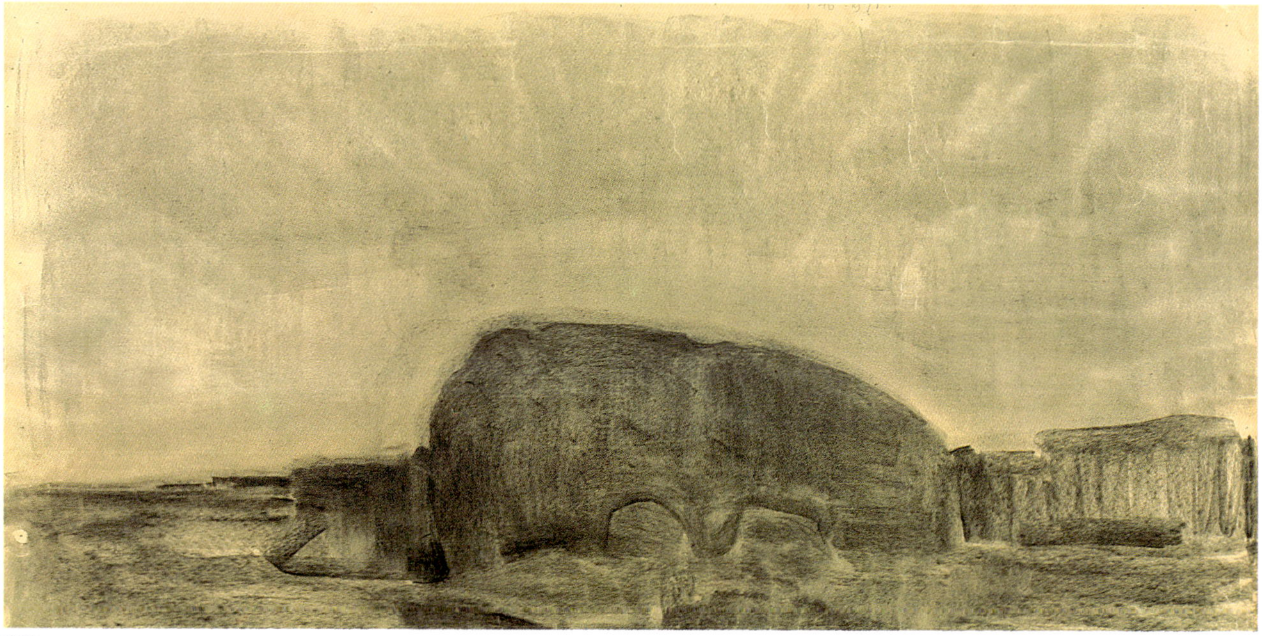
verso

40

Dredge (recto)

Haystack (verso)

1906/07
charcoal/crayon/paper
57 × 112 cm

inv.no. T46-1971
Blok 114

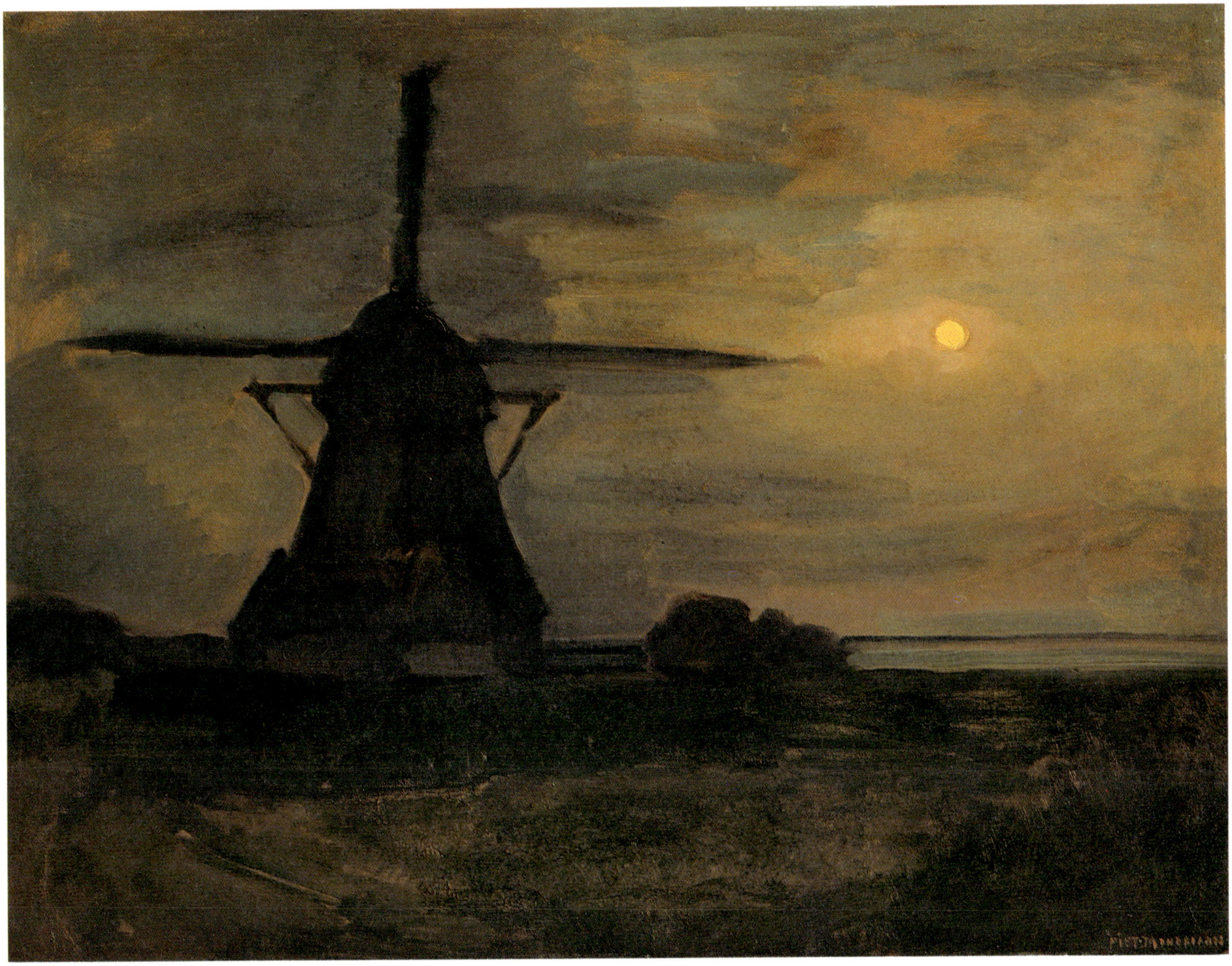

41

Mill in Moonlight

1906/07
oil/canvas
99.5 × 125.5 cm

inv.no.20-1939
Blok 117
Seuphor 23, c.c.104

Y—Yes indeed, rectangularity is *invariable* and thus expresses *calm.*

Z—This landscape is so calm because of the *plastic use* of the horizontal and vertical: the relationships of the planes, though not *in pure balance*, appear *in natural harmony.* The luminous sky stresses the vertical: the marked horizon the horizontal. The diagonal is eliminated. We would sense it though, if there were accents here and there. If, say, a tree stood out against the horizon, our glance would automatically trace a line from that tree to the moon: this diagonal would be out of balance with the vertical and horizontal of the landscape: the *great* calm would be destroyed.

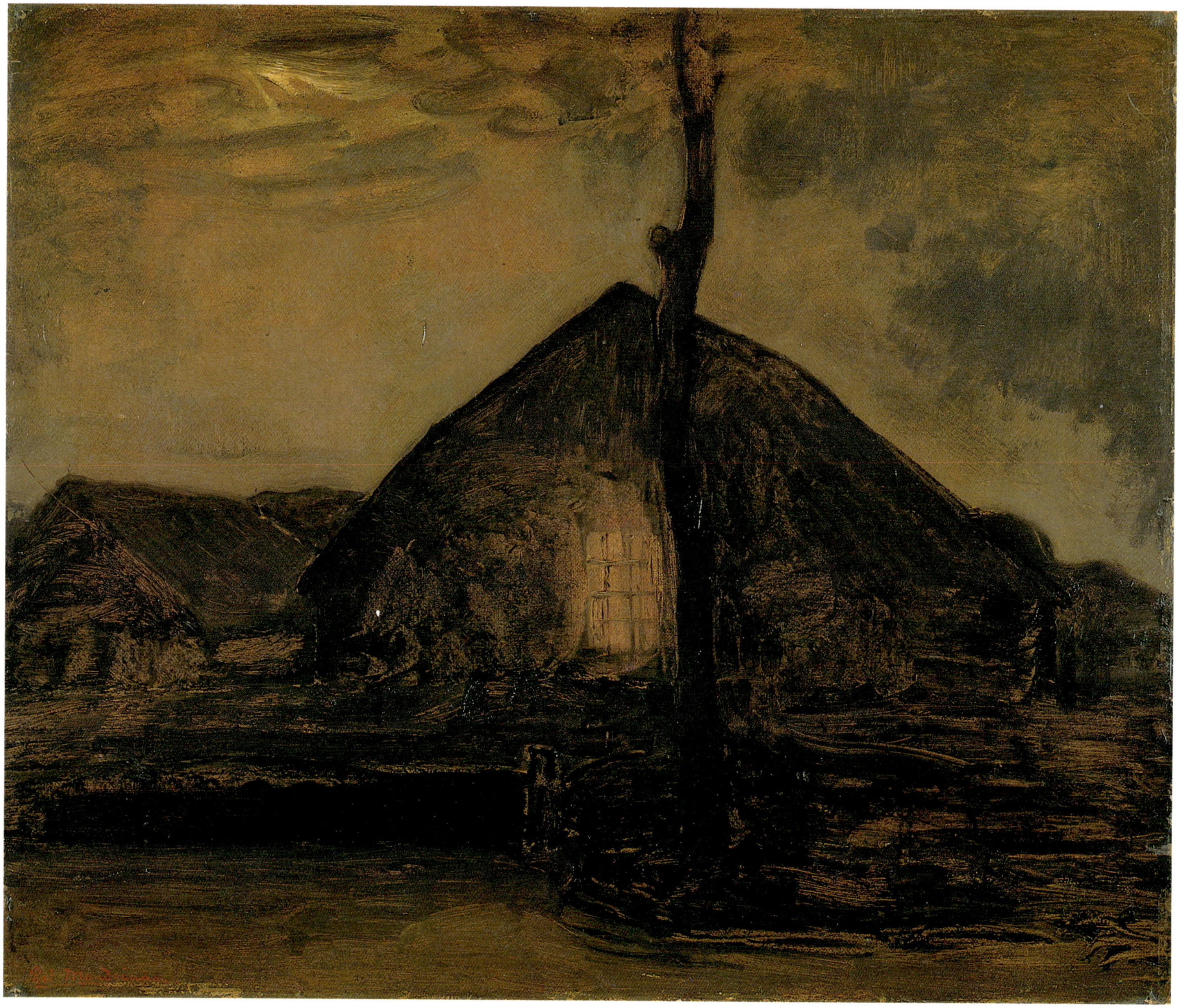

42

Farm in the Evening

1906/07
oil/cardboard
63.5 × 74.5 cm

inv.no. 95-1971
Blok 118
Seuphor 19, c.c.88

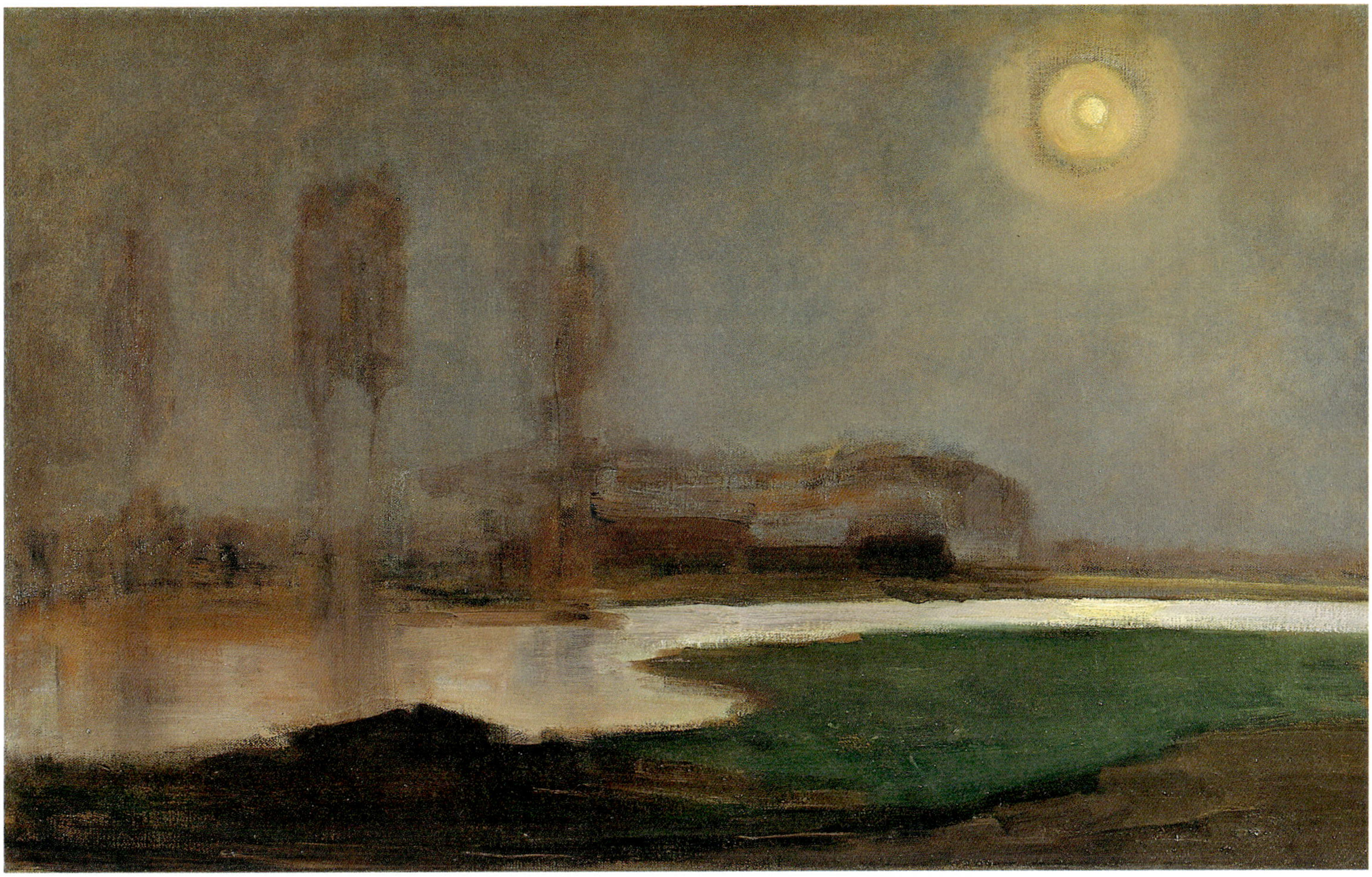

43

Summer Night

1906/07
oil/canvas
71 × 110.5 cm

inv.no.3-1967
Blok 120
Seuphor 207, c.c.50

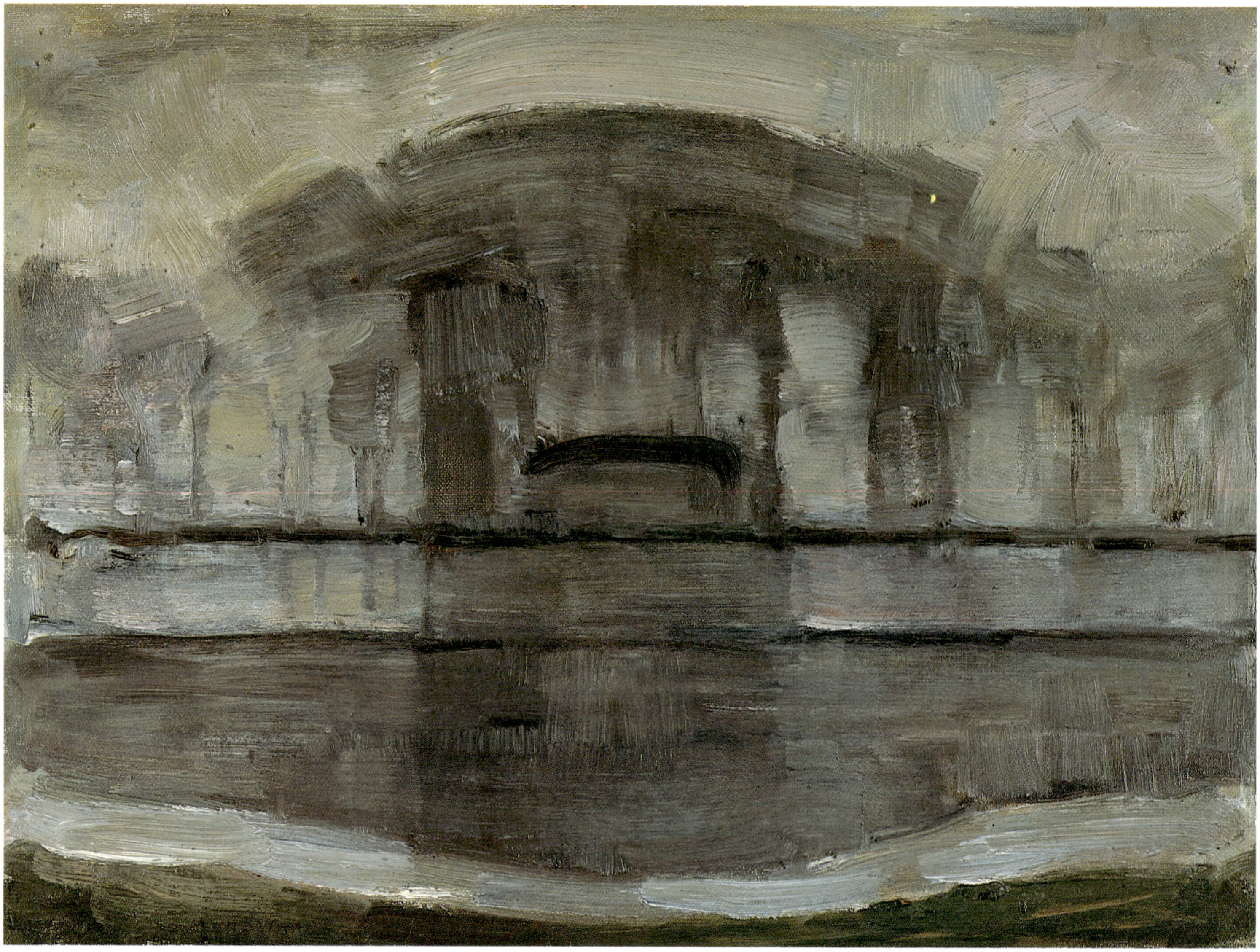

44

The Amstel: Haze

1906/07
oil/canvas
32.5 × 42.5 cm

inv.no.122-1971
Blok 122
Seuphor 181, c.c.75

X—Nature automatically makes me express relationships, but I am not very keen on depicting *solely* relationships. Take this landscape: I see the relationship of the bright moon, the sky and the earth; I also see that the moon's position in the landscape is a matter of relationship. But I fail to see why I should abstract everything for the sake of these relationships; naturalism makes relationships so *exciting* to me!

Z—It depends on how you look at things: to me the depiction of relationships is more exciting when *not* hidden by nature but occurring in planes and straight lines instead.

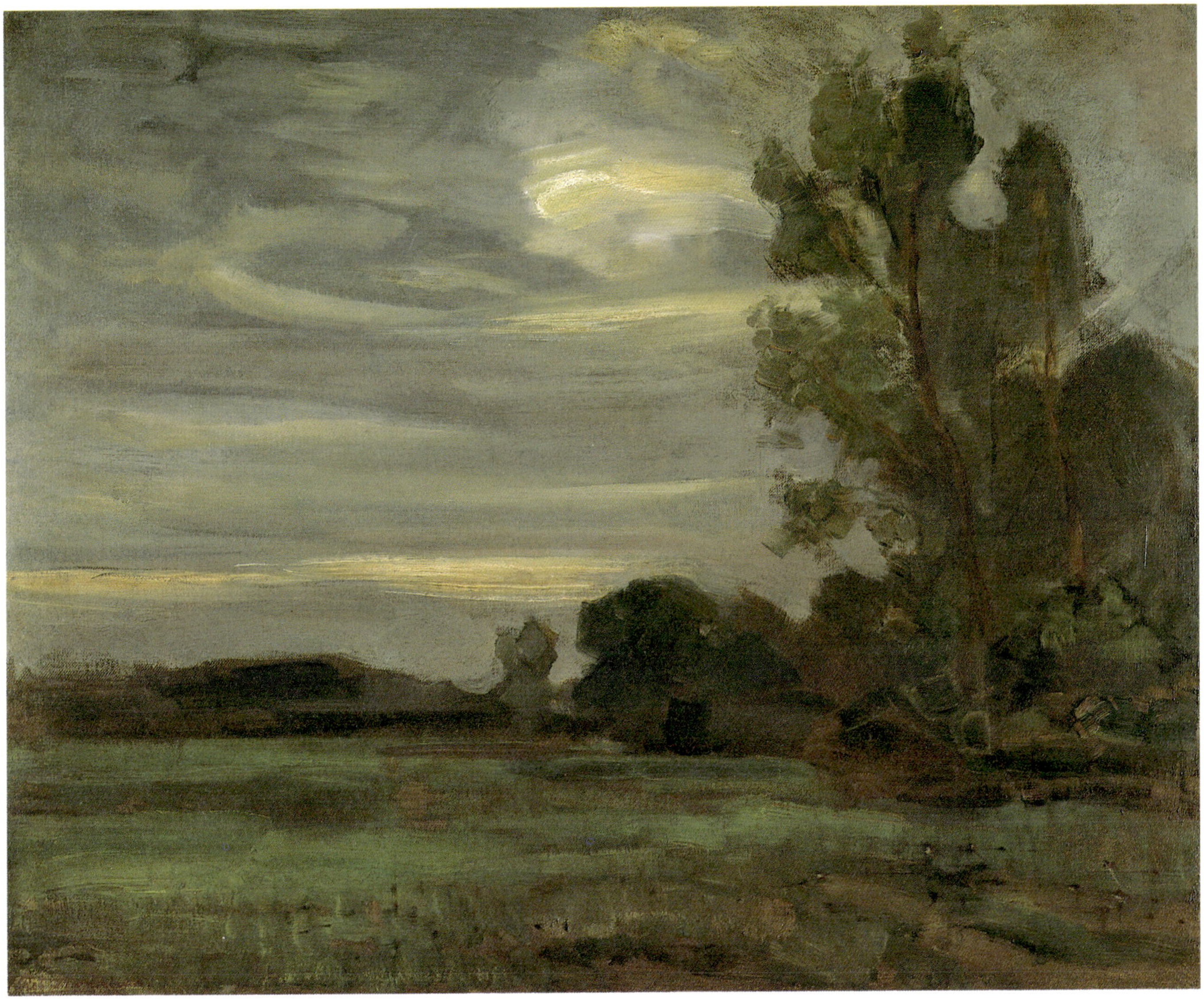

45

Landscape

1907
oil/canvas
78 × 91 cm

inv.no. 97-1971
Blok 129

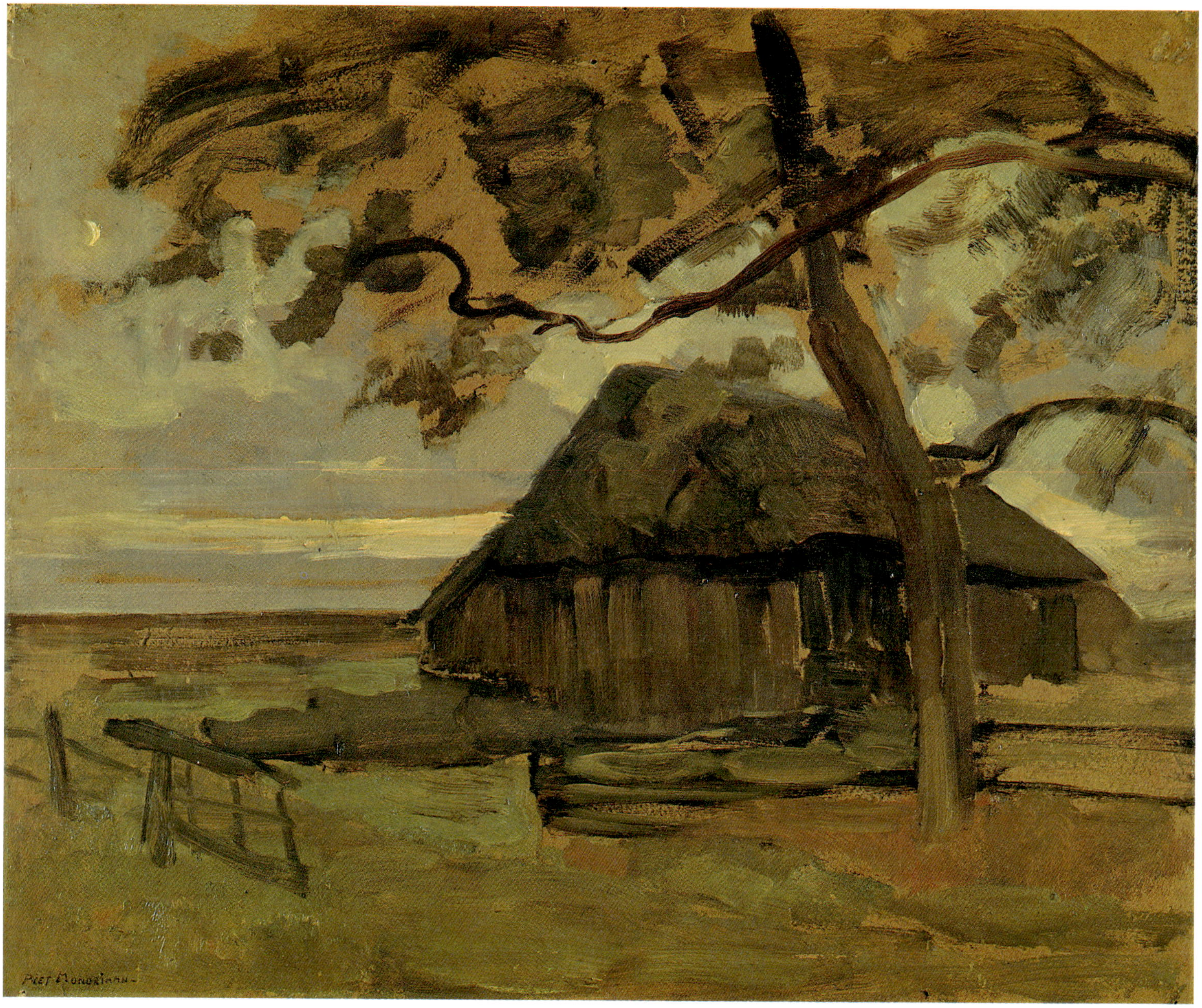

46

Farmhouse at Evening

1907
oil/cardboard
34.5 × 47.5 cm

inv.no.118-1971
Blok 132
Seuphor 195, c.c.100

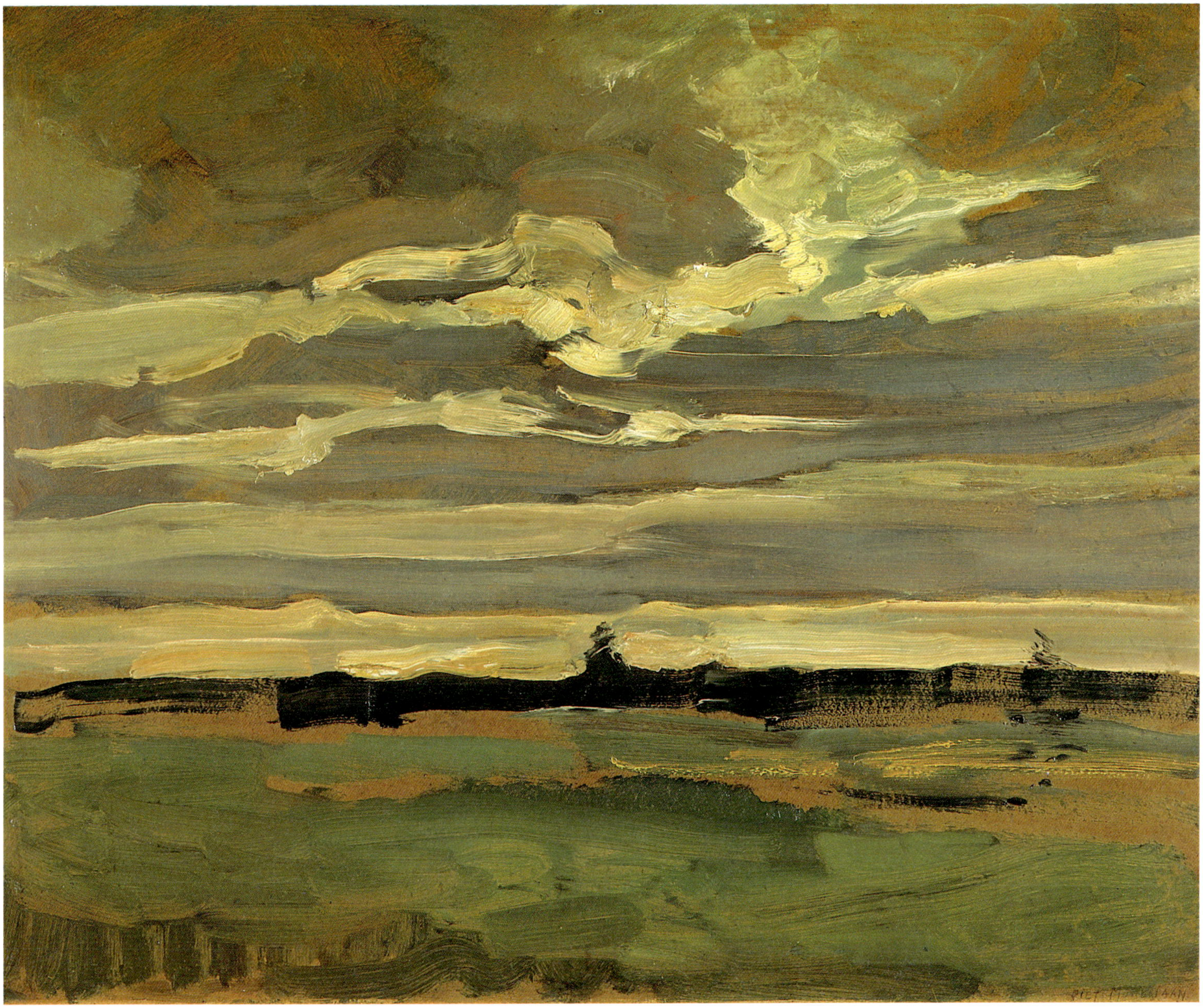

47

Landscape

1907
oil/cardboard
63.5 × 76 cm

inv.no.2-X-1967
Blok 133

Z — In this landscape the horizontal — from our viewpoint — is really only depicted by the *definition* of the horizontal line of the skyline. One direction is thus defined: however, neither its *opposite*, the *vertical*, nor any other line is depicted exactly in this landscape; height is depicted *as a plane*. The sky is shown as an indefinite plane, but the moon as *a point*, hence *exact*. The plane is defined *from this point to the horizon*: *defined* by a *vertical line*. Although it does not exist in nature, it is indeed there: and so if we draw it, the opposite of the horizontal is *defined*. We thus see that the relationship of directions, though not exact, does manifest itself plastically in nature. And the *balanced* relationship of directions — the rectangular confrontation of lines and planes — constitutes the plastic expression of *calm*.

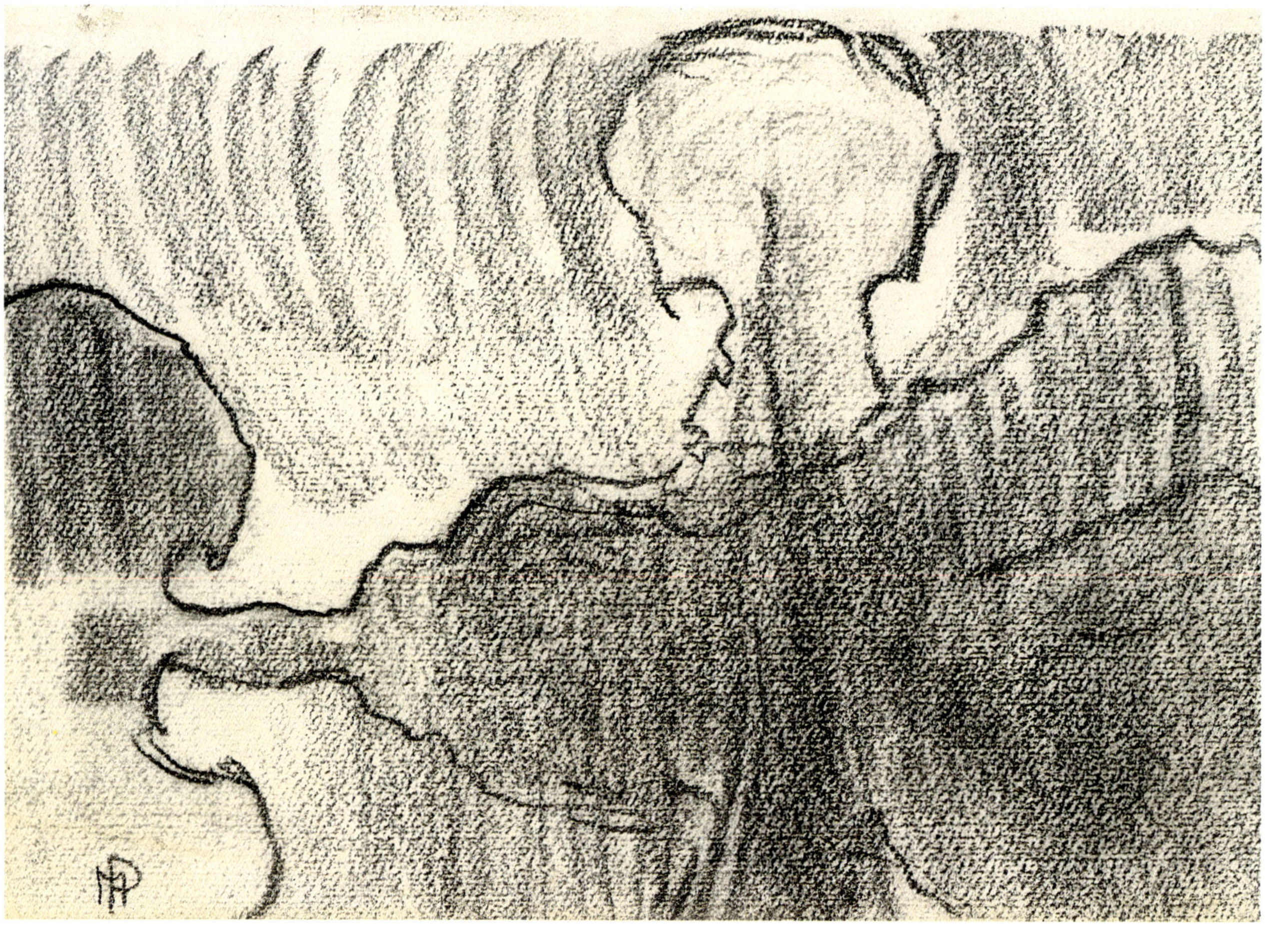

48

Solitary Tree

1907
crayon/paper
13.8 × 19 cm

inv.no.T98-1971
Blok 136

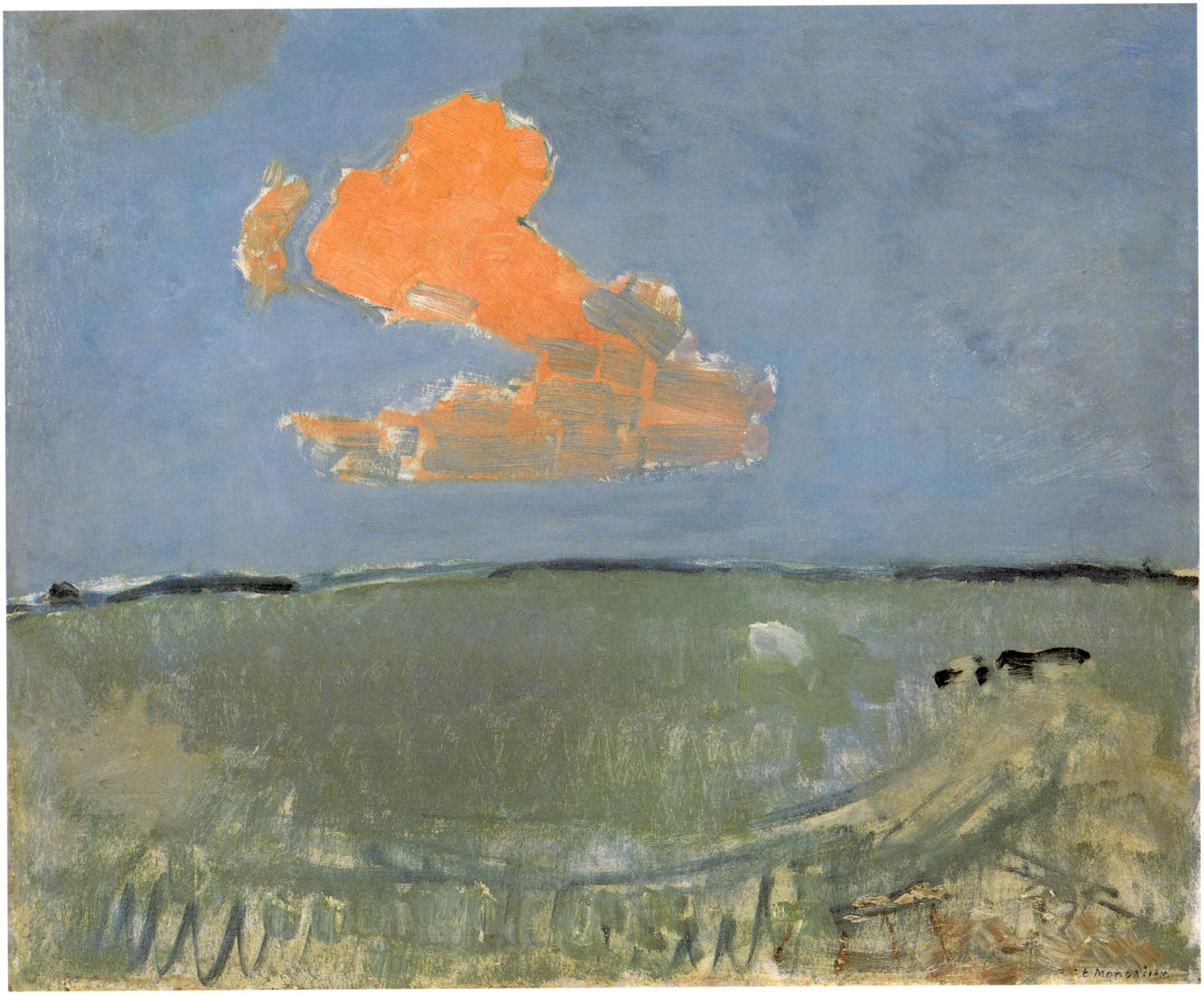

49

Red Cloud

1907
oil/cardboard
64 × 75 cm

inv.no. 23-1956
Blok 138

Y—Colour *itself* always affects me very strongly. Yellow on its own, a simple blue, opens up an entire world of beauty to me!

Z—To be sure, colour as colour enlivens things, and when colour is regarded purely it can rise to supreme heights, to the universal. But...colour as colour depicts the most external in such a dominating fashion that we are in danger, looking at it, of lingering on more external things and of vagueness, instead of *seeing* what is abstract.

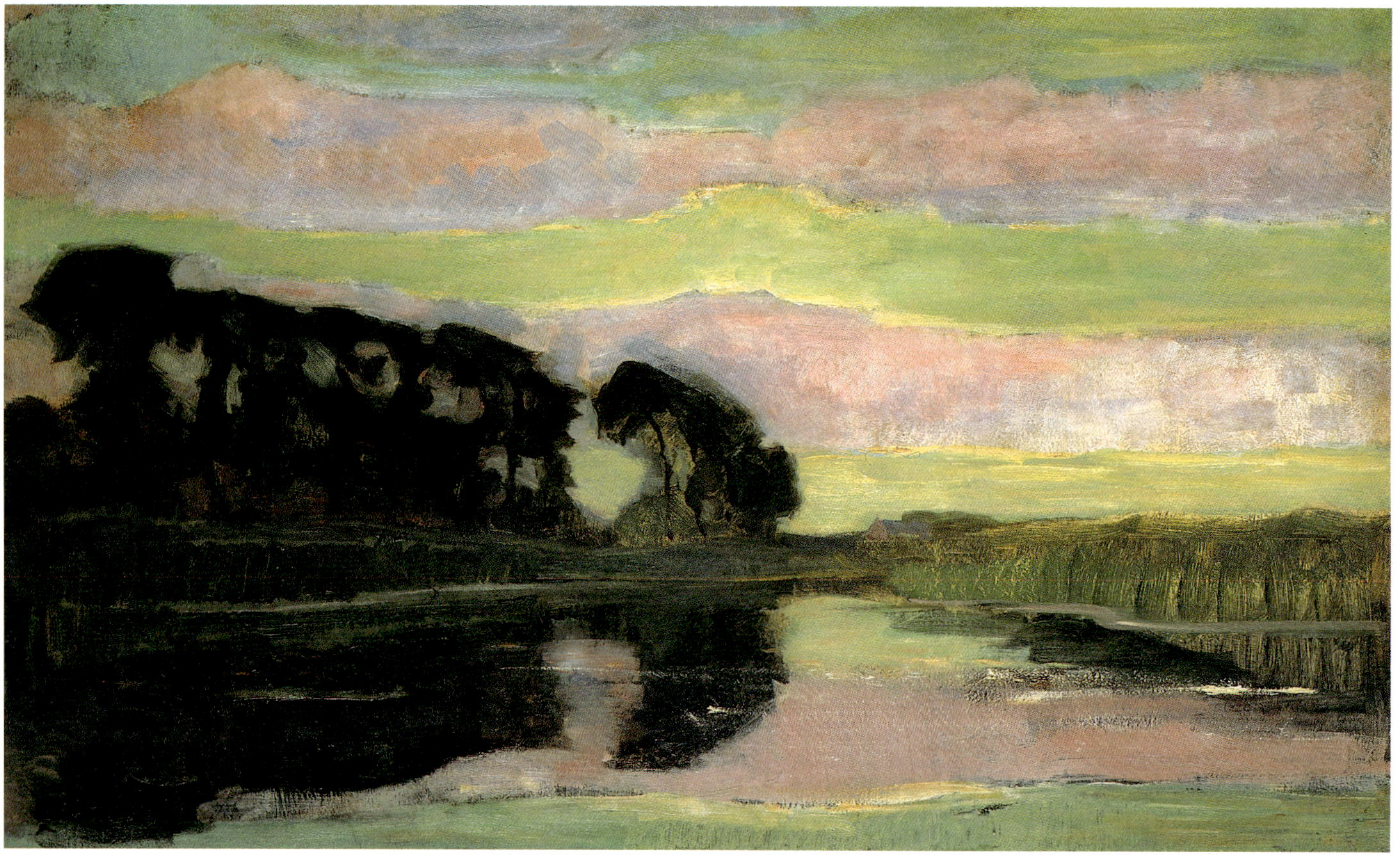

50

Large Landscape

1907
oil/canvas
75 × 120 cm

inv.no.111-1971
Blok 139
Seuphor 208, c.c.51

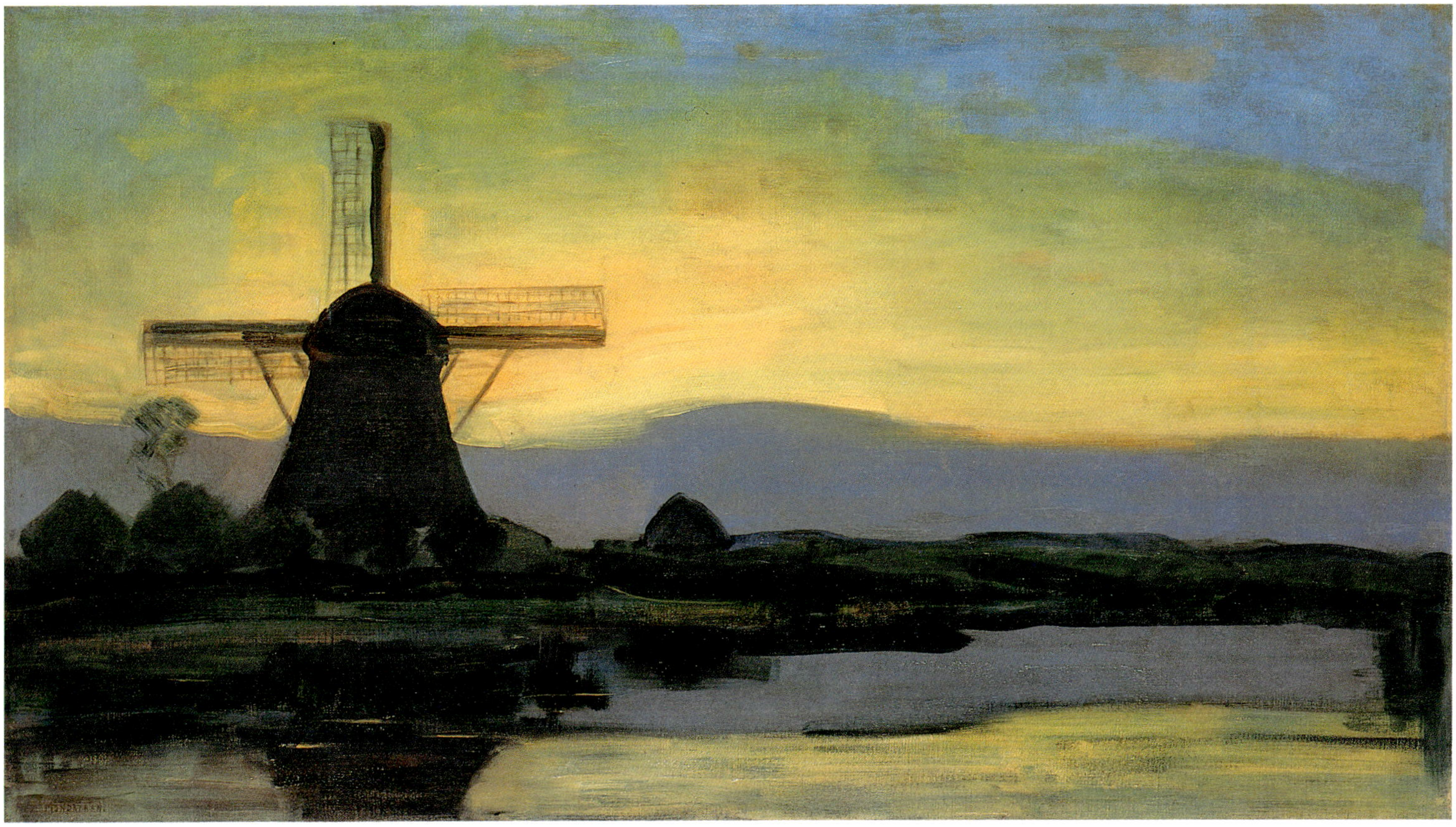

51

Mill in the Evening

1907
oil/canvas
67.5 × 117.5 cm

inv.no.75-1971
Blok 140

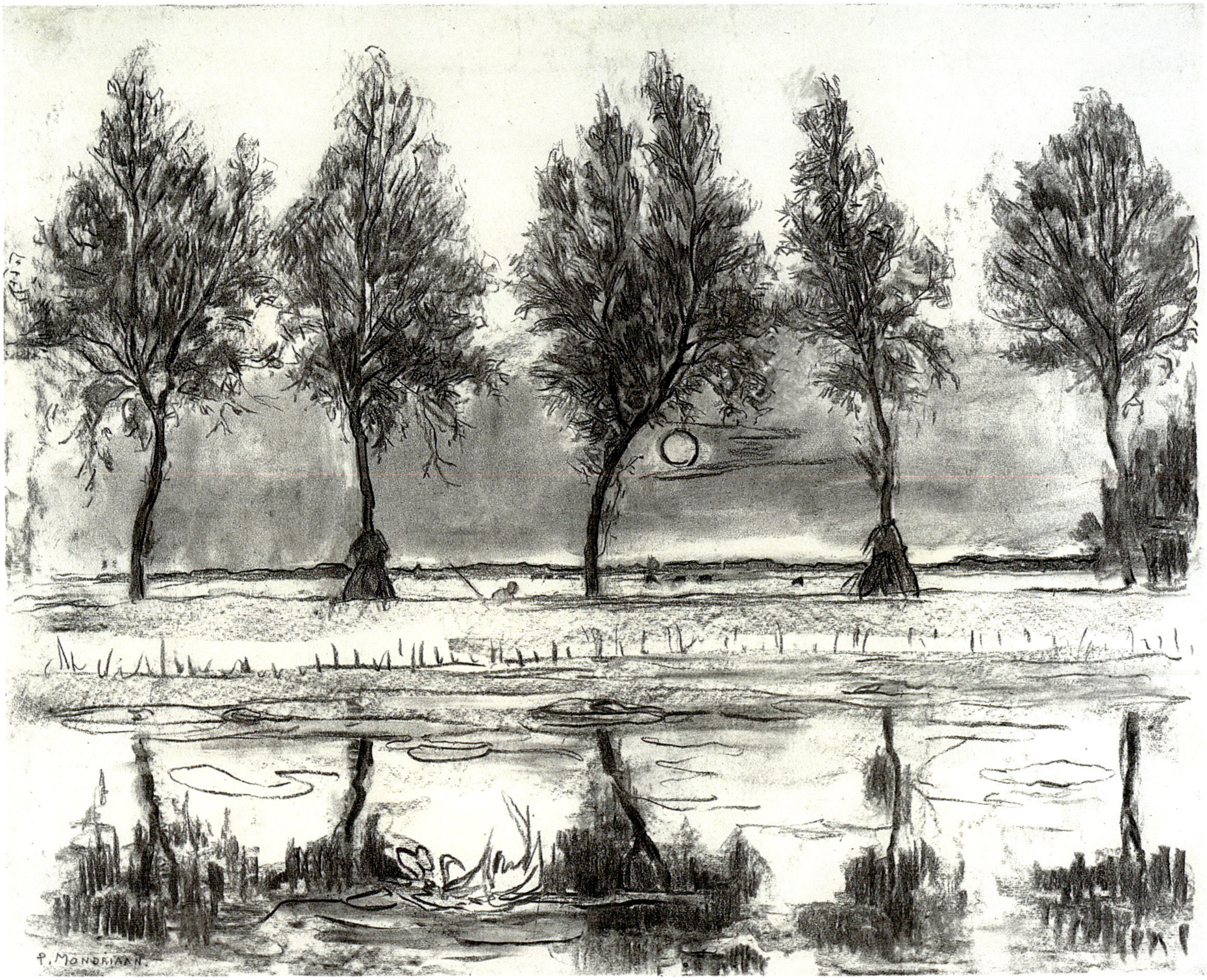

52

Trees on the Gein: Moonrise

1907/08
charcoal/paper
63 × 75 cm

inv.no.T106-1971
Blok 141
Seuphor 45, c.c.71

Z—The plane and the straight line must be the *means* of doing it...the artist must actually *do it.*

X—I agree with you there, but I'd rather stick to nature myself!

Z—(...)

X—Irregularity is beautiful.

Z—Beautiful but tragic; if you stick to nature you will only be able to ban tragedy from your art to a very slight extent. Naturalistic painting enables us to *sense* the harmony that transcends tragedy, but it fails to define it because it does not depict *solely balanced relationships.* The natural phenomenon, form, natural colour, natural rhythm, even in most cases natural relationships just depict *tragedy.*

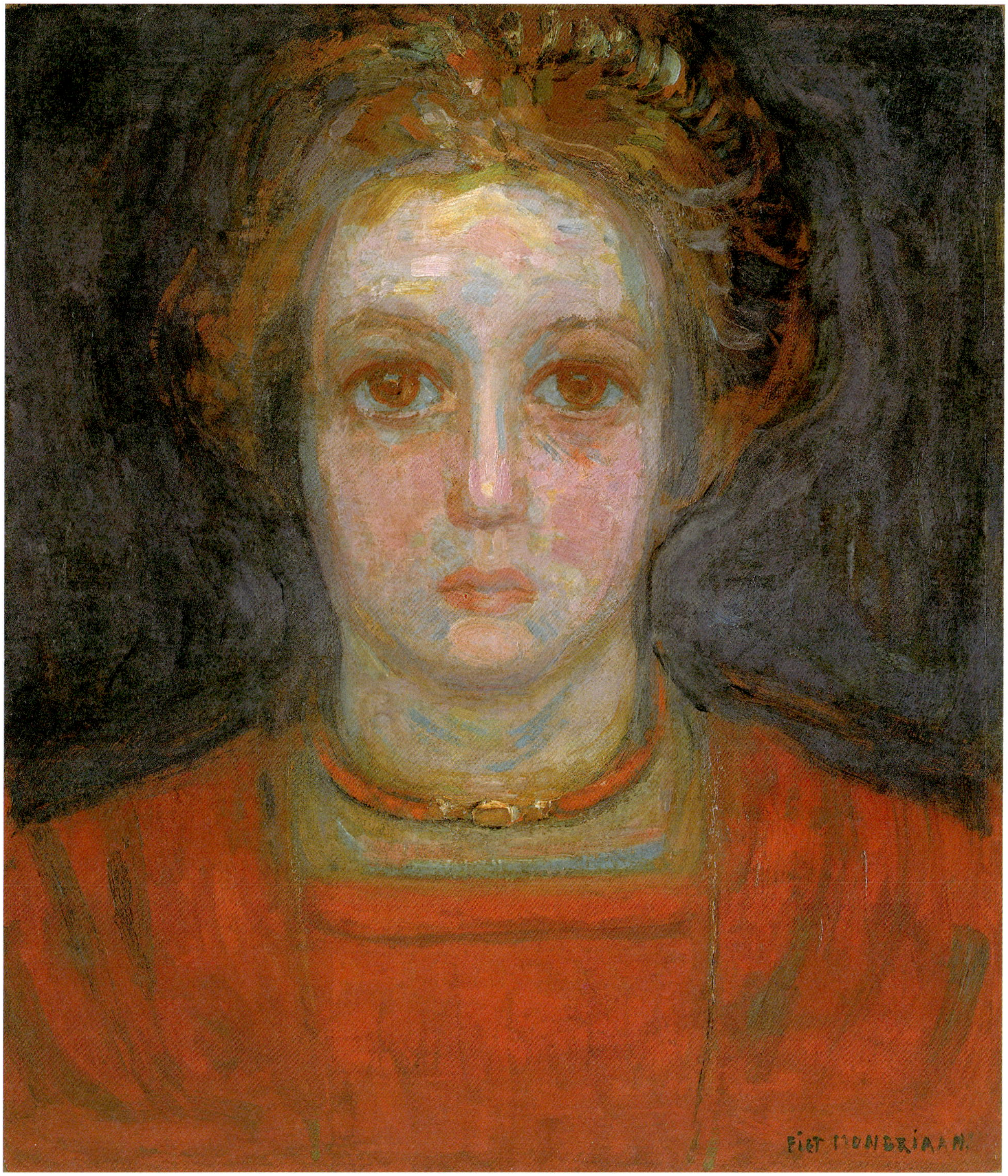

53

Portrait of a Girl

1908
oil/canvas/cardboard
49 × 41.5 cm

inv.no.129-1971
Blok 153
Seuphor 255, c.c.17

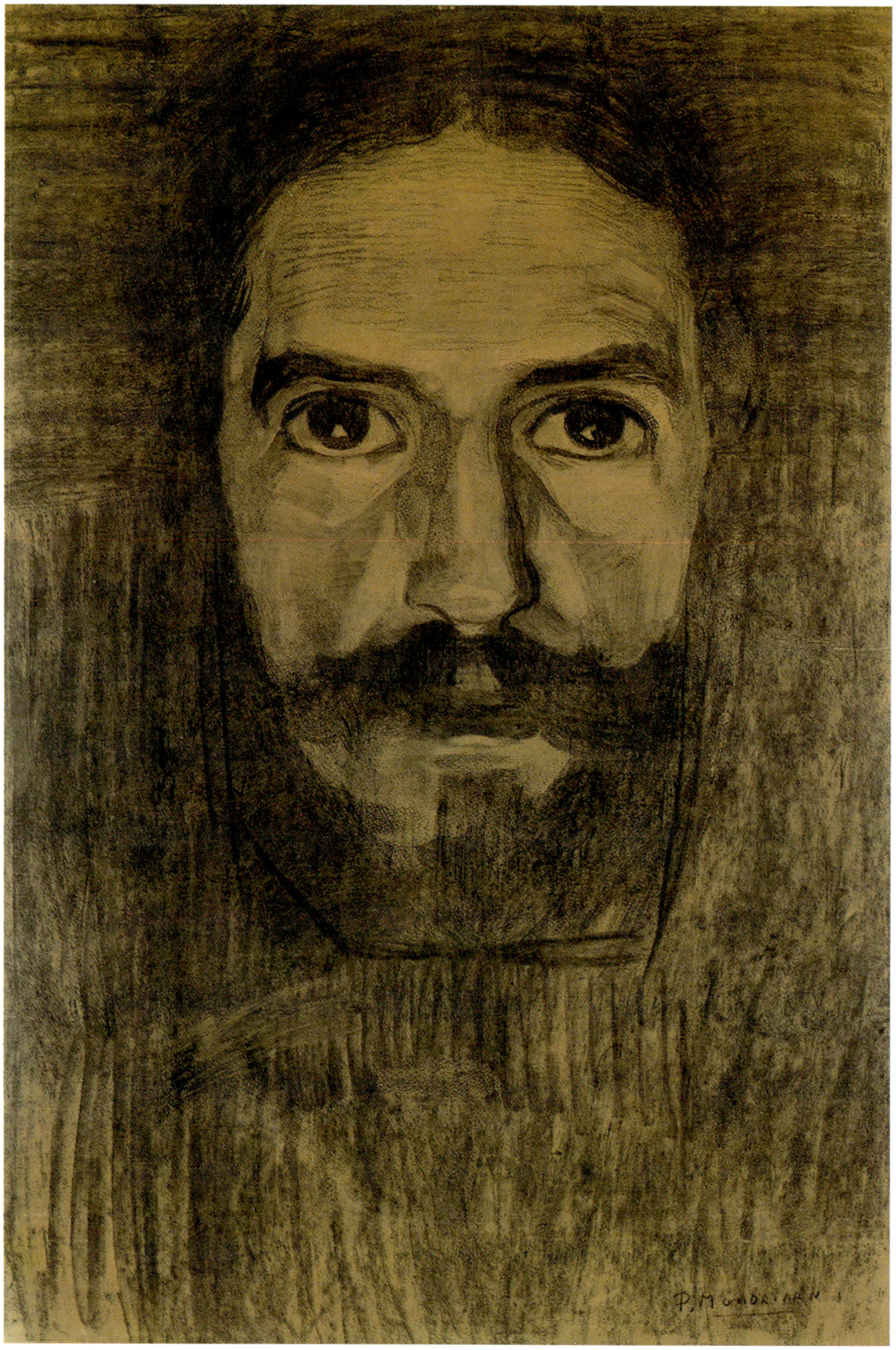

54

Self Portrait

1908/09
charcoal/crayon/paper
79.3 × 53 cm

inv.no.T48-1971
Blok 156
Seuphor 224, c.c.2

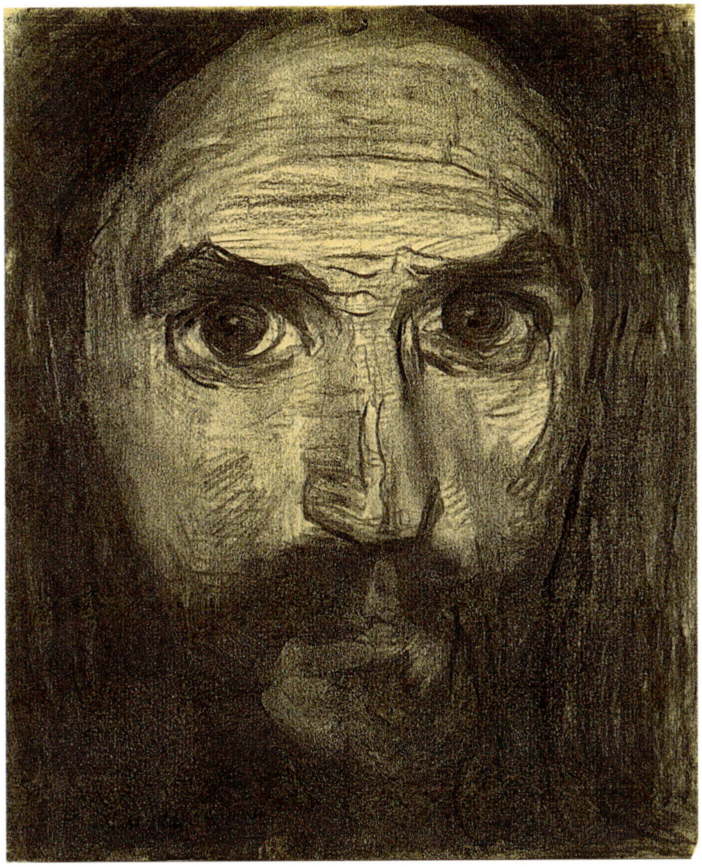

55

Self Portrait

1908/09
charcoal/paper
28 × 23.3 cm

inv.no.T52-1971
Blok 157
Seuphor 287

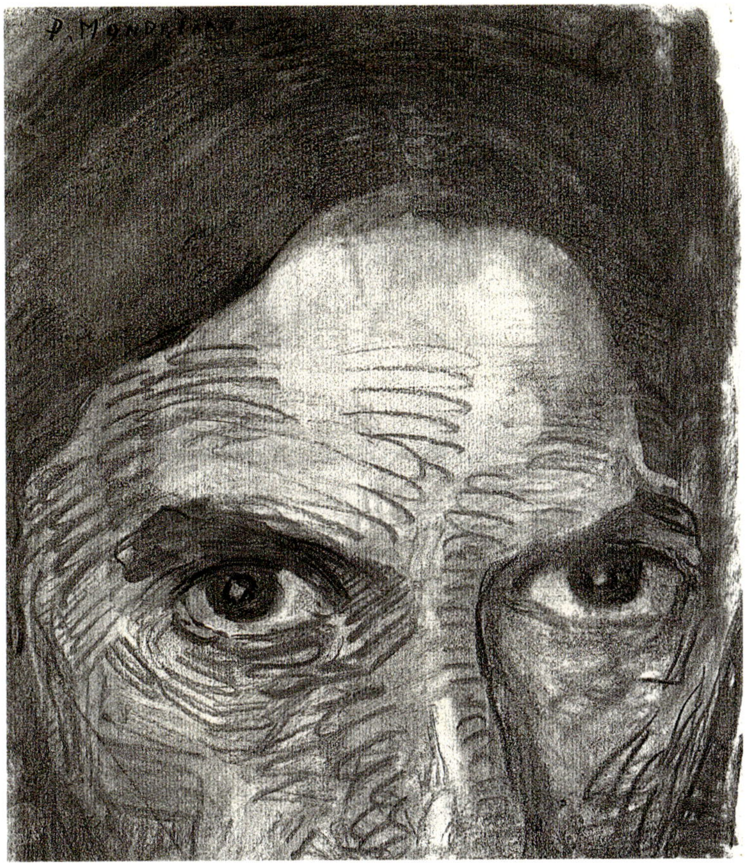

56

Self Portrait

1908/09
charcoal/paper
28.4 × 24.4 cm

inv.no.T53-1971
Blok 158
Seuphor 288

Z— If we take a naturalistic view of nature, there is no escaping tragic *interpretation*. A more profound interpretation is therefore necessary. *The sensation of tragedy can only be evaded by those who have learned, by developing purely plastic vision, to express the individual universally.*

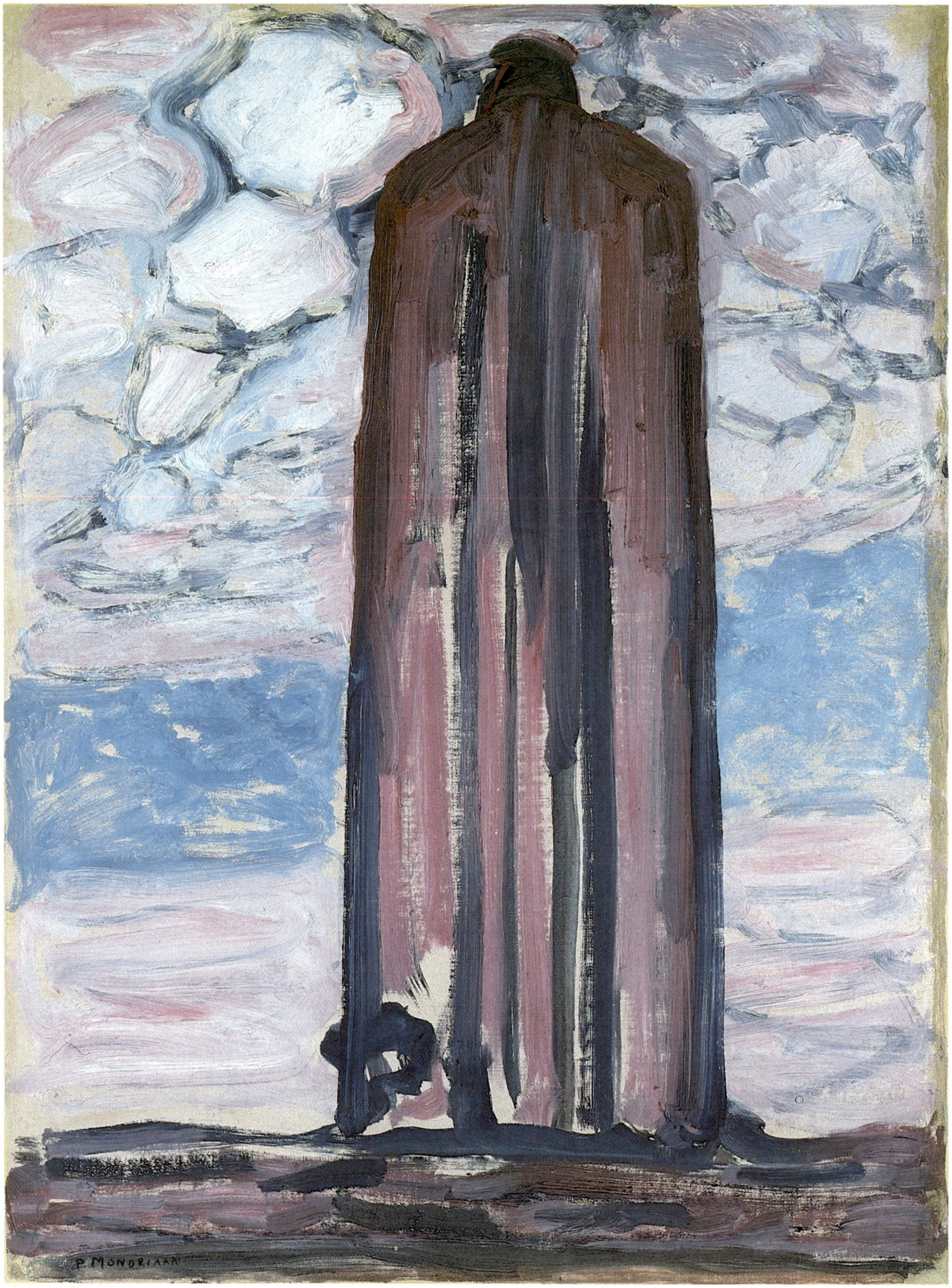

57

Lighthouse at Westkapelle

1908
oil/canvas
71 × 52 cm

inv.no.127-1971
Blok 160
Seuphor 312, c.c.242

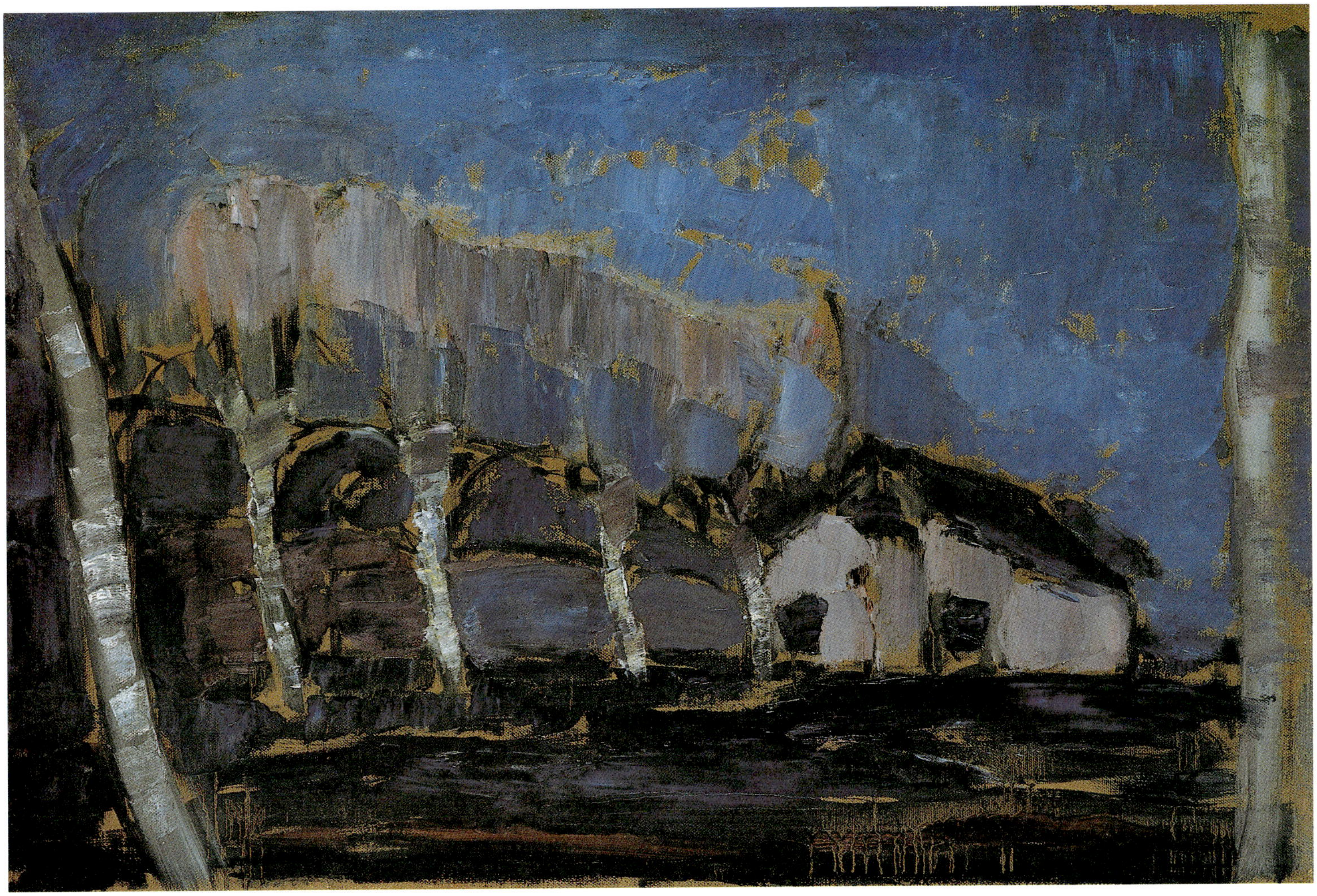

58

Landscape at Evening

1908
oil/canvas
64 × 93 cm

inv.no.54-1934
Blok 162
Seuphor 76, c.c.95

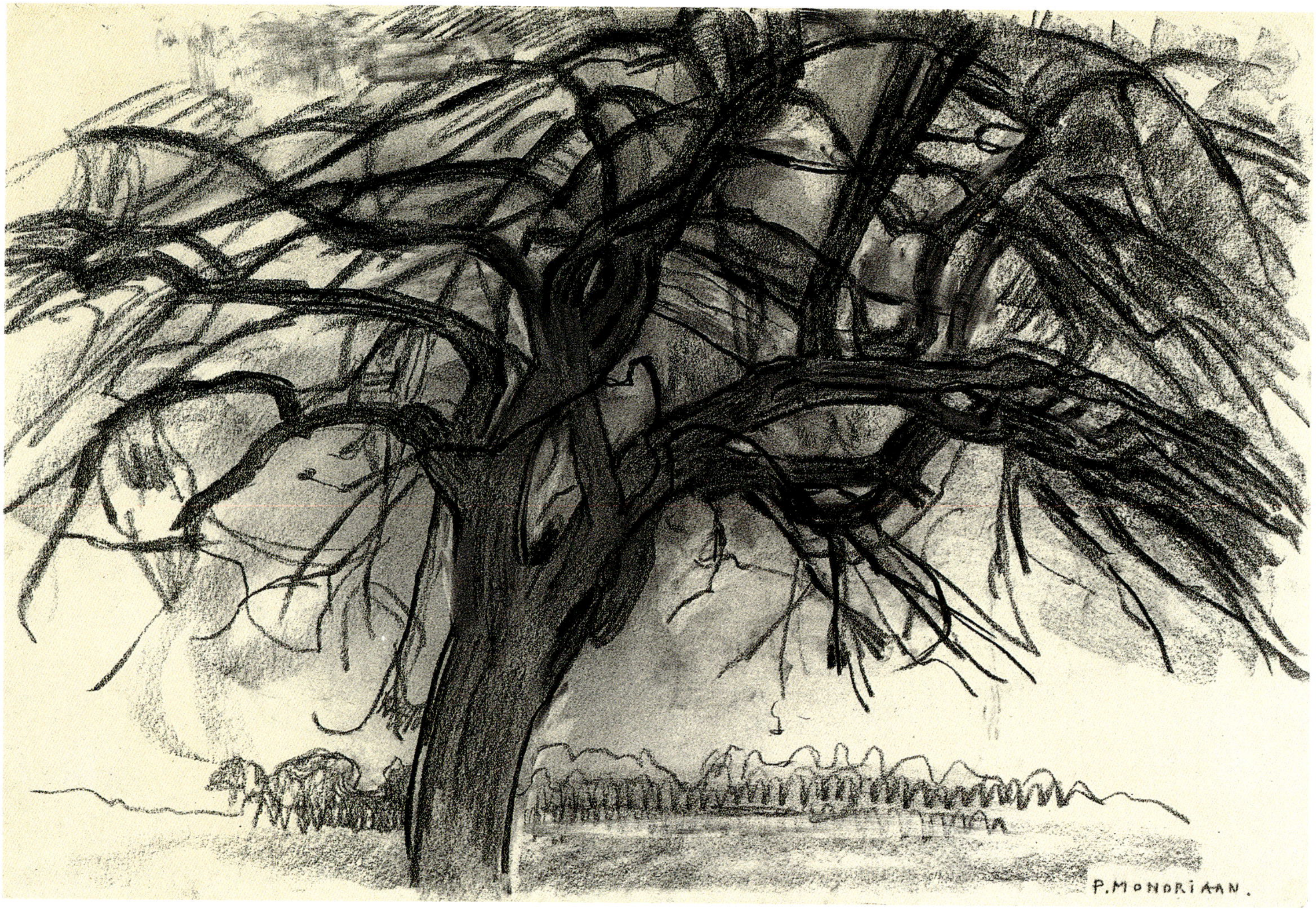

59

Tree I

1908/09
crayon/paper
35 × 43 cm

inv.no.T62-1958
Blok 164
Seuphor 282, c.c.169

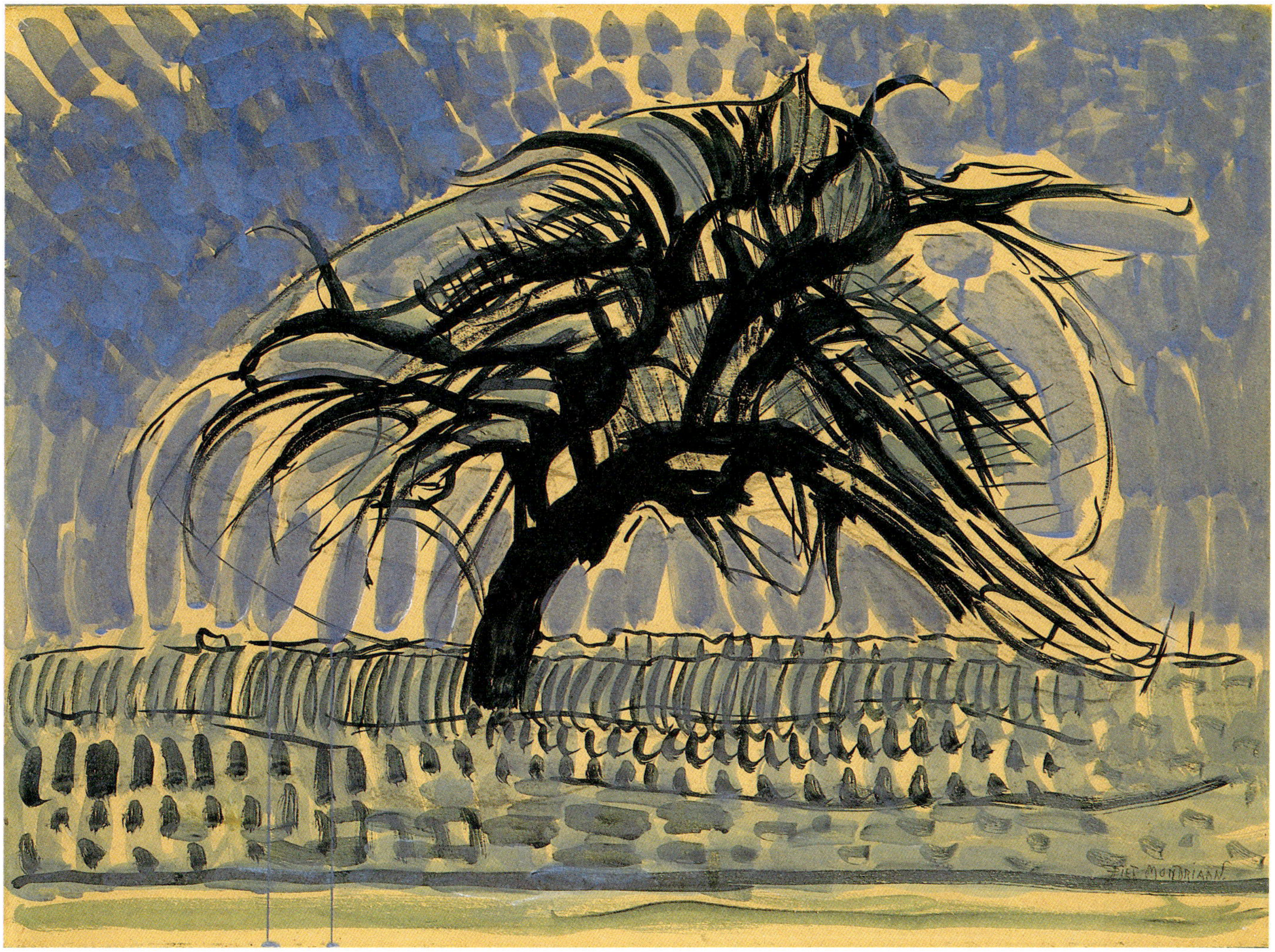

60

Blue Tree

1908/09
distemper/cardboard
75.5 × 99.5 cm

inv.no.T99-1934
Blok 165
Seuphor 284, c.c.172

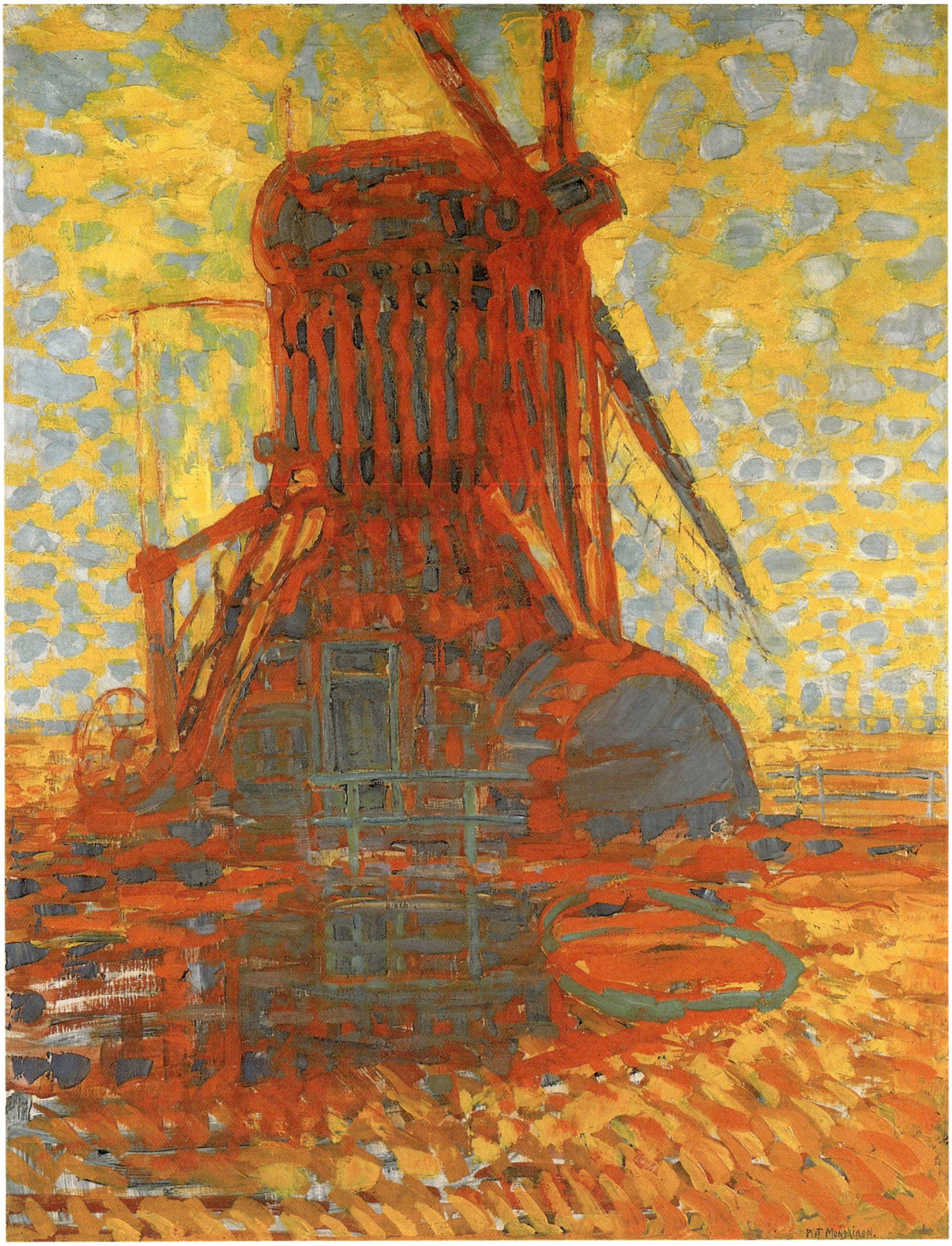

61

Windmill in Sunlight

1908
oil/canvas
114 × 87 cm

inv.no.130-1971
Blok 166
Seuphor 325, c.c.113

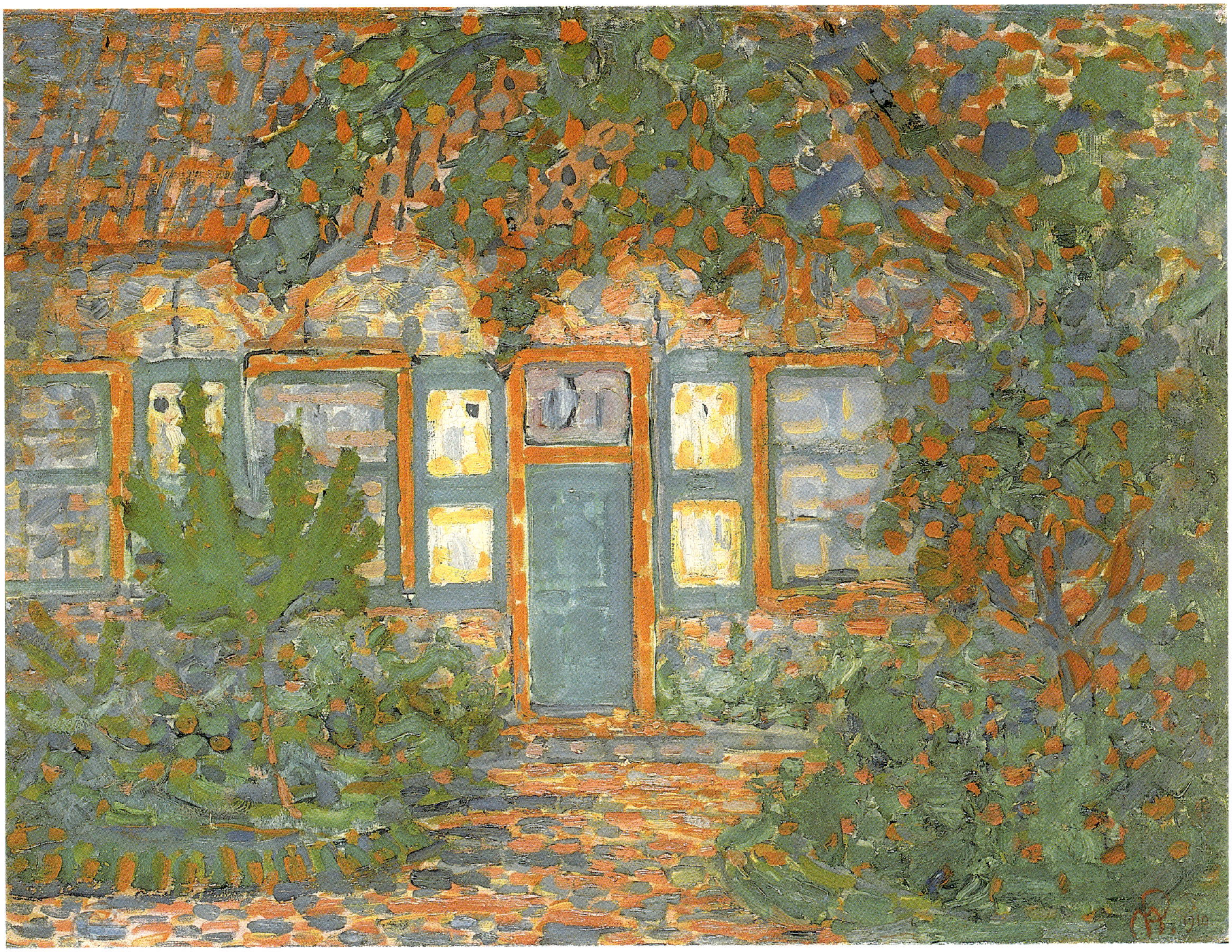

62

Farmhouse

1909
oil/canvas
52.5 × 68 cm

inv.no.106-1952
Blok 169
Seuphor 318

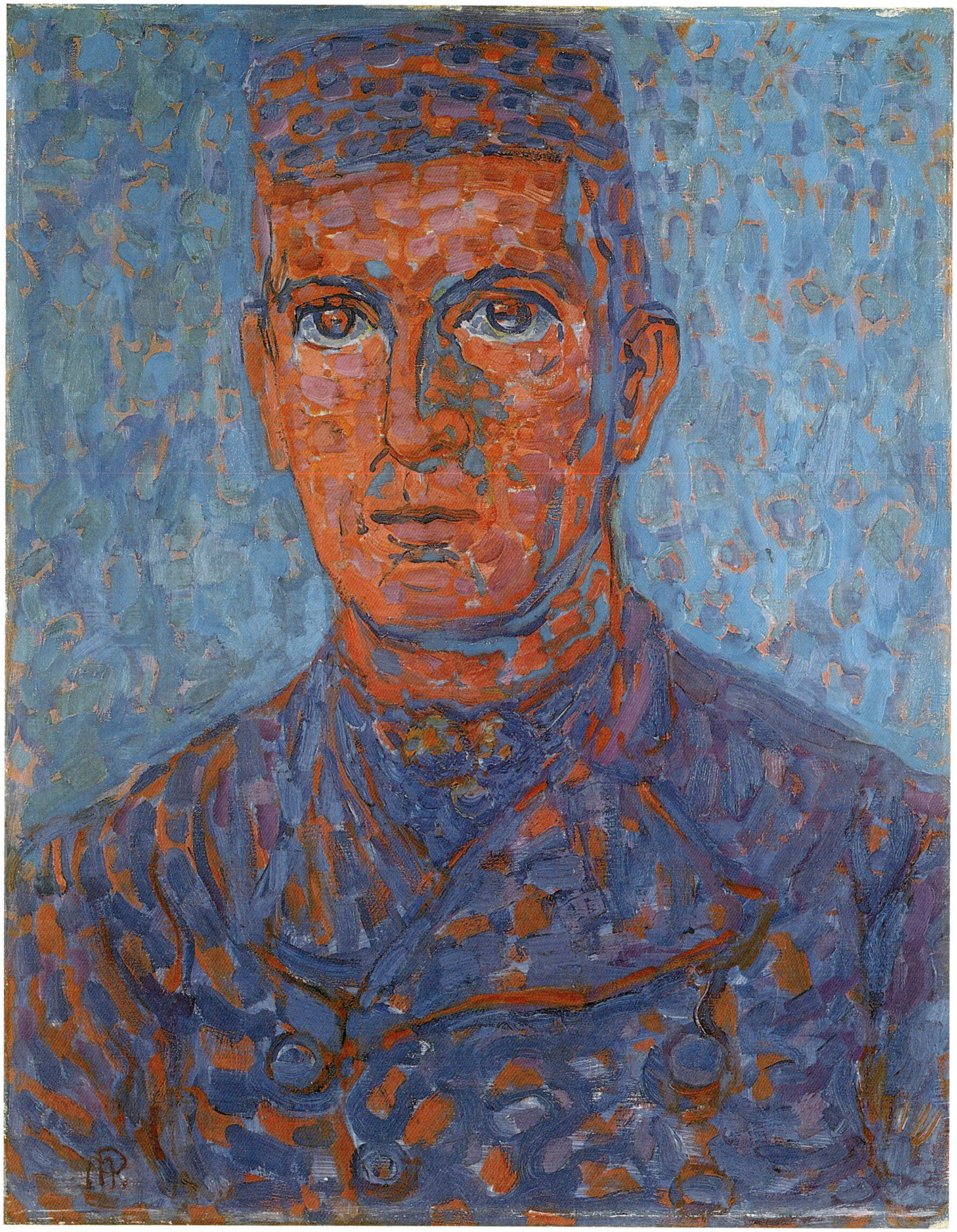

63

Zeeland Farmer

1909/10
oil/canvas
69 × 53 cm

inv.no.140-1971
Blok 170
Seuphor 225, c.c.15

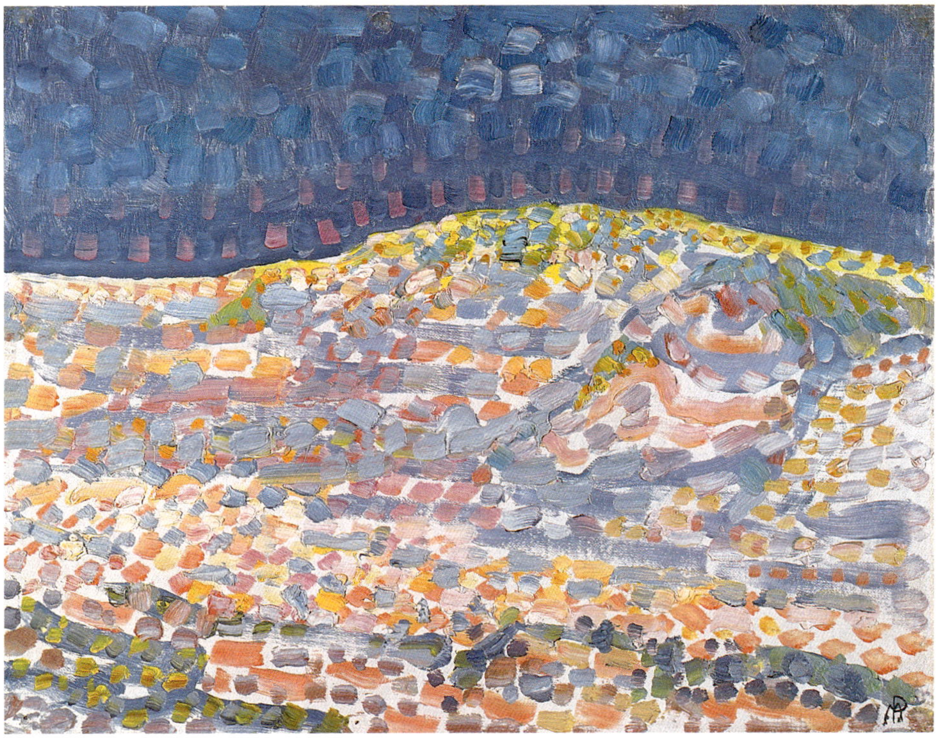

64

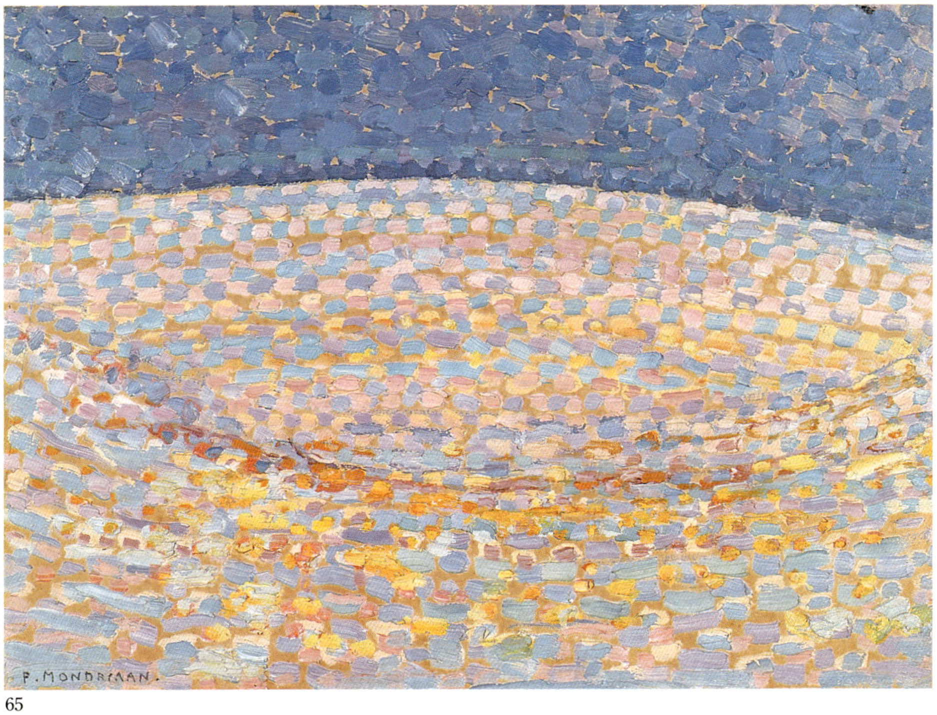

65

64

Dune II

1909
oil/canvas
37.5 × 46.5 cm

inv.no.134-1971
Blok 171
Seuphor 309, c.c.218

65

Dune III

1909
oil/cardboard
29.5 × 39 cm

inv.no.135-1971
Blok 172
Seuphor 310, c.c.219

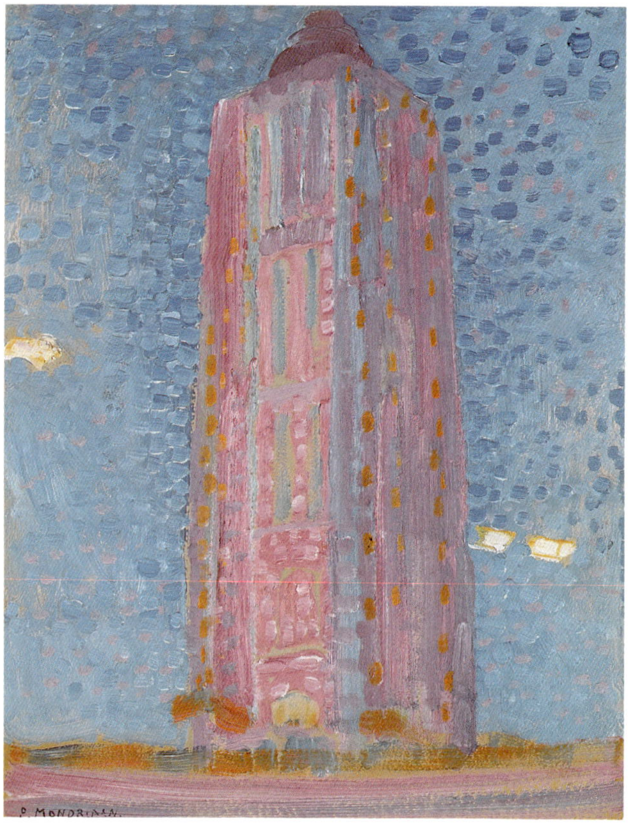

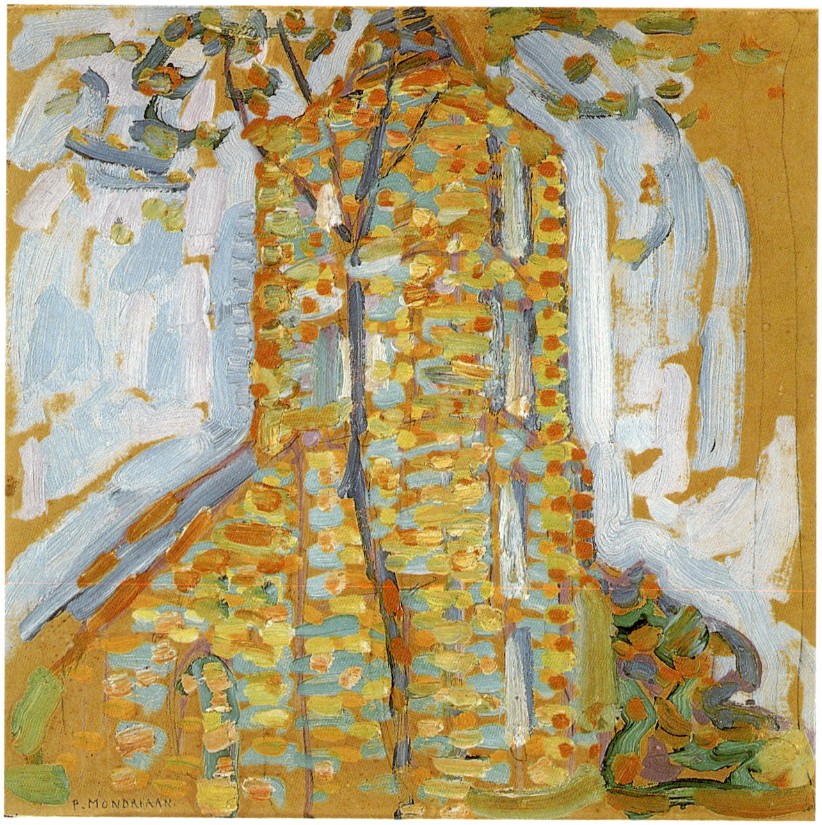

66

Lighthouse at Westkapelle

1909
oil/cardboard
39 × 29.5 cm

inv.no.137-1971
Blok 173
Seuphor 314, c.c.244

67

Church at Domburg

1909
oil/cardboard
36 × 36 cm

inv.no.136-1971
Blok 174
Seuphor 317, c.c.249

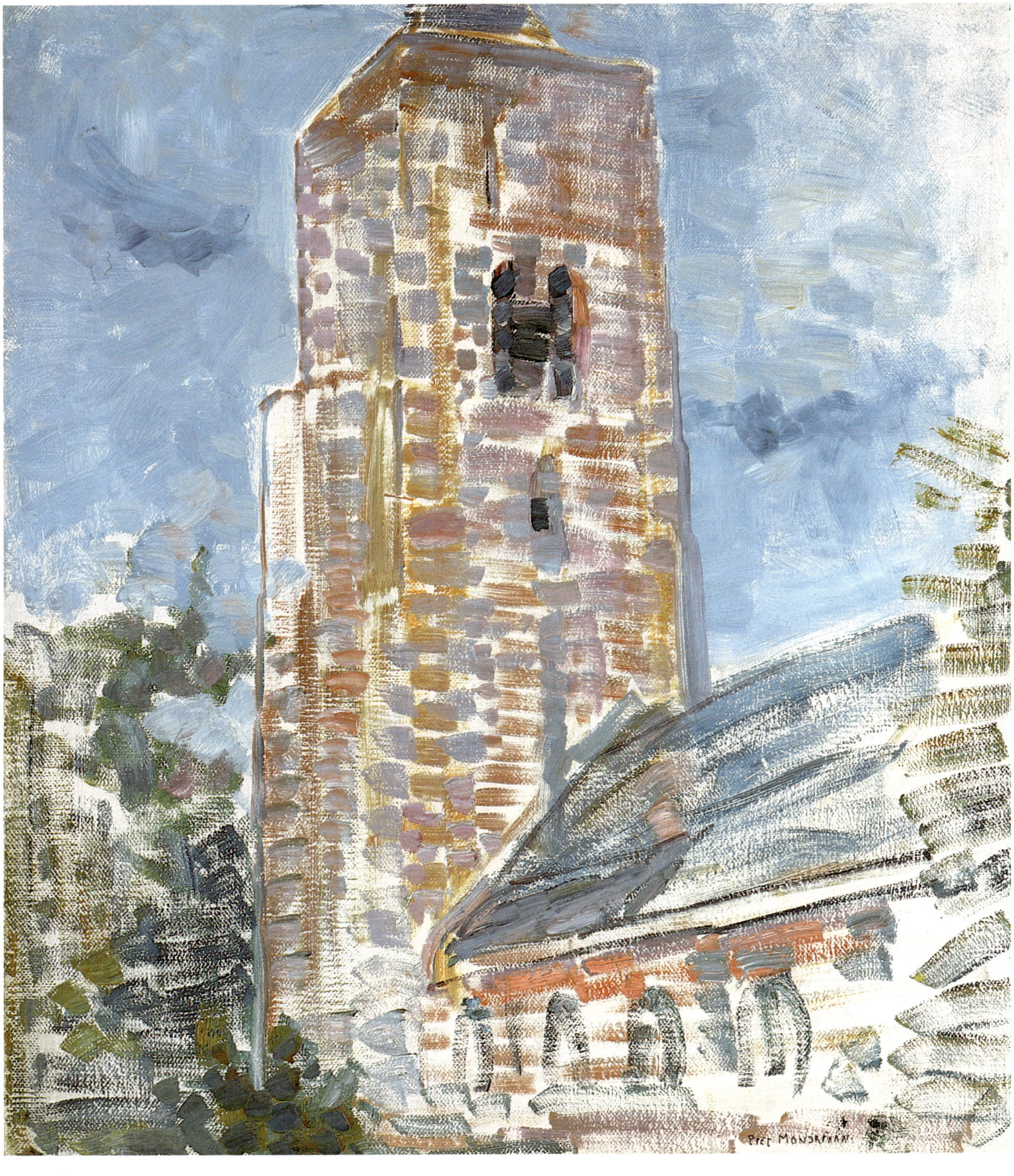

68

Church at Domburg

1909
oil/canvas
76 × 65.5 cm

inv.no.141-1971
Blok 175
Seuphor 316, c.c.248

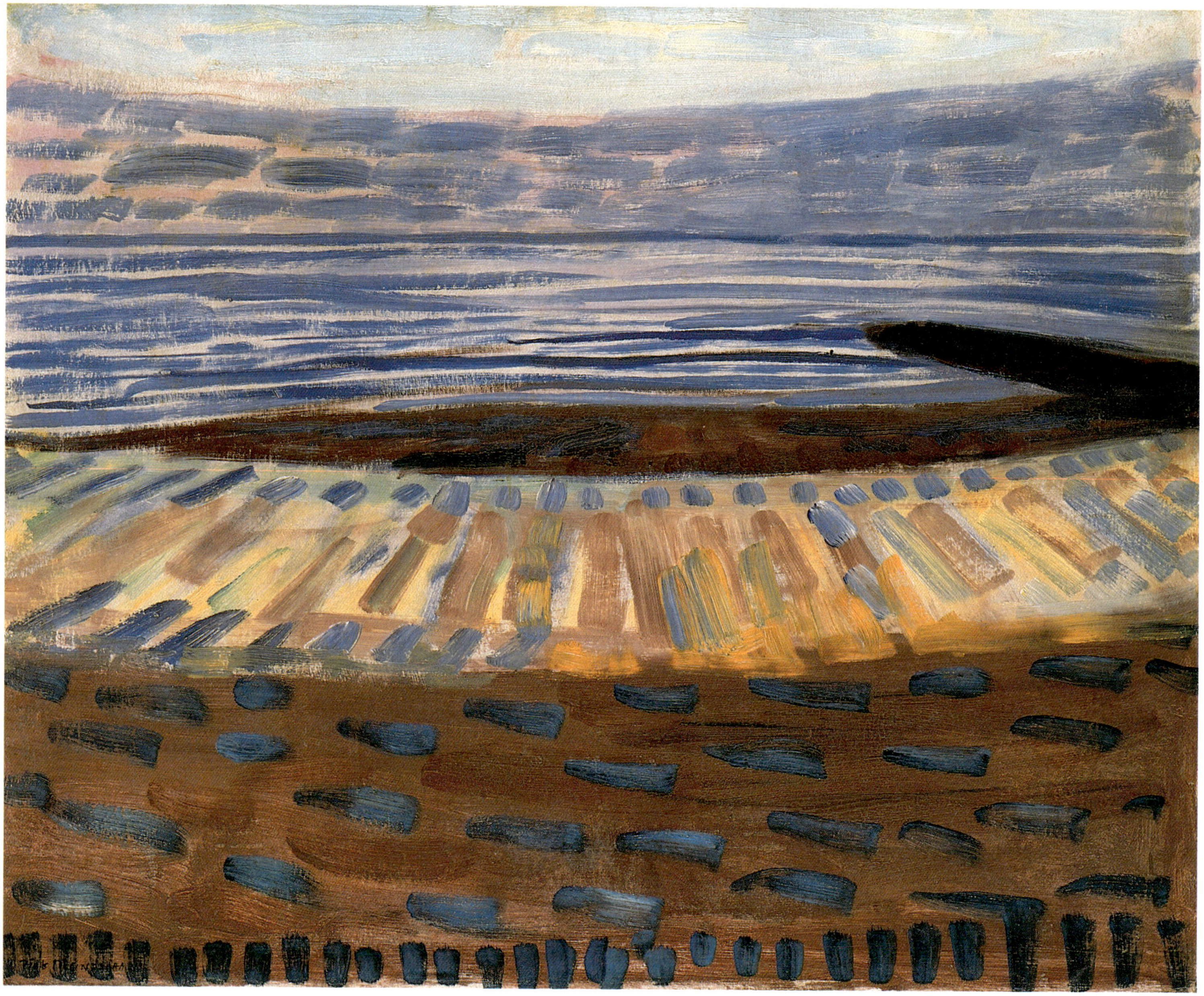

69

Sea after Sunset

1909
oil/cardboard/paper
63.5 × 76 cm

inv.no. 47-1963
Blok 177
Seuphor 278, c.c. 220

B — Form or illusion of form: whatever the case, colour must have a *fixed definition* if it is to convey anything to us. You are quite right in pointing out that in the transitional work of mine you just mentioned, the subject is neutralized by the free treatment of the colour; but you can also see that it is defined by the form, which is still practically faithful to nature. In order to create harmony of colour and form, the subject and hence *the form* are carefully *chosen.* Whenever it was my aim to depict *expanse, size,* for instance, the subject was *chosen.* The varied expression of the artistic idea depended on whether the subject was a group of dunes, the sea or a church.

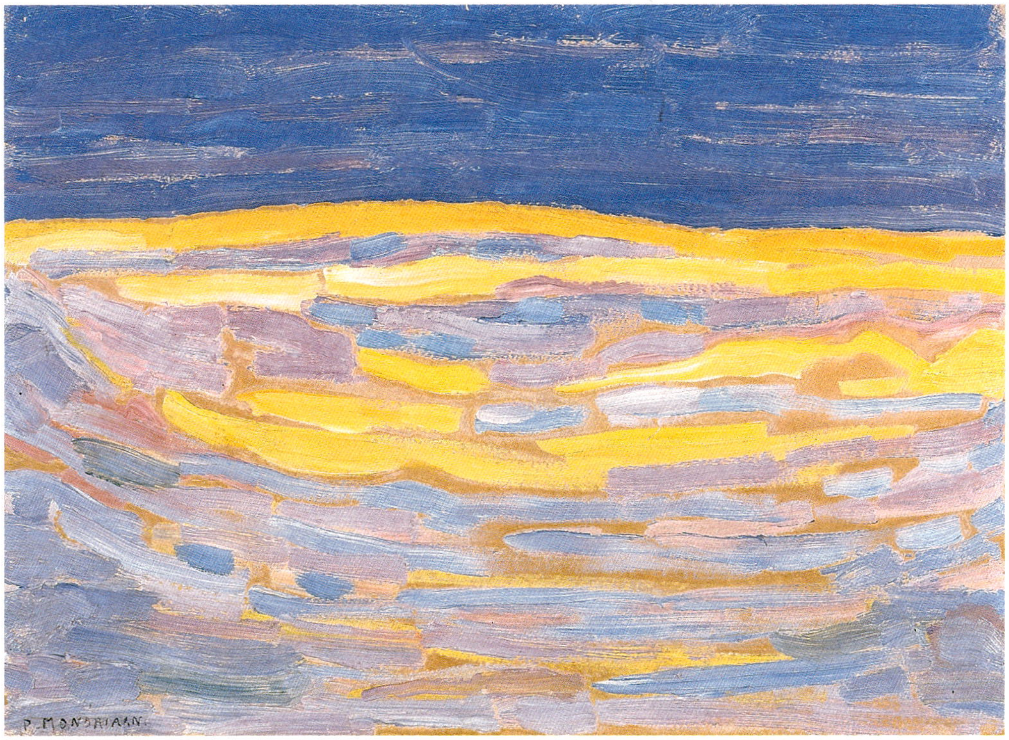

70

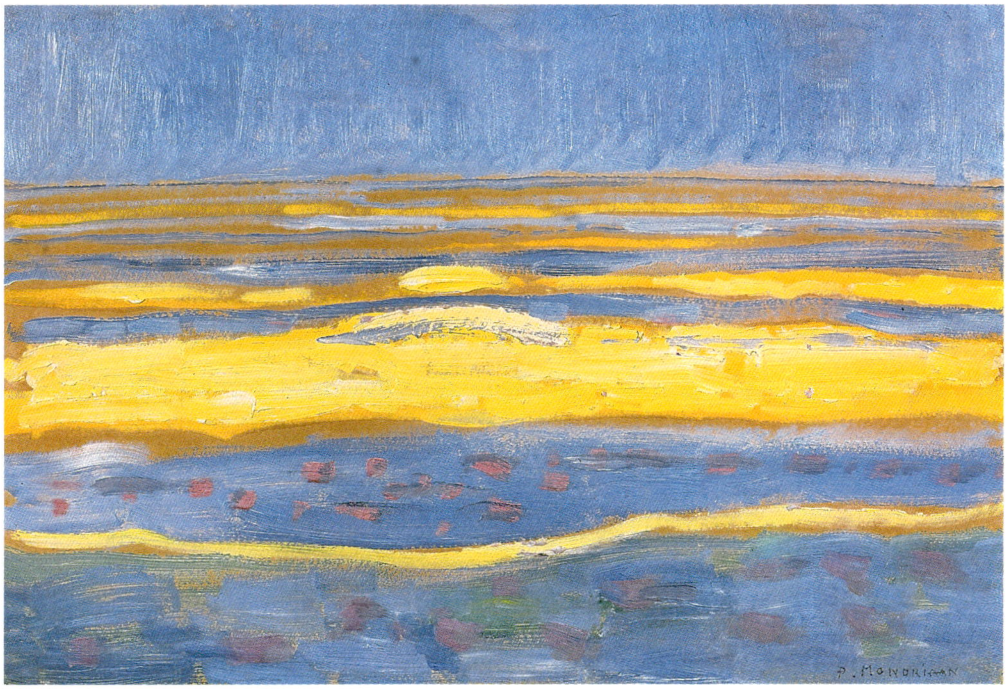

71

70

Dune I

1909
oil/cardboard
30 × 40 cm

inv.no.133-1971
Blok 179
Seuphor 205, c.c.213

71

Seascape

1909
oil/cardboard
34.5 × 50.5 cm

inv.no.132-1971
Blok 180
Seuphor 281, c.c.222

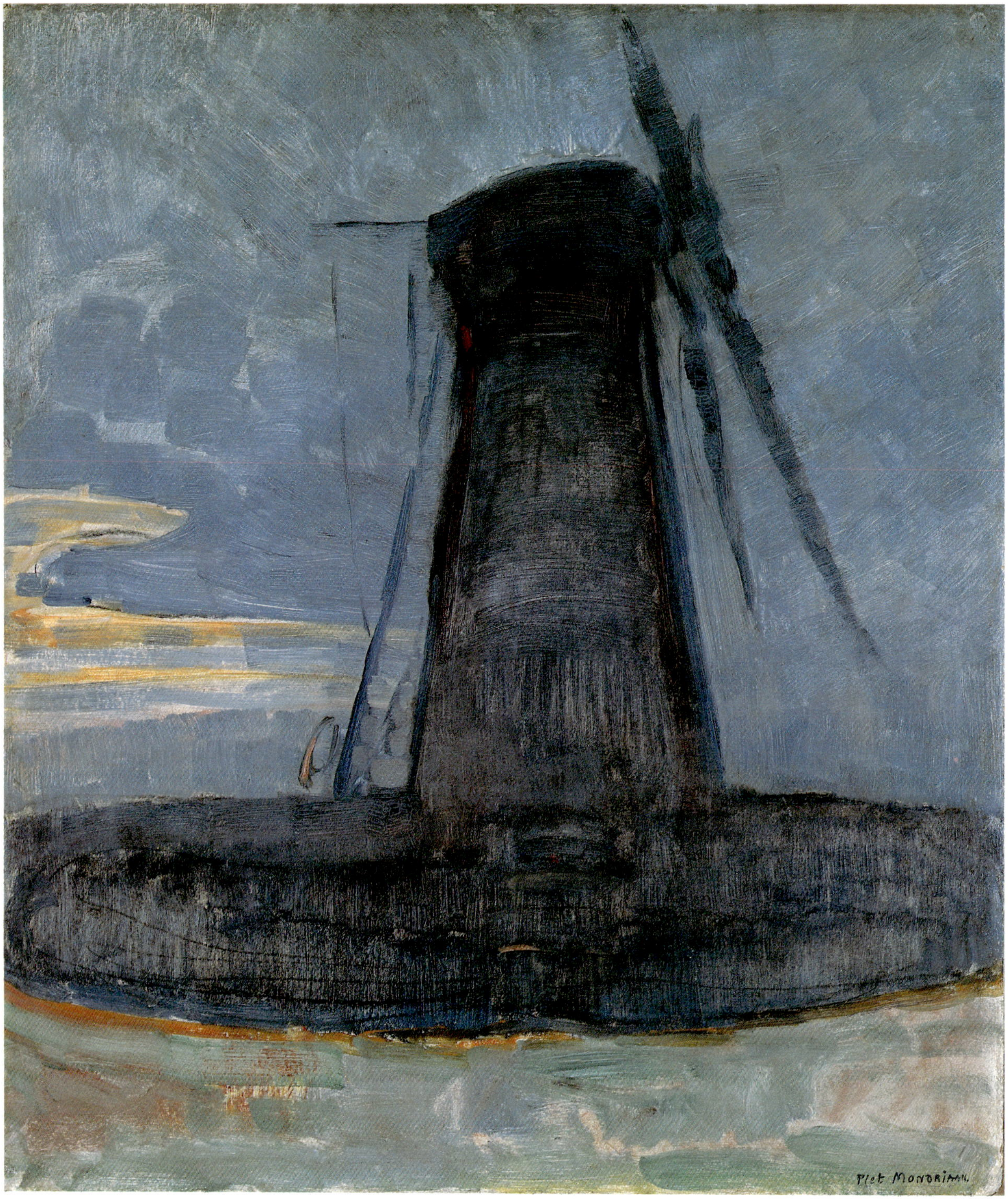

72

Mill at Domburg

1909
oil/cardboard
76.5 × 63.5 cm

inv.no.58-1957
Blok 181
Seuphor 275, c.c.111

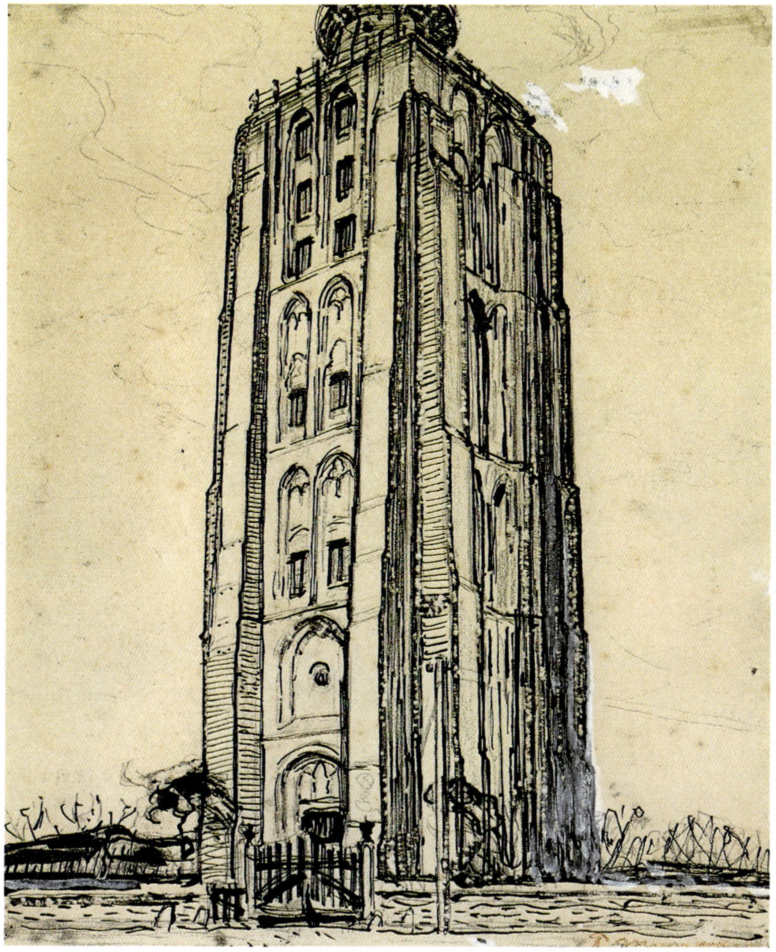

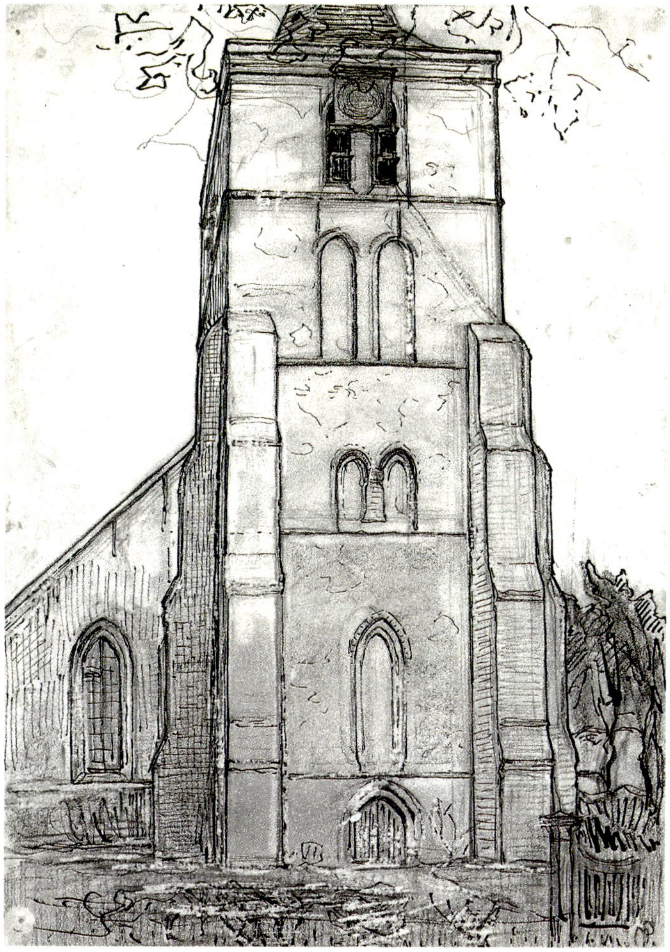

73

Lighthouse at Westkapelle

1909
ink/crayon/gouache/paper
30 × 24.5 cm

inv.no. T109-1971
Blok 182
Seuphor 271, c.c.240

74

Church at Domburg

1909
ink/paper
41.5 × 29 cm

inv.no. T110-1971
Blok 183
Seuphor 273, c.c.250

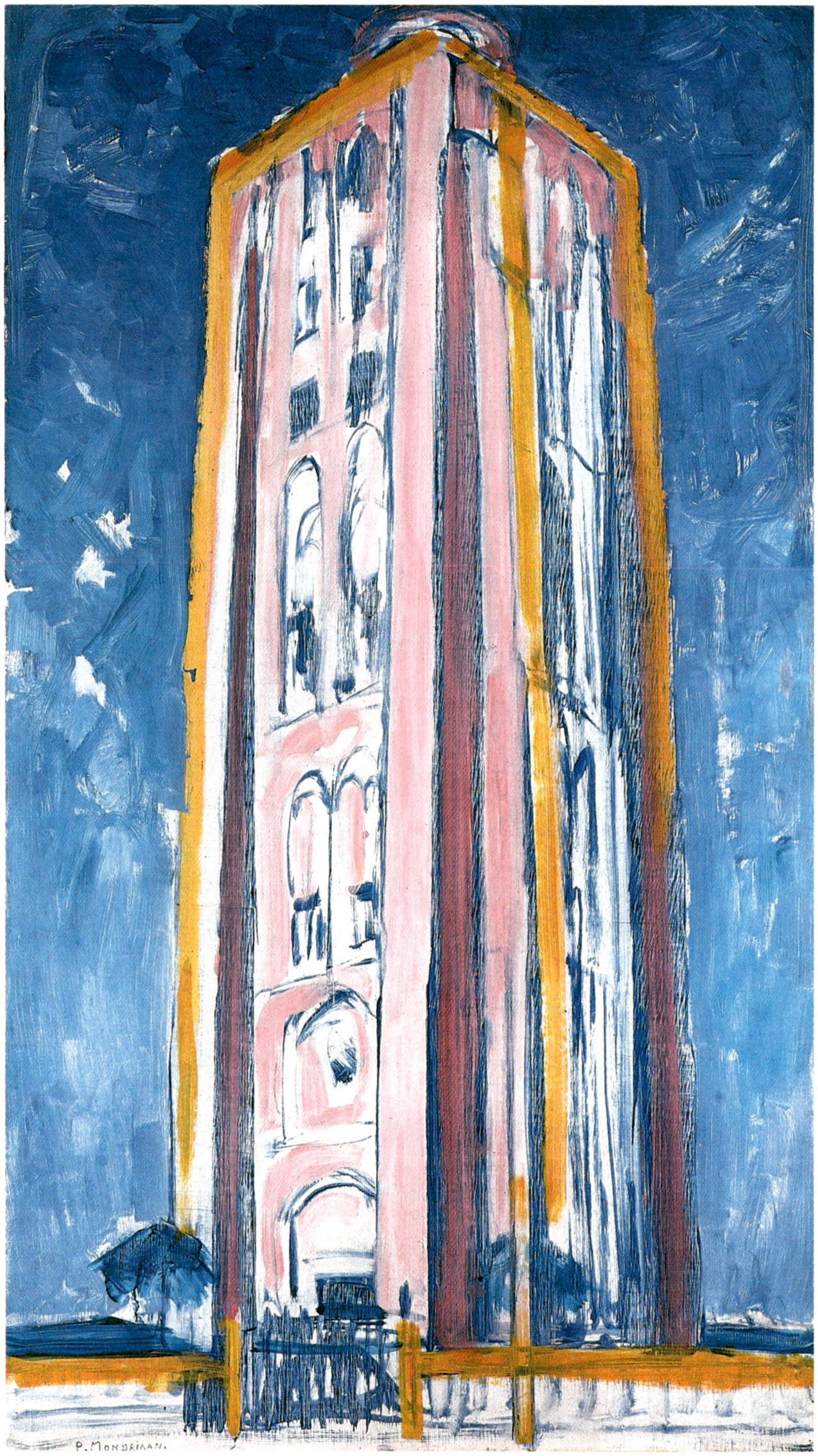

75

Lighthouse at Westkapelle

1909/10
oil/canvas
135 × 75 cm

inv.no.143-1971
Blok 186
Seuphor 272, c.c.241

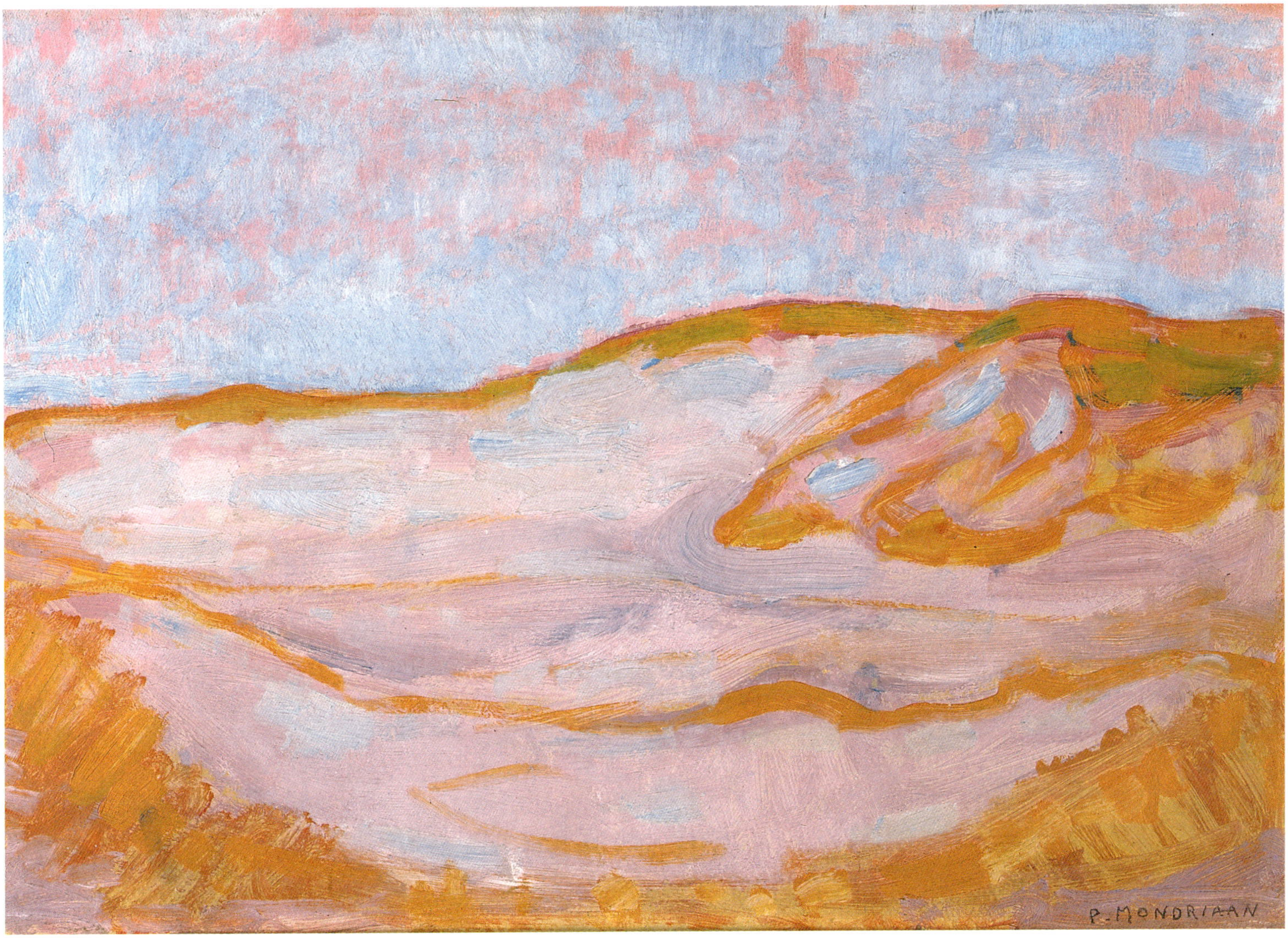

76

Dune IV

1909/10
oil/cardboard
33 × 46 cm

inv.no.144-1971
Blok 202
Seuphor 269, c.c.217

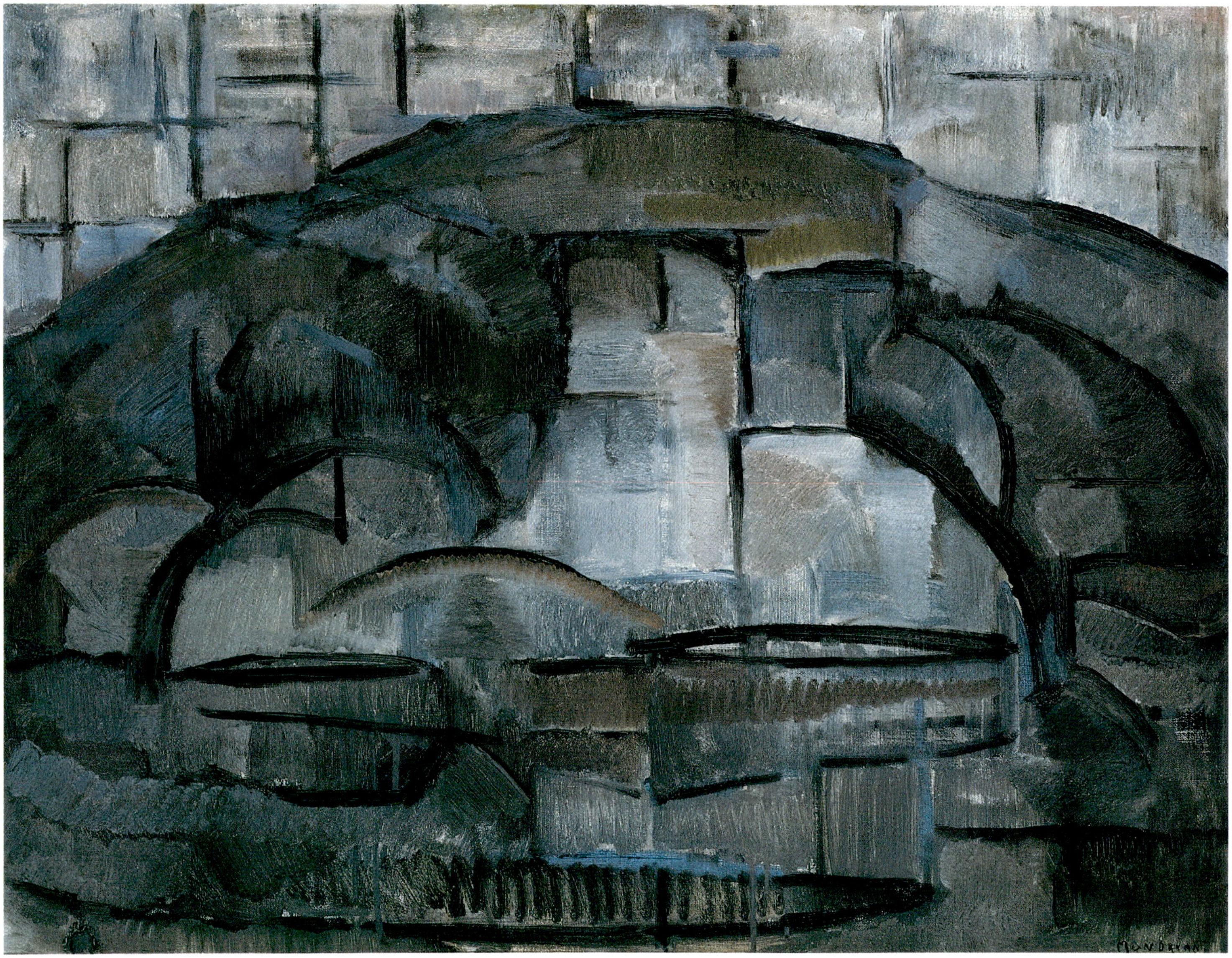

79

Landscape

1911/12
oil/canvas
63 × 78 cm

inv.no.150-1971
Blok 213
Seuphor 343, c.c.55

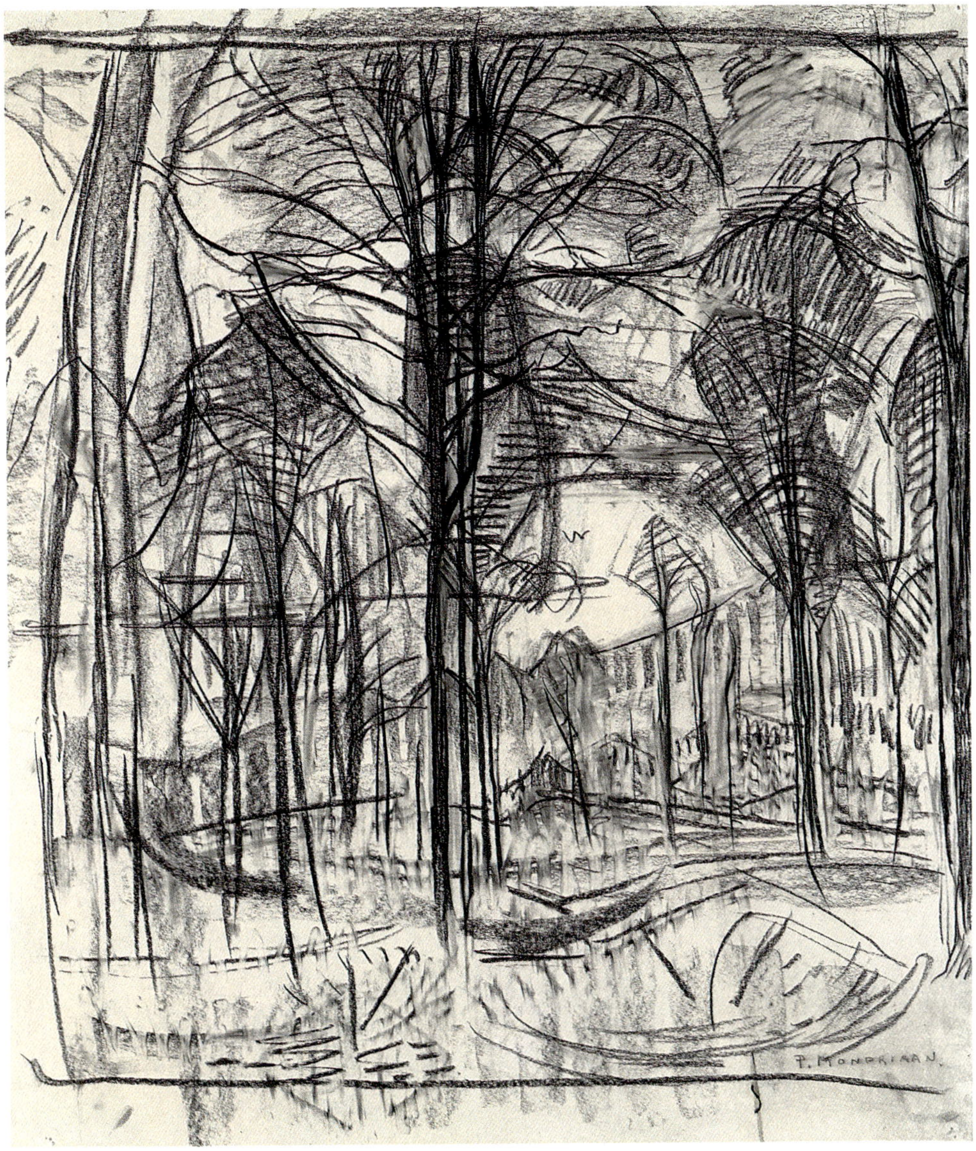

82

Forest

1912
crayon/paper
73 × 63 cm

inv.no.T63-1958
Blok 216
Seuphor 327, c.c.182

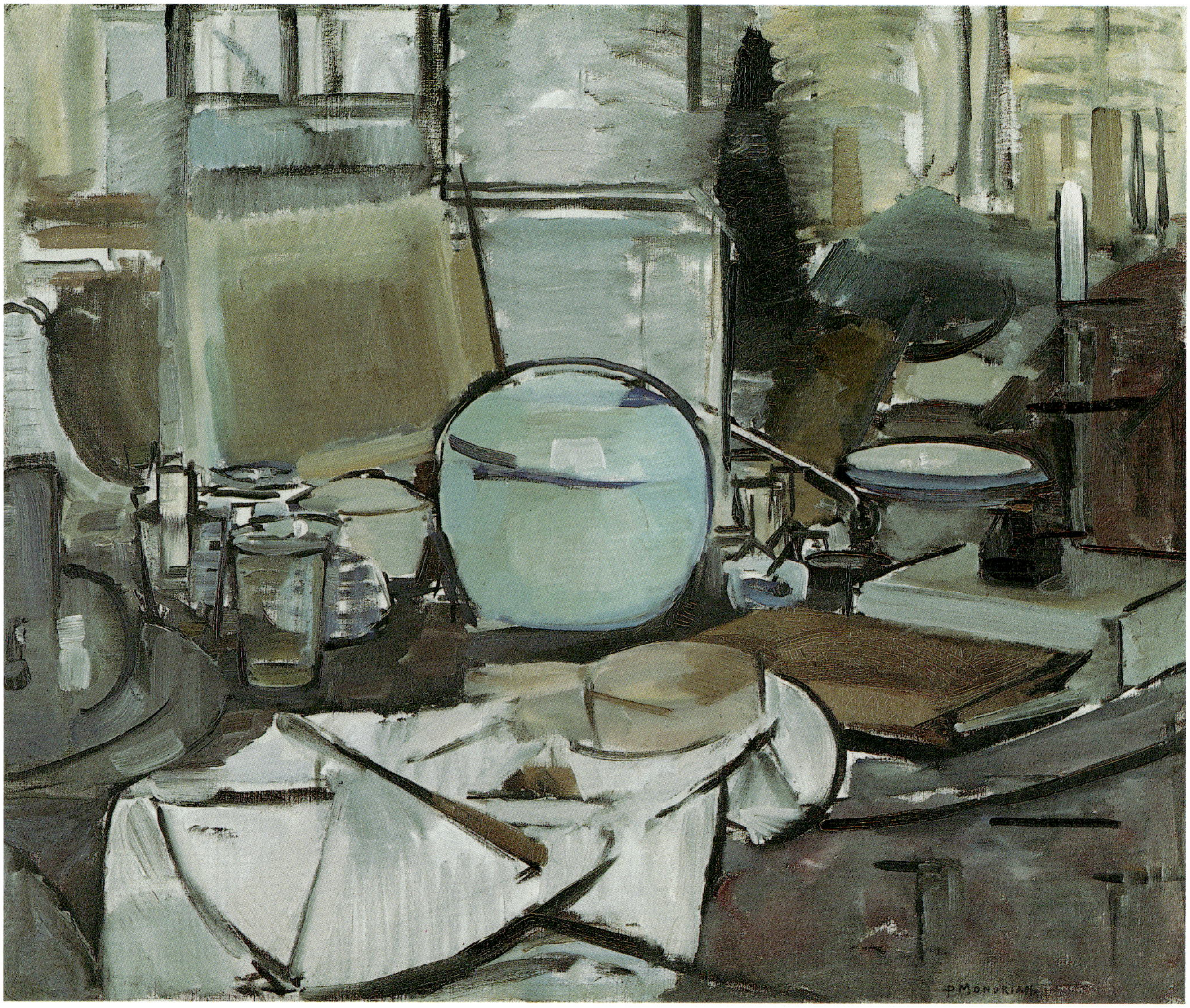

80

Still Life with Gingerpot I

1911/12
oil/canvas
65.5 × 75 cm

inv.no.154-1971
Blok 214
Seuphor 365, c.c.33

On loan to the Solomon R. Guggenheim Museum from the Haags Gemeentemuseum.

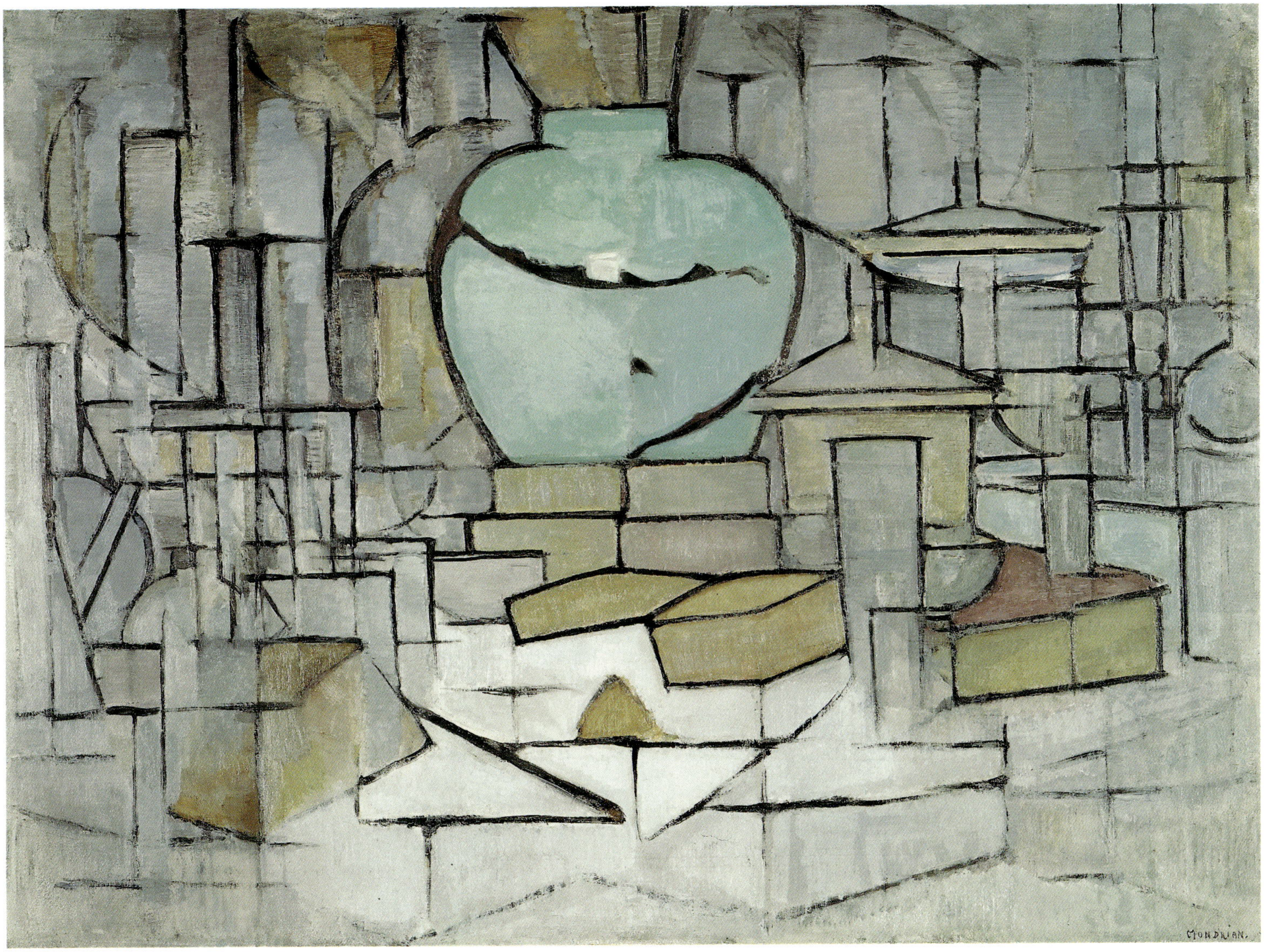

81

Still Life with Gingerpot II

1911/12
oil/canvas
91.5 × 120 cm

inv.no.155-1971
Blok 215
Seuphor 366, c.c.34

On loan to the Solomon R. Guggenheim Museum from the Haags Gemeentemuseum.

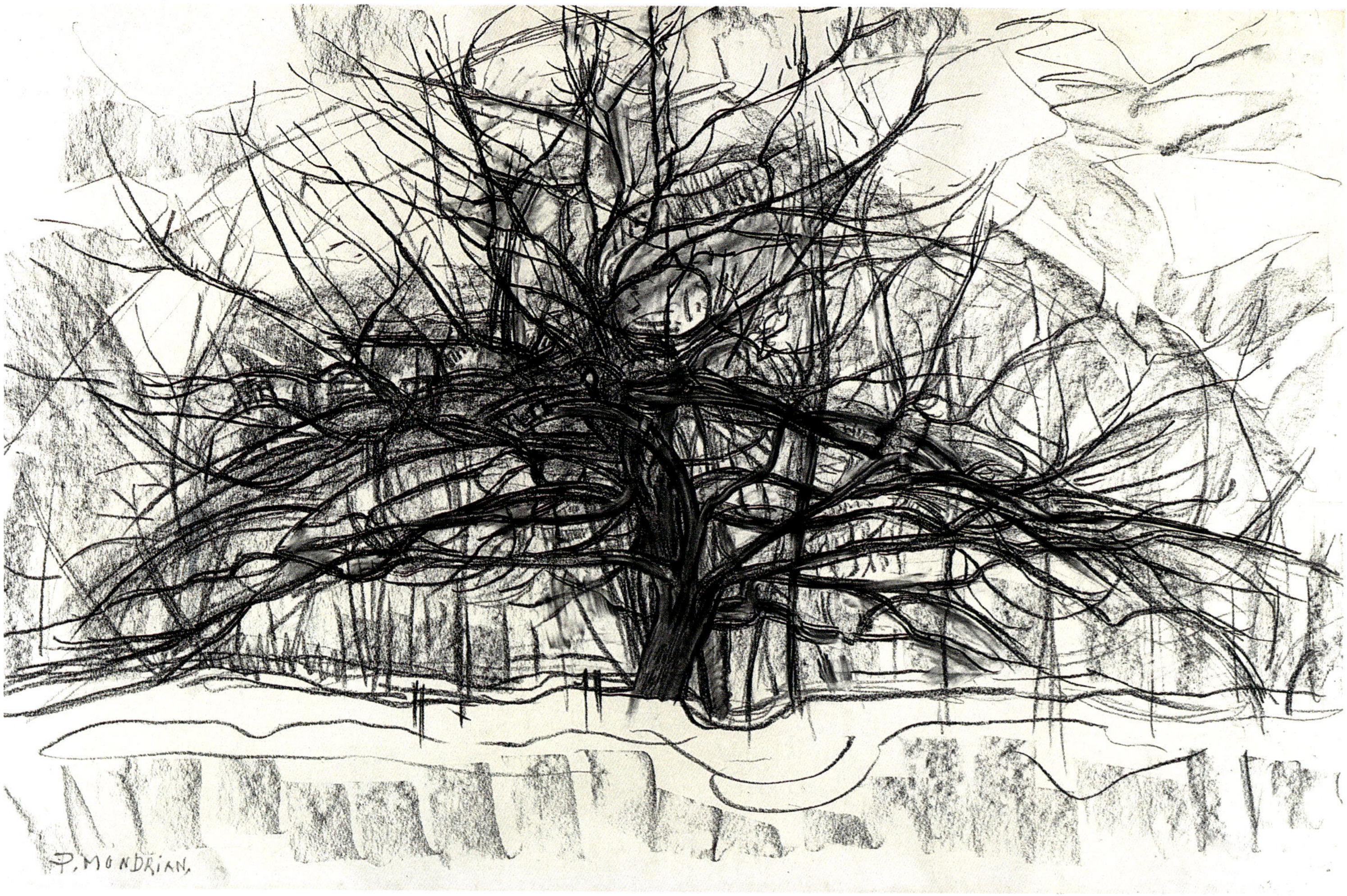

83

Tree II

1912
crayon/paper
56.5 × 84.5 cm

inv.no. T37-1971
Blok 217
Seuphor 322, c.c.175

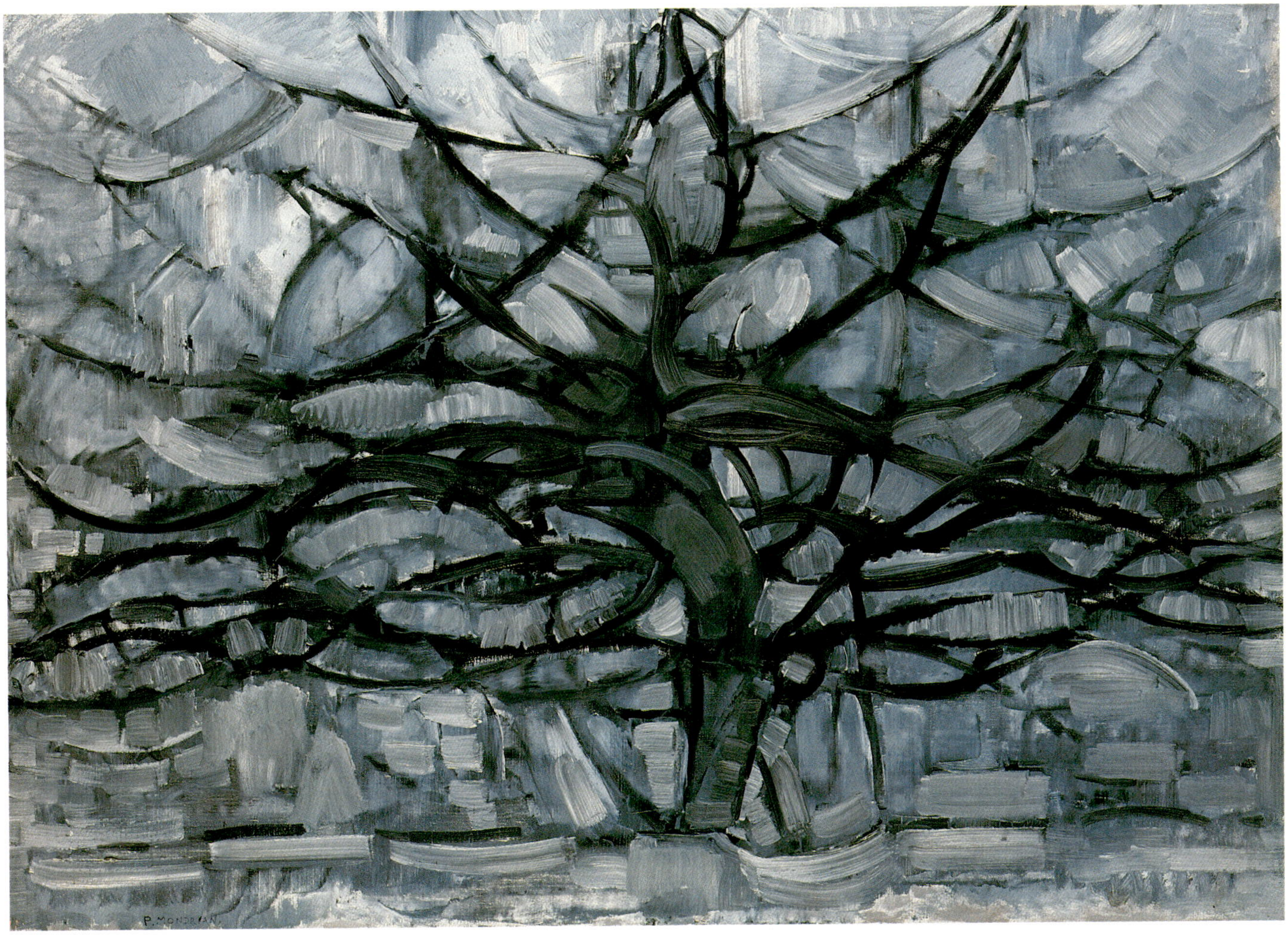

84

The Grey Tree

1912
oil/canvas
78.5 × 107.5 cm

inv.no.156-1971
Blok 218
Seuphor 335, c.c.177

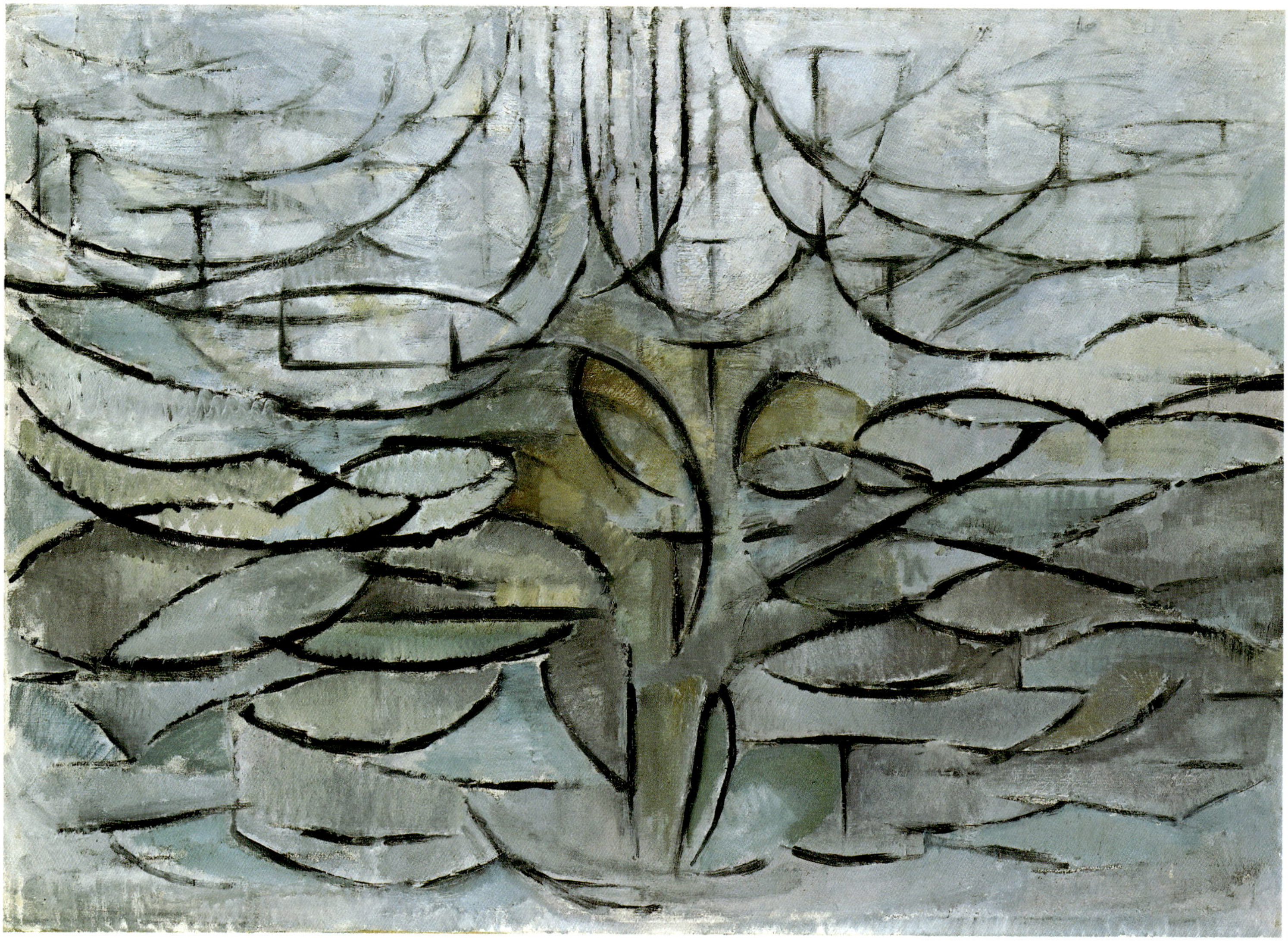

85

Flowering Apple Tree

1912
oil/canvas
78 × 106 cm

inv.no. 55-1934
Blok 219
Seuphor 345, c.c.179

A—Did this abstraction perhaps lead you to eliminate naturalism, representation and the subject?

B—Quite right: *While I was working.* The theories about this elimination which I just mentioned, occurred to me later. Consistent abstraction led to the elimination of the visibly concrete in my art. If you realize that when I painted a tree I increasingly abstracted the curves, you will see that not much of a 'tree' is left.

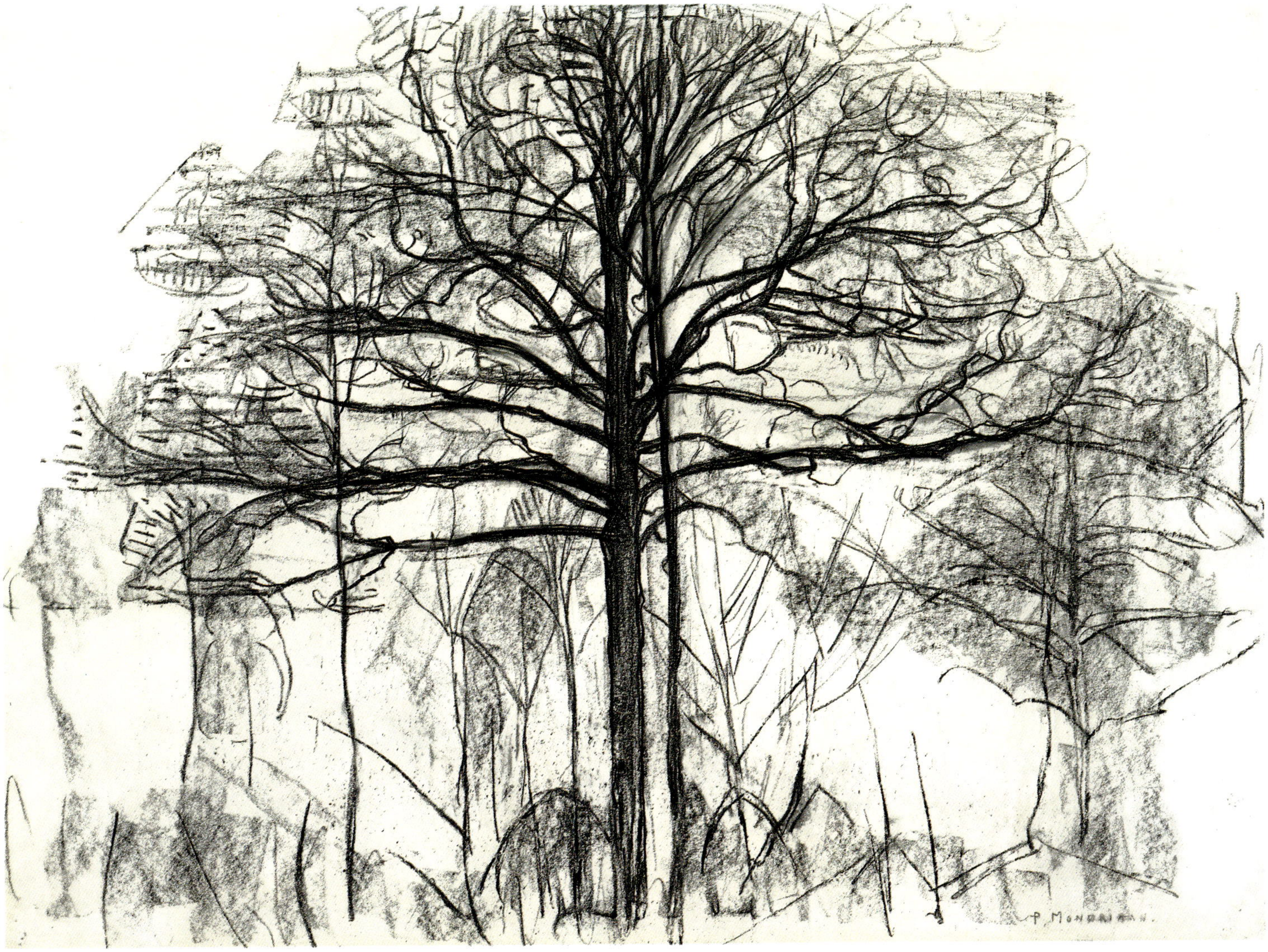

86

Study of Trees I

1912
crayon/paper
67.1 × 88.5 cm

inv.no.T65-1958
Blok 220
Seuphor 328, c.c.183

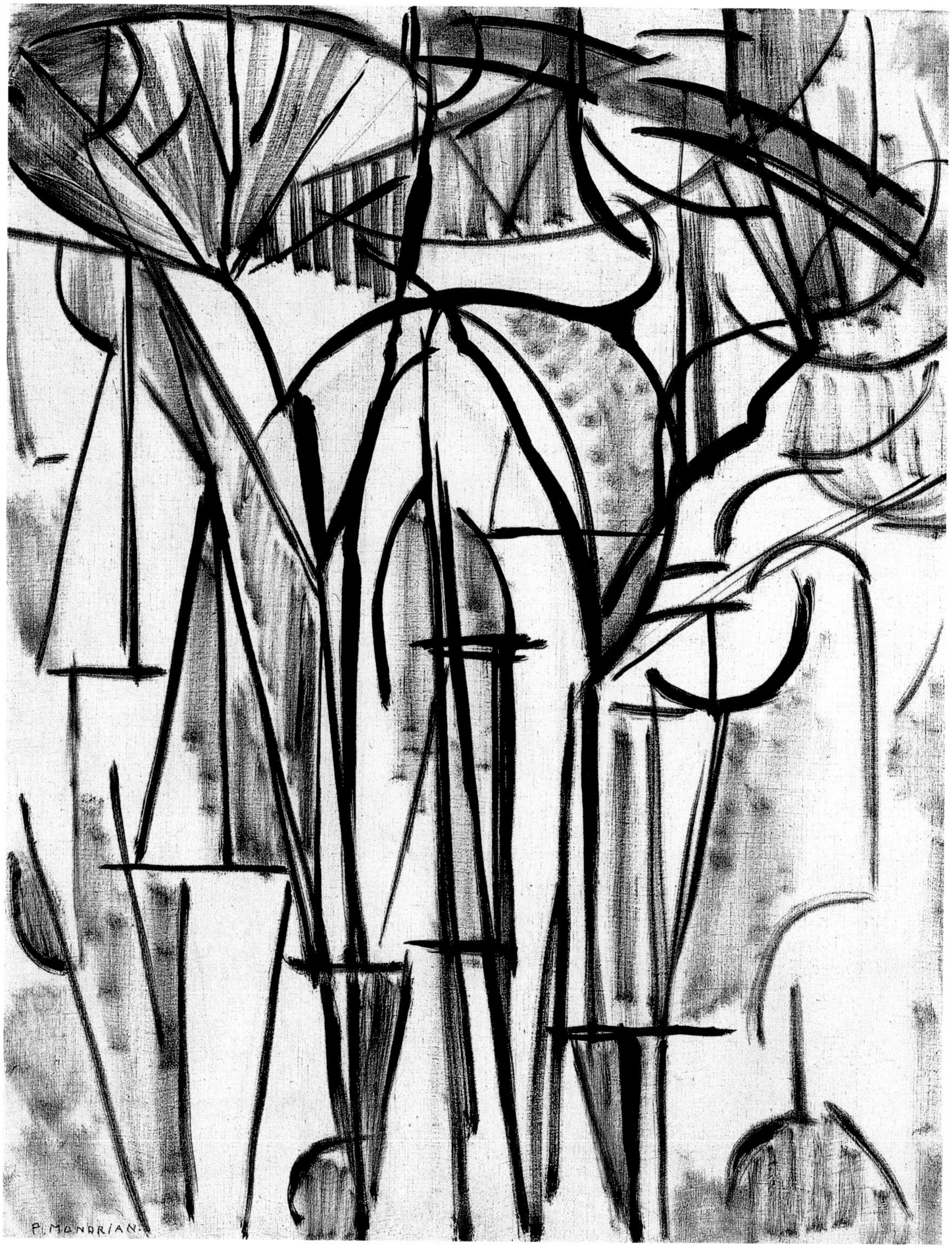

87

Composition: Trees I

1912
oil/canvas
81 × 62 cm

inv.no.157-1971
Blok 221
Seuphor 350, c.c.195

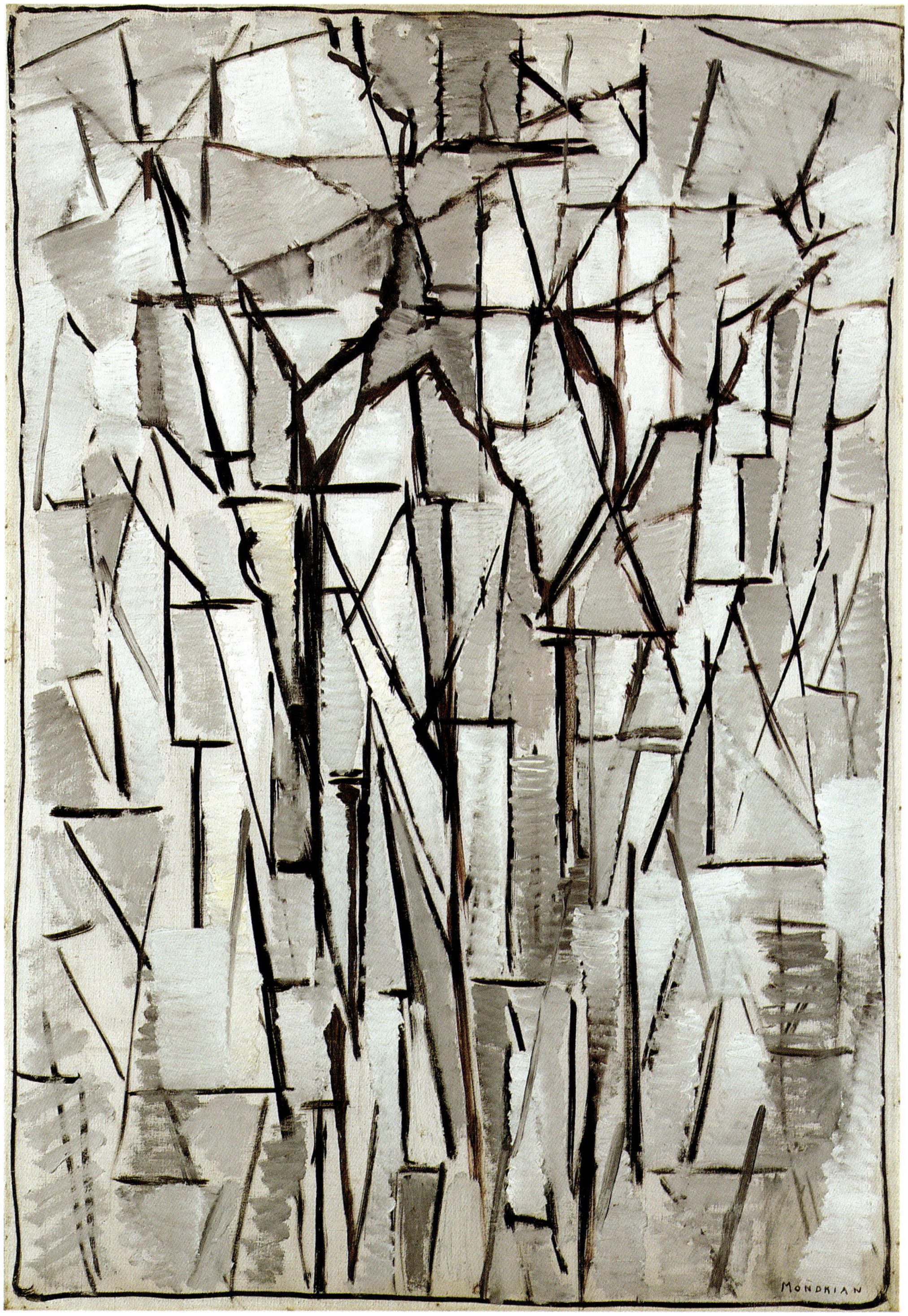

88

Composition: Trees II

1912
oil/canvas
98 × 65 cm

inv.no.158-1971
Blok 222
Seuphor 351, c.c.198

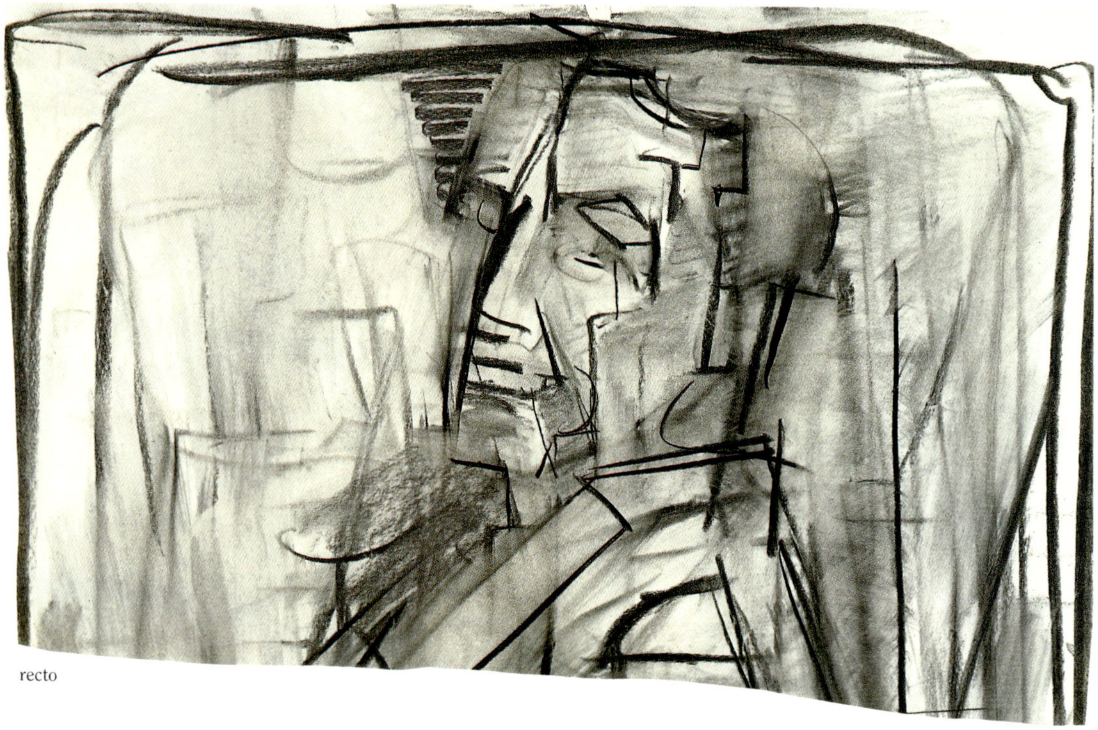

recto

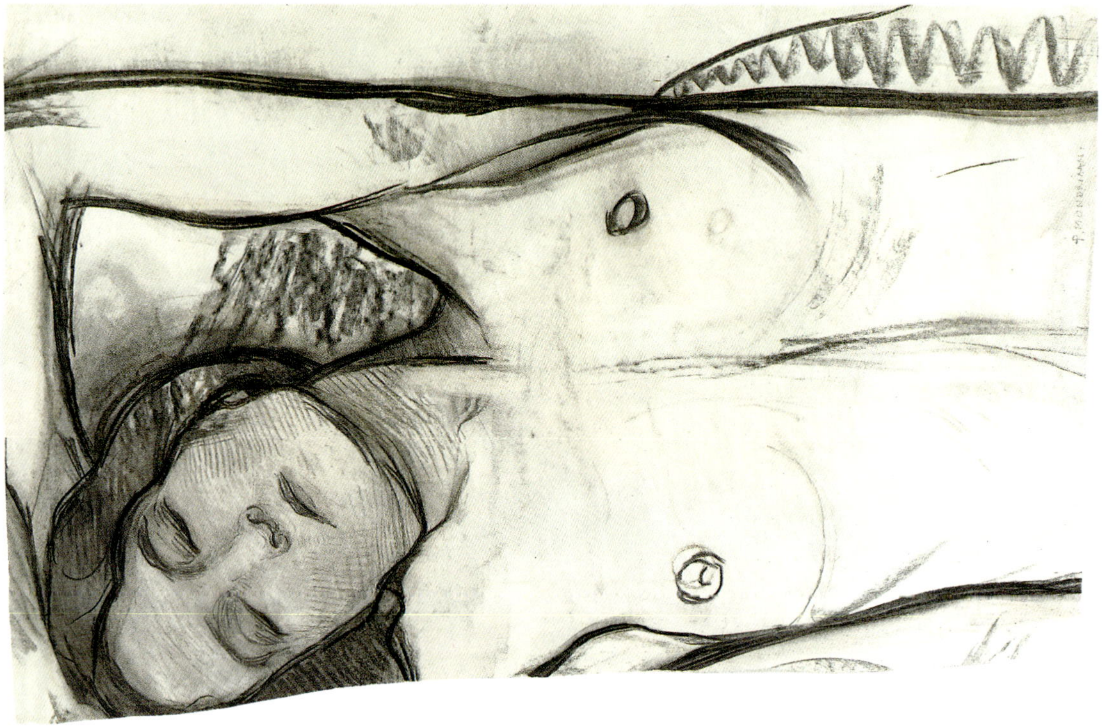

verso

89

Self Portrait (recto)

Nude (verso)

1912/13

charcoal/paper

49.5 × 73.5 cm

inv.no. T126-1971 (recto)

Blok 225 (recto)

Seuphor 323, c.c.5 (recto)

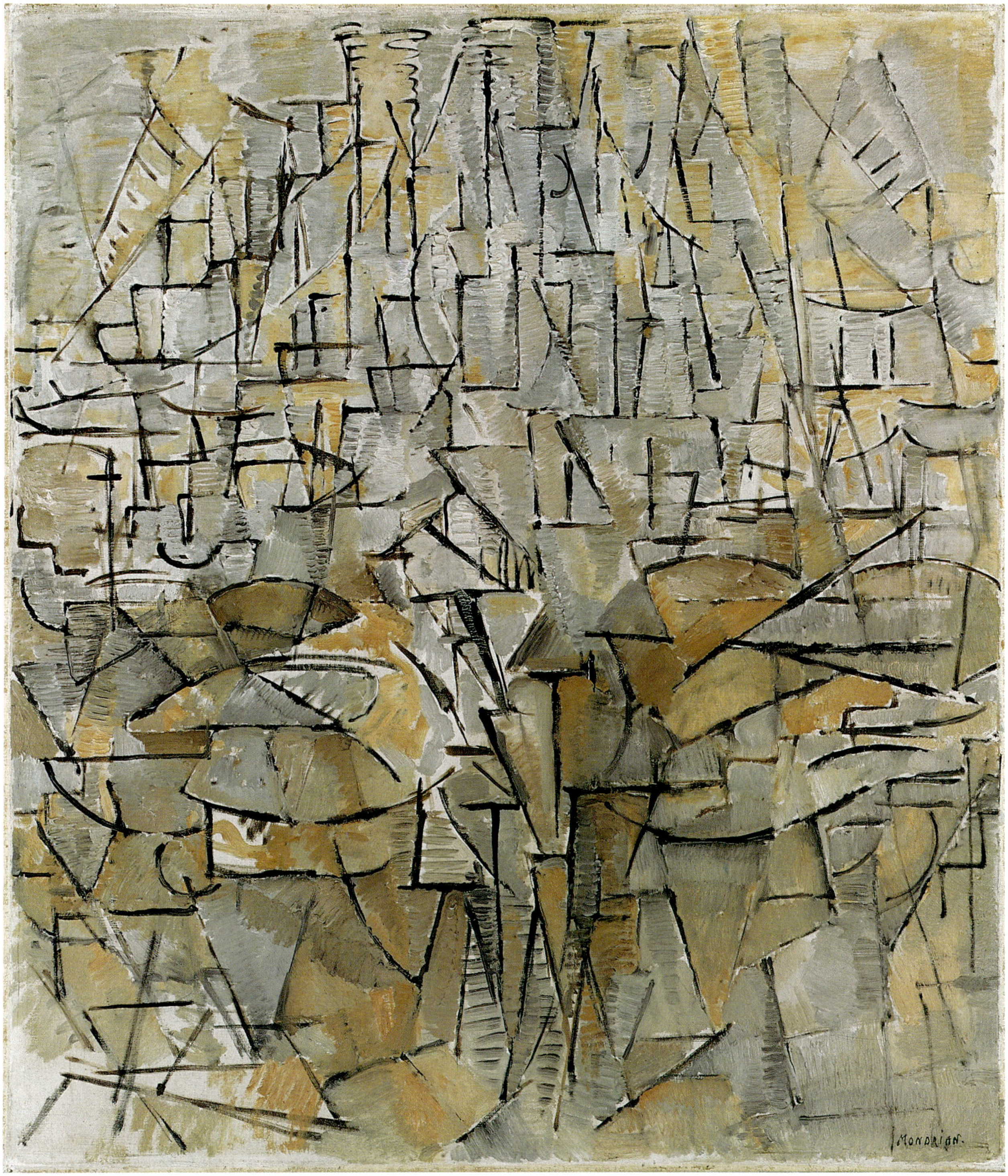

90

Composition no.3 (Trees)

1913
oil/canvas
95 × 80 cm

inv.no.159-1971
Blok 229
Seuphor 349, c.c.194

A—But I would think that a tree could surely be depicted in straight lines?

B—Perfectly true, and I now realize the flaw in my argument: *abstraction alone* is not enough to eliminate naturalism in art; it needs something *other* than the natural *application* of line and colour.

A—So what a painter calls composition changes as well?

B—Yes, an entirely different, more mathematical, though not symmetrical composition is needed for a *pure* depiction of balanced relationships. For simply depicting nature in straight lines still means depicting it *naturalistically*, even if it then makes a much stronger impression on us.

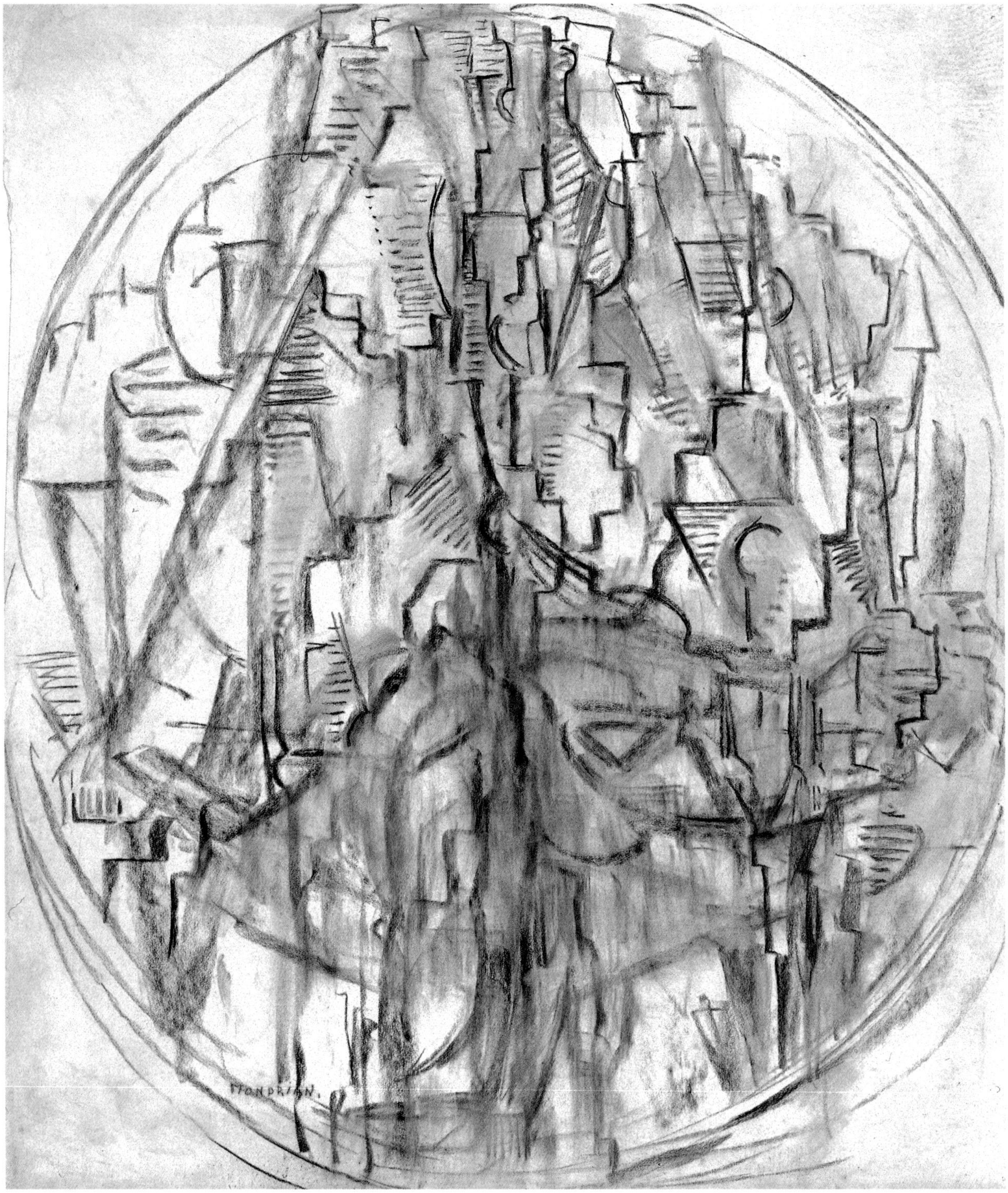

91

Oval Composition

1913
charcoal/paper
85 × 70 cm

inv.no.T125-1971
Blok 230
Seuphor 353, c.c.199

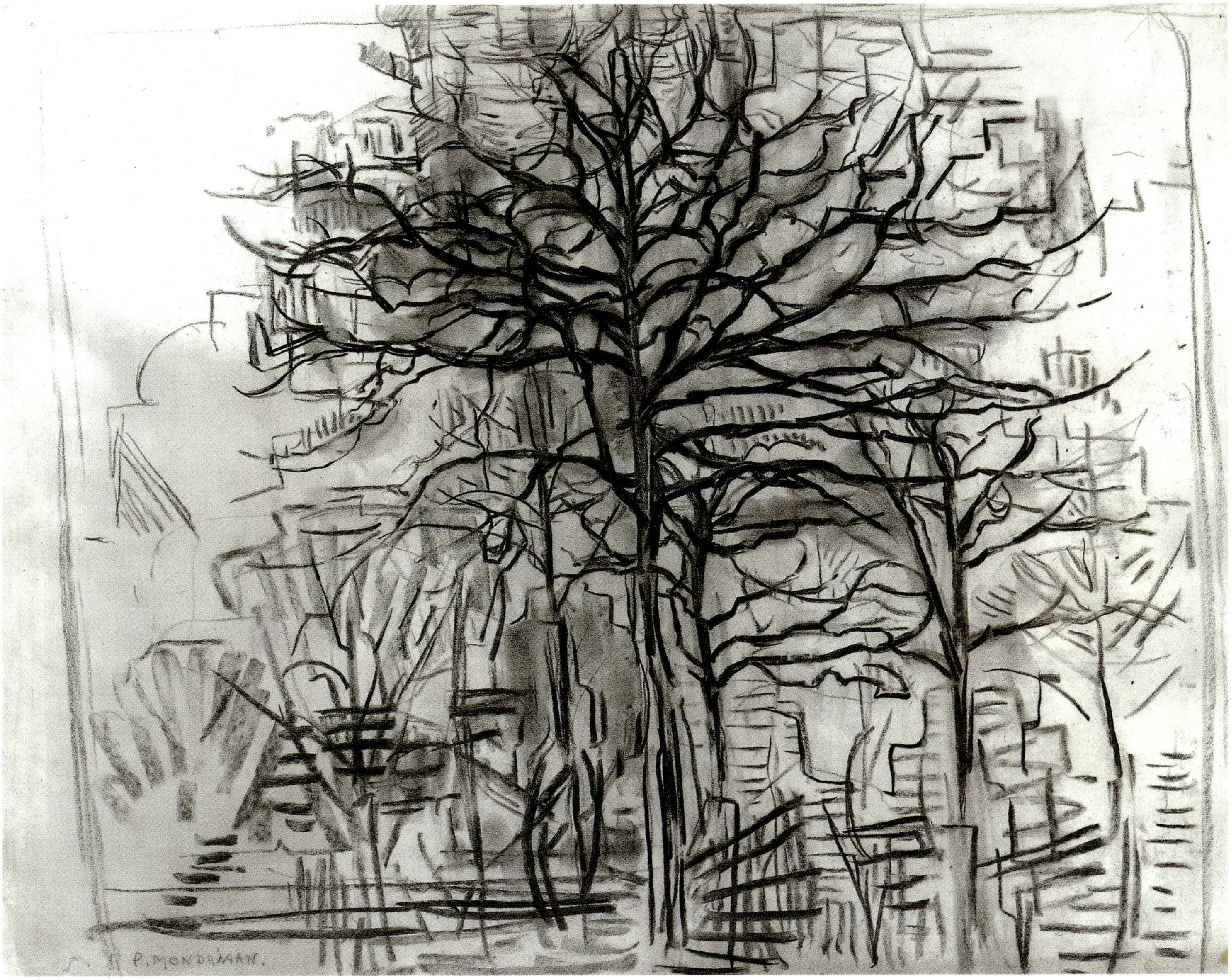

92

Study of Trees II

1913
charcoal/paper
65.5 × 87.5 cm

inv.no. T64-1958
Blok 232
Seuphor 329, c.c.184

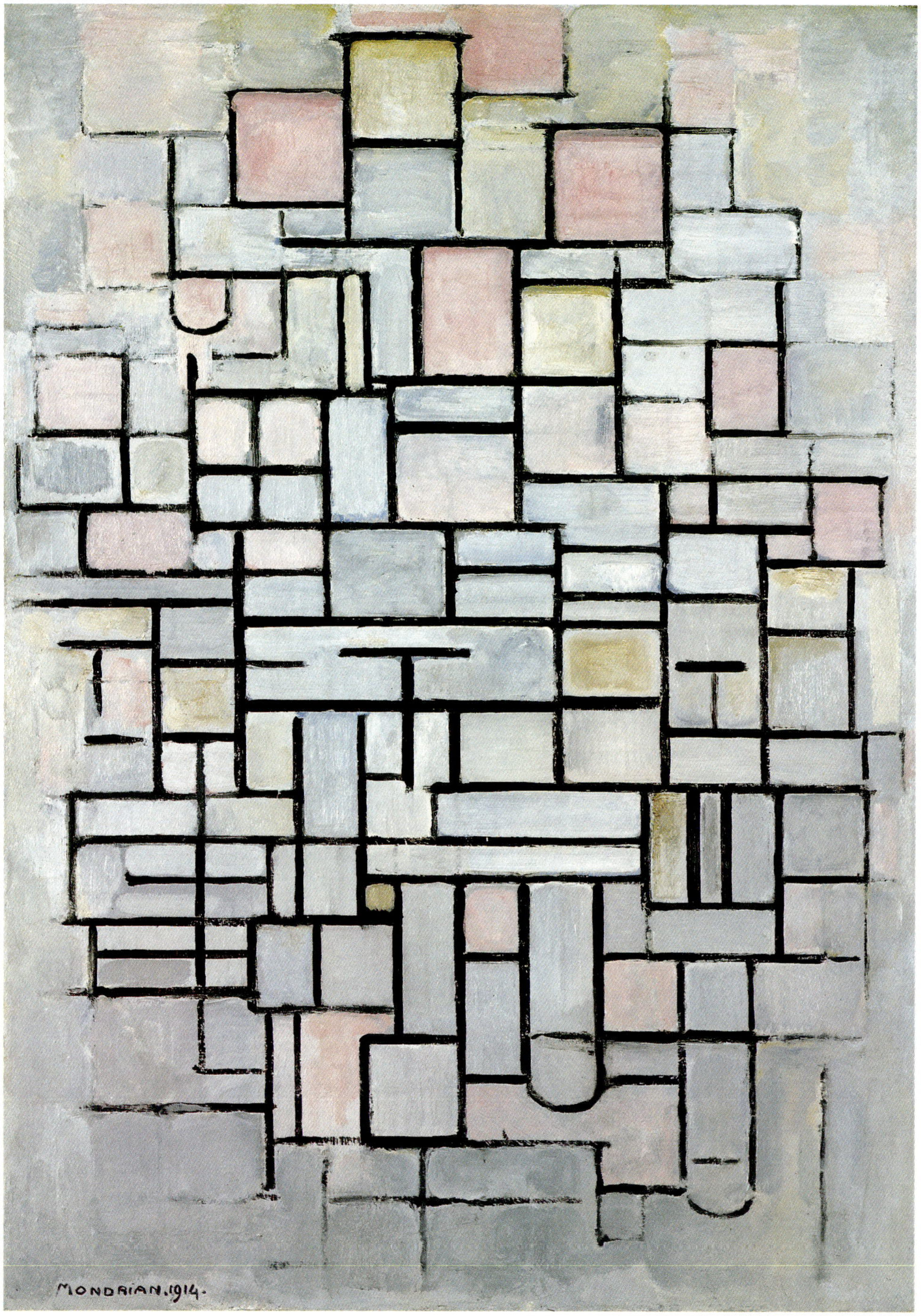

93

Composition no.6

1914
oil/canvas
88 × 61 cm

inv.no.161-1971
Blok 237
Seuphor 407, c.c.273

Y—The past survives for a very long time in buildings…

Z—It does, if nothing special happens to the building!

Y—This building takes me back to 'days of yore'…no matter how beautiful I think it is!

Z—Indeed. Once we have recovered, so to speak, from the first emotions which beauty arouses, we are reminded *of the past*. We see certain 'stylistic' forms which are not *our own*. Stylistic forms have something of the *descriptive* about them.

X—But can't description be beautiful too?

Z—It can be beautiful, but *purely plastic* beauty is harmed by description. *Description is time-bound and constantly changing. All appearance changes, everything moves, everything flows, as Antiquity already acknowledged. Everything changes, ourselves too…we are constantly changing.*

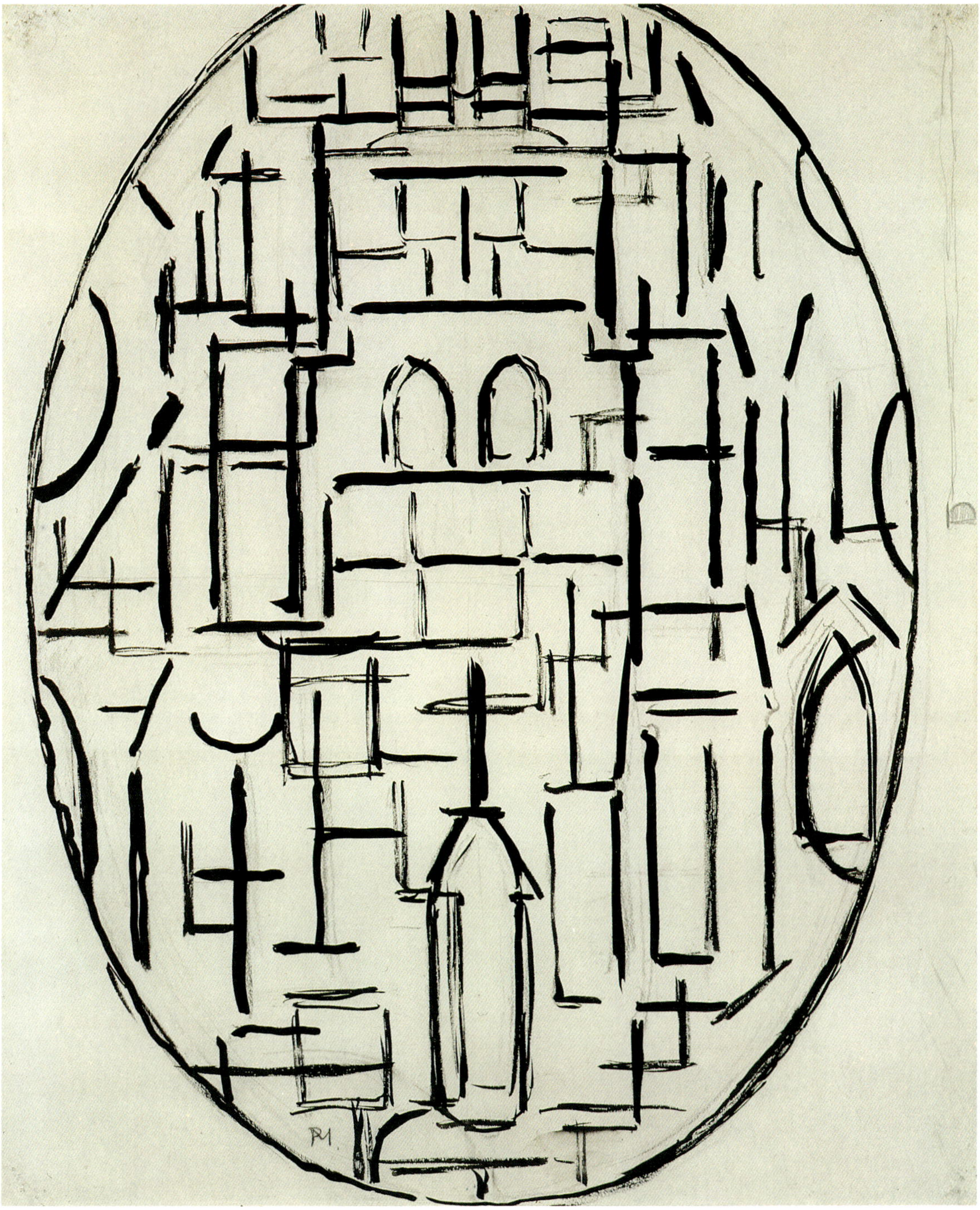

94

Church at Domburg

1914
ink/paper
63 × 50 cm

inv.no.T127-1971
Blok 240
Seuphor 387, c.c.254

Y—And if it is not form, it is ourselves who obscure these things! I remember your demonstrating that we ourselves transform what we see…like the stars, which we ourselves connect up into forms!

Z—To be sure; and a strange difference can be observed. With the starry sky we were less bound by the form, but tended to lapse into *creating* form. Our view of this church, though, is more influenced by the form, but makes it harder for us to create form. In the final analysis the difference is this: in the church we are bound by *another*, in the starry sky by *ourselves*!

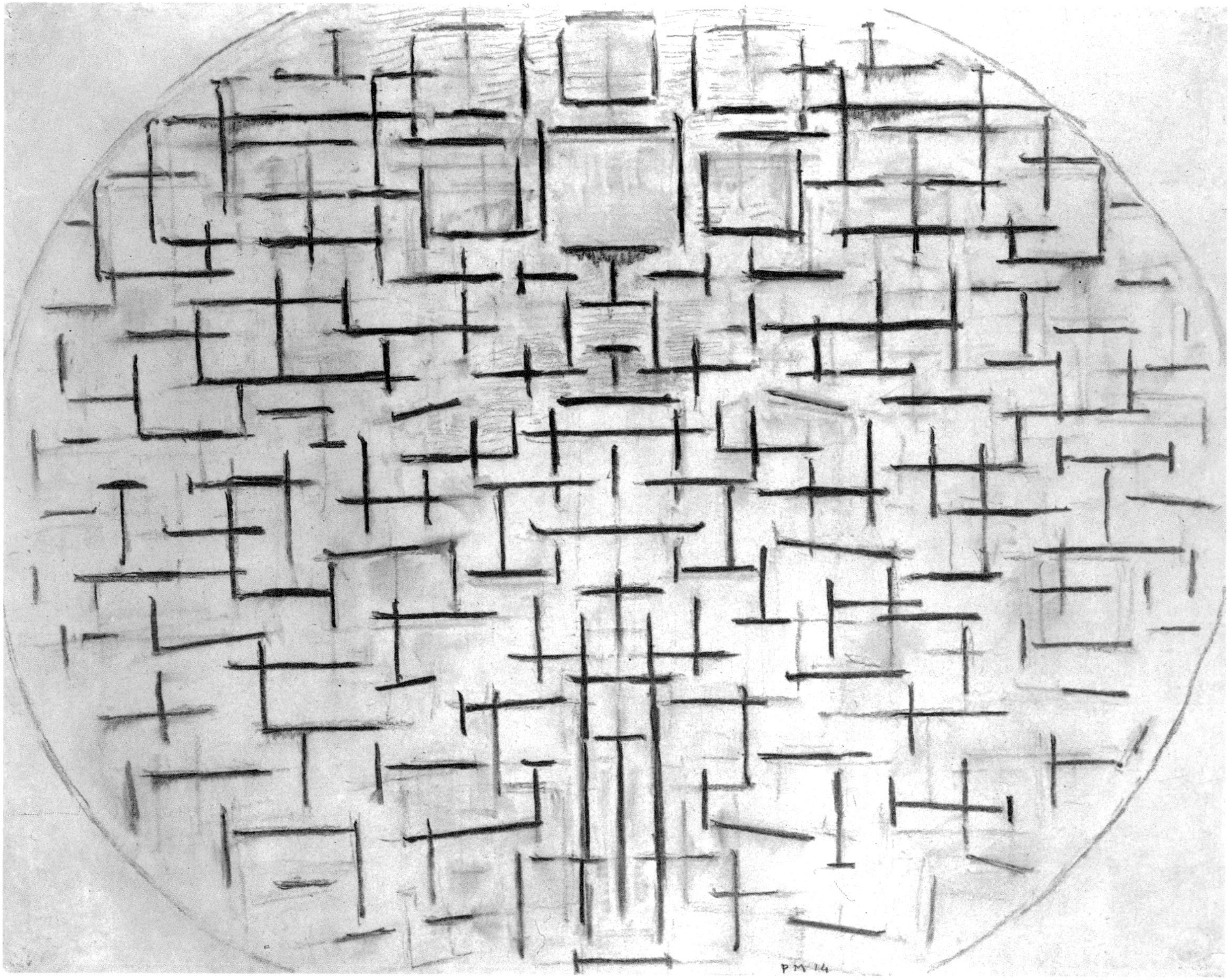

95

Sea (Starry Sky above the Sea)

1914
charcoal/paper
51 × 63 cm

inv.no.T128-1971
Blok 241
Seuphor 397, c.c.237

Z—Because the stars appear as *dots* they are *less eloquent about themselves and more eloquent about the original relationship*—at least if we are capable of seeing abstractly. Visually, though, the dot *in itself* only expresses something by virtue of its luminosity: *in itself* it depicts nothing. It does not remove limits, because it does not say anything definite about the universal. Visually, the dot in itself does not depict a relationship and can hence not annihilate our individuality. And it is this individuality that keeps on creating *form*: even where it is not directly manifest.

However, we do not see a *dot* but *dots*. And these *dots* create forms. The *line* mediates plastically between two dots, several lines between several dots. This starry sky shows us innumerable dots. They are not equally accentuated: some are brighter than others. And in their turn these unequal light-values produce *forms*. Think of stellar *constellations*: they, too, are forms. What I am trying to say is that *form is not removed from the starry sky when seen in its natural guise*.

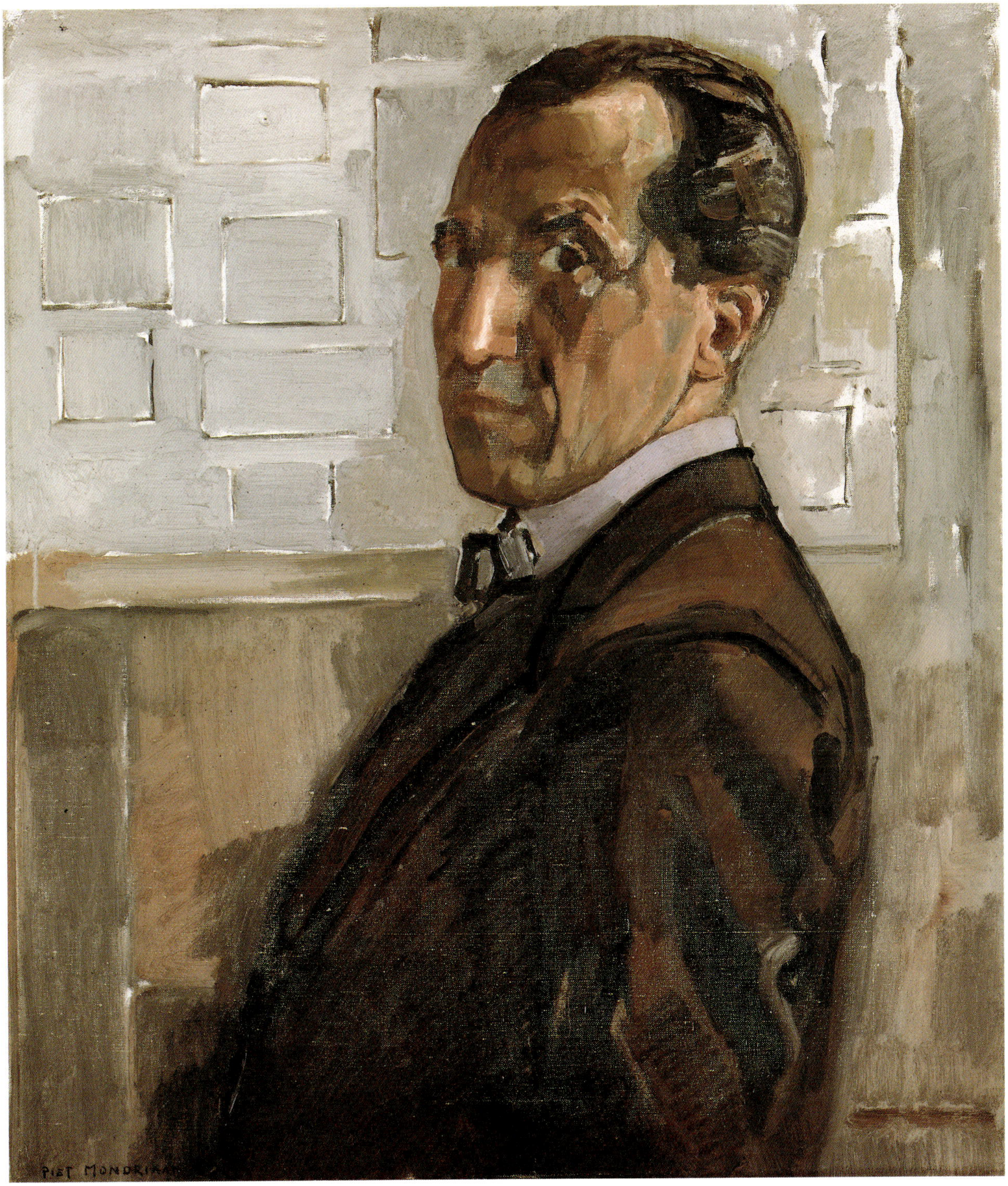

96

Self Portrait

1918
oil/canvas
88 × 71 cm

inv.no.166-1971
Blok 265
Seuphor 435, c.c.8

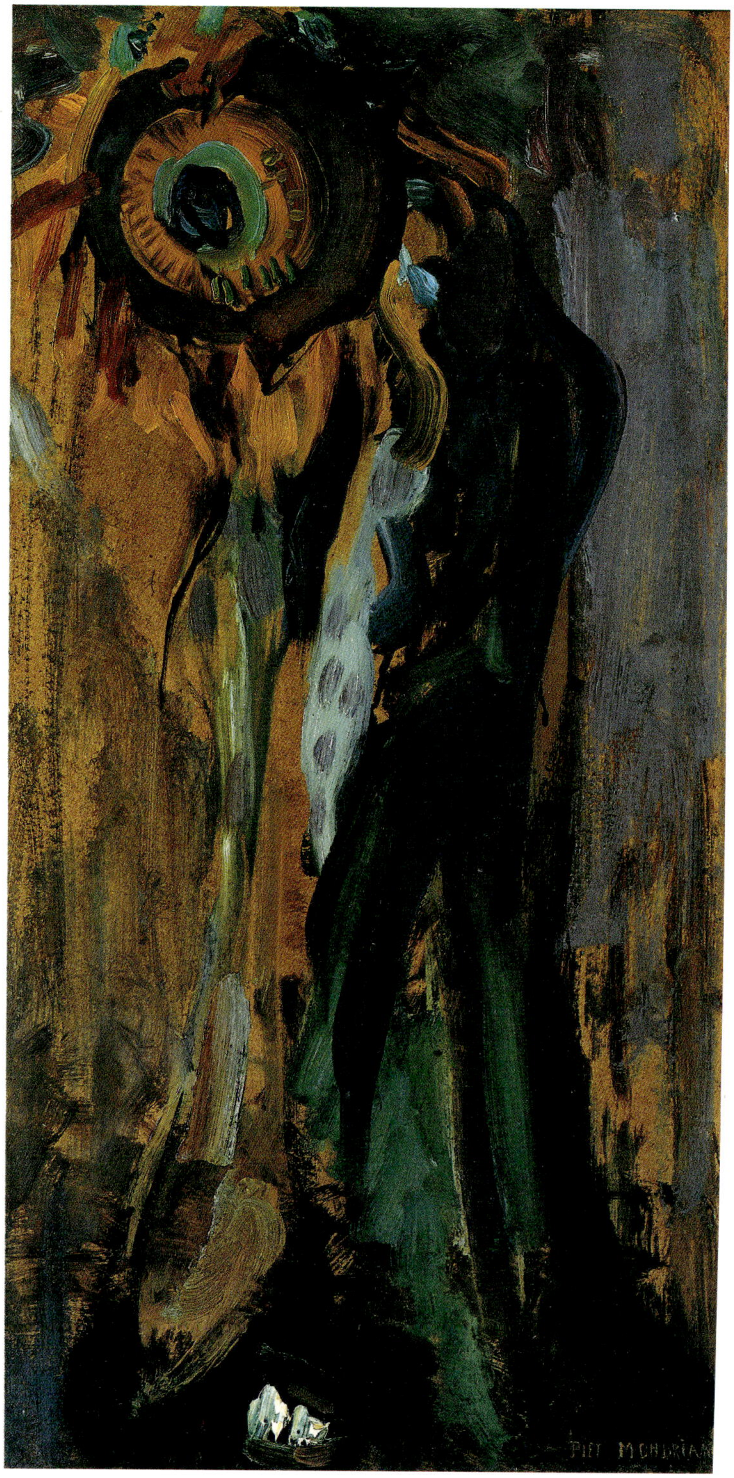

97

Sunflower I

1907/08
oil/cardboard
63 × 31 cm

inv.no.123-1971
Blok 146
Seuphor 299, c.c.156

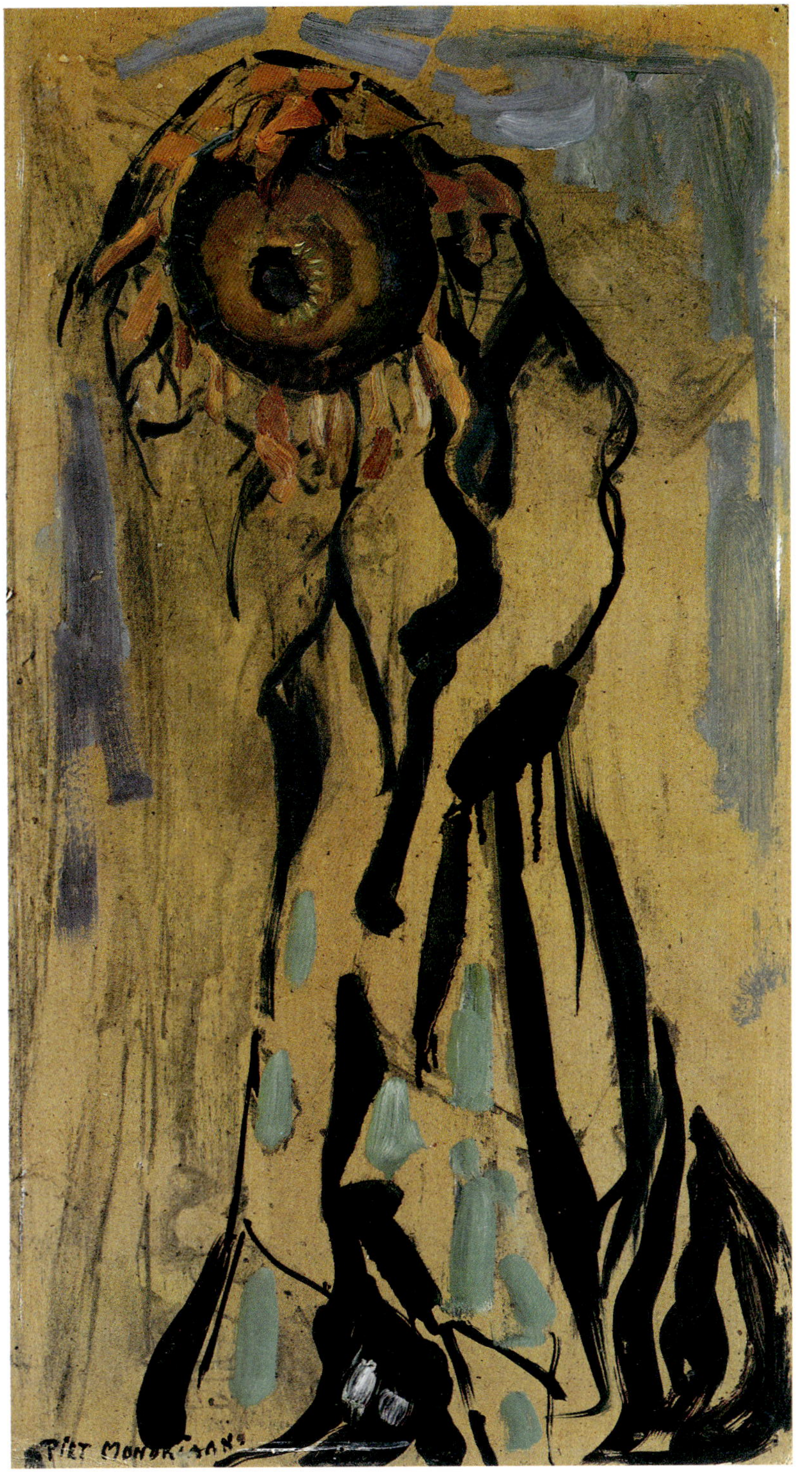

98

Sunflower II

1907/08
oil/cardboard
65 × 34 cm

inv.no.124-1971
Blok 147
Seuphor 201, c.c.155

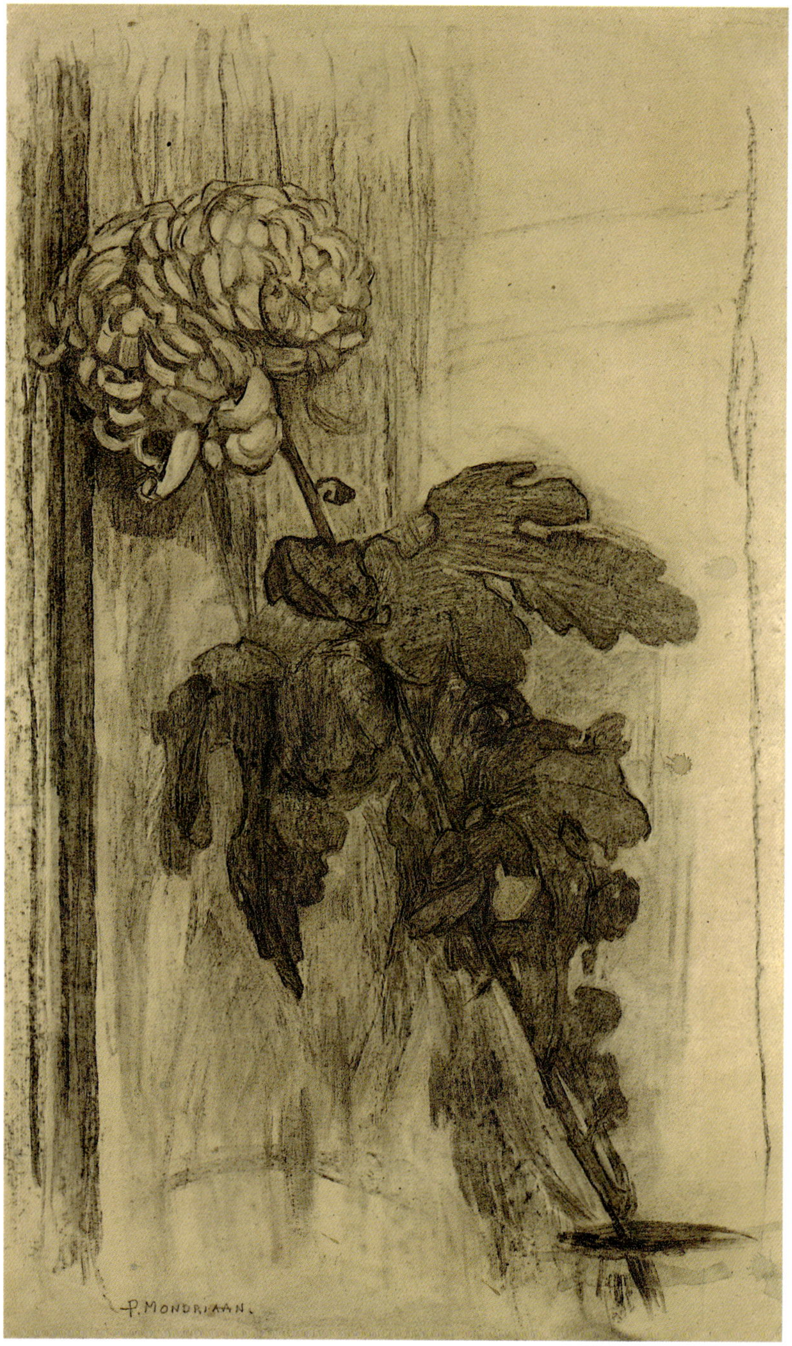

99

Chrysanthemum

1908
charcoal/paper
78.5 × 46 cm

inv.no.T115-1971
Blok 148
Seuphor 187, c.c.135

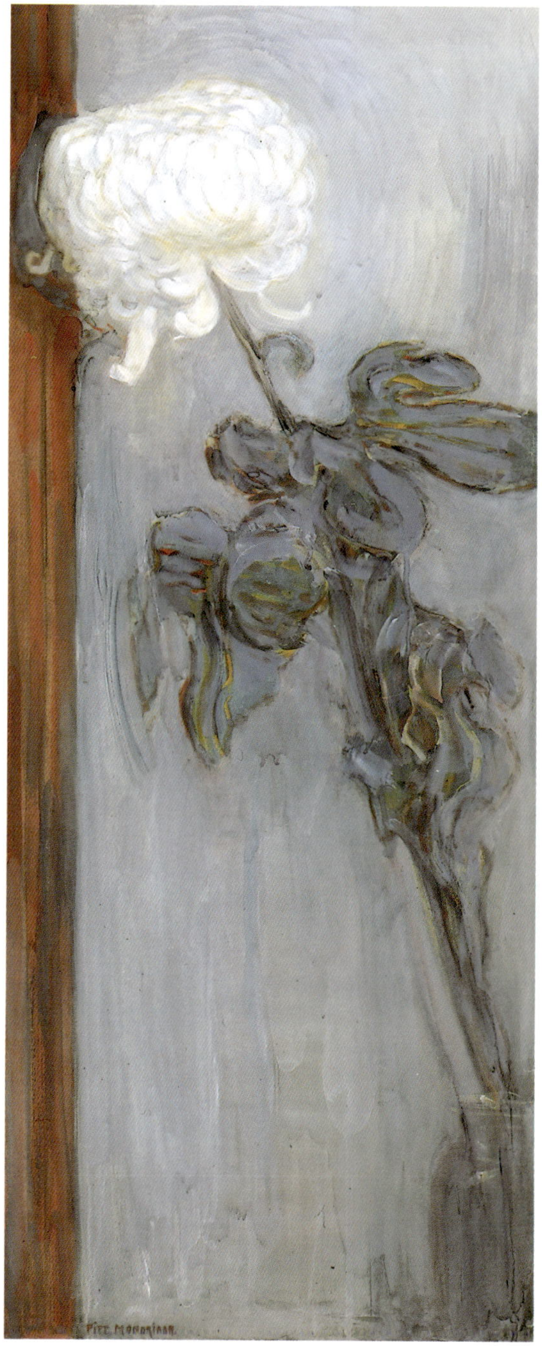

100

Chrysanthemum

1908
gouache/paper
94 × 37 cm

inv.no.T49-1971
Blok 149

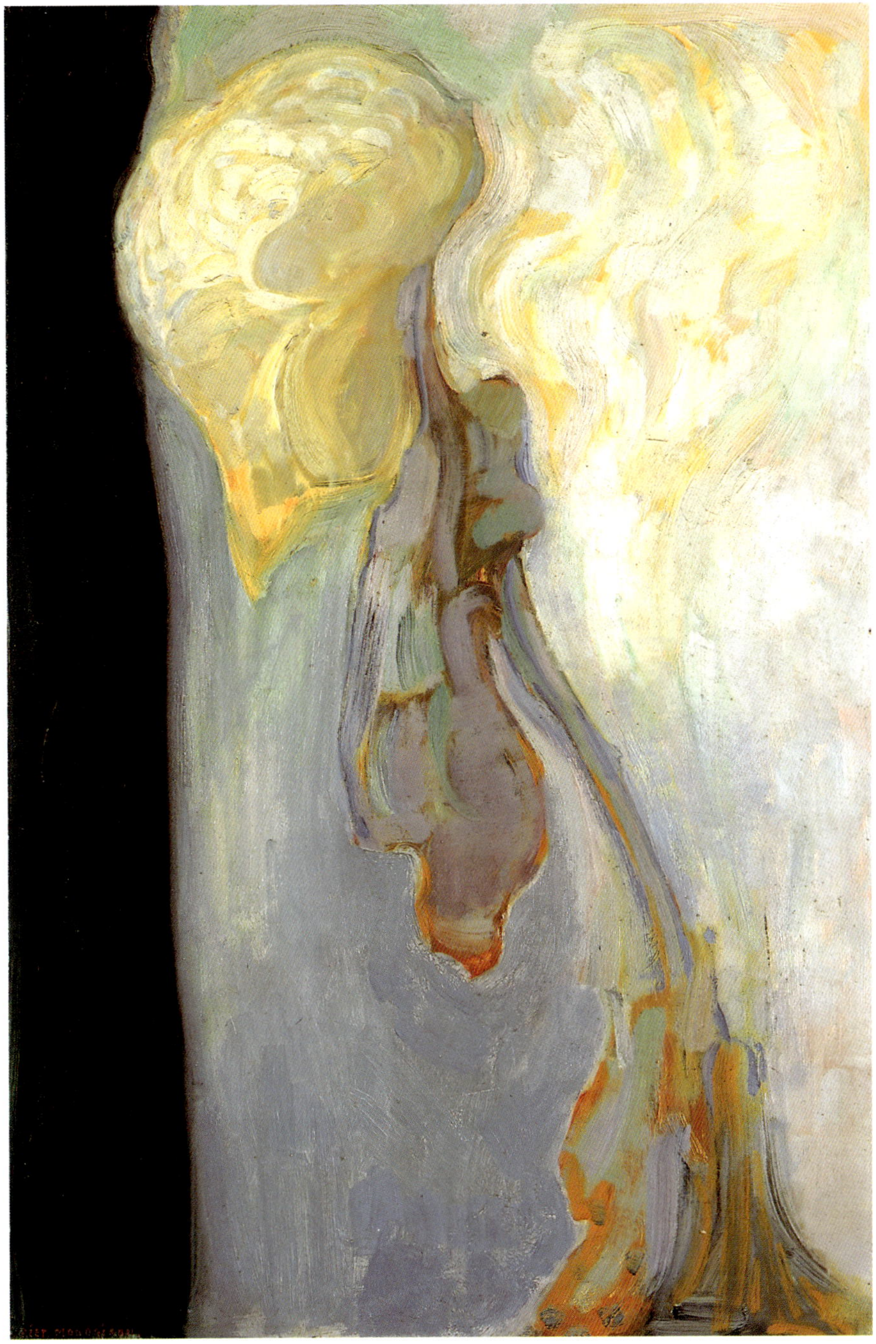

101

Dying Chrysanthemum

1908
oil/canvas
84.5 × 54 cm

inv.no.125-1971
Blok 150
Seuphor 199, c.c.136

A—I should like to continue our conversation...You want to depict *reality*: whereas I thought you wanted to express *the soul of things*.

B—Neither the one nor the other, really. If the outward *appearance* of things is what we call reality, it is not all that is depicted because man also consists of *inwardness*. i.e. soul and mind. Since he also consists of *outwardness*, though, more than *mere* inwardness can be depicted. Painting has always *more or less* adopted the middle path: but spiritual life is the life of human *feelings*. To depict the *soul of things* means expressing our *soul*. And that is not the *supreme* aim of art.

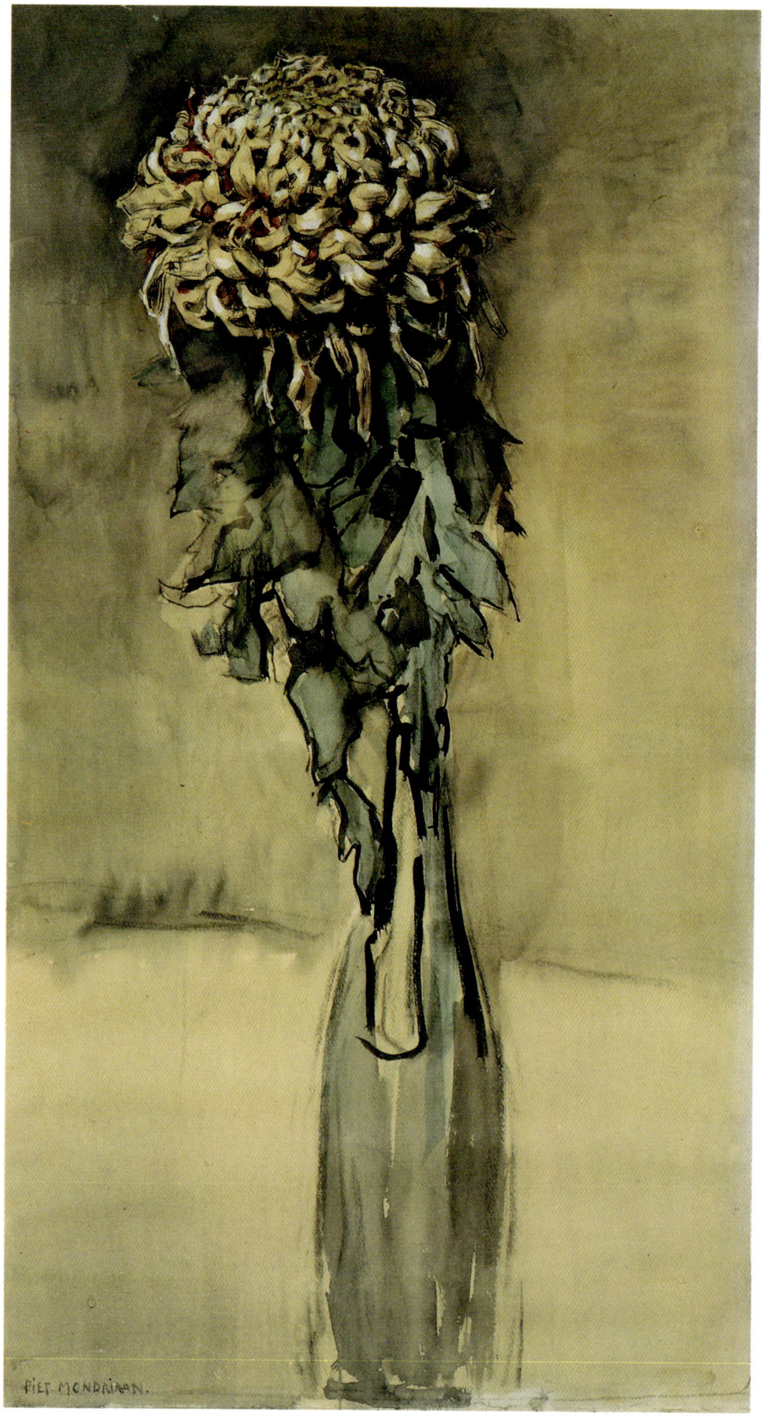

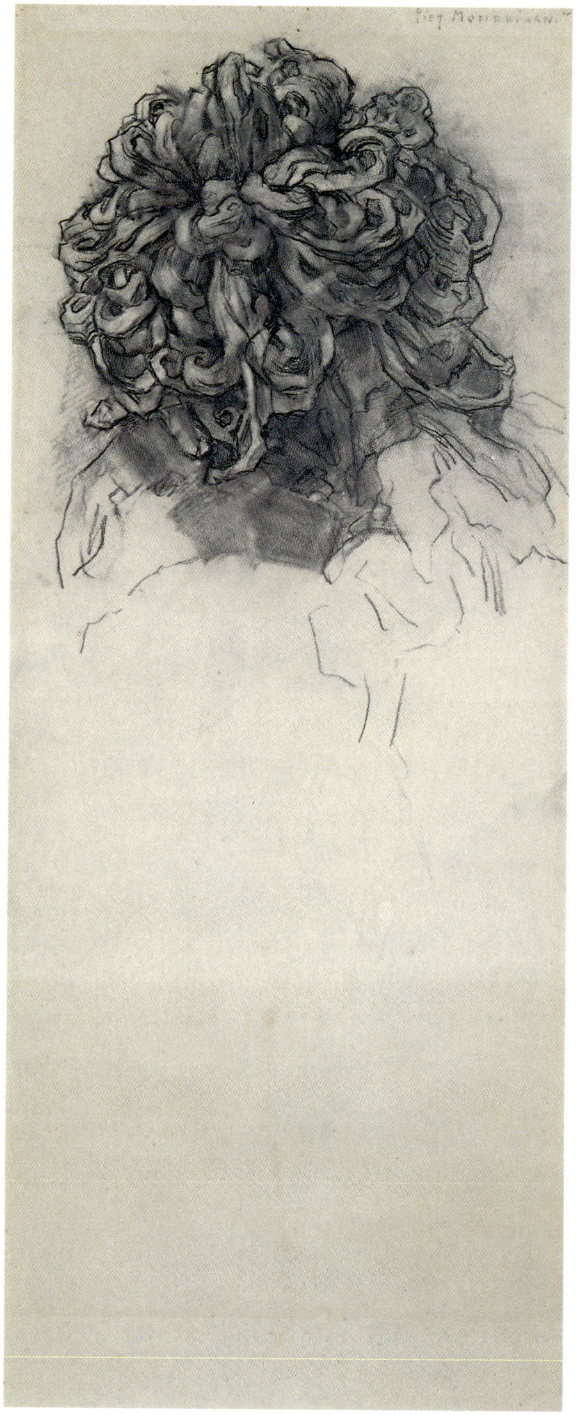

102
Chrysanthemum
ca.1909
watercolour/paper
72.5 × 38.5 cm

inv.no.T111-1971
Blok 187
Seuphor 178, c.c.129

103
Chrysanthemum
ca.1909
pencil/charcoal/paper
66 × 25.5 cm

inv.no.T112-1971
Blok 188

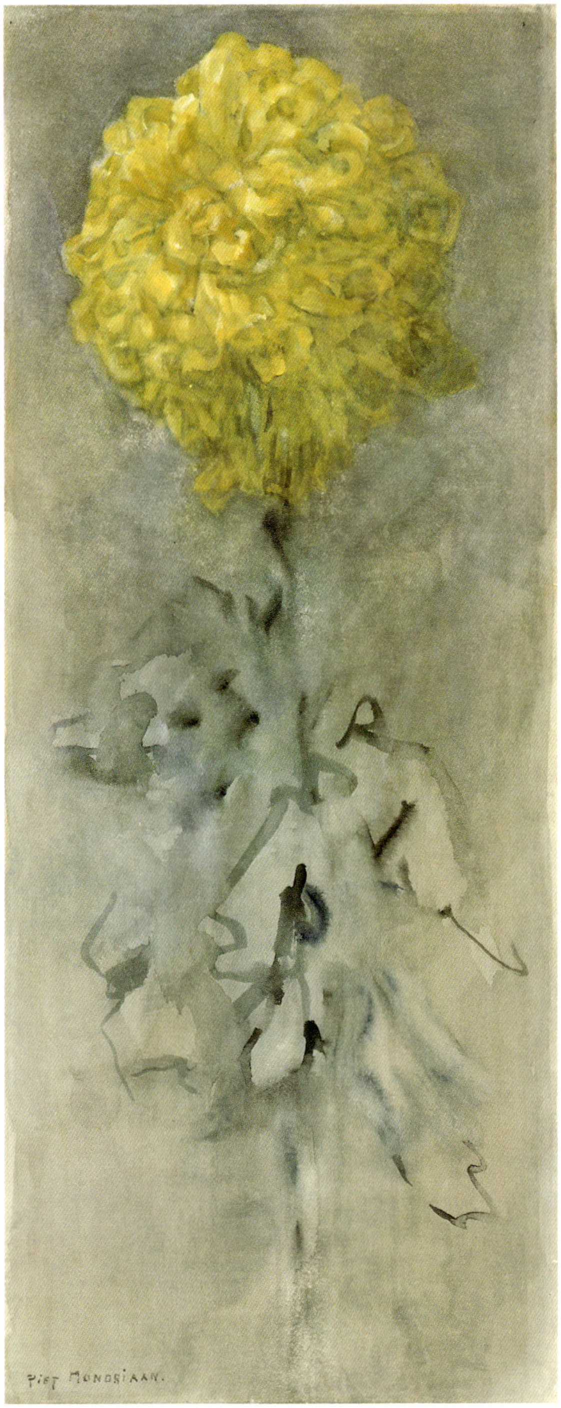

104
Chrysanthemum
1909
gouache/paper
69 × 26.5 cm
inv.no.T113-1971
Blok 190
Seuphor 177, c.c.128

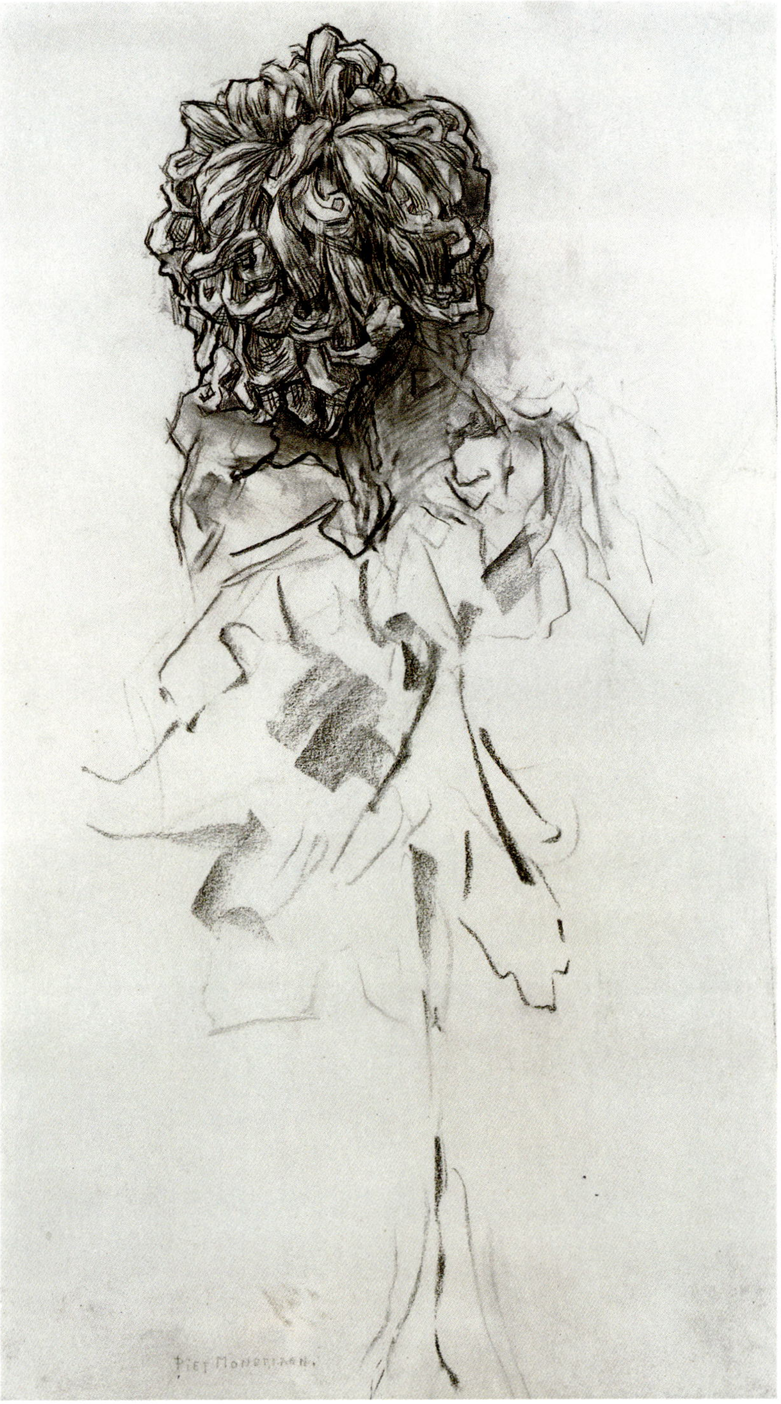

105
Chrysanthemum
ca.1909
charcoal/crayon/paper
72 × 47 cm
inv.no.T114-1971
Blok 191

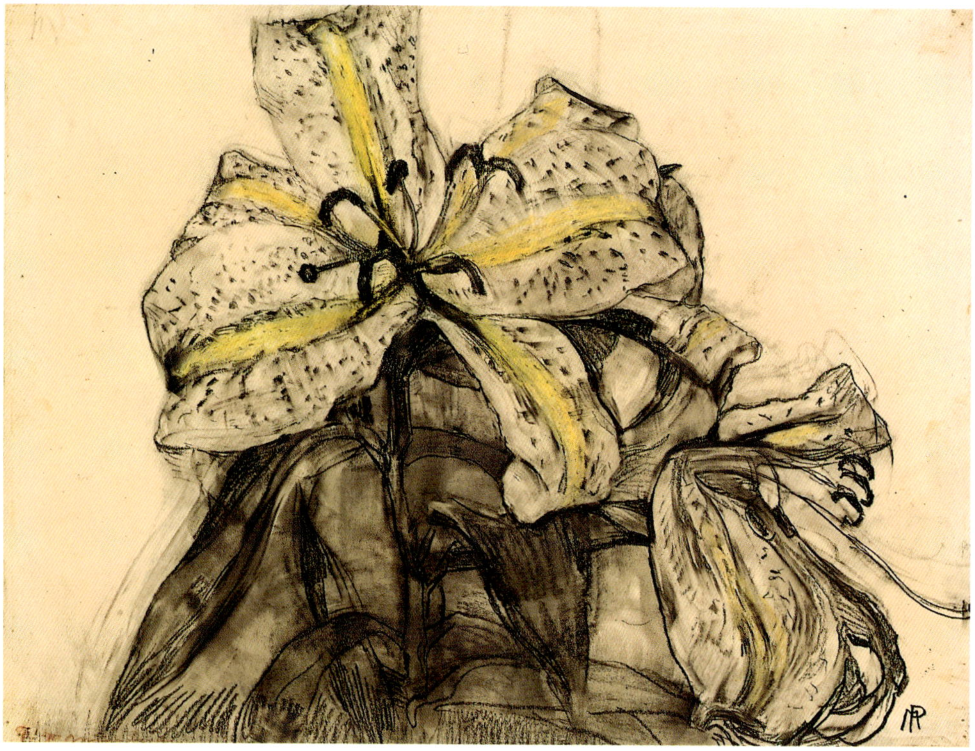

106

Tiger Lily

1909/10
charcoal/crayon/paper
35 × 44 cm

inv.no.T122-1971
Blok 198

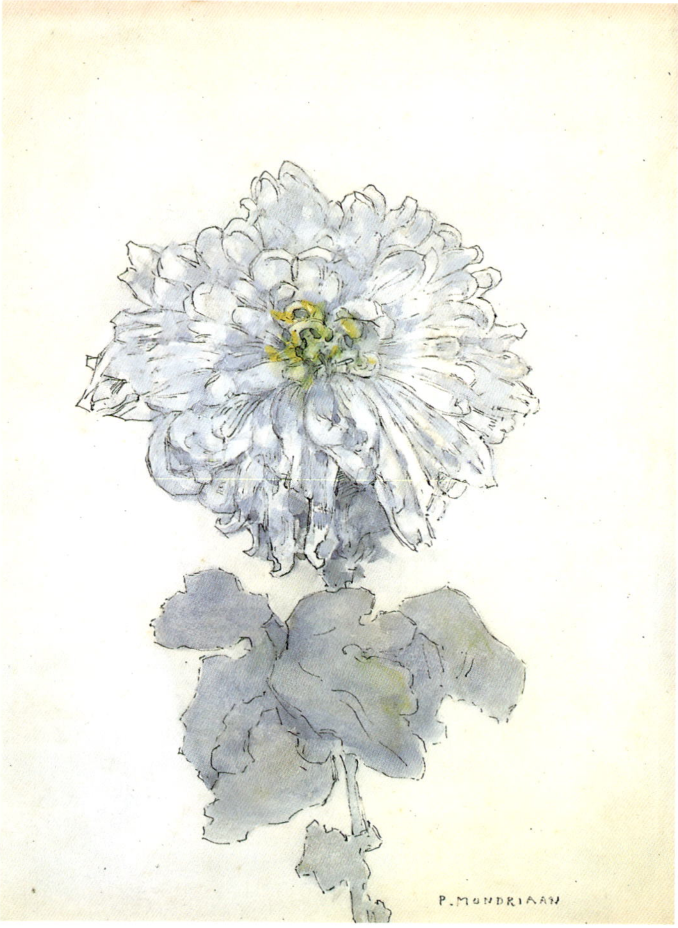

107

Chrysanthemum

after 1921
watercolour/paper
28.5 × 20.5 cm

inv.no.T33-1947
Blok 253

B—You recall my flowers; they, too, were 'chosen' from the many different kinds of flowers that exist. Didn't you think their 'expression' was different from my seas, dunes and churches?

A—Yes indeed: the flowers conveyed something of a more intimate nature, as it were, whereas the seas, churches and dunes suggested 'space' to me more.

B—And so you see how important form is. A closed form (like a flower) says something different from an open curved line (as in the dunes) and something different again from the straight line of a church or the radial petals of certain flowers, for instance. Comparison will show you that a certain form conveys a certain impression: that the line is potentially *plastic*, and that the tensest line depicts most purely the immutable, strength, size.

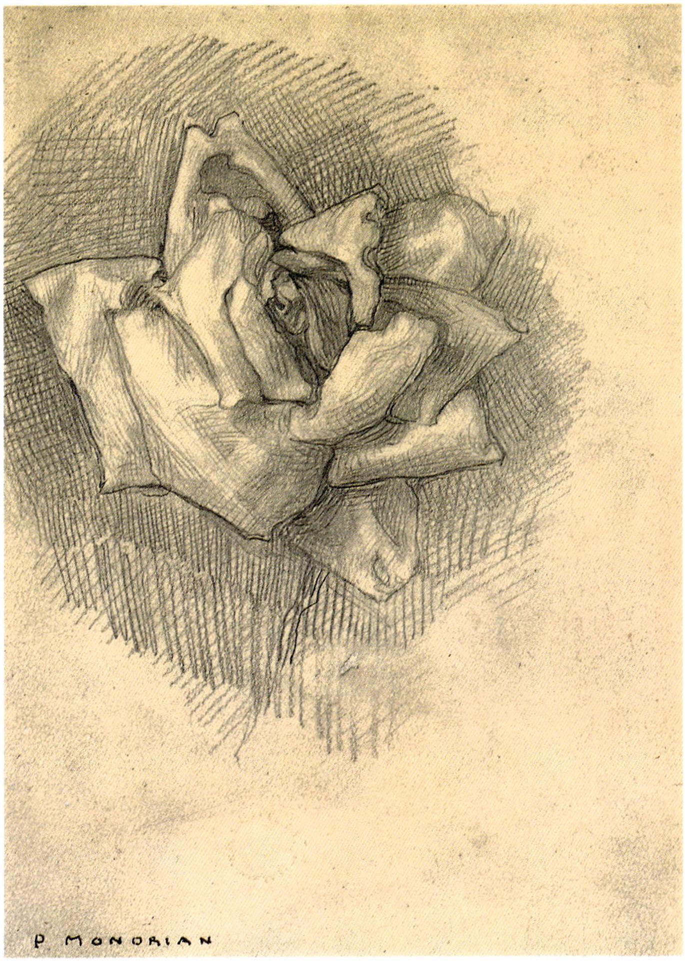

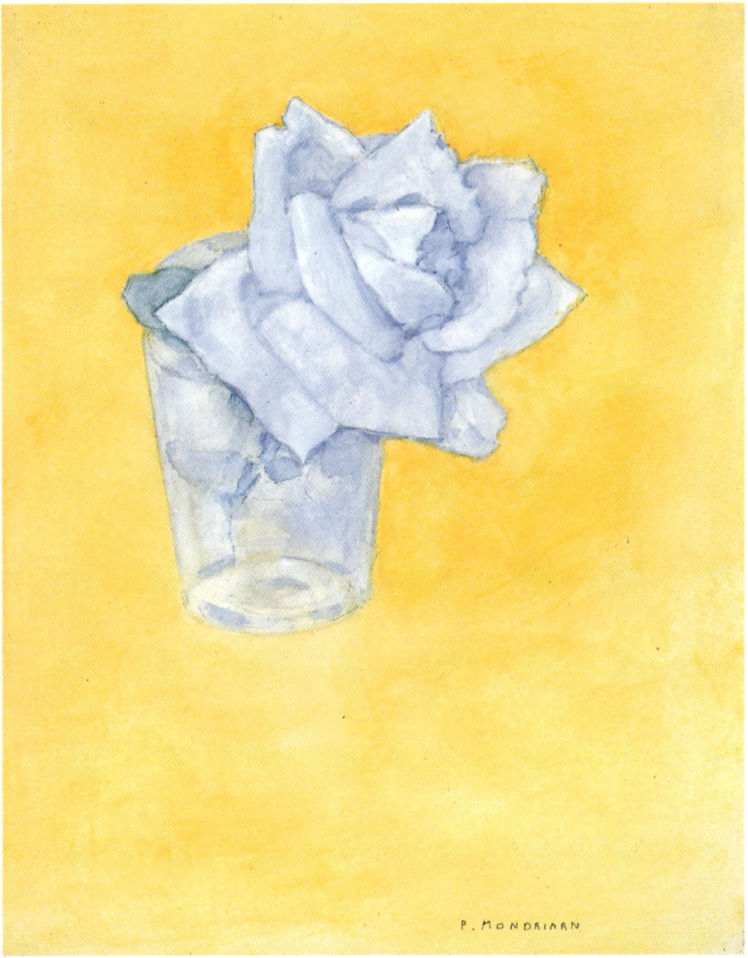

108

Rose

after 1921
pencil/paper
25 × 18 cm

inv.no.T71-1971
Blok 254

109

White Rose in a Tumbler

after 1921
watercolour/paper
27.4 × 21.3 cm

inv.no.T7-1971
Blok 255

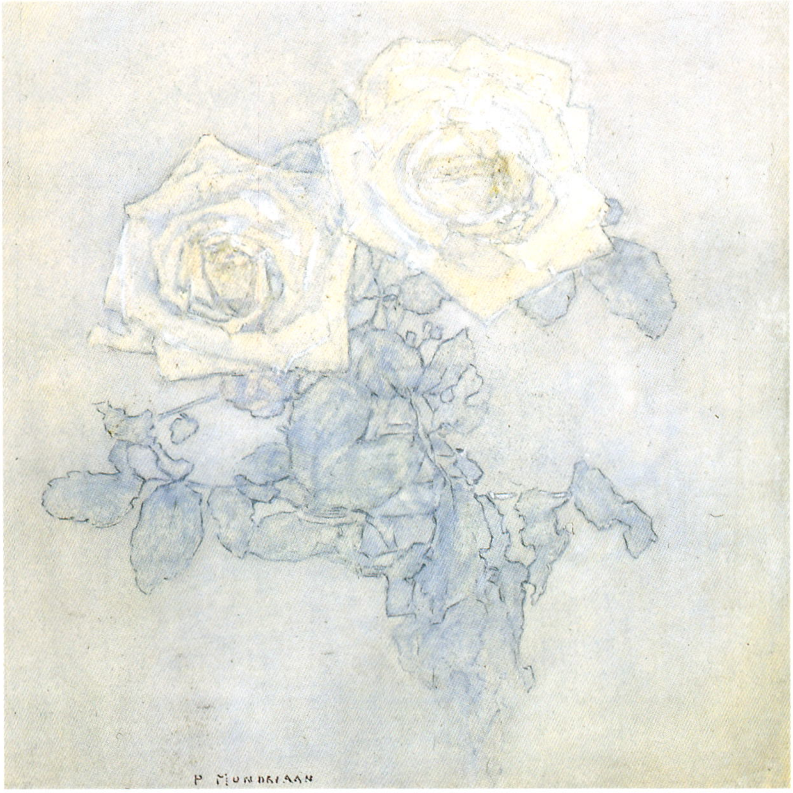

110

White Roses

after 1921
watercolour/colour pencil/paper
27.3 × 25.5 cm

inv.no.T70-1971
Blok 256

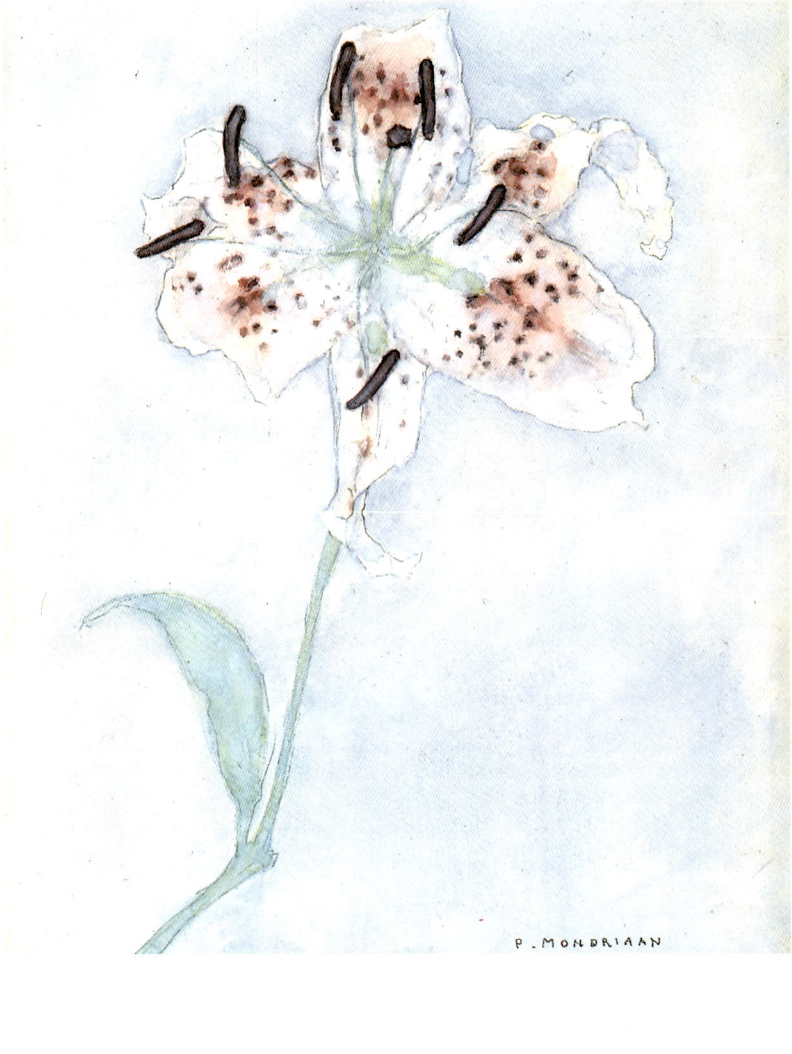

111

Lily

after 1921
watercolour/colour pencil/paper
24.9 × 19.3 cm

inv.no.T73-1971
Blok 258

Z—But at the aesthetic moment of contemplation, the individual is no longer the individual. *To render perceptible in colour and line the universal which then emerges* was the essence of all painting. And should future painting be characterized by the emphasis it places on the greater *definition* of the universal, breaking away from natural appearance, we ought to see this as the effect of the new spirit of the age which, with growing awareness, is increasingly capable of changing the *moments* of contemplation into *one moment,* into *permanent contemplation.*

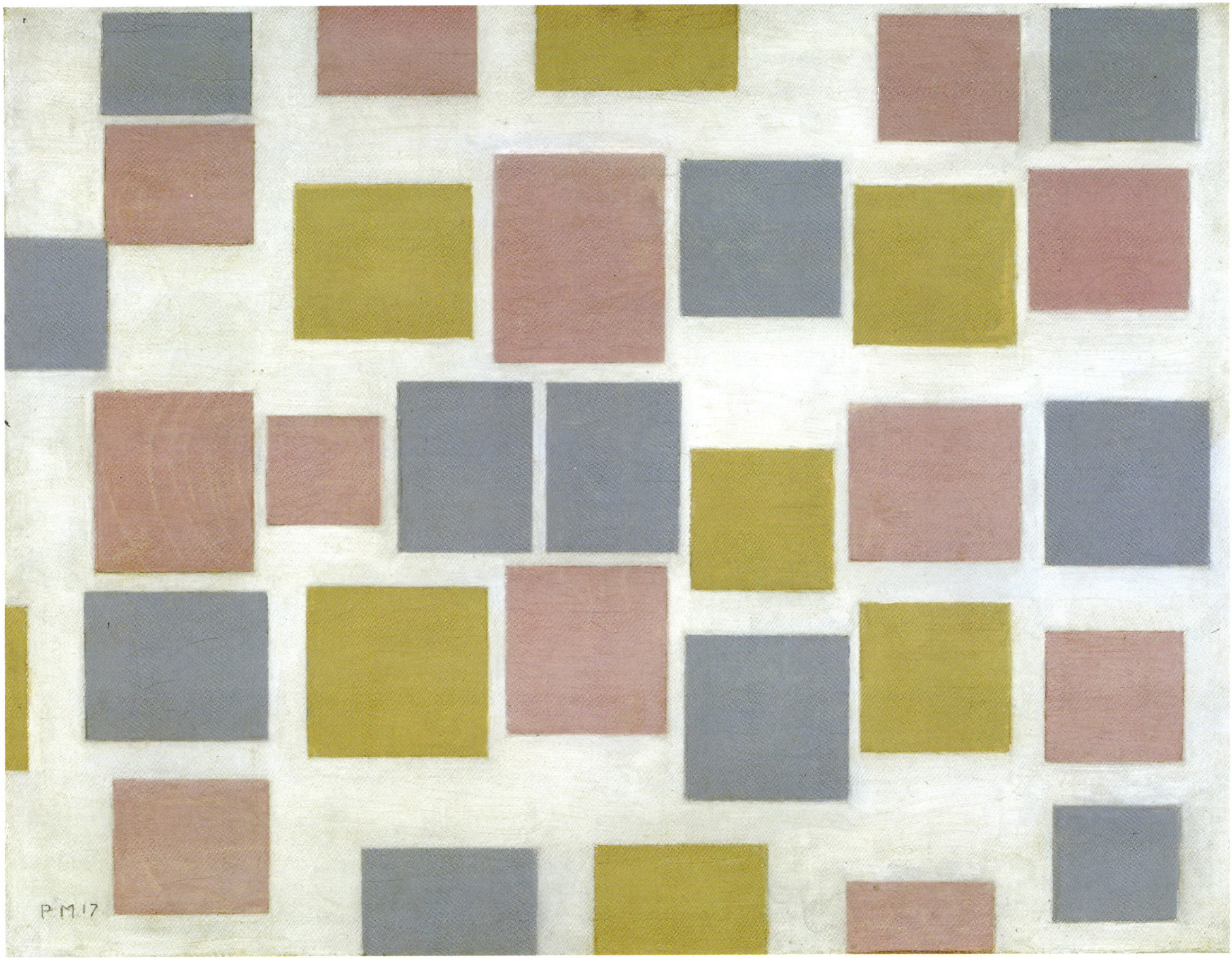

112

Composition no.3 with Colour Planes

1917
oil/canvas
48 × 61 cm

inv.no.31-1949
Blok 262
Seuphor 428, c.c.286

B—Truth is proclaimed by the straight line, and *eloquence*, in your sense, is not an artistic merit: eloquence makes art literary, tendentious. *Painting* must be purely *plastic*, and in order to achieve this it must use plastic means without individual eloquence. This justifies the use of rectangular areas of colour.

A—But is this motivated with regard to classical—indeed to all past art, which has always depicted the way things look?

B—If you really comprehend that the intention of all pure painting has always been *plastic*, the consistent application of that idea not only motivates *universal* plastic means, but even *necessitates* them. All naturalistic painting could not help paying too much attention to the *special*. Art must depict the *general*, though: that is what justifies Neo-Plasticism with regard to all painting.

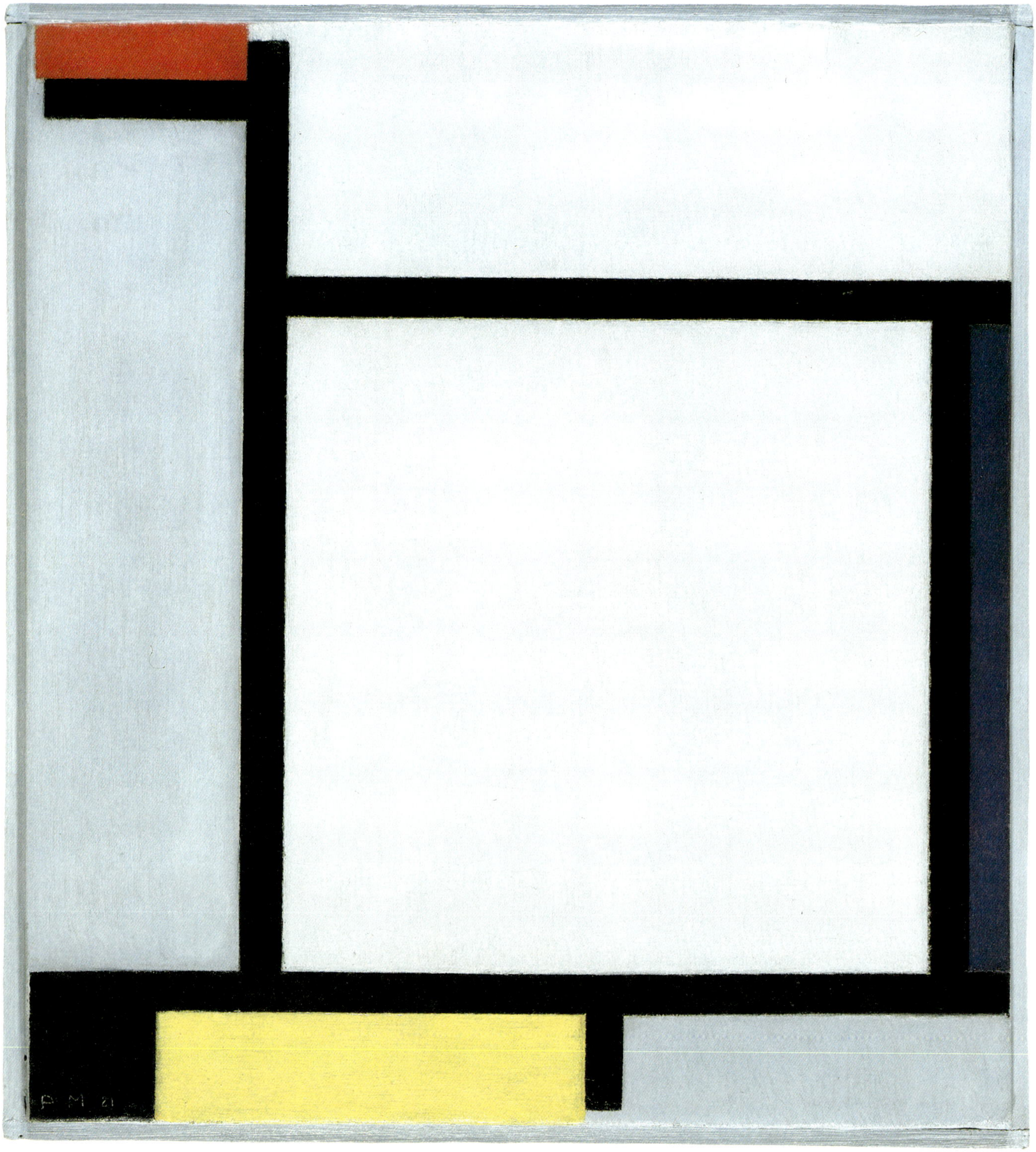

113

Composition with Red, Yellow and Blue

1921
oil/canvas
39.5 × 35 cm

inv.no.170-1971
Blok 274
Seuphor 464, c.c.321

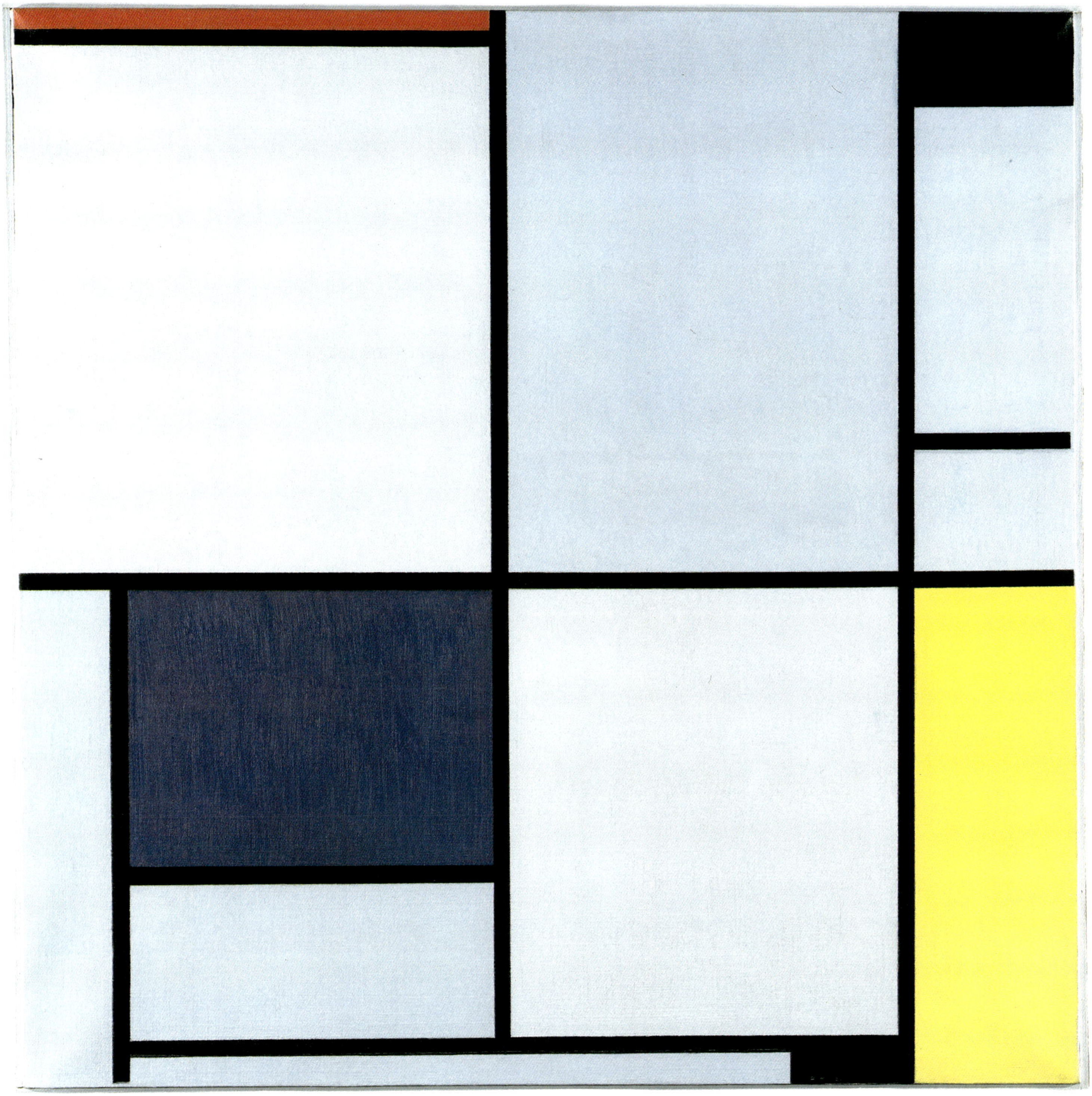

114

Composition I with Red, Yellow and Blue

1921
oil/canvas
103 × 100 cm

inv.no.169-1971
Blok 275
Seuphor 459, c.c.315

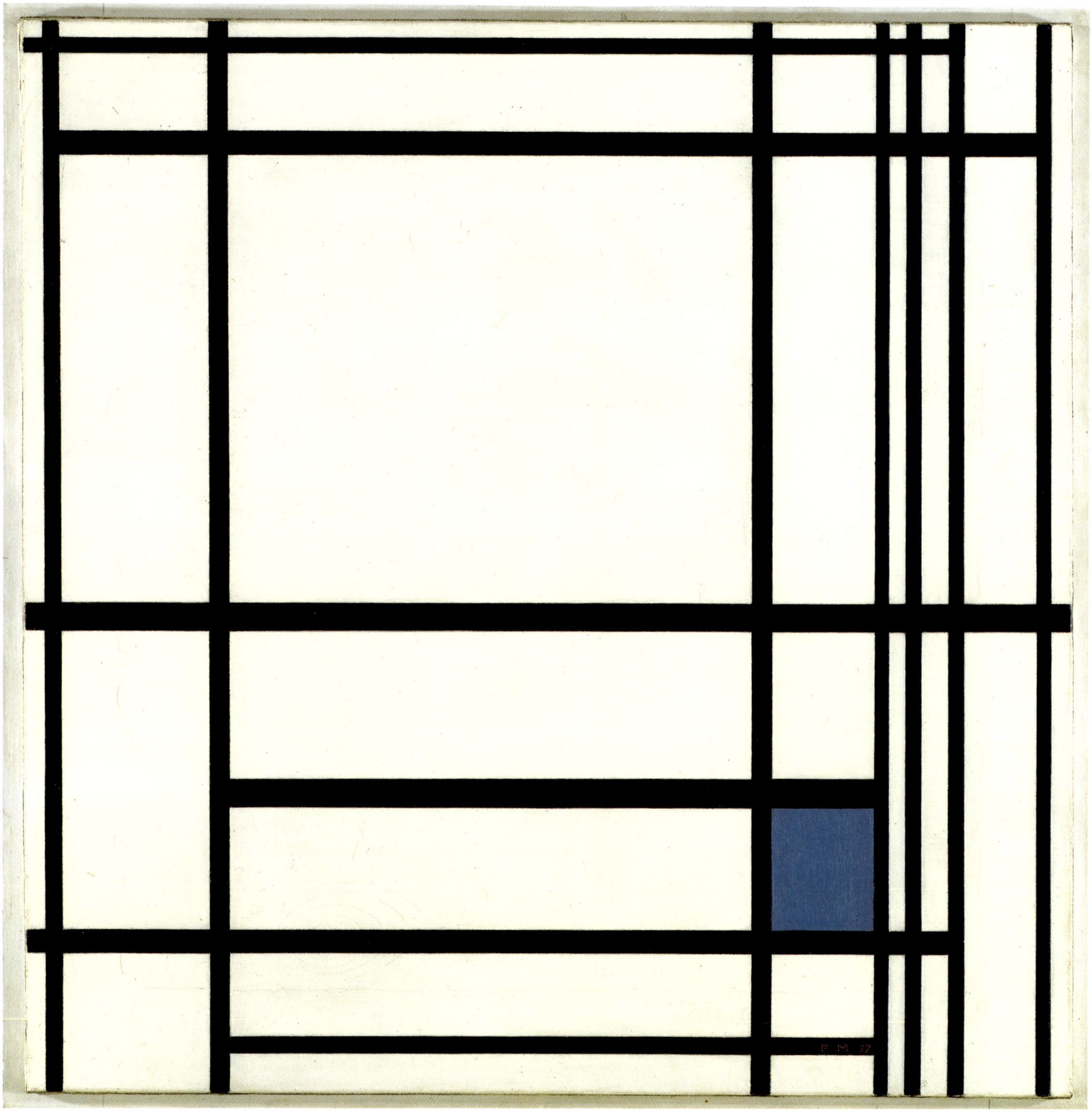

115

Composition with Blue

1937
oil/canvas
80 × 77 cm

inv.no.88-1967
Blok 284
Seuphor 564, c.c.395

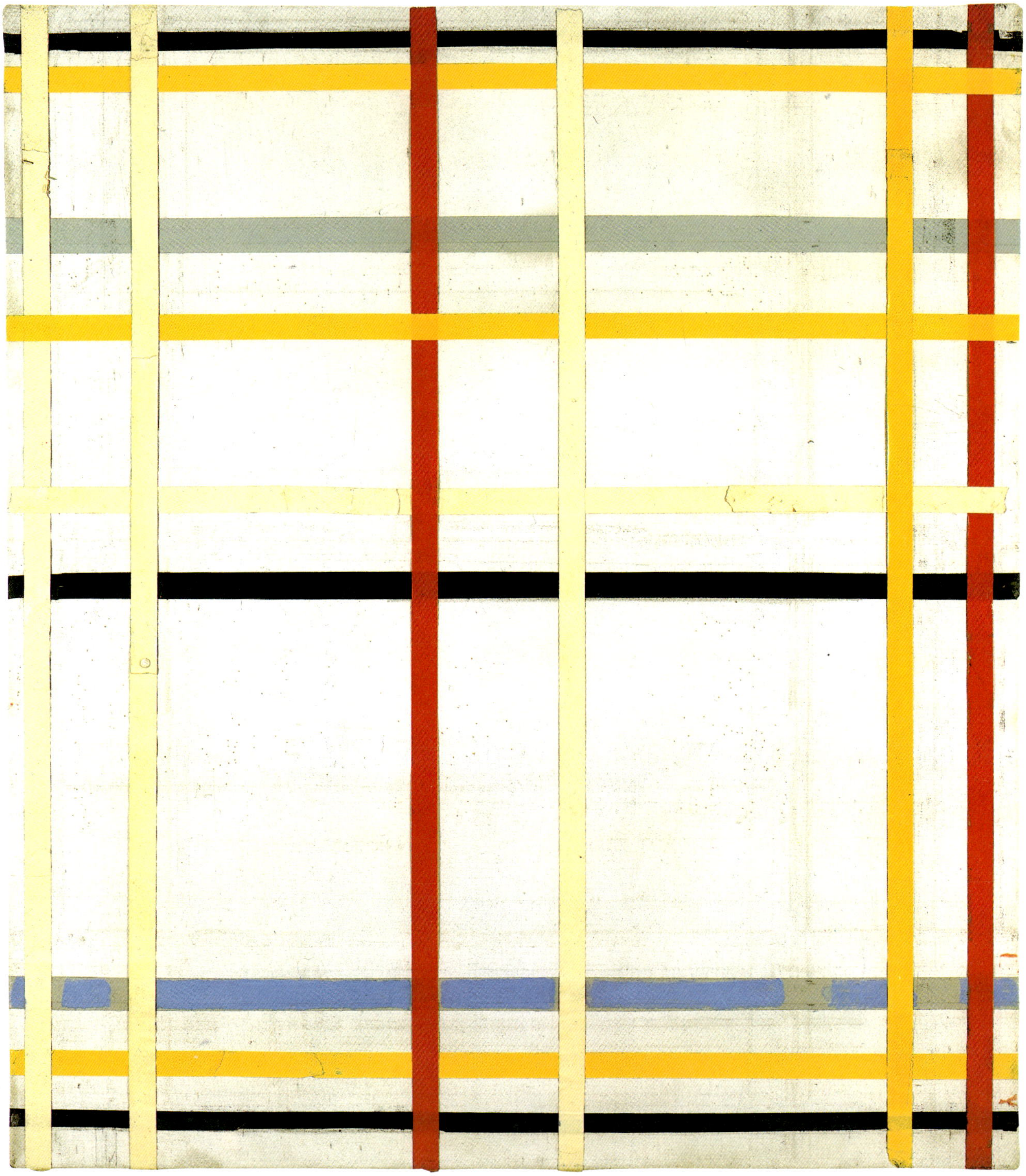

116

New York City III

1942-44
oil/tape/canvas
115 × 99 cm

Seuphor 586, c.c.436

Coll. Sidney Janis Gallery, New York

Mondrian in Winterswijk

herbert henkels

Mondrian himself spoke on two occasions of his training and first steps along the road towards becoming an artist. In 1907, at the invitation of F. Lurasco, Mondrian outlined his career up to that point as follows:
'Piet Mondrian, born on March 7th 1872 in Amersfoort, was first taught to draw by his father, who did a lot of drawing; at fourteen he learned to paint from his uncle, Frits Mondriaan of The Hague, who used to go to Winterswijk to paint outdoors; he obtained his elementary and secondary drawing certificates, studied for a while with Joh. Braedt van Uberfeldt and then attended the Amsterdam Academy for three years. After that he worked independently, painting figures and landscapes at first, later only landscapes. He has exhibited and sold successfully. Lives in Amsterdam'.
(F. Lurasco, Onze Moderne Meesters, Amsterdam 1907)

Thirty-seven years later the American journalist Jay Bradley published an interview with Mondrian which had taken place shortly before the artist's death and touched on his training: *'My father was always drawing', he* (Mondrian) *recalled in the conversation with this writer,' though it was only a hobby with him, and I began like everybody else. My father taught me at first and then my uncle who was a professional painter, gave me lessons. My serious drawing dates from the time I was about 14 years old. When it appeared that I wanted to devote my life to art, my father tried to discourage me. He lacked the money to pay for my studies and wanted me to get a job. But I clung to my art ambitions, and that was my father's sorrow. Another man paid for my studies for three years, sending me at 19 to the Amsterdam Academy of Fine Arts. At 22 began a very difficult time for me. To make a living I did many kinds of work—bacteriological drawings used for textbooks and in schoolrooms, portraits, copies of pictures in museums, and taught as well, and then I began to sell landscapes. It was a hard struggle but I managed to make a living and was glad to be able to make just enough money to be able to do what I wanted to do.'*
(J. Bradley, Piet Mondrian (1872-1944), in: The Knickerbocker Weekly, 14 Feb. 1944)

The following remarks about Mondriaan senior's drawing come from a letter from Carel Mondriaan (1880-1956), the painter's brother, to Sal Slijper, Mondrian's friend and major collector of his work:
'For the rest, Father drew nicely, sometimes pictures to celebrate certain events in the history of the House of Orange. I still have some of them. He had them printed by De Hoogh. One of father's brothers (uncle Frits) was an amateur painter without any qualifications, but his work sold well, even to the Russian court. Really saleable pictures, the Hague woods, etc. (...) Father also used to draw a lot for us, Louis and me. Splendid horses, cows, farmboys and girls, sometimes knights, too. He drew skillfully, I must say.'
(Carel Mondriaan to Slijper, 18.10.50, Slijper Archive HGM)
A curious item on the front page of the Nieuwe Winterswijkse Courant shows that there was occasionally some confusion about the activities of father and son:
'Mondriaan dead.
According to a press report, the well-known painter Mondriaan has died in New York. Older inhabitants will recall that Mondriaan once ran a school in the Ratumschestraat, opposite Ubbink's grocery. Even in those days he was famous for his fine drawings on cardboard.'
(Nieuwe Winterswijkse Courant, 27.11.1945)

This is not merely a case of mistaken identity, for as Carel Mondriaan pointed out in a letter to S. Slijper, Piet taught in his father's school in Winterswijk as well:
'The item in the Winterswijksche Courant is a half truth. In order to gain some 'teaching' experience (to which he was most averse), Piet gave older youths drawing and perspective lessons in the school in question on Ratumschestraat. It was father, though, who drew the pictures for children's Christmas parties at the Reformed Church. White chalk on black cardboard, the Holy Manger, for instance, or Simeon in the temple with the old Anna, the Flight into Egypt, etc. They were intended as decorations for the parties, where sandwiches, coffee and cocoa were served and the children were given books.'
(Carel Mondriaan to Slijper, 20.1.1946, Slijper Archive HGM)

Father Mondriaan's activities were thus not confined to the home but had a function outside it, at least in the small school; the aforementioned commemorative pictures were distributed more widely.
In the second part of this essay I shall pay special attention to the contact between Frits Mondriaan and his nephew Piet Mondrian, and attempt to show what Piet learned from Frits

and where the opinions of the two differed.
In the cited passage from the interview in the Knickerbocker Weekly, Mondrian referred to his uncle as a professional painter, whereas his brother Carel described his uncle's status as that of *'an amateur painter without any qualifications'.* Enlightenment is provided by Frits Mondriaan himself in the biographical notes which he sent to Lurasco in 1907:
'Frits Mondriaan, born in The Hague in 1853, was no longer young when he started to paint; he was mainly self-taught, but was also formed by Willem Maris and by his acquaintance with De Bock and Roermeester. His pictures found favour and were purchased by the Grand Duke of Saxe-Weimar for the 'Pinakothek' in his residence, by the Prague 'Kunstverein' for the Museum there, and awarded a prize in St. Louis. Frits Mondriaan chiefly paints woodland scenes and water views. He lives in The Hague'.
(Lurasco, Onze Moderne Meesters, Amsterdam 1907)

To some extent, then, both Frits Mondriaan and P.C. Mondriaan senior were esteemed in their own day for their drawings and paintings; both self-taught, they attained a certain standard which in Frits' case even led to his work being sold at home and abroad.

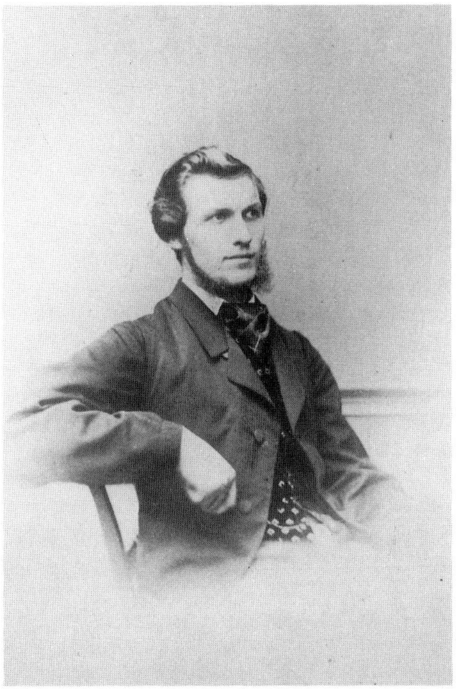

P.C. Mondriaan senior (1839-1921)

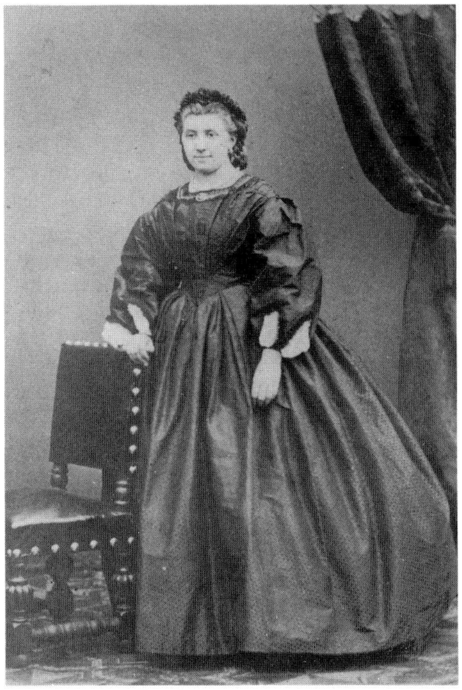

J.C. Mondriaan—de Kok (1839-1909)

P.C. Mondriaan senior , artist and activist (1839-1921)

Family

The Mondriaans are an old Hague family whose genealogy reaches back to the seventeenth century, albeit with slightly modified versions of their name—Monderiaan and Munterjan, for instance. From the late eighteenth and early nineteenth century they were known consistently as Mondriaan.
The forebear of the three Mondriaans with whom we are concerned was Fredrik Mondriaan (1809-1878), who married Petronella Hendrika Verment (1811-1856) in 1836. Seven children were born of this union, the oldest son, Willem Herman, dying at the age of eighteen, likewise two daughters in rapid succession in 1847. Four sons survived: Pieter Cornelis (1839-1921), Joh. Jacobus (1840-1901), Dirk Ernst (1847) and Frederik Hendrik (1853-1932), better known to us as Frits.
Family founder Willem Frederik was a member of the rising middle classes of The Hague. Shortly after his marriage he opened an exclusive hairdresser's shop which also sold wigs at 39 Lange Poten in The Hague. Wigs and their accessories were items for the upper-class market, being expensive. Making and dressing wigs demanded great experience; barbers and wigmakers consulted books of models which they often supplemented with their own designs and inventions.
Drawing these models was a laborious and painstaking task demanding a great deal of patience and precision. Willem Frederik ran a flourishing business in the heart of the smartest shopping district. His shop survived for many years, until about 1915. After the death of the eldest son, Willem Herman, at the age of eighteen, his brother Joh. Jacobus entered the business for a while. When father Willem Frederik died in 1878, however, it was taken over by Frits, who took up painting later. Only Pieter Cornelis and Dirk Ernst were trained as teachers.

Amersfoort

P.C. Mondriaan senior, educated in the eighteen-sixties at what became known as the first 'School van Groen' at 13 Nobelstraat in The Hague, was trained entirely by Groen himself and his followers, many of whom were members of the Réveil movement. Mondriaan senior not only trained as a teacher, but also qualified as headmaster and obtained certificates to teach French and drawing. He became an assistant teacher at the Nobelstraat school. His son Carel described his activities there:
'Father taught French and Dutch to all the bigwigs of the day, was picked up by coach and received several presents from the rich young people; one of them was Wassenaer van Opdam.'
(Carel Mondriaan to S. Slijper, 18.10.1950, Slijper Archive HGM)

It is quite likely that Mondriaan senior was already known in The Hague as a strong upholder of Groen's ideas. Not until he was appointed head of a denominational school in Amersfoort did he play a major part in spreading and propagating these ideas, firmly encouraged and actively supported by both Groen van Prinsterer himself and Abraham Kuyper, the leader of the anti-revolutionary camp, who gradually took over the banner from Groen.
In 1868, a local section of the Christian National Education Association was set up in Amersfoort, as in so many other towns. Its aim was to establish a denominational school there. Certain Amersfoort citizens of both liberal and strict Protestant persuasion, aided financially by a few wealthy sympathizers including the Scheltus family, purchased premises on the Kortegracht in Amersfoort in 1868. The two-family house was scheduled to be converted into a school in due course, one part being reserved for a teacher's flat.
On the recommendation of Rev. Donner of Leiden and the educator Van Lummel, Mondriaan senior was appointed headmaster of the newly opened school. He spent the next ten years of his life there, and played a cardinal role in Protestant circles.
In addition to the responsibilities for his grow-

The Kortegracht, Amersfoort; on the left the home of the Mondriaan family, (photograph ca.1885).

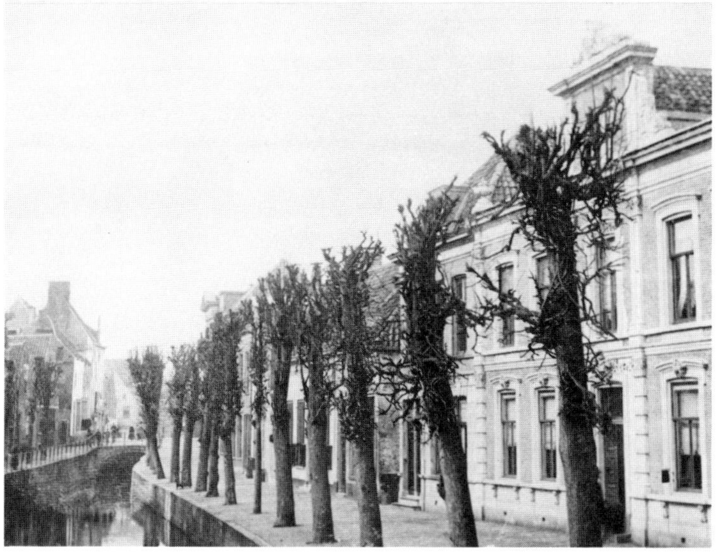

The Mondriaan children, 1890; from left to right: Carel, Pieter Cornelis, Johanna Christina, Willem Frederik and Louis.

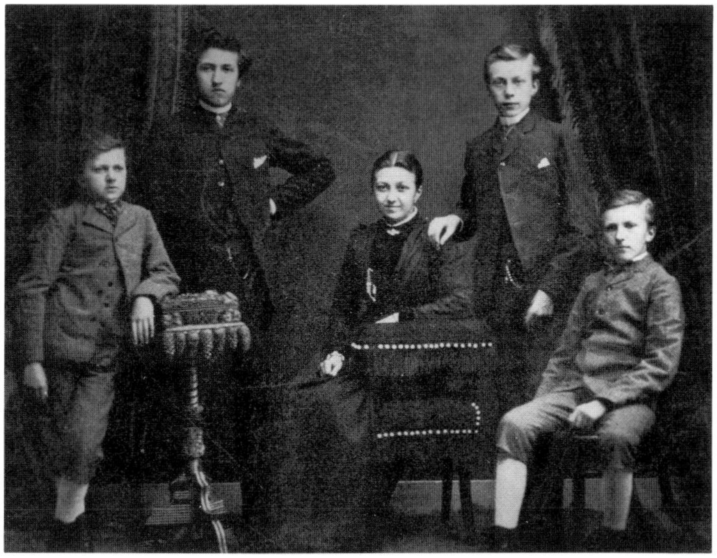

On the left the Mondriaan family house in Winterswijk; on the right part of the Christian primary school (photograph April 1979).

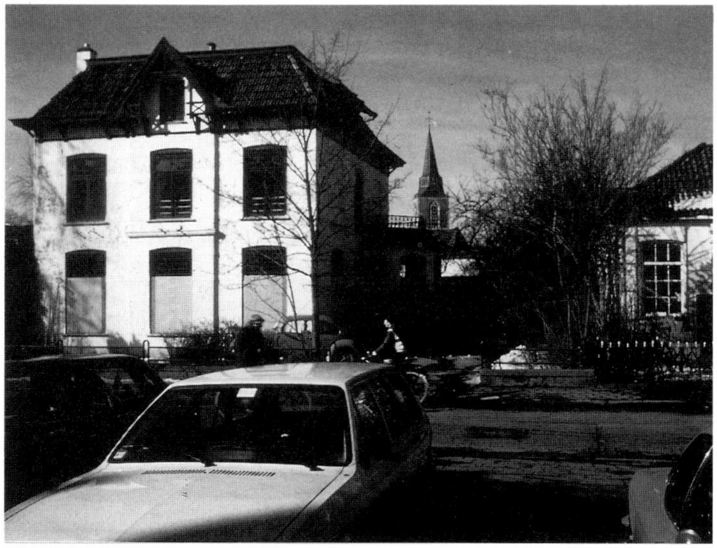

ing family—in 1870 his oldest daughter Johanna Christina was born, followed in 1872 by Pieter Cornelis junior, in 1874 by Willem Frederik and in 1877 by Louis Cornelis—he was given the task of mustering local Protestant forces with a view to recruiting election candidates not only for local government but also for parliament, where they would defend and disseminate Protestant policy. Mondriaan senior was right in the middle of the web of current politics, as it were. In 1878 the Board of the Anti-School Act Union decided to draw up a petition, leading to the mobilization of all those in favour of denominational education in the Netherlands. On May 2 1878 another petition was handed over to King William III in Loo Palace, requesting him not to sign the Kappeyne Bill, which had already been passed by the two Houses of Parliament. The petition was signed by the enormous number of more than 300,000 advocates of denominational education from both Protestant and Roman Catholic sections of the public. Although the king sympathized with the petition he could not violate the constitution, and had to enforce the proposals of the bill by signing it, to the acute disappointment of the confessional camp.

This all went to show, however, that a substantial portion of the Dutch population could be mobilized when properly organized. An important upshot of these events was the formal emergence of a new political party: the Anti-Revolutionary Party.

The discontent which Mondriaan senior had voiced in his letters to Kuyper in 1878, mounted in Amersfoort after the unsuccessful petition. The school board had always consisted of equal numbers of members of the liberal and strict Protestant churches. Some of Mondriaan senior's supporters on the board now resigned; feeling that he lacked sufficient backing, he decided to seek another position as quickly as possible. With the help of Kuyper he soon succeeded in obtaining a post in the distant village of Winterswijk.

Winterswijk

The Protestants formed a fairly large proportion of the population of Winterswijk around 1880. Due to the activities of a few people, Protestant principles had spread far beyond Winterswijk into the entire Achterhoek region.

The leading members of the community were the liberal Protestant minister Sipkes, the architect L.G. Richter, who was chairman of the school board from its founding in 1869 up to Mondriaan's departure in 1901, and Baron Th. Mackay, mayor of Winterswijk from 1874 to 1883, after which he played a prominent part in national politics.

Although Mondriaan senior continued his former activities during his early years in Winterswijk, writing articles for 'De Graafschapper', 'Het Wageningsch Weekblad' and 'De Standaard', the gap between him and religious groups in Winterswijk widened, especially after Baron Mackay left for The Hague in 1883. Despite applying for several posts, Mondriaan kept declining offers from A. Kuyper, first to edit 'De Standaard', and later the post of laboratory assistant at the newly established Free University in Amsterdam:
'As you know, I am a "schoolman", i.e. preferring to work and most at home in a large *primary school.'* (Mondriaan to Kuyper, August 29 1882)
In the long run, though, Mondriaan was quite content with his Winterswijk position, and made no further attempts to play a part in national denominational education by means of an appointment in one of the major cities.
Apart from the usual skirmishes between a headmaster and his Board, the directors were constantly complaining that the headmaster remained too aloof from the religious community and failed to attend church services regularly. It should be stressed, incidentally, that Mondriaan was not, as is often assumed, a member of the Reformed Church, but of the stricter 'Hervormd' church, and did not follow A. Kuyper into the dissenters' camp in 1886. However, Mondriaan senior's experience and other talents seem to have made a great impression on the school board and the Winterswijk Christian community. Among the skills which emerged notably during school festivities were his artistic bent and his knowledge of Dutch history. According to the minutes of a board meeting held after the celebrations marking the school's fifteenth anniversary in 1885: *'Then all those who had put down their names to attend the festive gathering and the communal meal, proceeded to the school, which due to the headmaster's extraordinary industry was decorated most tastefully and appropriately with well-chosen symbolic and historical representations, entirely in keeping with the significance of the celebrations, and transformed so artistically into a Christian national festive hall that the entire decoration provided fresh proof of the fine taste and Christian national artistic spirit of the skilled designer and executor.'* (Minutes of the school board meeting of 30.10.1885)

Mondriaan senior as an artist

Judging by their correspondence, there was a fundamental difference in the character of Mondriaan senior's relations with Abraham Kuyper and with Groen van Prinsterer.
To Mondriaan, Abraham Kuyper, who was pretty much the same age as himself, was a highly gifted leader and ally in the political struggle of the time, whereas Groen van Prinsterer was the revered teacher to whom the pupil owed his entire development. The undertone of Mondriaan's letters to Kuyper is much more direct and personal than he would have ever dared to adopt in his letters to Groen. Mondriaan formulated his reasons for feeling drawn towards Kuyper in the turbulent election of 1873: *'(...) for I am convinced that sitting idly when there is work to be done in these matters (especially at this juncture) is an abomination to the Lord. That is why I adhere to you. It is because of your work, your incomparable individuality in the intellectual field.'* The character of Mondriaan's relations with Groen emerges most clearly in a letter offering examples of his drawing skill:
'Dear Sir,
Were the sole purpose of that to which I have the honour to draw to your attention to provide proof of the gift of drawing with which the Lord has endowed me, I should not have the temerity to submit this work.
Among the host of masterpieces in your collection, it would cut a poor figure as a subject for artistic contemplation, although the publishers assure me that they have spared no pains or expense in giving it this appearance.
There is more, however. At my unforgettable school in the Nobelstraat I learned long ago to cherish and contemplate the History of our Fatherland as far as the sources and my strength permitted.
It hence became a necessity to me, in the days leading up to the 'Silver Coronation Celebrations'—so rich a subject for reflection!—to express in design and drawing what I felt and sensed. The enclosed concept of the picture will, I hope, be sufficiently clear to induce you to consider the various groups. The special interest which a leading light of our day has deigned to express in the design encourages me to hope—albeit not for all parties—that you will be glad that the development of a pupil at the aforementioned school into a teacher, has borne at least a little fruit.
I have not ventured to send you my 'Family Tree of the House of Orange-Nassau', available everywhere, with its accompanying 'Manual', fearing it to be too simple.
In the silent hope that I have been able to contribute to the well-being of the people so dear to your heart, I have the honour—with the assurance of my gratitude for what I received during my education—to dedicate to you the enclosed copy, which has not yet been published. I take this liberty in the conviction, shared with me by all, that in both the art and the history your original mind (your greatness, if I may say so) will see more than a simple student and enthusiast.

Your humble servant,
P.C. Mondriaan

Amersfoort, May 30th 1874'

Groen replied by return:
'June 3rd 1874

Thank you very much for sending me the Historic Picture. It does you credit. The plan and the execution seem excellent to me. I am always pleased when such celebrations can be combined with our national heritage. Nonetheless I must beg you not to rely solely on my approval in this matter. Leave me out of it entirely. To my mind your picture, with its memories of the past, glorifies the present too much; the representation is too much a kind of apotheosis. Amidst the exaggeratedly jubilant tones too little heed is paid to Da Costa's words: 'Be true!', too little thought for Oosterzee's 'No Dawn' and for his succinct criticism: 'sinking and singing Netherlands'. That is what I have to tell you. I must not be insincere, and it would be churlish to ignore your kind offering of what in my opinion is a successful picture.'

Mondriaan senior probably started drawing large numbers of historical commemorative pictures in 1870. Four of 1874 are extant; in 1878 he made one to commemorate the Union of Utrecht, another one, of 1884, commemorates the death of William the Silent. A 'Feestplaat ter gedachtenis aan Neêrlands onafhankelijkheid 1813-1888' (commemorating the Netherlands' independence 1813-1888) dates from 1888, in 1898 he made a 'Gedenk- en feestplaat' to mark Queen Wilhelmina's coronation, in 1901 another for her marriage; the last one known to me dates from 1913: a 'Gedenk- en Feestplaat ter herinnering aan Neêrlands Onafhankelijkheid 1813-1913', again commemorating the Dutch independence.
Examples of most of these prints are extant, but not of others, although it is very likely that Mondriaan senior drew more. Only the last picture (1913) is signed in full: P.C. Mondriaan; in the many others the initials P.C.M. are placed in a most inconspicuous position, often making attribution difficult. Mondriaan senior would rather not have signed them at all, judging by a letter he wrote to Abraham Kuyper:
'May I also ask you to indicate my signature P.C.M. somewhere on the picture, so that nobody can accuse me of being ashamed of it.' (Mondriaan to Kuyper 28.1.74)

The subjects were almost invariably taken from Dutch history, commemorating some event in

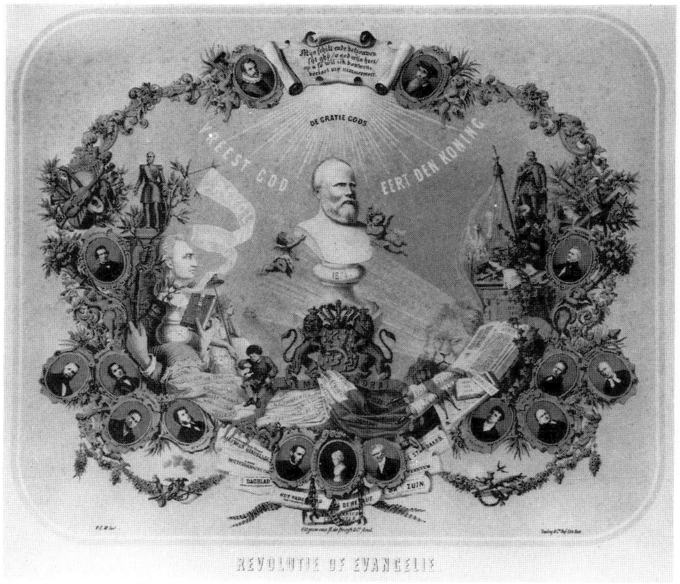

P.C. Mondriaan senior, Revolutie of Evangelie (Revolution or Gospel); 1874, lithograph, signed with initials on the left, printed by Tresling and Co., published by H. de Hoogh,Amsterdam; coll. Museum van Gijn, Dordrecht.

Details ; the garlands at the bottom left and right.

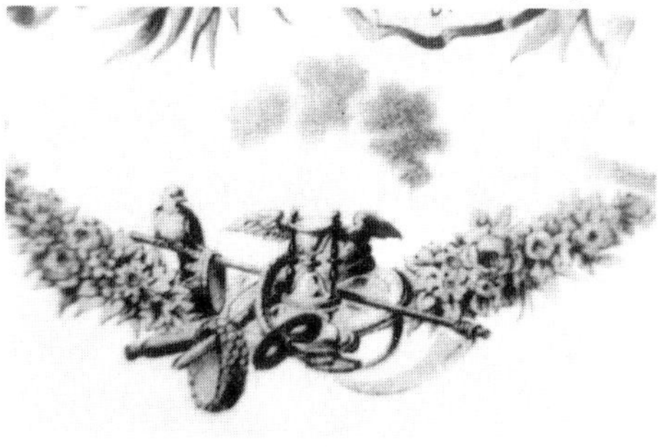

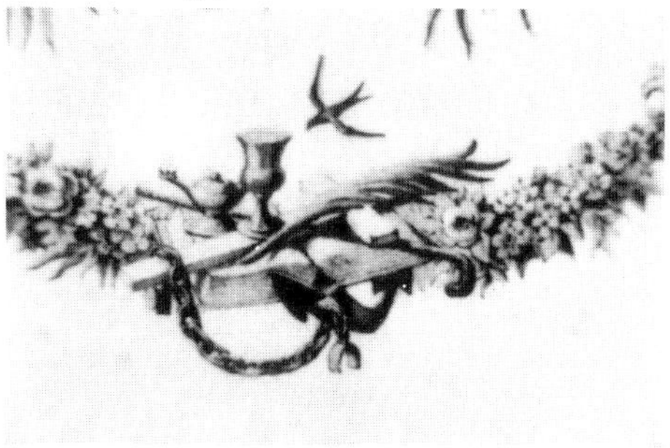

the Eighty Years' War, the remote or the more recent past, such as the unification of the Netherlands in 1813. The House of Orange always came in for generous treatment. The prints frequently feature the results achieved since unity was restored to the Netherlands in 1813.

The message conveyed by the prints, wholly in keeping with Groen van Prinsterer's spirit, is often the contrast between the benevolent and prosperous regime under the unity of the House of Orange and the threat posed to it by revolution, symbolized by Medusa's head. Accordingly, these prints may not be classified as mere commemorative pictures: they have an obvious moral.

This kind of illustration was particularly popular after 1850, and remained so up to the turn of the century. One of Mondriaan's prints, 'Leiden in 1574', which he made in 1874, was still available as a postcard in 1909 and was even reprinted in 1974! Distribution was wide, since several newspapers gave them away to their subscribers, and schools could get a reduction on bulk orders. The pictures were popular among teachers; many of them illustrated the major episodes of a particular historical event. They were invariably accompanied by an explanation providing a detailed description of the facts. This kind of picture played an important educational role in illustrating the nation's history. The composition of Mondriaan senior's pictures is always based on the same fundamental principle: the chief characters are invariably placed in the centre, surrounded by the most significant episodes of the story, generally separated or linked by garlands and ornaments bearing flags or other symbols; captions and appropriate verses complete the whole.

As a type, such pictures have much in common with the emblemata of the sixteenth and seventeenth centuries, which combined a picture with a caption, moralizing or otherwise, to express an adage in compressed form. These pictures, however, have nothing to do with adages, but interpret history. They always contain a moral lesson pointing out the blessings which God had showered on the Netherlands through the House of Orange ever since the country had been united up to the present. The illustrated scenes were frequently derived from existing paintings or prints by reputed masters. The special thing about them was that the various sections were often only linked by a framework of garlands.

Each little picture has its own construction and perspective, an extra dimension often added by the insertion of a copy of a painting. The individual scenes were usually drawn, although photographs were also used—as early as 1874 in the form of portraits, later, in 1913, whole scenes. This kind of picture may well be regarded as a prototype of the collage and later photo-montage, techniques which also combine different scenes, sometimes employing a variety of media. The collage, for instance, may juxtapose a drawing with a newspaper cutting or a photograph, and photo-montages combine parts of different photographs into a pictorial whole.

The finest of the extant pictures is a print of 1874 entitled 'Revolutie of Evangelie' ('Revolution or Gospel'). It is a highlight in Mondriaan senior's output, not only in its quality but still more for being not a commemorative picture with a moral, but conceived entirely as a topical political pamphlet. Existing documentation tells us something about the production and significance of this fine lithograph.

An advertisement in A. Kuyper's favourite paper, 'De Standaard', of January 2 1875, explains the title:

'We wish to draw your attention to the commemorative illustration De Revolutie en het Evangelie, *just published by the firm of De Hoogh en Co. The very idea of erecting a historical monument to Groen van Prinsterer's motto: The Gospel Against Revolution, is a splendid one'.*

Mondriaan himself had a different title in mind, though: *'I am almost ashamed of adding the titles I have considered to yours* (A. Kuyper's); *candour however impels me to inform you that I myself would have preferred 'Onze Tijd'* ('Our Time')...' (Mondriaan to A. Kuyper, May 25 1874)

The explanation in the newspaper advertisement illustrates the print's topical significance:

'The chief idea is that ever since 1813 our national institutions have been descending towards the revolutionary path, but that nonetheless from the old historical stem a young shoot has sprung which in accordance with the demands of our century perpetuates ancestral tradition; this is expressed in a rich yet not ornate allegory in such a fresh style, grouped around the bust of our beloved King who stands above all parties, that the opponent is not offended, nor the advocate over-adulated.'

The picture should be seen as a confrontation: on the left, revolution is symbolized as *'the*

revelation of unbelief in all its forms'; on the right, the path of the gospel is shown: *'the historical line of faith in cause and effect'.* At the right, under a portrait of William the Silent, an old man and his grandson, according to the explanation, symbolize religious freedom; further to the left a pelican is feeding its young with its own blood, a symbol of the self-sacrifice of the first Oranges.
On the right are portraits of Groen van Prinsterer, I. da Costa, Nic. Beets, Chantepie de la Saussaye *and* Dr. A. Kuyper! On the left are Thorbecke, Prof. Opzoomer, Tollens, De Genestet and A. Pierson. At the bottom are portraits of Bilderdijk, Prof. Brummelkamp and S. Gorter. The statue on the left is King William I, under it is a bust of William III with Medusa's head, the symbol of revolution, behind. The banderoles at the left and right list important events such as the draining of the Haarlemmermeer and the opening of the Yssel Bridge in 1860. At the top a verse of the Dutch national anthem is flanked by portraits of Calvin and Marnix van St. Aldegonde. The garlands on the left bear symbols meant to symbolize the fine arts; on the right the more practical and useful sciences such as architecture, mathematics and physics are depicted. An unusual feature is formed by the newspapers at the bottom, the confessional press on the right (De Standaard, De Wekstem, De Bazuin and De Heraut) and the more liberal, or revolutionary, press on the left (Algemeen Handelsblad, Nieuwe Rotterdamsche Courant and Het Dagblad voor Zuid-Holland). The broken fetters on either side of Bilderdijk's portrait indicate the freedom of the press. In the garlands at the lower left and right are two more groups of symbols which I shall discuss a little later.
Mondriaan senior evidently devised the composition together with A. Kuyper, discussing with him what symbols to use and which people to depict. Despite the advice he was given, Mondriaan held himself fully responsible for the final result: *'You will notice that I have had no aid whatsoever than my reason, eyes, hands and my faithful 13-year-old apprentice, who worked out a part of the border in the parts where there are no groups. Your book provided considerable help. Without it I should certainly not have had the idea.'* (Mondriaan to Kuyper, 18.1.1874)
Despite all his efforts, Mondriaan was not sure about the results:
"Vreest God eert den koning"("Fear God and honour the king") could be smaller. From all this you can see that the Lord has aided my undertaking. If only there are no complaints, the publisher can be satisfied.
I count on your strong support; for I do not know whether it is due to exhaustion; but I fear: (...) Several portraits could be better and I can do better if given time.

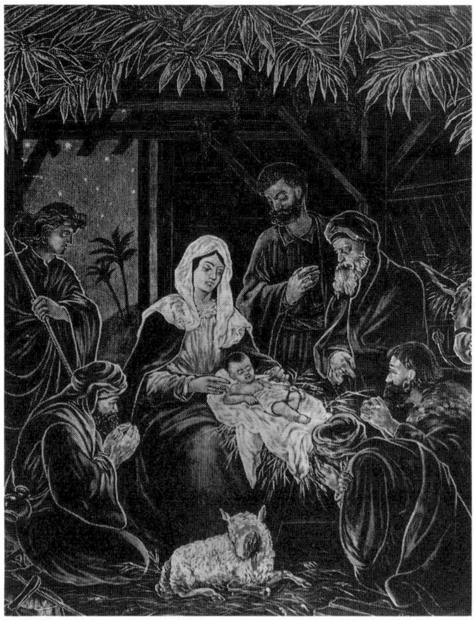
P.C. Mondriaan senior, the Adoration of the Sheperds; lithograph, 50 × 70 cm; private coll. Winterswijk.

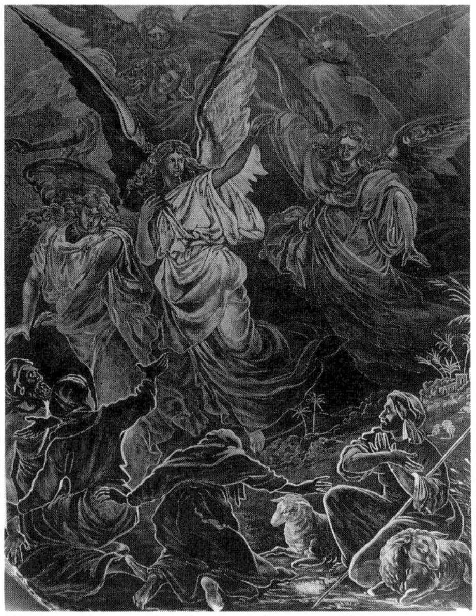
P.C. Mondriaan senior, the Annunciation to the Sheperds; lithograph, 50 × 70 cm, signed with initials; private coll. Winterswijk.

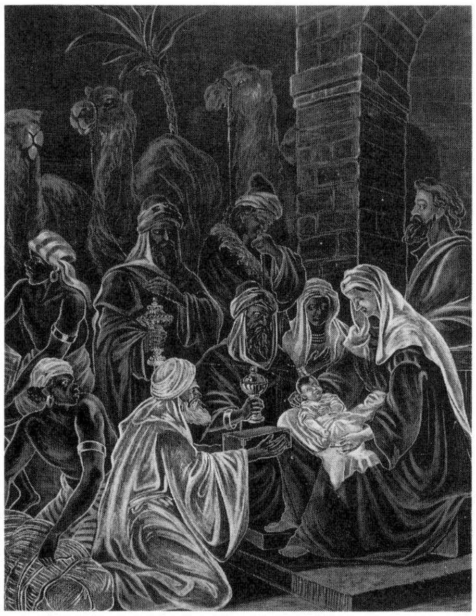
P.C. Mondriaan senior, the Adoration of the Three Kings; lithograph, 50 × 70 cm; private coll. Winterswijk.

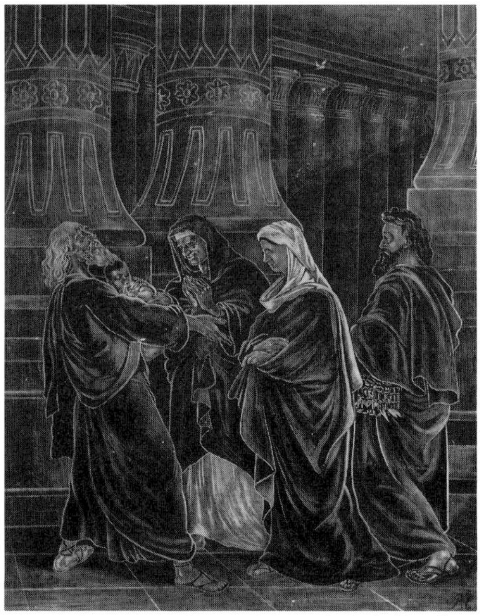
P.C. Mondriaan senior, Simeon giving praise in the Temple; lithograph, 50 × 70 cm; private coll. Winterswijk.

As it is, I have been sitting up until 3 or 4 o'clock in the morning. But, I thought, Dr. K(uyper) has done so much for me: let me do all I can to make him see that I can be of service where he needs me, doing something more than the schoolteaching I enjoy; which is why I did not go to The Hague for a single day, but stayed at school. Since I burn to know your opinion and what you expect of my success, I enclose a postcard. If you would just write a word on it to reassure me and my dear ones, I should be cheered and revived. If you would like other portraits, let me know. Also which ones could be better.
Your grateful P.C. Mondriaan
(in the margin of the letter)
Dear Sir! All now depends for our movement (in that direction) *on how the whole thing is executed. The Picture must conquer!'* (Mondriaan to Kuyper, 28.1.1874)

This last remark speaks volumes about the intended function of the picture, which was not the commemoration of a historical event but a political pamphlet mustering support for the anti-revolutionary movement.
Besides the already mentioned commemorative, festive and historical pictures, Mondriaan senior

drew Christmas pictures and illustrated Christian literature. I am not familiar with any examples of the latter. In 1874, a productive year, Mondriaan drew a Christmas picture which was apparently published: *'I designed a festive picture for Christmas which Gerretsson purchased for publication'.* (Mondriaan to Kuyper, 6.9.1874) It is not known what this picture looked like, but it was probably not much different in character from the four pictures illustrating episodes from the Nativity which a Christian primary school in Winterswijk still possesses. These four large scenes showing the adoration of the shepherds, the annunciation to the shepherds of the nativity, the adoration of the three kings and Simeon's joy in the temple, are evidently the pictures which Carel Mondriaan, and not only he, recalled in his letter to Slijper (20.1.1946, quoted above). Mondriaan himself only did the drawing, leaving the execution, the transference to the stone etc., to a specialized workshop. From 1878 on, however, he drew on stone directly: *'I have bought a small litho-press for 30 guilders and have engraved on stone what many regard as a meaningful, inoffensive and well-drawn picture to commemorate the Union.'* (Mondriaan to Kuyper, 16.4.1878) (By 'Union' he meant the Union of Utrecht, which took place in 1578).

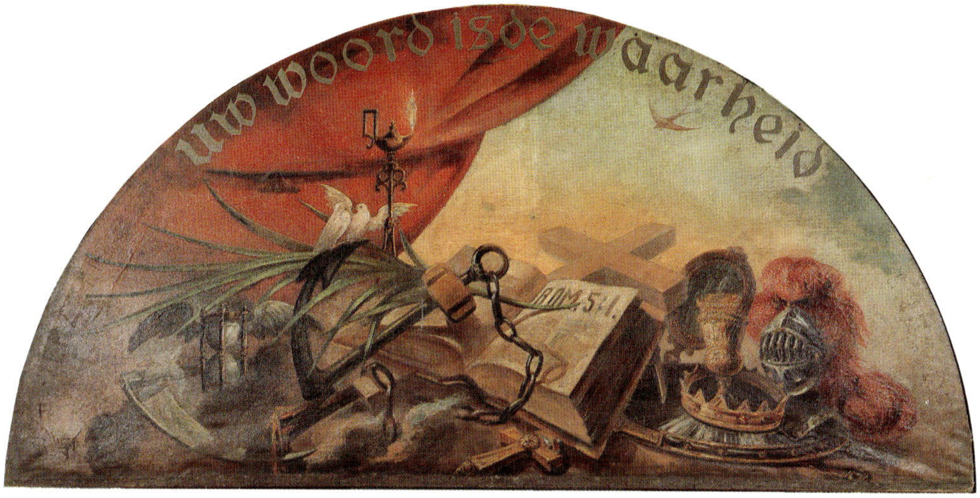

Piet Mondrian, 'Uw Woord is de Waarheid' ('Thy Word is Truth'); oil on canvas, 150 × 250 cm; private coll. Winterswijk.

'Thy Word is Truth'

For many years the Winterswijk Christian primary school of which Mondriaan senior was headmaster has had in its possession a painting which is thought to be his work. It is a practically semicircular painting of considerable size—150 by 250 centimetres. An inscription in Gothic lettering runs along the arc of the semicircle: 'Uw Woord is de Waarheid' ('Thy Word is Truth') Judging by its semicircular shape, the painting probably hung in an arched passage in the old school complex on Ratumschestraat, so that it could be seen by all the children and visitors.

At a first glance the meaning of the representation is obscure. In the middle of the composition is a Bible, its pages open at the text of Paul's epistle to the Romans, 5:1. To the left, on a ground reminiscent of clouds, are palm branches, a large anchor, a scythe, a winged hourglass, two doves and a burning oil lamp in front of a drawn-back curtain. Under the Bible is a large cross, with the handle of a sword protruding at the front; on the right are a helmet, a shield, a crown and a cup, reflected in a mirror. The silhouette of a swallow is painted above. On closer inspection it is obvious that the picture is the work of an experienced painter. Recent restoration confirms this on all counts. The colours are striking and bright, dominated by the red of the curtain and the green of the palm leaves. Under the words 'Uw Woord is de Waarheid' the naked eye can discern the vestiges of a text running from the lower left along the arc to the lower right. Close scrutiny of the entire painting in the Amsterdam Central Laboratory, using X-ray, infra-red fluorescent and ultraviolet photography, has facilitated the reconstruction of the text, most of which is covered by later overpainting. The words are: *'I am persuaded that neither life, nor things present nor things to come'*, and are a modified excerpt from Romans 8, verses 38/39: *'For I am persuaded that neither death, nor life, nor angels, nor principalities, nor powers, nor things present, nor things to come, nor height, nor depth, nor any other creature, shall be able to separate us from the love of God, which is in Christ Jesus our Lord.'*

There was obviously not enough room for the whole text in the painting. The artist opted for the phrases which he deemed most salient, assuming that the rest of the passage would not present too much of a problem to the Christian congregation of Winterswijk. More important, probably, is what prompted the painter to link this passage with the text in the middle of the composition from Romans 5, verse 1. What did the designer of the composition mean by all these details and texts?

In order to find a solution we must go back to the 'Revolution or Gospel' picture of 1874, which has already been discussed in detail. In the garlands on the left and right at the bottom of the picture are two representations which have much in common with this painting.

The key to the picture explains these symbols in detail: *'The small garland on the left supports a group which represents life. This is symbolized by a round mirror placed horizontally which reflects everything in its immediate neighbourhood. The winged hourglass indicates time, and the scythe from which the crown hangs represents death or life's end. The torch stands for enthusiasm and ardour. The serpent biting its own tail is eternity, which follows life as soon as the mask falls, the whole thing being completed by the white dove, symbol of sincerity. On the right-hand side, religion is depicted correspondingly. God's Word forms the basis, surmounted by the cross of faith. On it hang the anchor of hope and broken fetters, symbol of Christian freedom. The palm branch of victory, the staff of tranquillity or 'steady prop', the cup of sorrow, to be quaffed only by faith, hope and love—all have their place. The lamp's flame indicates the love that illuminates everything and which God Himself lit in the darkness of the heart. The swallow's restless wandering shows that true peace is not to be found here. It knows, however, where it has built its nest... No matter how dear we hold the Netherlands, the Christian knows a better Fatherland.'*

So much for the elucidation of the 1874 print; most of the symbols mentioned also occur in the painting, where they doubtlessly have the same significance. The 'Picture of Life' as expressed by these symbols is naturally a life permeated by the doctrine of Christianity. The two scenes from the print merge in the painting. By featuring the two passages from Romans, the artist indicates that this is the fundamental meaning of the entire representation. Romans 5, verse 1/2, reads: *'Therefore being justified by faith, we have peace with God through our Lord Jesus Christ: by whom also we have access by faith into this grace wherein we stand, and rejoice in hope of the glory of God.'* With these two texts Mondrian senior presents the beginning (5:1/2) and end (8:38/39) of a chapter which commentators regard as the most important that Paul ever wrote. It begins by justifying faith by grace and ends by stating that this faith and the love of God cannot be shaken by anything or anyone. A Christian

believer could not have professed his faith more clearly; moreover, the painting with its obvious message to the rising generation (in a Christian school) could not have had a more apt place.
A brief report of the celebrations marking the school's twenty-fifth anniversary contains the following passage: *'On the morning of Thursday, February 1st at half-past nine on the dot, the entire Board and Mr. Plette entered the school and proceeded to the two classrooms at the back, which were festively decorated through the good offices of Mr. Mondriaan. Greenery and bunting, a completely silver tree with four oranges hanging from it, one bearing a crown (symbols of the Royal family: Queen Wilhelmina, Queen Emma, Princess Sophia, Princess Marie). Birds perched on the tree, under which a musical box was concealed; there was a silver crown with candles, a centrepiece filled with paper flowers, similar flowers also lavishly adorning the greenery; Piet Mondriaan's lifesize portrait of Mr. Groen van Prinsterer, a portrait of William the Silent, a painting (allegorical) by Piet Mondriaan, the coats of arms of Winterswijk and Gelderland, the arms of Orange and Waldeck-Pyrmont on orange bunting, a silver lyre with golden strings, plants on the tables made especially for the occasion—such were the decorations.'* And a little further on: *'Mr. Mondriaan explained his son's paintings and recited a poem.'* (Minutes of the School Board Meeting, 31-1-1894) In my opinion, the above-mentioned allegory is identical to the painting "Uw Woord is de Waarheid' which still hangs in the school. An important argument in favour of Mondrian junior as the painter is the fact that Mondriaan senior always referred to himself as a 'drawer', as did others, including his son Carel; there is absolutely no evidence that father Mondriaan was able to paint.

Mondrian junior

As we saw in the introduction, Mondrian junior, when asked by Lurasco, said that his teachers had been his father, *'...who did a lot of drawing; at fourteen his uncle, Frits Mondriaan of The Hague, gave him painting lessons in Winterswijk, where he used to go to paint outdoors; he obtained his elementary and secondary drawing certificates, studied for a while with Joh. Braedt van Uberfeldt and then attended the Amsterdam Academy for three years.'*
J. Braet van Ueberfeldt (1807-1894) was a painter who when older, probably not before 1880, settled in Doetinchem, not far from Winterswijk. He is best known for the volumes of illustrations of Dutch regional costumes which he and Valentijn Bing published between 1850 and 1857. Carel Mondriaan also recalled Braet: *'He* (Mondrian junior) *would also occa-*

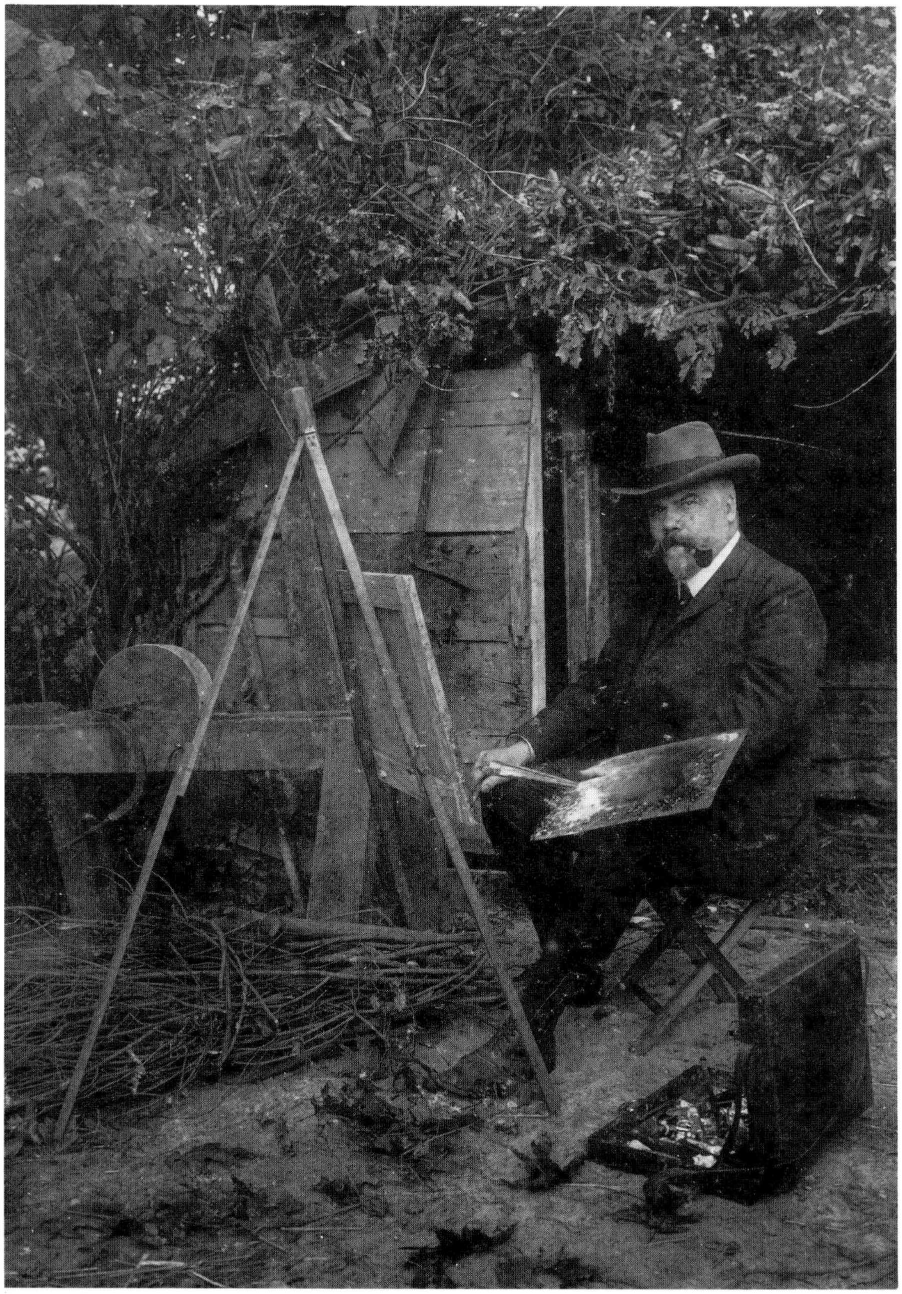

Frits Mondriaan (1853-1932).

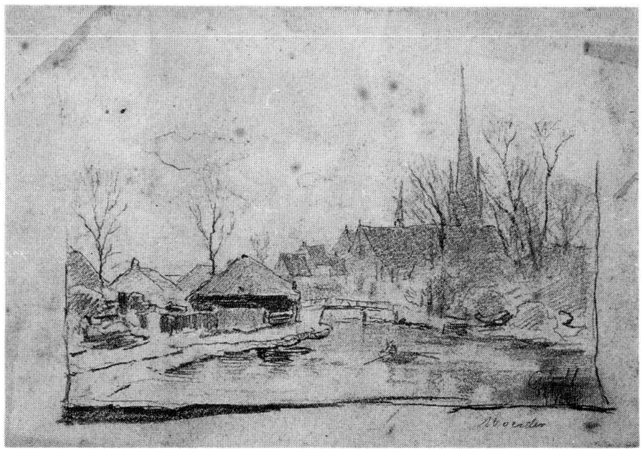

Frits Mondriaan, View of Woerden ; drawing, signed bottom right.

sionally take a local train to Doetinchem where an ancient painter lived with his sister Augusta and a large pet goat. This old gentleman was called Braet van Uberfelt. He was interested in Piet's work and gave him advice—not really lessons. He had the habit of cutting the prettiest pictures out of illustrations and storing them in large envelopes.

Piet usually brought home some of these portfolios, and we would while away the winter evenings looking at them and copying the ones that appealed to us.' (Carel Mondriaan to Slijper, 20.1.1946) Braet may well have proffered 'advice', for he had taught at an Amsterdam training college for art teachers; moreover, he and his colleague Bing had published a textbook on drawing tuition which dwelt particularly on perspective, ornaments and copying plaster models. These techniques were surely important to the young Mondrian, since he had to produce proof of experience in order to pass his drawing examinations. He obtained his certificate in October 1889. Carel Mondriaan remembers his brother drawing plaster models: *'He had converted our former "playroom" into a studio and studied at home. I can still see him coming back from the R.H.B.S.* [secondary school] *with a colossal arm of Moses in order to draw it at home.'* (Carel Mondriaan to Slijper, 29.11. 1945)

The said school was nearly opposite the Mondriaan family home. None of Mondrian's drawings of plaster models, quite normal practice in those days, have been found.

Frits Mondriaan (1853-1932)

In his appreciation of his teachers, Mondrian distinguished between his father as an amateur and his uncle Frits Mondriaan, whom he classified as a professional painter. The still sparse literature on Mondrian junior's early period, has paid scant attention to this observation—not so surprising, really, since Frits Mondriaan is best known for his fairly academic renderings of woodland scenes in the tradition of the Hague School; there is no survey of his further activities and work. The following remarks will show that there were indeed big differences between the two artists, but that they also had certain things in common, which makes it easier to understand what Mondrian junior meant by his remark about his uncle. Frits Mondriaan (1853-1932) was the youngest son of the Mondriaan forbear Willem Frederik. On his father's death in 1878 Frits took over the business, not only because his father had trained him in the shop, but because his other brothers had other occupations. Willem Frederik had built up a flourishing business at 39 Lange Poten in The Hague.

After a few years (1880) Frits moved the shop to

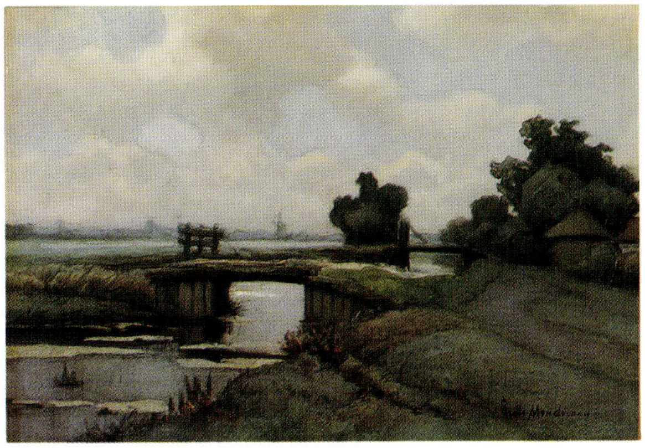

Frits Mondriaan, Waterway with Bridge ; watercolour, pencil, 20.5 × 29 cm, signed in full bottom right; coll. Haags Gemeentemuseum (donation 1987).

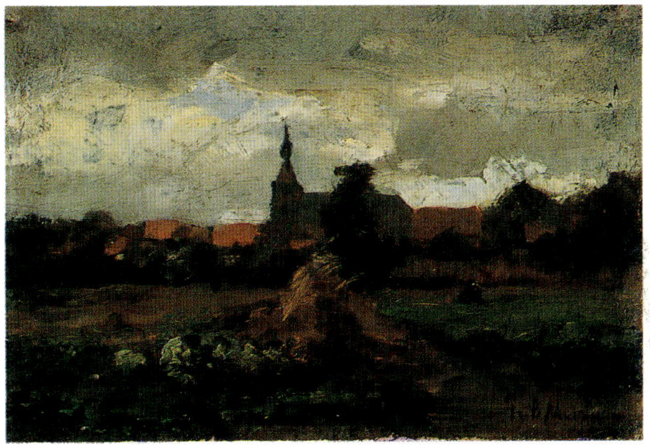

Frits Mondriaan, Village Scene ; oil on canvas, 20.5 × 30.2 cm, signed bottom right; coll. Haags Gemeentemuseum (donation 1987).

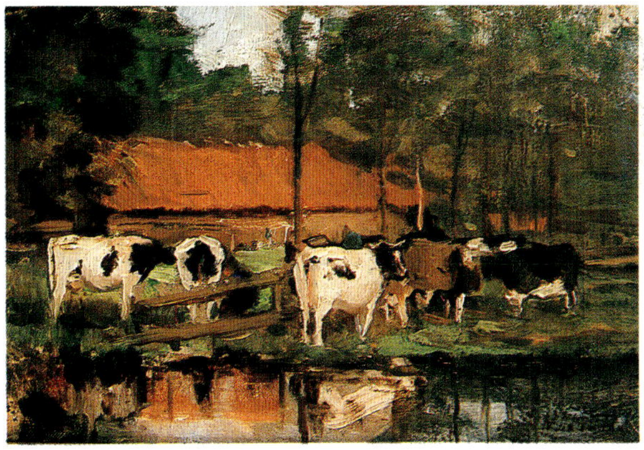

Frits Mondriaan, Cows at a Stream ; oil on canvas on cardboard, 15 × 22 cm, signed in full bottom right.

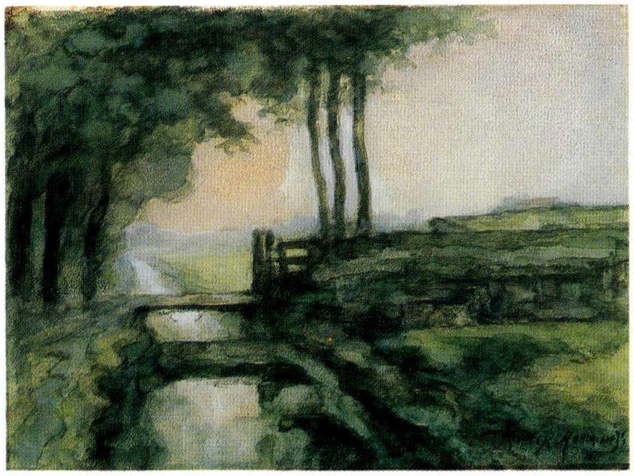

Piet Mondrian, Landscape with a Ditch ; ca. 1895, watercolour, 49 × 66 cm; signed bottom right; coll. Haags Gemeentemuseum.

45 Spuistraat, and enlarged it in 1887. He advertised as: 'F.H. Mondriaan, Hairdresser, specializing in wigs, toupets for Ladies and Gentlemen. Sale of Gentlemen's articles, perfumery, toiletries, travelling and bathing items, a large and refined selection of Cravats.' The directory of The Hague did not list F. Mondriaan as a painter until 1901, by which time his wife Joséphine Marie Destrée was running the business.

From 1909 Frits' son ran the shop on his own. For several years Frits had had a studio elsewhere in The Hague, and was now able to spend all his time painting.

Through a number of interviews with Frits Mondriaan's descendants, I have learned that his wife did indeed bear most of the business responsibilities while Frits devoted himself entirely to painting, at least during his latter years. From the second half of the eighteen-nineties Frits presented exhibitions of his work to the public. He seems to have gained rapid success with his sales, for according to Lurasco his reputation was already established by 1907. His exhibition activities peaked around 1900 and again, ten years later, around 1911, when his shows in Amsterdam and notably Rotterdam attracted the attention of the critics. The people who bought Frits Mondriaan's paintings and drawings belonged to the upper middle-class and aristocracy. His work was not only purchased by museums in Russia and Germany; a few pieces were also acquired by the Dutch court. Frits also painted the occasional portrait and still life, but the genre that appealed most to buyers was the landscape; he painted the woods near The Hague in all seasons and every conceivable light. Indeed, reviews often referred to him as the painter of the Hague woods. His most frequent subjects were the surroundings of The Hague, the Veluwe region and the countryside in the Achterhoek. Frits frequently spent long periods with his brother in Winterswijk and did a lot of painting in the area, often accompanied by his nephew Piet. *'Whenever Frits felt like going out to paint',* his descendants told me, *'he would shut up shop, hire a carriage and go off to Woerden or Wageningen to spend the day working outdoors.'* He was often accompanied by a fellow-painter, Théophile de Bock, for example. Most of his drawings and oil sketches were on-the-spot impressions which formed the basis for the larger formats which he composed in the studio.

Frits exhibited the direct impressions as well as the studio pieces. Most of the critics pointed out the considerable difference between these studies and the finished paintings.

N.H. Wolf, a critic with whom the painter was on friendly terms, had the following to say about a exhibition in the Van Delden gallery in Amsterdam in 1912: *'There is naturally a reason for Frits Mondriaan's success with the art-collection public. In the first place he is a man of taste who chooses his subject with discernment. Every little landscape, every woodland scene he puts on canvas, is splendidly framed, a perfect whole, delightful to behold. He is an experienced man and therefore knows that when all is said and done the public prefers a well-finished painting in a well-chosen frame. A self-taught painter, he is nonetheless a master of his technique, and his products are technically accomplished. To some, this is an added attraction. Even his studies and sketches are so sound that they might well pass for fully-fledged paintings. And those who are not so keen on paintings composed in the studio will not only be content with an outdoor 'study' that is fresh and juicy in colour, but may even prefer some of these outdoor studies to pictures painted in the studio.'* A little further on, Wolf expresses his opinion more clearly: *'If you would like to see the effect when a number of studies—for that is what they are—are composed into a paintings in the studio, look at no.28: "The large lake in the Forest". To a large number of collectors a painting like this is just what they want: a pleasing, agreeable example, something to look at, ... in short, a real drawing-room picture. Works like this will always find a buyer... But I prefer the study or the sketch from which this picture was painted, because I realize that even though the light is not distributed so well and the colours are perhaps a little more strident, rough, vivid, uneven, the original study conveys the first impression—the impression that fascinated the painter and inspired him to paint this picture; the study, obviously much more spontaneous than the painting and thus more buoyant, more genuine, more juicy, and hence more appealing to me. I do realize that the painting, too, has qualities—traits which I have already pointed out in my characterization of the painter himself.'* (N.H.W., Frits Mondriaan, in: De Kunst 1912/13, vol. V.pp.4-6)

Even a well-disposed critic like N.H. Wolf made obvious distinctions in his appreciation of Frits Mondriaan's work; he preferred the spontaneous studies to the modish academic works. In about 1900, ten years prior to this review, the climate had certainly been more propitious for such salon pieces, the Hague School having attained the pinnacle of esteem, whereas the work of, say, Van Gogh or the Impressionists had scarcely been noticed by a wider public; were these not the very painters who had constantly stressed spontaneity? By the early twenties, ten years after this review, appreciation of the Hague School had reached its lowest point and people were already talking about the good old days of the Hague School. By then Frits Mondriaan was over seventy. Wolf devoted a nostalgically retrospective article to him:

'Frits Mondriaan has complained at the public's lack of interest in what older painters regard as the only really good painting: that of the Hague, Amsterdam and Laren Schools (...) Frits Mondriaan recalled the good old days in Rotterdam, where—was he not born in Rotterdam?—in the Oldenzeel gallery of blessed memory he used to organize exhibitions regularly every three or four years and would sometimes sell his sound, solid paintings by the dozen for hundreds of guilders to wealthy Rotterdam and Hague collectors. Those were the days!' (N.H. Wolf, Frits Mondriaan, in: De Kunst 1925, p.447)

In the same way that developments were gaining momentum for art and artists around the turn of the century, ideas about the latest and most modern movements in contemporary art were changing fast. Critics invariably compared Frits Mondriaan's work with that of his nephew Piet. Notably in 1911/12, when several exhibitions of Frits' work were held, Piet, too, was attracting attention with shows of his latest work at the Moderne Kunstkring (Modern Art Circle), which had been founded in 1910. Wolf wrote: *'Things are somewhat different with Frits Mondriaan's nephew Piet Mondriaan. Last year he switched to cubism, and at the Modern Art Circle's exhibition which is due to open at the Stedelijk Museum tomorrow we shall probably be regaled with his newest creations. Due to a variety of activities—not the least of which was my interest in the Futurists—I have not yet had a chance to attend a preview of the Modernists...I shall therefore have to wait until tomorrow. But I venture to assert that nephew Piet's notions of art are still just as far removed from those of his uncle Frits as they ever were, perhaps even further!'*

(N.H. Wolf, Frits Mondriaan, De Kunst 1912/13, pp.4-6)

The scant interest in the great and minor masters of the Hague School ten years later was mainly blamed on the efforts of the ultra-modernists: *'He [Frits] eschews the ultra-modern trend cubist, futurist and expressionist. He also thinks that his nephew Piet and his followers, with the angles and crosses and lines which they claim to be 'art', have confused buyers an opinion shared by many non-ultra-modern painters, in other countries too, and for which, in view of the facts, there are some grounds of truth.'*

(N.H. Wolf, Frits Mondriaan, De Kunst, 1925, p.447)

In 1930, when Frits Mondriaan decided to stop painting—he was 77 at the time—his work again came to the notice of the public. The critic of the Nieuwe Rotterdamsche Courant summed up his appreciation, unable to resist a gibe at nephew Piet, with these words:

'Frits Mondriaan (not to be confused with his modernist name sake!) is certainly no stranger to lovers of Dutch painting. For more than thirty years his canvases have graced our important exhibitions; he has a resounding reputation in the artistic world. Mondriaan is one of the last to carry on the great tradition of our impressionistic landscape painting; however, while most of his predecessors and contemporaries took as their subject the Dutch meadows and lakes, or the picturesque heaths of the Gooi, Mondriaan, like De Bock, chose the woods and stately avenues of the Veluwe. He was a woodland painter par excellence.'
(N.R.C., 18 Jan. 1930)

Conclusion

From the above, it is clear that Frits and Piet Mondrian went their separate ways long before 1910. And yet there are indications that this had not always been the case. In the first place Piet Mondrian's statements leave no doubt about Frits Mondriaan's importance to him for having taught him how to paint and to work with paint and canvas.
Must we see this as a purely technical learning process, or can artistic ideas conceivably have driven the two apart? A closer examination of Piet Mondrian's training and some of his work of the eighteen-nineties ought to cast some light on the matter.

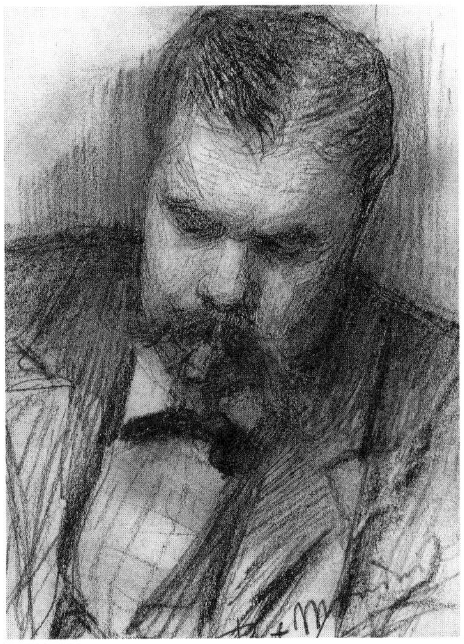

Piet Mondrian, Portrait of his Uncle Frits ; 1898, drawing, signed bottom right; coll. Haags Gemeentemuseum (donation 1987).

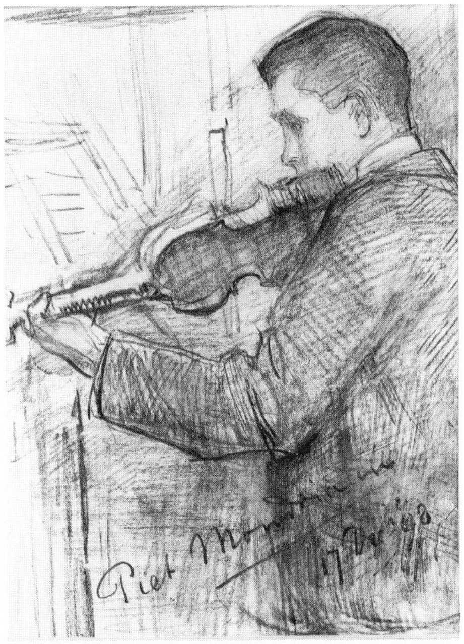

Piet Mondrian, Portrait of his Nephew Frits ; 1898, drawing, signed and dated bottom right; coll. Haags Gemeentemuseum (donation 1987).

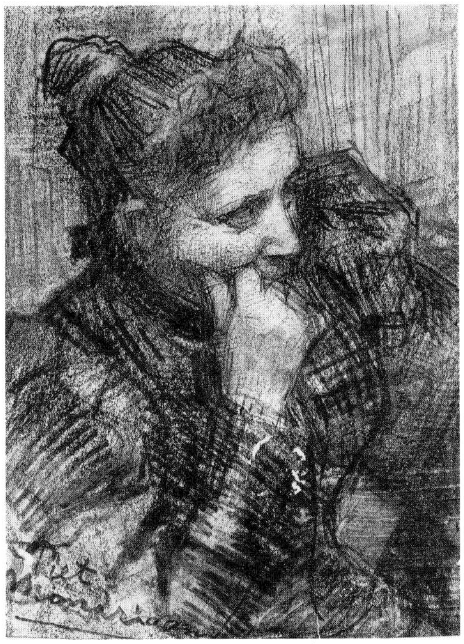

Piet Mondrian, Portrait of his Aunt J.M. Mondriaan-Destrée ; drawing, signed bottom left.

Piet Mondrian, 'Portrait of his Niece Johanna Mondriaan'; drawing, signed bottom right.

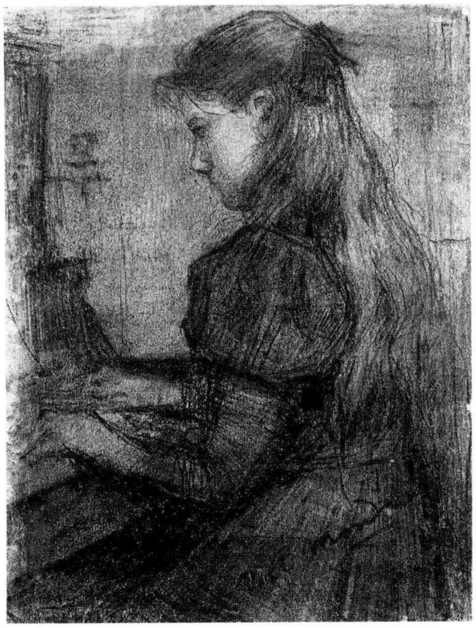

Piet Mondrian, 1892.

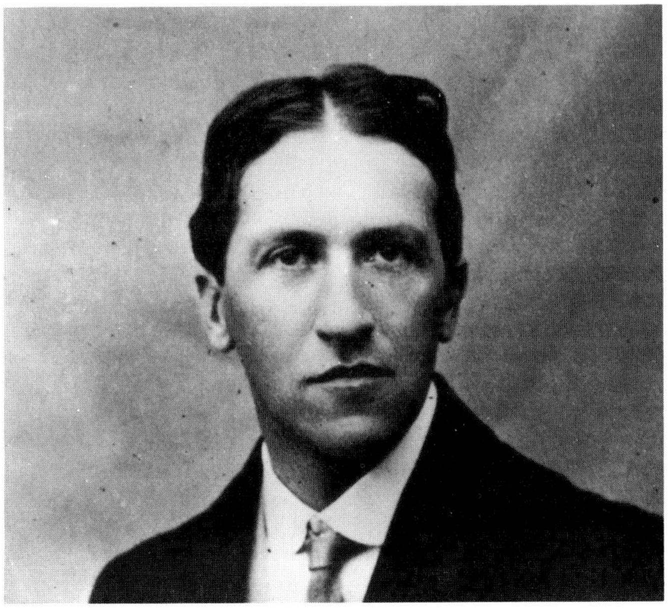

Piet Mondrian in Winterswijk

After obtaining the certificates which qualified him to teach drawing and thus to earth a living, a stipulation of his father's, the nineteen-year-old Mondriaan ventured the step towards becoming a genuine, i.e. independent artist.
The financial situation of the Mondriaan family, with four growing children, precluded any parental funding for the young Mondrian's start. Somebody else paid for his tuition at the Amsterdam Art Academy: *'Another man paid for my studies for three years, sending me at 19 to the Amsterdam Academy of Fine Arts.'* This period—how very strange that Mondrian said nothing about his time at the Academy!—was followed by hard times, which he described thus: *'At 22 began a very difficult time for me. To make a living I did many kinds of work—bacteriological drawings used for textbook and in schoolrooms, portraits, copies of pictures in museums, and taught as well, and then I began to sell landscapes. It was a hard struggle but I managed to make a living and was glad to be able to make just enough money to be able to do what I wanted to do.'* (J. Bradley, P. Mondrian, in: The Knickerbocker Weekly, 14.2.1944)
According to Mondrian's own testimony his prime concern in the first part of his time in Amsterdam was to keep on studying at the Academy as long as he could afford to, and to earn his living not by taking a permanent post as a teacher but by trying to obtain drawing and painting commissions.
During his first few years in Amsterdam, up to 1895, Mondrian had lodgings in the house of the Wormser family in Amsterdam's smartest shopping street, Kalverstraat. Wormser published Christian reading-matter for the Netherlands and in particular for South Africa; the firm had a bookshop in the Kalverstraat. Unlike his father, who had never become a member of Kuyper's church, Mondrian joined as soon as he went to Amsterdam, remaining a registered member for a long time. It was from this milieu—the Wormsers, too, were fervent Kuyper devotees—that Mondrian got his first commissions: to illustrate the Christian reading-matter published by the firm of Wormser. Mondrian was thus following in his father's footsteps! The extent of his father's influence on his drawing is apparent in a picture which the son drafted in 1901(!) to commemorate Queen Wilhelmina's wedding. It was never executed, unlike his father's design to mark the same occasion! As well as such assignments, he also earned money by accepting commissions from which he could learn something: copying famous painters and painting occasional portraits of friends and acquaintances. They didn't even have to sit for him: Piet Mondrian could paint a good likeness from a photograph. Some of these portraits still

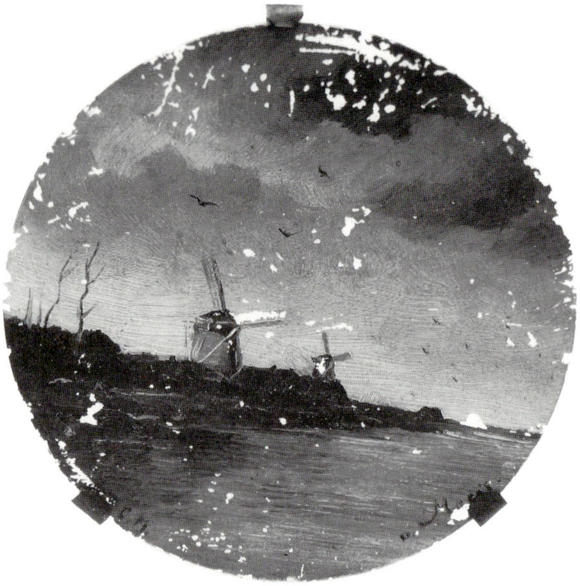

Piet Mondrian, painted tile; signed with initials bottom left; 'naar Maris' bottom right, 20 cm diameter.

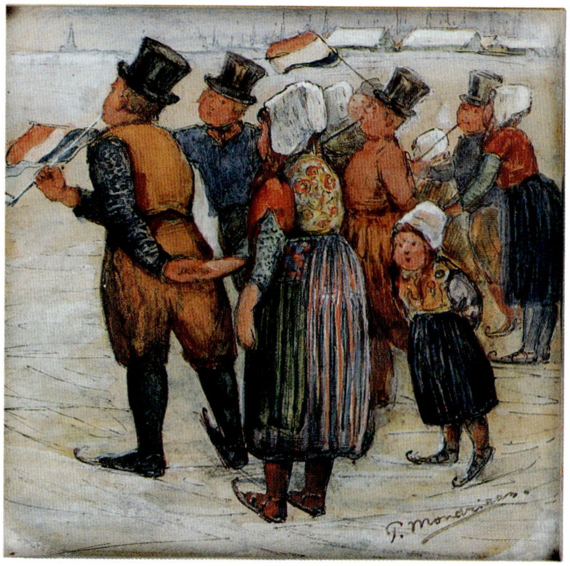

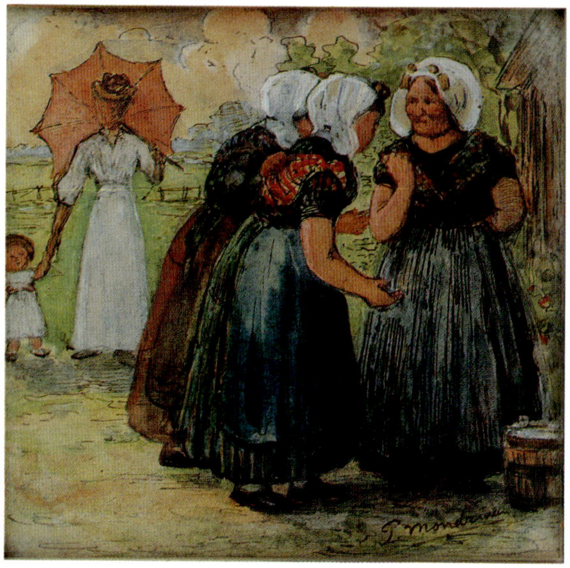

Piet Mondrian, two tile designs; watercolour, signed bottom right, 14.5 × 14.5 cm each; coll. J.P. Smid (Amsterdam).

exist, but the majority of his copies have not yet been traced.
Like his uncle Frits, Piet Mondrian rarely dated his early work, especially in the nineties. This presents serious problems to researchers, whose datings frequently differ by five or even ten years.
A striking feature in the above quotation is the distinction made by Mondrian himself between the various kinds of odd jobs, and the landscapes for which the public at times evinced an interest. Mondrian's work of the nineties can thus be divided into two categories: commissioned work which earned him a living, and works—landscapes in particular—which were not commissioned but which sold at a later date because of their artistic standard and their appeal to a certain public. Added to this is a third group of works which are quite separate, not only because they can be dated fairly accurately, but especially due to their common theme and to their content, which is quite different from the other two categories. I shall refer to this group henceforth as the 'Winterswijk group'.

Commissions

The first group of 'odd jobs' embraces a whole scale of subjects ranging from portraits of old men and married couples and even dogs, to painted tiles or designs for tiles. The art historian Welsh, one of the first to examine Mondrian's early period, speaks of a friend of Mondrian's who like him came from Winterswijk and was living in Amsterdam. The widow of this painter, who was called Dirk Voerman, recalls how her husband and Mondrian painted tiles with windmills to earn a living. Some of these tiles surfaced recently: they are copies of J. Maris, indeed with windmills, and of Du Chattel, painted directly over the glaze, so that the design is not very durable. Michel Seuphor, Mondrian's first biographer, also relates that Mondrian painted tiles as a wedding-present for his brother Willem, who had emigrated to the Transvaal in South Africa. Seuphor stresses that these tiles were painted before being fired. Two small, tile-sized watercolours with typically Dutch scenes may possibly be examples of this, in view of their provenance. The rapid and rather clumsy execution leads me to deduce that they were made in the mid-nineties. The bacteriological drawings mentioned by Mondrian were done in 1905 for Professor van Calcar, a lecturer at Leiden University in those days. Mondrian continued to do this work up to the 1914-1918 war. These drawings were purely functional, and intended as tuition material for lessons in the use of the microscope. They were generally pictures of bacteria, etc., enlarged several tens of times; the still existing pictures in the bacteriological institute at Leiden give absolutely no stylistic or other indication of the artist. Professor van Calcar's wife was one of the many ladies to whom Mondrian gave painting and drawing lessons. The others included Agaath Zethraeus, of whom Mondrian painted a portrait (now in the Stockholm National Museum), Mrs. Seelig and Mrs. Crabb. For the last two he made ex-libris plates, of which only a few are illustrated here. Mrs. Seelig and Mondrian were both featured in a group exhibition at 'Arti et Amicitiae' in Amsterdam in 1905. Mondrian accompanied Mrs. Crabb, who taught him English, to England, probably in 1898. He was so ill on his return that his father took him home to Winterswijk for a lengthy convalescence.
In addition to the exaggerated symbolism of the crab and the woman with a palette, both pictures contain symbols of the theosophical association: lotus blossom, stars and rising sun, and the exhortation 'Strebe zum Licht' ('aspire toward the light'). The Art-Nouveau stylization suggests that the pictures were drawn in about 1900-1905. Both Ex-Libris plates may be classified as odd jobs, although there is a wide gap between designing and painting tiles and these pictures.

Still Lifes and Landscapes

Soon after leaving Winterswijk and embarking on his studies in Amsterdam, Mondrian became a member of an artists' society in Utrecht, the Genootschap Kunstliefde. He exhibited there with his fellow-members as early as 1892, continuing to do so until 1909. Oddly enough, most of the pictures he submitted were not landscapes but still lifes. Three still lifes and one landscape drawing are listed in the 1892 catalogue, one still life in 1893, four still lifes and a 'Barn' in 1894 and one still life with apples and a portrait study in 1897. Due to the extremely general titles it is usually impossible to determine whether a catalogue title refers unambiguously to one particular work. One of the first still lifes that Mondrian sent to a Kunstliefde show a 'Still life with Herrings', signed and dated 'P.C. Mondriaan Jr. 1/93' (Stedelijk Museum, Amsterdam). It is a remarkable painting, not because of the obvious errors in perspective, for instance in the opening of the barrel on the left, but because both colour and composition display a well-considered and deliberate attempt to assess and balance forms in a single composition occupying the entire surface of the picture. The structure of the paint, especially in the light entering in the front at the left, enhances the intensity of the subject. By painting the letters A and N on a few pieces of broken wood in the background, Mondrian raises this still life above the traditionally composed still

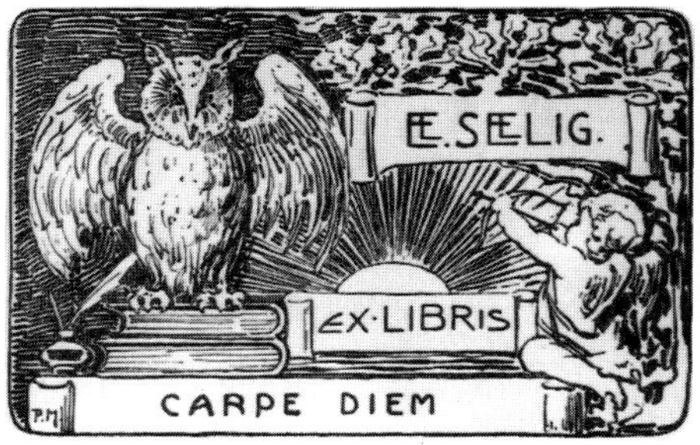

Piet Mondrian, Ex-Libris for E.E. Seelig 'Carpe Diem'; ca.1902, signed with initials bottom left; coll. Haags Gemeentemuseum.

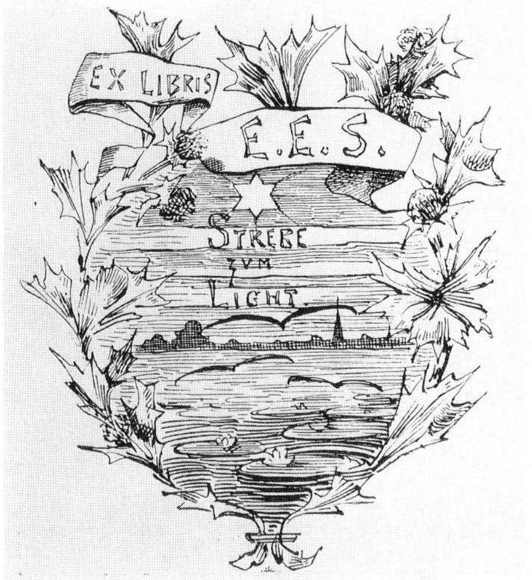

Piet Mondrian, Ex-Libris for E.E. Seelig 'Strebe zum Licht'; ca.1902, lithograph, 13.4 × 10.5 cm; coll. J.P. Smid (Amsterdam).

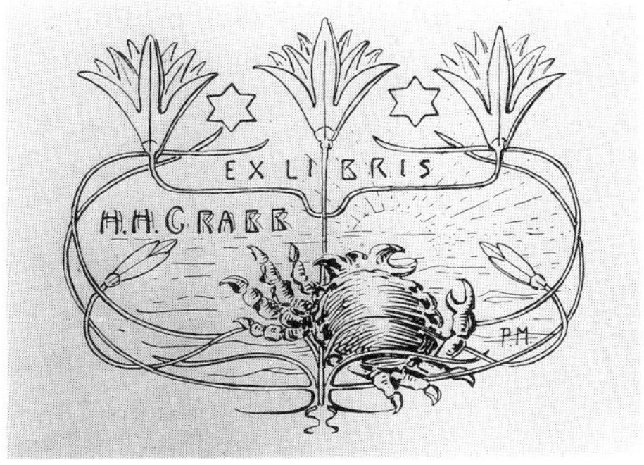

Piet Mondrian, Ex-Libris for H.H. Crabb; lithograph; 10.5 × 11.8 cm; coll. J.P. Smid (Amsterdam).

Piet Mondrian, Ex-Libris for E.E. Seelig 'Strebe zum Licht'; lithograph; coll. J.P. Smid (Amsterdam).

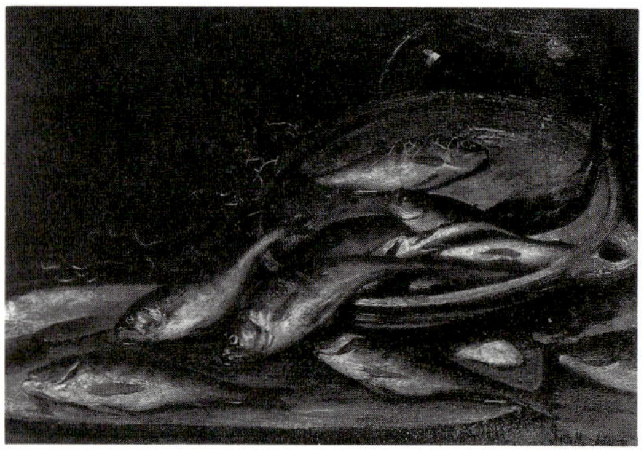

Frits Mondriaan, Still Life with Fish ; oil on canvas, signed bottom right in full, 61 × 43.5 cm.

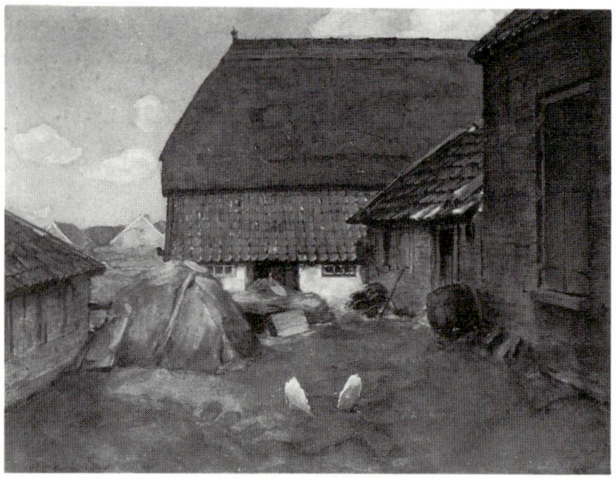

Piet Mondrian, Barn ; ca. 1894, watercolour, signed bottom left.

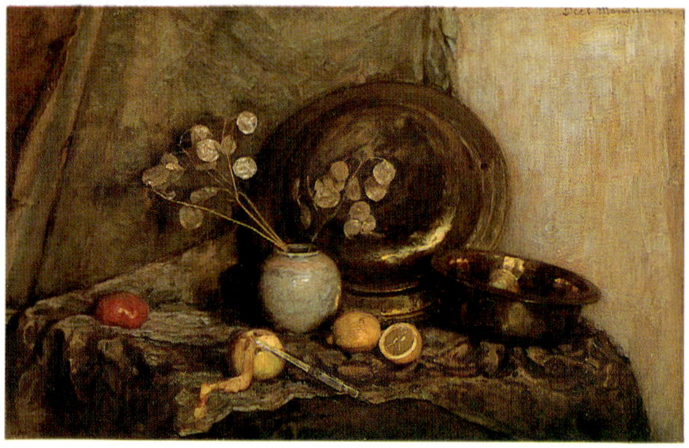

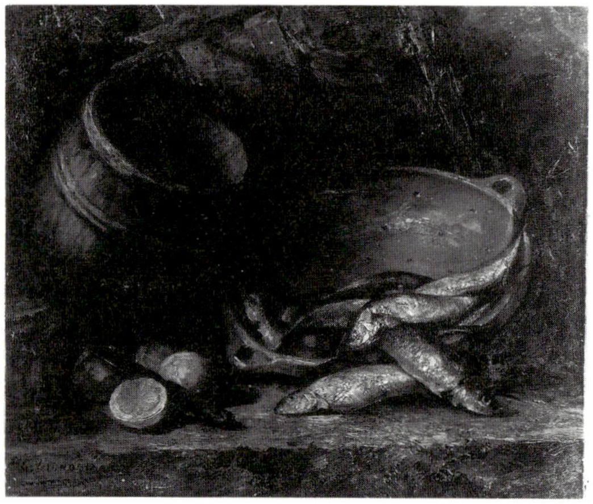

Piet Mondrian, Still Life with Herrings ; oil on canvas, 66.5 × 75.7 cm, signed and dated bottom left 'P.C. Mondriaan Jr. 1/93' ; coll. Sted. Museum (Amsterdam).

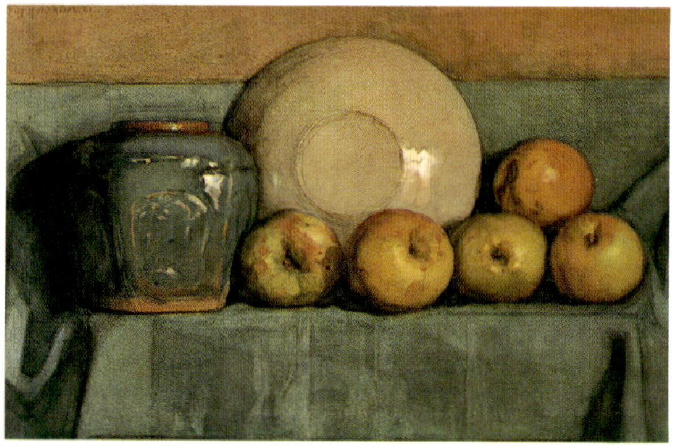

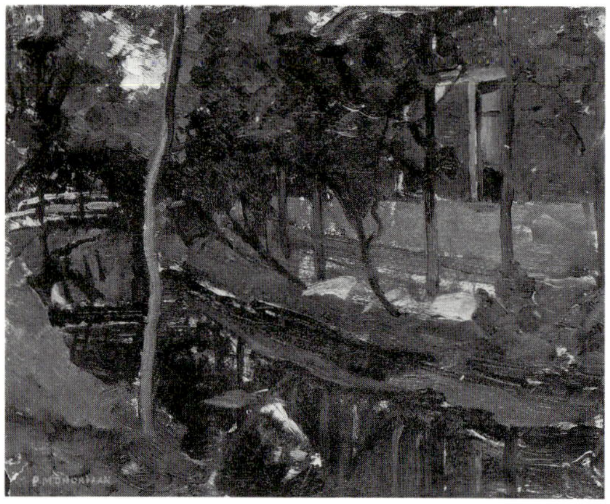

Piet Mondrian, Farms near a Ditch ; oil on paper, 26 × 32.5 cm, signed bottom left; coll. Haags Gemeentemuseum.

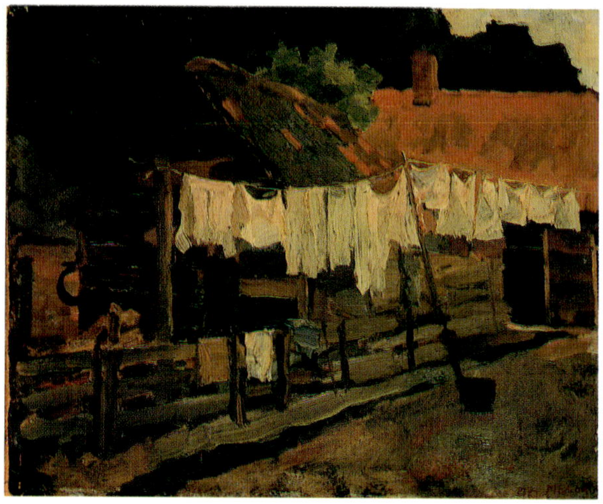

Frits Mondriaan, Still Life ; oil on canvas, 54.5 × 80 cm, signed and dated bottom left 'Frits Mondrian 1889'; coll. J.P. Smid (Amsterdam).

Piet Mondrian, Still Life with Moonwort ; ca.1905, oil on canvas, 87 × 79 cm signed in full top right, ca.1905; coll. J.P. Smid (Amsterdam).

Piet Mondrian, Still Life with Gingerpot ; watercolour, signed top left.

Piet Mondrian, Farmhouse with Clothesline ; 1895, oil on cardboard, 31.5 × 37.5 cm, signed bottom right; coll. Haags Gemeentemuseum.

life in which there was no place for details with a direct topical bearing or appeal to the imagination. Although it might be going too far to interpret this still life as a version of the seventeenth-century Vanitas pictures—the debris could indicate the transiency of seafaring life, likewise the cut lemon and herrings—it is clear that Mondrian wanted to depict more than a mere object of study in the form of a few herrings and a barrel. A comparison with another 'Still life with fish' by his uncle Frits emphasizes the contrast. Frits Mondriaan painted a traditional still life with a simple diagonal composition which does not create any tension; with its flowing rendering of the soft light and its inconspicuous brush-strokes, this still life's only virtue is as an illustration of a few objects.

Another of Frits Mondriaan's still lifes demonstrates his skill in painting soft light and material: nothing, not even the inconvenient brushstroke, can destroy the illusion of 'reality'. Piet Mondrian's other still lifes of this period, so far as they are extant, are more like studies in the genre encountered in Frits' work. Only in three still lifes dated around 1905 did Piet Mondrian overstep the traditional borders of the still life: his 'Still Life with a Plaster Head' and two 'Still Lifes with Moonwort' can only be understood when details such as the peeled apple, the thistles, the flowers and the light reflexes are interpreted as symbols of transiency. A closer examination of similar groups in Mondrian's later work is however beyond the scope of this essay. In the comparison of these two still lifes by Piet Mondrian and his uncle Frits, one is particularly struck by their different ideas about painting. There are also distinct resemblances, though, so much so that it is indeed often hard to be a hundred-per-cent sure whether Frits or Piet is the painter. Such is the case with a large group of works, in almost all of which the landscape motif occurs.

The critics' opinions of Frits Mondriaan's work, quoted above, plainly show that most of them noticed a big difference between his spontaneous nature studies, mainly of small format, and the studio pieces composed on the basis of these studies. Frits sold the finished paintings to museums and suchlike. Up to about 1905 not one of Piet Mondrian's paintings can claim the status merited by the studio paintings of Frits. True, dozens of Piet's studies exist which bear a similar character to Frits' impressions of nature. As we know, nephew and uncle worked together in the Winterswijk countryside; several of the titles suggest that even when Piet was studying in Amsterdam he would seek out similar spots to paint in the environs of Amsterdam and other towns, as was his uncle's wont. It is quite natural to assume that Frits and Piet often painted together on the Gein or in the surroundings of Arnhem, Abcoude or Watergraafsmeer. In the subjects of the usually small studies and their technical execution it is often hard to identify the characteristic differences which would identify the painter as Piet or Frits: the landscapes are similar with their cows, farms, small figures, canals or trees lining the water; so are the rapid brushwork and the sense of vivid colour contrasts.

Remarkably, this similarity of style, and of course of subject, is only apparent in the oil sketches which were presumably painted directly from nature. It has already been pointed out that Frits' other paintings were quite different in character from Piet's. Frits Mondriaan's drawings also differ too strongly in composition and conception to raise much doubt as to their author. Most of them feature a path or a ditch to lend depth to the composition, a horizon about a third of the way up the paper, and an occasional salient detail such as a church tower or windmill, suggesting a wide expanse of space. Piet Mondrian's early drawings are not so detailed, and represent a stage prior to the oil sketch.

We might end the comparison by saying that only the oil sketches display striking correspondences in the work of Frits Mondriaan and his nephew Piet; in their other work the differences are too great, so fundamental at times, indeed, that the ideas of Frits Mondriaan and Piet Mondrian diverged at an early stage, as early as the eighteen-nineties. Frits Mondriaan worked up his numerous impressions of nature into the only form of painting that really meant anything to him: the studio piece. In this he clung to academic practice as taught at the academies of the Netherlands and other countries. Piet Mondrian, just as skilled as his uncle in the rapid rendering of nature impressions, was after a different result in his painting, as demonstrated by his 'Still life with herrings' of the nineties, as well as by a number of works inspired by his observation of nature which he later worked up into pictures with a wholly different meaning. These works belong to the 'Winterswijk group'.

The Winterswijk Group

The Winterswijk group consists of works whose common link is their subject. Mondrian must have done a lot of work in Winterswijk and the surrounding countryside from his childhood up to about 1907, when he and a painter-friend were staying in Saasveld, near Hengelo. The two large series and two smaller ones discussed here illustrate the painterly problems which preoccupied Mondrian at that time. These works show that in the late nineties he was formulating certain problems of composition and content which were so fundamental that they continued to engross him for many years. The Mondriaan's house in Winterswijk was situated on the Zonnebrink, near the Ratumschestraat intersection. Zonnebrink had been one of the better Winterswijk districts ever since 1870, when large houses were built for the more prosperous citizens, and also because of the number of schools in the neighbourhood. Previously there had been the occasional small factory and small craftsmen's workshops. On the side of the Ratumschestraat intersection was the Christian primary school of which father Mondriaan was headmaster—the entrance to the school was in Ratumschestraat—with a pump, playground and garden; across the street from the teacher's residence, which was also built in 1869, was the secondary school, built in 1870, with living accommodation for the teaching staff next door. Nowadays the Zonnebrink bears scarcely any resemblance to its former appearance; demolition and rebuilding have completely changed the street's character. Master Mondriaan's old school is another recent victim of the demolition squad. 'De Batavier', a textile mill currently dominating the character of the Zonnebrink, started off in fairly large premises directly opposite the Mondriaan's house. It was called the 'Wevershuis' (Weaver's house). Two works by Piet Mondrian perpetuate this long-since vanished building. Architecturally it must have been an unusually fine structure, its facade regularly punctuated by two rows of windows, one above the other, with a framework of wooden timbering partly sunk into the wall. Piet Mondrian drew a small sketch of a corner of the building from his home. This drawing formed the basis for a gouache which is signed in full and dated: 'Piet Mondriaan '99'. Mondrian apparently gave or sold this gouache to a local inhabitant who, like so many other Winterswijk citizens in the second half of the nineteenth century, emigrated to New Zealand, where the picture has remained. There are a few striking differences between the two pictures. The composition of the drawing is very intense: there is plenty of tension between the forms of the wintry, vertical tree dominating the foreground and the articulation of the house's facade. No effort has been made to create an illusion of depth by means of perspective or the device of the repoussoir. In the gouache, which has a vertical format, Mondrian has added about a third again (proportionally) at the bottom with the purpose of enhancing the effect of depth.

The point of departure for the composition of the 'Lappenbrink' series is the space-creating motif of the road. The 'Lappenbrink' was a collection of winding streets in the centre of Winterswijk. Its character was determined by a few farms, labourer's cottages and small shopkeepers. One particular spot in the Lappen-

The Zonnebrink in Winterswijk: on the left the 'Weaver's House', on the right the garden of the Mondriaan-house (photograph ca.1900)

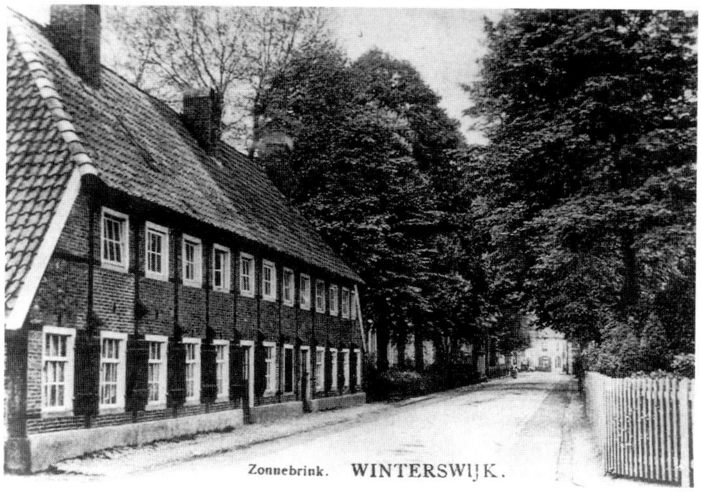

Piet Mondrian, The Weaver's House ; ca.1898; drawing, 11.5 × 16.6cm, signed with initials bottom right coll. J.P. Smid (Amsterdam).

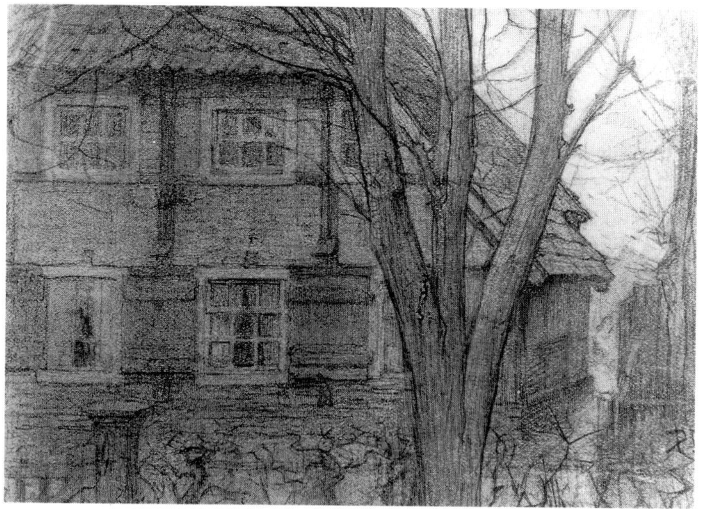

Piet Mondrian, The Weaver's House ; gouache, signed and dated bottom right 'Piet Mondriaan 1899'.

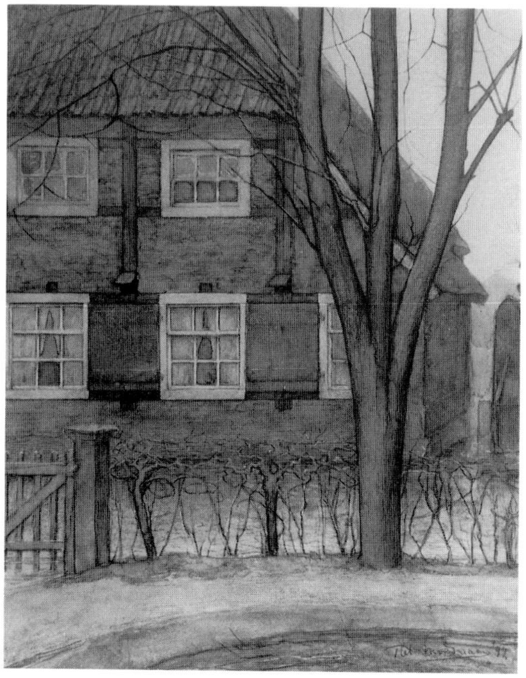

brink is the subject of all five works in this series; Mondrian first made sketches of one side of the street and then observed the same place from the opposite side. The tension between the 'empty' form of the S-shaped road and the structures of the houses pushed out towards the edge of the composition clearly show that in these works Mondrian was examining the elementary means of constructing a composition. The gouache, in which the road is occupied by the figure of the farmer's wife, forfeits much of the tension of the oil sketch. The motif of an object placed in the foreground and buildings behind, parallel to the picture plane, is an important compositional element in Mondrian's Winterswijk pictures.
An almost identical problem is tackled in three works which have the Winterswijk countryside as their theme. The oil study again features a curving country road. In the gouache, however, a ploughing farmer is added to the composition. In his 'View of Winterswijk', Mondrian has solved the problem of front and back in the composition by the traditional device of a winding road. A small drawing measuring 21 by 12 centimetres is the starting point for the 'Church at Winterswijk' series. A striking feature here, as in the sketchbook drawing of the 'Wevershuis', is that the deliberately chosen viewpoint of a nature motif determines the composition of the first sketch of a motif. The drawing for the etching plate shows an uninterrupted view of the church, the top half of the picture filled with the branches of a tree emerging at the right-hand side. Motifs from the first drawing and the preliminary study for the etching are combined in the gouache. The boughs of the trees appearing at the left and right-hand sides of picture fill the top half of the composition; the church is visible through the branches of the small apple tree in the middle. The trees are situated firmly in the foreground, emphasized still further by the hedge from the drawing of the 'Wevershuis'. A striking feature is the pattern formed by the twisted branches, occupying a good half of the composition. Comparison of this gouache with the first drawing clearly shows the work to be all construction, not rendered on the spot, but contrived. Its meaning is thus something other than the direct observation of nature, as Mondrian underlines with the poem he wrote on the back of the picture:

'—And the branches of the saplings
rejoiced
soaring to meet the others that hung down
from the tall trees
quietly in the grey sky and below
the silent green expanse—
And the church rose high above the village.
M'

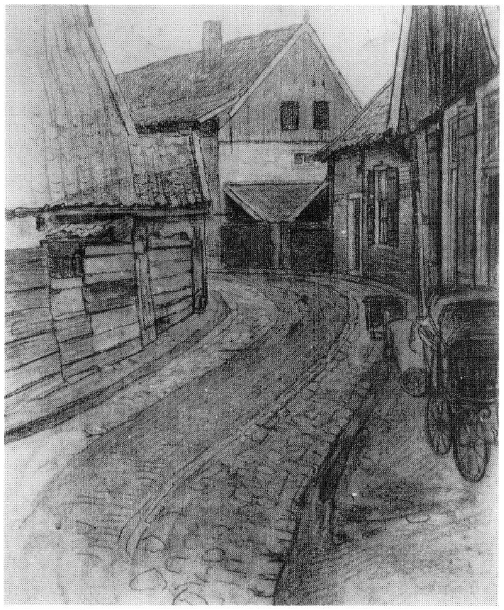
Piet Mondrian, The Lappenbrink ; ca.1898, drawing.

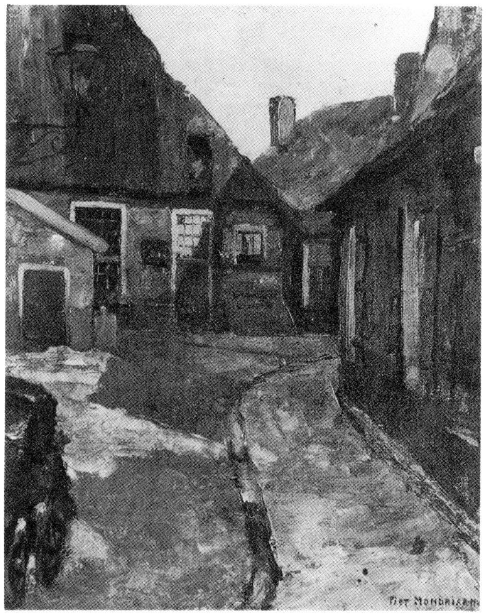
Piet Mondrian, The Lappenbrink ; ca.1898, oil on canvas.

Piet Mondrian, The Lappenbrink ; ca.1898, drawing.
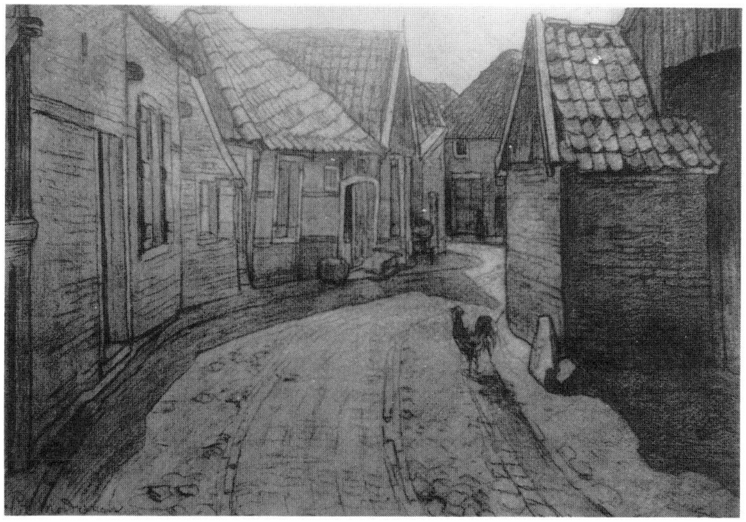

Piet Mondrian, The Lappenbrink ; ca.1898, drawing.
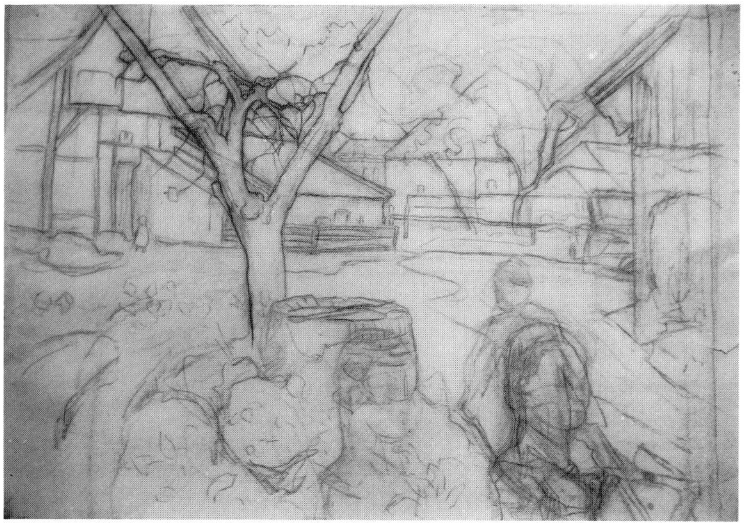

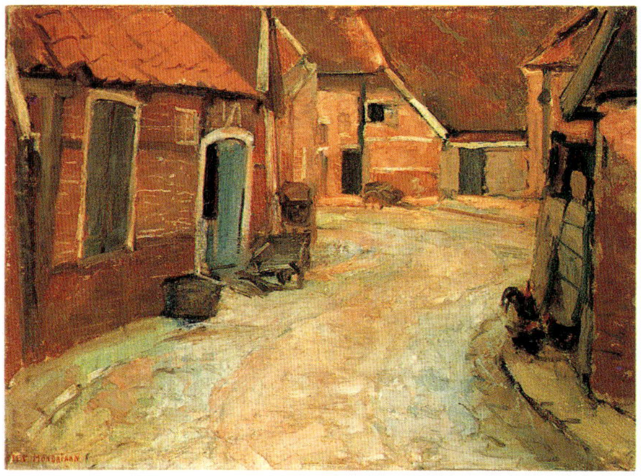

Piet Mondrian, The Lappenbrink ; oil on canvas, 32.5 × 44 cm.

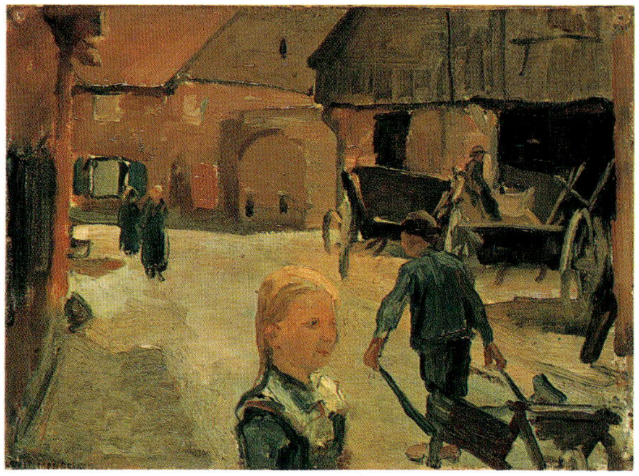

Piet Mondrian, 'The Lappenbrink'; oil on canvas on cardboard.

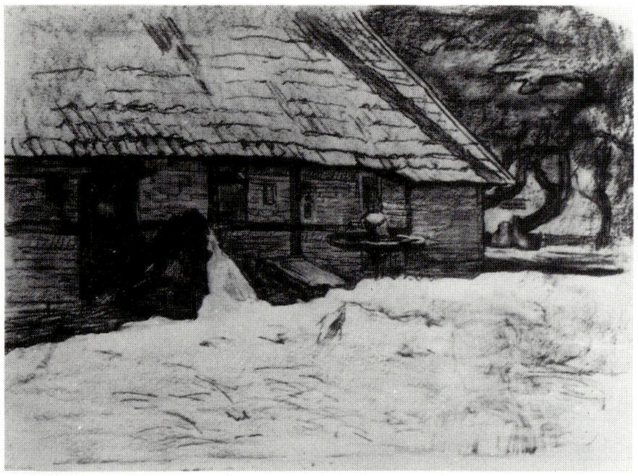

Piet Mondrian, Farm at Winterswijk with Farmer's Wife ; ca.1898, drawing.

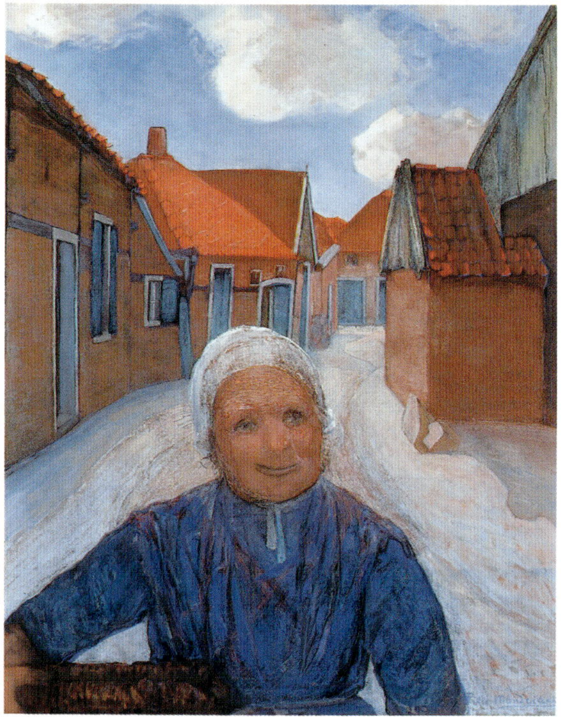

Piet Mondrian, The Lappenbrink with Farmer's Wife ; gouache, signed and dated bottom right 'Piet Mondriaan 1899'; coll. Haags Gemeentemuseum (on loan).

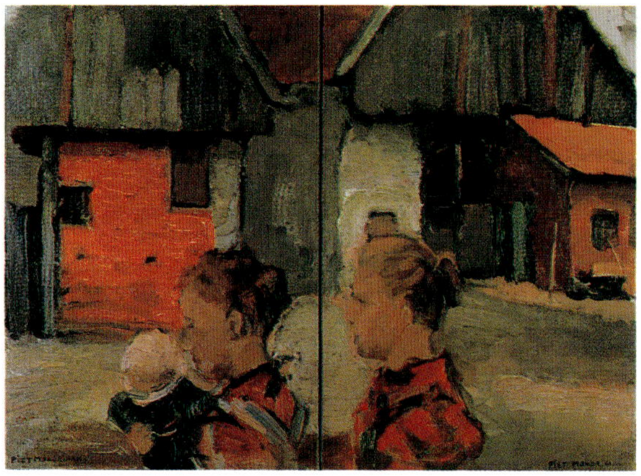

Piet Mondrian, Women with Child in front of a Farmhouse ; oil on canvas, 33.5 × 45 cm; coll. Haags Gemeentemuseum.

Piet Mondrian, 'Landscape near Winterswijk'; oil on canvas.

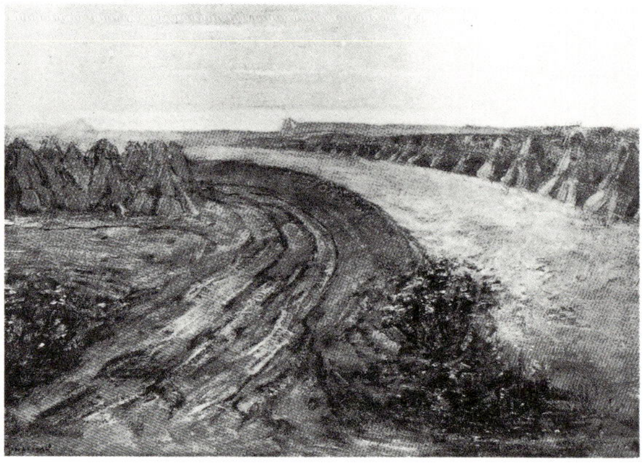

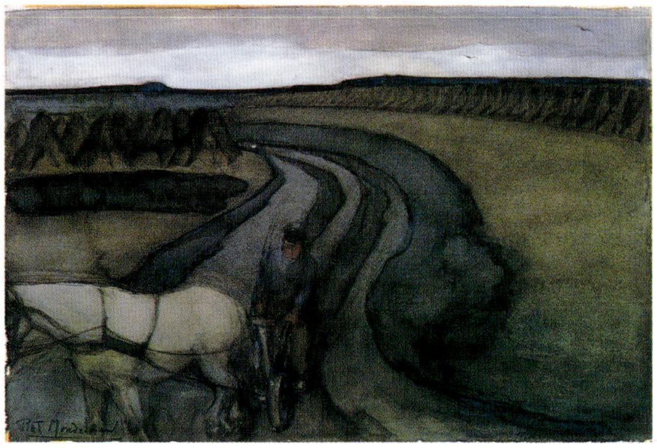

Piet Mondrian, At Work ; ca. 1898, gouache, 54 × 76 cm, signed at bottom left and right; coll. Haags Gemeentemuseum.

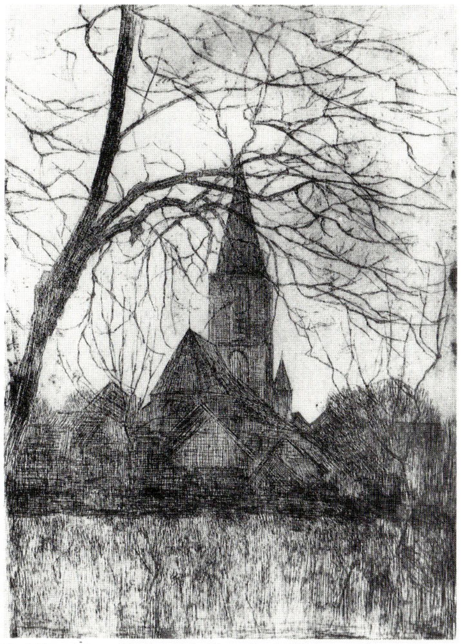

Piet Mondrian, St. Jacob's Church at Winterswijk ; etching, 37 × 26 cm; coll. Museum of Modern Art (New York).

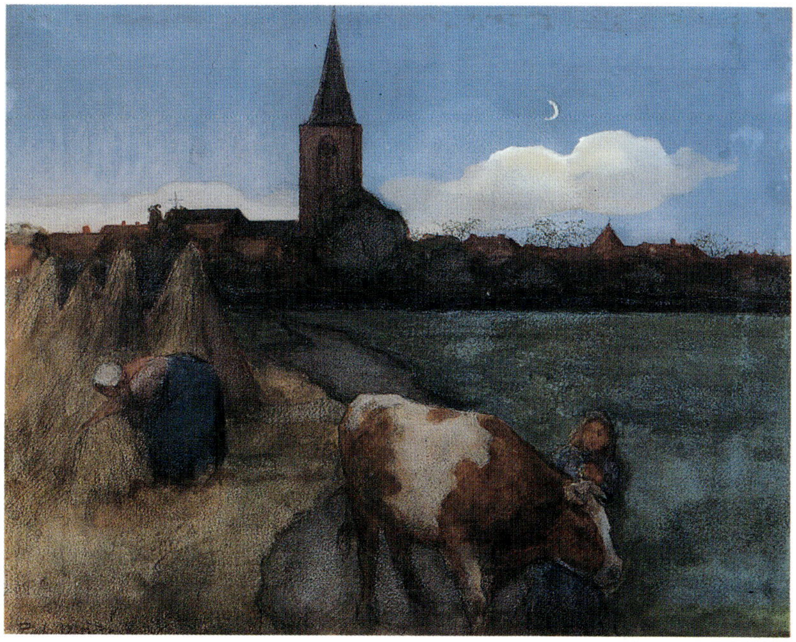

Piet Mondrian, View of Winterswijk ; 1898, 52 × 63.5 cm, gouache, 1898; signed bottom left 'Piet Mondriaan'; coll. J.P. Smid (Amsterdam).

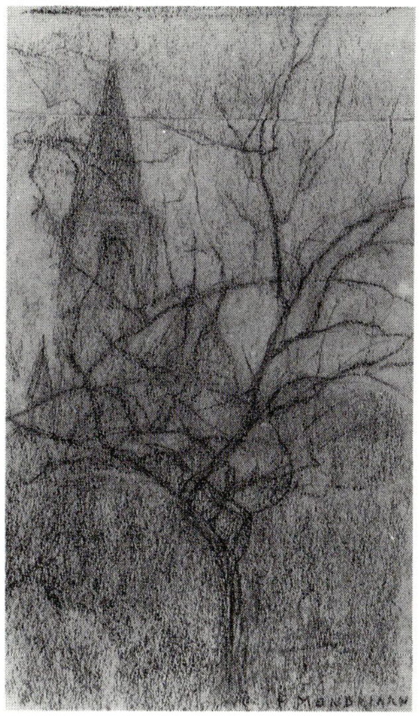

Piet Mondrian, St. Jacob's Church at Winterswijk ; ca.1898, drawing, 20.8 × 11.6 cm; coll. Haags Gemeentemuseum.

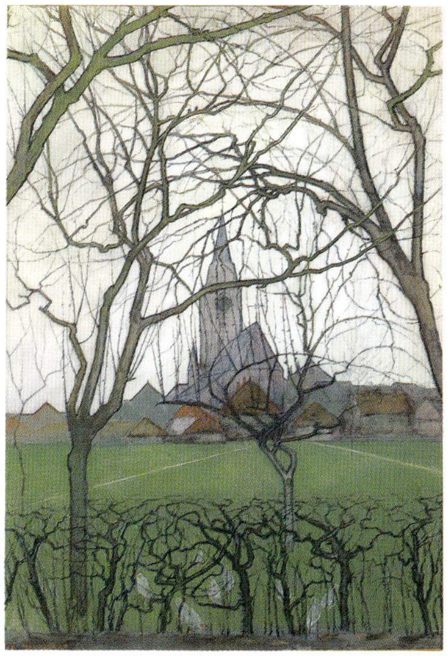

Piet Mondrian, St. Jacob's Church at Winterswijk ; ca.1898, gouache; 75 × 50 cm.

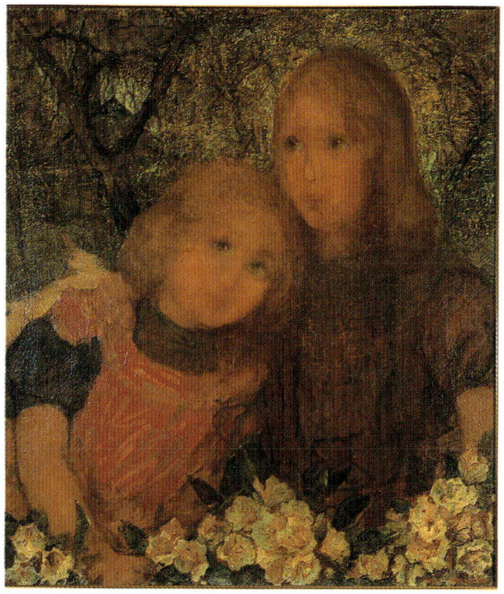

Piet Mondrian, Spring Idyll ; ca.1900, oil on canvas, 75 × 64 cm.

In 'Spring Idyll', a portrait of two girls, Mondrian repreated the motif of the 'Church at Winterswijk'. As in a collage, the motif is glued in the top left-hand corner of the painting. The flowers along the bottom edge, as in the gouache above, enhance the content of the poem. I think that Mondrian used this identifiable motif here not just in order to express the subtle, emotional meaning of the poem, but also to suggest a relationship between the two girls in the picture and Winterswijk. It seems quite likely to me that this double portrait was painted in the same period, 1899, in Winterswijk, as the result of a commission.

I have dwelt at some length on some of Piet Mondrian's works in order to convey an idea of how he achieved his compositions and what criteria he set himself. The main compositional features are (1) pictorial elements placed in the foreground: trees with buildings, or people with buildings; (2) a completely filled surface: skies or clouds are not important in these works; (3) the composition, as in the apple tree and the road, for instance, is concentrated in the centre of the picture; (4) perhaps the most important element in the works executed in the studio: the addition of certain elements charges the works with emotion. To express the essence of these works very briefly, we might say that Mondrian concentrated most intently during this period on the problem of organizing the picture surface and creating some correspondence between the organization of the surface and its emotional meaning. Obviously it is not so difficult in still lifes to add a few details in order to indicate that the maker wishes to endow the objects with greater meaning than they possess simply by virtue of their arrangement and depiction. In the landscapes discussed above the meaning given to them by the maker is represented by a changed notion of how the pictorial means themselves should be used. Professor H.

van der Waal has expressed the problem most aptly: *'The primary aspect of the structure of symbolic works of art is the disappearance of the perspective justification of space and the concomitant increase in the meaning of the surface.'* It is these very works of Mondrian's that clarify the transition from the observation of nature of works with added meaning. The depiction of space is the main problem in these works.

It will be clear that the works discussed above broach basic issues which were to preoccupy Mondrian for the rest of his life. I mention but a few: he elaborated the tree-and-building motif in his series 'Farm at Duivendrecht'; the 'horror vacui' or tendency to fill the entire picture surface occurs in several compositions, but with the greatest impact in the series of 'Red and Blue Trees', and of course the 'Apple Trees in Blossom' series; in the 'Cubist Landscape' of 1912 the composition still focusses on the tree. I cite these few examples in order to show that it was perfectly obvious that in the eighteen-nineties Piet Mondrian was already asking himself what painting in its widest sense meant to him. It will by now be apparent that his notions of painting differed fundamentally from those of his father and uncle.

Three artists

Three artists with close family ties have been presented here. All three gave meaning and function to the talent and interest with which they had been endowed and which they developed further. All three gave form to their ideas and presented them in completely different ways. The types they represent have a legitimate place in western art, and have coexisted for a very long time.

P.C. Mondriaan senior considered his drawing talent to be subordinate to the primary task of propagating his Christian beliefs by school-teaching, by adopting a political stance and by taking political action. The basis and function of his art are to be sought in his convictions and communal activities. His drawing was not just a hobby, then, but definitely functional. Abraham Kuyper frequently offered him jobs in which he could have done greater justice to his drawing skill, only to receive Mondriaan's invariable answer:

'As you know, I am a "schoolman", i.e. preferring to work and most at home in a large *primary school'.* (Mondriaan to Kuyper, 29.8.1882)

Father Mondriaan acquainted his children from an early age with his special interest in drawing. Many years later his youngest son Carel recalled:

'Father also used to draw a lot for us, Louis and me. Splendid horses, cows, farmboys and girls, sometimes knights, too. He drew skillfully, I must say.'

(Carel Mondriaan to Slijper, 18.10.50, Slijper Archive HGM)

Frits Mondriaan (1853-1932), like his brother, probably learned to draw in his father's shop, making designs for the wig model book. Frits must have started drawing and painting at an early age; his earliest known drawing is dated 1866, when he was thirteen. He did not take up drawing as a profession, but ran and continued his father's business. He kept on painting, though, consulting the 'real' painters of the Hague School for advice.

Not until the eighteen-nineties did he devote himself solely to painting; fairly soon he was a well-established artist with a particular reputation for his paintings of the Hague woods. Frits Mondriaan taught his nephew to paint during their country expeditions. To Frits, however, the epitome of painting was the constructed studio piece, conceived wholly in keeping with the fashion and taste of the day. After 1910 Frits Mondriaan's success faded. An anonymous critic of an exhibition held in 1913 supplied the following characterization:

'It is amazing to see the amount of talent around today! Geniuses are distributed sparsely over the centuries. Perhaps our own age does not possess a single great, pure genius in the field of painting, a spirit that embraces the forces of the past and present, elevating them and propelling them further, extending the limits on all sides and thus commanding the future. But minor and major talents jostle one another on the art market. (...) There is another Mondriaan who seeks—not beauty, but strange and curious things in a cubist or kaleidoscopic manner. In search of genius?... This one [i.e. Frits] is apparently satisfied with his talent.'

(Onze Kunst 1913, p.38)

Piet Mondrian (1872-1944) was indeed in search of a different kind of art. This was noticed by the outside world in 1910, but his independent attitude was evident from the very start, as we have seen. His constant pondering on the use of pictorial means and the meaning they ought to have is the hallmark of his art. In this context it is odd that although Piet Mondrian had been in contact with contemporary art from his childhood, there are few traces of any direct influence in his early work; he obviously learned from his uncle Frits to sketch outdoors in the manner of the Hague School.

The simple fact is that Mondrian cut himself off, more or less deliberately, from external influences. Only when he had achieved certain results was there an opening for 'influences' from outside. Mondrian later spoke about his art in no uncertain terms. The true nature of art is in constant development, evolution; the artist's position is parallel to this. The artist has a position of his own in society, comparable to that of the scientist; a place untrammelled by social convictions or the social norms of art production. That is the form that Piet Mondrian wanted to give to art.

Or, as he himself put it:

'One can rightly speak of an evolution in plastic art. It is of the greatest importance to note this fact, for it reveals the true way of art; the only path along which we can advance'. (Plastic and Pure Plastic Art, New York 1945, p.51). In the eighteen-nineties Mondrian was unable to formulate these terms. He later described the path he had travelled and the meaning he wanted to give art: *'Art is the expression of truth as well as of beauty.'*

Acknowledgements

Several libraries, antiquarian booksellers, municipal archives, official instances and private sources have aided my research. I wish to mention the following persons and institutions in particular:

The Central Laboratory, Amsterdam (E. Klusman, P. de Haan, J. van Broekhoven, V.R. Mehra, J. Voskuil); W. van Dam; Mrs. J.L. van Essen; the municipal archives of The Hague, Rotterdam, Arnhem, Amersfoort, Winterswijk; S. Honig junior; J.M. de Jong, Krimpen a/d Yssel; G.H. Rosenbrink; Mrs. Ligthart; M.J. Linssen; J.A. Oskamp; Dr. G. Puchinger; Th. Rechsteiner; H.C. Reinders; G. Ribbink; national archives, Arnhem; W. Scholtz; Mrs. Seelig; Mrs. Steneker; B. Wander; Dr. A. Wiersinga; Winkelaar b.v., Winterswijk.

Mondrian in his Studio

herbert henkels

I Introduction

My object here is to reflect, in brief, on certain aspects of the way Mondrian conceived of his role as an artist—aspects which, to my mind, have an essential bearing on both his thinking and his course of action. This essay may be seen, roughly, as a sequel to the previous article in which I attempted to describe the cultural and intellectual background against which the young Mondrian grew up. As a boy he was exposed to two very specific types of artistic practice: the socially committed graphic art of his father, and the so-called "indépendent" painting of his Uncle Frits.[1]
But the path that Piet Mondrian eventually chose to follow was a quite different one. Naturally this affected the way he drew and painted, and the way he lived in his studio, but the greatest difference lay in the way he thought about the artist's position in society and the nature of his relationship with Art. It was a very radical difference, for Mondrian believed in the virtually indissoluble link between notions such as society, art, the role of the artist, beauty, truth, the relationship between art and life, the relationship between the different arts (architecture, music, painting, literature). But it is the way Mondrian conceived of the purpose of the artist that lies at the core of all his thinking, and we shall see, in the following pages, how he sought to give form to his ideas on the practical level.
The self-awareness of the artist consists, in the main, of three images: the image of himself that he projects in his own mind, the image that he strives after, and the image he projects upon others. Obviously these three manifestations of the self-image are closely related, and very rarely can one component detach itself form the others. This same interrelatedness was emphasized in a recent article on the historical significance of biographical and autobiographical literature, by Dr. A.L. Constandse, in which he analyses the manners of image-projection employed in biographies, autobiographies, and other literary genres.[2]
Reading through the existing literature on Mondrian one cannot help noticing the tendency to treat Mondrian the artist as well as Mondrian the man as a figure of legendary proportions. I have pointed out elsewhere that he was, to some extent, a legendary figure in his lifetime among a limited number of people, but certainly all the ingredients were already there for the legend to grow and become widely known after his death.[3]
To my mind the reason that the development toward this "living legend" set in at such an early stage—in about 1910—and that it was fed and stimulated by the people in his direct surroundings, is that Mondrian was extremely successful in persuading those around him to accept the self-image that he strove after—i.e. that based on the complete integration of art and life—as the only image possible.
In his attempts to analyse this self-image created by the artist, the historian and art historian must rely, to a large extent, on a body of information consisting of letters, personal memories, interviews and so on, all of which confirm a specific pre-formed image. It is my aim in this essay to point out the basic structure of that self-image, and what its chief constituents are. In the course of this exploration it will become clear that this self-image exerted a considerable influence on Mondrian's manner of painting, in other words on the actual work in process.
The image that an artist forms of himself and strives after is not accidental, it is indeed based on and a product of the transmission and acceptance of the social patterns that were particularly pronounced in the social milieu in which the artist grows up. A self-image, in the strictest sense, can in fact emerge only as a result of a strong interaction, and often conflict, with the image that prevails in a particular social milieu. In Mondrian's case there was a pronounced cultural awareness in the circle in which the artist grew up, and this had an undeniable influence on the development of the artist's self-image. It seems an obvious assumption that Mondrian started out by adhering to the image of the artist that was considered right in his milieu. It was not until 1908—when also his ideas about art in general and about painting in particular started to change—that the final break with the image that his milieu had imposed upon him became clear. It was in this period, too, that Mondrian made the self-portraits that were to provide the basis, as far as content and composition were concerned, of nearly all his later self-portraits; and these same self-portraits, with the concentrated attention on the eyes, also have something to say about the role that Mondrian ascribed to art and to the artist.
Let me begin my exploratory tour with a brief outline of the facts of Mondrian's earliest period as an artist—a period in which he tried for the most part to mould himself according to the image of the artist that his milieu prescribed.

Not surprisingly, Mondrian soon proved incapable of and unwilling to live up to this idealized image of the artist, but it was several years before he succeeded in constructing his own idea of the artist's role (i.e. his own role as an artist). This look at Mondrian's early awareness of himself as an artist is followed by a section devoted to his newfound independence from his milieu, which is reflected not only in self-portraits but equally so in portraits, landscapes, still lifes and a number of figure compositions. Naturally his new conception of his role as an artist was complex. The definitive break with the milieu-imposed notion of the artist may be traced in the part that the theme of evolution began to play in Mondrian's philosophy of aesthetics. I use the term "philosophy of aesthetics" deliberately here, for Mondrian sought to express his ideas on the creation of an entirely new basis for art and for all artists in writings that were initially published in the journal *De Stijl*, and later in many European avant-garde periodicals. It would take us too far afield here to go into the intricacies of his aesthetic philosophy. I shall therefore restrict myself to pointing out all those passages in his writings that are of particular relevance to his role as an artist.[4]

In the third section of my essay I intend to examine how this notion of the artist's role affected his way of making art (i.e. mostly paintings, in the case of Mondrian). It will become evident that Mondrian's famous studio was not intended merely as an illustration or example of architecture of the future, or indeed of his own theories. The studio performed an essential function in the creative process. Mondrian's writing, (i.e. thinking) about art, the paintings he made and his concern for his studio played a major role in this important period of his life, and especially in the late twenties, when everything seemed to revolve around the actual work process. Evolution, which for Mondrian meant forward motion, an upward movement, aimed towards the future, was also tightly bound up with destruction, i.e. not just the destruction of obsolete traditional social or artistic norms, but also and more importantly the destruction within man himself, man constantly renewing himself in an uninterrupted process of destruction and creation. Applied to himself this meant that the artist must always be ready to leave behind and destroy what went before, since he aims at progress. Each next step was as necessary as the last (for "Truth" manifests itself always) on the road to a future paradise: and this, since it had been conquered wholly by mankind, would rest on a dynamic equilibrium which could only be attained, for the time being, by the artist in his painting. Artist and painting, in Mondrian's mind, were synonymous with his own artisthood and his own painting.

The image of the artist in Mondrian's formative years

In the mid-nineteen hundreds there was, in the Netherlands, a strong tendency on the part of the government and sections of the public to take a much keener interest in education. As a result of the development and differentiation of school systems, the teaching of drawing as a subject at different types of educational institutions received due attention, too. Small groups of people, inspired by liberal ideas or religious conviction, propagated the idea that much larger sections of the population should be engaged in the cultural and intellectual advancement of the nation. More and more rules and regulations were made—such as specifications of the size of classrooms, but they were especially concerned with both what was taught and how it was taught, and as a direct consequence, with what kind of training the teachers themselves should receive. This rather sudden upsurge of interest in all aspects of education not only greatly increased the burden of responsibility that was placed on teachers on all levels, it also brought about a far-reaching differentiation within the teaching profession. A glance at the history of education in the Netherlands shows that the generation of educationalists who received their training in the 1830s, and many of whom made important contributions to the reform of the educational system, were succeeded some thirty years later by a generation of teachers who were already differently equipped to start with, and who were entrusted with more specialized educational tasks.[5]

Naturally the development of drawing as a school subject followed this trend. Mondrian's father (1839-1921), who obtained a drawing teacher's diploma in the early 1860s, was probably largely self-taught as a candidate for the drawing master's examination, but he had enjoyed a special advantage in that, as a young boy, he had helped to make the drawings for the sample book of his father's wigshop. What is more important, though, is that he had come into contact, at an early age, with the art collection owned by the statesman Groen van Prinsterer (1801-1876). Some letters addressed to the wife of Groen van Prinsterer dating from the early 1870s mention the fact that Mondrian's father had received several small paintings from this collection as a gift.[6] Mondrian's father undoubtedly enlisted his son's help in preparing and executing the decorative and salutory propaganda drawings that Mondriaan senior used to make, both at his own initiative and at the request of others. A letter from Mondrian's father to A. Kuyper (1837-1920) reveals that, already in 1874, he was in the habit of engaging the services of a thirteen-year-old "student teacher" in drawing techniques the complicated ornaments and patterns that decorated his political plates.[7] It is amusing to think of Piet Mondrian as a young boy helping his father to make the instructive pictures of historical scenes, usually glorifying the unity of the Dutch nation as championed by the House of Orange. Besides practising the techniques of draughtsmanship, the young Mondrian must undoubtedly have thus become familiar with many works by famous Dutch painters of the nineteenth century and earlier.

Mondriaan senior often composed his memorial pictures out of a variety of scenes from the history of the Netherlands. These small scenes were for the most part borrowed from paintings by famous Dutch artists, such as Pieneman (1779-1853), whose *Battle of Waterloo* was copied several times by Mondriaan senior.[8] Also portraits of historical figures, scenes from the Bible and town views were recurrent features in the collage-like compositions of Piet Mondrian's father.

The most important thing that the young Mondrian undoubtedly learned from his father, besides technical skills, was that it was possible to communicate a message of spiritual or political import by composing a pictorial image, symbolical or otherwise (a good illustration is Mondriaan senior's *Revolution or Gospel* of 1874). A particularly interesting example of the collaboration between father and son is, in this connection, the painting entitled *Thy Word is Truth* (1894), a composition made in 1894, in which the symbolical elements were selected by the father while the actual composition and painting was done by the son.[9]

As we know from Mondriaan senior's own writings, he considered his drawing activity as merely one possibility—albeit an important one—out of many possibilities of propagating and disseminating his philosophy of life. So if it is fair at all to regard Mondriaan senior as an artist, he was surely only an artist in so far as he placed his art at the service of religious and social ends. In his personal philosophy his educational activities were more important than his art. Yet this does not entitle us to conclude that father Mondriaan made a fundamental distinction between the intellectural status of the school-teacher and that of the artist. Both professions, after all, were in his opinion wholly based on God-given talents and not on acquired skills. His belief in teaching as a "calling" is made clear in the following passage from an article written by him: "The true pedagogue, who knows that teachers are not made but born, and also that the talent, the desire to read and write is not acquired, but is a gift from above, it is quite clear that the modern ideas on education are much too materialistic to convince a thinking nation."[10] And, not surpris-

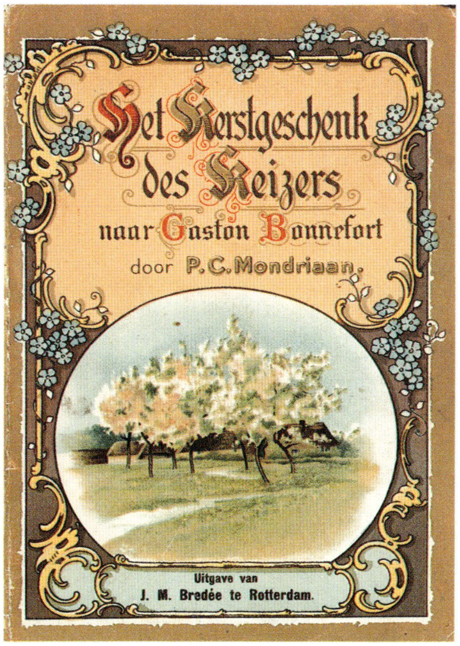

Cover of a book by P.C. Mondriaan senior, The Emperor's Christmas Gift, Rotterdam 1912.

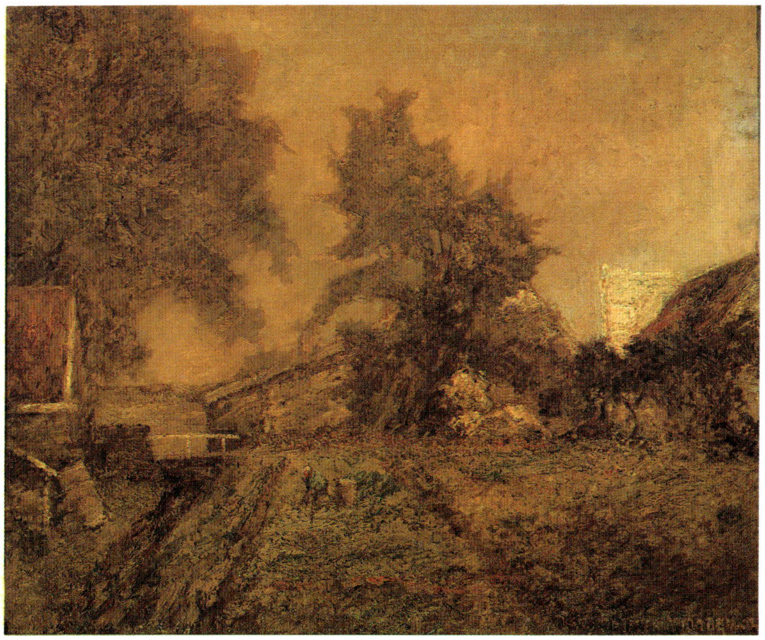

Piet Mondrian, Landscape; oil on canvas; 65 × 75 cm; 1893.

ingly, Mondriaan senior's ideas about art and artisthood ran along parallel lines.

In addition to his other work, Mondriaan senior also wrote short stories, based on a story by Gaston Bonnefont. The story is about a unique specimen of Austrian art of extreme value, namely an Austrian stove decorated with painted and glazed tiles. The stove is acquired by a cunning merchant from an impoverished man who is obliged to sell this household item (which has always been the pride of the family) for a small sum of money. The merchant, who knows that the Emperor is prepared to spend a lot of money on just such a stove, takes the object to the court, where the Emperor gladly adds it to his collection. The youngest son of the family, however, cannot bear the thought of losing the stove, because it gives him inspiration for his drawings: he spends nights on end copying the scenes depicted on the tiles. The budding artist—one cannot help seeing the parallel with the situation in the Mondriaan family!—therefore creeps into the stove before it is taken to the imperial court. Upon arrival there he emerges from his hiding-place and tells the Emperor the whole sad story of the sale of the stove, and his love for it as a work of art. The Emperor decides to test the boy by telling him that if he is able to draw the scenes on the tiles from memory, he will not only receive the stove as a reward but will also be admitted to the Imperial Academy to train as an artist. At this point in the story Mondriaan senior quotes one of his characters as saying: "That Tyrolean youth is a born artist, your Majesty! Never have I seen the like of this…it is not drawing that the boy does, it is magic! And all that from memory!" An explanation for such an abundance of talent follows: "Frans observed everything through eyes that were different to those of other children, for he was, as a born artist, receptive to the most exaggerated flights of fancy, both good and bad. How often do we not see in this world of ours that *God appears to tolerate evil while it is merely for the sake of the good that will come out of it.* The rest of the story of Frans Strehla clearly demonstrates that, just as in the life of our Dutch hero Michiel Adriaanszoon de Ruyter, the good eventually emerged victorious. Just as the story of the boyhood of this Christian hero of the seas cannot be offered as an example to our boys today, so this story fails to serve this cause—and yet it contains so many valuable signs concerning the conduct of man!"[11]

When Piet Mondrian had obtained his drawing master's degree at both ordinary and advanced levels, his father opposed the son's plans to further his artistic education at the Rijks akademie in Amsterdam. Mondriaan senior's opposition cannot have been rooted in a fundamental objection to artisthood, as we have seen in the above passages; it must have had a lot to do with the fact that the father could not afford to pay in full for his son's studies, and therefore feared an uncertain social position for his son, while Piet could be sure of a regular income if he were to accept a job as drawing master at a school.[12] The decision to obtain some teaching certificates first—they could always come in handy should he prove unable to earn a living by painting alone—turned out to have been a sensible one in the years directly following his departure from the Amsterdam Academy. For in those difficult years he was able to give private drawing lessons to young ladies and gentlemen from intellectual circles, and thus to earn a reasonable living.

There are records to show what kind of requirements candidates for the ordinary and advanced levels of the diploma were expected to meet.[13] The assignments given to examination candidates in August and September 1892—the year in which Piet Mondrian sat for his examination—were, as they usually were, of a highly practical nature. The practical part of the examination lasted five days, the theoretical part two days. The candidates had to draw after plaster models of part of a human body, and after a plaster ornament; they had to draw a still life as well as specific flowers and leaves in stylized form, by way of ornamentation. They were further expected to produce an architectural drawing, a geometrical drawing, drawings of mechanical devices, and perspective. The oral examinations were conducted along similar lines; the candidates' knowledge was tested in the fields of graphic projection, style and ornaments, anatomy, the methodology of teaching, and the techniques of freehand drawing.

So the professional training of Piet Mondrian prior to his enrolment at the Rijksacademie

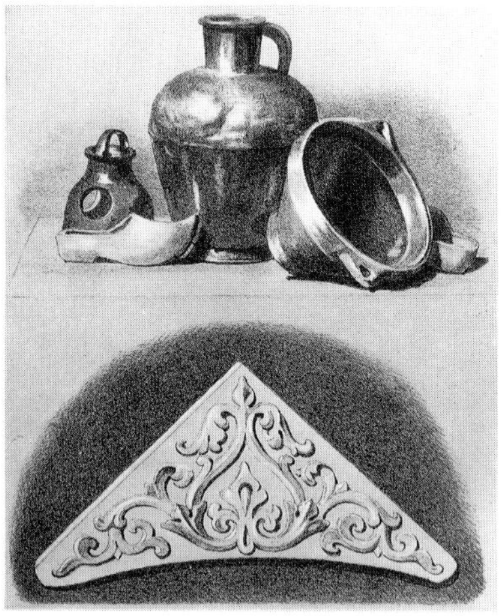

Illustration from: Braet van Ueberfeldt and V. Bing, Examples pour le Dessin d'après nature (examples for drawing after nature), 1866.

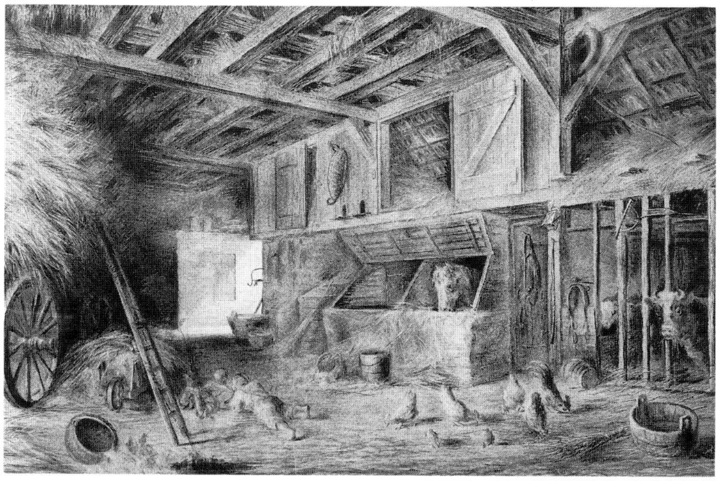

Piet Mondrian, Interior of a Stable; 1890, drawing, 57 × 83 cm.

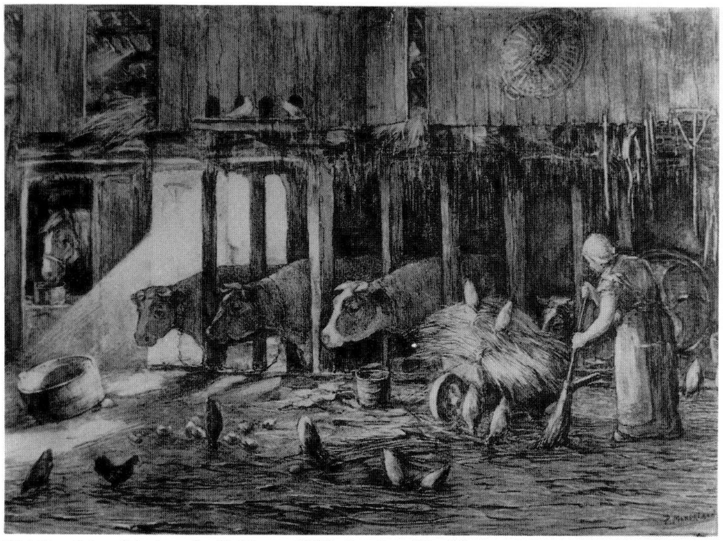

Piet Mondrian, Interior of a Stable; ca.1896, drawing, 65 × 90 cm.

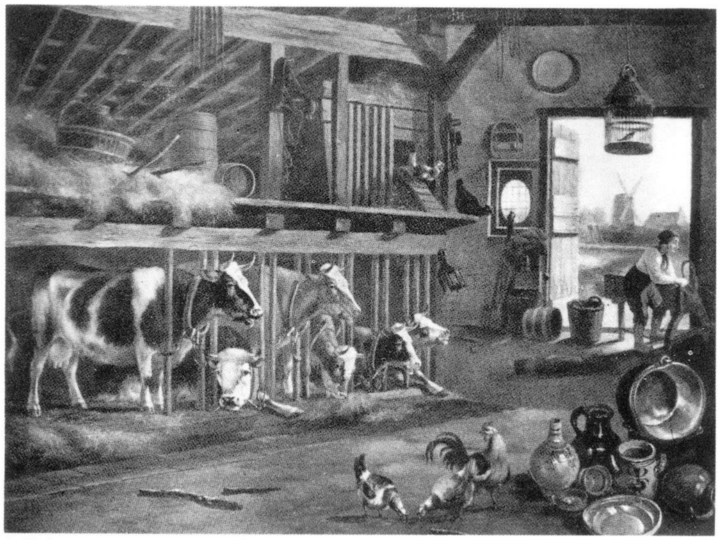

A. Verhoesen, Interior of a Stable; oil on canvas, 63 × 80 cm.

consisted largely of drawings of plaster casts of heads and hands, of plaster ornaments, or perspective drawing and architectural draughtsmanship.

As far as the preparatory studies for these exams was concerned the candidate was left largely to his own devices. For Mondrian it was an advantage that there was a secondary school, where drawing lessons were given, situated across from the house where he lived with his parents. Mondrian regularly borrowed the plaster casts that were used in that school, in order to make studies of them.[14] Another help in Mondrian's period of preparing himself for the diploma was the fact that there was a former drawing teacher living in Doetinchem not far from Winterswijk: his name was J. Braet van Uberfeldt (1807-1894), a well-known figure in the circles of art education. For many years he had been a teacher at a secondary school in Amsterdam, where he collaborated with his colleague V. Bing on the development of a new method of teaching drawing, based on the widely used method of the Frenchman Dupuis. This new method, too, was remarkable for the fact that the entire teaching programme consisted exclusively of drawing "from nature", based on the rules of perspective. Braet's curriculum was built up of six classes. It was not until the student had had sufficient practice with conventional drawing exercises that he was considered qualified to draw "from life", i.e. still-lifes of a small collection of pots and dishes, while the drawings of plaster casts (of ornaments, not parts of the human body) crowned the students' period of learning.[15]

Mondrian undoubtedly asked for and received much advice from this master in the teaching of the rules of perspective. Besides the practical advice on his preparation for the examinations, Mondrian's trips to Doetinchem had another purpose—for Braet owned a large number of paintings and drawings.[16] This was a unique chance for Mondrian to see the works of Théophile de Bock, Bosboom, Breitner, Du Chattel, Jozef Israels, Kever, Ten Kate, Koekkoek, Leickert, Mauve, Poggenbeek, Roelofs, Sadée, Springer and W. de Zwart—to name only the best-known artists represented in Braet's collection. Braet also had an extensive collection of reproductions of works by famous artists: Mondrian often borrowed these reproductions, not only to study them closely but also to make drawings after them, i.e. to copy them. Nearly all the works that Mondrian made before 1892 indeed have something of the nature of copies, even though it is often impossible to

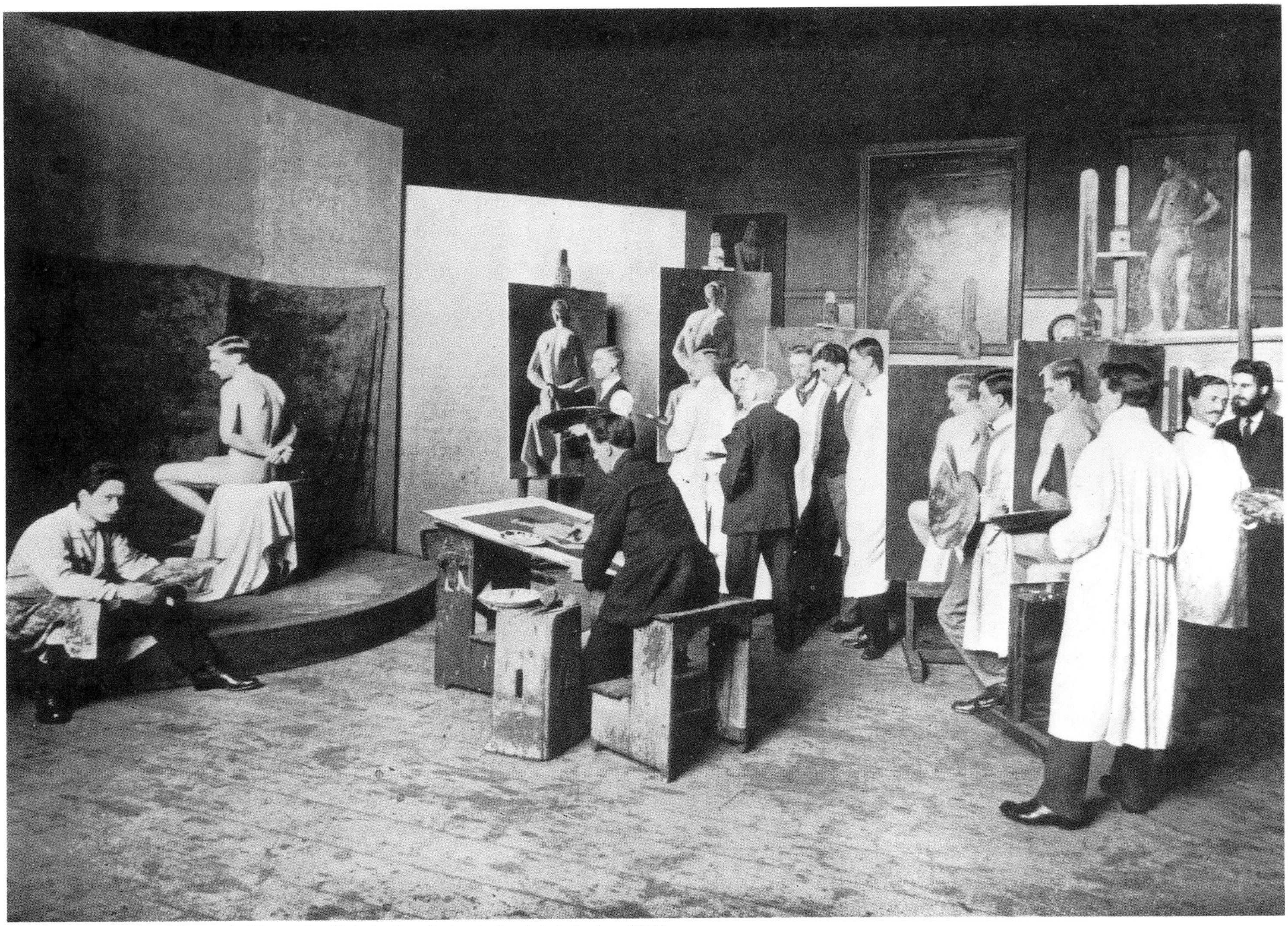

The drawingroom of Prof. N. van der Waay at the State Academy in Amsterdam (photograph ca.1913).

trace from which original works they may have been copied.[17] In some of the drawings he made of stable interiors the suggestion of imitation is particularly strong. The structure of the stable is very prominent, and the perspective is drawn strictly according to the rules of draughtsmanship; the animals are rather stiffly drawn, there is little indication of volume. This type of scene accords perfectly with the nineteenth century tradition of stable interiors, with A. Verhoesen (1806-1881) as its most popular representative. Braet van Uberfeld, too, is known to have had such a stable scene in his collection; it is extremely likely that Mondrian saw it, and quite possible that he copied it.

It was no problem for Mondrian to gain admittance to the Rijksakademie in Amsterdam in 1892; he was not required to pass any entrance examinations because he had already acquired his teaching diploma. Mondrian enrolled and paid tuition fees for all the classes that were given, but he concentrated his attention on the painting classes. He attended this class for two years—i.e. the academic years 1892-93 and 1893-94; the fee for the first year was paid by an unknown benefactor (Hfl. 100,-); for the second year Mondrian applied for, and received, a grant from the Royal Family. During the academic years 1896 and 1897 Mondrian only attended the evening drawing classes.[18] The Rijksakademie in Amsterdam had been established in 1870, as the successor to the Koninklijke Akademie voor Beeldende Kunsten (1820-70), and in fact offered the highest level of artistic training in the Netherlands, although the academy was not equated with the universities. Everyone excepting those who had obtained the "M.O." diploma had to pass an entrance examination, while at the end of each academic year exams were also held. There were six professors, who taught a variety of subjects. Prof. Auguste Allebé (1838-1927) taught the principles of proportion and "composition", Prof. Dake (1857-1918) taught perspective, proportion and drawing "from life"; Prof. Van der Waay (1855-1936) was the chief teacher of painting. He taught the students how to make "anatomical studies from life", the technical aspects of paint and, when Mondrian was an art student there, led the different painting classes. Prof. Stang gave a few lessons in engraving, while Prof. Leenhoff taught sculpture. But most important of all, to Mondrian, were undoubtedly the classes given by Prof. Six, who taught aesthetics and history of art.[19] What is particularly striking about the yearly teaching programmes is that the practical part concentrated almost entirely on studies of plaster casts, while some attention was also paid to the still life. Figure studies were all-important, but the landscape was wholly ignored. This is all the more remarkable because while we do not know of several still lifes done by Mondrian in this period, there are hardly any figure studies or compositions in which the human figure plays a central role. Even in this early period of his career as an artist Mondrian comes to the fore as a landscapist, despite the normal requirements set by the Academy. This discrepancy acquires even more significance when it is remembered that Mondrian twice sought official recognition of his art by participating in the Prix de Rome painting contests in 1898 and in 1901.[20]

Every Dutchman could enter for the Prix de Rome, although each candidate was expected to submit proof of his competence before taking part, e.g. a thorough knowledge of art theory, aesthetics, history of art, anatomy and perspective. In 1898 there were three candidates—P.C. Mondrian, H.J. Wolter and Martin Monnickendam (the latter had applied once before, in 1895, but had been turned down on that occasion). All three of them had studied at the Rijksakademie. Mondrian and Wolter were eventually excluded from candidacy on the grounds that their initial tests had not been satisfactory. Monnickendam, however, was considered a competent candidate, but the works he was assigned to execute (a nude study, a composition entitled "Before the Feast", and another on the subject "Rest after Work") did not satisfy the jury, which was chaired by Jozef Israels. Consequently no prize at all was awarded that year. The examination committee responsible for selecting the ultimate Prix de Rome candidate was made up of professors of the Rijksakademie. Mondrian gained very high marks for aesthetics, art history and perspective, but his drawings of parts of the human body and the nude model were considered far too poor for him to be accepted as a candidate.[21]

In May and June 1901 there were four artists who wished to compete for the Prix de Rome; A.H. Gouwe, M. Butter, P.C. Mondrian, and M. Monnickendam. This time all four were admitted to the candidacy. The most important part of the contest was a study of a nude figure, often life-size (ca.100 × 60 cm). The candidates were also required to paint two compositions measuring ca.40 × 30 cm, showing scenes from the Bible, notably "Jacob with Joseph's coat", and "Elisha with the widow's son." The jury's report notes that one candidate was turned down after this round: P.C. Mondrian. The reasons were given as follows: "The study of the nude model fails to meet reasonable requirements since neither form nor colour correspond with nature. The somewhat short but well-built and proportioned model is represented here in a shapeless and clumsy linear arrangement. The legs are far too heavy, and show little understanding of the human anatomy, while the dull colours and weak modelling make a no less unfavourable impression. Only the upper section of the torso suffers to a lesser degree from the aforementioned shortcomings. The sketch of "Elisha with the widow's son" attests to neither good taste nor soundness of principle. The dramatic treatment of the figures and the setting with the unnatural-looking ceremonial bed is not pleasing, nor is this lack compensated by other characteristics of artistic nature. Also the illumination, which is supposed to play an important part in this composition, is quite false. The composition of "Jacob with Joseph's coat" is equally unconvincing of the maker's talent for composition. The work is even lacking in veracity of the nature of the event. The scene looks like a group offering a gift, the more so since the aged Jacob does not look in the least surprised; on the contrary, he appears to stand there at the entrance to his tent well prepared for the Lord. Also the arrangement into groups is dull and unimaginative."[22]

A.H. Gouwe won the gold medal and a grant that enabled him to spend several years studying in Italy or Spain, and M. Monnickendam was awarded the silver medal. For the final test, each submitted a composition on the theme of "Boaz and Ruth". Gouwe's composition strikes me as a very traditional piece of work compared with the fashionable, vaguely erotic almost life-size composition of Monnickendam.[23]

It is not difficult to imagine how disappointed Mondrian must have been by the results of this competition; his father must have been bitterly disappointed, too, since he himself had made countless drawings (e.g. on the blackboard) of the same type of composition that his son had to make for the Prix de Rome.

So Piet Mondrian was not considered proficient in this particular genre, figure composition and figures in a landscape. Although he had earned a living since 1893 making portraits and copies of old masters in the Rijksmuseum and anything else that could fetch a sum of money, his failure for the Prix de Rome meant that he would neither receive official recognition nor a grant to enable him to spend several years working in the south of Europe.[24] His next objective was to secure a regular income by teaching and by finding a number of regular clients for his landscapes. In 1907 he submitted the following information for inclusion in the Lurasco book: "From then on he worked independently, first making figures and landscapes, then only the latter, with which he was successful at exhibitions as well as in terms of sales."[25] At this stage it looked as if Mondrian was going to follow in his uncle's footsteps by concentrating wholly on

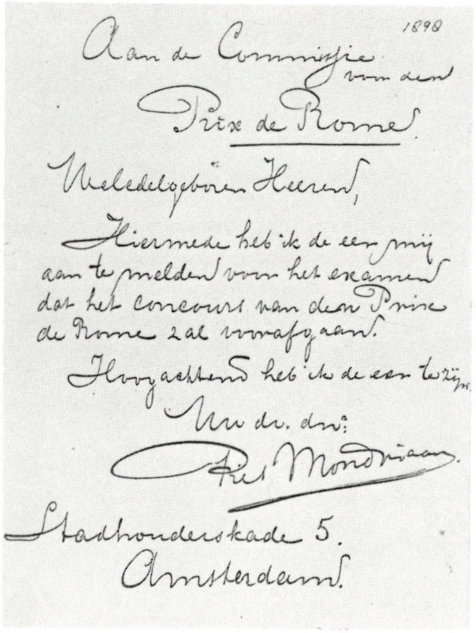
1898

Aan de Commissie van den Prix de Rome.

Weledelgeboren Heeren,

Hiermede heb ik de eer mij aan te melden voor het examen dat het concours van den Prix de Rome zal voorafgaan.

Hoogachtend heb ik de eer te zijn,

Uw dw. dn.:

Piet Mondriaan.

Stadhouderskade 5.

Amsterdam.

Letter by Piet Mondrian to the Committee of the 'Prix de Rome', 1898.

To the *Prix de Rome* Committee

Dear Sirs,

I have the honour to enter for the examination which will precede the Prix de Rome.

Yours respectfully,

Piet Mondrian

Stadhouderskade 5
Amsterdam

Piet Mondrian, Male Nude ; oil on canvas, 100 × 60 cm; coll. State Department for the Visual Arts (The Hague).

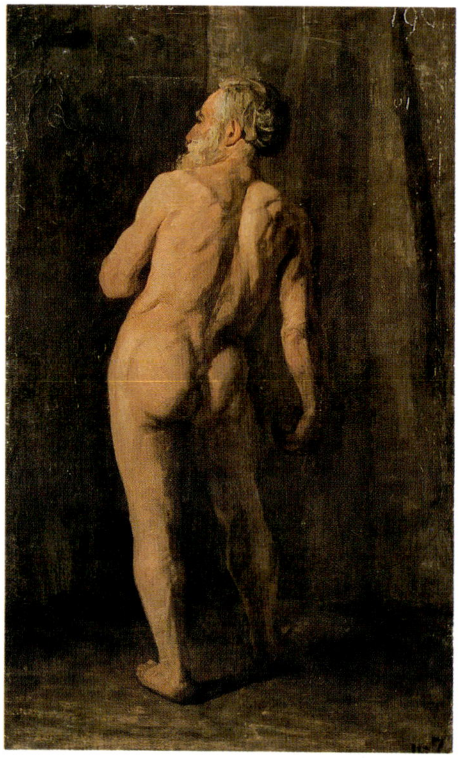

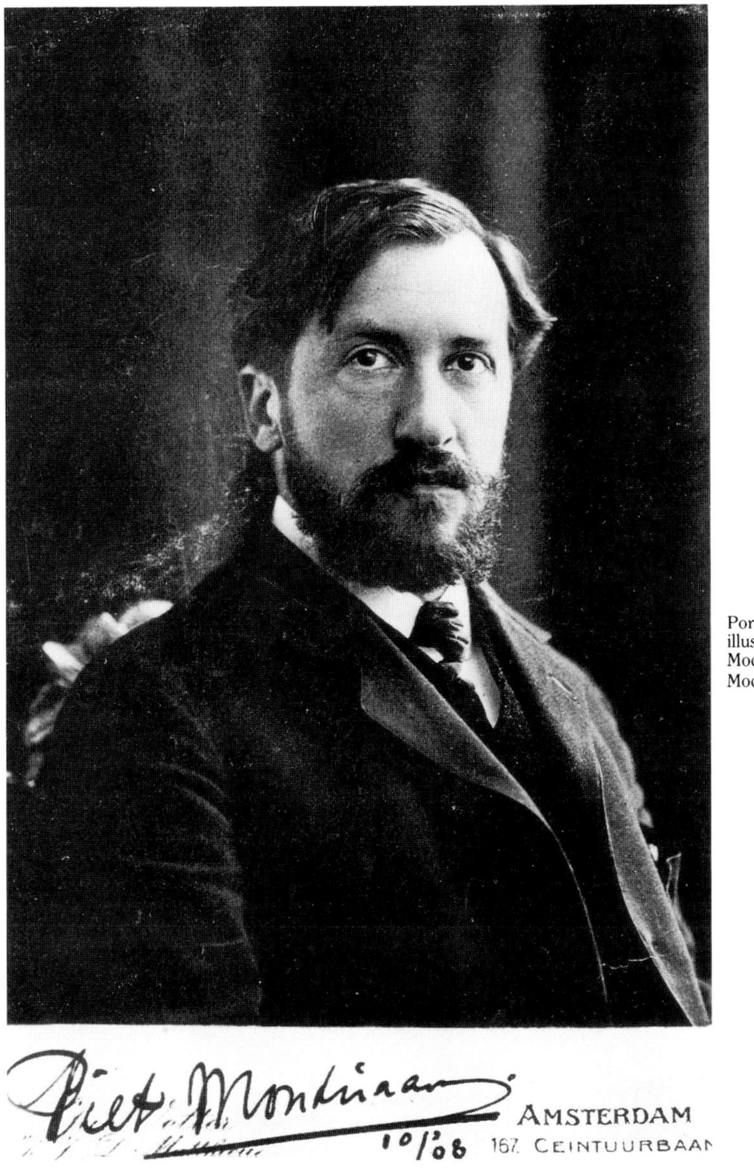

Portrait of Piet Mondrian, illustrated in F. Lurasco, Onze Moderne Meesters, 1907 (Our Modren Masters).

the landscape for which there was an almost insatiable demand.

Nine tenths of all the surviving works made before 1905 are landscapes. The few still lifes, compositions with flowers and of course the portraits, most of which were commissioned, represent only a fraction of his total output. As we shall see below, some of these early works are particularly important for a good understanding of Mondrian's art. The vast majority of the landscapes do not fall in the category of works for which the artist exerted himself to any extreme. Indeed, most of these early pictures are somewhat sketchily painted, and Mondrian himself was undoubtedly aware of this.[26] The typically nineteenth-century notion that several preliminary studies, both drawn and painted, were necessary before work on the definitive painting could commence, do not seem to have bothered Mondrian very much in those early years before 1905.[27] He was concerned, first and foremost, with finding regular buyers for his small oil sketches so that he could at least earn enough to live on as an "independent" artist.

The photograph of himself that Mondrian submitted for the Lurasco shows a dignified gentleman, in whom the prospective buyer could place his trust with respect to the quality of the goods once delivered. It is ironical that by the time the Lurasco book was at last published, that same dignified-looking artist had taken a completely different direction, and had dedicated himself wholly to the exploration of the foundations of art and painting. The large-format paintings that originated between 1906 and 1908, often preceded by preliminary drawings on the same scale and sometimes by countless oil sketches of varying size, show clearly that the intentions of the artist were quite different to those of the same artist a few years earlier. There are still some elements in those landscapes that reveal the lingering influence of nineteenth-century working methods.[28] The decision to use large formats in this period was not inspired by the desire to evoke the wideness of the Dutch landscape or to demonstrate his skilled "brushwork" on the immense skies. Mondrian's intentions were, indeed, in direct opposition to those of the Hague School.

This period of Mondrian's œuvre has been called the period of the "evening and night landscapes". The second generation of painters, following in the footsteps of the Hague School painters, often painted landscapes bathed in the glow of sunset. Both Théophile de Bock and Frits Mondriaan are known to have produced such evening landscapes.[30] But unlike these painters, who were specifically concerned with how the light affected the appearance of the landscape, Mondrian concentrated on the lightsource itself, details in the landscape disappear, trees and clouds are painted as large planes, i.e. with the emphasis on the contours. It is due to the light that the objects assume form. Mondrian's evening landscapes represent the onset of a development in which the light, conceived initially as a determinant of form—increasingly assumes a symbolic meaning as the origin of all that exists, and thus becomes the core and starting point of his painting and aesthetic philosophy.

It is almost impossible to ascertain exactly at which point in time certain essential changes take place in someone's life. Albert van den Briel, the main source of information on Mondrian's early years, states that significant changes occurred after Mondrian's stay in Uden, Brabant: "That too is when the abstract work started. I have some watercolours in which all the later work is already contained, also the horizontal and vertical lines. It was when he was living there (in Uden) that the change in him began."[31] I am adhering here to the date 1907 because at that time he still presented himself, via Lurasco's biographical notes, as an artist working in the traditional manner. Mondrian's starting point for making art was then already no longer determined by the norms of the art market: his norms and motivations are from then on to be found increasingly in the ideas. Mondrian himself developed concerning the meaning and value of art and of painting in particular.

It will be clear that at this point Mondrian turned his back on the starting points and function of painting that had been instilled in him in the course of his training and apprenticeship, and had after all secured him a reasonable position in society; naturally this resulted in a direct conflict with those who represented those

norms. Mondrian first presented a large number of works in which the change in his approach was obvious to everyone at the St. Lucas exhibition of 1909.[32]
Mondrian's uncle Frits, who must have felt responsible in some degree for Mondrian's embarking on a painter's career, aired his displeasure at the activities of his depraved nephew in no uncertain terms, and let all the critics know that he had nothing whatsoever to do with Piet anymore.[33] Indeed all the reviews of this exhibition as well as of all subsequent shows up to the 1920s remind the reader that Piet Mondrian should not be confused with his uncle Frits Mondriaan. In a letter to the art critic Bremmer, Mondrian explains his reasons for changing the spelling of his name by ommitting one a: "I have also left out the a because my Uncle felt that I was an embarassment to him as another artist with the same name."[34] Even Piet's father, after whom Piet had been named, considered it necessary to emphasize his identity as distinct from that of his son by adding "senior" to his name.[35] Mondrian's teachers at the Academy hastened to voice their fundamental opposition to their former student's "depravity". One of them, C.L. Dake, even started a crusade against the innovators, keeping up his invective until his death in 1918.[36]
The nature of these reactions to Mondrian's changed attitude to art make it abundantly clear that Mondrian had finally cut all the ties with those circles who had played, until about 1907, a dominant role in shaping his image of himself as an artist and, by extension, of his ideas on the role of art in society. The break manifested itself on nearly all social levels, and had far-reaching consequences for the development of the ideas that Mondrian was later to put forward concerning the role of the artist.

II "Toward the true vision of reality"

Of course Mondrian did not stand alone in his approach to painting: he was not the only artist to paint in a way that was directly opposed to the prevailing ideas about what a work of art should look like. In fact, since the appearance of Symbolism in the Netherlands in the 1890s, there had emerged a small group of artists who paid more attention to what was happening in Paris and Brussels, than to the situation of art at home, dominated as it was by the Hague School. Indeed, their rejection of the norms and standards of this great landscape school was in the first place a rejection of every form of nationalism as an artistic norm, leading to the rethinking of the really autonomous basis of art.
The small group of artists joined to form the "Moderne Kunstkring", whose members were not quite sure exactly which direction art should take, but who were nonetheless all convinced that art needed a much broader basis.[37]
They also agreed that a new type of artist was needed, as Toorop was reported to have said at the opening of the group's first exhibition: "He [Toorop] spoke on his own behalf, also on behalf of those who are convinced, like him, that only from a deeper and stronger understanding of the Eternal can the great, glad, strong soul and life-enhancing beauty be born, which the whole world sorely needs. He said that art can never become great, beautiful and holy as long as the artist as a man is small, un-beautiful and selfish."[38] For Toorop the basis of his art, since his conversion to Roman Catholicism in 1905, lay in his religious faith; his art was directly derived from that. For Mondrian his art was not connected with any particular religious conviction, for it transcended every religion in that the artist had a special mission to perform, namely to observe the most objective reality which underlies all its manifestations, and which determines all human thought and action. The artist (i.e. Mondrian) is merely one of the few who are capable of drawing aside the veils concealing life and who can give insight into the true evolution of man. Mondrian referred to this sense of mission as an artist time and again later on in his life, in his writings on a new aesthetic, the aesthetic philosophy of the future. Such notions about the avant-garde role of the artist had been expressed by socialist-utopians since the 1820s, and eventually became widespread among the artists who concerned themselves with the renewal of art.[39] In Mondrian's thinking, the principles of the new art did not lie primarily in the social role of art, but within the actual basis of art. However, the objective reality upon which art is based must necessarily also constitute the basis upon which the other arts, and also society as a whole, should rest. Mondrian's starting points are rooted in his belief in man's unification with the secular world *and* with the celestial spheres.
It is not surprising that Mondrian wished to found his religious convictions on as broad a basis as possible, in reaction to the severe and restricted dogmas with which he had been brought up. He therefore looked to the ideas that had, for centuries past, constituted the core of the aesthetic experience of poets and artists. Throughout the middle ages, from the Renaissance to the nineteenth century, we come across the Neo-Platonic theories concerning absolute beauty and pure light. But these could only be achieved in an ecstatic perception of the ultimate truths, and moreover only in a paradisal situation which would never be attainable in the secular world.
Mondrian came into contact with these ideas in several ways. An important contribution to the development of his thinking was undoubtedly the theosophical movement, but not to such an extent that Mondrian's art could be wholly explained by the principles or symbols of Theosophy.[40] Mondrian's symbols nearly all relate to eternity and transience, i.e. they were the same as those which were employed by many artists before him and also after him.[41]
I will return to this subject in more detail later in this essay. Until about 1912 Mondrian employed these symbols in the usual manner, i.e. a church represented eternity etc. Around this time Mondrian started asking himself not only how he should organize a painting, but even more what the meaning of the painting should be. In other words: Mondrian was not concerned with destroying the traditional kind of painting that refers to a reality outside the painting, nature for instance, or to a historical event, and with replacing it with a kind of art that refers only to itself.
On the contrary, Mondrian was concerned with finding a basis for art which would be broader, all-encompassing, greater, and which would refer more to universal truth than the traditional painting. Also the meaning, the symbols thus undergo a fundamental change. The "system" that Mondrian developed as the most universal is based on the horizontal and vertical line. Every conceivable pair of concepts that is felt to contain a universal opposition can be related to the opposition between horizontal and vertical. During the entire nineteenth century the need was felt to develop a scientifically-based aestheticism.[42] This need was most clearly expressed in the widely-read work of Charles Blanc *Grammaire des Arts du dessin* (1867). Blanc based his theories for a great deal on the writings of the first director of the Print Room at the University of Leiden, Humbert de Superville (1770-1849).[43]
In his study entitled *Essai sur les signes inconditionnels dans l'art* (Leiden, C.C. van der Hoek, 1827-1832), Humbert de Superville evolved a universally valid system of signs based on *le sentiment*, i.e. *conscience de soi-même*. The opening lines of this treatise provide the basis for all Humbert's ideas: «L'homme est droit et tourné vers le ciel. Il est droit, parce que l'axe de son corps en longueur, prolongement d'un rayon de notre globe, est perpendiculaire au plan d'horizon. Il est tourné vers le ciel, parce que la direction de cet axe lui indique le Zénith précisément au dessus du sommet de la tête: deux caractères contenus implicitement l'un dans l'autre, et rigoureusement distinctifs.
C'est donc, comme du centre de la terre que l'Homme semble s'élever jusqu'à la voûte des cieux, et remplir tout l'entre-deux de ses extrêmes. Sa force et sa dignité physiques, résultantes de sa marche droite, deviennent comme les garants de sa force et de sa dignité morales, et voilà tout l'Homme compris dans l'expression de son propre Axe, seule et unique

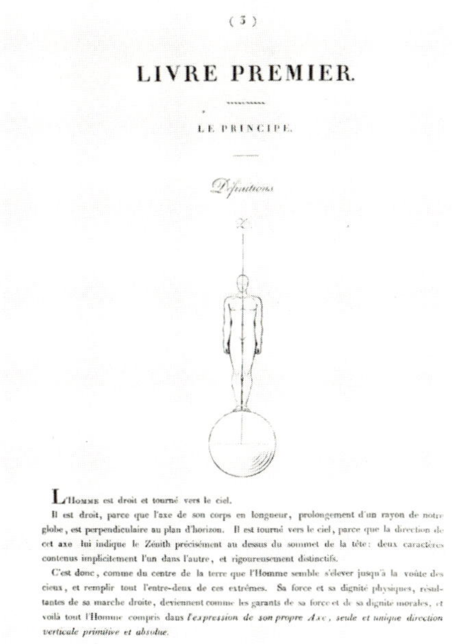
(3)

LIVRE PREMIER.

LE PRINCIPE.

Définitions

L'Homme est droit et tourné vers le ciel.

Il est droit, parce que l'axe de son corps en longueur, prolongement d'un rayon de notre globe, est perpendiculaire au plan d'horizon. Il est tourné vers le ciel, parce que la direction de cet axe lui indique le Zénith précisément au dessus du sommet de la tête: deux caractères contenus implicitement l'un dans l'autre, et rigoureusement distinctifs.

C'est donc, comme du centre de la terre que l'Homme semble s'élever jusqu'à la voûte des cieux, et remplir tout l'entre-deux de ces extrêmes. Sa force et sa dignité physiques, résultantes de sa marche droite, deviennent comme les garants de sa force et de sa dignité morales, et voilà tout l'Homme compris dans *l'expression de son propre Axe, seule et unique direction verticale primitive et absolue.*

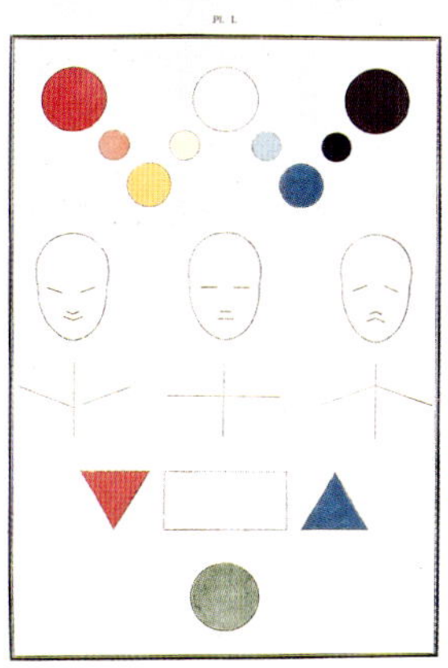

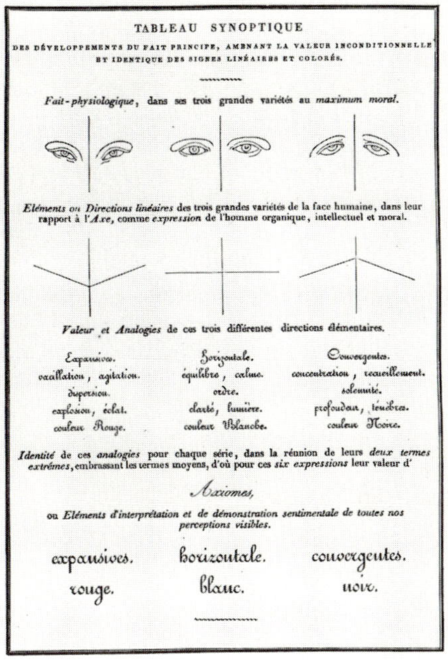
TABLEAU SYNOPTIQUE

DES DÉVELOPPEMENTS DU FAIT PRINCIPE, AMENANT LA VALEUR INCONDITIONNELLE ET IDENTIQUE DES SIGNES LINÉAIRES ET COLORÉS.

Fait-physiologique, dans ses trois grandes variétés au *maximum moral.*

Eléments ou Directions linéaires des trois grandes variétés de la face humaine, dans leur rapport à l'*Axe*, comme *expression* de l'homme organique, intellectuel et moral.

Valeur et Analogies de ces trois différentes directions élémentaires.

Expansives.	Horizontale.	Convergentes.
vacillation, agitation.	équilibre, calme.	concentration, recueillement.
dispersion.	ordre.	solennité.
explosion, éclat.	clarté, lumière.	profondeur, ténèbres.
couleur Rouge.	couleur Blanche.	couleur Noire.

Identité de ces *analogies* pour chaque série, dans la réunion de leurs *deux termes extrêmes*, embrassant les termes moyens, d'où pour ces *six expressions* leur valeur d'

Axiomes,

ou *Eléments d'interprétation et de démonstration sentimentale de toutes nos perceptions visibles.*

expansives.	horizontale.	convergentes.
rouge.	blanc.	noir.

Three illustrations from D.G.B. Humbert de Superville, 'Essai sur les signes inconditionelles dans l'art', 1827-32.

direction verticale primitive et absolue.»[44] The vertical line is accompanied by another constant sign: the horizontal. The numerous lines that are possible between these two extremes either follow an upward direction (approaching the vertical) or a downward direction (approaching the horizontal). Such lines are a sign of unstable expression, in facial expressions they are a sign of happiness or sadness. Only the perpendicularly placed horizontal and vertical are a sign of complete eqilibrium, and of divine inner harmony. Humbert illustrates this with examples of facial expressions. In the same way Humbert approaches the constancy of the expression of colours and planes. The two figures shown here clarify the correlation between colour, line and plane, as well as their external expressive value.

So there is a considerable correspondence between the thinking of Humbert de Superville and that of Mondrian, as is further demonstrated in the following description of a moonlit night—a theme Mondrian treated in several paintings;

«Gardons-nous donc, pour en revenir au grand spectacle de la nature, de comprendre un seul instant la Lune dans celui du firmament. Disque périodique et changeant, mais trahissant toujours dans toutes des apparitions le cercle limité dans l'espace, la Lune dépare les cieux et n'embellit fortuitement que la terre, où les objets qu'elle éclaire faiblement et les ombres qu'elle leur fait projeter prennent une teinte mystérieuse, avec laquelle sympathise l'âme sensible, sans l'élever néanmoins jamais au dessus d'une sensualité épurée, ou la porter au delà d'une vague mélancolie; et plus d'une femme aimable, se consultant de bonne foi elle-même dans ces moments, se trouverait fort embarrassée pour rattacher au Ciel les sensations et l'espèce d'émotion qu'elle éprouve alors. Cause d'effets et d'applications en définitive donc toujours matériels et terrestres, c'est la Lune, ou tout autre corps errant semblable, qui a sans doute inspiré le premier culte. Cause d'effets toujours exclusivement sursensibles, c'est le Firmament ou ciel uniquement étoilé, dont les ténèbres solennellement visibles ont fait placer le trône de celui qui est sans commencement et sans fin au centre de l'inaccessible solitude des ténèbres sans limites.»[45]

The main difference between de Superville's and Mondrian's "system", however, is that Mondrian sees the basis of the union of his art with the universal truths as contained in the relationship between two extremes, i.e. in a dynamic equilibrium, and not in the static equilibrium proposed by Humbert.[46]

A large number of Mondrian's paintings and much of his thinking is directly traceable to important aspects of Neo-Platonic thought that he encountered in the theosophical movement, and also in the writings of Humbert de Superville.[47]

Mondrian's thoughts on art are characterized on the one hand by a high degree of spiritualization, introversion of art, and on the other hand by his claim that he applied the most universal and therefore truest laws that exist. I have used the term "laws", but perhaps "principles" would be a better word, because the use of "laws" suggests that Mondrian believed in the laws of mathematics as providing the basis of art, which would be entirely incorrect. On the contrary, that most elusive property, which is exclusive to only a few chosen initiates—intuition—provided the basis of Mondrian's art: "Intuition always finds the way of progress, which is continuous growth toward a clearer establishment of the content of art: the unification of man with the universe."[48]

Mondrian started writing down these ideas in about 1911, initially in the form of personal notes, and later on for publication.[49]

In the same years that Mondrian was recording his ideas on art and in the course of doing so developing them further, his painting was passing through a highly critical phase, during which the individual painting no longer led spontaneously to a follow-up work. We do not know whether Mondrian already wrote about art before his personal involvement with art became problematical to him: very few written documents by Mondrian dating from that early period survive. Still, many of his early works show clearly that he was deeply concerned with the fundamentals and content of art.

Eternity and transience are the two concepts that constitute the recurrent theme in the work of Mondrian. In the painting *Thy Word is Truth* (Psalms, 119: 160) and in the originally legible text taken from Romans 8:38, it is clear that all the symbols that compose the "still life" refer to the Christian message of salvation from the trials of wordly life by the intervention of the Almighty.[50]

A similar kind of symbolism is contained in the work known as Spring Idyll (ca.1899).

And the same starting points are to be seen, once again, in a few still lifes that Mondrian made in roughly the same period, i.e. ca.1902. The half cut and peeled orange, the satin-flowers and the mirrored reflections are the symbols of the transience of all wordly things. This becomes even more obvious if we examine the other still life.[50a]

The question imposes itself here whether this work should be qualified as a still life at all. Of course the painting does show an arrangement of various objects, such as thistles, satin-flowers, a peacock feather and a polished metal dish. But in the centre of the composition stands a plaster cast placed "en profile". All the objects in the composition appear to gravitate towards the bust. The light comes from above (the source is not in view) and illuminates the face of the bust, while the left-hand side of the face is to be seen as a distorted reflection in the dish. Due to the manner of illumination, which creates strong light-and-shade contrasts and emphasizes the modelling of the bust, the viewer's attention is inexorably drawn to the determined stance of the eyes.[51] All this creates the impression of a painting that is not a still life in the usual sense of the word, but rather a portrait. The objects grouped around the portrayed figure serve to clarify the artist's specific intentions in painting this portrait, rather than to express a meaning independently from the bust. Before going any further it is necessary to know who the figure portrayed as a bust actually was, and why he was important to Mondrian.

As we have seen in the first section of this essay, a considerable part of the training at the Rijksakademie consisted in making drawings of plaster casts. Ever since 1881 the Rijksakademie had allocated part of its rather restricted budget to the purchase of plaster casts of the most famous statues in the European history of art, ranging from Greek and Roman statues to the most famous examples of Dutch seventeenth-century sculpture. These heads were used for the art students to practise drawing, but they also served as models for the examination of candidates for the drawing teacher's diploma. It is very likely that Mondrian first set eyes on this bust when he sat for his M1-examination, since it was very often used for these candidates to draw because of its universally praised high quality.[52] In the report of the examinations held in the year 1886 the candidates' assignments were described as follows: "Mr. Dysselhof of Amsterdam has produced a number of pen-drawings of the heads, ornaments and some of the still lifes that were given as examples to the candidates. We are pleased that the pen drawings and the reproductions have turned out so well that we are able to offer the readers of our journal two plates of excellent quality. The candidates for M1 were requested to draw one of the heads E, G, two outstanding casts of Italian sculptures dating from the late fifteenth century. To carry out the assignment the candidates were allowed two days (three hours in the morning, and three in the afternoon)."[53] "Head G" is the bust we are concerned with here. The above excerpt shows that the identity of the portrayed figure was not known at the time. But a few years later the man's identity was established in a publication by R. Becker. Not only was it now known in Amsterdam who the man was, also that the statue was not a magnificent Quattrocento bust as had been assumed, but a work by the Italian sculptor Bastianini (1830-1868), which had been "discovered" by an art dealer in Paris in 1864 as being an indisputably original work of the Italian Renaissance and which had been sold as such to the Louvre in 1866.[54] The following year an art dealer in Florence, by the name of Freppa, declared that he personally had commissioned Bastianini to make this portrait bust in 1864. Comte de Nieuwerkerke, the minister responsible for the purchase, who was convinced by the high quality of the bronze bust that it was an original fifteenth-century work, challenged Bastianini to prove, by producing another bust, that he possessed sufficient talent to have created such a work. Bastianini complied with this request, and just before his death in 1868 the Louvre recognized the greatness of Bastianini's talent, and the bust was, from then on, considered his work.

The Florentine art dealer Freppa had commissioned Bastianini to make a bust of Girolamo Benivieni, by whose features Freppa had been struck when he saw a seventeenth-century engraved portrait of the man. To discover what Mondrian's intentions could have been in making such a portrait of Girolamo Benivieni it is necessary to know a little more about this poet and philosopher.

Girolamo Benivieni (1453-1542) was a Florentine gentleman of noble birth: he was a familiar figure in the circles of Lorenzo de Medici, and a good friend of the famous poets and philosophers of the day: Marsilio Ficino (1433-1499), Angelo Poliziano and Pico della Mirandola (1463-1494). He was a faithful supporter of Savonarola, whose treatise *De simplicitate vitae christianae* (On the Simplicity of Christian Life) he translated into Italian.[55] But Benivieni appears to have had the greatest affinity with Pico della Mirandola: at his own request he was buried under the same marble tablet as Pico in the S. Marco in Florence. Ficino and Pico della Mirandola were the leading representatives at the court of the Medicis of the revival of classical philosophy, in particular of the works of Plato and Plotin, which were also translated by Ficino. The influence that this group of poets and philosophers had on the artists of the day,

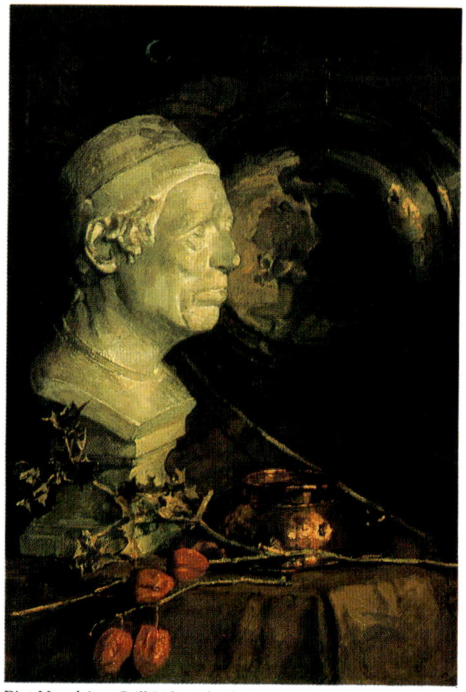

Piet Mondrian Still Life with plaster portrait of G. Benivieni ; 1902, oil on canvas, 73.5 × 61.5 cm; coll. Groninger Museum van Stad en Land.

G. Bastianini Portrait bust of G. Benivieni ; 1864, terracotta; coll. Louvre (Paris).

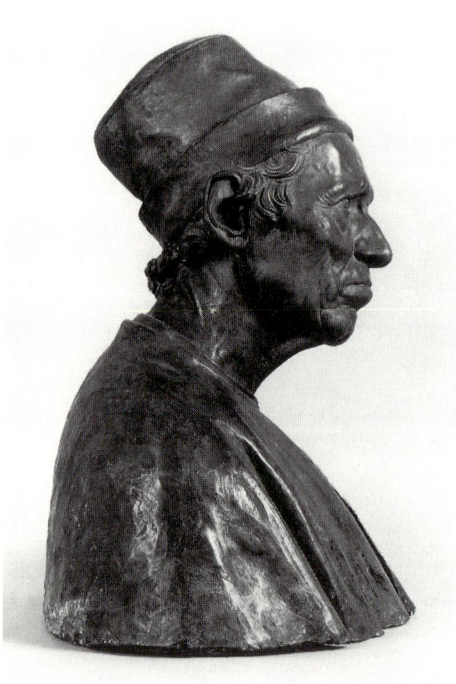

such as Botticelli, was considerable.[56]

Benivieni is generally characterized as a poet who wished to follow the great example of Dante and Petrarch. Some poems by him eulogizing the Neo-Platonic, divine and celestial love became famous because Pico della Mirandola discussed them at length in a written exposé of his philosophy. The poem *La canzone dell'Amor celeste divino col commento del Conte G. Pico* (Song of the Celestial and Divine Love with commentary by Count G. Pico della Mirandola), consisting of nine verses, describes how the divine love descends into the human soul and how the human soul aspires to the divine. The human soul ascends, via the lowest level of the sensual world, to the level of reason and eventually to that of the intellect (the highest level of knowledge that could be attained by the human mind) and was ultimately able to perceive the divine beauty of the universe.[57] As an illustration of Benivieni's way of thinking, a few verses from his poem are cited below, in the prose translation of S.J. Salchenberger:

"Stanza V

As the eternal mind has being, life, and understanding from the first good, so the soul understands, moves and shapes, unfolds and depicts through the [angelic mind] that sun which illuminates the divine breast [of the angelic mind]. Then, [the soul] scatters that which the pious breast [of the angelic mind] conceives and holds, and then that which moves and feels [i.e., potentially], moved marvellously through the soul, feels, lives, and brings about all its effects [i.e., actually]. As from the heaven [Venus is born] into the intellect, so from [the soul] Venus is born down here, whose beauty shines in the heavens, lives upon the earth, shadows the world. Just as the [celestial Venus] (who mirrors herself in the sun, in the shade of [the angel] who, because of her, accustoms himself to contemplation), takes all her riches from the living sun that shines in [the angel], so does she grant her light to this [Venus], and as celestial love depends on the former, so vulgar love follows the latter."

"Stanza VII

The heart feeds upon a sweet error, looking upon the beloved object within itself as upon its own offspring. Sometimes then re-forming it (a rare and celestial gift) in the divine light which is impressed within it, then raising itself from grade to grade, it returns to the uncreated sun, whence is formed that which is expressed in the beloved object. Through three fulgid mirrors one sun [coming] from the divine face itself rekindles all beauty that adorns the mind, the spirit, and the body. From here the eyes, then through the eyes where its other handmaid dwells, the heart takes the ornate wrappings [which have been] re-formed in [the handmaid],

Piet Mondrian, Ex-Libris for E.E. Seelig 'Strebe zum Licht'; lithograph, 8.6 × 11.7 cm; coll. J.P. Smid (Amsterdam).

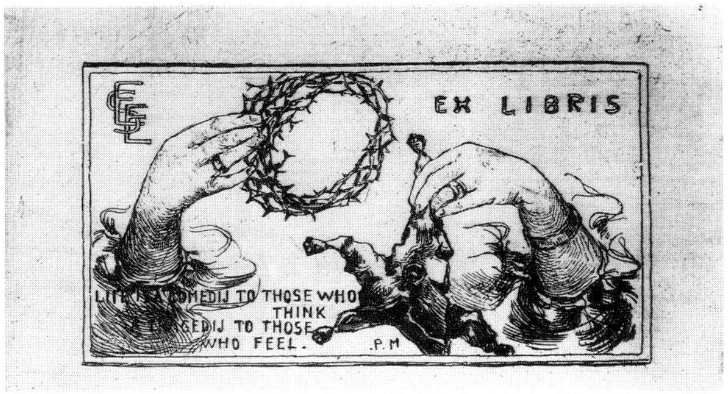

Piet Mondrian, Ex-Libris for E.E. Seelig 'Life is a comedy to those who think, a tragedy to those who feel'; etching, 17 × 8.8 cm; coll. J.P. Smid (Amsterdam).

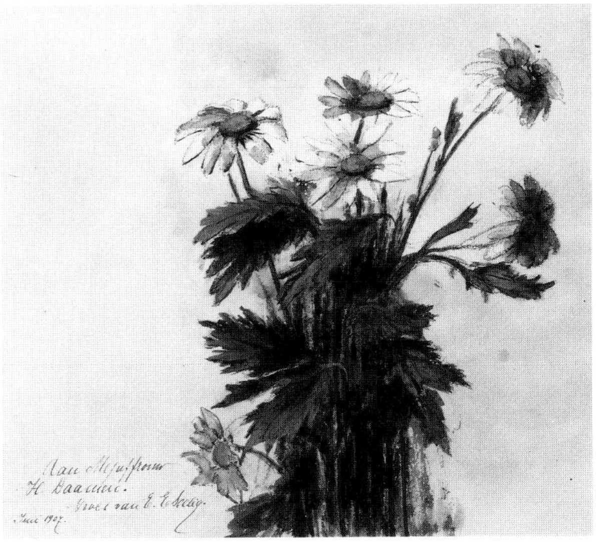

E.E. Seelig, Flowers ; pencil/watercolour; 23.2 × 26.5 cm, dated July 1907.

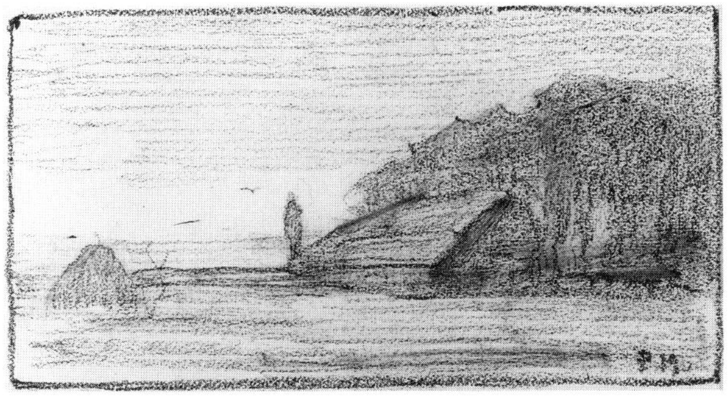

Piet Mondrian, Sheep pen ; 1907, drawing, 23.2 × 26.5 cm.

but not expressed; thence, of various and numerous beauties freed from the body, it forms a concept in which that which nature had divided into many it depicts and shapes into one."[58]

So much for Benivieni, who was much admired by Mondrian (his is symbolized by the peacock-feather in the "still life"). The painting is better described as a "homage to Girolamo Benivieni, poet of the divine light".[59] The painting was sold during an exhibition in the Amsterdam Arti society in 1903 for 200 guilders, to a lawyer by the name of Mr. W. Bakker G. Gz, himself an amateur artist who collected paintings and drawings. The only work by Bakker that I have been able to trace is a self-portrait in a mirror.[60]

How important the symbolic value of light was to Mondrian in the first decade of this century is further attested in a number of particularly handsome ex libris plates which he designed for one of his drawing students, Emmy Seelig.[60a] In one of them Emmy is shown sitting in the foreground, her face turned to the setting sun. The contact between Emmy Seelig and Mondrian is also documented in the visitors' book of a mutual acquaintance, in which Emmy Seelig made a beautiful drawing of flowers dated July 1907, and to which Mondrian contributed a good sketch of a "landscape with sheep-pen".

A work that may be described as a true "ode to the sun" is the landscape that is known by the title *Woods near Oele* (1908). Several naturalistic drawings of this subject are known—but how different they are to this ambitious painting. The full attention of the viewer is immediately drawn to the upper right of the painting. The paintstrokes hardly appear to represent more than simply that: of the tree only the vertical, uprising bare trunks are suggested; the details which are still very meticulously included in the drawings, have disappeared almost completely—they are only present at the crown of the trees, which are lit up by the bright sunlight. Especially remarkable is the foreground, which although it is supposed to serve as a *repoussoir*, is extremely interesting because of the almost complete autonomy of the brushstrokes which hardly even cover the surface of the canvas. In the small preparatory oil sketches Mondrian often made on location, he already demonstrated how he handled the paintbrush in a free-flowing, yet still disciplined, movement. In this work, however, the physicality of the action of painting seems to take over.

Another recurrent theme in the work of Mondrian is the "mill in the evening"—a theme that was, for obvious reasons, also very popular among the painters of the Hague School.[60b] In Mondrian's Mills—the enormous machines that dominated much of the Dutch landscape and towns at the beginning of this century—we are continually struck by the opposition between

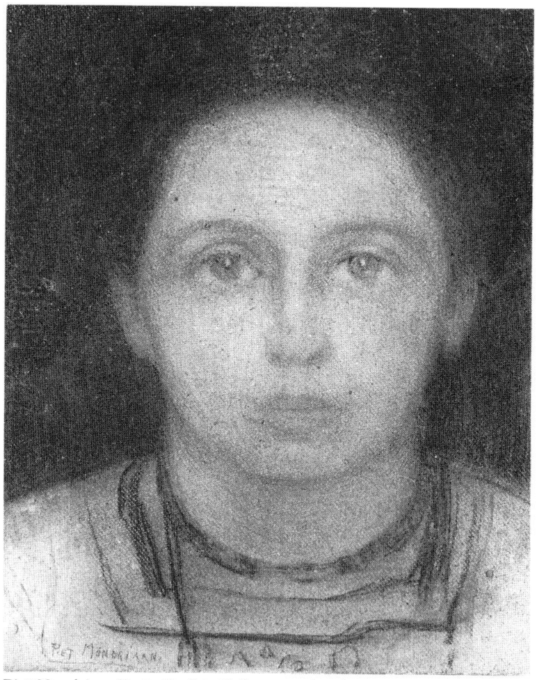

Piet Mondrian, Portrait of A. Zethraeus; drawing, 40×31cm; coll. National Museum (Stockholm).

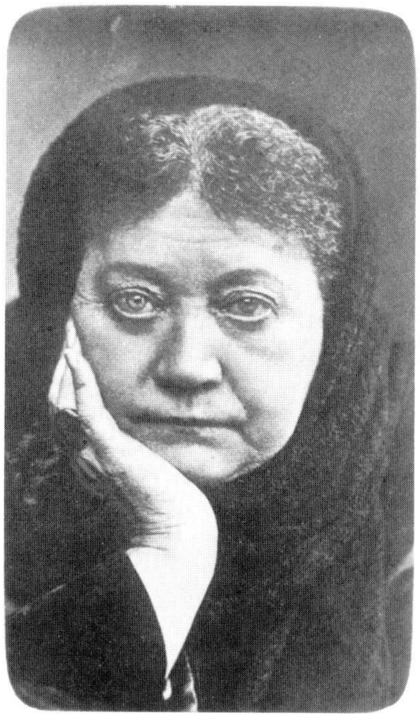
Portrait of H.P. Blavatsky (1831-1891).

the cross symbol formed by the vanes, symbolizing the unchanging, the everlasting, and the cyclical, constantly changing aspect of nature. Later, when Mondrian had abandoned the use of symbols, he also spoke out about this cross-symbolism, emphasizing that in the neoplastic works the intersecting lines should definitely not be interpreted as symbols; "Indeed: I find this windmill very beautiful. Particularly as we are too close to it now to view it in *normal perspective* and therefore cannot see it or draw it *normally*. From here it is very difficult merely to reproduce what one sees: one is compelled toward a *freer mode of representation*. In my early work, I tried repeatedly to represent things seen from close by, precisely because of the grandeur they then attain. At that time, in the case of the windmill, I was particularly struck by the cross formed by its arms. Now, however, I discerned the perpendicular in everything and the arms of the windmill are not more beautiful to me than anything else. *Seen plastically*, they actually have a disadvantage. To the shape of the cross, particularly when in the upright position, we readily attach particular, rather *literary* ideas. The cross form, however, is constantly destroyed in the New Plastic."[61]

And elsewhere he wrote: "Ancient wisdom represented the fundamental inward-outward relationship by the cross. Neither this *symbol*, however, nor any other symbol, can be the plastic means for abstract-real painting: the symbol constitutes a new limitation, on the one hand, and it is *too* absolute, on the other."[62]

Mondrian is here referring in particular to the so-called "Red Mill", a narrow vertical composition in which the severely schematized vanes become an almost abstract cross-symbol.[62a] As in the *Woods near Oele*, the attention is immediately focussed on this cross-symbol, which occupies roughly one quarter of the canvas, while the rest of the canvas is hardly detailed.

The same manner of composition and the same symbol of eternity lies at the basis of the "evolution triptych". Mondrian used the somewhat unusual form of the triptych to demonstrate his ideas: his intention was that the three parts should hang side by side, while the centre panel, which is slightly larger than the lateral ones, should hang slightly higher. This particular form of triptych, although essentially derived from the religious panel paintings of the Middle Ages, was entirely Mondrian's own invention, and are based on the importance he wished to give to the central panel.[63]

Another difference from the traditional form of the triptych is that the panels are intended to be "read" in the following order: first the one on the left, then the one on the right, while the central panel represents the "conclusion". In this way Mondrian further strengthened the symbolic intent, namely that the three panels represent ascending stages of "inner vision".

The central panel, however, addresses the viewer the most directly, thereby creating the impression that the two lateral panels are a somewhat literary complement to the central one. The two lateral panels are, more "natural-

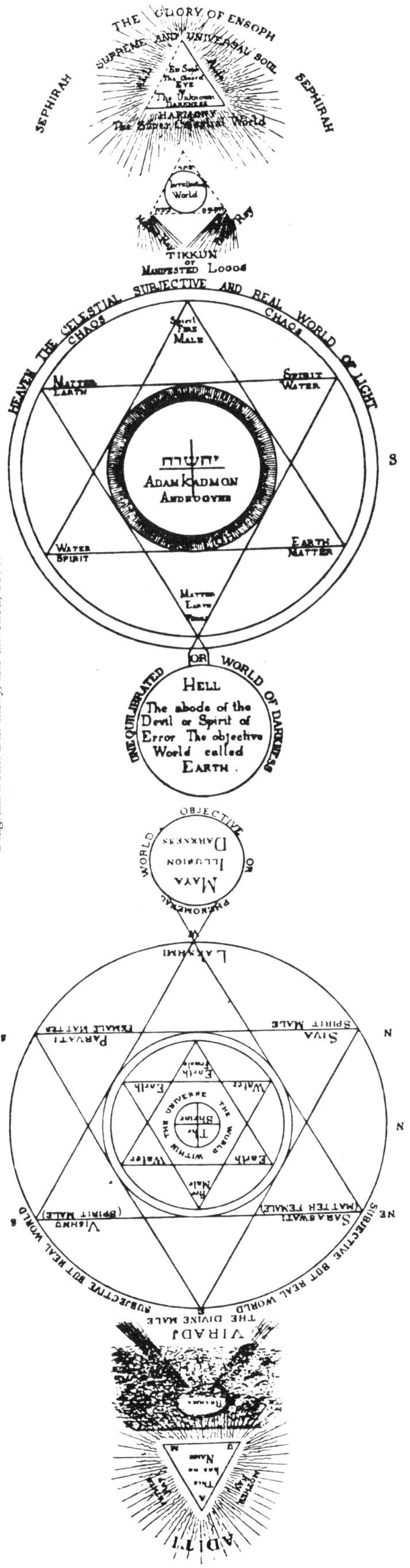

Diagram from: Blavatsky, Isis unveiled, 1877.

istic" than the central panel. For Mondrian had previously portrayed a female figure in combination with several symbols indicating inner spiritual concentration. The triptych as a whole is intended to symbolize the journey that the soul must make in its efforts to free itself from the material world (left panel), via inner contemplation (right panel) to the perception of the divine light, more or less in the same way Benivieni described in his poem. The symbols that Mondrian uses are to a large extent traceable to the theosophical diagrams of Madame Blavatsky, which she described as "representing the chaotic and the formative periods, before and after pure universe began to be evolved. From the esoteric brahmanical, buddhistic and chaldean standpoints, which agree in every respect with the evolutionary theory of modern science."[64] But Mondrian also encountered the ideas about the perception of the divine in Schuré's *Les Grands Initiés*, a book he kept and read throughout his life. The fact that Mondrian chose a female figure to personify these symbolic truths is not so surprising when it is remembered that the Greeks—"the ancients" as he often referred to them—attributed the power to communicate with the divine to the priestesses in particular. The initiates are those who are able to perceive the ecstatic understanding of the mysteries, the "epopteia": «Les initiés apprenaient que la divine Perséphône, qu'ils avaient vue au milieu des terreurs et des supplices des Enfers, était l'image de l'âme humaine enchaînée à la matière dans cette vie, ou livrée dans l'autre à des chimères et à des tourments plus grands encore, si elle a vécu esclave de ses passions. Sa vie terrestre est une expiation ou une épreuve d'existences précédentes. Mais l'âme peut se purifier par la discipline, elle peut se souvenir et pressentir par l'effort combiné de l'intuition, de la raison et de la volonté et participer d'avance aux vastes vérités dont elle doit prendre possession pleine et entière dans l'immense au-delà. Alors seulement Perséphône redeviendra la pure, la lumineuse, la Vierge ineffable, dispensatrice de l'amour et de la joie.—Quant à sa mère Cérès, elle était, dans les mystères, le symbole de l'intelligence divine et du principe intellectuel de l'homme, que l'âme doit rejoindre pour atteindre sa perfection.»[65]

As so often in Mondrian's œuvre we are here confronted with several works which—as far as the plastic form is concerned—are closely related to the triptych. In a study of a nude we encounter the same attitude of the arms and concentration on the face, while in the "Passionflower" we find the attitude of the head and the symbolic flowers beside the female figure, who is this time dressed. The same angle of the head is also to be seen in a watercolour portrait-study. A drawing that Mondrian made of a

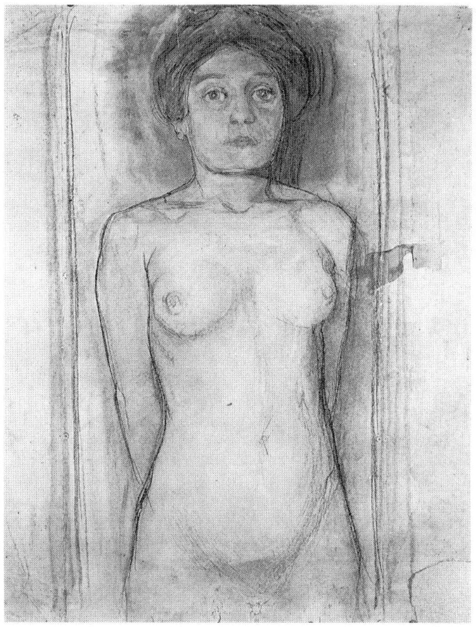

Piet Mondrian, Study of a Female Nude; drawing, 86 × 42 cm; coll. Haags Gemeentemuseum.

Piet Mondrian, Passionflower; 1908-09, watercolour/ink; 72.5 × 47.5 cm; coll. Haags Gemeentemuseum.

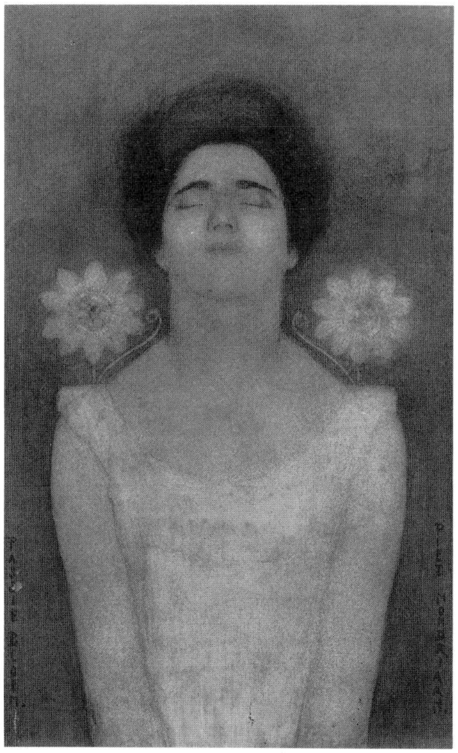

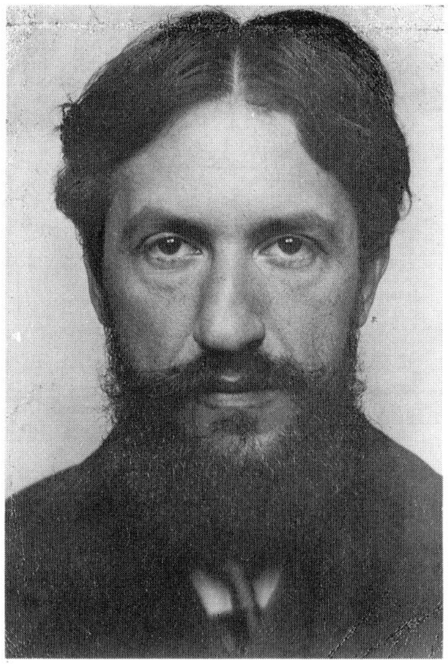

Piet Mondrian, Photographic Self-Portrait, 1908.

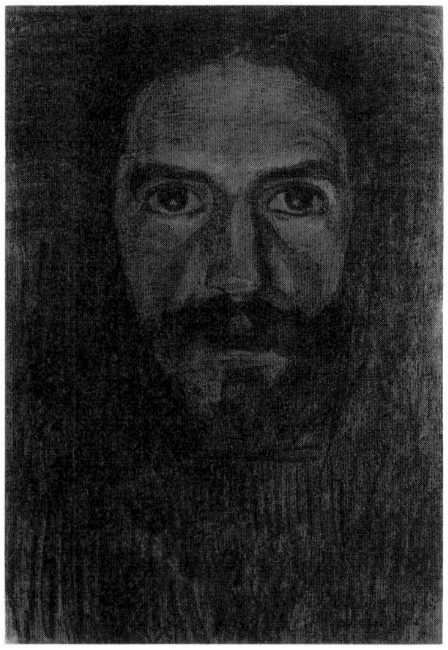

Piet Mondrian, Self-Portrait; drawing, 79.5 × 53 cm; coll. Haags Gemeentemuseum.

Jan Toorop, Portrait of Christ; 1912, lithograph, 50 × 36.5 cm.

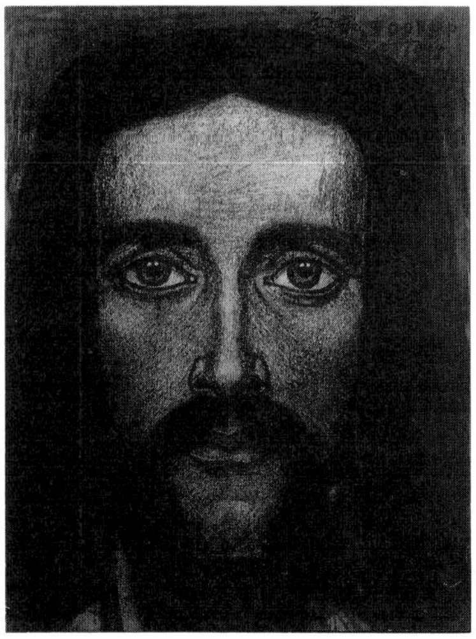

shall go there in January."[69b] A few days later, however, Mondrian decided to persevere in his attempts to realize his ideas: "I simply could not come to terms with my decision to accept my friend Van Eck's offer. I had already decided, as you said, but I have changed my mind. I would rather lead an uncertain existence here than an easier life there in the south. When I had decided this (i.e. to stay) I visited Rosenberg again. He told me that I should certainly be able to sell my work in the future, and that I was his greatest artist. It was a matter of persevering, just like during the war."[70] Mondrian is here referring to the uncertainties facing him at the time when he painted the self-portrait. The aforementioned article in *De Stijl*, in which he accuses his fellow artists of weakness, included a photograph of him in his studio which, as far as pictorial structure is concerned, bears a striking resemblance to the self-portrait; it assumes even greater significance when compared with the self-portrait painted by Max Liebermann (1847-1935) in 1909-1910 likewise at a time when the maker was uncertain about his possibilities as an artist.[71]

The role of the artist as set forth in Mondrian's writings is especially analogous to the first group of self-portraits discussed above. As we have seen, the role of the artist is a key concept in Mondrian's theories. The artist, i.e. Mondrian himself, is he who, after lengthy and tortuous searching, ultimately discovers a little of "the" truth. What is particularly remarkable about Mondrian's theories concerning the position of his own art is not so much that Mondrian saw his own paintings as the culmination of all art, but rather that he saw them as part of an uninterrupted flow of development.

The historical importance claimed by Mondrian in the development of art is critical: after all it is he who, as an "instrument" of his time, succeeded in exposing and visualizing the great truths underlying all art more clearly than any other artist before him. The artists who succeeded him would indeed need to do little other than give a personal rendering of the "system" discovered by Mondrian.[72] An essential point is that he found, in his *Nieuwe Beelding* (neo-plasticism), that law, i.e. in the Neo-Platonic sense that one truth that underlies the exterior world (nature) and the world of the soul: "Formerly one only perceived either the outward or the inward: the world was divided into the profane and the (so-called) believers. Modern man, however, is capable of seeing the inward in equilibrium with the outward, and conversely: through relationship he knows both opposites. Precisely in this way, truly modern man sees things *as a whole* and accepts *life in its wholeness*: nature and spirit, world and faith, art and religion—man and god, as *unity*."[73]

Mondrian explains this further in a letter to Arnold Saalborn: "I think the ordinary human being seeks beauty in material life, but I believe the artist should not do this. He should wish for nothing from the material world: he must be alone and stand alone. He must create on a level that is immaterial: that of the intellect. And if he simply obeys that creative urge, and keeps himself as free as possible for that purpose, he is doing enough. And as a consequence he will mean very much to mankind. I am rereading what you wrote on that subject: being alone is very wrong, especially for the great and noble among us. I must state here that I should maintain the opposite. Being alone means (to the *great*) turning to the inner self, to self-knowledge, knowledge of humanity, of the man-god and the divine, ultimately. So this amounts to growing greater, more conscious—and in the end to reach the divine. How could this ever be wrong? But perhaps I have read your intentions wrongly, and so I think it is best if we have another talk on the subject at some time in the future."[74] By searching his soul and meditating, therefore, the artist could come into contact with that one universal truth. At about the same time that this letter was written, probably around 1910, Mondrian practised meditation techniques on the beach in Domburg: "Do you recall how beautiful it was, and funny old Mondrian sitting in his Buddha positions in the middle of the beach?"[75]

In the ancient world it was a prerogative of kings, priests and those who had been initiated into the mysteries of the universe to perceive the eternal truth and to act accordingly. The masses followed these spiritual leaders, and after the death of one of these initiates the masses disintegrated into individuality, until a new "initiate" arose to give form to the "universal" truth. In Mondrian's view this knowledge of the universal truth was passed on in the course of time by high-ranking men down to the broader levels of society, which would explain why Mondrian himself with his middle-class background was capable of transmitting these great truths further. This reflects a democratic orientation in Mondrian's thinking that is closely related to his conception of the position of art in society and also to his idea that art, although in the vanguard of the development of mankind, would ultimately (i.e. thousands of years hence) no longer exist, for art and life would be identical in the paradise on earth that man would create for himself.[76]

From about 1908 onwards a recurrent theme in private conversations as well as in his writings was that art is not just another occupation that anyone can pursue so long as he receives proper training. Mondrian was not satisfied with the bourgeois notion that art is merely a peripheral phenomenon in the history of man. Perhaps he

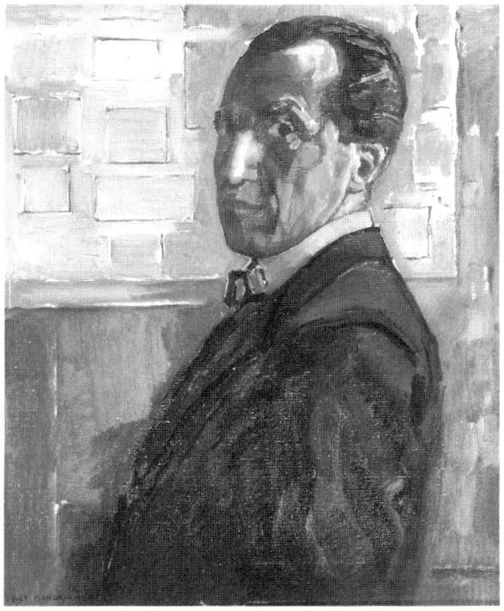

Piet Mondrian, Self-Portrait; 1918, oil on canvas, 88 × 71 cm; coll. Haags Gemeentemuseum.

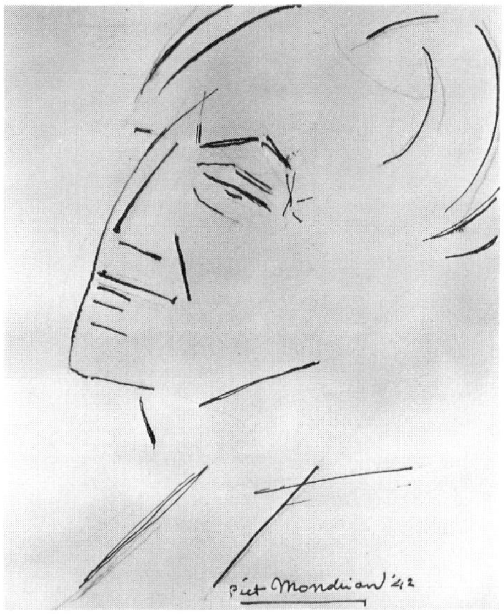

Piet Mondrian, Self-Portrait; 1942, drawing, 29.8 × 22.8 cm.

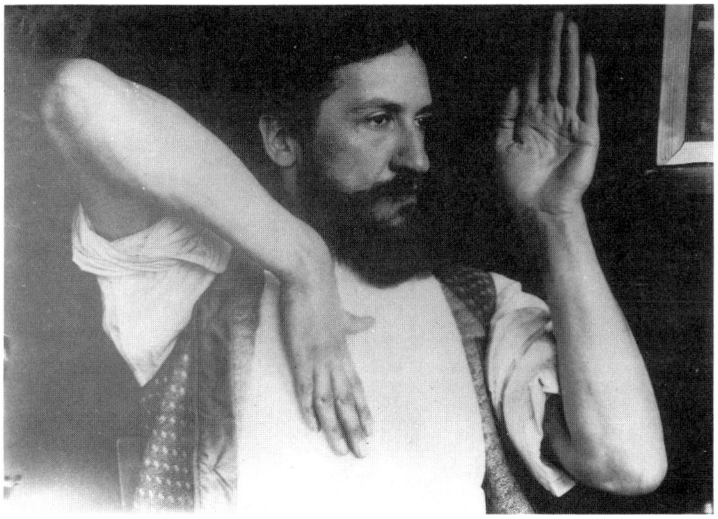

Mondrian meditating, 1909.

Mondrian in his studio, 1922 (published in De Stijl, 1924).

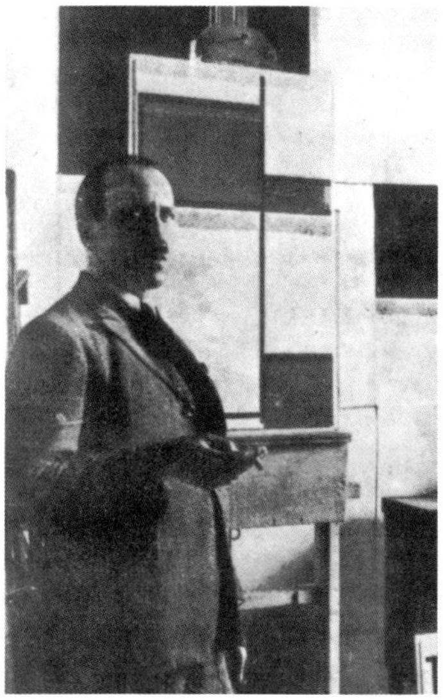

M. Liebermann, Self-Portrait; 1909/10, oil on canvas, 112 × 92.5 cm; coll. Kunsthalle (Hamburg).

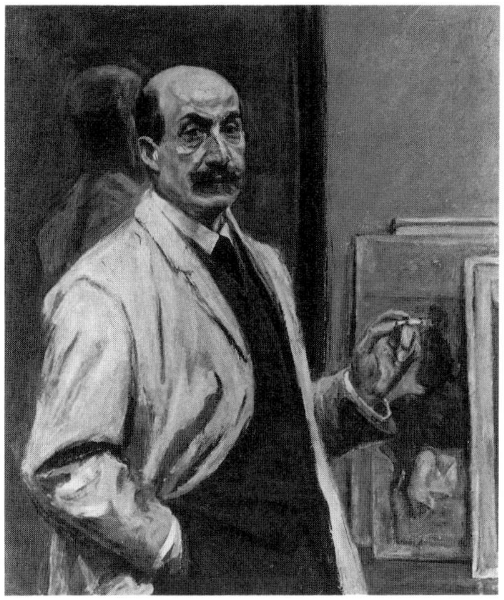

was over-reacting somewhat when he posited that art, and more especially the artist, is not only unique but also the sole possible leader of mankind. The importance that was formerly attributed to the great philosophers is now attached to the artist. Mondrian himself frequently used images that had always been associated with the great importance of philosophical thinking in the past. In an etching that must date from the same period as the ex-libris plates, i.e. around 1908, Mondrian re-emphasizes that the man of wisdom is able to raise himself above the level of everyday occurrences and thus to concentrate wholly on more elevated matters: "Life is a comedy to those who think, a tragedy to those who feel." This quote from Horace Walpole (1717-1797) may be seen as the starting point of Mondrian's writings on art, and was elaborated some ten years later by Mondrian in a somewhat literary piece of prose published under the title "De groote boulevards" (The Great Boulevards, 1902).[77]

«Les grands boulevards», the French expression which Mondrian translated rather prosaically and literally into Dutch, represented to Mondrian the theatre of the world, a metaphor for life. In short sentences he tried to give an impression of the tremendous confusion of exceptional phenomena: the text is interspersed with remarks intimating that only those who are able to detach themselves from the exceptional are able to perceive the universal truth underlying all these phenomena: "To annihilate the particular is to achieve unity, say the philosophers." Mondrian's painting is ahead of society, for: "An image images something: colour and form alone image something—what? Where is truth in truth?—the particular disappears in the plastic image; does it in society too? The plastic image can be a bit ahead of us." And it is the artist who is capable of liberating himself from the confines of detail: "The artist gives the universal universality." The boulevard, which swallows up all and everyone, inspires the artist-philosopher to reflect on the universal truths: "The boulevard is more concentrated. [...] The boulevard is the physical turning outward and the spiritual turning inward." The boulevard, as part of the city, is one of the most advanced manifestations of the development of the human intellect, and it is to be preferred above nature, it is an initial step on the path that humanity must, according to Mondrian, travel in order to attain the unification of art and life: "On the boulevard there is already much artifice, but it is not yet 'art'." Mondrian wrote this brief impression of the role he envisaged for himself as an artist, a few months after returning to Paris from his native country, where he spent the war years during which he laid the foundations for his new art. The impressions that the main arteries of a city can make on an artist are reflected in the work of French painters of the nineteenth century, but also in statements based on largely the same ideas as Mondrian's. Fantin-Latour (1836-1904), who came from the provincial town of Grenoble and settled in Paris in 1854, also stressed the transitory and sensory impressions of the street, and how difficult it is for the artist to resist being diverted by them from his purpose: "I desire everything here, in this Parisian life—it is a woman going by, it is a horse galloping, it is a carriage rolling along: here are all the vanities which prevent me from pursuing my studies, and from putting myself into making a serious study of all I do not know."[78] Anton Chekhov refers to the same theme in *The Seagull* of 1895. In that play Dorn, a doctor who often plays the role of philosopher and interpreter of Chekhov's own ideas on life and art, describes his reasons for liking the city of Genoa as follows:

"Medviedenko: If I might ask you, Doctor, which city do you like best of all those you've seen abroad?

Dorn: Genoa.

Trepliov: Why Genoa?

Dorn: Because there's something very fine about the street crowds there. You go out of your hotel at night, and the whole street is packed with people. You just wander among them aimlessly, anywhere you like, up and down, you live with them, become part of the crowd spiritually, and you end by almost believing that a world-soul can really exist—something like the world-soul in your play, the one Nina Zaryechnaia acted in some time back."[79]

In the passage Dorn is referring to here Chekhov uses a metaphor that is traceable to Plato's Simile of the Cave in his *Republic*; there he characterizes the unique role of the philosopher as the only human being capable of escaping the illusions of the world and hence of seeking the eternal truth.[80] Chekhov uses the image of a well instead of the cave: "Like a prisoner cast into a deep and empty well, I know not where I am, or what awaits me here. All I know is that I am destined to struggle with the Devil, and in cruel and stubborn battle to conquer the principle of material force, after which matter and spirit will merge in beautiful harmony and the Kingdom of Cosmic Will will come into being. But this will only happen after a long succession of millennia during which time the moon, bright Sirius, and this earth will have been gradually turned to dust. Until then horror, horror..."[81]

In Plato's view the philosopher had to return to the cave, i.e. to the world of illusions where he had to guide his fellow prisoners, even though the notion might seem abhorrent to him. Chekhov, however, saw the struggle that was to culminate in the eternal harmony of matter and spirit as lasting thousands of years, but as ultimately successful. Mondrian uses both images. On the one hand he as an artist occupies the same position as the philosopher in Plato's thinking, on the other hand Mondrian is just as sure of the realization of his "super-realistic" world as Chekhov. In an article written in 1930, Mondrian once more expressed his unshakeable faith in his own art and in neo-plasticism as the only true path to the future paradise man shall create for himself.[82] Again Mondrian uses the old metaphor which is so characteristic of the creator of neo-plasticism: the struggle between light and dark:

«L'oppression de ce tragique—un sentiment de souffrance sans fin, nous le subissons à l'aube: émotion éprouvée par tout artiste et, en peinture, exprimée par le peintre paysagiste.

A l'aube, la nuit domine encore. La lumière faible essaye de la vaincre. On sent l'oppression du déséquilibre nuit-jour, clair-obscur. C'est l'aspiration vers l'équilibre. L'espoir-désespoir. L'absence de certitude. C'est l'attente du plein-jour: unité par équivalence de clarté et d'ombre. La nuit: le passé. Plein-jour: l'avenir—l'homme et la nature unifiés. Le présent: l'aube, la fin de la nuit. L'aube: l'évolution.

Toutefois, la nuit est quelquefois éclaircie par la lumière blafarde de la lune: reflet de la lumière du jour. Quelquefois même au point d'atteindre une harmonie féerique. Et c'est ainsi que nous devons comprendre les belles œuvres classiques du passé: comme autant de choses créées dans la lumière harmonieuse de pleine-lune. Leur création n'est pas possible dans la lumière du grand-jour. Que de telles œuvres puissent encore être produits aujourd'hui, à l'aube, c'est à cause du reflet de la nuit et que la conception du grand-jour n'est pas encore claire. Mais, comme la lumière artificielle vainc de plus en plus la nuit, l'homme du grand-jour la vaincra. La nuit: non représentable et sans expression plastique. Le jour: non représentable avec une expression plastique inexacte, confuse. Nuit-jour: nature, non représentable et avec une expression plastique inexacte, comment, en art, la suivre afin d'aboutir à une expression exacte, claire, qui exprime notre sensation et notre conception du grand-jour? Ne tâchons pas de la reproduire. Créons. En art, créons une expression plastique en opposition avec la forme de l'unité apparente nuit-jour. Car les formes variées elles-mêmes réalisent le tragique (le déséquilibre) que le grand jour palpable vainement tâche de vaincre et ne réussit qu'à neutraliser. La réalité de la forme, même au grand-jour, n'est pas réelle pour nous qui vivons dans un grand-jour de notre conception et d'un équilibre exact. Aucune forme même créée par l'homme ne réalise le vrai contenu du grand-jour, cet équilibre absolu. Sa réalisation la plus approximative, l'homme seulement la peut atteindre en créant une superréalité des rapports. Aujourd'hui à l'aube, vivons déjà par l'esprit au grand jour qui approche. A la fin de l'aube notre conception du grand-jour n'est plus un idéal spéculatif. Car la lumière, assez forte déjà, la réalise. Faisons déjà le travail du grand-jour—fortifiés par le sommeil du passé, rassasiés du tragique de l'aube. Attendons ainsi le grand-jour—l'avenir. Attendons notre maturité.»[83]

In the years between 1908 and 1920 Mondrian developed an image of the artist as he saw it, and as he wished to see himself. This comes to the fore in the drawings and paintings as well as in his writings. The artist is, in Mondrian's view, one of the few seers of the true reality, the most universal reality. Mondrian was not the only artist to entertain such thoughts. The portrait of Mondrian made by the photographer Arnold Newman in 1942 is once again similar in composition to the portraits that Mondrian made of himself around 1908, and indeed also shows him in the role of seer, of one of the "initiated". The portrait made by the Dutch photographer P. Huf of Vordemberge-Gildewart, an artist who had some affinity with Mondrian, has the same pictorial structure. Vordemberge too is seen in the role Mondrian envisaged for the artist: "Object-less art is engaged in clarifying the face of humanity in virtually all world problems, and in this light, one may describe Vordemberge-Gildewart as one of the most important 'illuminati' of our time, an eminent guide in the world of science, in particular the psychology of colour and metapsychology, inasmuch as the latter aspires to the status of science. The word 'art' has acquired a quite different meaning to that which it had in the pre-abstract period."[84] This image of the artist is, however, not exclusive to artists working in the abstract manner, it stands firmly in an age-old West-European tradition, as I have attempted to demonstrate in the above.

III The studio

After Mondrian had expounded his theories on neo-plasticism in the early issues of *De Stijl* in a philosophical, reflective manner, he summed up his ideas and how he arrived at them—partly as a response to various criticisms of his work and his ideas—in two colloquies. The second of these, which Mondrian called a "Trialogue", deals with Mondrian's own development from landscapist to designer of a wholly new architectural environment. This new environment was epitomized by Mondrian's studio.[85]

From the fifteenth century onwards paintings of artists' studios (usually those of painters) were an expression of the importance the artist attached to his art and to his theories on the foundation and meaning of art. This is particularly evident in the countless pictures of artists'

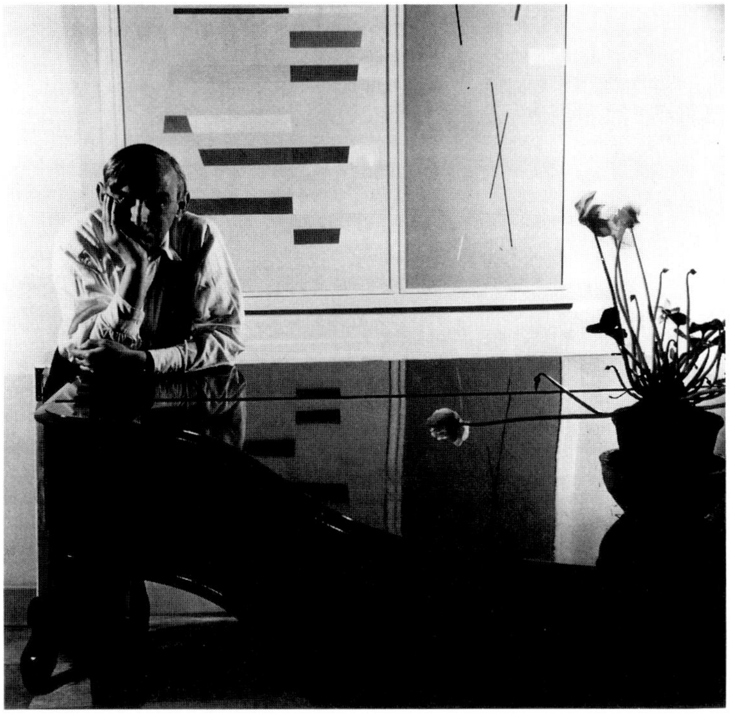

P. Huf, Portrait of the artist Vordemberge-Gildewart, 1948.

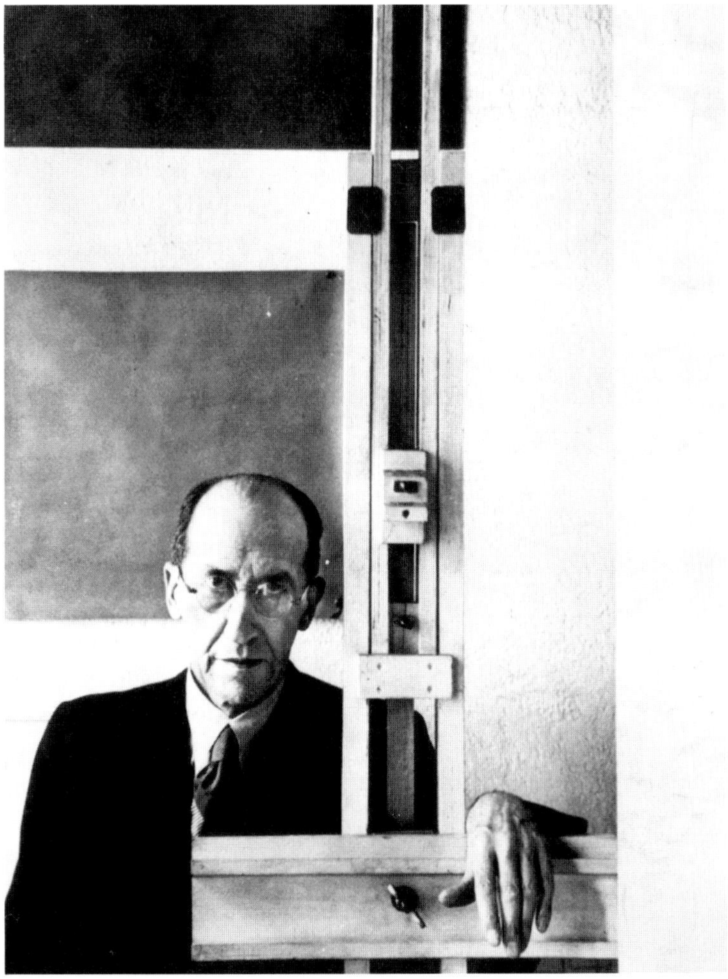

A. Newman, Portrait of P. Mondrian, 1942.

studios by the German Romantics, but the most outstanding example is undoubtedly the portrait Courbet painted of his studio as a manifesto of his relation to his art.[86]

Not only can paintings of studios epitomize the artist's relation to art in the widest sense, as in the case of Courbet, also the actual studio in which an artist lives and works can materialize his ideas. Goethe himself had already declared, in *Wilhelm Meisters Wanderjahre,* that artists should live like the kings and gods who are their patrons. In contrast with this, is the image of the ideal study as an island of peace in the midst of chaos—only in his cell could the artist be himself: »Hier bleibe es Ordnung, wenn die Unordnung draussen auch noch so gross wird.«[87] However, towards the end of the nineteenth century the artist's studio had become a large, appropriately appointed reception-room that accorded with the status of the artist.

So for Mondrian his studio represented a break with tradition, just as he had broken away from the traditional image of the artist. Undoubtedly Mondrian was thinking of his uncle Frits' studio in this description of the traditional painter's studio: "Most painters advance the cultivation of the old and like to surround themselves with antique furniture, old paintings, carpets and so on. [...] I think it's retardatory for an artist to work on a new concept of beauty and at the same time to turn his studio or house into a kind of museum of ancient art—and not usually of the best at that. This creates an atmosphere unsuited to the new, clinging to the old. The layman follows the example of the artist. The contemporary artist must go with his own time in everything. This studio gives something of the idea of the New Plastic."[88]

Indeed Uncle Frits had filled his studio with cupboards, carpets, furniture and pottery made in the heyday of the Golden Age—there again this reflected his own position as an artist of the Hague School, which was after all supposed to be the renaissance of that same Golden Age. In this way Frits Mondriaan's studio was a very truthful representation of his relation to art.

So the artist's studio constitutes the most favourable environment in which to view and appreciate a work of art. Consequently the studio, being where the artist makes his works of art, acquires a special significance. The greater the importance that is attached by the artist to the function of art and the artist within the development of human thought and action, the more important and special the studio becomes, since that is where the artist creates his unique contributions to culture.

Mondrian's studio is an excellent example. At a very early stage visitors to Mondrian's studio were impressed by its austerity, and some of them wrote about the striking difference between Mondrian's and most artists' studios [see:

At Piet Mondrian's three interview s page 24-33]. A correspondent of the newspaper *Het Vaderland* described his impression of Mondrian's studio as follows (this was at the time when Mondrian was publishing his views on the importance of the studio in *De Stijl*) "Close by the ancient ramparts (where the poorest of the poor pluck their spring flowers) is where Piet Mondrian lives. A street with picturesquely neglected gardens, a verdant courtyrad, a dark staircase—and the painter comes towards me in his overall. What a difference to Kees van Dongen's house. True, both have furnished their own apartments, but at Van Dongen's one is staggered by a drunken riot of colours and cushions through which it takes a while to distinguish in the blue cigarette smoke the graceful lines of a Parisian gesture. Mondrian's, however, is a severe, businesslike room flooded with limpid, cool light, where the painter, deaf to the Whitsuntide jollity around him, grapples with his material in monklike solitude in his quest for his lofty, highly controversial ideal.
On an easel in the middle of the studio is a square canvas, the painter's most recent work. It is divided into rectangular fields painted in the principal colours of bright red, blue, black. It does not represent anything. No regularity can be discerned in the figure. And yet there is a not unpleasing balance about it, the painter says, and having said so, promptly turns the canvas round in order to keep it steady...
While I recover from my initial surprise in a cubic cane chair, the painter discloses the name of his creation: Foxtrot. It has the same modern, rhythmic feeling, the regular steps to and fro. I myself have often danced the foxtrot at Van Dongen's, and am amazed to find the artistic essence of this profane activity in Mondrian's ascetic cell. However, the painter goes on to explain in succinct terms how the foxtrot led to his depiction, or transformation, and how the mundane representation has mysteriously and totally vanished".
After giving a lengthy account of Mondrian's development as an artist, the author explores the relationship between his paintings and his studio: "Yet how does the artist intend to enclose, to frame, to place his work—which in itself seems unenclosed—in an interior? Surely the days of the easel painting are over? Mondrian does not need to reply to this question: the studio speaks on his behalf. The walls of this room, which incidentally is of pleasing proportions, are divided spatially by unpainted or primed canvases, so that each wall in itself forms a sort of abstract painting enlarged several times." But the writer mentions relief at finding himself back in the everyday world after his visit to Mondrian's sterile laboratory. Still, he could see some echoes of Mondrian's ideas in certain aspects of life in a metropolis: "For

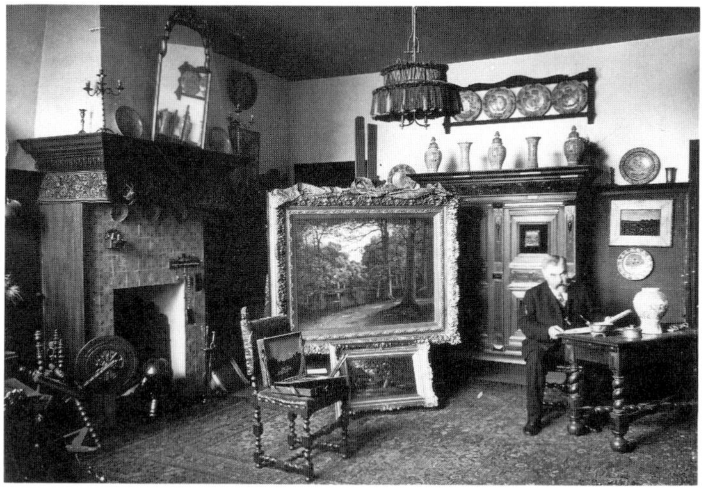
Frits Mondriaan in his studio, 1930.

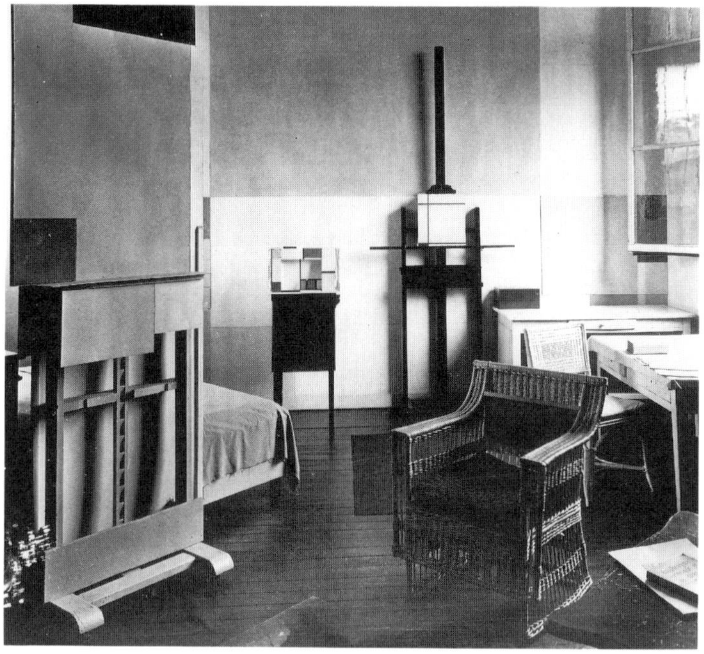
P. Delbo, Mondrian's studio at 26 rue du Départ, Paris, 1926.

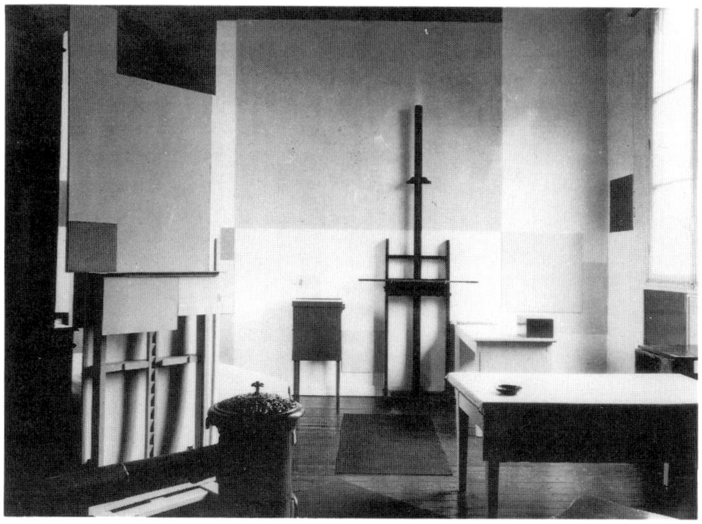
P. Delbo, Mondrian's studio at 26 rue du Départ, Paris, 1926.

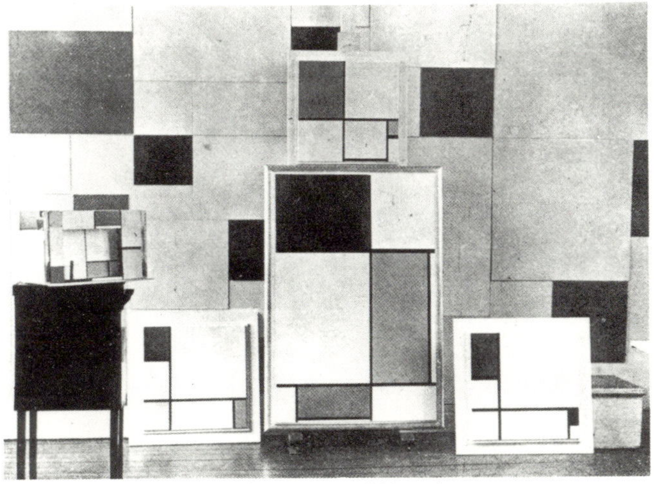

Mondrian's studio at 26 rue du Départ, Paris, ca.1930; on the left the maquette of M. Seuphor's play, 'L'éphémère est éternel' by Piet Mondrian.

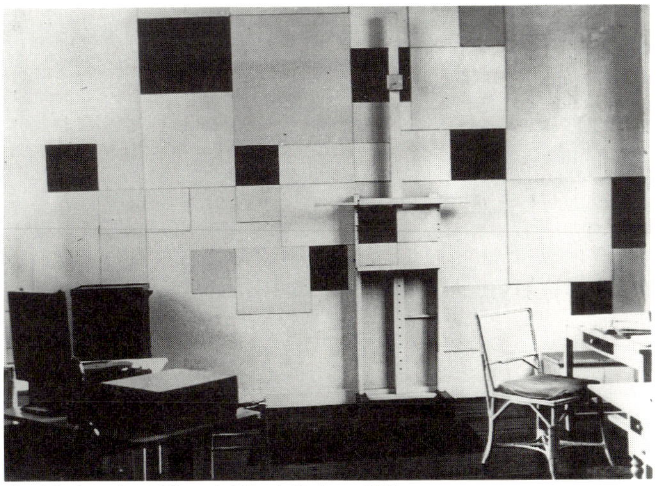

Mondrian's studio at 26 rue du Départ, Paris, ca.1930.

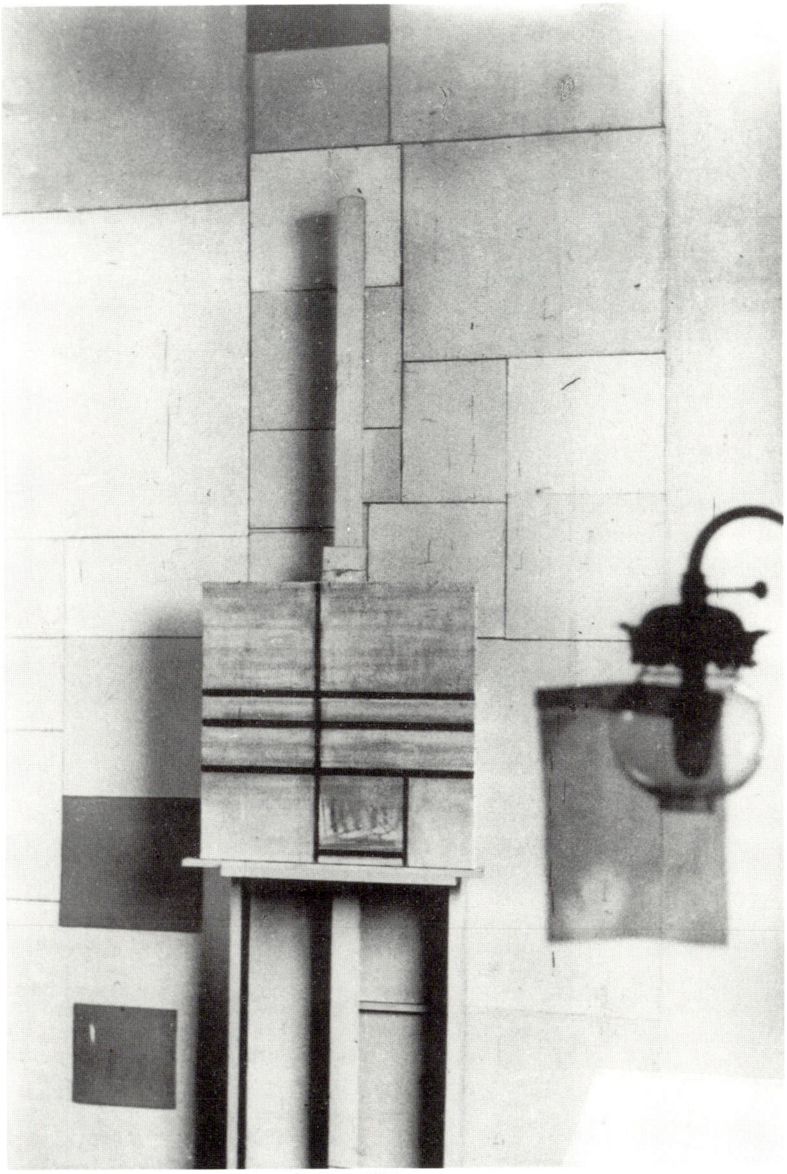

Mondrian's studio at 26 rue du Départ, Paris, ca.1935.

when I descend into the cavern of the metro station, then I find living beauty there also, and suddenly it seems to me as if Mondrian's laboratory tests have been transformed into reality in those rectangular long tunnels, rectangular trains sliding in and out, and even the rectangular walls are divided into colour planes by means of red and green advertisements—almost according to Mondrian's recipe."[89] When the same journalist visited Mondrian again a few years later, this time in his studio in the Rue du Départ, he experienced the same sensation of contrast between exterior world and interior harmony. "Yet indoors the oppressive aspect of modernity has been tamed, order has been brought into chaos, while the simplicity of the forms and colours create an atmosphere of Apollonian peace".[90] Similar feelings were expressed by virtually all the people who visited Mondrian in his studio during those years.[91] Several artists even went so far as to change their own studios into reflections of their abstract work, as for instance Jean Gorin and Marlow Moss did.

In the foregoing at least two reasons came to the fore for arranging a studio in a certain way: the first being that the studio was considered an expression of the ideas of the artist and his position in society; the second reason lies at the root of Mondrian's thinking about art, which can exist only in surrogate form in this world, in other words, in this essentially "tragic" life art is obliged to lead a separate existence, whereas in the distant future art and life will merge into one, i.e. there will be no more distinctions between the different arts and life itself. However, it is curious that these theories of Mondrian's about a future obsolescence of art did not lead him to break down the old academic division of the arts into separate disciplines of painting, sculpture and architecture, but that he, on the contrary, reasserted these distinctions. It is a fairly well-known fact that Mondrian also attempted to apply his neo-plastic ideas to language; he soon had to admit that this was not possible. More or less the same happened with music. Initially Mondrian admired the composer Van Domselaer for having realized his ideas in terms of music, though quite independently from him, but later on he became convinced that Van Domselaer was taking a wrong direction. He was equally opposed to futuristic music which, in his opinion, was still too tied down to melody, rather than merging into pure sound and absence of sound. Mondrian believed that only jazz music (he was a jazz enthusiast throughout his life) contained the rhythmical movements and counter-movements which would, in that distant future, lead to a neo-plastic kind of music.[92] A dominant theme in his paintings of this period is "the city". The two themes "city" and "music" are unified in the painting entitled *Broadway Boogie-Woogie*. Jazz, and especially the boogie-woogie, may be seen as the best musical expression of Mondrian's neo-plasticism. *Victory Boogie-Woogie* may indeed be interpreted as the victory of neoplastic music,[93] i.e. pulsating rythm.

Mondrian tried to relate the ideas he had developed within his own art of painting to a variety of fields. This was a logical consequence of the universal nature that he attributed to his theories—universal not only with respect to the arts, but also and even more so to life in its entirety. The nineteenth-century theory of the *Gesamtkunstwerk* held no appeal for Mondrian, since the only *Gesamtkunstwerk* he recognized was life itself.

Although Mondrian continually predicted the ultimate obsolescence of art, his whole life as an artist was devoted to working towards the absolute within his own art, which found its sole and exclusive form in painting. Indeed his texts are full of references to his belief that neoplasticism can only exist in painting, and when Mondrian uses the term painting he means his own canvases. To Mondrian painting ranked above all other arts.

In the city, the metropolis, Mondrian saw several of his ideas already realized, while the "true" city as Mondrian conceived it was still thousands of years away. Returning to Paris from a visit to a suburb with Roth the architect, Mondrian fell asleep, not from exhaustion but because the urban environment was so oppressive to him![94] The extreme tension between the reality in which art needs to be made, and the remote future in which art no longer has a function, is in fact another element in the interaction between painting and studio.

Up to the end of his life Mondrian saw his studio as a testing ground for an architecture of the future. In an interview by J.J. Sweeney he said: "And I feel that painting can become much more real, much less subjective, much more objective, when its possibilities are realized in architecture in such a way that the painter's capabilities are joined with constructive ones. But then the constructions would become very expensive; they would require a pretty long time for execution. I have studied the problem and practiced the approach with removable color and non-color planes in several of my studios in

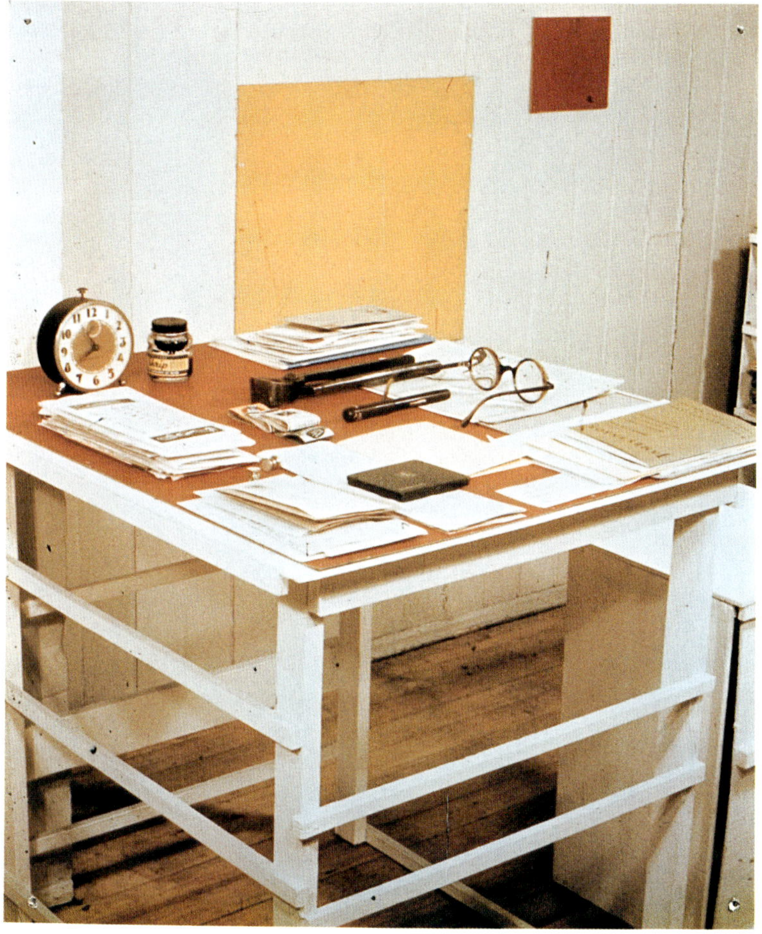

F. Glarner, Mondrian's studio at 15 E.59th Street, 1944.

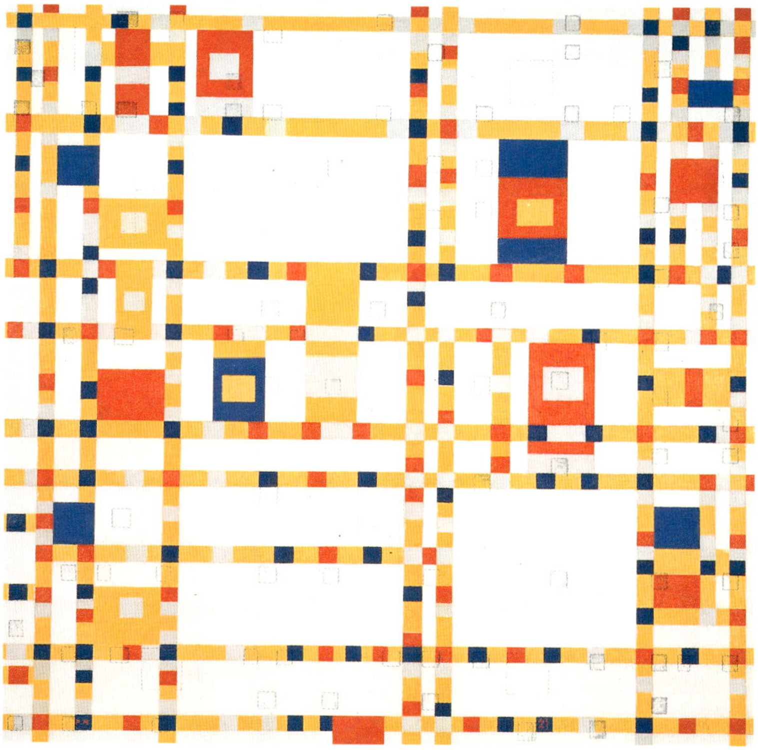

Piet Mondrian, Broadway Boogie-Woogie; oil on canvas, 150 × 150 cm; coll. Museum of Modern Art (New York).

Europe, just as I have done here in New York."[96] So Mondrian mentions his own studio as a place where he "studied the problem"; he forgot to mention, though, that he had submitted designs for the neo-plastic renovation of a room for Mrs. Ida Bienert in Dresden in 1926. Mondrian made several sketches for this room, but the project was never realized. In a letter he wrote to the architect Oud, with whom he had nearly quarelled some years previously over the difference between Mondrian's ideas of a future architecture and those of the rather less Utopian architect Oud, Mondrian mentions how difficult it was for him to make these designs, and also the function of the studio in this respect: "I have been busy for some time on the plans for a library-room in Dresden, I am only getting 150 marks for it, but it is an interesting assignment, although very hard. Without the exercise of creating my own interior I would have been unable to do it at all. I hope to send you the photographs later on, or to show them to you when you are here."[97] And soon afterwards he wrote: "No, I'm not doing too badly. That room in Dresden has turned out well (the design), but it wasn't financially justifiable to go there myself to supervise the work. And I don't think anyone else could take care of that part."[98]

It was at this time that Mondrian had several photographs taken of his studio by the photographer Delbo. But what the photographs show and don't show was entirely Mondrian's decision. The objects in the room are arranged in such a way that their forms suggest a certain relationship between them. It is very curious to see how, in the foreground of these photographs, a table or stove introduces a diagonal into the composition, thus serving a purpose rather like that of the old-fashioned *repoussoir.* The studio as portrayed in these photographs looks like a huge still life. The empty chairs, empty tables, the absence of the painter's tools are all intended to evoke a certain image in the mind of the viewer. Both Michel Seuphor and Louis Saalborn mentioned that the human element was alien to the studio, as the latter was to observe. Later: "His entire studio was furnished like one of his paintings, chairs, tables and easels were arranged in the space in a contrived, emphatic way; sterile and object-less as his paintings, an environment in which the artist himself in his dark suit struck an almost jarring note."[99] Mondrian wanted the photographs to strengthen the image of his studio as a "cell", "laboratory", in which the environment of the future is researched.

The studio was an experiment, just like the Dresden designs. Mondrian was not very interested in the realization of his ideas. One of the photographs shows a stage-model of Seuphor's «L'éphémère est éternel». Here again Mondrian's attitude was that of a scientist in his laboratory: the project was a tentative experiment. In a letter to Oud he wrote, "Well, Vantongerloo read somewhere that M. Stevens was going to give a lecture on theatre, and he wrote him a letter asking him if he knew that I was involved etc. A fortnight after Vantongerloo had left he showed up, was very friendly (just like Van Doesburg at first), took a good look round and wanted to have photographs of the stage model to make slide projections for his lecture. I let him have them: of course some of the ideas will be pinched, but it's even possible that I might myself one day realize them. Personally I am not making any particular effort in that direction, but Seuphor (Bercelaers) has his connections. I built the model for a play of his that is being put on in Lyons (it's not really a play but rather a criticism of the theatre, very good) but there's no money there for décors. Still, I'm glad I made it, because now I can see a whole new field of possibilities."[100] Mondrian's visions of an ultimate fusion of art into a total harmonious environment were indeed idealistic, speculative. He himself saw the few designs of this nature that he made as experiments, the realization of which he was not very eager to undertake. Even so Mondrian persisted, also later in life, in his claim that he was the only artist capable of designing the architecture of the future. He saw himself as a sort of chief supervisor of the planning and ultimate realization. He had already imagined himself in that capacity in 1921,[100a] when he was engaged by the art-dealer Rosenberg, but his ideas on this score are even more obvious from a letter he wrote to Moholy-Nagy in 1939: "I am very glad you do like my statement that I published in *Circle.* However, I think it will be good to explain to you my ideas more clearly. Perhaps this is superfluence, but I don't know if you see my relation to Architecture and industry. I see in your letters that you are thinking that I could do good work at the Bauhaus in the future. But why did you not think of me firstly? I am, among the different artists, perhaps the most free from 'art' and the most near to the 'reality' and its esthetic construction; the most near to architecture and industry. I have studied the most consequently that which only create reality's true beauty, that is pure relations of planes, lines and colours. [...] Nice architecture and nice objects must be created: not nice forms. Nice drawings are useless. That is why I see the usefulness of an artist at the Bauhaus only in this way that he is able to teach how to make more perfect the material constructions. A 'painter' and a 'sculptor' are of no use at the Bauhaus: well their capability to teach all about forms, colours and their relations.

'Art' must be forgotten: beauty must be realized... By this fact I have seen that you are creating a 'new' Bauhaus. I heard from Helion also that you intended to create a workshop for architecture and were looking for an architect. Why should you not go a new way and take an engineer with an esthetic collaborator. This latest must be an artist, but an artist free from 'art'. But all this is perhaps not possible now. You know that better as I do."[101] Indeed, Mondrian did not get an opportunity to put his ideas concerning the new architecture into practice at Moholy-Nagy's New Bauhaus in Chicago. Apart from the two aforementioned designs, which were made in the twenties, no actual designs for an environment or an architectural construction by Mondrian are known; Mondrian's conception of a future architecture did not evolve in the course of actual commissions but in his painting. It is the paintings with the meaningful titles *Place de la Concorde, Trafalgar Square, New York,* and *New York City,* that visualize the ideals of modern architecture and point to a future art-environment.[101a] Mondrian projected his ideas concerning the future obsolescence of art on the basis of the gradual evolutionary process that his own work was going through; each step ahead represents an evolution towards the following stage. Mondrian had a photograph album with pictures of works which, in his opinion, were of essential importance in his own development.[101b] It is possible to divide Mondrian's abstract works into groups (as Seuphor did in his biography of Mondrian) according to certain characteristics. One can see that there is a certain development from one problem to the next. But how exactly this development takes its course and what determines the transition from one group to the next is often unclear. And this cannot indeed become clear if we start out from the notion that Mondrian developed certain formal problems from one *work* to the next. On the contrary, Mondrian tried out solutions to a certain problem in several works in a relatively short space of time, followed by a "period of rest". Then work on a subsequent group of works could commence. In all this the studio continued to play an important role. After the very lean years of 1921 and 1922, when Mondrian was almost forced to abandon art altogether, he found a source of income in producing "flowers" on commission. The turning-point came around 1924-25; the esteem for Mondrian's work grew, and he was able to spend more and more time on his painting. During this period he was very prolific. Late in 1926 Mondrian was working on a large series of paintings which represented, for him too, an important "evolution". In another letter to Oud, who had tried to help him in many ways during the preceding difficult years, he described the disaster that befell him:

"One month ago I had twenty canvases done, and I was to exhibit them in the l'Esthetique,

Boulevard de Montparnasse: then some people from that new Dutch artist's society De Klomp came to ask me to show my work there one evening. I agreed (it was on a Saturday), but when I returned the following Monday as arranged to fetch my canvases, the room had been emptied by the French staff (there wasn't a Dutchman in sight) and my paintings had been stacked in such a way that the nails that projected from the backs of the stretchers had sunk into the paint, which was still soft; one was even torn. Excepting the latter, I over-painted all the others, which took me another month, and now I console myself with the thought that the canvases are now better than they were before."[102] So after having spent months working on twenty paintings at the same time, he did not hesitate to start work on them all over again to repair the damage. When he had finished these twenty paintings he entered into a "period of rest" of nearly one year during which he did not paint. The period between the completion of one series of canvases and the commencement of a new one was a time of inactivity that gradually led to a new creative period lasting several months. The "period of rest" was in fact a period of reflection on what had been achieved in the finished works, of the "destruction of the past" as Mondrian put in, and of "revitalization", of preparation for the next step ahead.

The studio figured prominently in the creative period as well as in the period following it. In a letter to Oud dated a few months later Mondrian wrote: "It is in the nature of my work that it is so difficult to sell despite my growing reputation etc. I sometimes even worry that I might have to make those flowers again on the side. I can sell a watercolour of flowers in Holland, but I have been impractical again, and instead of making some of them after I had finished my canvases, I have been busy with my studio, it looks quite good now and I would very much like you to see it, ah well..."[102a]

Some time later he adds: "But at first I was so busy getting my ambiance right: I have now also done the little room and the kitchen."[103] By the end of that same year, 1927, Mondrian had apparently entered into a new phase. He became wholly preoccupied with setting down his ideas in writing: "It will be a whole series, a sort of artistic-philosophical treatment of neoplasticism. I had hoped to postpone this because it all takes so much time. Especially this initial period of getting started has kept me terribly busy, but I couldn't resist doing it now, and it's all right because who knows if I will ever have the opportunity again later."[104]

The studio, then, has a very distinct function within the creative process. But this function is different in the next period, that of writing, which is concerned with reflection on the position of art in society, for instance; in effect, it is the theoretical counterpoint to his painting. On the one hand the arrangement of the studio serves a kind of supportive function while he is working on a group of paintings, on the other hand the studio is immediately re-arranged when the paintings are completed, and the theme is apparently exhausted.

The relation between completed painting and studio is indeed that between a wholly unstructured space and a perfectly balanced structure. It is also remarkable that new elements in the paintings, such as the introduction of double lines, are not reflected in the arrangement of the studio. It was not until he was living in New York that the actual furniture etc. in his studio played a more important role as part of his living environment, but vis-à-vis the completed paintings the studio continued to serve as a large testing-ground, a space in which all possibilities are in essence contained. The end-product, the painting, represents the top of a pyramid of creativity, which always has the studio as its base.[105]

So apart from serving as a visiting-card of the modern painter's intentions, the studio has a very basic function in the creative process as a whole. From amidst the relatively unformed "chaos" of the studio the paintings emerge as carefully cut, pristine crystals. Mondrian in his studio personifies the artist concentrating all his powers on evolution, on renewal: "If we cannot free ourselves, we can free our vision."[106]

This statement, once again, contains that duality of body and soul. The soul can, by means of that "vision" ascend to higher levels of consciousness. Growth of consciousness is a pre-condition of evolution in the artist's work. Only those who have the kind of vision that runs parallel with that of the artist are capable of really "seeing" his art.[107] It is also this vision that enables them to experience the eternal truths. Mondrian's self-image may be compared to that of the poet-philosopher, who evolves, in the course of his lifetime, from the twilight of chaotic impressions towards the light, the eternal truth.

Notes

In the course of my research for this essay I have been fortunate in receiving the help and support of many colleagues, friends, and organizations, for which I am very grateful. Special thanks are due to:
Yve-Alain Bosi, Paris; Dr. A. W. Boschlo and staff, Kunsthistorisch Instituut, Leiden; A. Braaksma, The Hague; Fondation Custodia, Paris; dr. J. Gaborit, Musée du Louvre; Dr. C. van Hasselt, Paris; Prof. dr. H.L.C. Jaffé, Amsterdam: A. van der Jagt, Paris; Dr. W. Kloek, Amsterdam; Dr. Oort, Amsterdam. Dr. Overdiep, Groningen: Dr. H.C. van Rheeden, Haarlem; staff of Rijksdienst voor Kunsthistorische Dokumentatie, The Hague; staff of Provinciaal Rijksarchief, Haarlem; Prof. Nancy Troy, Baltimore; Dr. P.I.M. Vries, Groningen.

1 For Mondriaan's early period see R. Welsh, *Mondrian's Early Career, the naturalistic period.* New York 1977; H. Henkels, *Mondriaan in Winterswijk*, The Hague 1979.

2 Dr. A.L. Constandse, 'De betekenis van de biografie voor de geschiedenis, de historische betekenis van biografie en autobiografie', *De Gids* 1/1979, pp.32-38.

3 H. Henkels,'Mondriaan Legendes,' *Kunstschrift*, Openbaar Kunstbezit 21e jrg. 1977-3, pp.138-142.

4 A recent analysis of Mondriaan's aesthetic philosophy is not available; dr. H.L.C. Jaffé, *De Stijl 1917-1931, the Dutch contribution to modern art,* Amsterdam 1956; chapter 4 discusses the ideas and aesthetic conceptions of Mondriaan. See also C. Blok. *Piet Mondriaan, een catalogus van zijn werk in nederlands openbaar bezit,* Amsterdam 1975, pp.59-64.

5 D. Lako, *Overzicht van de Geschiedenis van het Teekenonderwijs in Nederland*, Tiel 1899.

6 *Groen van Prinsterer Schriftelijke Nalatenschap* published by dr. C. Gerritsen and dr. A. Goslinga, fourth volume 1866-1876, edited by A. Goslinga and completed by Mrs. J. L. van Essen, The Hague 1967, pp.605-606; correspondence Mondriaan-Groen, letter dated 30 May 1874, Rijksarchief, The Hague (published in: H. Henkels, *Mondriaan in Winterswijk*, p.20); see also: letter Mondriaan to A. Kuyper, 4 Jan 1876, Kuyper archives, Vrije Universiteit, Amsterdam: 'After that I very soon received a sweet letter from Mrs. Groen with two striking little paintings.'

7 Letter Mondriaan-Kuyper 18. 1. 1874, Kuyper archives, Vrije Universiteit, Amsterdam.

8 P.C. Mondriaan sr., instructions for the plate *The Orange Tree*, 1874.

9 See for a more detailed interpretation: H. Henkels, *Mondriaan in Winterswijk*, The Hague 1979, pp.25-30. It is important to note that Mondriaan undoubtedly read the articles his father's friend A. Kuyper wrote on the subject of art: dr. A. Kuyper, *Het calvinisme en de kunst, rede bij de overdracht van het rectoraat der Vrije Universiteit op 20 Oct.1888*, Amsterdam J.A. Wormser 1888; dr. A. Kuyper, *The Antithesis between Symbolism and Revelation, lecture delivered before the historical presbyterian Society in Philadelphia, Pa.* Amsterdam 1899, Höveker and Wormser; for an account of Kuyper's discussion on the importance of the literary group known as the 'Tachtigers', see: J.C. Rullman, *A. Kuyper-bibliografie*, Kampen 1936, dl. II, pp.38-47; 57-58; 236-265; dl. III, p.146; 168-309; 366-375; for the authoritarian view of society taken by Kuyper: K. van Weringh, *Het Maatschappijbeeld van A. Kuyper*, Assen 1967.

10 P.C. Mondriaan sr., 'Schoolstrijd in Amersfoort' *De Standaard* 27.12.1874; published in H. Henkels, op.cit., p.15.

11 P.C. Mondriaan sr., *The Emperors Bringing Christmas Gifts*, after G. Bonnefont, published by J. Bredee, Rotterdam 1912; the two illustrations in this volume are not by father Mondriaan; it is not certain who designed the cover shown here; flowering trees are a theme that Piet Mondriaan was particularly interested in ca.1905.

12 Piet Mondriaan told J. Bradley ('Piet Mondrian', *The Knickerbocker Weekly* 14. 2. 1944): 'Another man paid for my studies for three years sending me at 19 to the Amsterdam Academy of Fine Arts.' However, only one year's tuition fees were paid by this unknown benefactor. The fee for taking all the courses was Hfl.100.— per year, archives Rijksacademie, Prov. Rijksarchief Haarlem.

13 Archives Rijksacademie van Beeldende Kunsten, Prov. Rijksarchief Haarlem; dossier teaching programmes; requirements for the various teaching diplomas were published in *Maandblad gewijd aan de belangen van het teekenonderwijs*

en de kunstnijverheid in Nederland, September 1892.

14 letter from Carel Mondriaan to S. Slijper, 20.1.1946, Slijper archives, Haags Gemeentemuseum.

15 Braet van Uberfeldt and V. Bing, *Handleiding tot het teekenen naar de natuur en de beginselen der Doorzichtkunde*, 2 vols, Amsterdam 1866.

16 'Catalogue des Tableaux Modernes provenant des successions de feu M. J. Braet van Uberfeldt, décédé à Doetinchem, et autres, vente publique le mardi 26 Févr. 1895, C.F. Roos et Cie.'; the auction comprised 166 items. no.160 was: A. Verhoesen, 'Des poules, et une fille dans un intérieur—Deux pièces.'

17 C. Blok, *Piet Mondriaan, een catalogus van zijn werk in nederlands openbaar bezit*, Amsterdam 1974, nos 1 and 3; R. Welsh, *katalogus Piet Mondriaan*, The Hague 1966, no.2; Up to 1913 Mondriaan made copies of the following works in the Rijksmuseum in Amsterdam:
26 January 1895: P.J.C. Gabriel, *In the Month of July*, inv. no.A 1505
12 June 1895: B. J. Blommers, *Women Knitting*, inv.no. A 1327
15 June 1895: P. van der Velden, *Double Blank*, inv. no. A 1327
8 July 1898: N. Maes, *The Spinning-Woman*, inv.no. C 176
24 August 1898: J. Steen, *Cage with Parrot*, inv.no. A 386
15 February 1905: N. Maes, *The Endless Prayer*, inv.no. C 176
14 August 1911: Frans Hals (copy), *The Jester*, inv.no. A 134
24 August 1911: Cornelis Kruseman, *Count Johannes van den Bosch*, inv.no. A 2166
29 July 1913: Jan Kieft. *Portrait of G.M. Cort Heyligers*, inv.no. A 2356
9 August 1913: Adriaan Beeldemaker, *The Hunter*, inv.no. A 750
Thanks are due to drs. W. Kloek of the Rijksmuseum for this information.

18 Archives Rijksacademie, Prov. Rijksarchief Haarlem; register of students.

19 Archives Rijksacademie, Prov. Rijksarchief Haarlem; 'Programma der lessen aan de Rijksacademie van Beeldende Kunsten te Amsterdam.' Amsterdam P.N. van Kampen; of special importance to Mondriaan were the following: *'Drawing:* the drawing course is divided into two sections. In the first section lessons are given in: a. drawing from plaster casts, b. proportions of the human image; c. (principles of) anatomy, skeleton, muscles and tendons. In the second section: a. drawing from plaster casts, b. drawing from a nude model and from animals, c. comparative proportions. d. anatomy (applied to character and expression), e. linear perspective, f. modelling, g. history of the different styles in the fine arts. *Painting*. This course too is divided into two sections. The first comprises the following: a. the principles of painting (copies and still life from nature), b. painting from nude and dressed live models and from live animals, c. the theory of light and brown, and aerial perspective, d. the theory of the harmony of colours, e. comparative anatomy, f. art history. In the second section: a. higher painting (composition, style, characterization, expression) b. history of art, c. aesthetics.'
Mondriaan obtained the highest marks for aesthetics in 1898 and in 1901, archives Rijksacademie, Prov. Rijksarchief Haarlem.

20 The landscape reproduced here must have been painted around 1893 or earlier. Mondriaan gave this painting as a token of gratitude to the Wormser family, with whom he had lodged for several years at Kalverstraat 152; the Wormser family, publishers and booksellers, were involved with the anti-Revolutionary newspaper *De Standaard;* Mondriaan's father knew Wormser quite well. One of Wormser's sons (roughly of the same age as Mondriaan), became a well-known architect of the Amsterdam School, see: G. Fanelli, *Moderne Architectuur in Nederland 1900-1940*, the Hague 1978.

21 Archives Rijksacademie, Prov. Rijksarchief; dossier competitions, see also note 19.

22 Archives Rijksacademie, Prov. Rijksarchief Haarlem; dossier competitions; these studies have not yet been recovered.

23 A.H. Gouwe (1875-1965) continued to paint quite competently in this style until about 1914, when he adopted the Neo-Impressionist style; he emigrated to Tahiti in 1927, where he died. M. Monnickendam (1874-1943) continued to paint in the same fashionable style, taking no notice of developments in other directions; he is only important as a teacher.

24 It was either at this time, i.e. around 1901, or, which is less likely, around 1906-1907, that he took a short trip to Spain in the company of the painter Simon Maris.

25 F. Lurasco, *Onze Moderne Meesters*, Amsterdam 1907.

26 The affinity with his uncle Frits is most obvious in the sketches made in this period, i.e. from ca.1898 to 1904; see also C. Blok, *op. cit.*, pp.12-13.

27 For the relationship between sketch and completed painting in France see A. Boime, *The Academy and French Painting in the Nineteenth Century*, New York 1971.

28 Particularly the subjects 'Pond near Saasveld' and 'Trees along the Gein'; certain features of the landscape were painted from several different angles; the subject and location remain the same. Mondriaan worked out his subjects in series of canvases. On the serial nature of his production see: D. Lewis, *Piet Mondriaan*, London 1967; J. Coplans, 'Serial Imagery' *Artforum* 7-2 1968; J. Elderfield, 'Mondrian, Newman, Noland; two notes on changes of style', *Artforum* 10, no. 4 1971, pp.48-53.

29 C. Blok, *Mondriaan in de collectie van het Haags Gemeentemuseum*, 1968.

30 Cat. Atelier Frits Mondriaan, Sept. 1930, Van Marle and De Sille, Rotterdam, no.160: *Nigth with Moon*, 233. *Evening in Heelsum*, 234. *Evening in the Haagsche Bosch*, 235, *Eventide*, etc.

31 Dossier Van den Briel, Haags Gemeentemuseum.

32 A.B. Loosjes-Tersptra, *Moderne Kunst in Nederland 1900-1914*, Utrecht 1957.

33 To add to the confusion, both Frits and Piet Mondriaan held exhibitions at about the same time, the former being the better-selling artist in about 1911. See H. Henkels, *Mondriaan in Winterswijk*, The Hague 1979; both the reviews of both Piets' and Frits' exhibitions constantly remind the readers to bear in mind that Frits and Piet should certainly not be confused; for Frits see H. Henkels, *op. cit.*, pp.34ff.; the art historian M. D. Henkel showed a discerning eye in a review of the St. Lucas exhibition in *Zeitschrift für Bücherfreunde:* 'Unter den hier vertretenen jüngeren Künstlern ist wohl Piet Mondriaan—nicht zu verwechseln mit seinem ebenfalls malenden, aber belanglosen Onkel Frits Mondriaan—der bedeutendste;...'

34 Letter from Mondriaan to Bremmer, 8. 4. 1914, published in: J. Joosten, 'Documentatie over Mondriaan, 26 brieven van Mondriaan aan L. Schelfhout en H.P. Bremmer 1910-1918,' in *Museumjournaal* 13 (1968), pp.208-215.

35 The title page of *The Emperors Bringing Gifts* acknowledges Piet's father's contribution as being by 'P.C. Mondriaan sr.'; the distinctive 'sr.' was also added to his name as author of several other stories.

36 C.L. Dake and E. Wichmann, *Nieuwe richtingen in de schilderkunst (cubisme, expressionisme, futurisme etc.)*, Baarn 1914.

37 A.B. Loosjes-Tersptra, *Moderne Kunst in Nederland 1900-1914*, Utrecht 1957, pp.108ff.

38 M. Viola, 'Moderne Kunstkring', *Van Onzen Tijd* 1911-12, no.1, p.13.

39 The most exhaustive survey in: M. Calinescu, *Faces of Modernity; Avant Garde, Decadence, Kitsch* Indiana University Press, Bloomington/London 1977.

40 Mondriaan's friend A. van den Briel described this contact as follows: 'He (Mondriaan) came from a strictly religious Calvinist background (his father was a friend and supporter of A. Kuyper) and, although he had long since gone his own way (was living with two brothers at Ringdijk, Diemermeer), he had still not shaken off the influence of his childhood. He had to be able to develop his personality in complete freedom, and in that process of liberating himself he came across the theosophical movement. Mondriaan was receptive to the greatness of this world-view, out had a strong antipathy to the way the theosophists manifested themselves in clubs and societies, as the rather superficial gatherings in Amsterdam ('theosophical misses'). He may have been a member of the Theosophical Society for some years, but he did not attach much importance to that membership. Strictly speaking he cannot be said to have been a theosophist in those days. He was always an artist first and foremost, searching for a way to express what he felt and thought. For that reason it was not very likely that a concrete religious conviction could ever take hold of him. In a more general sense, however, his view of life (and work) ran to a considerable extent (but not on the most essential points) parallel with the theosophical persuasion. In this period of transition theosophy did deepen his spiritual life, but he had no time for studying, and always his art claimed priority, and as he became freer himself his own personality became more dominant, and the link with theosophy became looser. [...] The great lines that he formerly perceived in theosophy, and the awareness that the real truth underlying the material world he now found within himself, and it was his duty as an artist to express it.' Dossier Van den Briel, Haags Gemeentemuseum. See also: R. Welsh, 'Mondrian and Theosophy', in cat. Mondrian-Centennial, Guggenheim Museum 1972, pp.35-51; Ch. von Wiegand, *The Oriental Tradition and Abstract Art*, New York 1957, pp.55-68.

41 R. Rosenblum, 'Notes on Mondrian and Romanticism,' in: cat. Mondriaan, The Hague/Toronto 1966, pp.17-21.

42 A. Chastel, 'L'interpretation esotérique de l'art de la renaissance à la fin du siècle dernier,' in: *Umanesimo e Esoterismo* (see note 55), pp.439-448; for the influence of these ideas on Van Gogh and Gauguin: E. van Uitert, 'Vincent and Gogh and 'Paul Gauguin': a creative competition,' in: *Simiolus* vol.9, 1977 no.3, pp.149-168.

43 On Humbert de Superville: J. Knoef, 'Humbert de Superville,' *Elseviers Geill. Maandschrift* 1939, pp.361-376; B.M. Stafford, 'Les deux Edifices—The new Areopagus and a spiritual trophy: Humbert de Superville's Vision of Utopia,' in: *The Art Quarterly*, spring 1972; B. Stafford, 'Medusa or the physiognomy of the earth; H. de Superville's cosmological aesthetic,' in: *The Warburg Journal* 1972, vol.35; B. Stafford, 'Mummies, Herms and Colossi: Easter Island and the origin of Sculpture,' in: *The Art Quarterly*, summer 1973.

44 Humbert, *op. cit.*, p.3.

45 Humbert, *op. cit.*, pp.21-22: Mondriaan also evoked the image of the moonlit night in Trialoog' *(De Stijl.* vol.2 no.10, August 1919), but here the emphasis is on the stars; Mondriaan illustrated his text with a reproduction of one of his recent abstract compositions. Mondriaan again used this image in 'The Great Boulevards' (see note 77): 'On the

boulevard one thing succeeds another, but also merges with it. A quiet moonlit night gives more opportunity for everything.'

46 This essay is not concerned with the origins and meaning of Mondrian's art theories; in order to avoid a common misconception it is necessary to emphasize here that the *dynamic equilibrium* constitutes an essential aspect of these theories; Mondrian undoubtedly consulted the writings of the Dutch Neo-Hegelian philosopher G.J.P.J. Bolland, *Eenheid van Tegendeelen,* Amsterdam 1900, and *Zuivere Rede,* Leiden 1904; Mondrian quotes Bolland in *De Stijl* 1. 7. 1918 (p.73), 1.8. 1918 (p.90), 1.9.1918 (p.103).

47 Mondrian quotes Humbert in *De Stijl* 1.9. 1918 (p.108).

48 P. Mondrian, *Essays,* New York Wittenborn 1945, in: 'A New Realism,' p.17.

49 See for a list of Mondrian's writings: C. Blok, *Piet Mondriaan, een catalogus van zijn werk in nederlands openbaar bezit,* Amsterdam 1974, p.190.

50 See for a more detailed interpretation: H. Henkels, *Mondriaan in Winterswijk,* The Hague 1979, pp.25ff.
50a H. Henkels, *Mondriaan in Winterswijk,* ill. 61; R. Welsh, *Mondrian's Early Career,* ill.102.

51 A hand-written inventory (ca.1903) of the casts at the Rijksacademie gives the year of acquisition a 1881 (archives Rijksacademie, Prov. Rijksarchief Haarlem); H. van der Smagt, *Katalogus der Verzameling afgietsels van beeldhouwwerken van de Rijksacademie,* Amsterdam 1913, p.261, gives a detailed description of this bust, its maker and the man portrayed.

52 It is not known exactly which bust was used in each year; around 1890 there were about thirty casts in the collection of the Rijksacademie roughly one third of which were casts of Italian sculptures. Mondrian is known to have had a cast of a head of Dante in his studio (see note 91).

53 *Maandblad gewijd aan de belangen van het teekenonderwijs en de kunstnijverheid in Nederland,* III no.10, 1 March 1887.

54 R. Becker, 'Die Benivieni-Büste des Giov. Bastianini' *(Schriften des wissenschaft. Vereins zu Breslau),* Breslau 1889; this treatise was present in the library of the Rijksacademie. For a survey of the Benivieni bust by Bastianini and the casts made of it, see: J. Schuyler, *Florentine Busts. Sculpted portraiture in the 15th century,* New York, Garland 1976, passim.

55 *Enciclopedia Italiana,* s.v. Benivieni; C. Re, G. Benivieni, Naples 1906; G. Pico della Mirandola, *Ausgewählte Schriften, übersetzt und eingeleitet von Arthur Liebert,* Leipzig 1905; N.A. Robb, *Neoplatonism of the Italian Renaissance,* London 1935; R. Klein, ‹L'Enfer de Ficin›, in: *Umanesimo e Esoterismo, Archivio di Filosofia,* Anno 1960 no.2-3, Padua 1960, pp.47-84; E. Cassirer, *Individuum und Kosmos in der Philosophie der Renaissance,* Leipzig/Berlin 1927; R. Assunto, *Die Theorie des Schönen im Mittelalter,* Dumont, Cologne 1963.

56 E. Gombrich, 'Botticelli's Mythologies, a study in the neoplatonic symbolism of his circle,' in; *Symbolic Images, studies in the art of the Renaissance,* London 1972, pp.31-82.

57 E. Panofsky, 'Neo-platonic movement in Florence and North Italy,' in: *Studies in Iconology,* Harper Torchbooks New York 1962, pp.144-145, gives a detailed comparison of the systems devised by Ficino and Pico.

58 S. J. Salchenberger, *The Commentary of Giovanni Pico della Mirandola on a love song of Girolamo Benivieni,* translated with introduction and notes, Ph. D. diss. Johns Hopkins University Baltimore 1967 (typescript); E. Garin, *Giovanni Pico della Mirandola: Vita e dottrina* (Publicazioni della R. Università degli studi di Firenze, III Serie, vol.V), Florence 1937.

59 J.J.N. Timmers, *Christelijke symboliek en iconografie,* Bussum 1974, s.v. *pauw* (peacock); the peacock is often used as a symbol of immortality.

60 On the bequest of Bakker (1845-1919) to the Groninger Museum in 1919, see inventory in archives of the Groninger Museum; the bequest comprised dozens of paintings by lesser masters, many watercolours mostly by 19th century Dutch masters, miniatures, drawings, and other art objects.
60a Henkels, *Mondriaan in Winterswijk,* ills.58, 59, 60.
60b C. Blok, *Mondriaan, een catalogus van zijn werk in nederlands openbaar* bezit, 1974; e.g. ills.110, 140.

61 P. Mondriaan, "Trialoog', *De Stijl* III. 2. 1919, p.16.

62 P. Mondriaan, 'De nieuwe Beelding in de schilderkunst,' in: *De Stijl* I. 7. 1918, p.74
62a C. Blok, *Mondriaan,* 1974, ill.206.

63 K. Lankheit, *Das Triptychon als Pathosformel,* Heidelberg 1959; it is interesting to compare Mondrian's triptych with that of Mark Rothko in Houston, Texas, Rothko Chapel, ill. in: R. Rosenblum, *Modern Painting and the Northern Romantic Tradition, Friedrich to Rothko,* London 1975, p.217.

64 Blavatsky, *Isis Unveiled, a master-key to the mysteries of ancient and modern science and theology,* 1896, II, p.266.

65 E. Schuré, *Les grands initiés,* Libr. Académique Perrin Paris 1960, p.504; on E. Schuré and his contacts with Madame Blavatsky: G. Jeanclaude, *Edouard Schuré,* Libr. Fischbacher Paris 1968.

66 Dr. H.L.C. Jaffé, 'Een preekstoel naar ontwerp van Mondriaan,' in: *Nederlands Kunsthistorisch Jaarboek,* 1981: Prof. Jaffé was so kind as to draw my attention to this work and to permit reproduction of this detail.

67 Dossier A. van den Briel, Haags Gemeentemuseum.

68 A. Dürer, Self-portrait 1500, Alte Pinakothek, Munich: ill. in: S. Holsten, *Das Bild des Künstlers, Selbstdarstellungen,* Hamburg 1978, p.84.

69 M. Seuphor, *Piet Mondrian, sa vie et son œuvre,* Paris Flammarion 1970, p.57.
69a P. Mondrian, 'De huif naar den wind,' in: *De Stijl* VI, 6/7. 1924, pp.86-88
69b Mondrian to Oud, 6.12. 1921, Oud archives, Fondation Custodia Paris.

70 Mondrian to Oud, 10.12. 1921, Oud archives, Fondation Custodia, Paris.

71 For an interpretation of the self-portrait by Max Liebermann: S. Holsten (note 68).

72 P. Mondrian, 'De nieuwe Beelding in de schilderkunst', in: *De Stijl* I. 11. 1918, p.128: 'The modern artist performed the arduous task of creating a mode of expression for the future generation, after destroying that of the previous one. The artist of the future will not have to follow the path of gradual liberation from natural form and colour: the way has been cleared for him; the mode of expression is ready; he has only to perfect it.'

73 P. Mondrian, 'De nieuwe Beelding in de schilderkunst,' in: *De Stijl* I. 9. 1918, p.103. See also G.J.P.J. Bolland, *Aesthetische Schoonheid,* Leiden 1907.

74 Mondrian to A. Saalborn, undated letter, probably 1911 or later, documentation Haags Gemeentemuseum; the growth of spiritual awareness (evolution) is a key concept of Mondrian's theories, (see note 106).

75 Letter from Charley Toorop to C. Spoor, published in: L. van Ginneken and J. Joosten, 'Documentatie: kunstenaarsbrieven aan Kees Spoor (2),' in: *Museumjournaal* 15 (1970), no. 5, p.262.

76 Dr. H.L.C. Jaffé, 'Mondrian's Utopian Vision', *Symposium Mondriaan Centennial,* Guggenheim Museum 1972; neoplasticism already gives an impression of that paradise: 'Today, man's individual consciousness is maturing, and the lost harmony can be rediscovered. No longer obstructed by individuality, the *universal (in nature)* can exist *universally—independently,* and *perceptible* to man. Abstract-real painting images this regained harmony.' *(De Stijl* I. 8. 1918, p.90)

77 Horace Walpole (1717-1797) to the Countess of Upper Ossory 16 August 1776, Oxford Dictionary of Quotations, 3rd edition 1979; instead of 'life' Walpole wrote: 'this world is a...'; J. Schwencke, *Exlibriskunde, een nieuwe kunstwetenschap met een beschrijvende bibliografie van het Ex Libris in Nederland en Belgie 1837-1946.* Amsterdam 1947. P. Mondrian, 'De groote Boulevards,' *De Nieuwe Amsterdamner* 27. 3. 1920, pp.4-5; 274, 3. 4. 1920, p.5; quoted at length in *De Telegraaf* 18. 3. 1920, 'Parijs in Blokjes'; for Mondrian's literary aspiration see: C. Blotkamp, "Mondriaan als literator,' in: *Maatstaf,* April 1978, pp.1-23.

78 E. Lucie-Smith, *Fantin-Latour,* London 1977, p.13 (no references).

79 Chekhov, *The Seagull,* Penguin Classics, Harmondsworth 1978, p.170.

80 Plato, *The Republic,* Penguin Classics, Harmondsworth 1979 (515); Iris Murdoch, *The Fire and the Sun, why Plato banished the artists, based upon the Romanes Lectures 1976,* Oxford University Press 1978.

81 Chekhov, *op.cit.,* p.130.

82 Sometimes the activities of the constructivists went too fast to Mondrian's taste. He suggested to Seuphor that he should name the new journal (which Torres-Garcia and Seuphor published later under the title *Cercle et Carré)* "Stop": 'Pour la revue, qu'est ce que tu penses du mot "Stop" parce que l'on va trop vite... route.' (published in: H. Henkels [ed.], *M. Seuphor,* Antwerp 1976, p.88).

83 P. Mondrian, ‹L'Art réaliste et l'art superréaliste (la morphoplastique et la néoplastique)›, in: *Cercle et Carré* no 2., 15 April 1930.

84 H. Buys, 'Vordemberge Gildewart', in: *Elsevier Geill. Maandschrift,* 1939, pp.237-243; the image is built up of elements that are also to be found in Mondrian: flower (nature), piano (music), abstract composition (primacy of painting).

85 Mondrian describes the importance of his studio in: 'Trialoog,' *De Stijl* II. 5. 1920; see also notes 91 and 95. After his arrival in Paris in June 1919 Mondrian had studios at the following addresses: June 1919—November 1919 Rue du Départ 26; November 1919—1 November 1921 Rue de Coulmiers 5; 1 November 1921—4 March 1936 Rue du Départ 26; March 1936—21 September 1938 Boulevard Raspail 278.

86 J. Baticle, P. Georgel, N. Wilk-Brocard, *L'Atelier, technique de la peinture,* éd des Musées Nationaux, Paris 1976; a report on research to date concerning Courbet's studio is given by Kl. Herding (Hrsg), *Realismus als Widerspruch—die Wirklichkeit in Courbet's Malerei,* Frankfurt 1978.

87 K.L. Immermann, *Die Epigonen,* 1836, quoted in: F. Würtenberger, ‹Das Maleratelier als Kultraum im 19. Jahrhundert›, in: *Festschrift L. Bruhns, Miscellanea Bibl. Hertzianiae,* Vienna 1961, pp.502-509; Goethe, *Wilhelm Meisters Wanderjahre,* II Buch, 8 kap.: ‹Bildende Künstler müssen wohnen wie Könige und Götter, wie wollen sie denn sonst für Könige und Götter bauen und verzieren.›

88 P. Mondrian, 'Trialoog', in: *De Stijl* III. 6. 1920, p.54; On

30 September 1930 the contents of Frits Mondriaan's studio were put up for auction: in addition to about 140 works by him there were 85 items of blue and coloured china, pottery and glass; also brass, pewter, curios, arms and furniture. *Catalogus Atelier Frits Mondriaan*, auction Van Marle and De Sille, 30 September 1930.

89 'Een bezoek bij Piet Mondriaan, van onzen correspondent' *Het Vaderland,* 9 July 1920, Avondblad A; the interviewer is therefore describing the studio in the Rue de Coulmiers!

90 *Het Vaderland,* 17.10. 1924, 'Het Neo-Plasticisme in Schilderkunst, Bouwkunst, Muziek en Literatuur, Van onzen correspondent.'

91 For various reactions of visitors, see; N. Troy, 'Piet Mondrian's Atelier,' *Arts Magazine,* December 1978, pp.82-88. Troy also gives a reconstruction of the studio in the Rue du Départ 26; the studio in Amsterdam at the Sarphatipark is discussed in the autobiographical novel by L. Saalborn, *De vader en de zoon.* Querido Amsterdam 1934. Saalborn describes Mondrian in his studio in 1911, when Saalborn was a student at the Rijksacademie (he was enrolled for the period of one year: 1911-12). In a short article in *Het Nieuws van de Dag* 6. 4. 1955, Saalborn again mentioned that he drew the head of Dante at the studio. The most straightforward and interesting description of Mondriaan in his studio (both at Rue de Coulmiers 5 and Rue du Départ 26) is given by the correspondent of *Het Vaderland* and *Nieuwe Rotterdamsche Courant,* notably in *Het Vaderland,* 9 July 1920 and 17 October 1924, and *Nieuwe Rotterdamsche Courant* 23 March 1922. *De Telegraaf* 12 September 1926. a direct impression is given by the artist Piet Zwart in a letter to his wife N. Cleyndert in August 1926: 'After dinner I visited Piet Mondrian, whom I found at home. We are always as happy as children to see each other again. His studio in the middle of Montparnasse is very beautiful. All dimension has, so to speak, been eliminated, and I blurted out: "...it's always as if I am being admitted to the Lords's house when I visit you." We both laughed heartily at this. He told me that a French young lady had after a silence of a quarter of an hour or more, suddenly said «Mais monsieur, chez vous on ne peut pas avoir du chagrin.» And indeed, this careful man has created an environment for himself that is immune to care.' (Piet Zwart archives, The Hague). Other descriptions are to be found in: M. Seuphor, *Les Evasions d'Olivier Trickmansholm,* Paris 1939, p.142 (reprinted in: H. Henkels, *Michel Seuphor.* Antwerp 1976, pp.182-183); H. A. van Anrooy, 'Piet Mondriaan,' in: *Forum, Maandblad voor architectuur en gebonden kunsten,* 1 April 1946; M. van Loon, 'Mondriaan zoals hij leefde te Parijs', *De Groene Amsterdamer* 7. 12. 1946: A. Roth, *Begegnung mit Pionieren,* Basel/Stuttgart 1973: see also notes 95, 96, 99, and 106.

92 The compositions of Jakob van Domselaer (1890-1960) convinced Mondrian for the first time that the Neo-Plastic principles could also be applied in music. 'In the spring of 1915 Van Domselaer gave a recital in the lounge of the Concertgebouw; after the interval he played his own compositions, a sonata and two elaborations of a chorale, one of which is the first piece in the collection *Proeven van Stijlkunst.* The concert was followed by a heated discussion in the audience, during which Mondrian defended the innovations in Van Domselaer's music.' (Kaspar Niehaus, 'Bij het overlijden van Van Domselaer,' in: Van Domselaer archives, Haags Gemeentemuseum). Van Domselaer published the seven compositions in 1916, with the comment: 'the pieces should be played in such a way that "the standing element" (harmony) occupies the foreground and that the "movement" (melody) can proceed unhindered and peacefully, despite the dominance of the standing element.' (J. van Domselaer, *Proeven van Stijlkunst* nos. I-VII, 1913-1916, Uitgave van Den Nieuwen Kring 1916). After his rejection of the music of the futurists, Mondrian considered jazz to be the form of music closest to neo-plasticism; P. Mondrian, 'De jazz en de neo-plastiek,' *i 10,* 1927.

93 The title *Victory Boogie-Woogie* has been interpreted by some as a homage to the victory of the allied armies in 1944. However, not only did Mondrian never use titles that referred to events, the name also originated two years earlier, in 1942, see: 'Interview with Ch. von Wiegand' in: cat. Mondrian Centennial, Guggenheim Museum 1972, ill. p.82; E.A. Garmean, *Mondrian: the Diamond Compositions,* Washington 1979, p.66, interprets this work as a hommage to New York, a theme Mondrian had already honoured in *New York* (private coll. New York), and in the series entitled *New York City.* It is therefore more likely that Mondrian intended his painting as a homage to the boogie-woogie.

94 A. Roth, *Begegnung mit Pionieren,* Basel/Stuttgart 1973.

95 J.J. Sweeney, *Mondrian,* ed. The Museum of Modern Art 1948, p.16.

96 N. Troy, *De Stijl's Collaborative Ideal: the colored abstract Environment 1916-1926,* Ph. D. diss. Yale University 1979; N. Troy is preparing a contribution for *The Art Bulletin* on the subject of this room.

97 Letter from Mondrian to Oud, undated, ca. March 1926, Oud archives, Fondation Custodia, Paris.

98 Mondrian to Oud, [22. 5. 1926], Oud archives, Fondation Custodia, Paris.

99 L. Saalborn, 'Mondriaan,' *De Telegraaf* 6. 4. 1955; M. Seuphor, 'Christen-Calvinist,' in: *Opbouwen,* October 1937 (reprinted in: H. Henkels, *M. Seuphor,* Antwerp 1976, p.176).

100 Mondrian to Oud, 20. 12. 1926, Oud archives, Fondation Custodia, Paris.
100a Mondrian to Oud, 9. 4. 1921, Oud archives Fondation Custodia, Paris: 'I told Does that I think it would only be possible if you and Does make a plan together, and with me there as advisor.'

101 R. Kostelanetz, *Moholy-Nagy,* London 1971, pp.176-177.
101a Illustrations in M. Seuphor, *Mondrian,* 1970.
101b Dossier Van den Briel, Haags Gemeentemuseum; also: H. Van Loon, 'Piet Mondriaan 70 jaar,' *Nieuwe Rotterdamsche Courant* 6. 3. 1942.

102 Mondrian to Oud, [March 1927] Oud archives, Fondation Custodia, Paris.
102a Mondrian to Oud, 19. 6. 1927, Oud archives, Fondation Custodia, Paris.

103 Mondrian to Oud, undated [December 1927], Oud archives, Fondation Custodia, Paris.

104 Mondrian to Oud, 4 December [1927], Oud archives, Fondation Custodia, Paris.

105 H. Holtzman, 'Piet Mondrian 1872-1944, Some notes on Mondrian's method: the late drawings,' in: cat. *Mondrian: the process works,* the Pace Gallery April 1970. This is the only friend or visitor to Mondrian's studio to realize the tremendous importance of the studio for the actual realization of the paintings.

106 P. Mondrian, Essays, New York Wittenborn 1945, in: 'Toward the true vision of reality,' p.15; in 1918 Mondrian expressed it as follows: "The *plastic artist realizes* visual insight: he constantly destroys it—he constantly realizes truth more purely. He lives by *perception*—by inward as well as outward perception." Piet Mondrian, De Nieuwe Beelding, *De Stijl* 1. 11. 1918, p.127.

107 P. Mondrian, 'De nieuwe Beelding in the Schilderkunst', *De Stijl* I. 11. 1918, p.127; see also M. Seuphor, *Les Evasions d'Olivier Trickmansholm,* Paris 1939, p.142 (reprint see note 91).

Mondrian: a life in pictures 1872-1944

herbert henkels

1872

Pieter Cornelis Mondriaan was born on 7 March in Amersfoort, on the Kortegracht. His father, Pieter Cornelis Mondriaan (1839-1921) and mother, Johanna Christina de Kok (1839-1909) had married in 1869, in The Hague, where the former had trained at a Protestant teachers' training college. He moved in the circles of the Dutch statesman Groen van Prinsterer (1801-1876), whose ideas he continued to propagate in speach and writing throughout his life. P.C. Mondriaan was qualified to give French and freehand drawing in addition to the normal primary school subjects. Between 1872 and 1913 he made innumerable 'historical' memorial plates, and also published several short stories. In 1869 he was appointed headmaster of a Protestant primary school in Amersfoort. Besides his teaching duties P.C. Mondriaan was actively engaged in disseminating the Christian ideals with respect to education; this brought him into close contact with dr. A. Kuyper (1837-1920), the leading Protestant politician of the day.
Mondriaan had three brothers and one sister: Johanna Christina (1870), Willem Frederik (1874-1944), Louis Cornelis (1877-1942), Carel (1880-1957). Willem Frederik trained to be a primary school teacher, but he left for the West Indies (Surinam) in 1895, and emigrated to South Africa five years later; Louis was also a teacher, and worked at the progressive 'Humanitarian School' of Prof. J. van Rees in Blaricum and Laren from 1914 to 1918; Carel held various posts in the civil service.

1880

In April of this year P.C. Mondriaan accepted a post as headmaster of a Protestant school in Winterswijk. The Mondriaan family lived in the teachers' residence on the Zonnebrink next to the school, the main entrance of which was on the Ratumschestraat. Also in that street there was a neutral 'Hogere Burger School' (secondary school) with teachers' residences adjoining the premises. Across from the Mondriaan's house stood the 'Weevershuis', of which Mondrian made at least one drawing. The Zonnebrink contained mainly patrician houses and small home industries. Mondrian portrayed several sites in Winterswijk in drawings, paintings and one etching, the most important subjects being the 'Lappenbrink' and the Protestant church of St. Jacob.
At an early age Mondrian started helping his father in carrying out the designs for the historical memorial plates that his father made, either in commission for publishers or on his own initiative. He attended his father's school, after which he set about obtaining the diploma necessary for giving drawing lessons at primary schools.

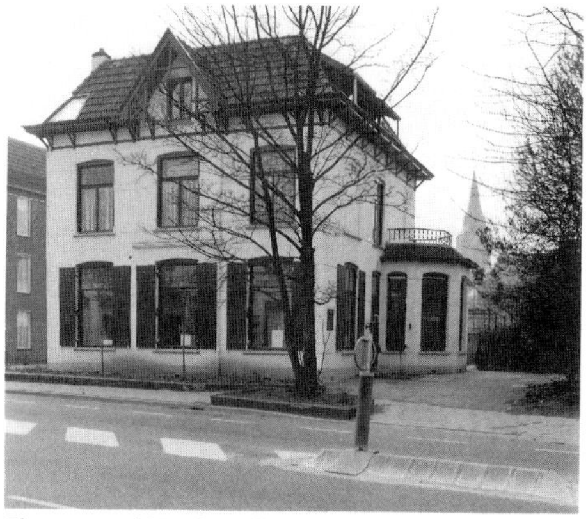

The renovated Mondriaan-house in Winterswijk (photograph 1987).

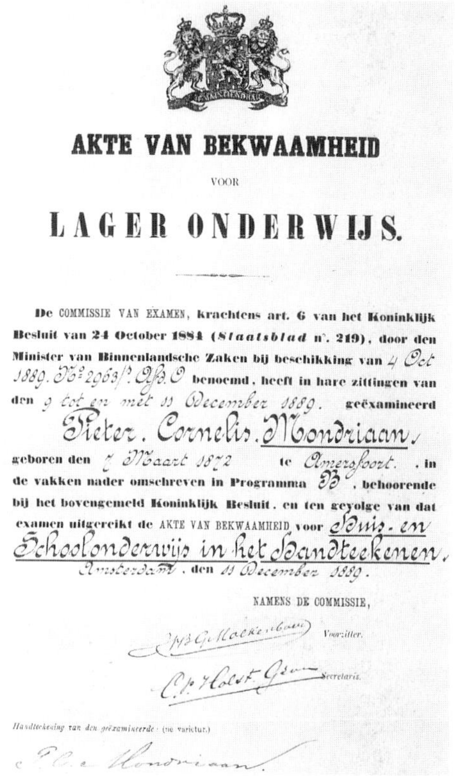

AKTE VAN BEKWAAMHEID

VOOR

LAGER ONDERWIJS.

De COMMISSIE VAN EXAMEN, krachtens art. 6 van het Koninklijk Besluit van 24 October 1884 (*Staatsblad* n°. 219), door den Minister van Binnenlandsche Zaken bij beschikking van 4 Oct 1889. No. 2963/1°. Afd. O benoemd, heeft in hare zittingen van den 9 tot en met 11 December 1889. geëxamineerd

Pieter. Cornelis. Mondriaan,

geboren den 7 Maart 1872 te Amersfoort. in de vakken nader omschreven in Programma B, behoorende bij het bovengemeld Koninklijk Besluit, en ten gevolge van dat examen uitgereikt de AKTE VAN BEKWAAMHEID voor Huis- en Schoolonderwijs in het Handteekenen.

Amsterdam, den 11 December 1889.

NAMENS DE COMMISSIE,

Voorzitter.

C.P. Holst Gzn — Secretaris.

Handteekening van den geëxamineerde: (ne varietur.)

P.C. Mondriaan

The diploma that gave Mondrian the right to teach at primary schools, 1889.

The diploma that gave Mondrian the right to teach at secondary schools, 1892.

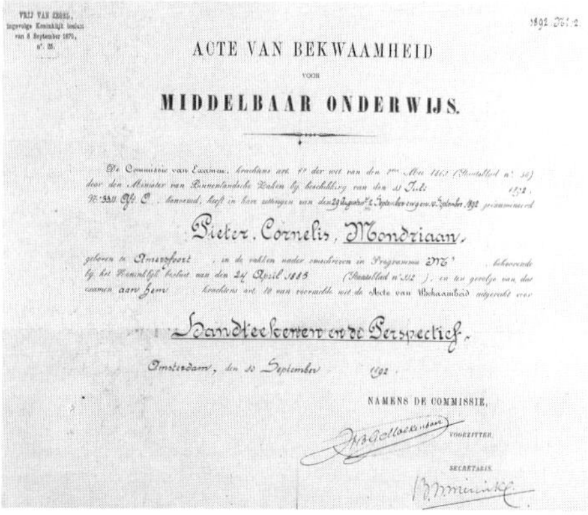

ACTE VAN BEKWAAMHEID

VOOR

MIDDELBAAR ONDERWIJS.

Pieter. Cornelis. Mondriaan,

geboren te Amersfoort, in de vakken nader omschreven in Programma

Handteekenen en de Perspectief.

Amsterdam, den 10 September 1892.

NAMENS DE COMMISSIE,

VOORZITTER.

SECRETARIS.

1889

Mondrian obtained his first drawing master's diploma, and frequently went to Doetinchem near Winterswijk to visit Braet van Uberfeldt, a former drawing master, to study the latter's collection of plates and paintings. He taught drawing at his father's school.
Uncle Frits Mondriaan (1853-1932) paid regular visits to Winterswijk and environs to paint.

1892

As soon as he had obtained his intermediate drawing diploma, which entitled him to teach at secondary schools, he enrolled at the Rijksakademie in Amsterdam. The register gives the following comments about Mondrian as a student: '1892/93 Painting class, very industrious, progress quite good; 1893/94, Painting class, very industrious, progress good; 1894/95 Evening drawing class, industrious, progress quite good; 1896/97 Evening drawing class, industrious, progress fair'. The painting classes were given by Prof. N. van der Waay, drawing classes by Prof. C.L. Dake, and aesthetics and art history by Prof. J. Six. The curriculum centred on figure study, from live models, plaster casts, and parts of the human body, as well as on perspective and proportion. The fees for the first year were paid by an unknown benefactor, the second year Mondrian was given a Royal grant, and after that he earned a living with portraits and copies of paintings in the Rijksmuseum, and with a variety of commissioned work.
Throughout his life there was a certain tension between commissioned work and his 'own' painting. Mondrian lived till 1895 at 154 Kalverstraat with the Wormser family, who were acquainted with his father.

1898

Mondrian became increasingly involved in the artistic life of Amsterdam. In 1892 he became a member of 'Kunstliefde', an association of painters in Utrecht, where he exhibited in 1892,

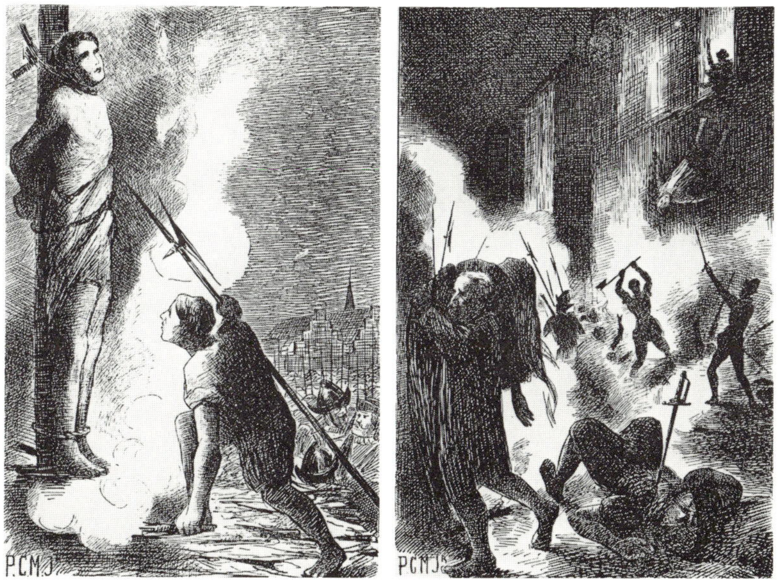

Two of the numerous illustrations Mondrian made for Calvinistic books published by the Wormser publishing house, 1894.

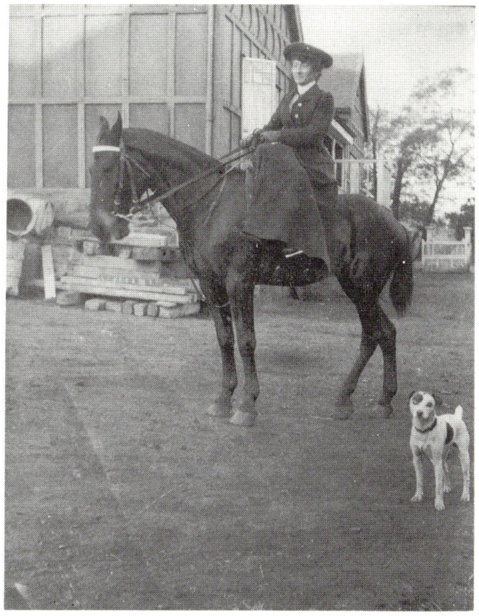

Mrs. Crabb on horseback with Mondrian's dog, 1897.

The pulpit of the English Reformed Church 'de Begijnhof' (Amsterdam) with details of the decoration. Mondrian made the design for the compositions, 1898.

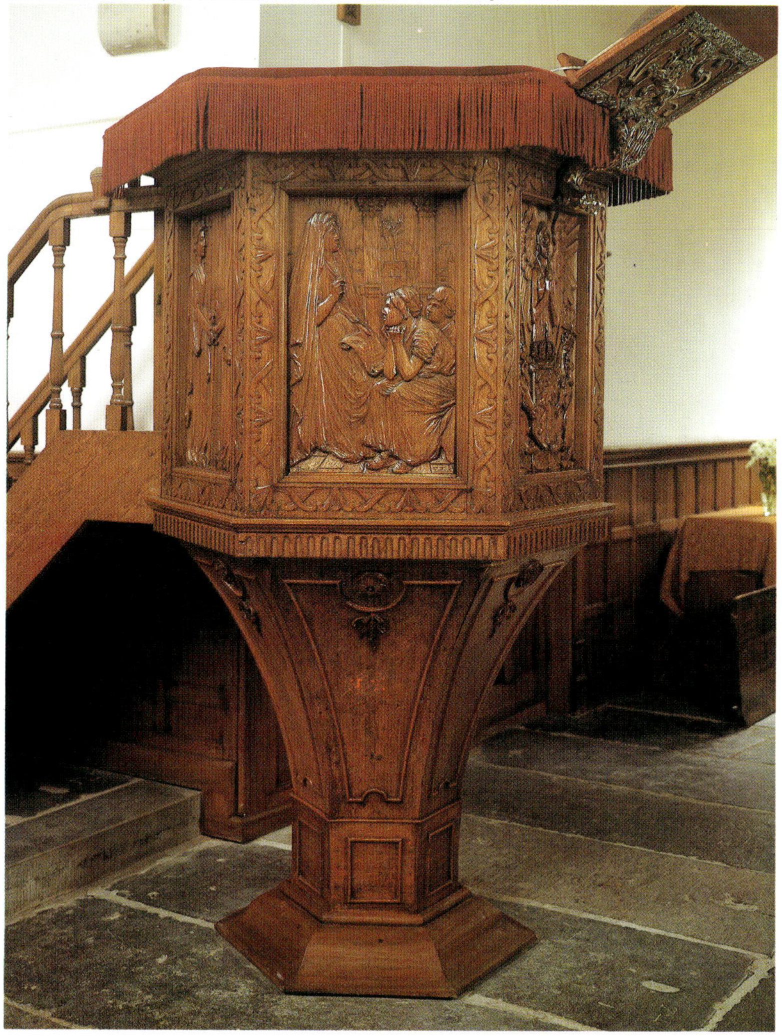

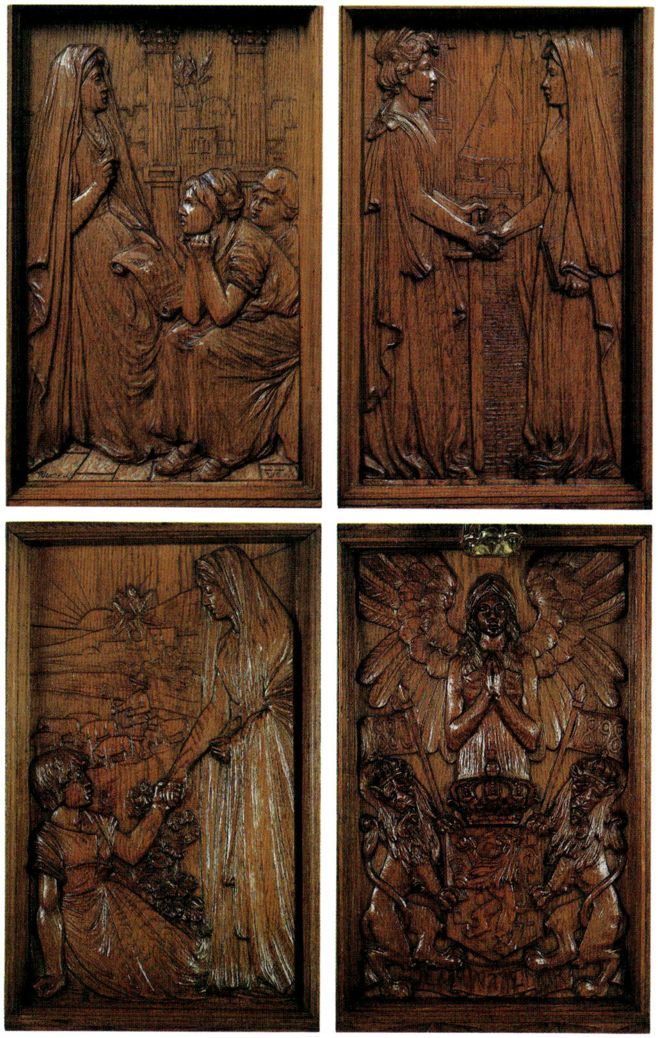

1893, 1894, 1900 and 1909. In 1897 he joined the Amsterdam society of St. Lucas and 'Arti et Amicitiae', where he exhibited regularly between 1897 and 1910. Most of the works he showed at these exhibitions were still lifes. In 1894 he produced a painting known as *'Thy Word is Truth'*, at the request of his father. Mondrian made designs for a pulpit in Amsterdam, and in 1899 he was commissioned to decorate a ceiling in a house in Amsterdam. By entering the Prix de Rome contests Mondrian hoped to obtain official recognition as an artist, but his attempts—in 1898 and again in 1901—were unsuccessful. He detached himself increasingly from his strictly Protestant upbringing, becoming more and more interested in esoteric ways of thinking (notably theosophy). His acquaintance with Albert van den Briel brought him into contact with the ethical pantheism of Dr. Hugenholtz, which had such a profound influence on the later writings of Dr. Schoenmaeckers.

In 1895 Mondrian lived at 75 Ruysdaelkade, from 1895 to 1897 at 180 Eerste Ooster Parkstraat, in 1897 at 128a Ringdijk, in 1897 and 1898 at 5 Stadhouderskade.

1904

After his second unsuccessful bid for the Prix de Rome in 1901, the most important theme in his work became the landscape. He also made views of Amsterdam, but was especially often to be found in the environs of the city: Watergraafsmeer, Abcoude and along the small river Het Gein, often in the company of other painters such as A.M. Gorter and Simon Maris. 'De Vink', a pub situated along the Gein, was a meeting place of painters from Amsterdam. Also a regular visitor to these parts was his uncle Frits, whose way of sketching landscapes Mondrian took over. In 1900 or thereabouts Mondrian went on a trip to Cornwall in the company of a teacher of English, Mrs. Crabb. Mondrian started giving private lessons in drawing and painting, e.g. to the son of the famous actor Willem Royaards. Due to tensions in his private life Mondrian decided—at the advice of his friend A. van den Briel—to spend some time in a village in the south of the Netherlands. There, in Uden and in the neighbouring villages, Nistelrode and Hilvarenbeek, where was also staying A. van den Briel, Mondrian came into close contact with the local population. As a result of this comparative isolation Mondrian reflected at length on the nature and meaning of art for him as an artist. From 1898 to 1904 Mondrian showed his work each year at St. Lucas and Arti. From 1898 to 1903 he lived at 158 Albert Cuypstraat, in 1903 at 55 Ringdijk, and in 1904 in the Stationsstraat in Uden (N. Brabant).

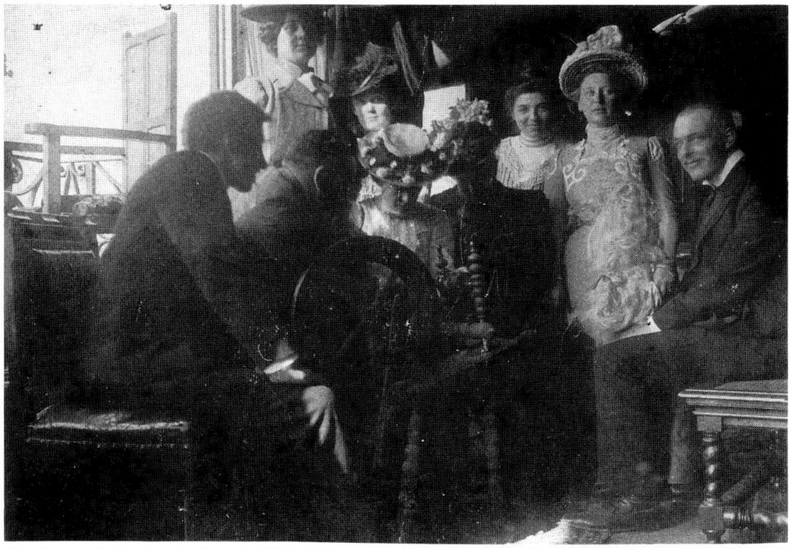

Mondrian with his friends, June 8 1901; sitting from left to right: Mondrian, Simon Kroon, Lizzy Ansingh, Georgine Schwartze, Chris Huidekooper; standing from left to right: Th. Peizel-Ansingh, Nelly Bodenheim, J. Hendriks (unidentified).

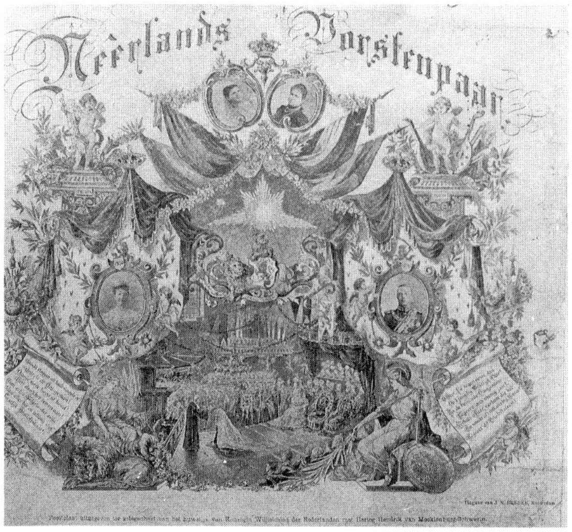

P.C. Mondriaan senior, Neerlands Vorstenpaar (Commemoration plate for the wedding of Queen Wilhelmina), lithograph, edition by J.M. Bredée, Rotterdam, 1901.

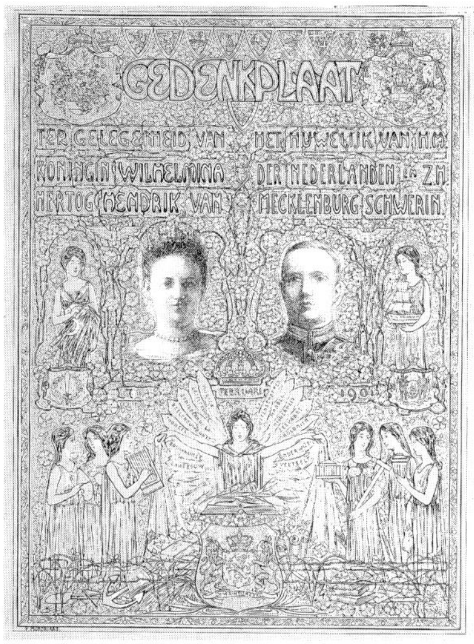

Piet Mondrian, Gedenkplaat, (Commemorative plate for the wedding of Queen Wilhelmina); 1901, pencil, signed lower left, 50 × 85 cm; coll. Haags Gemeentemuseum.

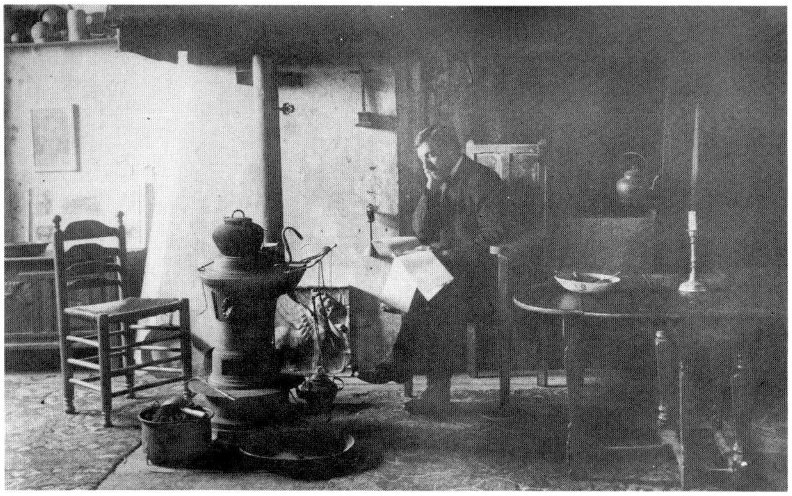

Mondrian in his studio, 1903.

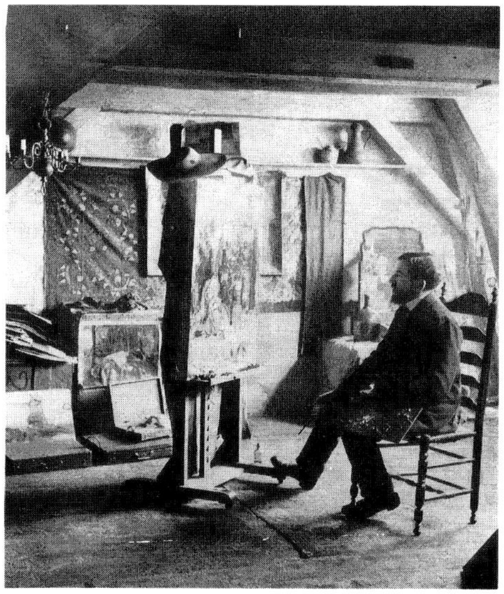

Mondrian in his studio in Amsterdam, 1905.

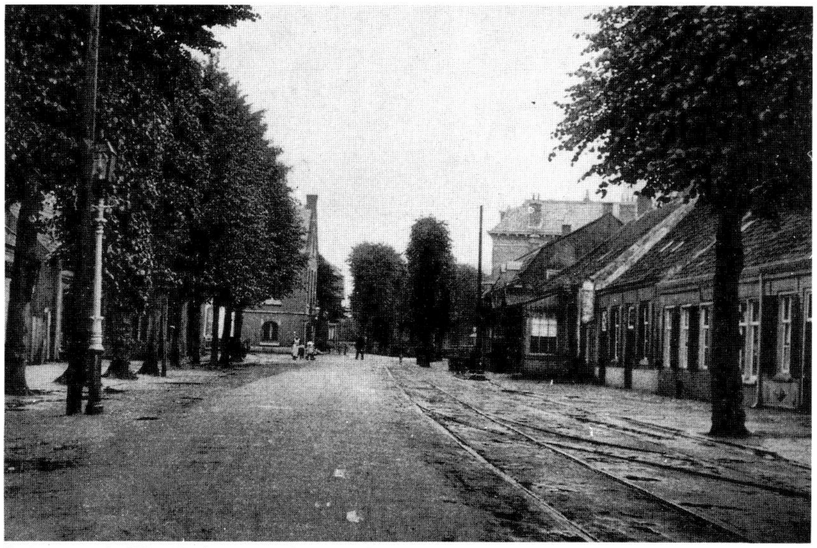

St. Jansstraat in Uden (Brabant): Mondrian's studio is the second house from the right.

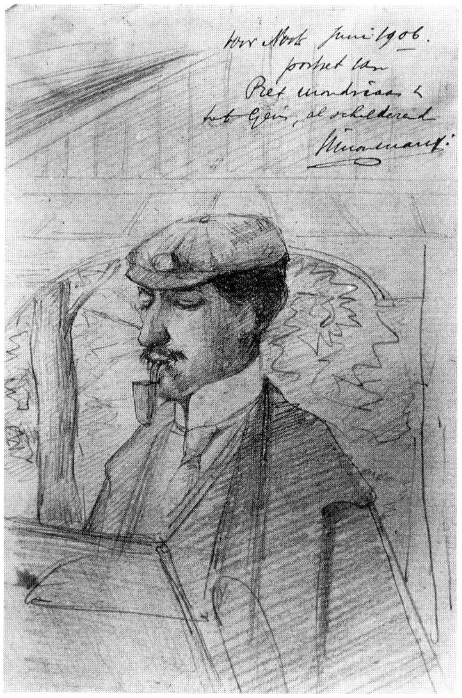

S. Maris, Portrait of Piet Mondrian, painting at the Gein river, June 1906; drawing, 18 × 11.5 cm; coll. Haags Gemeentemuseum.

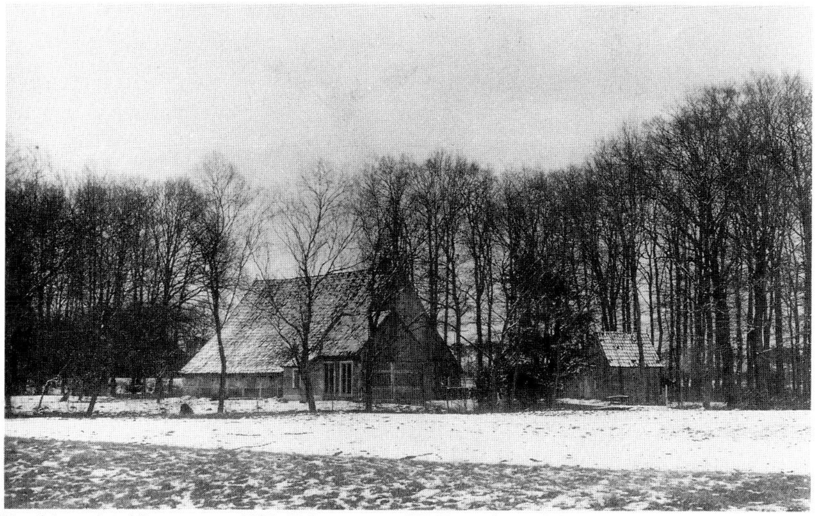

Mondrian painted from autumn 1906 till the summer of 1907 together with his friend Hulshoff Pol near Saasveld; they lived in a farmhouse: the frontpart of this farmhouse was the studio.

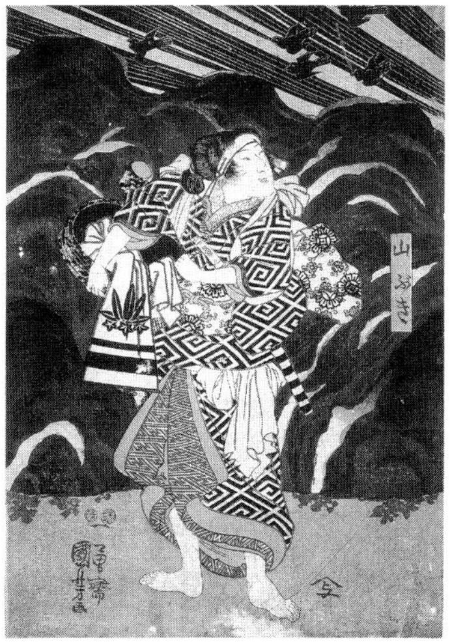

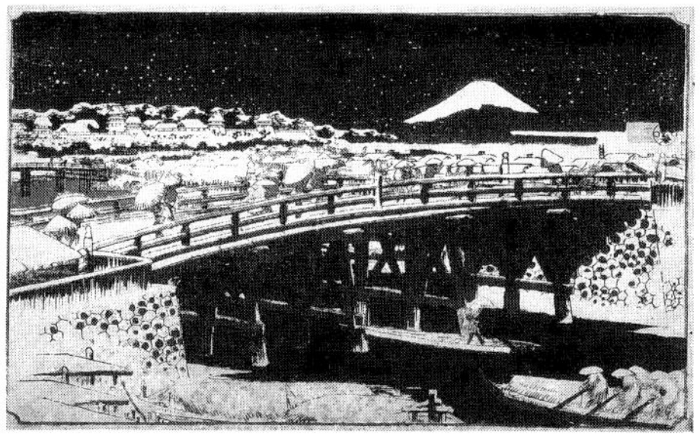

Hiroshige, Morning snow on the Nihombashi, ca. 1843-46.

Recently a series of Japanese prints were located which were in the collection of Mondrian before he went to Paris in 1912.

Kuniyoshi, Middle page of a triptych, ca. 1847-50.

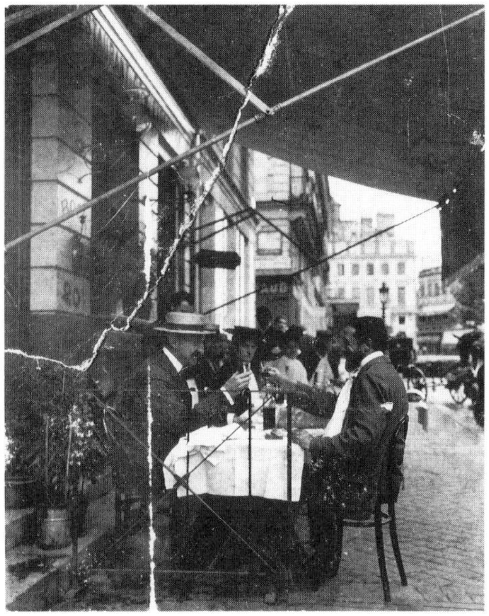

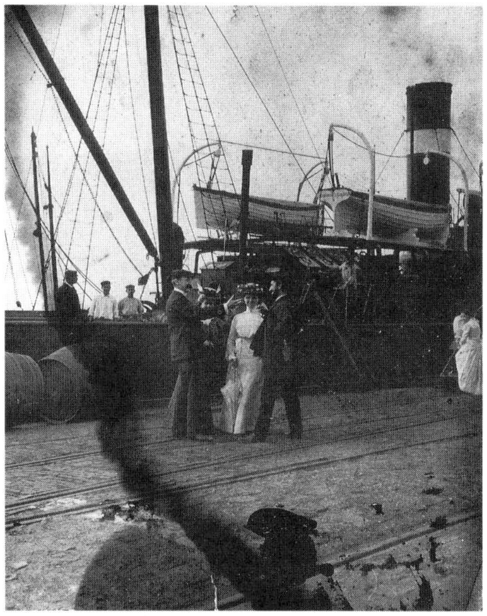

Probably in 1908 Mondrian made a short trip with his friend Simon Maris to Spain; these two photographs were taken in Bordeaux.

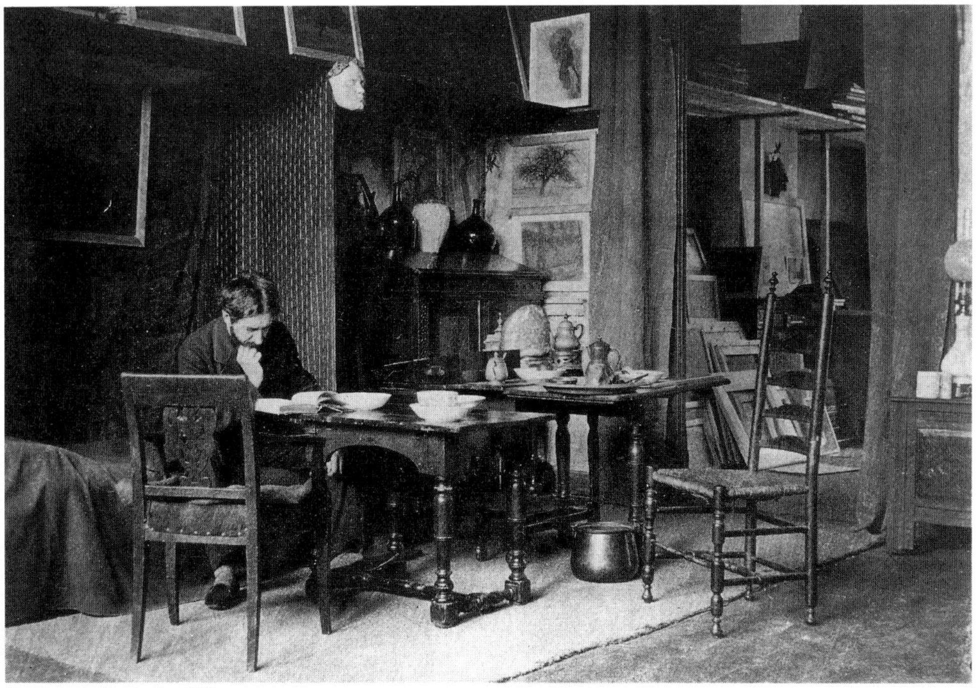

Mondrian in his studio, 1909.

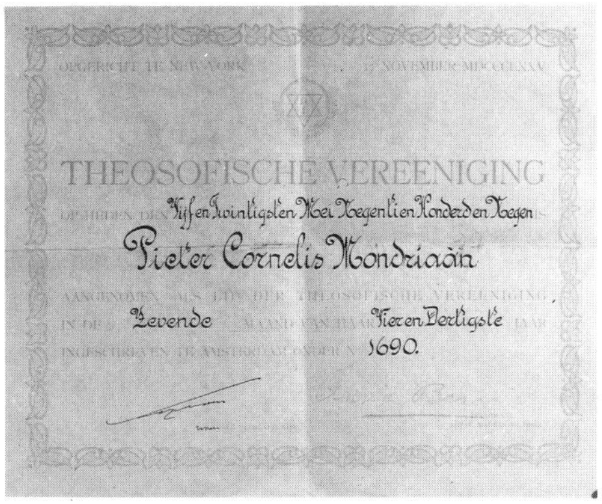

THEOSOFISCHE VEREENIGING
Vijf en Twintigsten Mei Negentien Honderd en Negen
Pieter Cornelis Mondriaan
Zevende Vier en Dertigste
1690.

Membership certificate of the Theosophical Society, 25 May 1909.

1909

From 1905 on, light—both sunlight and moonlight—played a very important role in Mondrian's work. In the series of "evening and night landscapes" the details gradually dissolved, and the contours of large planes determined the image; many drawings and small oil studies culminated in a number of large paintings; the painterly element became increasingly dominant, manifesting itself especially in a very light touch and great tonality, which after 1908 developed into strong colour contrasts.
In 1906 Mondrian and four other artists were awarded the Willink van Collen prize: he spent the winter of 1906-07 with the painter A.G. Hulshoff Pol on a farm belonging to the latter's family in Oele, a village in the east of Holland not very far from Winterswijk. The confrontation with the work of V. van Gogh, Otto van Rees, Kees van Dongen and Jan Sluyters aroused Mondrian's interest in developments in painting in Brussels and Paris.
During a visit in September 1908 to the seaside resort of Domburg in Zeeland, Mondrian joined a group of internationally-orientated artists, of whom Jan Toorop was the best informed.
In May 1909 he became a member of the Theosophic Society in Amsterdam. In January 1909 Mondrian, Jan Sluyters and C. Spoor exhibited in the Stedelijk Museum in Amsterdam—the first time a large number of works by Mondrian, mostly of the past five years, were shown together. This exhibition made it clear to everyone, friend and foe, that Mondrian was concerned with giving form to a highly individual conception of art. A letter to the art critic Is. Querido contains Mondrian's earliest written explanation of his motives. He spent most of the autumn and winter of 1909-10 in Domburg. Light-houses, dune landscapes, church facades and seascapes are the main themes of this period.

1910

To: Schelfhout

Domburg [postmarked October 3 1910]

Dear Schelfhout,

My address is Domburg for the next two weeks. I have done a lot of work here and feel I have made some progress. In November I have to draw more 'bacteria' in Leiden, because I am not selling anything of course.
I wish you would tell me something about this Union Int. des Beaux Arts et des Lettres, Alcassar d'Eté, Champs Elysées. Please let me know what *kind* of work is on show, whether it

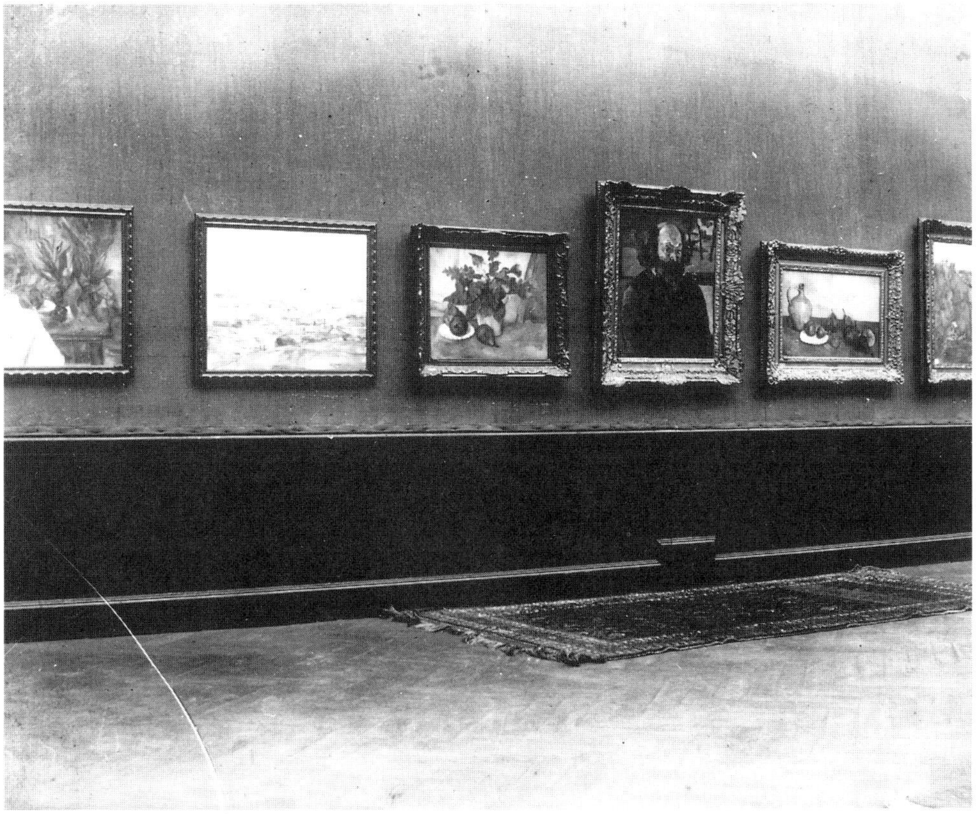

Two views of the rooms with the Cézanne pictures from the 'Modern Art Circle' exhibition, 1911.

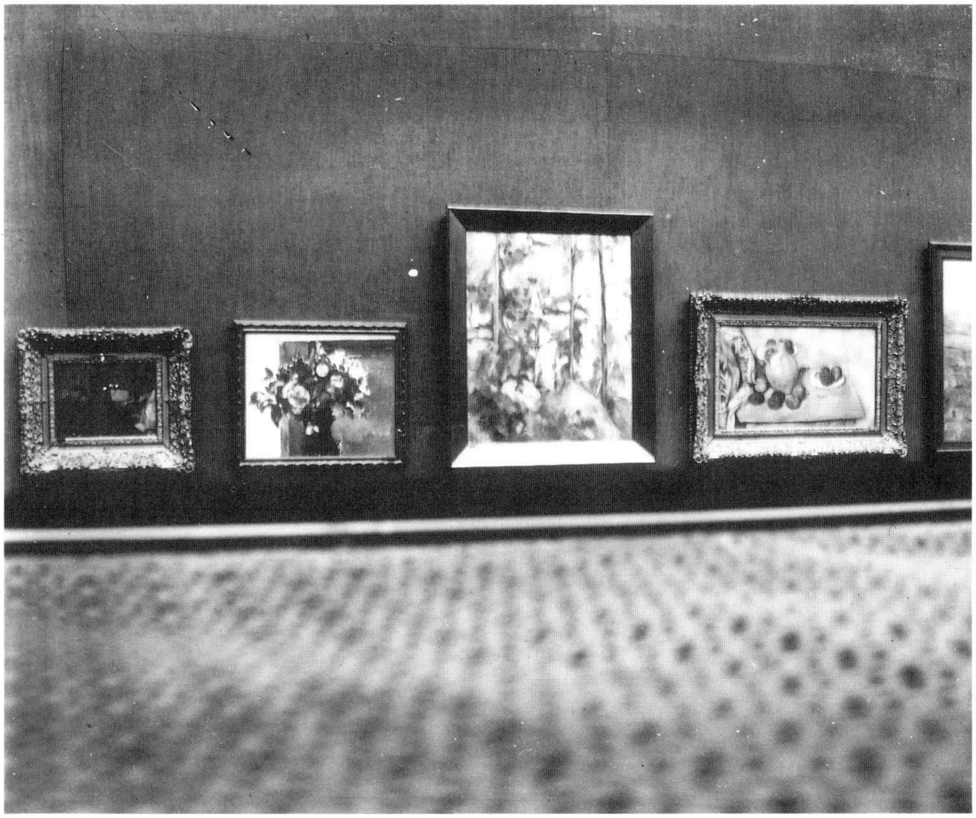

is our kind of work or not. Jan Sluyters sent me a postcard saying that van den Tonge (who paints interiors in the Dutch manner) was also invited. In think it is very strange of them to invite me as well after seeing my exhibition in Brussels.
Kikkert warned Sluyters about this association, Sluyters tells me. I had written to Sluyters that the Salon d'Automne had refused me, and now he writes that he doesn't understand why I call the Salon conventional, because (according to him!) it is frightfully modern. I don't know whether I can rely on Sluyter's judgment, which is why I am writing to you. Go and take a look at the Automne and let me know what is hanging there: I mean whether the kind of work we like is on show. You would be doing me a great favour.

Best wishes from Piet Mondrian.

1912

In 1910 C. Kikkert, Jan Sluyters and Mondrian founded the Moderne Kunstkring, with Jan Toorop acting as chairman. The group intended to mount annual exhibitions of work by the most progressive artists, following the example of the Salon d'Automne in Paris. The first of these exhibitions was held in late 1911, and comprised the work of Cézanne, Braque, Picasso, Derain and Le Fauconnier as well as their own. Mondrian showed his most recent works. He held his last exhibition at Arti in October 1909, and at St. Lucas in April of that year. He spent August, September and October of 1910 working in Domburg and in July 1911 he stayed in Veere. Mondrian exhibited a 'Soleil' at the Salon des Indépendants in Paris, and took part in the first exhibition of the colony of artists at Domburg. Esoteric writings, especially those of Madame Blavatsky and Rudolf Steiner, inspired Mondrian to several works, of which the programmatic 'Evolution Triptych' was the most important.
Early in 1912 Mondrian moved to Paris, first taking residence at 33 Avenue du Maine, then in one of the studios at 26 Rue du Départ. He soon became acquainted with the fairly large colony of Dutch artists in Paris at the time, which included Kees van Dongen, Schelfhout, Otto van Rees and the composer Jacob van Domselaer. He exhibited at the Salon des Indépendants, the Moderne Kunstkring in Domburg and at the Sonderbund in Cologne.

1913

He spent considerable time in Domburg again, and took part in the exhibition at the Moderne Kunstkring in Amsterdam, and in the Erster

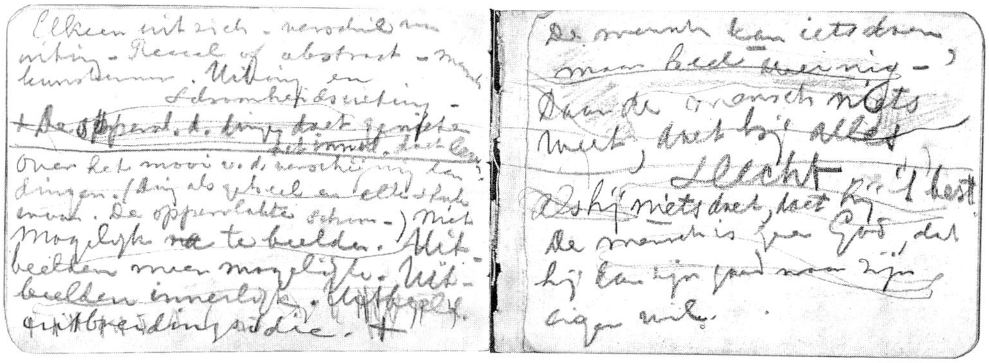

Everyone expresses himself
— differences in expression —
real or abstract — man (or) artist.
Expression and expression of beauty.

Concerning beauty in the appearance of things. [the object as a whole and (in) all its parts. The surface is beautiful].

(This) Cannot be transcribed into form.
(It is) Sooner possible to express in form.
To express in form (concerns) the inner sphere.
To express in form extension idea.
The surface of things causes pleasure, their inner character bring life.

Man *can* accomplish something, but very little.
Because man understands nothing, he does everything **badly**.
When he does *nothing*, he does best.
Man is not a God, who can achieve goodness according to his own will.

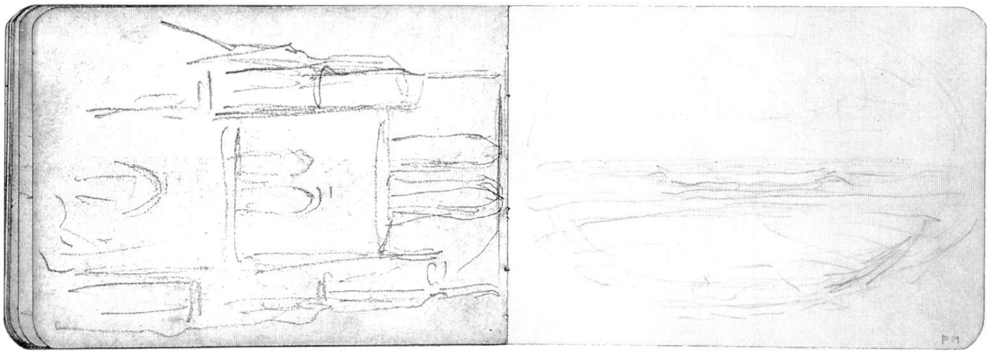

Four pages of Mondrian's sketchbooks, 1911-14.

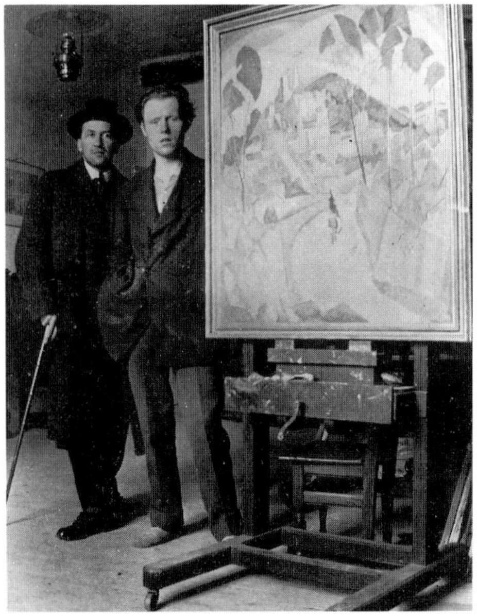

Mondrian and his painter friend Lodewijk Schelfhout—his 'View of Villeneuve-les-Avignon', 1912 on the easel—in the studio 26 rue du Départ, Paris.

Deutscher Herbstsalon organized by Herwarth Walden in Berlin.

1914

The outbreak of the First World War caught Mondrian by surprise during one of his regular visits to his native country, and prevented him from returning to Paris. Interest in his work in the Netherlands was growing; an exhibition of recent work was mounted by the progressive art dealer Walrecht in The Hague.

To: H. P. Bremmer

26 rue du Départ Paris 29/1 '14

Dear Sir,

In answer to your letter I hasten to reply that I greatly appreciate your opinion of my work, and have no objections to your reproducing two pictures. While on the subject of my work, perhaps you might like to hear *my* attitude to it. Most people think my work is rather vague: the nicest thing they say is that it reminds them of music. Well, I don't mind that, but I do take exception to their going on to say that my work is thus outside the scope of visual art. For I construct lines and colour combinations on a flat surface in a deliberate attempt to depict *general beauty*. Nature (or what I see) inspires me, giving me, like any other painter, a sensation which produces an urge to make something, but I want to approach truth as closely as possible, which is why I abstract everything until I arrive at the fundament (still an external fundament!) of things. To me it is a form of truth that by not saying *anything particular*, one expresses something very particular indeed, which is in fact the truth (of great comprehension). To me the architecture of Antiquity is the highest art. I allege that by constructing horizontal and vertical lines *consciously* but not *calculatingly*, and guided by great intuition, arranging them in harmony and rhythm, I allege that with these basic forms of beauty—with the addition, if necessary, of other straight or curved lines, it is possible to create a work of art which is as powerful as it is true.—There is therefore nothing vague about it to a more profound observer: it is only vague to the superficial observer of nature. *Chance* must be as remote as *calculation*. I also think it is necessary to interrupt a horizontal or vertical line continually: for if these directions are not opposed by others, they might start to express something 'definite' and hence something human. And the point I am trying to make is that people should not try to express anything

human in art.
By not expressing anything human, by complete self-negation, a work of art emerges which is a monument to beauty: far transcending everything human and yet extremely human in its profundity and generality! I am convinced that this is the art of the future. Futurism, although a stage further than naturalism, is too concerned with human sensations. Cubism (the content of which is still far too firmly based on earlier products of beauty and hence far modern than Futurism), has taken the great step towards abstraction and for that reason is nonetheless both of this age and of the future: modern, then, *not* because of its content but because of its effect.— For my part I do not subscribe to either, but feel the spirit of the times in both, and in myself.
If you would like to see some of my earlier work, an acquaintance of mine will gladly show it to you. In that period, as now, I sought monumentalism, and tried to achieve abstraction by converting natural colours into a few exaggerated colours. Later, though, I became convinced that this work was too external and, although good of its kind perhaps, not 'constructed' enough. Finally, I was influenced by seeing Picasso's work, which I *greatly* admire. I am not ashamed to mention this influence, for I think it is better to have room for improvement than to be satisfied with attained perfection and to think this makes one more original! As do many painters.— Besides, I am sure that I am quite different from Picasso, as is generally said.
The address of my acquaintance is van Beuningenstraat 112, The Hague, Miss de Bruin. When I went to Paris this lady was so kind as to keep some large canvases for me, some of which she has even sold already. If you would care to go and see them, you might also be able to recommend a potential customer. Please excuse my practical presumption: staying alive is a vital issue!

Thanking you for your consideration,
Yours faithfully,
Piet Mondrian

To: L. Schelfhout

Paris, June 12 '14

Dear Loe,

It was nice of you to write, and I have a few more remarks to make. It seems to me that a lack of understanding or vision was responsible for the infrequency of our contact in Paris. As my actions have often demonstrated, I am not a professional recluse, and like you, I must see a bit of life. But a 'pseudo-life' like the Kikkert circle was not the life for me, which is why I preferred nothing. Things were also very hard for me at the time because I was searching for my own form of expression, and I was quite upset to hear in a letter from Kikkert that you imagined I was not doing any work, etc.— whereas I was seriously searching, but had little to show for it. It was 2 years ago, I think, when K. was in Zandvoort and you were still here. He also wrote that *if* he were to show me letters (nice of him *not* to) I would know who my friends were and who were not. You and he: he the friend, of course, not you. Anyhow, I didn't pay much attention, but think you ought to know. He also told me that you had fallen off the sofa laughing when you saw my work at the first M.K.K.! I didn't think that was very kind, because it was very serious work, although it had to change. Anyhow, I have often been disturbed at a kind of disdain on your part, because I knew I had something, even if the results of my work were not so good. But despite everything I know that you had a certain respect for my work, especially on seeing it for the first time, and that you thought my work from the blue tree period very good, just as K. told me that you thought I was the only one in A'dam. That's all well and good, but if one has something it doesn't suddenly change, and so I thought you were being inconsistent. From my last letter, however, you will realize that I now understand how it all happened, and that in your circumstances a little exaggeration is sometimes necessary. You write: I cannot be a Theosophist—well, perhaps I agree with you if you mean Theosophists in general. But that doesn't alter the fact that I think the Th. doctrine very wise, and that it leads to clarity in mental development. We agree on that point, then.
It seems to me that consciousness is paramount for every human being. To my mind Catholicism can lead to something vague, but Theosophy, a mental science, never can. Last winter I wrote a long article on Art and Theosophy for a Theosophical magazine, but it was too revolutionary for them, and they refused to print it. Perhaps that is in the article's favour.
As you wrote, we can fully appreciate each other's work and still pursue our own ways. It's the same with me and Verhoeven, who works so differently from me, and yet we still respect one another. He and I had a show in Zurich, but didn't sell anything. I also exhibited a few times in Germany, again without selling anything. I hope to sell something in The Hague, if only to pay the next bills! It is probably too far for you to go and see: Smidsplein 4, The Hague, and it opens on June 15, I think. I see what you mean about your wife. I only met her once but she made a very sympathetic impression on me. The same goes for what you wrote about K. Kikkert is *too* superficial to be a real friend. I don't *entirely* agree with what you write about Alma: I don't think you can expect genuine *friendship* in a deeper sense from him. Well, dear Loe, that's all for now. I shall come and see you in August, but I won't have any time to stay. I'll let you know beforehand. Best greetings to you both from Piet.

1917

To: H.P. Bremmer

7-3-17 Laren N.H.

Dear Mr. Bremmer,

Thank you for the postal order, which arrived safely. It was the 12th and the time is therefore up in which *you* paid me and *I* did not send a single work. I have already sent you a partial explanation. The main reason, however, is this: I have spent much of this year working and searching; a lot of my old work had to be changed. I was looking for a more pure form of depiction: that is why nothing satisfied me up to now.
I now think I have found a good form of depiction; I say this having finished a small canvas for you with which I am satisfied. You will understand that this is all in the nature of my work: you put me in a better position to carry on working (although I still had to take some orders), but in the end the delay was a help, because it takes 'time' to improve.
At the end of the year, then, my sincerest thanks: you will have to judge the result; *personally* I am satisfied.
Because the museum is closed, the exhibition I wrote about has been postponed, probably until mid-April. I therefore wanted to keep the things here until then: afterwards I shall send you the ones you have chosen. If you decide to stop my monthly allowance for the time being* until you have made your choice I shall perfectly understand; if you continue to send it, it will be better for me.
I have also altered the big black and white canvas, but wish I hadn't, because it would have been better to leave it and make something new. But when you are *searching* you don't know *how* beforehand. I think that is all I wanted to write.
Yours sincerely, Piet Mondrian

* (if you had been planning to continue it for more than one year)

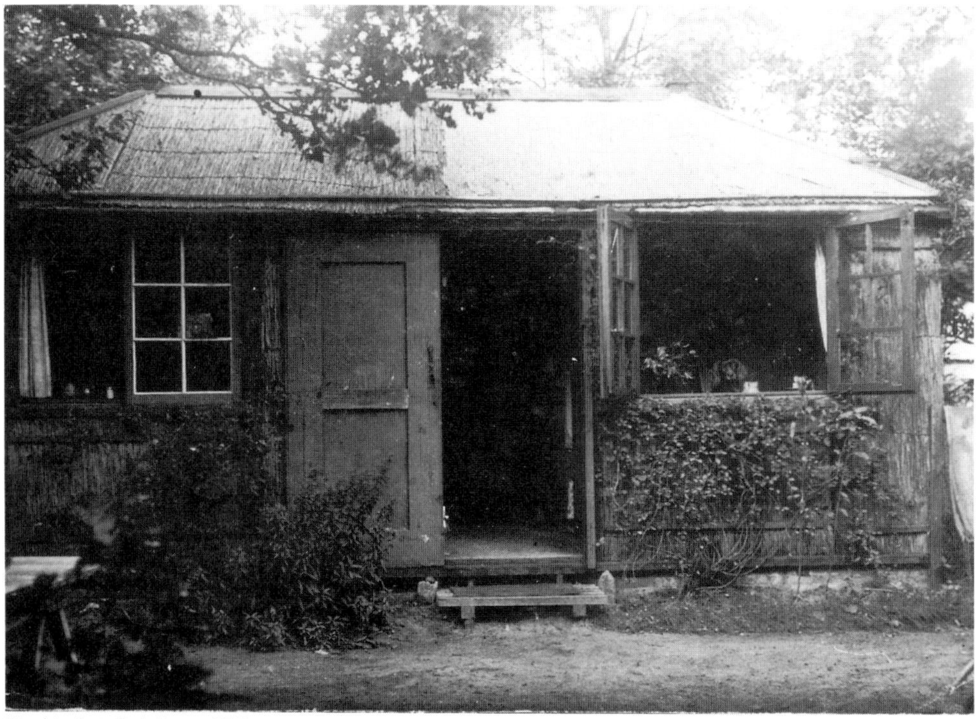

Mondrian's studio in Laren, 1915

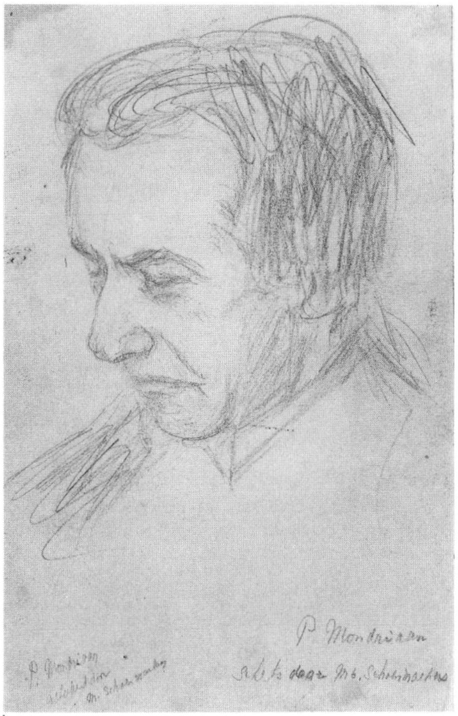

Mathieu Schoenmaekers, Portrait of Piet Mondrian, drawing. 1915

DE STIJL (no.1)

INTRODUCTION

This review is intended to form a contribution to the development of a new awareness of beauty. It aims at making modern people receptive to the new in art. It aims at confronting archaic confusion—modern "baroque"—with the logical principles of a maturing style based on the pure relationship of the spirit of the age and expressive means. It aims at uniting current ideas about neo-plasticism which, though basically the same, have developed independently.

The Editors will attempt to attain the above goal by providing a platform for the truly modern artist, who can contribute to the reform of aesthetic awareness and the consciousness of plastic art. Where the public is not yet ready for the neo-plastic aesthetic, it is the task of the expert to arouse the layman's sense of beauty. The truly modern i.e. conscious artist has a double vocation. First, to produce purely plastic art; second, to render the public susceptible to the beauty of pure plastic art. This calls for a review of an intimate nature, the more so because public criticism has failed to compensate for the lack of susceptibility towards the beauty of the abstract art revelation. The Editors themselves will appoint experts to cope with this task.

This little review will hence create a closer contact between artist and public and between those practising the various plastic arts. By allowing the modern artist to speak about his own profession, the prejudiced view that the modern craftsman works according to pre-established theories will vanish. On the contrary, we shall show that the new work of art does not emerge from a priori theories, but that conversely the principles emerge from plastic work.

This will pave the way for a more profound artistic culture based on the common embodiment of the new awareness of plastic art. As soon as artists from the different plastic professions realize that they are basically equal, that they have a common language, they will cease to cling anxiously to their individuality. They will serve the general principle beyond a limiting individuality. Serving that general principle, they will automatically engender an organic style. For the dissemination of beauty, a spiritual, not a social, community is needed. A spiritual community, however, cannot exist unless ambitious individuality is sacrificed.

Only if these principles are consistently applied can, through the artist's new relationship to society, neo-plastic beauty manifest itself in all objects as style.

Cover of the first issue of 'De Stijl', Oct.1917; the vignette was designed by V. Huszar.

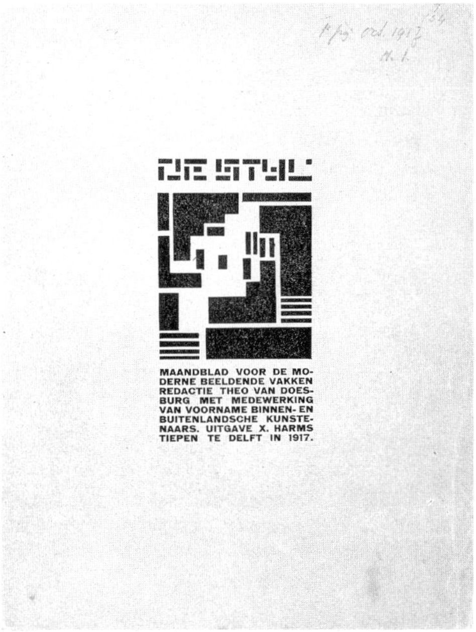

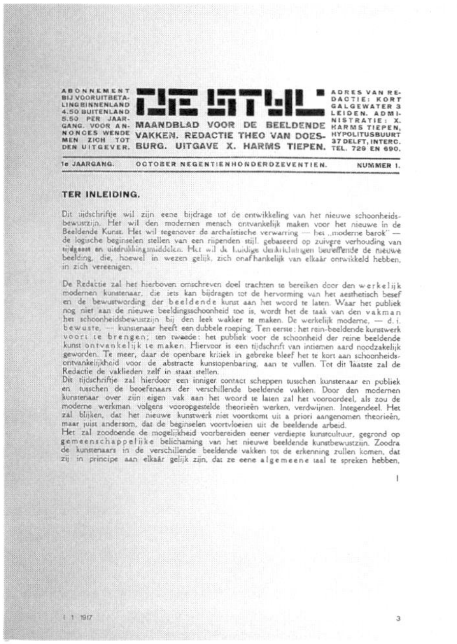

ABONNEMENT BIJ VOORUITBETALING BINNENLAND 4.50 BUITENLAND 5.50 PER JAARGANG. VOOR ANNONCES WENDE MEN ZICH TOT DEN UITGEVER.

DE STIJL

MAANDBLAD VOOR DE BEELDENDE VAKKEN. REDACTIE THEO VAN DOESBURG. UITGAVE X. HARMS TIEPEN.

ADRES VAN REDACTIE: KORT GALGEWATER 3 LEIDEN. ADMINISTRATIE: X. HARMS TIEPEN, HYPOLITUSBUURT 37 DELFT, INTERC. TEL. 729 EN 690.

1e JAARGANG. OCTOBER NEGENTIENHONDERDZEVENTIEN. NUMMER 1.

TER INLEIDING.

Dit tijdschriftje wil zijn eene bijdrage tot de ontwikkeling van het nieuwe schoonheidsbewustzijn. Het wil den modernen mensch ontvankelijk maken voor het nieuwe in de Beeldende Kunst. Het wil tegenover de archaïstische verwarring — het „moderne barok" — de logische beginselen stellen van een rijpenden stijl, gebaseerd op zuivere verhouding van tijdgeest en uitdrukkingsmiddelen. Het wil de huidige denkrichtingen betreffende de nieuwe beelding, die, hoewel in wezen gelijk, zich onafhankelijk van elkaâr ontwikkeld hebben, in zich vereenigen.

De Redactie zal het hierboven omschreven doel trachten te bereiken door den werkelijk modernen kunstenaar, die iets kan bijdragen tot de hervorming van het aesthetisch besef en de bewustwording der beeldende kunst aan het woord te laten. Waar het publiek nog niet aan de nieuwe beeldingsschoonheid toe is, wordt het de taak van den vakman het schoonheidsbewustzijn bij den leek wakker te maken. De werkelijk moderne, — d. i. bewuste, — kunstenaar heeft een dubbele roeping. Ten eerste: het rein-beeldende kunstwerk voort te brengen; ten tweede: het publiek voor de schoonheid der reine beeldende kunst ontvankelijk te maken. Hiervoor is een tijdschrift van intiemen aard noodzakelijk geworden. Te meer, daar de openbare kritiek in gebreke bleef het te kort aan schoonheidsontvankelijkheid voor de abstracte kunstopenbaring, aan te vullen. Tot dit laatste zal de Redactie de vaklieden zelf in staat stellen.

Dit tijdschriftje zal hierdoor een inniger contact scheppen tusschen kunstenaar en publiek en tusschen de beoefenaars der verschillende beeldende vakken. Door den modernen kunstenaar over zijn eigen vak aan het woord te laten zal het vooroordeel, als zou de moderne werkman volgens vooropgestelde theorieën werken, verdwijnen. Integendeel. Het zal blijken, dat het nieuwe kunstwerk niet voortkomt uit a priori aangenomen theorieën, maar juist andersom, dat de beginselen voortvloeien uit de beeldende arbeid.

Het zal zoodoende de mogelijkheid voorbereiden eener verdiepte kunstcultuur, gegrond op gemeenschappelijke belichaming van het nieuwe beeldende kunstbewustzijn. Zoodra de kunstenaars in de verschillende beeldende vakken tot de erkenning zullen komen, dat zij in principe aan elkaâr gelijk zijn, dat ze eene algemeene taal te spreken hebben,

1

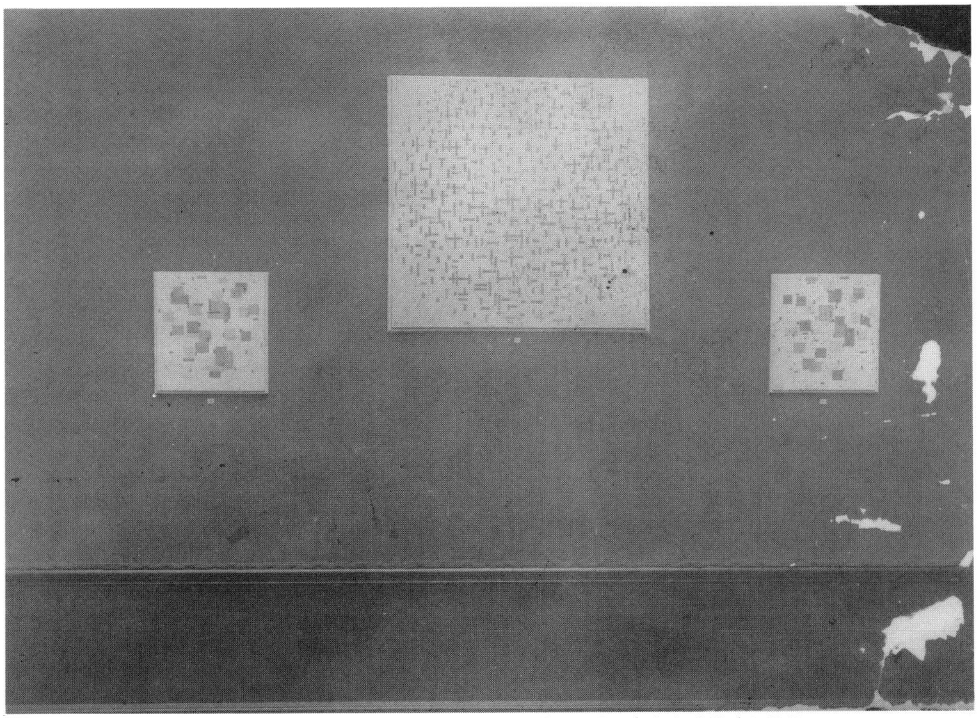

Three Mondrian pictures at the exhibition of the 'Hollandse kunstenaarskring' (Dutch Artists' Circle), 1917.

Piet Mondrian, Composition, 1918 (whereabouts unknown).

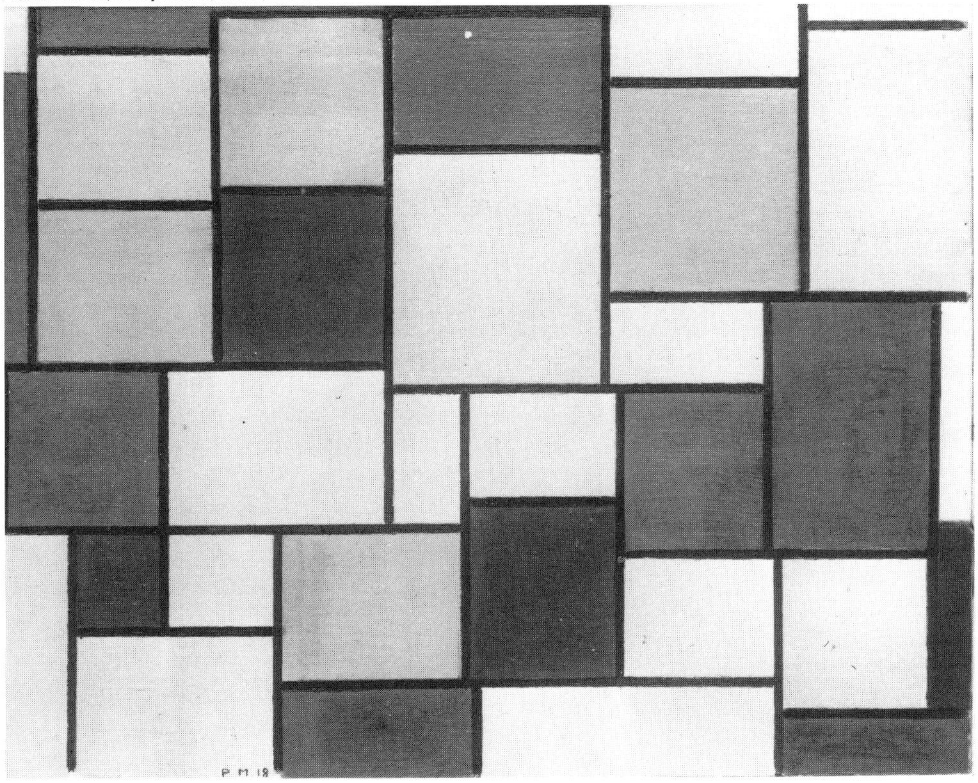

1919

As a result of the intensive interaction between thinking about the basis of art, writing about art, and making art, Mondrian became increasingly convinced that his art was the truly consistent concretization of all painting before him. He developed his ideas in conversations with the composer Van Domselaer, with whom he lived for some time in the Pijlsteeg, Laren, and with the 'Christosoph' Dr. M.H.J. Schoenmaekers, who had a large number of articles and several books to his name, the most important being *Het geloof van den nieuwen mensch* (1st impression 1907, revised edition 1914). *Het nieuwe wereldbeeld* (1915) and *Beginselen der Beeldende Wiskunde* (1916).

Although Mondrian agreed with Schoenmaekers on many points, he continued to read widely, e.g. the writings of the Dutch Neo-Hegelian philosopher G. J. P. J. Bolland and leading art theoretical writings such as Charles Blanc's *Grammaire des Dessins* (1867).

Mondrian wrote down his ideas, and also read them out loud to his friends. The journal *Theosophia* invited him to publish his views, but withdrew the invitation after reading the manuscript. It was probably towards the end of 1913 that he came into contact with H.P. Bremmer, who acted as artistic advisor to the wealthy family of industrialists, Kröller-Müller. Bremmer guaranteed Mondrian a fixed monthly sum in return for a number of paintings annually. This meant that he no longer had to spend a large proportion of his time on producing copies on commission of paintings in different Dutch museums, or making replicas of his own, earlier, naturalistic works. In 1915 he met Theo van Doesburg, another painter, who had for some time entertained ideas of starting a progressive journal, and he was introduced to Salomon Slijper in Laren, who was to prove a welcome buyer of his works in the years that followed.

Mondrian worked in Laren, where his younger brother Louis taught at Prof. van Rees' Humanitaire School, and lived in Amsterdam. In Laren he met Bart van der Leck, whose paintings with their large, flat primary colours he found inspiring.

In January/February 1915 Mondrian exhibited together with Peter Alma and Le Fauconnier in Rotterdam and Groningen, and late in that year in the Stedelijk Museum in Amsterdam together with Schelfhout, Sluyters, Gestel, Le Fauconnier and Van Epen. Works were also shown at exhibitions of the Hollandsche Kunstenaarskring in Amsterdam in 1916 and 1917.

The first issue of *De Stijl* was published in October 1917, and edited by Theo van Doesburg. 'The Book' that Mondrian had worked on for many years, and in which he formulated his art-theoretical views, figured prominently in the

issues of *De Stijl* up to and including 1920. 'New Plasticism' became the motto of the journal. After the period of abstracting naturalistic points of departure such as trees, facades, and the series of drawings and paintings now generally known under the title 'Pier and Ocean' (many of these works are abstract representations of a pier in the sea under a bright starry sky) Mondrian turned in 1917 to the exploration of the expressive force of plastic means such as planes and lines without direct reference to a naturalistic starting-point. The experiments culminated in a number of works based entirely on a regular division of the plane, e.g. *Losangique with Grey Lines* (Gemeentemuseum, The Hague), the compositions in light colours, and *Composition with Dark Colours* (both at the Gemeentemuseum, The Hague). During 1919 Mondrian exhibited both at the Hollandsche Kunstenaarskring in Amsterdam and at the gallery of the art-dealer Walrecht in The Hague.
In June of that year he returned to Paris, where he lived at 26 Rue du Départ; before the end of the year he moved to a studio at 5 Rue de Coulmiers (from November 1919 to November 1921).

To: Th. van Doesburg

18/4 19 Laren N.H.

Dear Does,

Many thanks for the reproductions and your letter. I appreciate your various objections. It is true that a regular arrangement carries the danger of repetition, but that can be counteracted by contrast. Everything can become a system, irregular and regular arrangement alike. It all depends on the solution.
When I compare that work of mine you reproduced in De Stijl with, say, the rhomboids which you (and I) prefer, I clearly see that the latter are better composed. The size of the subdivisions could differ more, but that doesn't bother me. It took *me* a long time to discover this method, as you can plainly see in the photo I sent you last year; the one you have just reproduced in fact forms the transition to regular arrangement. I think we ought to make our own choices and work things out for ourselves; the one will achieve more with *this*, the other with *that*. The main thing is to adhere to the principle. The same applies to starting with an item of nature or not. Your description is a little narrow, I think. I agree with the main issue of destroying the natural aspect and reconstructing it according to the spirit, but we ought to take this too strictly. After all, the natural aspect need not be a

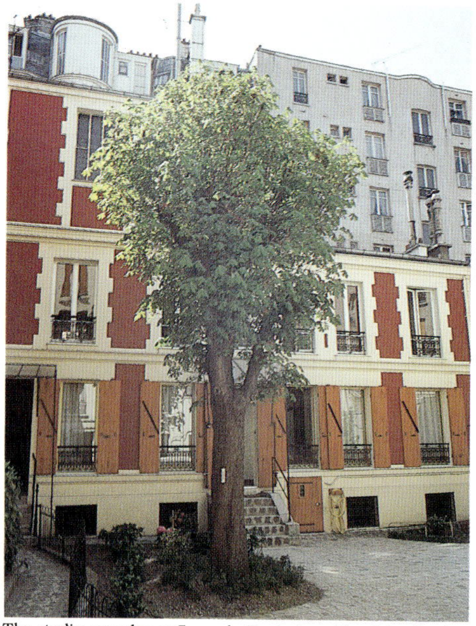

The studio complex at 5 rue de Coulmiers; Mondrian lived on the first floor from November 1919 to November 1921. (photograph 1984)

particular representation. At present I am working on something that is a reconstruction of a starry sky, but I'm doing it without resorting to nature. The man who claims he starts from nature can be right, and so can someone who claims he starts from nothing! I'm just trying to demonstrate the danger of assuming a system.
In the long run I don't think you will have any objection to *my* method, whatever it may be. I have no further news. I have to leave here on June 1st and will probably stay on in A'dam to visit friends, etc. etc. I shall come to Leiden first of all. I think I can finish 5 pictures.
Of course Valoir Plast. interests me. What serious work, compared with natural painting. *Ours* is much better, I think. When will you start on the Dutch issue? I think you ought to supply a brief description like the one for the Cubists. If any space is left it would be better to fill it with a translation of a short article by me, and by, say, an architect, better than those French verses by Salmon, for example! Who's paying for the reproductions? Let me know some time how many of the French numbers I should send you. Is any more expense involved, and how much? So long, Does. I'm going to Arnhem for Easter.

Best regards from your friend Piet.

To: S.B. Slijper

Picture postcard: Panorama des Sept Ponts, postmarked 24.6.1919

Dear Sal, I arrived safely. On Saturday I was sent back from Roosendaal to Rotterdam for my passport, and couldn't leave until Sunday morning. I enjoyed the journey. More later. For the time being best wishes. Your friend Piet.

To: Th. van Doesburg

1 Aug. '19 Paris.

Dear Does and Lena,

Here at last is the copy; the photo will follow soon. You know I thought it might be a good idea to accompany this article with a reproduction of the last thing I showed you, or put it in the next number if necessary, because it was prompted by a starry sky. I believe it would be better to touch up the print with chalk.
Anyhow, you know my intentions because we discussed them and I showed you a poor reproduction. The article has taken so long because I have had a lot of bother; you'll appreciate that there was so much to do. I read this article to you before, but I've changed and modified so much since then that it is now too long. I'm sending you the first half now, and the second half will follow at the end of the month. I believe I have thought up some nice things, such as the bit about rhythm, which I had not treated that way before. I hope you're satisfied. Don't hesitate to send it back with any remarks you may have; I should prefer that if it's necessary, even if it would be too late for the next issue. If you're careful we needn't have to read proofs. As far as I could see there was *one* small mistake in the last number on p.87, 14th line from the top, where "gemaskeerde" [masked] was printed instead of "gemarkeerde" [marked] horizon. I hope that Does has fully recovered. It was probably overexertion. I hope to hear good news about that very soon. As to things here: I hope to keep going. Everything is much dearer than before the war of course, but the same applies to Holland. And my rent hasn't gone up, which is most unusual. Rivera moved to a larger studio (also at N°26) some time ago and had to pay so much more rent that he moved out. I went to his old studio first and saw "Tour Donas" on the door. The caretaker had already told me that this was a *lady*, not a gentleman! The way they always go in for intrigue here. I asked Rivera about her. He didn't know who she was, but said that Archipenko had presented her as a man in order to make a better impression (at least so he *thought*!) He said that people would have less confidence in a woman! This might be true. In any case it was unfair of Archip., but don't write to him about it. One of

these days I shall visit this *Mister* Tour Donas and see for myself. I wasn't *very* keen on that last reproduction of hers in De Stijl. Not that I am criticizing it: I just mean that I don't have very high expectations. Even Rivera disappointed me more than I had expected: I always knew he was more of a *follower* than a real cubist. He has now completely abandoned cubism and paints pictures you could hang in the Louvre. Very clever but not at all modern. He himself said that the war had restored a lot of what was not abstract. I wasn't very pleased to hear that; anyhow, he's moved now. I also went to the Picasso exhibition. Old and new work, not much changed, but I thought his latest work less serious, less convincing. I hear he is doing other work, not to make money but *because he wants to be versatile*!! That's right: his work can't be convincing then, can it? Like most of the Cubists he is on contract to Rosenberch, at whose brother's he exhibits other work, serious portraits, I hear. The Ros. are Jews, but the galleries in the Rue de Baume are very good and exclusively Cubist. I should like to exhibit there later if possible. I won't undertake anything until I have enough work ready. The pieces I was working on are in Laren; I am considering having them sent, although it would cost 25 guilders per 100 kilos. When things get back to normal perhaps you might exhibit there too. I was not enamoured of the Picasso show, then, although it is marvellous that that sort of thing goes on, however irresolutely, and that there is an exhibition gallery for it, which is not the case in Holland. At Rosenb. I saw a good painting by Léger, who has made great progress I think. Summing up, the new is carrying on and we, working, wait. I therefore have nothing special to write about Paris for De Stijl; keep what I have written to yourself.
How are things with the Italian?
I am longing for the new issue of De Stijl. How nasty of Huszar: I shall pretend he doesn't exist in future. I blame him most for being in league and collaborating with weak characters. Isn't that what you told me?
Well, Does and Lena, you won't lose heart, nor shall I. I look forward to hearing from you soon and remain, as ever, your *friend* Piet.
I am glad to be back here, because I feel the seriousness of the metropolis very strongly. Everything is so juvenile in Holland.

To: Th. van Doesburg

4 Dec. '19

Dear Does and Lena, thanks for your letter and the issues of De Stijl. It is due to your efforts that it can carry on. I have only *glanced* at the new number because I'm so busy with a new article, but I read your last articles about Rol. Holst and Expressionism carefully and I think they are *extremely* good; perhaps the one could be slightly more impersonal in places, but maybe that's the way it ought to be. My new article is about, among others, the decorative aspect with regard to my studio here, where I have been experimenting a bit. I couldn't work on the wall and had to confine myself to putting up a few sheets of painted cardboard. However, I now realize that it is quite feasible to have N.P. in a room in this way. I had to paint the furniture too, of course. I don't regret the effort, because it has a favourable effect on my work. I have produced something that I like better than all the previous stuff. Of course I don't mean that this is due to the studio! (I've been working on it for months.) It took a long time to think up, ever since I've been here. I wish I could *send* you a photo of it, but I'd rather leave it as it is for a while before applying the final coat of paint, and see how it behaves. I am working on about 6 pictures. It was good to hear that you have made a good thing, and also about your studio! *White is beautiful, sure, but colour is important too, Write to me later saying whether you agree with all my ideas, it will all go into the next article.* I'm glad you are pleased with this article: so was I. It is really fine to collaborate like this with a common goal! I fully agree with what you wrote. There is more to it than that group of it Hoff's thinks! I think it's strange to use the craftsman to "turn things upside down" and then see what one can do oneself. What is the result? Unfinished business; *when* they really need it, there's no reason for them to work. When it's really necessary to turn things upside down I'm all in favour; you'll agree that things have to change. But I've no confidence in the v.H. group, and agree with you that they are too superficial. A pity, because they could have been good workers.—To return to my article: might it not be better to send it back with your remarks? Perhaps I could change a few small details. For instance, you could see whether I have used *palpably*—real properly; it's so hard to find a term to distinguish *N.P. in a building* from *N.P. in a painting*. If there are only minor corrections you could just send a few pages and the proofs, for example, so that I can check them. So will you send me your remarks soon? Perhaps you might risk unregistered mail; all letters have arrived safely. But you can register it if you like, since it will be delivered to the door in any case. At worst I have a copy here, but it's much corrected and hard to survey.—I agree with you that we stand completely alone, surpassing the foreigners by far. I saw the exhibition at Rosenberg's here but the standard is below ours. I was even disappointed in Léger's and other people's work. I enquired about their Revue, but it isn't out yet; the gallery attendant didn't know anything about it. I also went to see the famous "Courbet studio". (Kikkert goes there nearly every day! He thinks it extraordinary!!!) Of course it's *good*, but just as good as a Rembrandt is *good*. Anyhow, there is really *nothing* here. How nice that you may be coming. Lena will come too, of course; the two of you can use my room and I'll move into the studio. You'd better bring a blanket. It's good to hear that you're going to give a lecture in Belgium. Perhaps the soil is fertile there. At any rate De Stijl seems to work well there. I have not had time to go to Archip. I don't see anyone these days really, and I think it's better that way at present. I've been thinking about Severini—I saw his work at Rosenberg's—what a difference! I think I'll wait. He seems a bit "half" to me. Yes, the Italians are real people. But like you said, too mystical etc. I think the way you're treating them is right. It is very nice of you to mention a small remuneration but don't bother: De Stijl needs it and I can manage. I only mentioned it in connection with van 't Hoff in order to point out that a man like that could be useful financially, and that we suffer from striking out on our own!

So long, warm greetings from your *friend* Piet.

1920

Together with his boyhood friend Dr. van Eck, Mondrian translated a resumé of the latter's 'New Plasticism' into French; the translation was dedicated 'aux hommes futurs' and was published under the title 'Le Néo-plasticisme' by the art-dealer Léonce Rosenberg. From then on Mondrian abandoned his attempts to apply his ideas concerning neo-plasticism in order to apply his ideas concerning neo-plasticism to language. However, he did try to realize his neo-plastic ideas, as described in his contribution to *De Stijl*, in his studio at 5, Rue de Coulmiers and after November 1921 in his studio at 26, Rue du Départ.
In this year Mondrian showed his work at an exhibition in his native country (Hollandsche Kunstenaarskring and 'Section d'Or' in The Hague) and in England (Brighton Public Art Galleries).

To: Th. van. Doesburg

5 août 20, Paris—Dada—

Dear Does and Lena DADA.

I received your letter this afternoon. I was revising my article for van Eck because he wants to try to translate something in between his own work. I hope something comes of it, but he always has so much to think of himself. While I was revising I noticed that part of it was rather *thick*, which is why what I am sending you is slightly altered; don't you think this version is better? The first sentences look all right to me, so I left them as they were. I thought you would more or less agree with me about it all. I don't think it need be in Dutch and French; if it is to be an appendix, just French will do. I thought of an appendix because it would fill an entire issue of De Stijl or even be too long for one number. So a separate brochure, just in French. But ought we to let the subscribers have it for nothing? Perhaps it would be better just to announce the brochure in De Stijl and try to sell it mainly here in Paris. We might cover our expenses then. Anyone in Holland wanting to read it can read it in French, don't you agree? It sounds a good idea, putting it on the new volume as you suggested. Could it be longer, like this:
Wouldn't it be better
to make the N.B.* more
noticeable by
making it black and De Stijl red?

Yes, we shall go on fighting as long as we can, Does!

[see illustration]

Maybe N.B. would be better in red after all.

[see illustration]

Linked letters are always less readable.
I'm just fooling around, but it might help you hit on the right proportions.

* Translator's note: N.B. refers to "Nieuwe Beelding", the Dutch for Neo-Plasticism, abbreviated elsewhere as N.P.

1921

Financial problems with the art-dealer Rosenberg induced Mondrian to consider abandoning his painting altogether and moving to the South of France. However, several commissions for copies and watercolours and drawings of flowers enabled him to keep his head above water. Various friends in Holland, notably the architect Oud, helped him to obtain commissions in Holland. His father died.

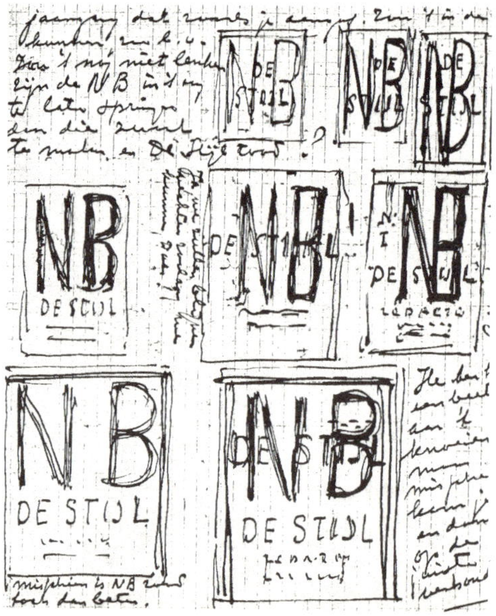

"De Stijl" cover, 1921

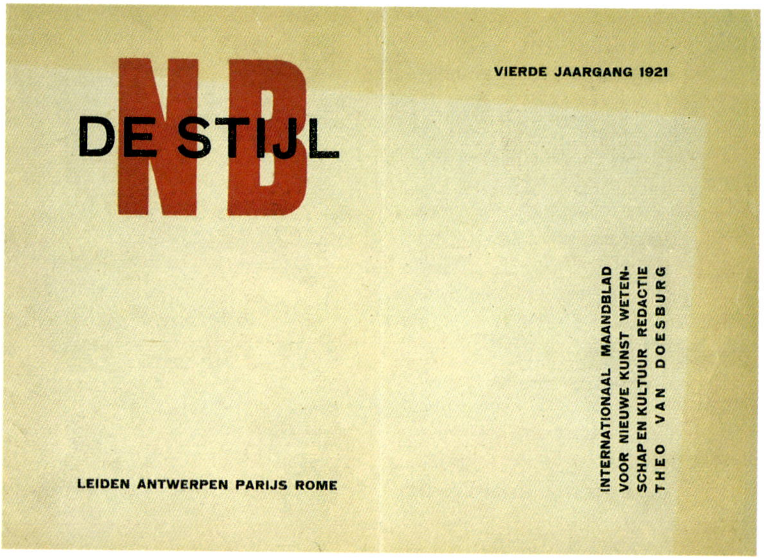

View of the room of the exhibition 'Maîtres du Cubisme' at the Rosenberg Gallery, Paris, 1921.

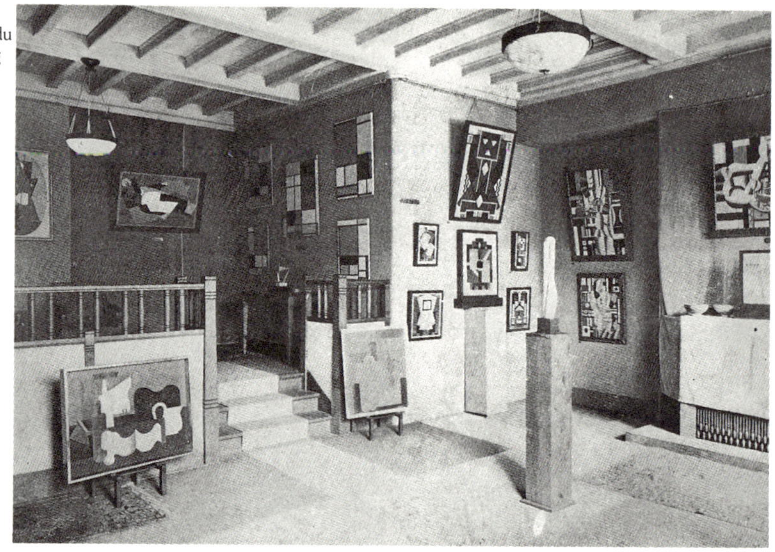

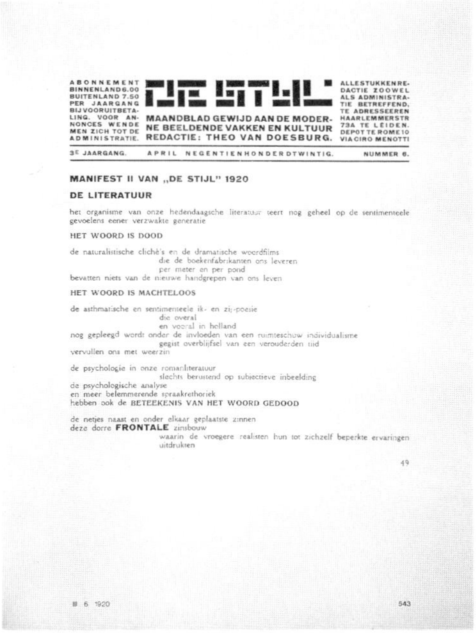

ABONNEMENT BINNENLAND 6.00 BUITENLAND 7.50 PER JAARGANG BIJ VOORUITBETALING. VOOR ANNONCES WENDE MEN ZICH TOT DE ADMINISTRATIE.

DE STIJL

MAANDBLAD GEWIJD AAN DE MODERNE BEELDENDE VAKKEN EN KULTUUR
REDACTIE: THEO VAN DOESBURG.

ALLE STUKKEN REDACTIE ZOOWEL ALS ADMINISTRATIE BETREFFEND, TE ADRESSEEREN HAARLEMMERSTR 73A TE LEIDEN. DEPOT TE ROME 10 VIA CIRO MENOTTI

3E JAARGANG. APRIL NEGENTIENHONDERDTWINTIG. NUMMER 6.

MANIFEST II VAN „DE STIJL" 1920

DE LITERATUUR

het organisme van onze hedendaagsche literatuur teert nog geheel op de sentimenteele gevoelens eener verzwakte generatie

HET WOORD IS DOOD

de naturalistische cliché's en de dramatische woordfilms
die de boekenfabrikanten ons leveren
per meter en per pond
bevatten niets van de nieuwe handgrepen van ons leven

HET WOORD IS MACHTELOOS

de asthmatische en sentimenteele ik- en zij-poesie
die overal
en vooral in holland
nog gepleegd wordt onder de invloeden van een ruimteschuw individualisme
gegist overblijfsel van een verouderden tijd
vervullen ons met weerzin

de psychologie in onze romanliteratuur
slechts berustend op subjectieve inbeelding
de psychologische analyse
en meer belemmerende spraakrethoriek
hebben ook de BETEEKENIS VAN HET WOORD GEDOOD

de netjes naast en onder elkaar geplaatste zinnen
deze dorre **FRONTALE** zinsbouw
waarin de vroegere realisten hun tot zichzelf beperkte ervaringen uitdrukten

49

III 6 1920 543

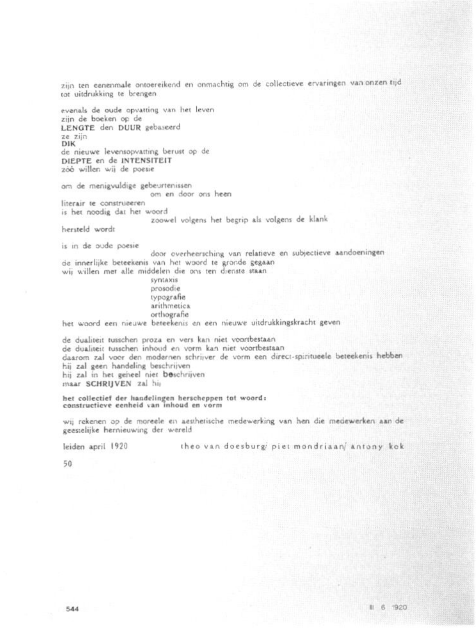

zijn ten eenenmale ontoereikend en onmachtig om de collectieve ervaringen van onzen tijd tot uitdrukking te brengen

evenals de oude opvatting van het leven
zijn de boeken op de
LENGTE den DUUR gebaseerd
ze zijn
DIK
de nieuwe levensopvatting berust op de
DIEPTE en de INTENSITEIT
zóó willen wij de poesie

om de menigvuldige gebeurtenissen
om en door ons heen
literair te construeeren
is het noodig dat het woord
zoowel volgens het begrip als volgens de klank
hersteld wordt

is in de oude poesie
door overheersching van relatieve en subjectieve aandoeningen
de innerlijke beteekenis van het woord te gronde gegaan
wij willen met alle middelen die ons ten dienste staan
syntaxis
prosodie
typografie
arithmetica
orthografie
het woord een nieuwe beteekenis en een nieuwe uitdrukkingskracht geven

de dualiteit tusschen proza en vers kan niet voortbestaan
de dualiteit tusschen inhoud en vorm kan niet voortbestaan
daarom zal voor den modernen schrijver de vorm een direct-spiritueele beteekenis hebben
hij zal geen handeling beschrijven
hij zal in het geheel niet beschrijven
maar SCHRIJVEN zal hij

het collectief der handelingen herscheppen tot woord:
constructieve eenheid van inhoud en vorm

wij rekenen op de moreele en aesthetische medewerking van hen die medewerken aan de geestelijke hernieuwing der wereld

leiden april 1920 theo van doesburg/ piet mondriaan/ antony kok

50

544 III 6 1920

Two pages of the III.6.1920 issue of 'De Stijl' with the Literature's Manifesto .

DE STIJL (vol.III, no.6)

MANIFESTO II OF "DE STIJL" 1920

LITERATURE

the organism of contemporary literature is still feeding
on the sentimental feelings of an enfeebled generation

THE WORD IS DEAD

the naturalistic clichés and the dramatic word-films
delivered by the manufacturers of books
by the metre and by the pound
contain nothing of the new handles in our life

THE WORD IS IMPOTENT

the asthmatic and sentimental I and she poetry
which everywhere
and particularly in Holland
is still perpetrated under the influence of an
agoraphobic individualism
the putrefied remains of an obsolete age
fill us with disgust

the psychology of our novels
based solely on subjective imagination
psychological analysis
and other hampering linguistic rhetoric
have also KILLED THE MEANING OF THE WORD

the sentences placed neatly side by side and one
above the other
this arid FRONTAL syntax
in which the former realists expressed
their own experiences
are once and for all inadequate and powerless to
express the collective experience of our age

like the old views of life
books are based
on LENGTH and DURATION

they are
THICK
the new view of life is based on
DEPTH and INTENSITY
that is how we want our poetry to be

in order to construct the manifold events
around and in us
in a literary fashion
it is necessary for the word
in terms of meaning and sound
to be restored

while in old poetry
due to the domination of relative and
subjective afflictions
the inner meaning of the word has been destroyed
we wish with all the means at our disposal
syntax
prosody
typography
arithmetic
orthography
to invest the word with new meaning and new
expressive power

the duality of prose and verse cannot continue to
exist
the duality of content and form cannot continue to
exist
form will therefore have a directly spiritual meaning
to the modern writer
he will not describe an action
he will not describe at all
but WRITE

re-create the collective actions into word:
the constructive unity of content and form

we are counting on the moral and aesthetic
cooperation of those
involved in the spiritual renewal of the world

leiden april 1920
theo van doesburg/piet mondrian/antony kok

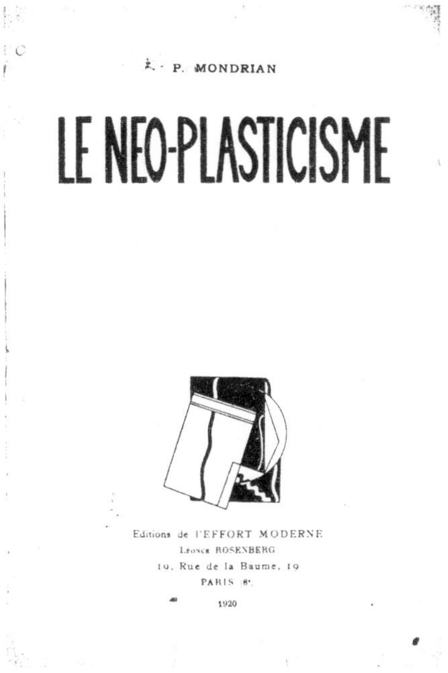

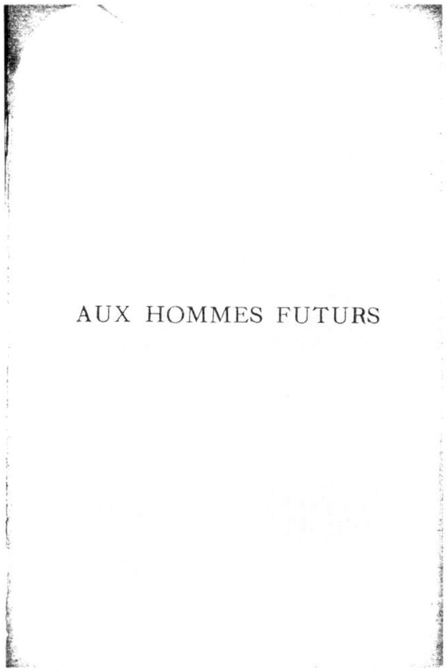

Cover of Piet Mondrian, Le Néo-Plasticisme, ed. L. Rosenberg (Paris), and first page 'Aux hommes futurs' (To the people of the future), 1920.

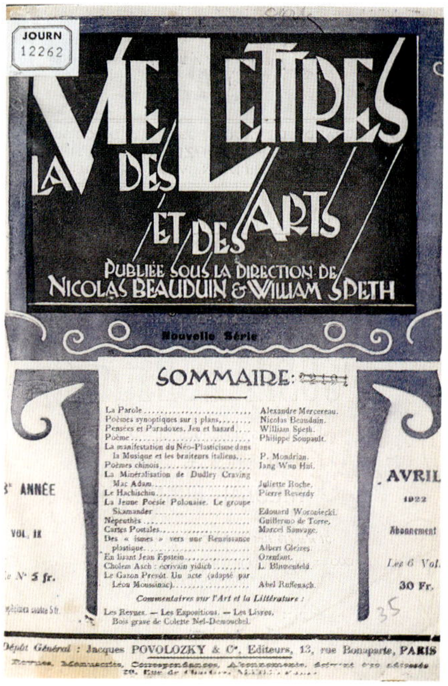

JOURN 12262

LA VIE DES LETTRES ET DES ARTS

PUBLIÉE SOUS LA DIRECTION DE NICOLAS BEAUDUIN & WILLIAM SPETH

Nouvelle Série

SOMMAIRE:

La Parole	Alexandre Mercereau.
Poèmes synoptiques sur 3 plans	Nicolas Beauduin.
Pensées et Paradoxes. Jeu et hasard	William Speth.
Poème	Philippe Soupault.
La manifestation du Néo-Plasticisme dans la Musique et les bruiteurs italiens	P. Mondrian.
Poèmes chinois	Iang Wun Hui.
La Minéralisation de Dudley Craving Mac Adam	Juliette Roche.
Le Hachischin	Pierre Reverdy
La Jeune Poésie Polonaise. Le groupe Skamander	Edouard Woroniecki.
Nèpenthès	Guillermo de Torre.
Cartes Postales	Marcel Sauvage.
Des « ismes » vers une Renaissance plastique	Albert Gleizes.
En lisant Jean Epstein	Ozenfant.
Cholem Asch : écrivain yidich	L. Blumenfeld.
Le Gazon Prevôt. Un acte (adapté par Léon Moussinac)	Abel Ruffenach.

Commentaires sur l'Art et la Littérature :

Les Revues. — Les Expositions. — Les Livres.
Bois gravé de Colette Nel-Dumouchel.

3e ANNÉE — VOL. II — Le N° 5 fr.

AVRIL 1922 — Abonnement — Les 6 Vol. 30 Fr.

Dépôt Général : Jacques POVOLOZKY & Cie, Editeurs, 13, rue Bonaparte, PARIS

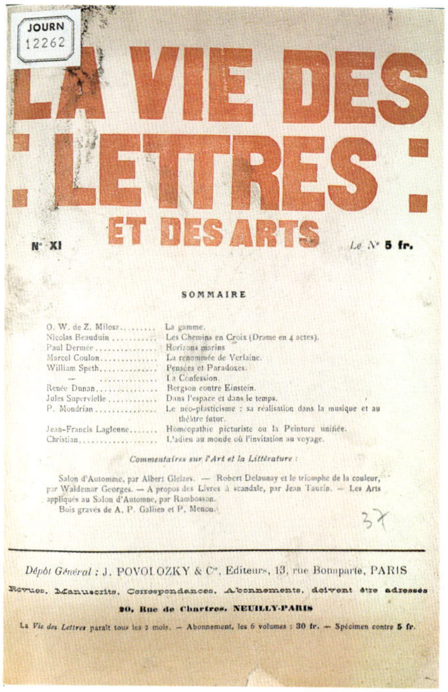

JOURN 12262

LA VIE DES LETTRES ET DES ARTS

N° XI — Le N° 5 fr.

SOMMAIRE

O. W. de Z. Milosz	La gamme.
Nicolas Beauduin	Les Chemins en Croix (Drame en 4 actes).
Paul Dermée	Horizons marins
Marcel Coulon	La renommée de Verlaine.
William Speth	Pensées et Paradoxes.
—	La Confession.
Renée Dunan	Bergson contre Einstein.
Jules Supervielle	Dans l'espace et dans le temps.
P. Mondrian	Le néo-plasticisme : sa réalisation dans la musique et au théâtre futur.
Jean-Francis Laglenne	Homéopathie picturiste ou la Peinture unifiée.
Christian	L'adieu au monde où l'invitation au voyage.

Commentaires sur l'Art et la Littérature :

Salon d'Automne, par Albert Gleizes. — Robert Delaunay et le triomphe de la couleur, par Waldemar Georges. — A propos des Livres à scandale, par Jean Tauzin. — Les Arts appliqués au Salon d'Automne, par Rambosson.
Bois gravés de A. P. Gallien et P. Menon.

Dépôt Général : J. POVOLOZKY & Cie, Editeurs, 13, rue Bonaparte, PARIS

Revues, Manuscrits, Correspondances, Abonnements, doivent être adressés

20, Rue de Chartres, NEUILLY-PARIS

La *Vie des Lettres* paraît tous les 2 mois. — Abonnement, les 6 volumes : 30 fr. — Spécimen contre 5 fr.

Cover of the magazine 'La Vie des Lettres et des Arts', April 1922 and August 1922, containing Mondrian's articles on Music: 1. The Manifestation of Neo-Plasticism in Music and the Italian Futurists', 2. 'Neo-Plasticism and its Realization in Music.'

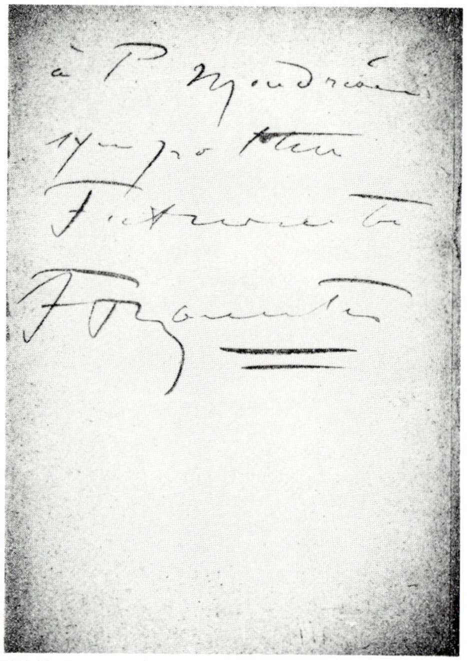

F.T. Marinetti sent his book 'Parole in Libertà' (Words in Freedom') with this dedication to Mondrian, 1922.

To: J.J.P. Oud

9/4 '21 Paris rue de Coulmiers

Dear Bob,

Thanks for your postcard of the bulb fields. You surely got my letter. Does told me that you kindly offered to fetch the picture yourself. With regard to the money, could I have a first instalment at the end of May, if you can't manage it all at once? Please ask, because my rent is due on June 1st. You've heard of Rosenberg's big plan. It seems somewhat impracticable to me because there is no Stijl group as a unit yet, nor a Stijl group at all, really. Rosenberg mentioned various architects to me, including v. 't Hoff. He seems to think all those people are still with De Stijl. I told Does that I think it can only work if you and Does draw up a plan together and engage me as advisor. If we get that far, others might join in or cooperate or suggest alternatives. That would result in *a whole*. Perhaps you could even collaborate with v. 't Hoff, although I don't know if he is able. I told Does that the scale model ought really to be made of wood and tin or cardboard and not plaster, but later I said it would be far too expensive and time-consuming and that it might be feasible to have a model in the form of a plaster sketch, with which he agreed.
For my part I take the decoration very seriously and have told Does that I couldn't supply designs for nothing. It would be a gigantic undertaking. I believe Does sees things differently and may be prepared to take a risk. Anyhow, he is in charge, and you'll have to discuss things with him. You know how I stand, though. I'd like to help as much as possible, but I won't promise to design or execute. If you need to know anything else, do write. Goodbye Bob, best wishes to Annie

your friend Piet

To: J.J.P. Oud

26 rue du Départ
6 Dec. '21

Dear Bob,

Thanks for your kindness and encouragement. I don't think I'm going to manage. This cold spell has shown me how much money one needs. Not a single artist is selling anything. All the good artists are retracting: making concessions. *I'd* rather stop. My friend van Eck has offered me a gardening job on his farm down south. I think I might go there in January. With the picture for van Lohuizen I enclose a recent picture for you too, which is at Rosenberg's at present. You have paid for most of it; if you feel like sending any more later it would be nice. What about another 50 francs? Later, I mean, in spring if necessary, when I'm there. *Thanks for your sympathy and friendship.*
As for Doesburg, he hasn't said anything to me but I can understand from what you write that he has the wrong idea about you. I almost had the impression myself that you did not consider *N.P.* suitable for that kind of use. I know you were bothered about "society" (from which I must now withdraw!) but that you were convinced about N.P. That is why I've started on an article that will clarify everything. I shall finish it in the country and send it to you. I think I shall continue to write for De Stijl etc. All good wishes to you both from Piet.*

* *Translator's note: Neo-Plasticism.*

1922

Mondrian submitted works to the exhibition mounted by Léonce Rosenberg under the title 'Du cubisme à une renaissance plastique'. Some of Mondrian's friends in Holland including Oud, the artist Peter Alma and S. Slijper, organized a retrospective exhibition of work at the Hollandsche Kunstenaarskring Amsterdam.
A performance of futuristic music in Paris prompted Mondrian to write a series of articles in *De Stijl* on the application of Neo-plastic principles to music.

P. Mondrian

Blown by the wind

Those familiar with the powerful innovatory movement in painting and sculpture in prewar Paris will be doubly irritated—if they are in favour of the new—at the current "lull" and retrogression. The action of breaking with the old and preparing ground for the new is slackening in the majority of cases, apart from a few staunch exceptions. As we know: reaction follows action, the latter being rendered almost unfeasible by outward, material circumstances. These are presently making it practically impossible to work in a new fashion. Financial and moral exhaustion in all countries since the war is the prime cause. The confusion of new art with inadequate and abortive social reforms has had a daunting effect.

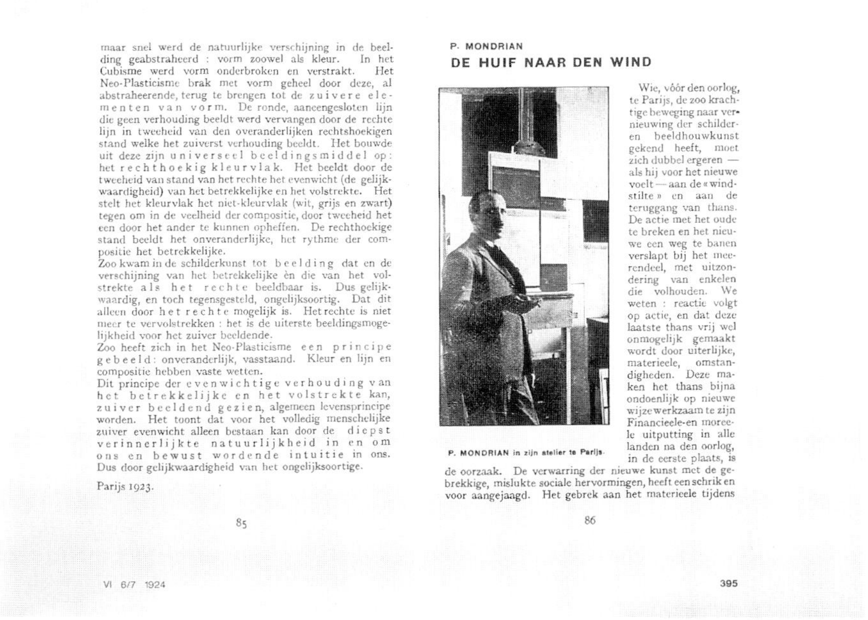
maar snel werd de natuurlijke verschijning in de beelding geabstraheerd : vorm zoowel als kleur. In het Cubisme werd vorm onderbroken en verstrakt. Het Neo-Plasticisme brak met vorm geheel door deze, al abstraheerende, terug te brengen tot de zuivere elementen van vorm. De ronde, aaneengesloten lijn die geen verhouding beeldt werd vervangen door de rechte lijn in tweeheid van den overanderlijken rechtshoekigen stand welke het zuiverst verhouding beeldt. Het bouwde uit deze zijn universeel beeldingsmiddel op: het rechthoekig kleurvlak. Het beeldt door de tweeheid van stand van het rechte het evenwicht (de gelijkwaardigheid) van het betrekkelijke en het volstrekte. Het stelt het kleurvlak het niet-kleurvlak (wit, grijs en zwart) tegen om in de veelheid der compositie, door tweeheid het een door het ander te kunnen opheffen. De rechthoekige stand beeldt het onveranderlijke, het rythme der compositie het betrekkelijke.
Zoo kwam in de schilderkunst tot beelding dat en de verschijning van het betrekkelijke èn die van het volstrekte als het rechte beeldbaar is. Dus gelijkwaardig, en toch tegensgesteld, ongelijksoortig. Dat dit alleen door het rechte mogelijk is. Het rechte is niet meer te vervolstrekken : het is de uiterste beeldingsmogelijkheid voor het zuiver beeldende.
Zoo heeft zich in het Neo-Plasticisme een principe gebeeld: onveranderlijk, vasstaand. Kleur en lijn en compositie hebben vaste wetten.
Dit principe der evenwichtige verhouding van het betrekkelijke en het volstrekte kan, zuiver beeldend gezien, algemeen levensprincipe worden. Het toont dat voor het volledig menschelijke zuiver evenwicht alleen bestaan kan door de diepst verinnerlijkte natuurlijkheid in en om ons en bewust wordende intuitie in ons. Dus door gelijkwaardigheid van het ongelijksoortige.

Parijs 1923.

85

VI 6/7 1924

P. MONDRIAN

DE HUIF NAAR DEN WIND

P. MONDRIAN in zijn atelier te Parijs.

Wie, vóór den oorlog, te Parijs, de zoo krachtige beweging naar vernieuwing der schilder- en beeldhouwkunst gekend heeft, moet zich dubbel ergeren — als hij voor het nieuwe voelt — aan de « windstilte » en aan de teruggang van thans. De actie met het oude te breken en het nieuwe een weg te banen verslapt bij het meerendeel, met uitzondering van enkelen die volhouden. We weten : reactie volgt op actie, en dat deze laatste thans vrij wel onmogelijk gemaakt wordt door uiterlijke, materieele, omstandigheden. Deze maken het thans bijna ondoenlijk op nieuwe wijze werkzaam te zijn Financieele-en moreele uitputting in alle landen na den oorlog, in de eerste plaats, is de oorzaak. De verwarring der nieuwe kunst met de gebrekkige, mislukte sociale hervormingen, heeft een schrik en voor aangejaagd. Het gebrek aan het materieele tijdens

86

395

Two pages of the VI.6/7.1924 issue of 'De Stijl' with Mondrian's attack on the attitude of his fellow-artists 'De Huik naar den Wind' ('Blown by the Wind').

To: J.J.P. Oud

le 25 Fevr. '22
rue du Départ 26

Dear Bob and Annie, very nice of you to think of me. Warmheartedness is so rare; it did me good. Thank you for your despatch. It arrived this afternoon just when I was working on a couple of little watercolours. Someone recently ordered a flower (naturalistic) from me for 100 fr. They liked it so much that I was then asked to do two watercolours for 50. I agreed because there's always room for improvement; if things always went like that I'd stop painting! The day before yesterday I was at an exhibition at Rosenberg's. He came up to me and said he'd like to show the same work again in April. He also wanted to come and take a look in my studio but what with all my worries, moving house and the commissions I've nothing finished, although plenty in progress. I sent those two big pictures to A'dam at the invitation of the Dutch Artists' Circle (of which I ceased to be a member a long time ago), or perhaps Alma; I've no other explanation for their interest. They are even paying half the transport costs. I think it will be mid-March, but you'll probably see it in the papers or somewhere. You will go and look, won't you? Maybe a buyer will go too. Miss Tak v. Poortvliet, who used to buy my work but later thought it too abstract, has ordered a recent watercolour. She wrote that she had a portfolio of drawings from which I definitely ought not to be missing. A strange compliment, don't you think? Anyhow, she advanced the 400 fr. I'm constantly amazed at how I always manage to scrape along. In January I needed a lot of money to move into the studio, which meant another expensive deposit and a rent increase of 600 fr. per annum, but it's all paid for and the studio is now in my name. My friends couldn't help because of financial obligations. I'll tell you all about it in detail later; it took a lot of planning to get everything organized. I've also written another article for De Stijl; the one about architecture isn't finished yet. I'm still working on the paintings for v. Lohuizen and you. Marinetti sent me another book in which he wrote "à l'auteur de Néo-Plasticisme avec sympathie". (I'd sent him my brochure on receiving his first despatch.) I thought that was nice of him. Well, dear Bob and Annie, I have to do some cooking for tomorrow, so I'll stop.

Thanks again, and best wishes from your friend Piet.
That Kamerlingh Onnes is a nice fellow, but terribly green and not at all "new", is he?

To: A. Kok 5/12/1922

Dear Antony, thanks for your letter; this morning I received notification from the Bank. It's always agreeable and reassuring to have some money for eventualities and in times of need; I now have enough to get by on, from painting flowers. I'd much rather earn money some other way, just as you have a job that has nothing to do with art. But I never learned anything else. I shall try to stay here and see what happens. Life in the country doesn't appeal to me. Everything evolves differently, but slowly, old chap. Long live the futurists! (with their urge for speed). The last piece I wrote for De Stijl has already been translated, but the second, about music, was not even placed. And the whole abstract movement is stewing (only on the surface, thank goodness) in materialism and naturalism. Does is persevering staunchly; I realize that he has to interpret the Neo-Plastic idea very broadly, because practically nobody is willing to take the consequences. It's nice that there are a few who are.
Your second picture will have to wait. Someone will probably come by in the spring and bring it to you, together with the other one that is ready. Well, so long, Antony. Greetings from Piet.

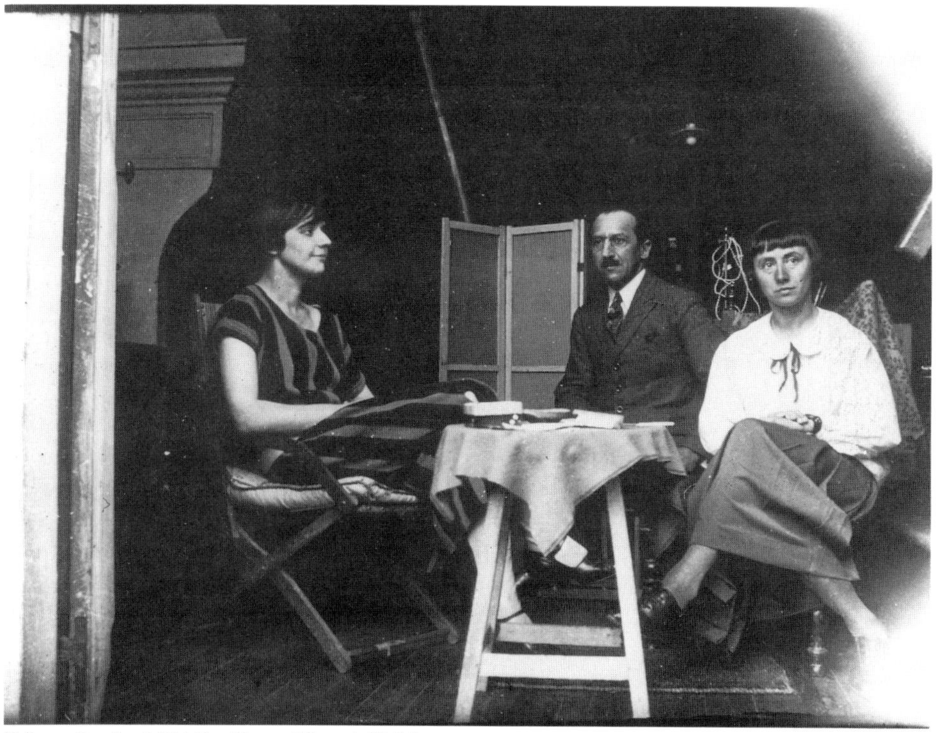

Nelly van Doesburg, Piet Mondrian and Hannah Höch in Van Doesburg's studio in Clamart, 1924.

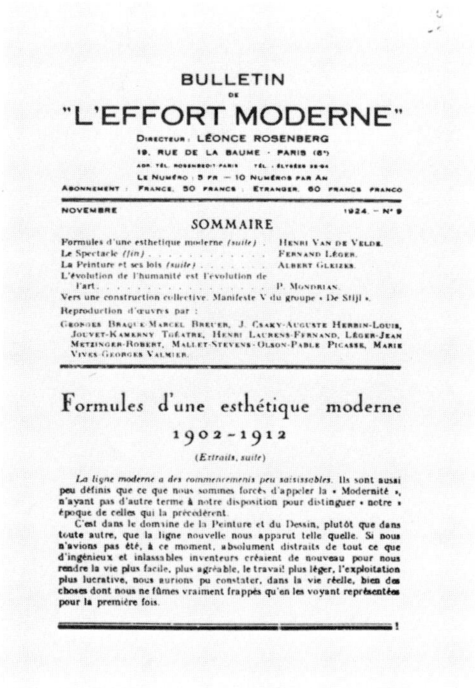

BULLETIN
DE
"L'EFFORT MODERNE"

DIRECTEUR : LÉONCE ROSENBERG
19, RUE DE LA BAUME · PARIS (8e)
ADR. TÉL. ROSENBEDIT-PARIS TÉL. : ÉLYSÉES 39-04
LE NUMÉRO : 5 FR — 10 NUMÉROS PAR AN
ABONNEMENT : FRANCE, 50 FRANCS ; ETRANGER, 60 FRANCS FRANCO

NOVEMBRE 1924. — N° 9

SOMMAIRE

Formules d'une esthetique moderne *(suite)* . . . HENRI VAN DE VELDE.
Le Spectacle *(fin)* . . . . FERNAND LÉGER.
La Peinture et ses lois *(suite)* . . . . ALBERT GLEIZES.
L'évolution de l'humanité est l'évolution de l'art. P. MONDRIAN.
Vers une construction collective. Manifeste V du groupe « De Stijl ».
Reproduction d'œuvres par :
GEORGES BRAQUE-MARCEL BREUER, J. CSAKY-AUGUSTE HERBIN-LOUIS JOUVET-KAMERNY THÉATRE, HENRI LAURENS-FERNAND LÉGER-JEAN METZINGER-ROBERT MALLET-STEVENS-OLSON-PABLO PICASSO, MARIE VIVES-GEORGES VALMIER.

Formules d'une esthétique moderne
1902-1912
(Extraits, suite)

La ligne moderne a des commencements peu saisissables. Ils sont aussi peu définis que ce que nous sommes forcés d'appeler la « Modernité », n'ayant pas d'autre terme à notre disposition pour distinguer « notre » époque de celles qui la précédèrent.

C'est dans le domaine de la Peinture et du Dessin, plutôt que dans toute autre, que la ligne nouvelle nous apparut telle quelle. Si nous n'avions pas été, à ce moment, absolument distraits de tout ce que d'ingénieux et inlassables inventeurs créaient de nouveau pour nous rendre la vie plus facile, plus agréable, le travail plus léger, l'exploitation plus lucrative, nous aurions pu constater, dans la vie réelle, bien des choses dont nous ne fûmes vraiment frappés qu'en les voyant représentées pour la première fois.

1

First page of the 'Bulletin de L'Effort Moderne', Nov. 1924; Mondrian published his article 'L'évolution de l'humanité est l'évolution de l'art' ('The Evolution of Humanity is the evolution of Art') in this issue.

On Sunday afternoons Mondrian used to visit the Colin family in Clamart, near Paris, to dance: Mondrian (third from the left) with members of the Colin family in the garden of their house in Clamart.

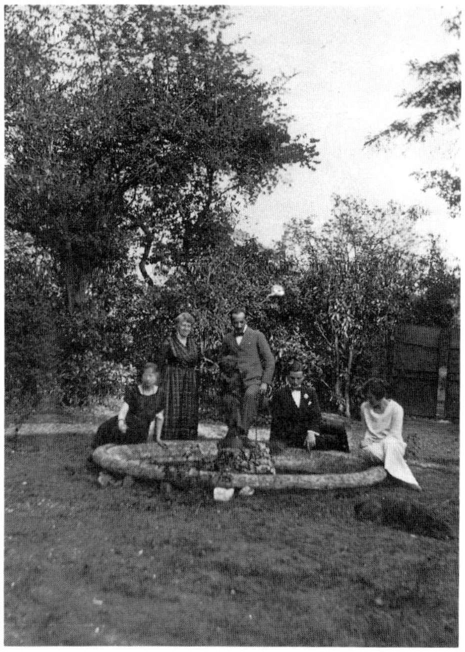

Mondrian published in 'Manomètre', 6, August 1924 his article: 'Les Arts et La Beauté de notre ambiance tangible' ('The Arts and the Beauty of Our Tangible Surroundings').

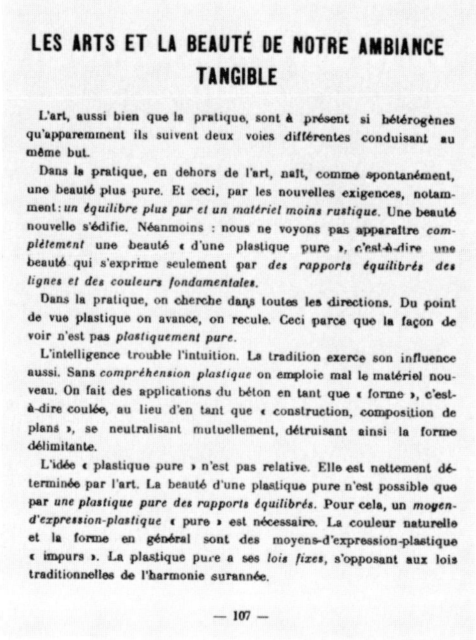

LES ARTS ET LA BEAUTÉ DE NOTRE AMBIANCE TANGIBLE

L'art, aussi bien que la pratique, sont à présent si hétérogènes qu'apparemment ils suivent deux voies différentes conduisant au même but.

Dans la pratique, en dehors de l'art, naît, comme spontanément, une beauté plus pure. Et ceci, par les nouvelles exigences, notamment: *un équilibre plus pur et un matériel moins rustique.* Une beauté nouvelle s'édifie. Néanmoins : nous ne voyons pas apparaître *complètement* une beauté « d'une plastique pure », c'est-à-dire une beauté qui s'exprime seulement par *des rapports équilibrés des lignes et des couleurs fondamentales.*

Dans la pratique, on cherche dans toutes les directions. Du point de vue plastique on avance, on recule. Ceci parce que la façon de voir n'est pas *plastiquement pure.*

L'intelligence trouble l'intuition. La tradition exerce son influence aussi. Sans *compréhension plastique* on emploie mal le matériel nouveau. On fait des applications du béton en tant que « forme », c'est-à-dire coulée, au lieu d'en tant que « construction, composition de plans », se neutralisant mutuellement, détruisant ainsi la forme délimitante.

L'idée « plastique pure » n'est pas relative. Elle est nettement déterminée par l'art. La beauté d'une plastique pure n'est possible que par *une plastique pure des rapports équilibrés.* Pour cela, un *moyen-d'expression-plastique* « pure » est nécessaire. La couleur naturelle et la forme en général sont des moyens-d'expression-plastique « impurs ». La plastique pure a ses *lois fixes,* s'opposant aux lois traditionnelles de l'harmonie surannée.

— 107 —

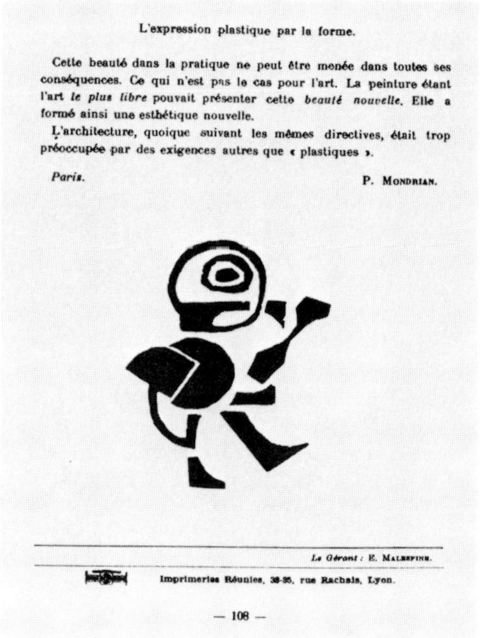

L'expression plastique par la forme.

Cette beauté dans la pratique ne peut être menée dans toutes ses conséquences. Ce qui n'est pas le cas pour l'art. La peinture étant l'art *le plus libre* pouvait présenter cette *beauté nouvelle.* Elle a formé ainsi une esthétique nouvelle.

L'architecture, quoique suivant les mêmes directives, était trop préoccupée par des exigences autres que « plastiques ».

Paris. P. MONDRIAN.

Le Gérant : E. MALESPINE.

Imprimeries Réunies, 33-35, rue Rachais, Lyon.

— 108 —

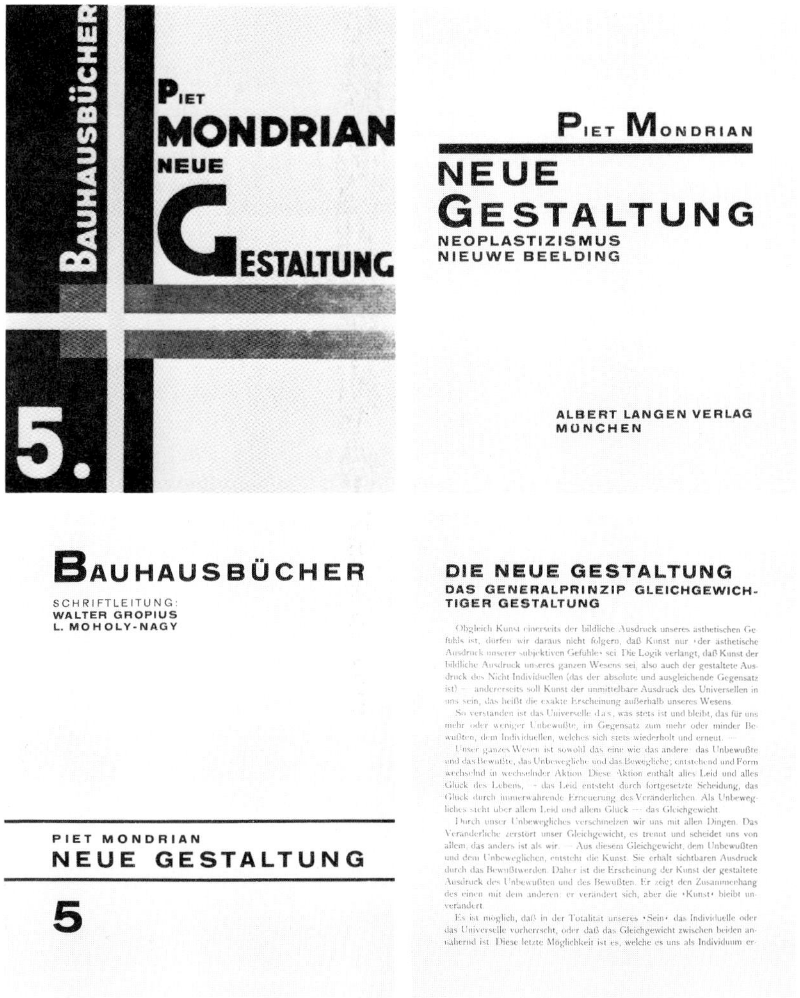
BAUHAUSBÜCHER

5.

PIET MONDRIAN NEUE GESTALTUNG

PIET MONDRIAN

NEUE GESTALTUNG

NEOPLASTIZISMUS
NIEUWE BEELDING

ALBERT LANGEN VERLAG
MÜNCHEN

BAUHAUSBÜCHER

SCHRIFTLEITUNG:
WALTER GROPIUS
L. MOHOLY-NAGY

PIET MONDRIAN
NEUE GESTALTUNG

5

DIE NEUE GESTALTUNG

DAS GENERALPRINZIP GLEICHGEWICHTIGER GESTALTUNG

Obgleich Kunst einerseits der bildliche Ausdruck unseres ästhetischen Gefühls ist, dürfen wir daraus nicht folgern, daß Kunst nur »der ästhetische Ausdruck unserer subjektiven Gefühle« sei. Die Logik verlangt, daß Kunst der bildliche Ausdruck unseres ganzen Wesens sei, also auch der gestaltete Ausdruck des Nicht Individuellen (das der absolute und ausgleichende Gegensatz ist) — andererseits soll Kunst der unmittelbare Ausdruck des Universellen in uns sein, das heißt die exakte Erscheinung außerhalb unseres Wesens.

So verstanden ist das Universelle das, was stets ist und bleibt, das für uns mehr oder weniger Unbewußte, im Gegensatz zum mehr oder minder Bewußten, dem Individuellen, welches sich stets wiederholt und erneut. —

Unser ganzes Wesen ist sowohl das eine wie das andere: das Unbewußte und das Bewußte, das Unbewegliche und das Bewegliche; entstehend und Form wechselnd in wechselnder Aktion. Diese Aktion enthält alles Leid und alles Glück des Lebens, — das Leid entsteht durch fortgesetzte Scheidung, das Glück durch immerwährende Erneuerung des Veränderlichen. Als Unbewegliches steht über allem Leid und allem Glück — das Gleichgewicht.

Durch unser Unbewegliches verschmelzen wir uns mit allen Dingen. Das Veränderliche zerstört unser Gleichgewicht, es trennt und scheidet uns von allem, das anders ist als wir. — Aus diesem Gleichgewicht, dem Unbewußten und dem Unbeweglichen, entsteht die Kunst. Sie erhält sichtbaren Ausdruck durch das Bewußtwerden. Daher ist die Erscheinung der Kunst der gestaltete Ausdruck des Unbewußten und des Bewußten. Er zeigt den Zusammenhang des einen mit dem anderen: er verändert sich, aber die »Kunst« bleibt unverändert.

Es ist möglich, daß in der Totalität unseres »Sein« das Individuelle oder das Universelle vorherrscht, oder daß das Gleichgewicht zwischen beiden annähernd ist. Diese letzte Möglichkeit ist es, welche es uns als Individuum er-

Cover and first pages of Piet Mondrian, Neue Gestaltung, published by the Bauhaus; design by L. Moholy-Nagy; (Neo-Plasticism), 1925.

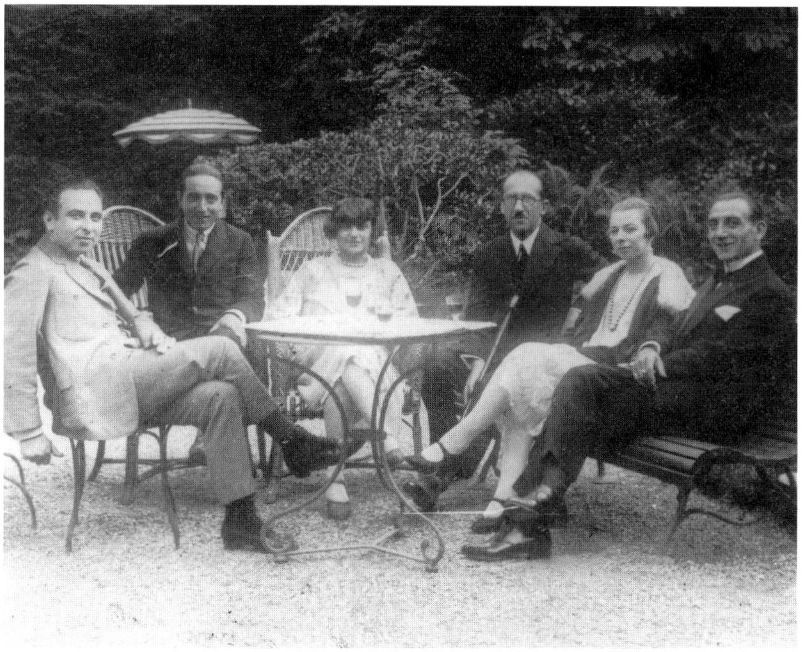

Mondrian with his friends the musician Paul F. Sanders, Mr. and Mrs. Tas, and his friends Tine and George Vantongerloo in St. Germain-en-Laye, 1925.

1923

Rosenberg mounted an exhibition devoted exclusively to *De Stijl*; Mondrian submitted several works.

After the period from 1919 to 1921, during which the compositions were dominated by multiple planes, often of highly subtle colouring, Mondrian reduced his compositions to a few planes painted in primary colours, with few gradations white and black.

1925

Theo van Doesburg introduced what he called 'Elementarism' in his new works: composition based on the diagonal. Mondrian, who had regarded Van Doesburg as one of the few people with whom he had a close spiritual affinity, was bitterly disappointed by Van Doesburg's failure to understand the dynamic equilibrium of opposites as he had set forth in *De Stijl*. The artistic break with Van Doesburg was definitive; on a personal level, however, they resumed contact some time later. Mondrian's work was becoming increasingly well-known, he even had buyers and admirers in Germany and Switzerland. This enabled him to devote himself entirely to his abstract work without the frustration of having to produce works on commission simply to survive. In this year Mondrian had an exhibition at Kühl and Kühn in Dresden, and at the Rotterdamsche Kring. 'Le Néo-Plasticisme' was published as 'Die Neue Gestaltung' in the series of Bauhaus-Bücher.

Mondrian was represented at the following exhibitions: 'De Onafhankelijken' 1925, 1926, 1927; Potsdamer Kunstsommer 1925 (50 Jahre holländische Malerei); l'Art d'Aujourdhui (Art plastique non-imitatif) in the Chambre Syndical, Paris 1925/26 (this exhibition was held partly in protest at the exclusion of De Stijl at the international exhibition of decorative arts in 1925); De Bron, The Hague 1925/26 (with, among others, Jacoba van Heemskerck, Lissitzky, Jawlensky and Vlaminck); De Branding, Rotterdam (in a former post office) Jan. 1926; Grosse Berliner Kunstausstellung 1926; International Exhibition of the Société Anonyme, Brooklyn 1926 (through the intervention of Katharine Dreier, whom he had met in Paris); Salon des Tuileries 1927; A.S.B.; Stedelijk Museum Amsterdam 1928; Holländische Kunst Düsseldorf 1928; E.S.A.C.; Stedelijk Museum, Amsterdam and Pulchri Studio, The Hague, both 1929.

1926

Numerous artists and admirers visited Mondrian in his studio. He had engaged the photographer Delbo to photograph his studio from

various angles; these photographs served to give an impression of Mondrian's ideas concerning the Neo-plastic interior. In the same context he made designs for a library for Mrs. Ida Bienert in Dresden, which were never carried out. El Lissitzky, whose wife had sold a lot of work on Mondrian's behalf in Germany, started an 'abstract cabinet' in the Landesmuseum in Hannover, which included three works by Mondrian (destroyed in 1936). A small model for a play by Mondrian's friend Michel Seuphor, 'L'éphémère est éternel', was Mondrian's last experiment in this direction.
From this year on Mondrian published numerous short articles in various European avant-garde periodicals, including *Vouloir, Cahiers d'art, i 10.*

To: J.J.P. Oud

Paris 22 May 26

Dear Bob, Thanks for your letter. About that magazine of Müller-Lehning's, it seems a good idea to me. M.L. is an anarchist, but the paper won't be an *anarchist party* paper. I'm not acquainted with all the different parties, but I do know that he is very broad-minded and of all directions *in our direction* (i.e. against convention, capital-in-the-wrong sense, bourgeoisie, etc.). It *won't* be devoted exclusively to art, which is a good thing. I myself plan to write about Neo-Plasticism *in society,* something I have intended to do for a long time. Being human is no. *one* priority, then art or (no "art") follows automatically, doesn't it. I'm simplifying things, but you know what I mean. M.L. (between you and me) was not too keen on having Stam on the board, since Stam makes no bones about being a Communist. M.L. (like me) wants to help build a pure society by means of *ideas.* I think it would be a good thing for you to accept. It won't involve a lot of work: no more than you'd be prepared to undertake. He wants you because you're straight and in favour of what's new, plain-speaking and yet generous to others. After you, he had Van Eesteren in mind. I recommended you. I get on well with M. Lehning and his wife. They have been interested in my work for, I think, 2 years, and go to see it. I don't see them very often, or anyone else; but when I do find them congenial. Of course I can't tell you exactly what they're like: I don't know them well enough for that. There seems to be enough money to run the paper without a profit for a time.
The idea sounds good to me, and M.L. seems practical enough to carry it out. Yes, I'm not doing too badly. The room in Dresden was approved (the design), but I wasn't offered

[continued on page 216]

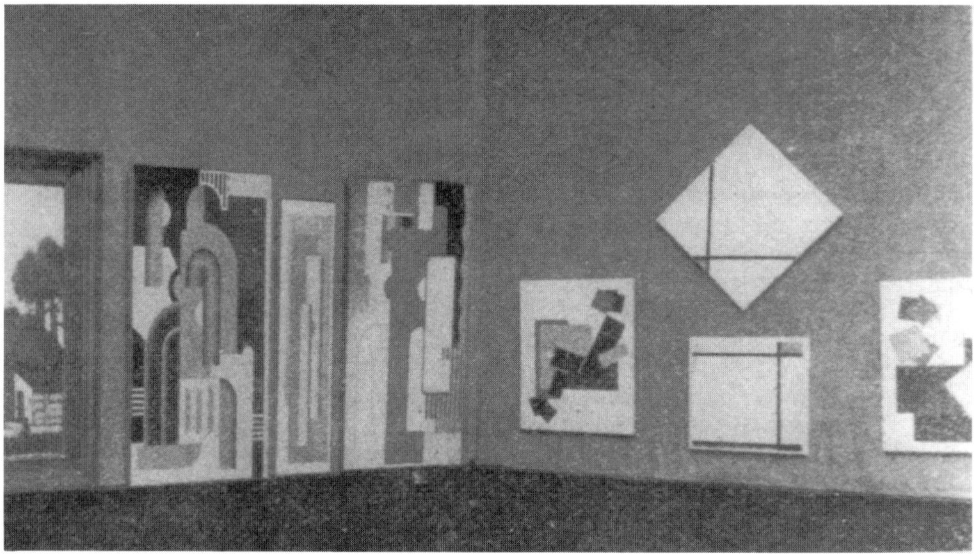

A view of the exhibition 'De Onafhankelijken' ('The Independent Artists'), Sted. Museum (Amsterdam), with two Mondrian pictures, 1926.

From left to right: M. Seuphor, Tysliava, Mondrian, L. Saalborn, 1927.

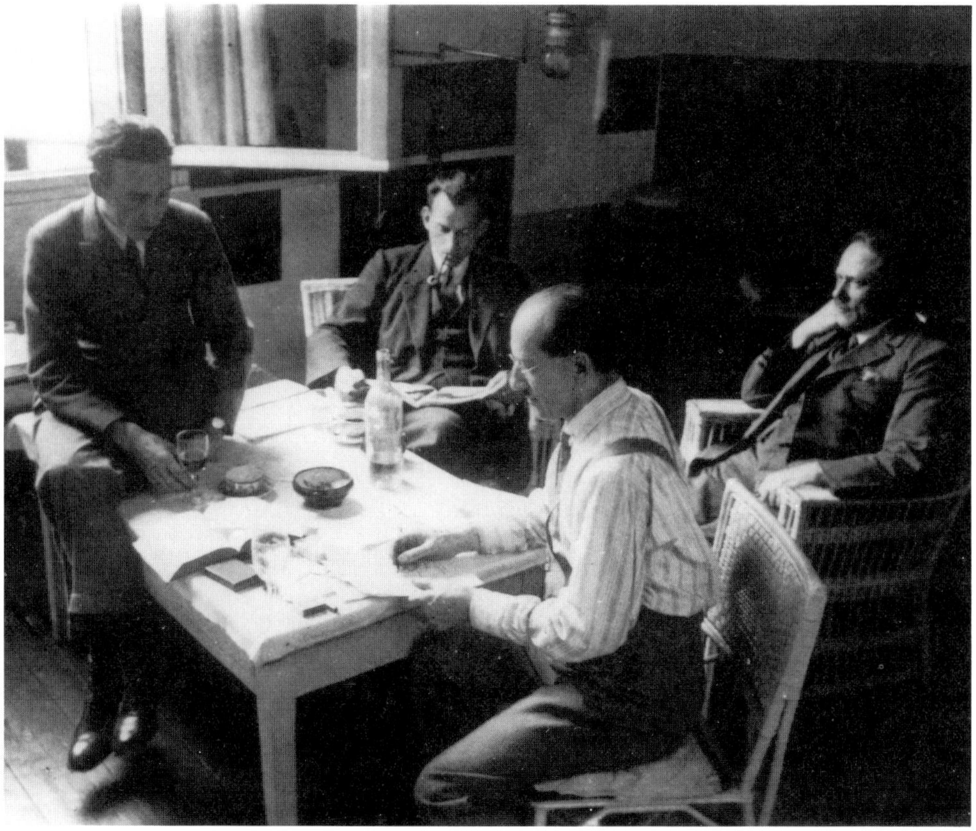

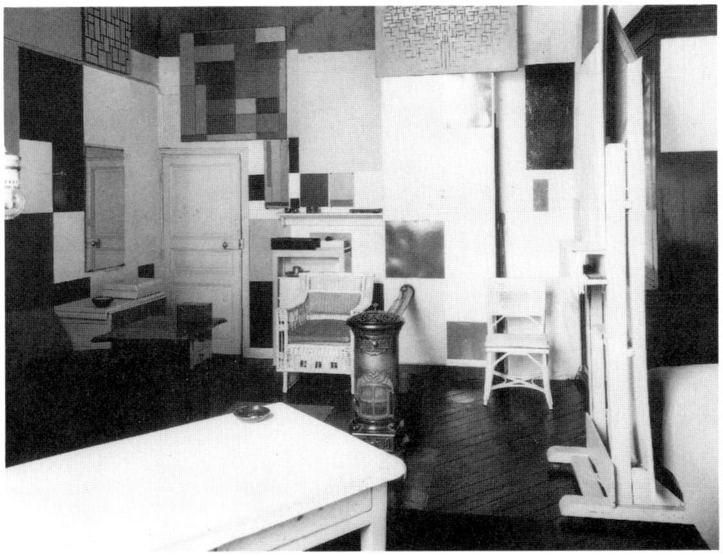

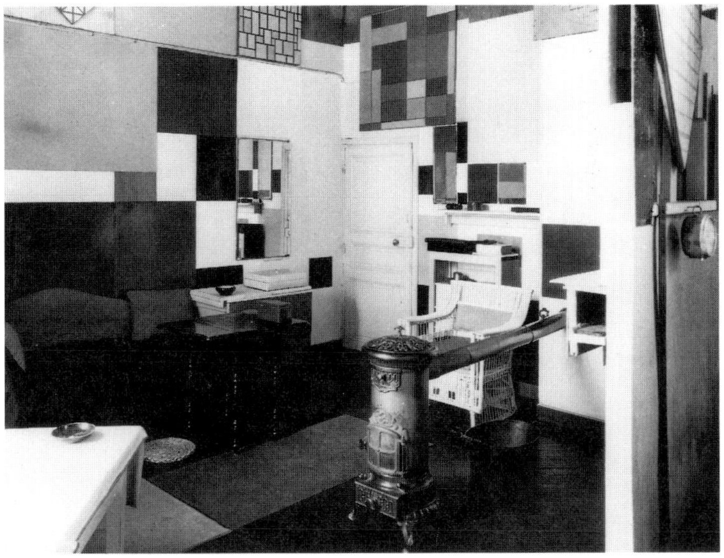

P. Delbo, Mondrian's studio, 1926.

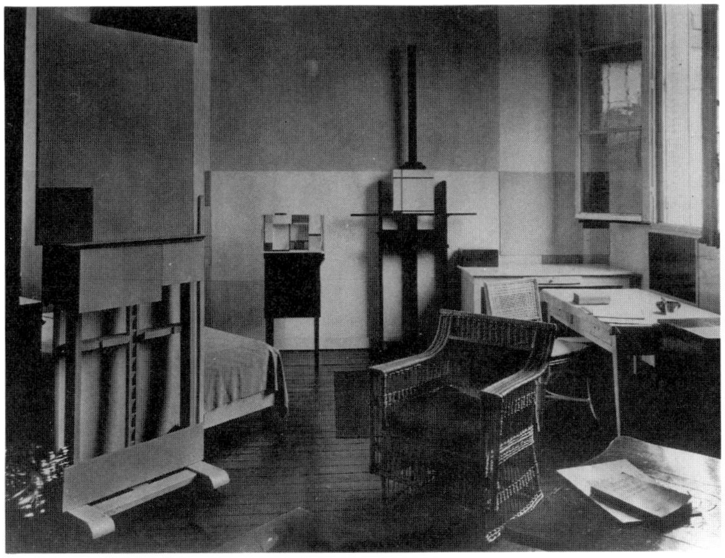

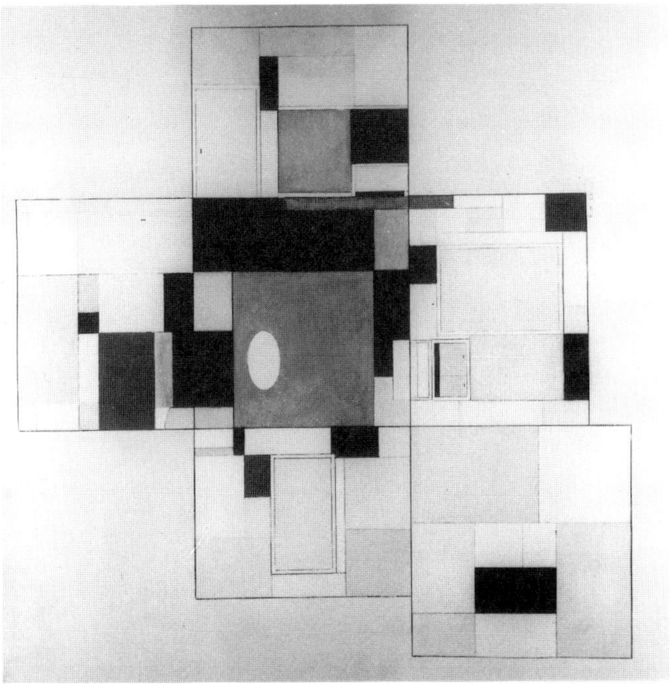

Piet Mondrian, Three designs for Mrs. Bienert's Studio-Library at Dresden; coll. Kupferstichkabinett (Dresden).

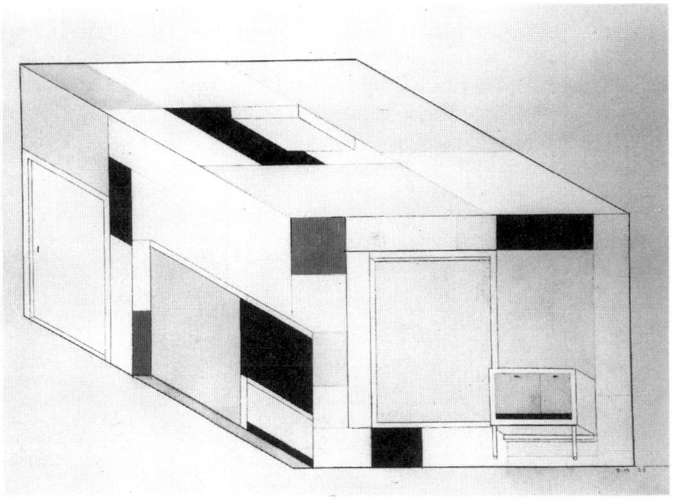

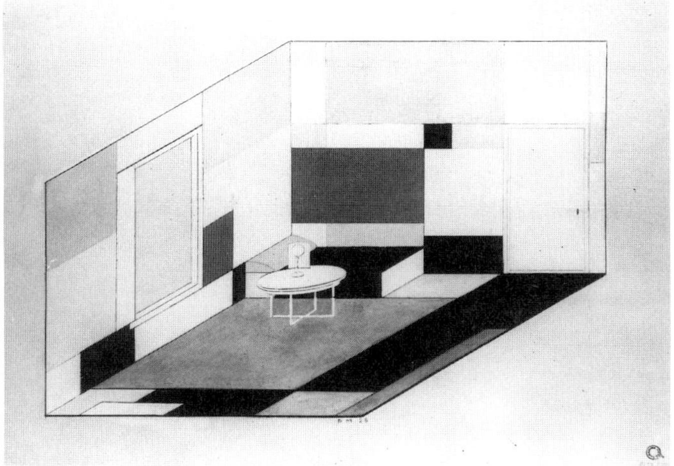

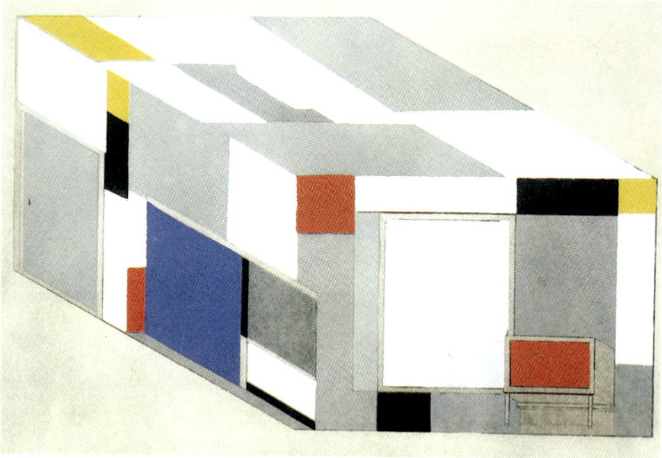

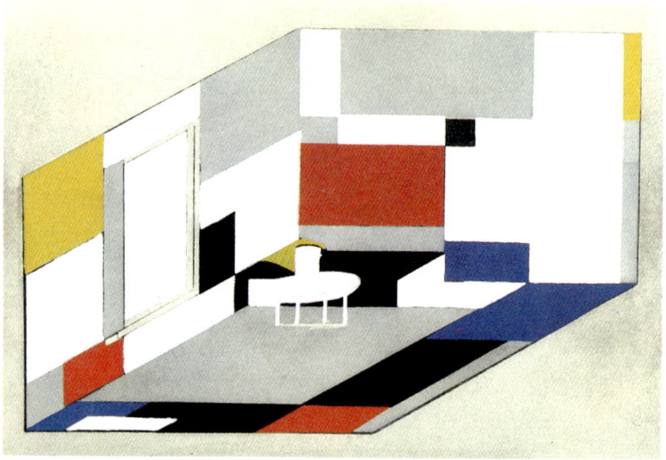

Piet Mondrian, Design for Mrs. Bienert's Studio-Library at Dresden: 'Vouloir' (no.Ambiance), 1927, published two of Mondrian's designs in colour: 'Piet Mondrian, Architecte à Paris'.

To : W. Baumeister

P. MONDRIAN
Rue du Départ, 26

Dear Sir,
I shall be very pleased to see you here tomorrow at 3 o'clock. My friend Seuphor and some other artists will be there too.

P. Mondrian

Staircase I, IIIrd floor

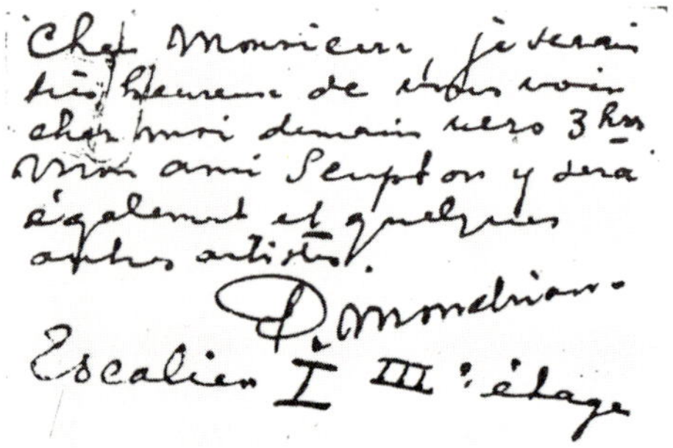

Cher Monsieur, je serai
très heureux de vous voir
chez moi demain vers 3 hrs.
Mon ami Seuphor y sera
également et quelques
autres artistes.
P. Mondrian.
Escalier I III: étage

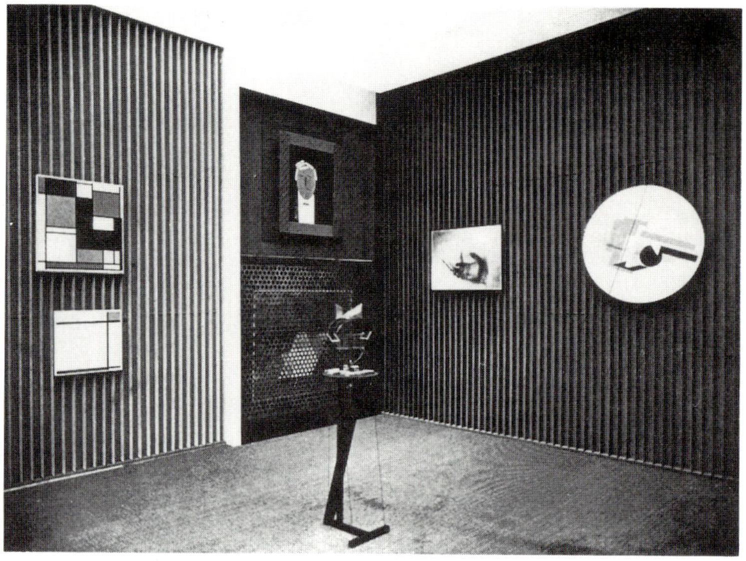

Three views of 'Das Abstrakte Kabinett' ('The Abstract Room') designed by El Lissitzky for the Museum in Hannover with three pictures by Mondrian (destroyed 1936).

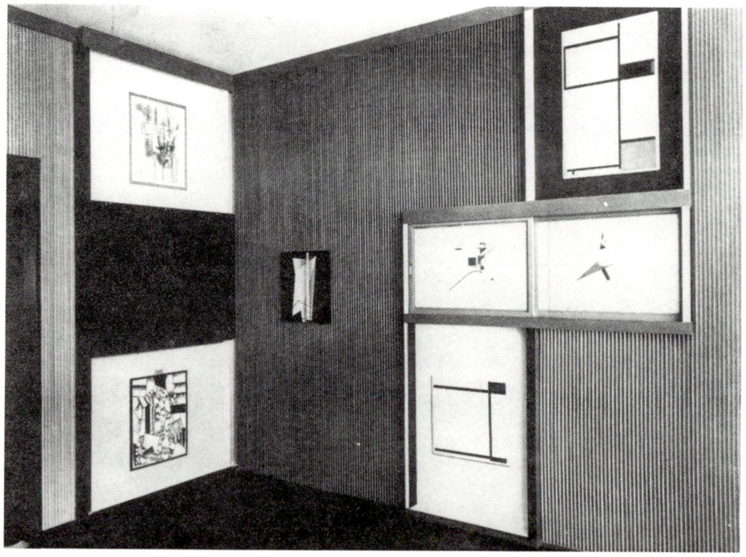

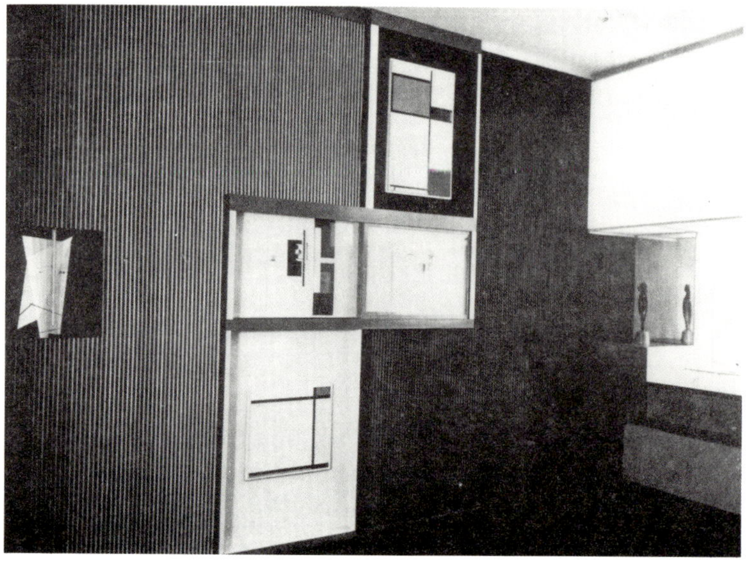

THE INTERNATIONAL ARCHITECTS' ASSOCIATION IN JAPAN

Manifesto

I. On the basis of human life we wish to examine the development of architecture closely.
II. We wish to build in the style that emerges from the evolution of human life.
III. With the solution of the problems of architecture in Japan in mind, we wish to collaborate with like-minded architects of all nations towards a common goal.

Programme

1. In constructing style we should not imitate traditional forms nor adhere to nationality in the strict sense, but develop building from the situation, nature and needs of our times.
2. Our work embraces research and products in the field of all human life, with architecture at the centre.
3. In order to implement our principles and claims, not only should exhibitions and lectures be organized but an Institute for research and training be established too.

Kyoto, September 23, 1927
Kikuji Ishimoto, Masabumi Itô, Séigo Motono, Famotsu Naka, Taneo Shimmô, Isaburo Uéno.

Two pages of the VII.79/84.1927 issue of 'De Stijl' with a manifesto by Japanese architects.

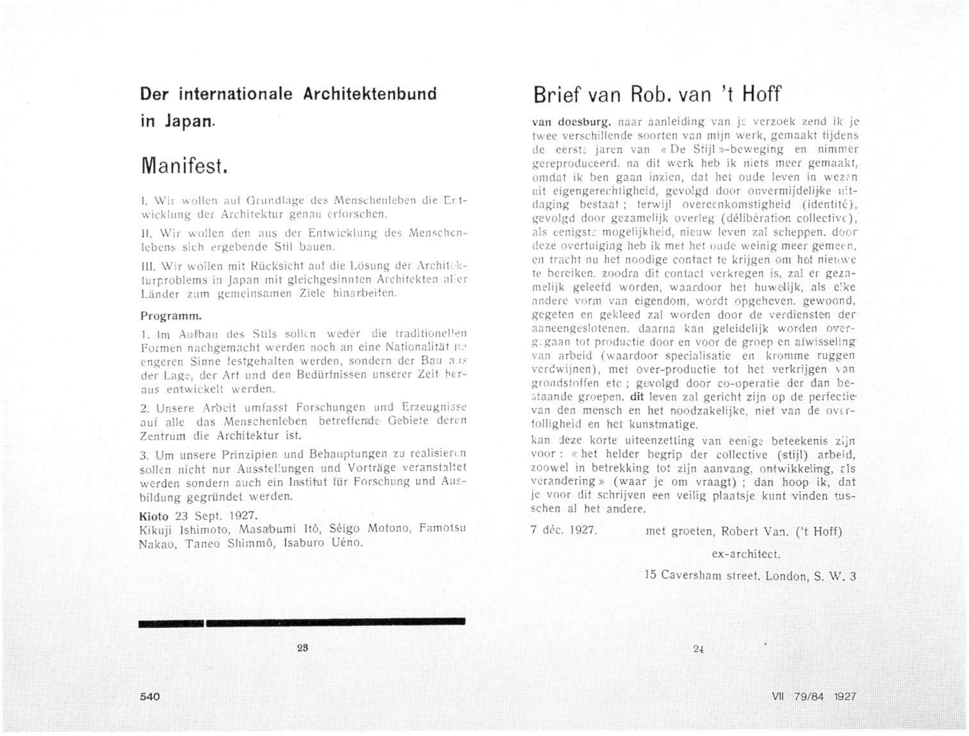

Der internationale Architektenbund in Japan.

Manifest.

I. Wir wollen auf Grundlage des Menschenleben die Entwicklung der Architektur genau erforschen.

II. Wir wollen den aus der Entwicklung des Menschenlebens sich ergebende Stil bauen.

III. Wir wollen mit Rücksicht auf die Lösung der Architekturproblems in Japan mit gleichgesinnten Architekten aller Länder zum gemeinsamen Ziele hinarbeiten.

Programm.

1. Im Aufbau des Stils sollen weder die traditionellen Formen nachgemacht werden noch an eine Nationalität im engeren Sinne festgehalten werden, sondern der Bau aus der Lage, der Art und den Bedürfnissen unserer Zeit heraus entwickelt werden.

2. Unsere Arbeit umfasst Forschungen und Erzeugnisse auf alle das Menschenleben betreffende Gebiete deren Zentrum die Architektur ist.

3. Um unsere Prinzipien und Behauptungen zu realisieren sollen nicht nur Ausstellungen und Vorträge veranstaltet werden sondern auch ein Institut für Forschung und Ausbildung gegründet werden.

Kioto 23 Sept. 1927.
Kikuji Ishimoto, Masabumi Itô, Séigo Motono, Famotsu Nakao, Taneo Shimmô, Isaburo Uéno.

23

Brief van Rob. van 't Hoff

van doesburg. naar aanleiding van je verzoek zend ik je twee verschillende soorten van mijn werk, gemaakt tijdens de eerste jaren van « De Stijl »-beweging en nimmer gereproduceerd. na dit werk heb ik niets meer gemaakt, omdat ik ben gaan inzien, dat het oude leven in wezen uit eigengerechtigheid, gevolgd door onvermijdelijke uitdaging bestaat; terwijl overeenkomstigheid (identité), gevolgd door gezamelijk overleg (délibération collective), als eenigste mogelijkheid, nieuw leven zal scheppen. door deze overtuiging heb ik met het oude weinig meer gemeen, en tracht nu het noodige contact te krijgen om het nieuwe te bereiken. zoodra dit contact verkregen is, zal er gezamelijk geleefd worden, waardoor het huwelijk, als elke andere vorm van eigendom, wordt opgeheven. gewoond, gegeten en gekleed zal worden door de verdiensten der aaneengeslotenen. daarna kan geleidelijk worden overgegaan tot productie door en voor de groep en afwisseling van arbeid (waardoor specialisatie en kromme ruggen verdwijnen), met over-productie tot het verkrijgen van grondstoffen etc; gevolgd door co-operatie der dan bestaande groepen. **dit** leven zal gericht zijn op de perfectie van den mensch en het noodzakelijke, niet van de overtolligheid en het kunstmatige.
kan deze korte uiteenzetting van eenige beteekenis zijn voor: « het helder begrip der collective (stijl) arbeid, zoowel in betrekking tot zijn aanvang, ontwikkeling, als verandering » (waar je om vraagt); dan hoop ik, dat je voor dit schrijven een veilig plaatsje kunt vinden tusschen al het andere.

7 déc. 1927. met groeten, Robert Van. ('t Hoff)
ex-architect.
15 Caversham street. London, S. W. 3

24

540 VII 79/84 1927

Piet Mondrian
Neo-Plasticism

The Dwelling—The Street—The City

In both past and present the dwelling is man's true "refuge". If dwelling and street are not treated equally there is no harmony, no unity in the city. This is partly due to the climate, partly due to the differences between individuals. It is quite natural for people to flee from one another because of their mutual differences. The cause of all disharmony, though, is to be sought in the individual himself: as long as man remains as he is at present in the mass, he is incapable of creating harmony in his surroundings.

The present city is unharmonious due to the lack of homogeneity in dwelling and street. Neo-plasticism points the way to unity by being based on the pure plastic aesthetic of the pure relation of pure line and colour.

First page of Mondrian's article on 'Jazz and Neo-Plasticism' in the avant-garde magazine 'i 10', 1927.

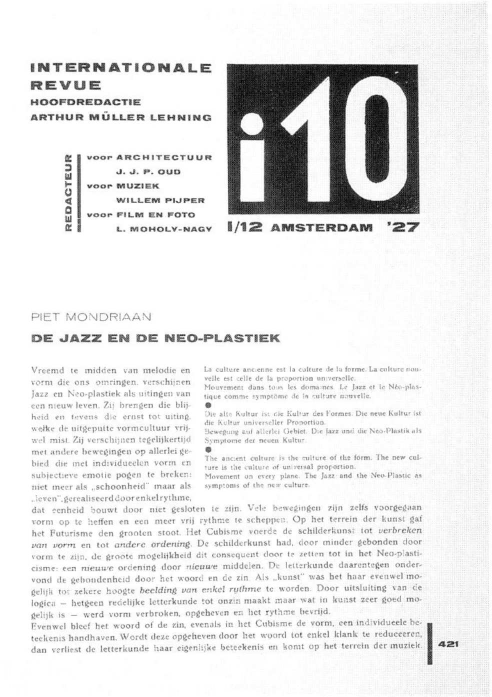

INTERNATIONALE REVUE
HOOFDREDACTIE
ARTHUR MÜLLER LEHNING

REDACTEUR
voor ARCHITECTUUR J. J. P. OUD
voor MUZIEK WILLEM PIJPER
voor FILM EN FOTO L. MOHOLY-NAGY

i10
I/12 AMSTERDAM '27

PIET MONDRIAAN

DE JAZZ EN DE NEO-PLASTIEK

Vreemd te midden van melodie en vorm die ons omringen, verschijnen Jazz en Neo-plastiek als uitingen van een nieuw leven. Zij brengen die blijheid en tevens die ernst tot uiting, welke de uitgeputte vormcultuur vrijwel mist. Zij verschijnen tegelijkertijd met andere bewegingen op allerlei gebied die met individueelen vorm en subjectieve emotie pogen te breken: niet meer als „schoonheid" maar als „leven", gerealiseerd door enkel rythme, dat eenheid bouwt door niet gesloten te zijn. Vele bewegingen zijn zelfs voorgegaan vorm op te heffen en een meer vrij rythme te scheppen. Op het terrein der kunst gaf het Futurisme den grooten stoot. Het Cubisme voerde de schilderkunst tot *verbreken van vorm* en tot *andere ordening*. De schilderkunst had, door minder gebonden door vorm te zijn, de groote mogelijkheid dit consequent door te zetten tot in het Neo-plasticisme: een *nieuwe* ordening door *nieuwe* middelen. De letterkunde daarentegen ondervond de gebondenheid door het woord en de zin. Als „kunst" was het haar evenwel mogelijk tot zekere hoogte *beelding van enkel rythme* te worden. Door uitsluiting van de logica – hetgeen redelijke letterkunde tot onzin maakt maar wat in kunst zeer goed mogelijk is – werd vorm verbroken, opgeheven en het rythme bevrijd.
Evenwel bleef het woord of de zin, evenals in het Cubisme de vorm, een individueele beteekenis handhaven. Wordt deze opgeheven door het woord tot enkel klank te reduceeren, dan verliest de letterkunde haar eigenlijke beteekenis en komt op het terrein der muziek.

La culture ancienne est la culture de la forme. La culture nouvelle est celle de la proportion universelle.
Mouvement dans tous les domaines. Le Jazz et le Néo-plastique comme symptôme de la culture nouvelle.

●

Die alte Kultur ist die Kultur des Formes. Die neue Kultur ist die Kultur universeller Proportion.
Bewegung auf allerlei Gebiet. Die Jazz und die Neo-Plastik als Symptome der neuen Kultur.

●

The ancient culture is the culture of the form. The new culture is the culture of universal proportion.
Movement on every plane. The Jazz and the Neo-Plastic as symptoms of the new culture.

421

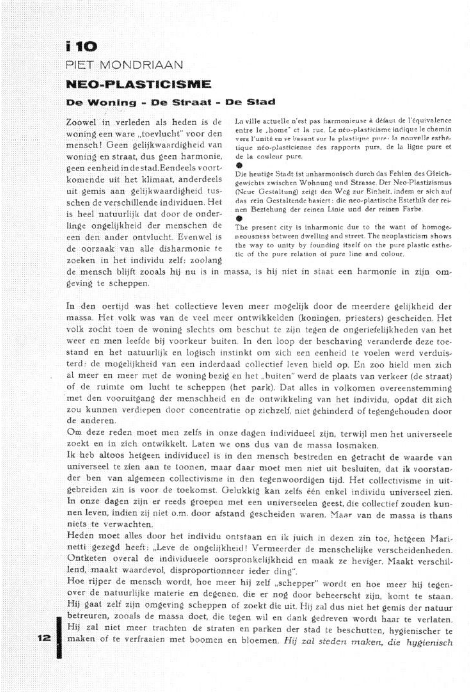

i 10

PIET MONDRIAAN

NEO-PLASTICISME

De Woning - De Straat - De Stad

Zoowel in verleden als heden is de woning een ware „toevlucht" voor den mensch! Geen gelijkwaardigheid van woning en straat, dus geen harmonie, geen eenheid in de stad. Eendeels voortkomende uit het klimaat, anderdeels uit gemis aan gelijkwaardigheid tusschen de verschillende individuen. Het is heel natuurlijk dat door de onderlinge ongelijkheid der menschen de een den ander ontvlucht. Evenwel is de oorzaak van alle disharmonie te zoeken in het individu zelf: zoolang de mensch blijft zooals hij nu is in massa, is hij niet in staat een harmonie in zijn omgeving te scheppen.

La ville actuelle n'est pas harmonieuse à défaut de l'équivalence entre le „home" et la rue. Le néo-plasticisme indique le chemin vers l'unité en se basant sur la plastique pure: la nouvelle esthétique néo-plasticienne des rapports purs, de la ligne pure et de la couleur pure.

●

Die heutige Stadt ist unharmonisch durch das Fehlen des Gleichgewichts zwischen Wohnung und Strasse. Der Neo-Plastizismus (Neue Gestaltung) zeigt den Weg zur Einheit, indem er sich auf das rein Gestaltende basiert: die neo-plastische Estethik der reinen Beziehung der reinen Linie und der reinen Farbe.

●

The present city is inharmonic due to the want of homogeneousness between dwelling and street. The neoplasticism shows the way to unity by founding itself on the pure plastic esthetic of the pure relation of pure line and colour.

In den oertijd was het collectieve leven meer mogelijk door de meerdere gelijkheid der massa. Het volk was van de veel meer ontwikkelden (koningen, priesters) gescheiden. Het volk zocht toen de woning slechts om beschut te zijn tegen de ongeriefelijkheden van het weer en men leefde bij voorkeur buiten. In den loop der beschaving veranderde deze toestand en het natuurlijk en logisch instinkt om zich een eenheid te voelen werd verduisterd: de mogelijkheid van een inderdaad collectief leven hield op. En zoo hield men zich al meer en meer met de woning bezig en het „buiten" werd de plaats van verkeer (de straat) of de ruimte om lucht te scheppen (het park). Dat alles in volkomen overeenstemming met den vooruitgang der menschheid en de ontwikkeling van het individu, opdat dit zich zou kunnen verdiepen door concentratie op zichzelf, niet gehinderd of tegengehouden door de anderen.
Om deze reden moet men zelfs in onze dagen individueel zijn, terwijl men het universeele zoekt en in zich ontwikkelt. Laten we ons dus van de massa losmaken.
Ik heb altoos hetgeen individueel is in den mensch bestreden en getracht de waarde van universeel te zien aan te toonen, maar daar moet men niet uit besluiten, dat ik voorstander ben van algemeen collectivisme in den tegenwoordigen tijd. Het collectivisme in uitgebreiden zin is voor de toekomst. Gelukkig kan zelfs één enkel individu universeel zien. In onze dagen zijn er reeds groepen met een universeelen geest, die collectief zouden kunnen leven, indien zij niet o.m. door afstand gescheiden waren. Maar van de massa is thans niets te verwachten.
Heden moet alles door het individu ontstaan en ik juich in dezen zin toe, hetgeen Marinetti gezegd heeft: „Leve de ongelijkheid! Vermeerder de menschelijke verscheidenheden. Ontketen overal de individueele oorspronkelijkheid en maak ze heviger. Maakt verschillend, maakt waardevol, disproportionneer ieder ding".
Hoe rijper de mensch wordt, hoe meer hij zelf „schepper" wordt en hoe meer hij tegenover de natuurlijke materie en degenen, die er nog door beheerscht zijn, komt te staan. Hij gaat zelf zijn omgeving scheppen of zoekt die uit. Hij zal dus niet het gemis der natuur betreuren, zooals de massa doet, die tegen wil en dank gedreven wordt haar te verlaten. Hij zal niet meer trachten de straten en parken der stad te beschutten, hygienischer te maken of te verfraaien met boomen en bloemen. *Hij zal steden maken, die hygienisch*

12

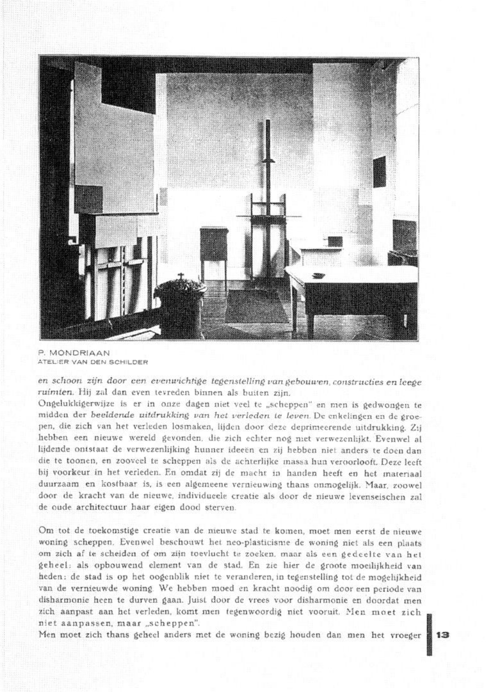

P. MONDRIAAN
ATELIER VAN DEN SCHILDER

en schoon zijn door een evenwichtige tegenstelling van gebouwen, constructies en leege ruimten. Hij zal dan even tevreden binnen als buiten zijn.
Ongelukkigerwijze is er in onze dagen niet veel te „scheppen" en men is gedwongen te midden der *beeldende uitdrukking van het verleden te leven.* De enkelingen en de groepen, die zich van het verleden losmaken, lijden door deze deprimeerende uitdrukking. Zij hebben een nieuwe wereld gevonden, die zich echter nog niet verwezenlijkt. Evenwel al lijdende ontstaat de verwezenlijking hunner ideeën en zij hebben niet anders te doen dan die te toonen, en zooveel te scheppen als de achterlijke massa hun veroorlooft. Deze leeft bij voorkeur in het verleden. En omdat zij de macht in handen heeft en het materiaal duurzaam en kostbaar is, is een algemeene vernieuwing thans onmogelijk. Maar, zoowel door de kracht van de nieuwe, individueele creatie als door de nieuwe levenseischen zal de oude architectuur haar eigen dood sterven.

Om tot de toekomstige creatie van de nieuwe stad te komen, moet men eerst de nieuwe woning scheppen. Evenwel beschouwt het neo-plasticisme de woning niet als een plaats om zich af te scheiden of om zijn toevlucht te zoeken, maar als een gedeelte van het geheel; als opbouwend element van de stad. En zie hier de groote moeilijkheid van heden: de stad is op het oogenblik niet te veranderen, in tegenstelling tot de mogelijkheid van de vernieuwde woning. We hebben moed en kracht noodig om door een periode van disharmonie heen te durven gaan. Juist door de vrees voor disharmonie en doordat men zich aanpast aan het verleden, komt men tegenwoordig niet vooruit. Men moet zich niet aanpassen, maar „scheppen".
Men moet zich thans geheel anders met de woning bezig houden dan men het vroeger

13

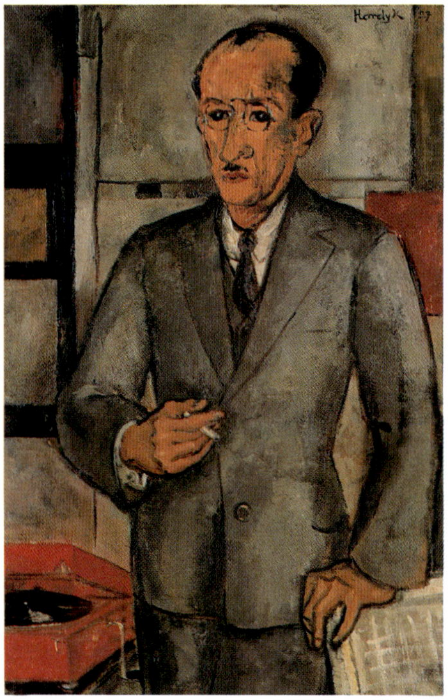

G. Hordijk, Portrait of Piet Mondrian, oil on canvas, 115 × 73.5 cm; coll. Haags Gemeentemuseum.

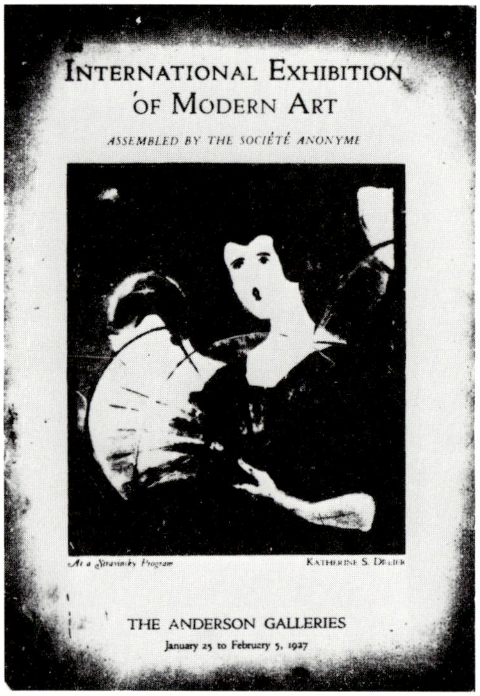

INTERNATIONAL EXHIBITION OF MODERN ART

ASSEMBLED BY THE SOCIÉTÉ ANONYME

At a Stravinsky Program

KATHERINE S. DREIER

THE ANDERSON GALLERIES

January 25 to February 5, 1927

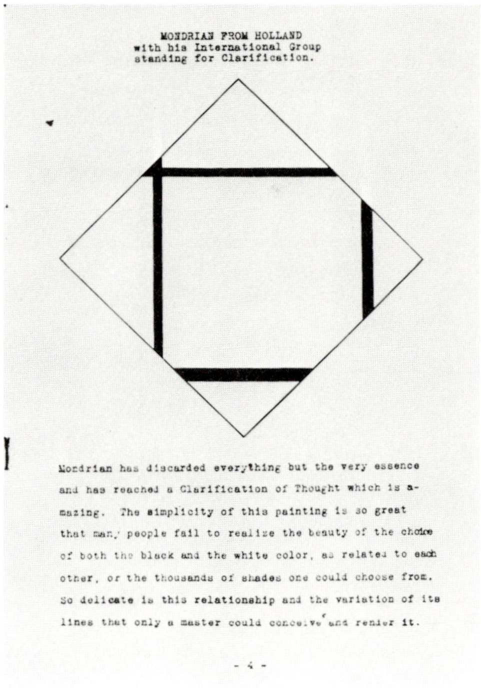

MONDRIAN FROM HOLLAND
with his International Group
standing for Clarification.

Mondrian has discarded everything but the very essence and has reached a Clarification of Thought which is amazing. The simplicity of this painting is so great that many people fail to realize the beauty of the choice of both the black and the white color, as related to each other, or the thousands of shades one could choose from. So delicate is this relationship and the variation of its lines that only a master could conceive and render it.

- 4 -

Cover of the Catalogue of 'The International Exhibition of Modern Art, Assembled by the Société Anonyme', the Anderson Galleries, Jan.25-Feb. 5, 1927, and page 4 on 'Mondrian from Holland' of this catalogue.

At Paul Dermée's home; from left to right: Michel Seuphor, Piet Mondrian, Vantongerloo, Russolo, Voronca, Dermée, Tysliava; seated: Céline Arnauld, Raffalowski, Stazewski, 1927.

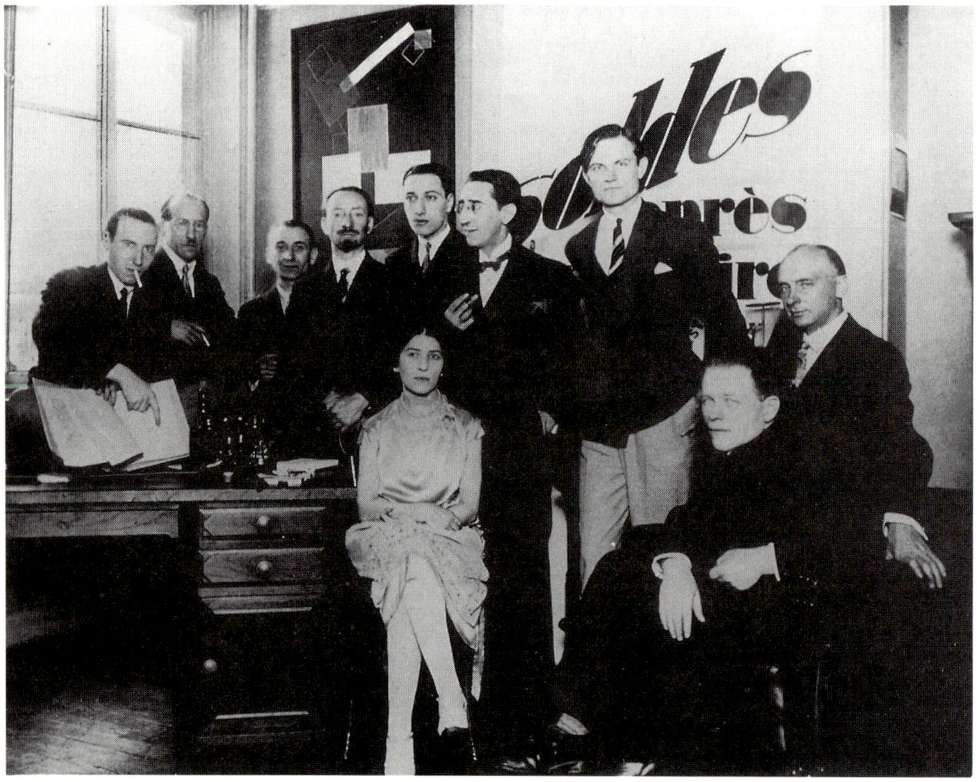

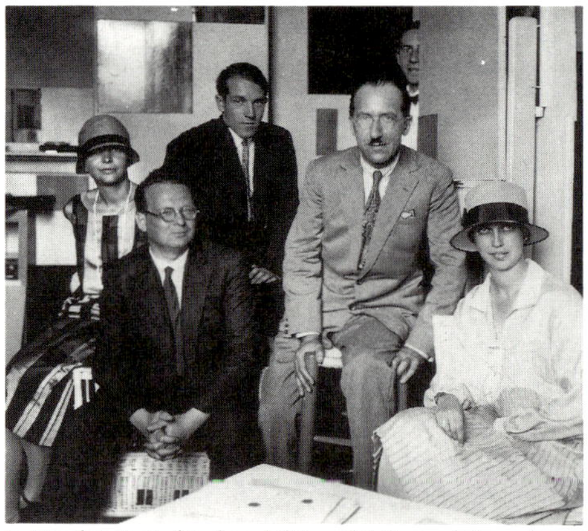

In Mondrian's studio; from left to right: Gertrud Stemmler, Willi Baumeister, Herburger, Mondrian, Michel Seuphor, Margret Baumeister, 1927.

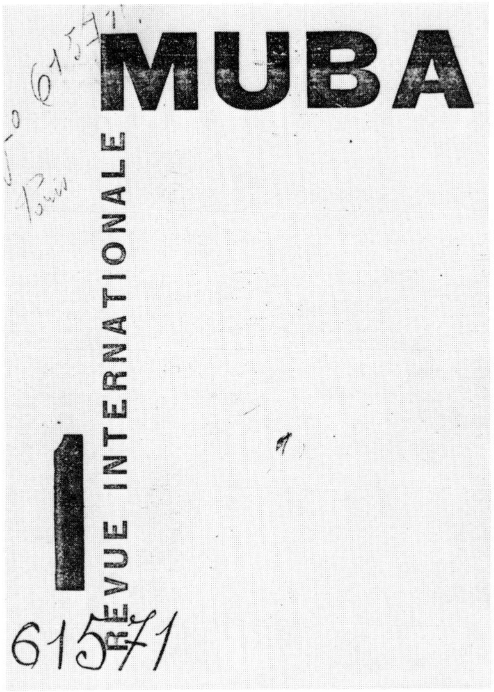

MUBA

REVUE INTERNATIONALE

1

61571

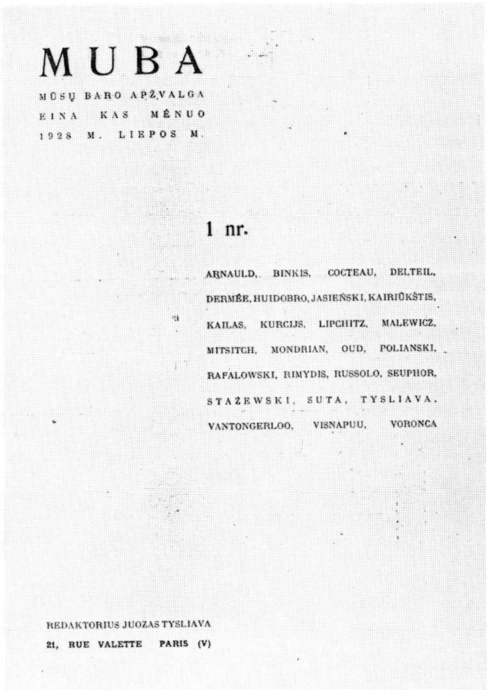

MUBA

MŪSŲ BARO APŽVALGA

EINA KAS MĖNUO

1928 M. LIEPOS M.

1 nr.

ARNAULD, BINKIS, COCTEAU, DELTEIL, DERMÉE, HUIDOBRO, JASIEŃSKI, KAIRIŪKŠTIS, KAILAS, KURCIJS, LIPCHITZ, MALEWICZ, MITSITCH, MONDRIAN, OUD, POLIANSKI, RAFALOWSKI, RIMYDIS, RUSSOLO, SEUPHOR, STAŻEWSKI, SUTA, TYSLIAVA, VANTONGERLOO, VISNAPUU, VORONCA

REDAKTORIUS JUOZAS TYSLIAVA

21, RUE VALETTE PARIS (V)

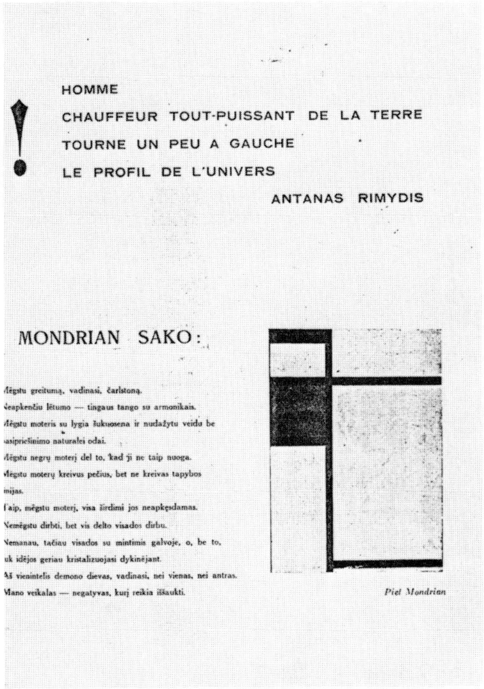

!

HOMME

CHAUFFEUR TOUT-PUISSANT DE LA TERRE

TOURNE UN PEU A GAUCHE

LE PROFIL DE L'UNIVERS

ANTANAS RIMYDIS

MONDRIAN SAKO:

Mėgstu greitumą, vadinasi, čarlstoną.
Neapkenčiu lėtumo — tingaus tango su armonikais.
Mėgstu moteris su lygia šukuosena ir nudažytu veidu be
asipriešinimo naturalei odai.
Mėgstu negrų moterį del to, kad ji ne taip nuoga.
Mėgstu moterų kreivus pečius, bet ne kreivas tapybos
mijas.
Taip, mėgstu moterį, visa širdimi jos neapkęsdamas.
Nemėgstu dirbti, bet vis delto visados dirbu.
Nemanau, tačiau visados su mintimis galvoje, o, be to,
uk idėjos geriau kristalizuojasi dykinėjant.
Aš vienintelis demono dievas, vadinasi, nei vienas, nei antras.
Mano veikalas — negatyvas, kurį reikia iššaukti.

Piet Mondrian

Cover and two pages from 'MUBA'

MUBA, an avant-garde review intended for avant-garde circles in Lithuania, published a few brief statements by Mondrian 1928.

' They say:
he likes speed and hence the Charleston.
he hates slowness hence the slow accordeon tango.
he likes women with bobbed hair and make-up, while hating natural complexions.
he likes negresses, as they are not so naked.
he is unity-god-demon-but neither one nor the other.
his ideas crystallize (are born) while he is shaving.
he does not think all the same he has ideas (thoughts).
he does not like work—all the same he is always working.
he likes Woman while detesting her.
a work by Mondrian is a developing plate.
he likes sloping shoulders in a woman, but he does not like sloping lines in art.'

Mondrian (second from right) with fellow artists, 1928.

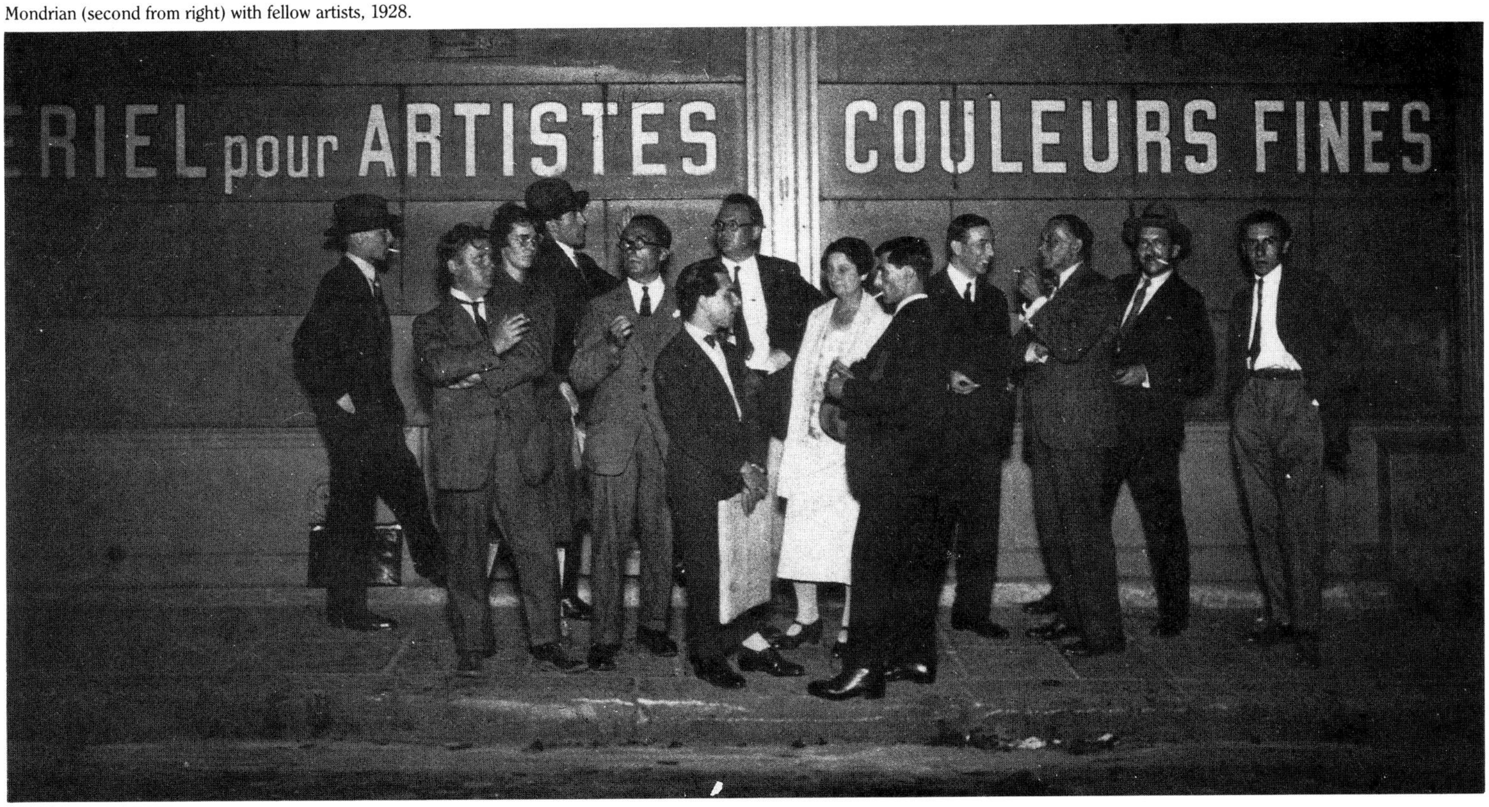

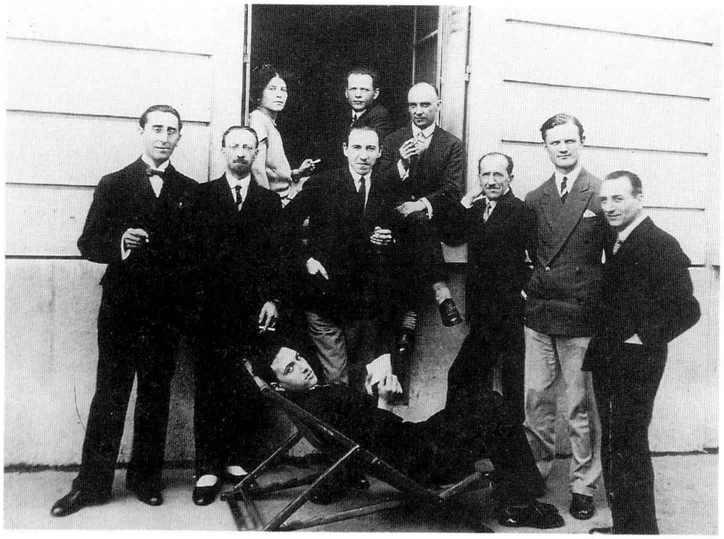

From left to right: Paul Dermée, Russolo, C. Arnauld, Voronca, Raffalowski, Seuphor, Stazewski, Mondrian, Tysliava, Vantongerloo, 9 June, 1928; photograph by Londynski.

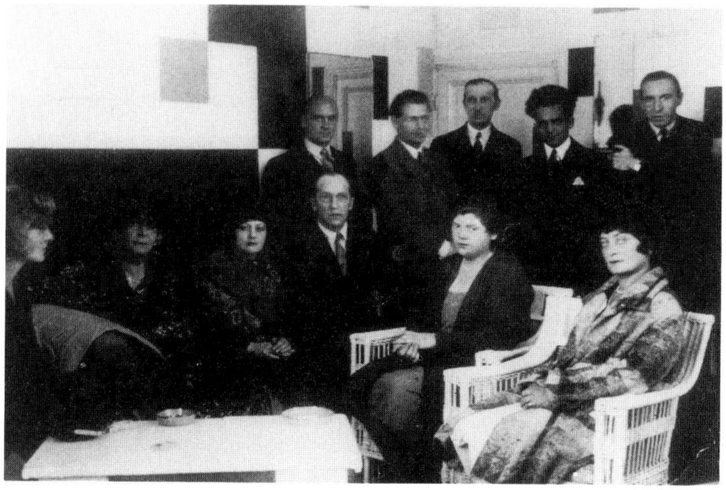

In Mondrian's studio; from left to right: Ingeborg Bjarnasson, Alexandra Exter, Véra Idelson, Mondrian, Lucy Glarner, Madame Martini; standing: Stazewski, Fritz Glarner, Arturo Martini, Lancelot Ney, Michel Seuphor, 1928.

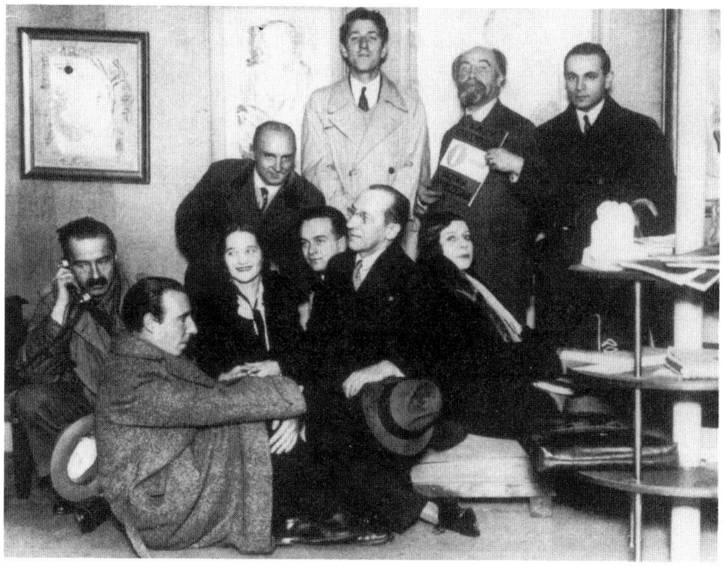

From left to right: Zawoyski, Michel Seuphor, Mrs. Graborwska (Later Mrs. Léger), Henryk Stazewski, Brzekowski, Mondrian, Florence Henri; two unidentified; photograph S. Londynski, 1929.

enough money to go and execute it. I don't think anyone else could supervise it. I have 4 pictures in Dresden, one in Berlin, 2 are going to America and 2 are at the A'dam Independent. You'll probably be going there.
Due to all these exhibitions I haven't had time to paint a picture for those acquaintances of yours like the one you have. I have very little colour in A'dam: it looks like some kind of evolution to me, but I do also use 3 colours. My price is a little higher nowadays, but for those people it is still 150 gld, as I wrote (a painting the same size as the one you have). So, Bob and Annie, write to me when you've seen the picture in A'dam. Best wishes to you both from your friend Piet.
(The photos of the Dresden room are bonmarché and therefore not good, I'll show them to you here later)

I don't have anything for you yet: I don't have a canvas in the house right now. Nothing has come back from Germany. I sell one occasionally.

1929

To: J.J.P. Oud

rue du Départ 26
7 Sept [1929]

Dear Bob and Annie,

I was so pleased with the letter I received from Bob such a long time ago. I can't think why I didn't answer sooner. But something's always coming up; you know how it is. At present I am terribly busy with exhibitions. I sent 4 things to Zurich, four are off to an exhibition that Van Doesburg has organized in A'dam, and then there's the stuff for A.S.B. in Amsterdam. I have also sent something to Spain. I've been on speaking terms again with Van Doesburg for some time now: despite his faults he is still almost the only one, apart from me, who does purely abstract painting. I sold a few things in Frankfurt in the spring, one to Stam, who is earning some money there with his buildings. And that's what I'm still living on, in the hope of more sales. I've been able to keep on working, fortunately, but am only just managing to make ends meet. I'm lucky to be so healthy, unlike you. You wrote that you were not fully recovered and were having to stay in the country this summer. That's why I'm sending this to Kijkduin, in the hope that Bob is better now. It's very hot here, which is more annoying than pleasant with all the work I have. But it's splendid for people on holiday.

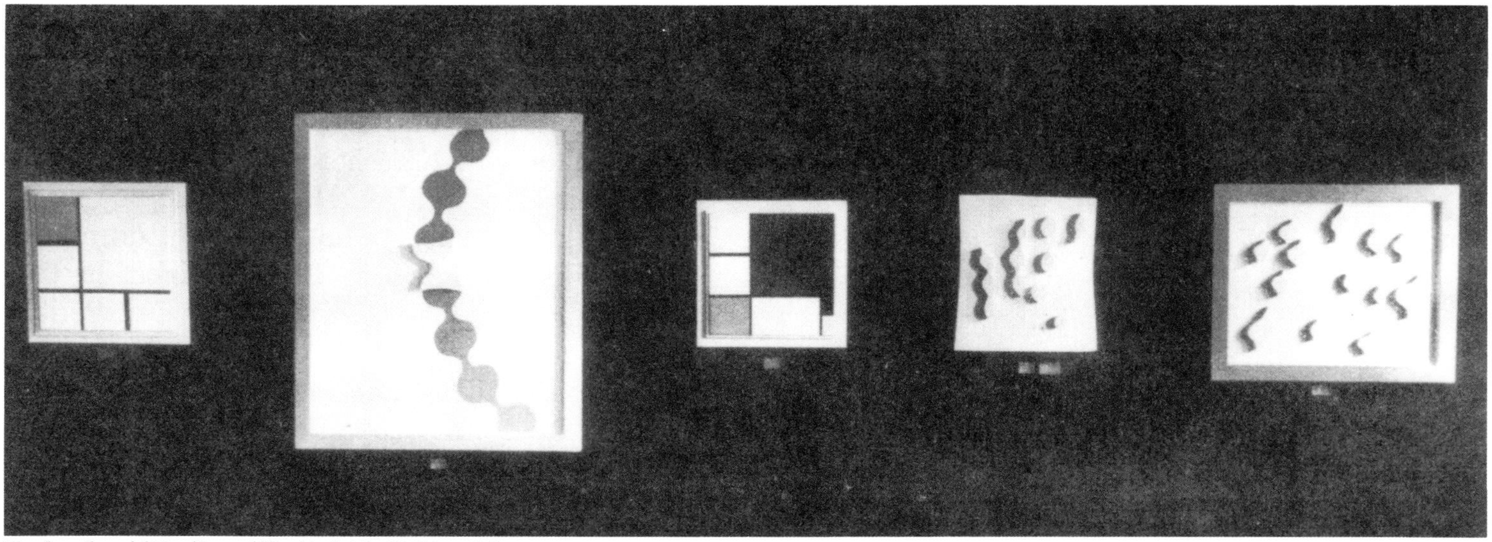

View from the exhibition 'Arp and Mondrian' at the Wolfsberg Gallery, Zürich, 1930.

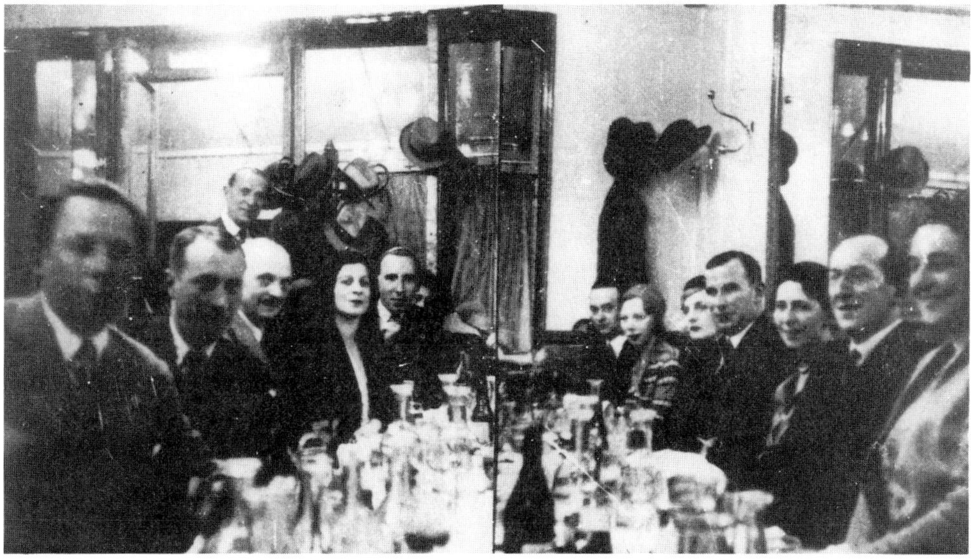

In the 'Restaurant Voltaire' (Paris); from left to right: Robert Delaunay, Jean Arp, Stazewski, Florence Henri, Michel Seuphor, Brzekowski, Mrs. Vantongerloo, Mr. and Mrs. Werner, Sophie Taeuber-Arp, Mondrian, Sonja Delaunay, 1930.

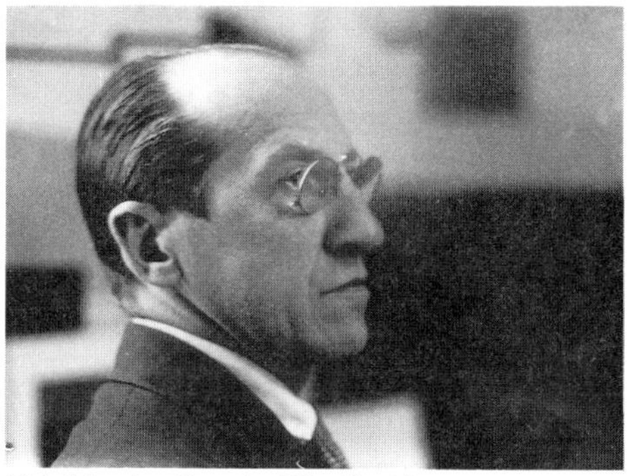

Michel Seuphor, Portrait of Piet Mondrian.

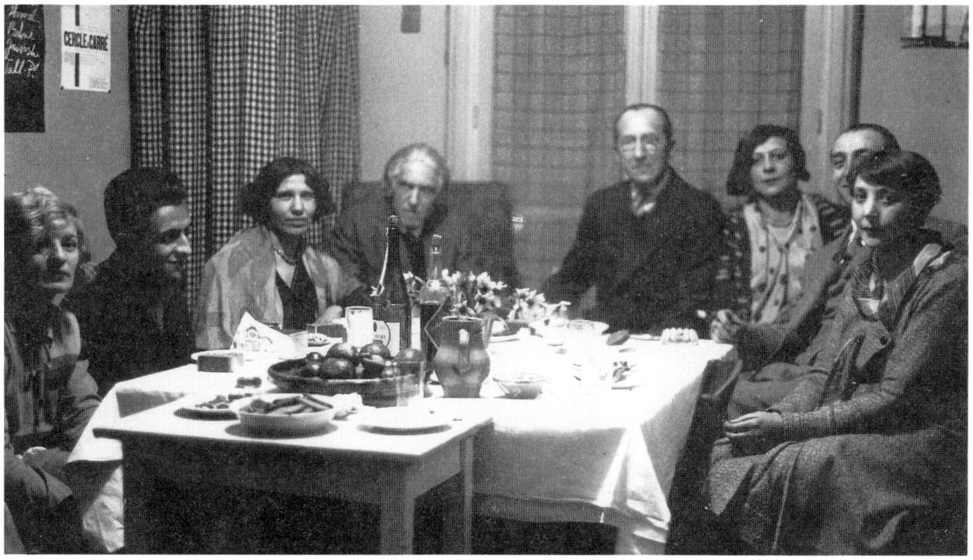

Michel Seuphor, A meeting in his studio with (from left to right) I. Bjarnasson, Honegger, Mrs. Torres-Garcia, Torres-Garcia, Mondrian, Florence Henri, G. Vantongerloo, Tine Vantongerloo, 1930.

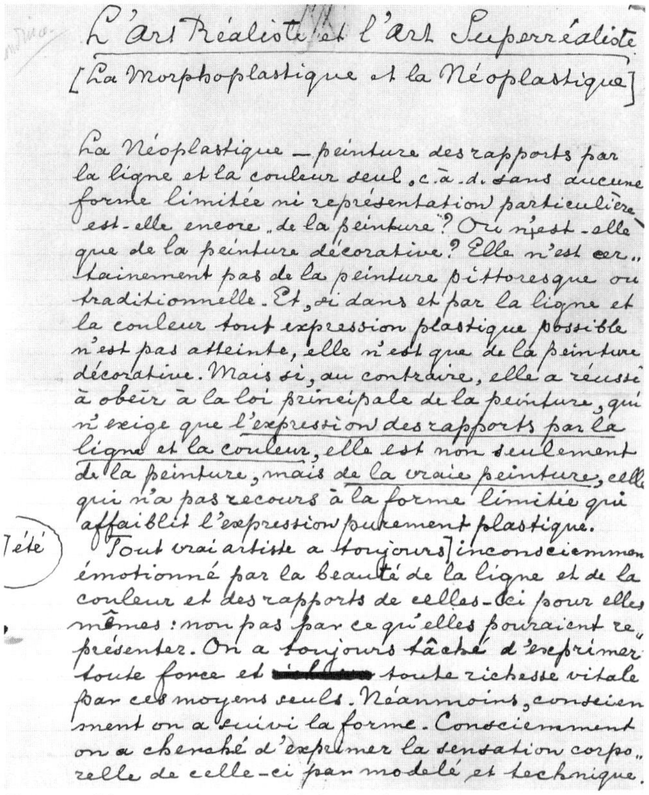

L'Art Réaliste et l'Art Superréaliste
[La Morphoplastique et la Néoplastique]

La Néoplastique — peinture des rapports par la ligne et la couleur seul, c.à.d. sans aucune forme limitée ni représentation particulière est-elle encore „de la peinture"? Ou n'est-elle que de la peinture décorative? Elle n'est certainement pas de la peinture pittoresque ou traditionnelle. Et, si dans et par la ligne et la couleur tout expression plastique possible n'est pas atteinte, elle n'est que de la peinture décorative. Mais si, au contraire, elle a réussi à obéir à la loi principale de la peinture, qui n'exige que l'expression des rapports par la ligne et la couleur, elle est non seulement de la peinture, mais de la vraie peinture, celle qui n'a pas recours à la forme limitée qui affaiblit l'expression purement plastique.

été

Tout vrai artiste a [toujours] inconsciemment émotionné par la beauté de la ligne et de la couleur et des rapports de celles-ci pour elles mêmes: non pas par ce qu'elles pourraient représenter. On a toujours tâché d'exprimer toute force et toute richesse vitale par ces moyens seuls. Néanmoins, consciemment on a suivi la forme. Consciemment on a cherché d'exprimer la sensation corporelle de celle-ci par modelé et technique.

First page of the manuscript of the article for 'Cercle et Carré', 1930.

For the second issue of 'Cercle et Carré' ('Circle and Square') Mondrian wrote one of his most important articles 'L'Art Réaliste et l'Art Superréaliste' ('Realist and Superrealist Art: Morphoplastic and Neo-Plastic'), 1930.

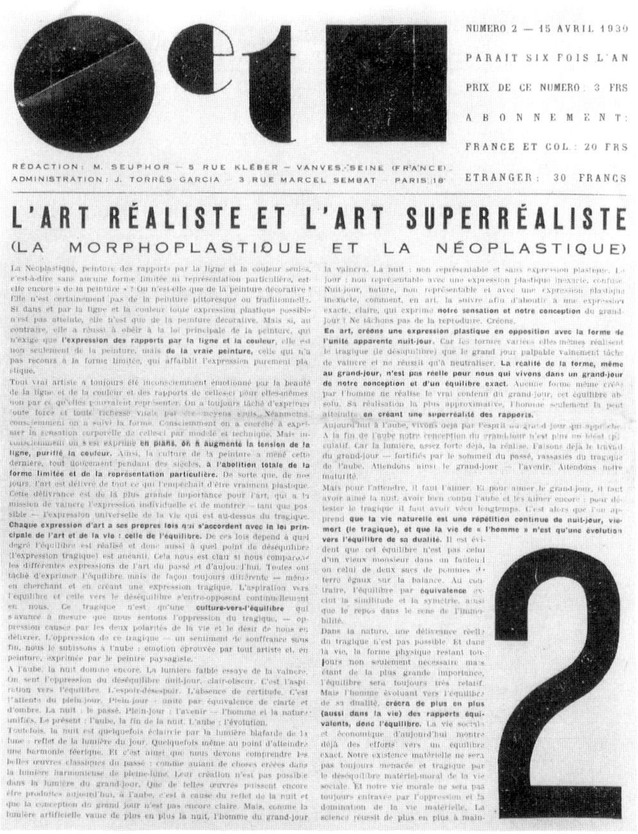

NUMERO 2 — 15 AVRIL 1930
PARAIT SIX FOIS L'AN
PRIX DE CE NUMERO : 3 FRS
ABONNEMENT :
FRANCE ET COL. : 20 FRS
ETRANGER : 30 FRANCS

RÉDACTION : M. SEUPHOR — 5 RUE KLÉBER — VANVES-SEINE (FRANCE)
ADMINISTRATION : J. TORRÈS GARCIA — 3 RUE MARCEL SEMBAT — PARIS 18e

L'ART RÉALISTE ET L'ART SUPERRÉALISTE
(LA MORPHOPLASTIQUE ET LA NÉOPLASTIQUE)

La Néoplastique, peinture des rapports par la ligne et la couleur seules, c'est-à-dire sans aucune forme limitée ni représentation particulière, est-elle encore « de la peinture » ? Ou n'est-elle que de la peinture décorative ? Elle n'est certainement pas de la peinture pittoresque ou traditionnelle. Si dans et par la ligne et la couleur toute expression plastique possible n'est pas atteinte, elle n'est que de la peinture décorative. Mais si, au contraire, elle a réussi à obéir à la loi principale de la peinture, qui n'exige que **l'expression des rapports par la ligne et la couleur**, elle est non seulement de la peinture, mais **de la vraie peinture,** celle qui n'a pas recours à la forme limitée, qui affaiblit l'expression purement plastique.

Tout vrai artiste a toujours été inconsciemment émotionné par la beauté de la ligne et de la couleur et des rapports de celles-ci pour elles-mêmes, non par ce qu'elles pourraient représenter. On a toujours tâché d'exprimer toute force et toute richesse vitale par ces moyens seuls. Néanmoins, consciemment on a suivi la forme. Consciemment on a cherché à exprimer la sensation corporelle de celle-ci par modelé et technique. Mais inconsciemment on s'est exprimé **en plans, on a augmenté la tension de la ligne, purifié la couleur.** Ainsi, la culture de la peinture a mené cette dernière, tout doucement pendant des siècles, **à l'abolition totale de la forme limitée et de la représentation particulière.** De sorte que, de nos jours, l'art est délivré de tout ce qui l'empêchait d'être vraiment plastique. Cette délivrance est de la plus grande importance pour l'art, qui a la mission de vaincre l'expression individuelle et de montrer — tant que possible — l'expression universelle de la vie qui est au-dessus du tragique. **Chaque expression d'art a ses propres lois qui s'accordent avec la loi principale de l'art et de la vie : celle de l'équilibre.** De ces lois dépend à quel degré l'équilibre est réalisé et donc aussi à quel point le déséquilibre (l'expression tragique) est anéanti. Cela nous est clair si nous comparons les différentes expressions de l'art du passé et d'aujourd'hui. Toutes ont tâché d'exprimer l'équilibre mais de façon toujours différente — même en cherchant et en créant une expression tragique. L'aspiration vers l'équilibre et celle vers le déséquilibre s'entre-opposent continuellement en nous. Ce tragique n'est qu'une **culture-vers-l'équilibre** qui s'avance à mesure que nous sentons l'oppression du tragique, — oppression causée par les deux polarités de la vie et le désir de nous en délivrer. L'oppression de ce tragique — un sentiment de souffrance sans fin, nous le subissons à l'aube : émotion éprouvée par tout artiste et, en peinture, exprimée par le peintre paysagiste.

A l'aube, la nuit domine encore. La lumière faible essaye de la vaincre. On sent l'oppression du déséquilibre nuit-jour, clair-obscur. C'est l'aspiration vers l'équilibre. L'espoir-désespoir. L'absence de certitude. C'est l'attente du plein-jour. Plein-jour : unité par équivalence de clarté et d'ombre. La nuit : le passé. Plein-jour : l'avenir — l'homme et la nature unifiés. Le présent : l'aube, la fin de la nuit. L'aube : l'évolution.

Toutefois, la nuit est quelquefois éclaircie par la lumière blafarde de la lune : reflet de la lumière du jour. Quelquefois même au point d'atteindre une harmonie féerique. Et c'est ainsi que nous devons comprendre les belles œuvres classiques du passé : comme autant de choses créées dans la lumière harmonieuse de pleine-lune. Leur création n'est pas possible dans la lumière du grand-jour. Que de telles œuvres puissent encore être produites aujourd'hui, à l'aube, c'est à cause du reflet de la nuit et que la conception du grand jour n'est pas encore claire. Mais, comme la lumière artificielle vainc de plus en plus la nuit, l'homme du grand-jour la vaincra. La nuit : non représentable et sans expression plastique. Le jour : non représentable avec une expression plastique inexacte, confuse. Nuit-jour, nature, non représentable et avec une expression plastique inexacte, comment, en art, la suivre afin d'aboutir à une expression exacte, claire, qui exprime **notre sensation et notre conception** du grand-jour ? Ne tâchons pas de la reproduire. Créons.

En art, créons une expression plastique en opposition avec la forme de l'unité apparente nuit-jour. Car les formes variées elles-mêmes réalisent le tragique (le déséquilibre) que le grand jour palpable vainement tâche de vaincre et ne réussit qu'à neutraliser. **La réalité de la forme, même au grand-jour, n'est pas réelle pour nous qui vivons dans un grand-jour de notre conception et d'un équilibre exact.** Aucune forme même créée par l'homme ne réalise le vrai contenu du grand-jour, cet équilibre absolu. Sa réalisation la plus approximative, l'homme seulement la peut atteindre **en créant une superréalité des rapports.**

Aujourd'hui à l'aube, vivons déjà par l'esprit au grand jour qui approche. A la fin de l'aube notre conception du grand-jour n'est plus un idéal spéculatif. Car la lumière, assez forte déjà, la réalise. Faisons déjà le travail du grand-jour — fortifiés par le sommeil du passé, rassasiés du tragique de l'aube. Attendons ainsi le grand-jour — l'avenir. Attendons notre maturité.

Mais pour l'attendre, il faut l'aimer. Et pour aimer le grand-jour, il faut avoir aimé la nuit, avoir bien connu l'aube et les aimer encore : pour détester le tragique il faut avoir vécu longtemps. C'est alors que l'on apprend **que la vie naturelle est une répétition continue de nuit-jour, vie-mort (le tragique), et que la vie de « l'homme » n'est qu'une évolution vers l'équilibre de sa dualité.** Il est évident que cet équilibre n'est pas celui d'un vieux monsieur dans un fauteuil ou celui de deux sacs de pommes de terre égaux sur la balance. Au contraire, l'équilibre par **équivalence** exclut la similitude et la symétrie, ainsi que le repos dans le sens de l'immobilité.

Dans la nature, une délivrance réelle du tragique n'est pas possible. Et dans la vie, la forme physique restant toujours non seulement nécessaire mais étant de la plus grande importance, l'équilibre sera toujours très relatif. Mais l'homme évoluant vers l'équilibre de sa dualité, **créera de plus en plus (aussi dans la vie) des rapports équivalents, donc l'équilibre.** La vie sociale et économique d'aujourd'hui montre déjà des efforts vers un équilibre exact. Notre existence matérielle ne sera pas toujours menacée et tragique par le déséquilibre matériel-moral de la vie sociale. Et notre vie morale ne sera pas toujours entravée par l'oppression et la domination de la vie matérielle. La science réussit de plus en plus à main-

2

At the opening of the exhibition of the group 'Cercle et Carré' ('Circle and Square'); in the middle Torres-Garcia, behind him Piet Mondrian, 1930.

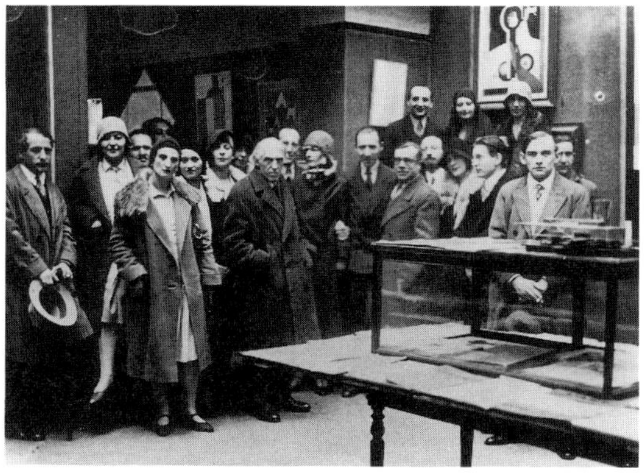

At the opening of an exhibition with works by the Swiss painter Buchet at the Zak Gallery, Mondrian at the right with Florence Henri; M. Seuphor at the left, 1930.

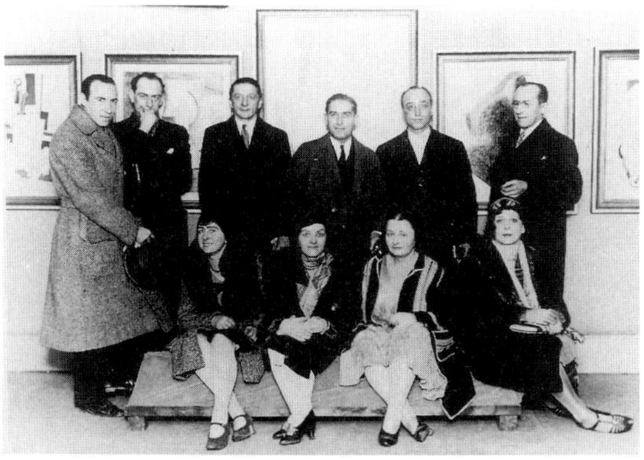

Three paintings by Mondrian in his studio, 1930.

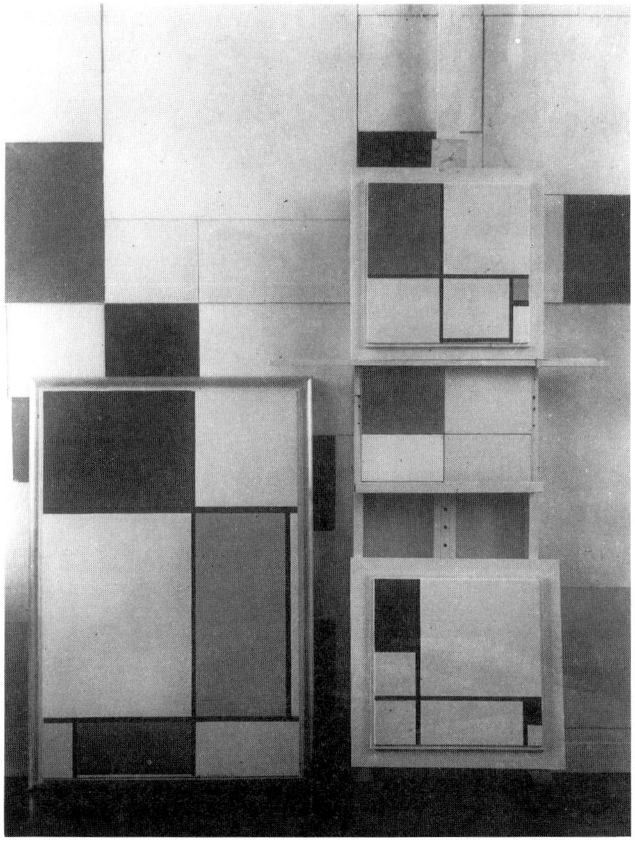

You wrote about that Witteveen. I haven't seen him since, but Stam and Van Eesteren told me same as you did. Of course the Hoyacks are acquainted with the better side that he's bound to have: at any rate he sometimes seems quite affable. He said very nice things to me about you. I hope, Bob, that you will give those lectures in America in 1930. New stuff is coming slowly. This summer I sold another painting to Miss Dreier, who was over from New York. Will I hear from you again soon?

Your friend Piet.

1930

For some time Mondrian had been working on a summary of his ideas concerning art and society; this essay was to be entitled 'L'Art et la Vie'; he was to work on the project for several years before it was ready for publication at last. Mondrian took part in the group exhibitions of 'Cercle et Carré' and 'Abstraction et Création'. His contacts with American art collectors grew. Work by him was also shown at exhibitions in Stockholm, Brussels and in the Netherlands.

1931

To: A. Roth

10-11-31

Dear Friend,

I was very pleased to hear your news. And that you–like me–are enthusiastic about the new life. My brochure has grown into a small book: I hope that you and Mr. Backlund like it. The corrections are almost finished. As soon as I find the means I shall have it copied and send you an example. (If you move, you will let me know your new address, won't you?) The matter of a modern museum has been postponed because of the poor economical climate. I myself have not submitted a project for the museum (not being an architect), but I have suggested how it could be organized. Anyhow, that will come later. Please convey my regards to the Gidéons when you see them. I think they are most congenial. Also to Mr. Backlund, whose humanitarian mentality I admire very much. "L'Abstraction-Création" will resume work on the 30th of the month. I shall send you the papers after that date, when there will be a meeting. I shall show them your house project, which I like very much.
I was glad to hear about the progress of the school movement at Geneva.

Goodbye, dear Friend, and kind regards,

Piet Mondrian

About Arp
I think the work (the flat reliefs) is very close to my own. True, it does not go so well with the architecture, but the spirit and rendering are good. I like Arp's things very much: I feel that he is the only "pure" artist since néo-plasticism.

To: S.B. Slijper

13.11.31

Dear Sal, If you can sell a picture I shall gladly paint another one for you. It will remain between ourselves. I thought of the windmill with water on the Gein from Fr. Muller's catalogue, but I have already returned it to you. So see if you can find anything. Let me know what size you want. The farmhouse would do as well, but it's so well known. With regard to the price, I thought 200 guilders would not be too much; perhaps you can delay ordering until you have sold that other picture, otherwise I think 200 guilders too high a price. If you want me to start on it immediately it could be finished by the end of the year or the beginning of January. But I have to buy canvas and paints, because I don't use those colours any more, as you know. So you might send me 10 guilders or more now, because it will be a month before I get paid for a picture which I've just finished and sold but which is not dry yet. I shall write again telling you who I sold it to, etc. It's rather strange, because as you know there's not much being sold these days. Things are just as bad in other countries. Still, my expenses are not high and so I manage to scrape along. Regarding that watercolour for Dr. d'Eck, I did it in A'dam; it is a view of the prison on Stadhouderskade with a boat in front, from the time before it was the Hôtel Américain. It is a dark painting, grey and brown, a gloomy day. It is, I think, bigger than that farmhouse of mine which you have. With glass and a white frame. I've no idea how it will survive the journey. I don't want any trouble, and the thing seems to be here in Paris, probably in storage since d'Eck left. It will be up to d'Eck to get you to buy it. It's annoying because I don't want to be blamed if the thing doesn't suit. I thought it good at the time, and it was on show at an Arti exhibition. Although it is painted in broad lines, it is properly finished.
Otherwise the situation is as follows. D'Eck published a book for a business in which a friend of mine—a writer—is involved.
D'Eck is constantly in financial trouble and lives in style; the printing costs came inopportunely, which is why he wrote to my friend asking whether he could sell a watercolour of mine that was in Paris. The friend consulted me but I wanted no part of it; later, though, I let d'Eck have your address. He seemed inclined to ask more, but I wrote to him that you wouldn't pay more than 200 guilders if it appealed to you. I heard nothing further apart from what you have told me. I don't know what I should advise you to do.
And now about publishing. I have just finished writing a book in French which is being corrected, and am gradually looking for a publisher. I could translate it into Dutch if you can think of a publisher, and would only take my percentage after defrayment of the costs. Of course I can't afford any expenses myself. What do you think about waiting until the French version is out?
Well, Sal, this is a real business letter. It doesn't look as if you will be coming over this year. So long, Piet.

I haven't heard anything about that book on Dutch painters for years, nor seen it.

You can't send me that painting of yours because it is liable to high tax which is only waived when sending *from* here.

1932

To: M. Seuphor from P. Mondrian
June 14 1932

Dear Nant,

Thank you very much for what you sent me, and for your efforts to ensure the success of the edition of 'L'Art et la Vie'. At the moment, though, I dare not promise anything; I shall try and find some money, but it will have to come [...] and I do not see it yet. I hope I can profit from M. Michon's fine offer when the occasion arises.
I shall write again as soon as possible. I have been looking at my manuscript again and have found some things which were not quite clear or exact. Therefore, if you have any room for fragments let me know, so that I can let you have another copy. I have already read a part of your Flemish book, and enjoyed it.

A bientôt, I hope,

Piet

August 18 [1932]

Dear Nant,

Please forgive me for not writing sooner. I am very sorry that you are no longer at the printer's and especially that you have such a job, but it won't be for ever; I hope that you will be delivered from it one day. You have the advantage of still being young, so that you can afford to lose a little time—no, it's never wasted: one can always learn something. I am so glad that you are there now and can work and even be with [...] friends, I especially like Moholy very much; I don't know Baumeister so well but he seems very nice too. I should be very pleased if Moholy came to Paris, and send him and his wife my best wishes , Baumeister and my other friends too. It is very nice of everyone to think of me and to send their greetings. I am well now, and the result is that I have redecorated my studio: I could no longer stand seeing my painting [...] when I entered. But it was hard work, which is why I did not write before.
The Hoyacks have returned from Holland. While they were there I corresponded with him about his book "De Tijdgeest" (nice name!!) [The Spirit of the Times] He talks about art too; I find it all badly [seen?], even the profound Hindu wisdom—I told him so politely and we are still friends.
Later he came to Paris with his editor and his Dutch wife [?], who stayed here for a fortnight. He and Ella came to see me; they are as nice as ever, but what an "icy" friendship! Anyhow, they are "icy" and believe they have fire—even light! They invited me to their place but I didn't accept. I shall go later, for the day. They are at the same address: Avenue d. Mar. Foch 141, until September.
I think you will feel strange in this [...]
When you are in Paris I hope to see you. I did not go to the Lilas on Friday because it is not the place to talk freely with you. Later, on Monday and Tuesday, you didn't come; I understand you were prevented.

Best wishes from Pierre.

I went twice to the Vantongerloos while they were at the old address. I sent a card afterwards, but I haven't heard anything.
His new abode is more important than an old friendship!!!

P.T.O.

1935

The compositions, dominated primarily by the relationship between lines and (often) a single plane, became increasingly complex in structure. The impending demolition of the studios at the Rue du Départ forced Mondrian to move, this time to 278, Boulevard Raspail, where he lived until his departure for England in 1938. He published an important essay in a book of the English Constructivist group *Circle* entitled 'Plastic Art and Pure Plastic Art' (1937). Interest in his work increased steadily in England, but especially in the United States, among both collectors and fellow-artists. In September 1938 Mondrian took up residence in Hampstead, 66 Parkhill Road, in a studio next-door to the studios of Gabo and Nicholson. He took a lot of unfinished work with him from France, some of which was not completed until he moved to the United States several years later.

A.E. Gallatin, Portrait of Piet Mondrian.

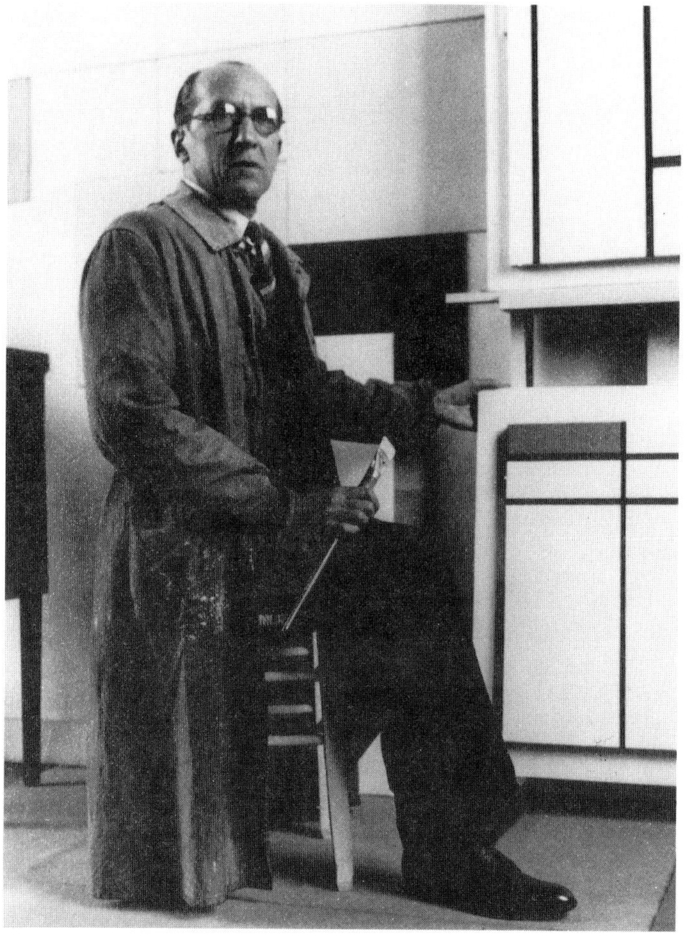

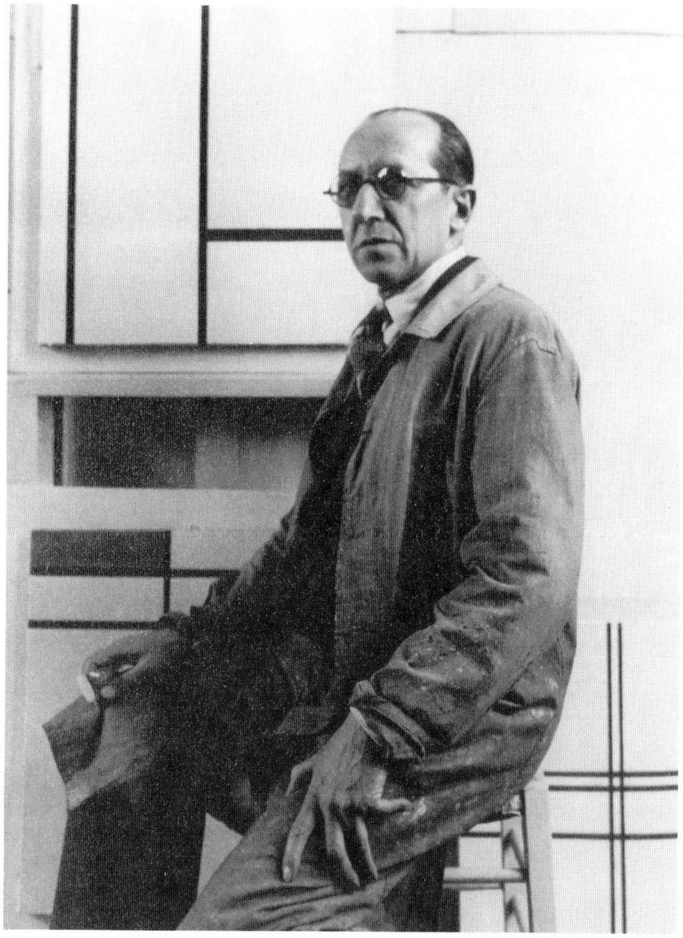

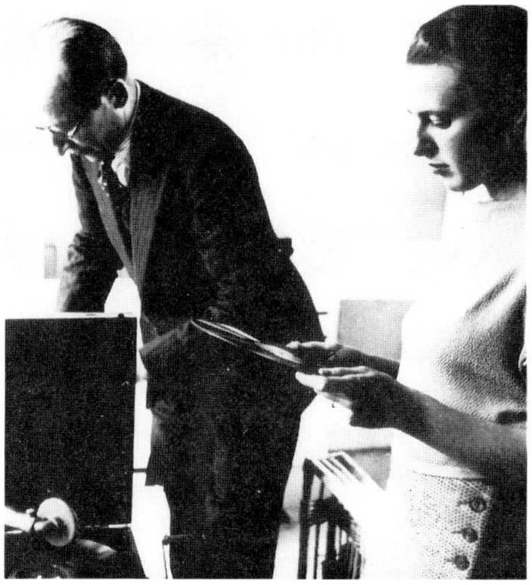

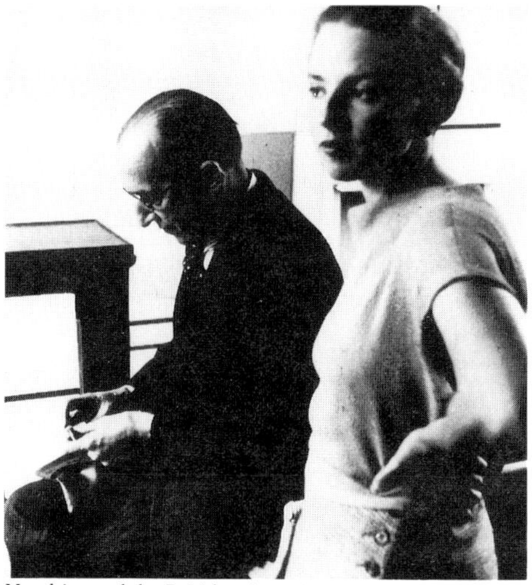

Mondrian and the British painter Gwen Lux, 1935.

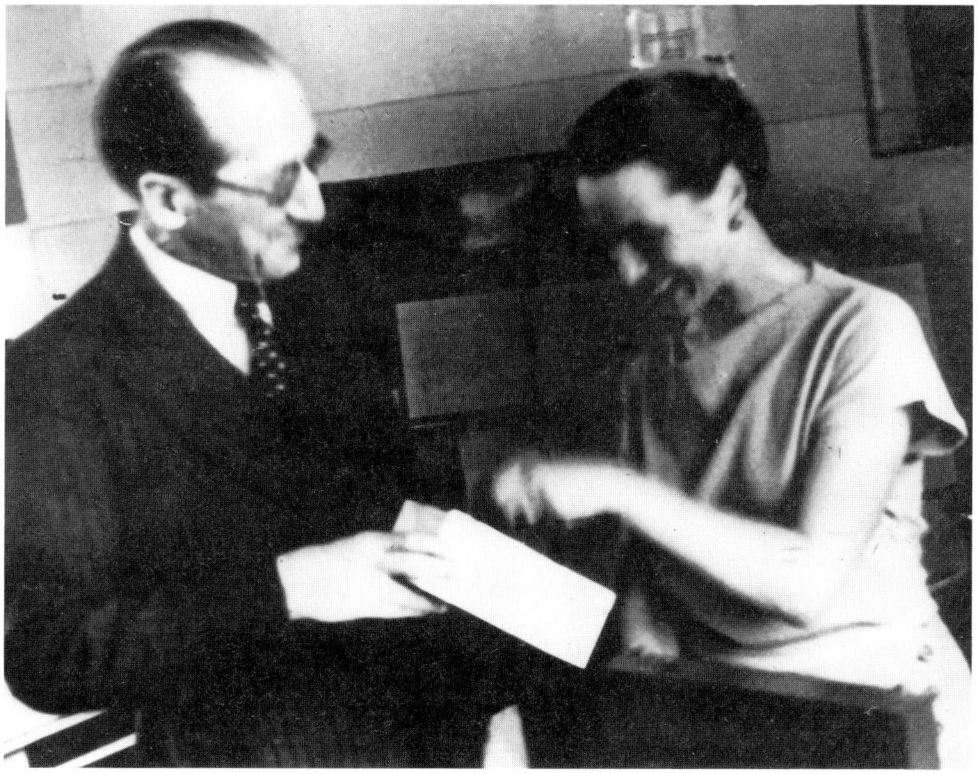

Mondrian offering Gwen Lux a delicacy, 1935.

Selection of Works by 20th century Artists, the Renaissance Society of the University of Chicago, directed by J. J. Sweeney, 1935.

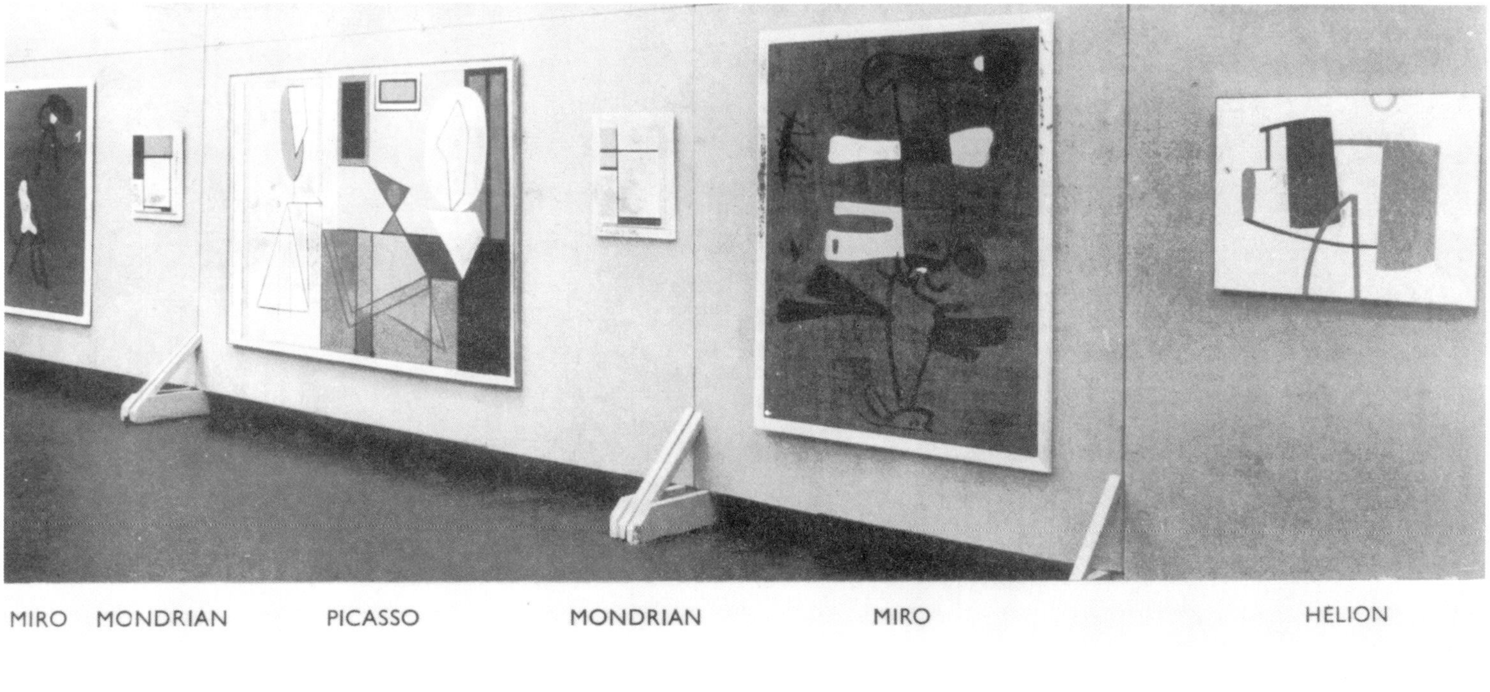

MIRO MONDRIAN PICASSO MONDRIAN MIRO HELION

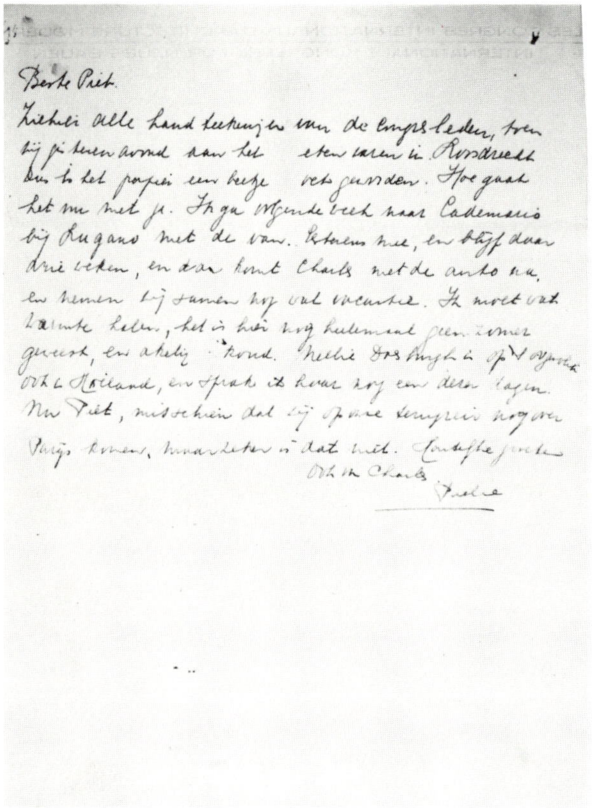

Beste Piet.
Hierbij alle handteekeningen van de congresleden, toen wij gisteren avond aan het eten waren in Loosdrecht dus is het papier een beetje vet geworden. Hoe gaat het nu met je. Ik ga volgende week naar Cademario bij Lugano met de van Eesterens mee, en blijf daar drie weken, en dan komt Charles met de auto na, en nemen wij samen nog wat vacantie. Ik moet wat warmte hebben, het is hier nog heelemaal geen zomer geweest, en akelig koud. Nellie Doesburg is op 't oogenblik ook in Holland, en sprak ik haar nog een deze dagen. Nu Piet, misschien dat wij op onze terugreis nog over Parijs komen, maar zeker is dat niet. Hartelijke groeten
ook van Charles
Paulie

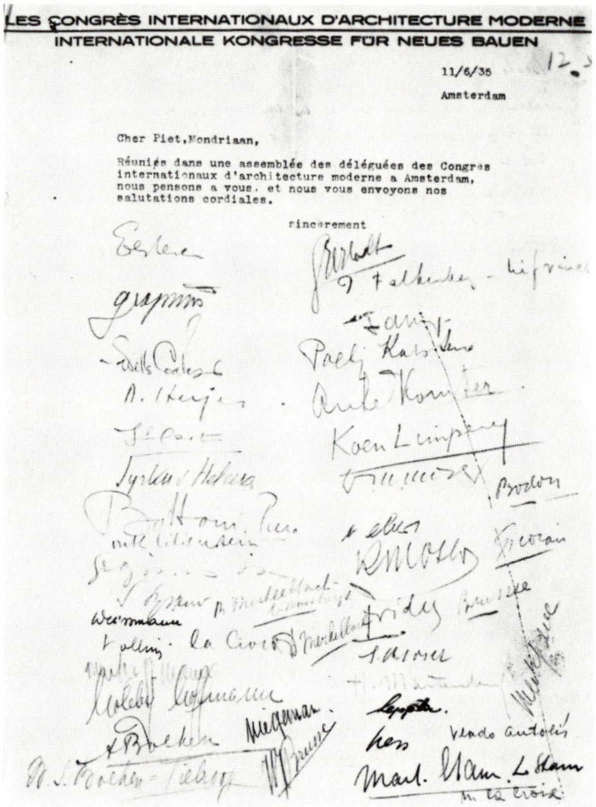

LES CONGRÈS INTERNATIONAUX D'ARCHITECTURE MODERNE
INTERNATIONALE KONGRESSE FÜR NEUES BAUEN

11/6/35
Amsterdam

Cher Piet,Mondriaan,

Réunies dans une assemblée des déléguées des Congres internationaux d'architecture moderne a Amsterdam, nous pensons a vous, et nous vous envoyons nos salutations cordiales.

sincerement

Letter of sympathy to Mondrian, 1935.

Dear Piet,

Here are all the signatures of the congress delegates at yesterday evening's dinner in Loosdrecht. The paper is a little greasy. How are you. I am going to Cademaris near Lugano with the van Eesterens next week, and shall spend three weeks there; Charles will follow by car and we shall have a short holiday together. I must have warmth, there are no signs of summer here yet, and it's terribly cold. Nellie Doesburg is also in Holland at the moment; I spoke to her a day or two ago.

Well Piet, perhaps we shall pass through Paris on our way back, but it's not certain.

Best wishes, also from Charles, [Karsten]
Paulie

Dear Piet Mondrian,
Gathered together in an assembly of delegates at the International Congress of Modern Architecture in Amsterdam, we are thinking of you and send cordial greetings.

Sincerely,

signatures

left column
C. van Eesteren
Walter Gropius
Wells Coates
A. Herjer
J.L. Sert
Helena Syrkus
Piero Bottoni
Ruth Lilienstein
Isa Gropius
S. Syrkus
R. Merkelbach-Van Doesburgh
Weissmann
Gino Pollini
Willy la Croix
B. Merkelbach
Josef Hoffmann
Holeby Hoffmann
A. Boeken
Johan Niegeman
W.S. Boeken-Tielrooy
H.J. Brusse

right column
G.H. Holt
I. Falckenberg-Liefrinck
Charles Karsten
Auke Komter
Koen Limperg
W.M. Moser
S. Giedion
Fridy van Eesteren
Wim Brusse
S. Moser
H. Mastenbroek
H. Leppia
Miek Greve
Vlado Antolis
Hess(e)
Mart Stam
Lotte Stam-Beese
M. la Croix

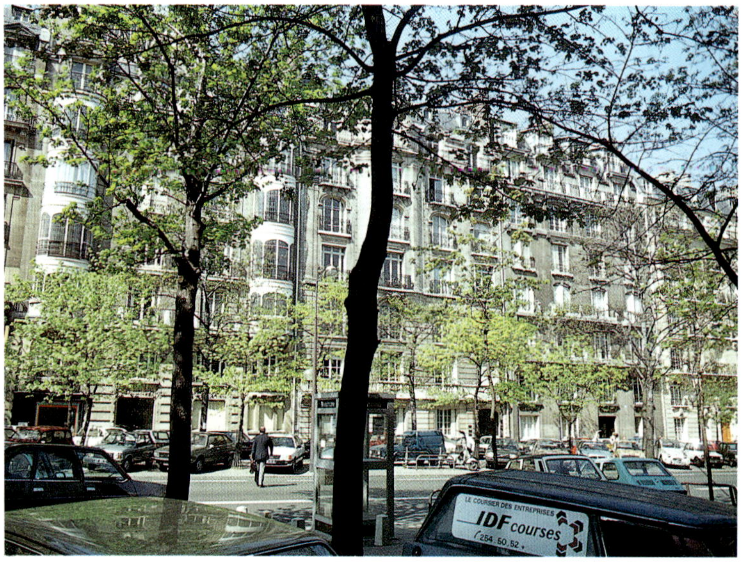

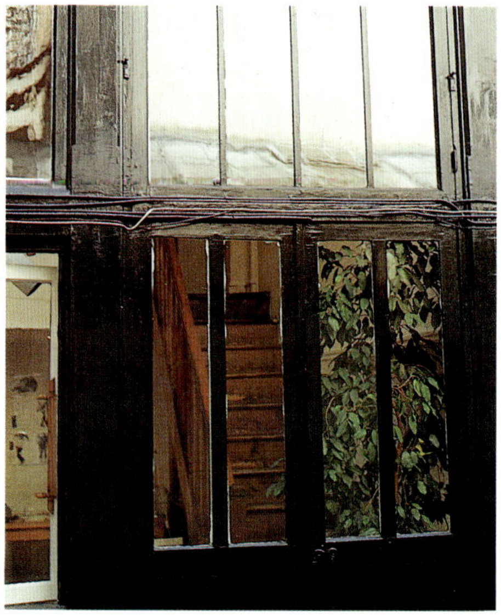

Mondrian's studio at 278 Boulevard Raspail; Mondrian lived here from March 1936 till September 1938. (photograph 1984)

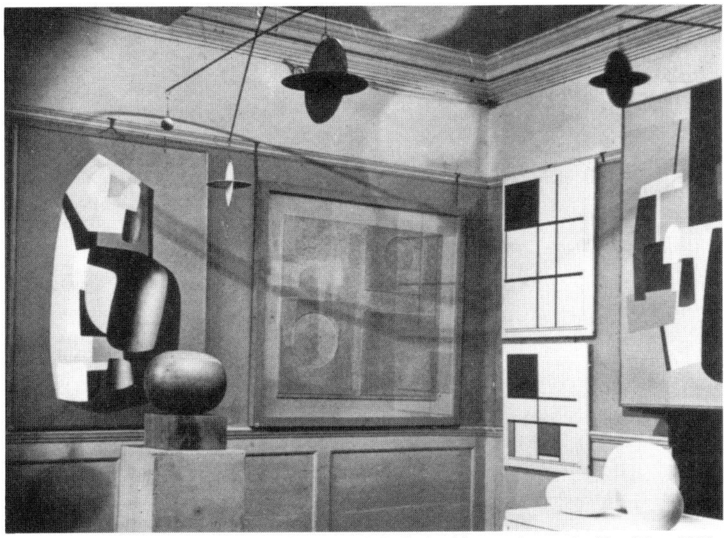

View from the exhibition 'Abstract and Concrete', Oxford, with two pictures by Mondrian, 1936.

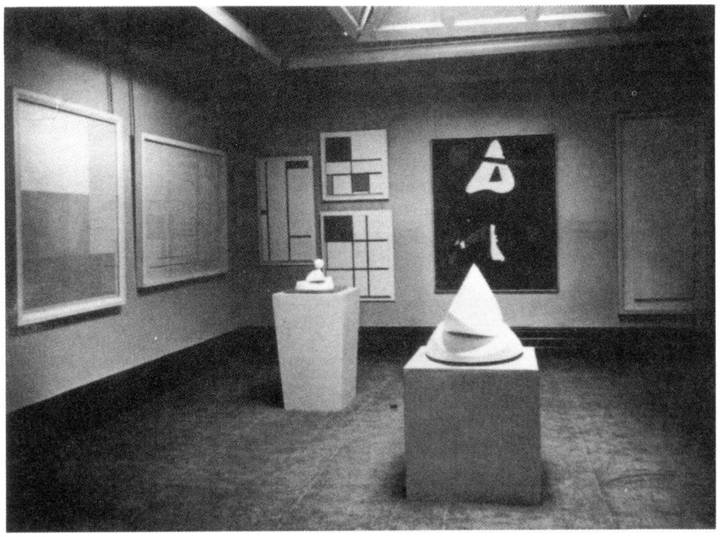

View of the 'Abstract and Concrete Exhibition', London, with three paintings by Mondrian, 1936.

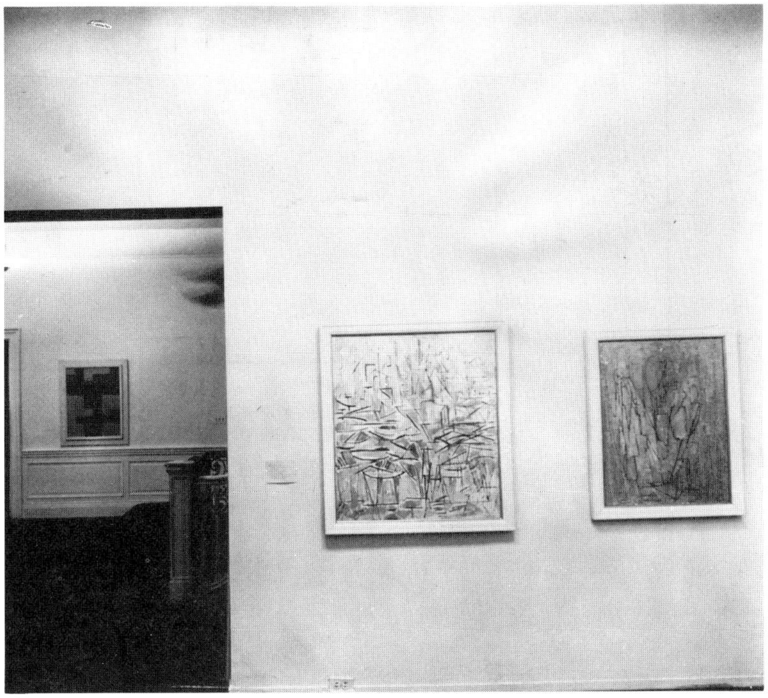

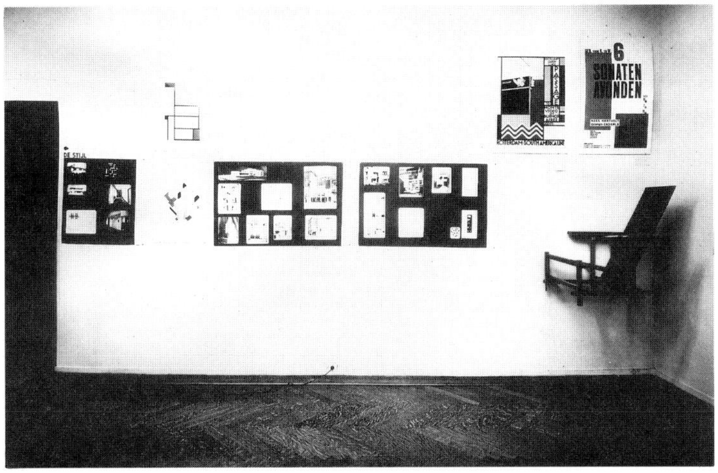

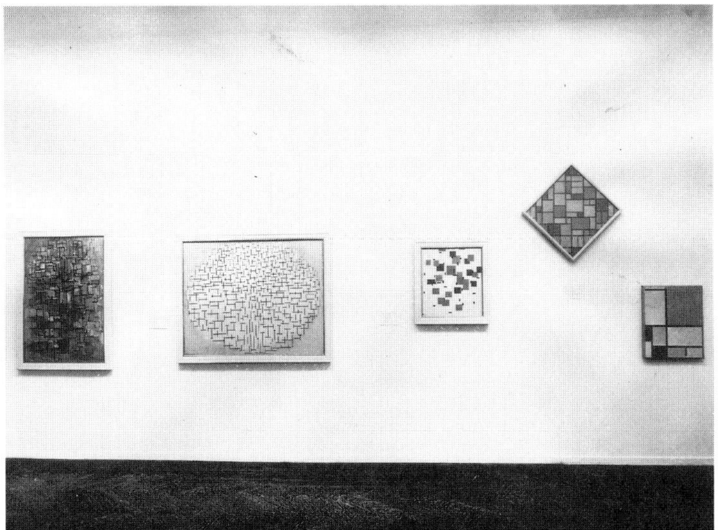

Installation Views from Alfred Barr's 'Cubism and Abstract Art' exhibition, March 2-April 19, 1936, Museum of Modern Art (Courtesy the Museum of Modern Art): two views with work by Mondrian, the third one gives a view of the introductory panels, with a lithograph of Mondrian's 'Tableau I', made by the Bauhaus in 1924.

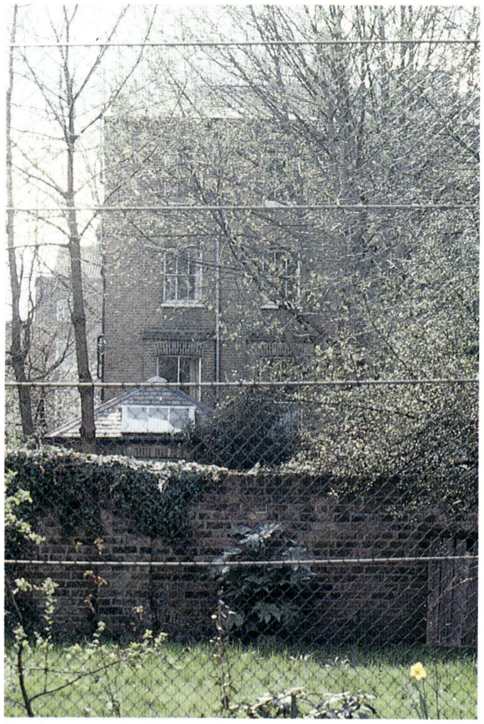

Mondrian's studio at 60 Parkhill Road
Mondrian lived here on the first floor from September 1938 till September 1940. (photograph 1986);

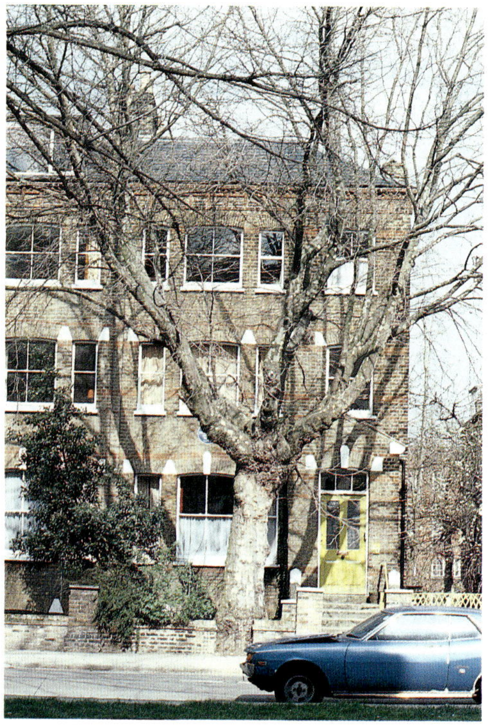

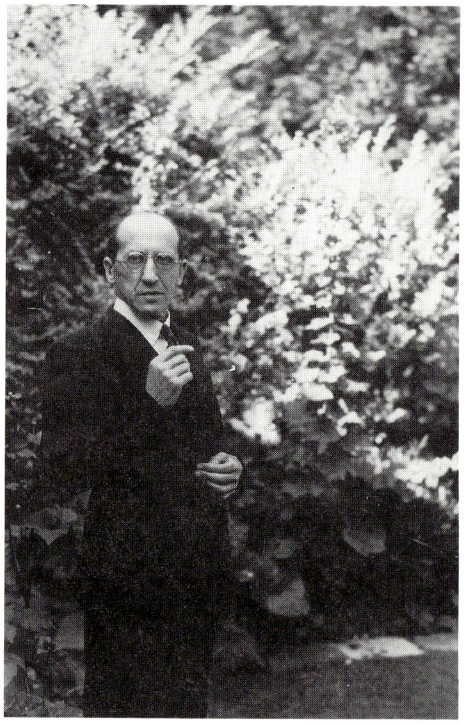

Cecil Stephenson, Portrait of Mondrian at the Mall studios.

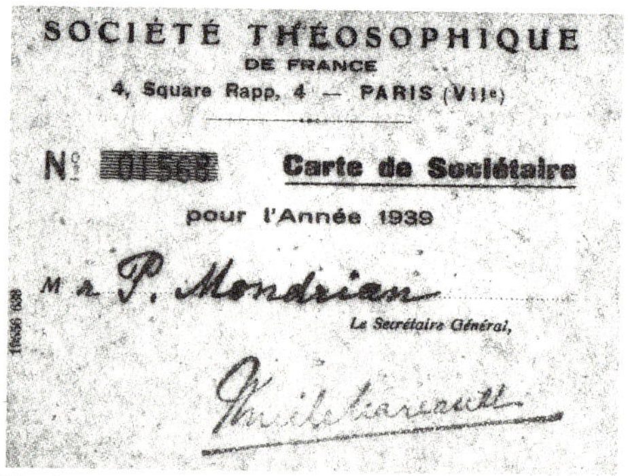

SOCIÉTÉ THÉOSOPHIQUE
DE FRANCE
4, Square Rapp, 4 — PARIS (VIIe)

N° 01568 Carte de Sociétaire

pour l'Année 1939

M r P. Mondrian

Le Secrétaire Général,

Mondrian's membership certificate of the Theosophical Society in Paris. for the year 1939

Michel Seuphor, 60 Parkhill Road, drawing (1938)
Mondrian's room at the first floor and Ben Nicholson's studio in the garden.

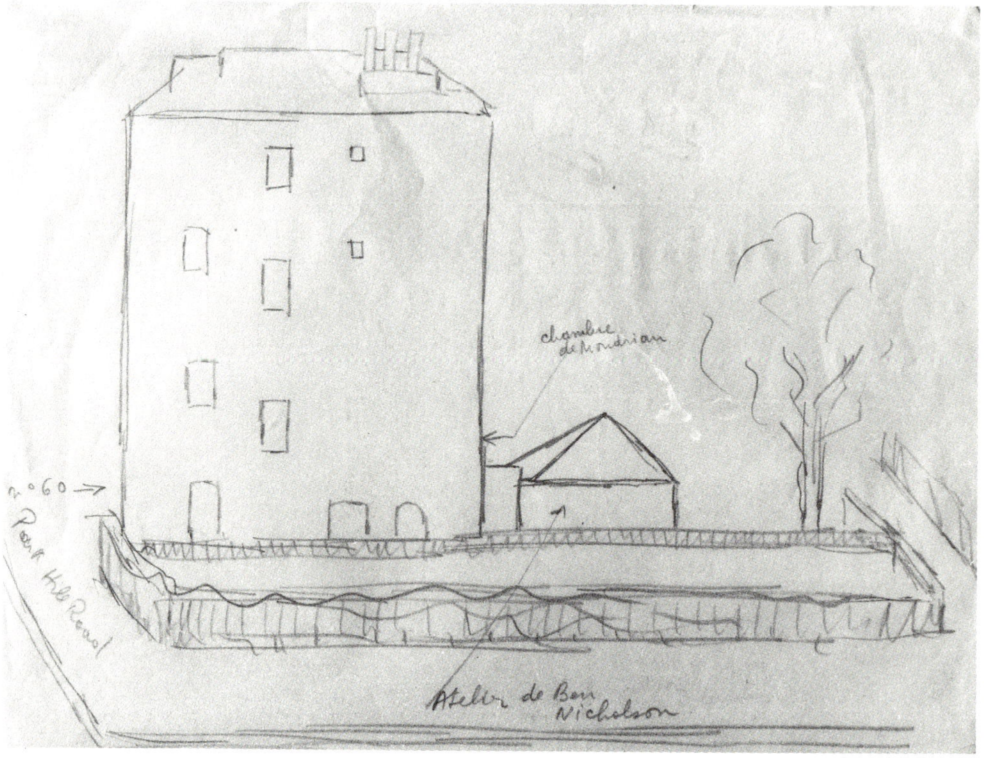

1939

To: Mrs. & Mr. Hoyack [postmark 4.4.39]

60 Parkhill Rd.
London N.W.3.

Dear Ella and Louk,

From London this year my very best wishes for April 5th, Ella's memorable birthday. Didn't the three of us had a good time in St. Cloud? Things are *different* now, but no "worse", are they? I was glad to get Louk's long letter—for which I admire him, for I'm no longer up to it and my letters are always short. I see that Louk was and is as active as ever. Ella's letter apparently never got written, but I know she meant well. Now that she is sculpting—according to Harry—for Louk didn't mention it—I realize that work is keeping her occupied. I actually wanted to write yesterday evening but couldn't tear myself away from my work, which means that this may not reach you by the morning of the 5th.

My room is now white, as always; I mean its contents, such as cupboard, seats, etc. I had the walls whitewashed when I moved in. White with the odd patch of red. It suits me very well here, but who knows for how long? The international situation is more and more menacing. At any rate I should like you to keep me posted with your address, so that we can exchange the occasional word. Louk wrote "temporary address", so maybe you are somewhere else by now. I hope this reaches you. Things are not as bad as they have been in Paris lately, but it's better not to read the papers too much. Bombs etc., and preparations for war. I expect it's the same in Rome. Fortunately we know that the way of the world is good in the end: greater perfection. I have already exhibited here, but not sold anything. Luckily I sold a few things in America. Goodbye for now, and very best wishes from Piet.
Thank goodness my health continues to improve.

1940

The American artist Harry Holtzman, who had visited Mondrian in 1934 in Paris to hear about his theories in person, persuaded Mondrian to move to New York. Many European artists had already preceded him. First he took a studio at 353 East 52nd Street and a few months before his death he moved into a new studio at 15 East 59th Street. Several years before his arrival in the United States plans for an exhibition of his work in that country had been discussed. One-man shows of his work were held in 1942 and 1943 at Valentine Dudensing Gallery, and he was represented at several group exhibitions. His contacts with numerous young American artists resulted in a wide dissemination of his ideas. The enormous 'evolution' that is to be seen in his work from about 1935 continued up to his death on 1 February 1944. The main characteristic of his work in this last period is the balanced, complex structure of his compositions, executed exclusively in coloured lines or coloured planes or combinations of both, in which the dynamic vitality of his art reached levels of unprecedented intensity.

Page of sketchbook with addresses in New York and drawing of painting; coll. the Pace Gallery, New York.

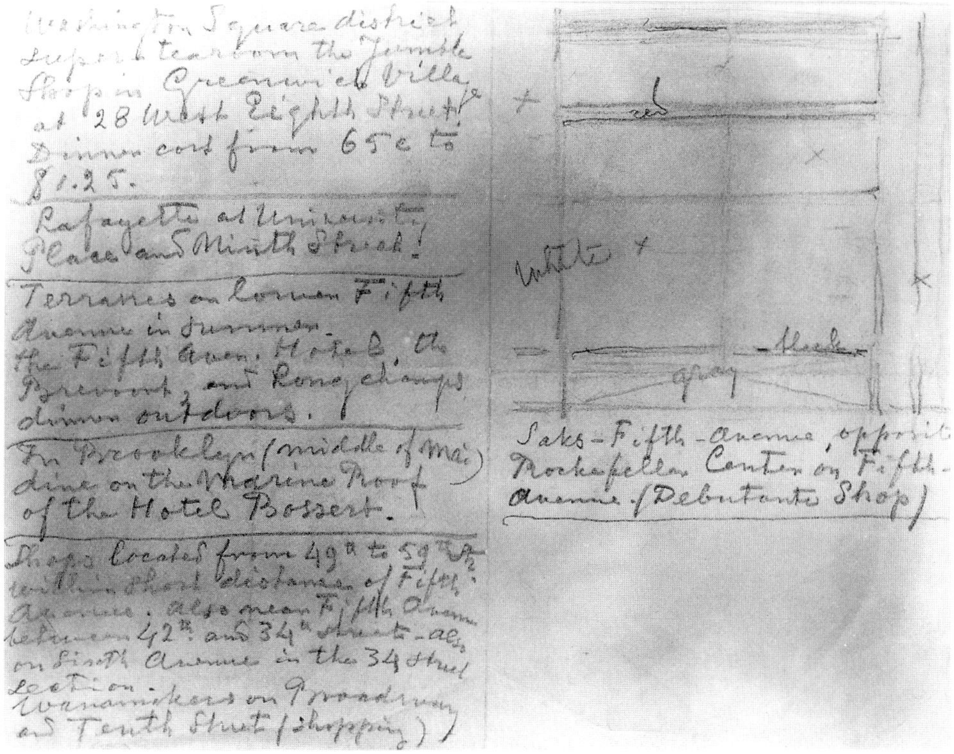

Entrance to Mondrian's first New York studio at 353 E 56th Street; Mondrian lived here till October 1943.

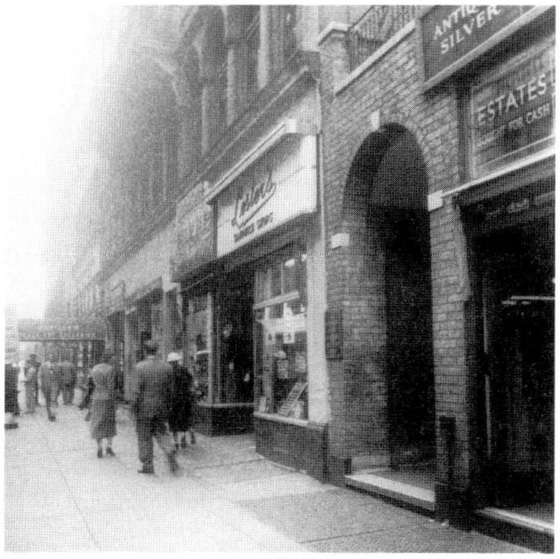

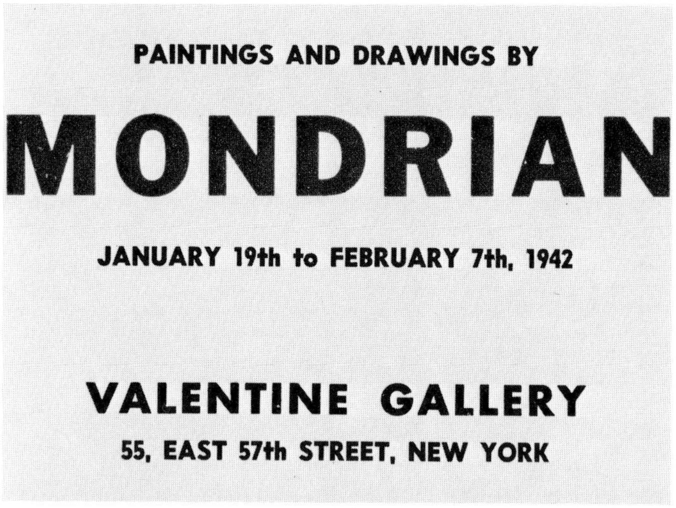

PAINTINGS AND DRAWINGS BY

MONDRIAN

JANUARY 19th to FEBRUARY 7th, 1942

VALENTINE GALLERY

55, EAST 57th STREET, NEW YORK

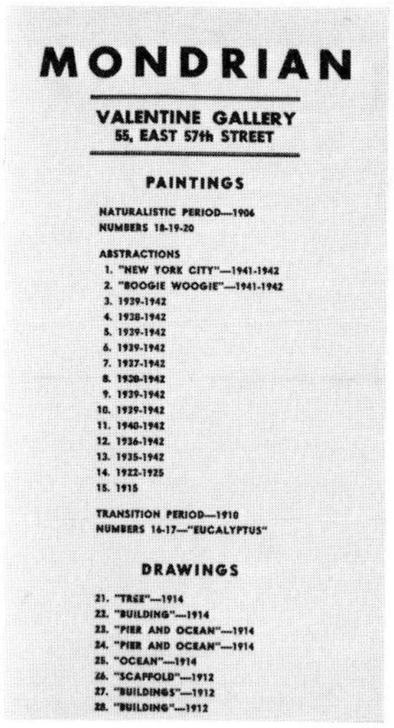

MONDRIAN

VALENTINE GALLERY
55, EAST 57th STREET

PAINTINGS

NATURALISTIC PERIOD—1906
NUMBERS 18-19-20

ABSTRACTIONS
1. "NEW YORK CITY"—1941-1942
2. "BOOGIE WOOGIE"—1941-1942
3. 1939-1942
4. 1938-1942
5. 1939-1942
6. 1939-1942
7. 1937-1942
8. 1930-1942
9. 1939-1942
10. 1939-1942
11. 1940-1942
12. 1936-1942
13. 1935-1942
14. 1922-1925
15. 1915

TRANSITION PERIOD—1910
NUMBERS 16-17—"EUCALYPTUS"

DRAWINGS

21. "TREE"—1914
22. "BUILDING"—1914
23. "PIER AND OCEAN"—1914
24. "PIER AND OCEAN"—1914
25. "OCEAN"—1914
26. "SCAFFOLD"—1912
27. "BUILDINGS"—1912
28. "BUILDING"—1912

Catalogue of Mondrian's first New York one-man show, 1942.

European artists in exile; first row: Matta, Zadkine, Yves Tanguy, Max Ernst, Chagall, F. Léger; second row: André Breton, Mondrian, A. Masson, Ozenfant, Lipchitz, Tchelitchew, Kurt Seligmann, Eugène Berman, 1942.

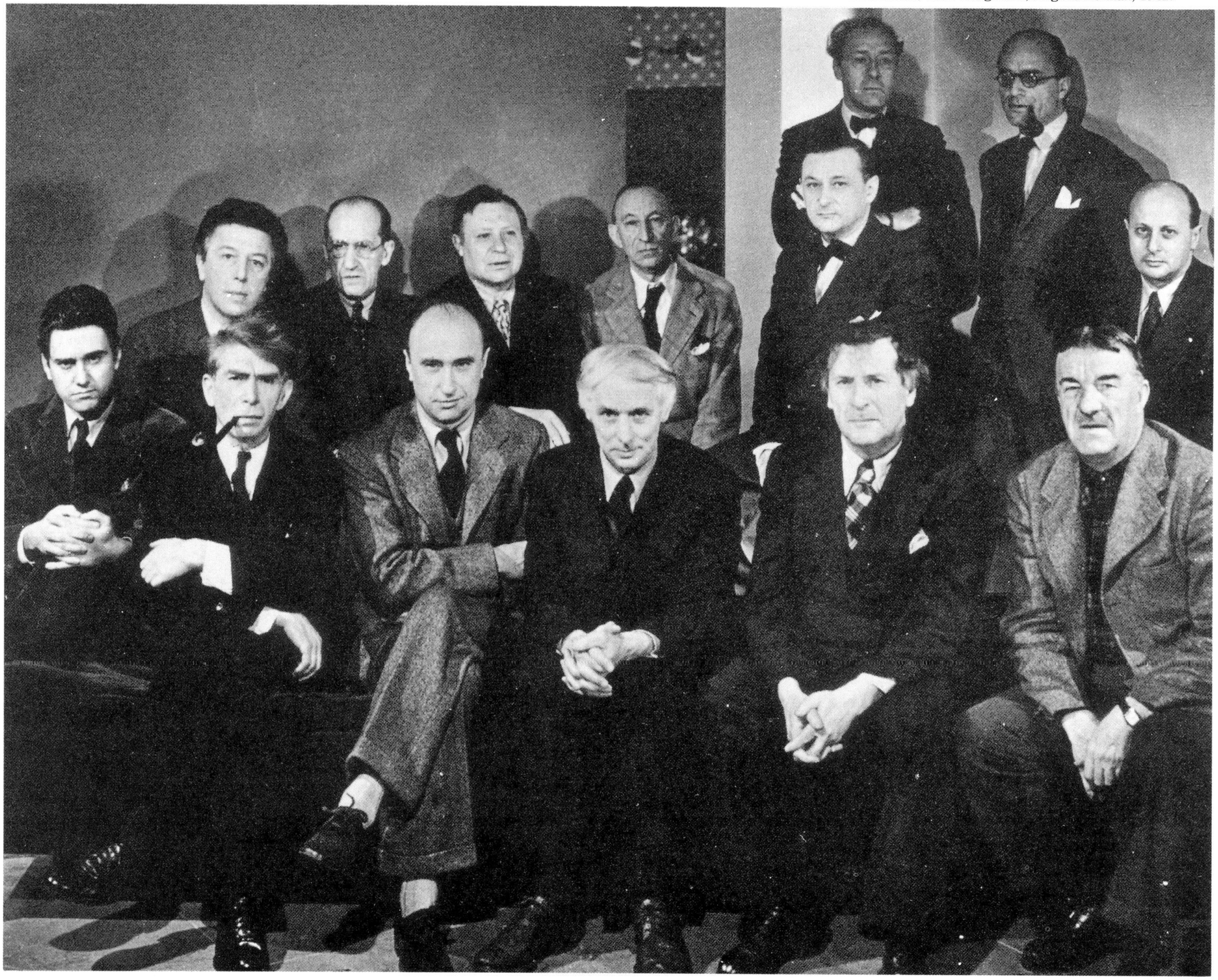

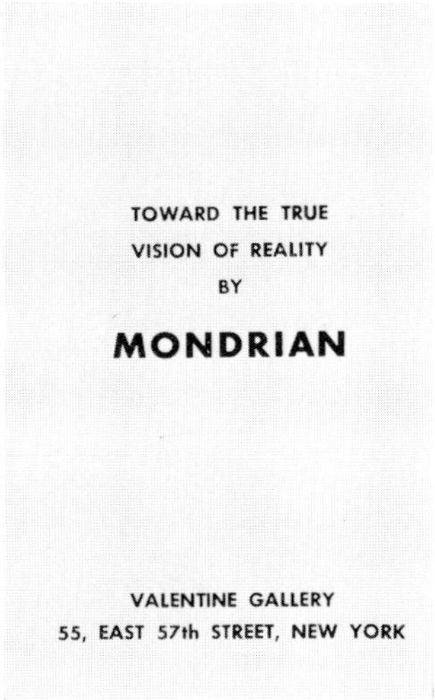
TOWARD THE TRUE
VISION OF REALITY
BY

MONDRIAN

VALENTINE GALLERY
55, EAST 57th STREET, NEW YORK

The Valentine Gallery issued an article by Mondrian,' Toward the true vision of Reality,' 1942.

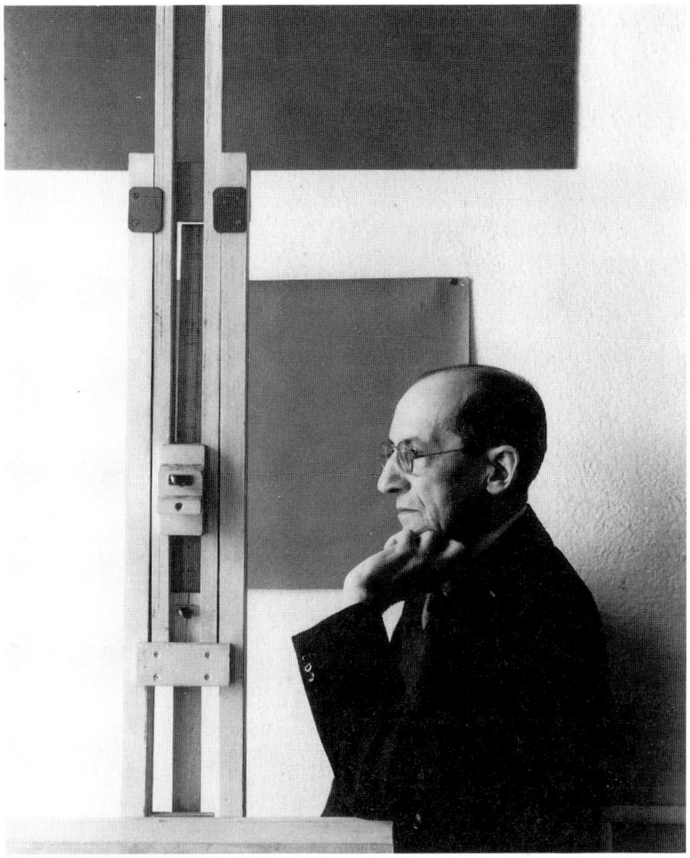

A. Newman, Three portraits of Mondrian in his studio, 1942.

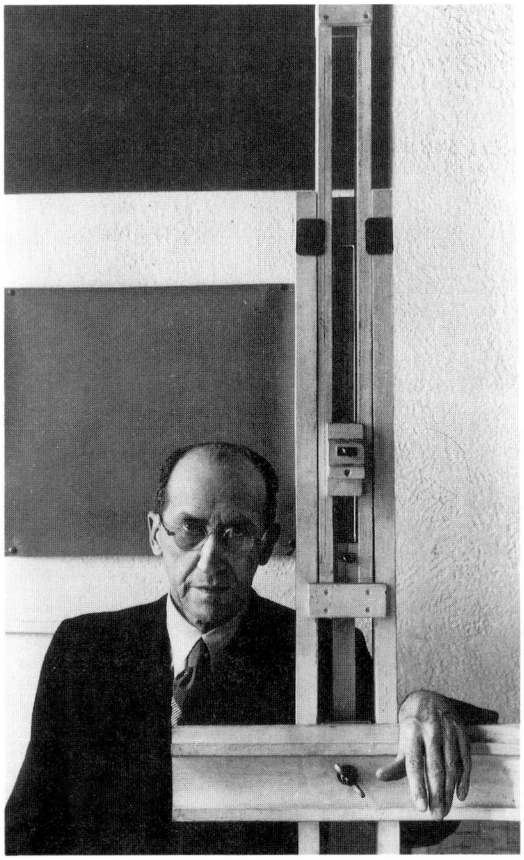

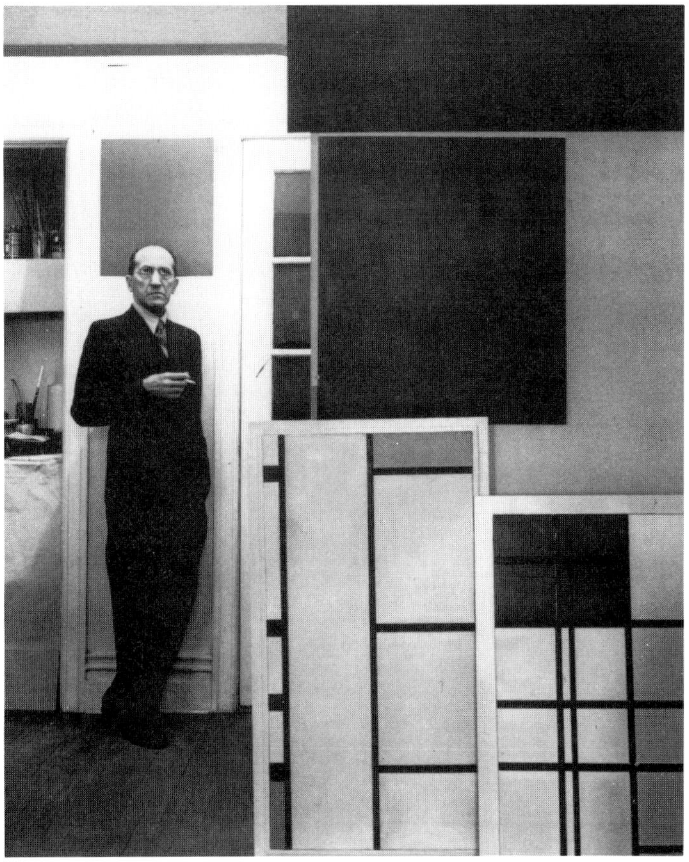

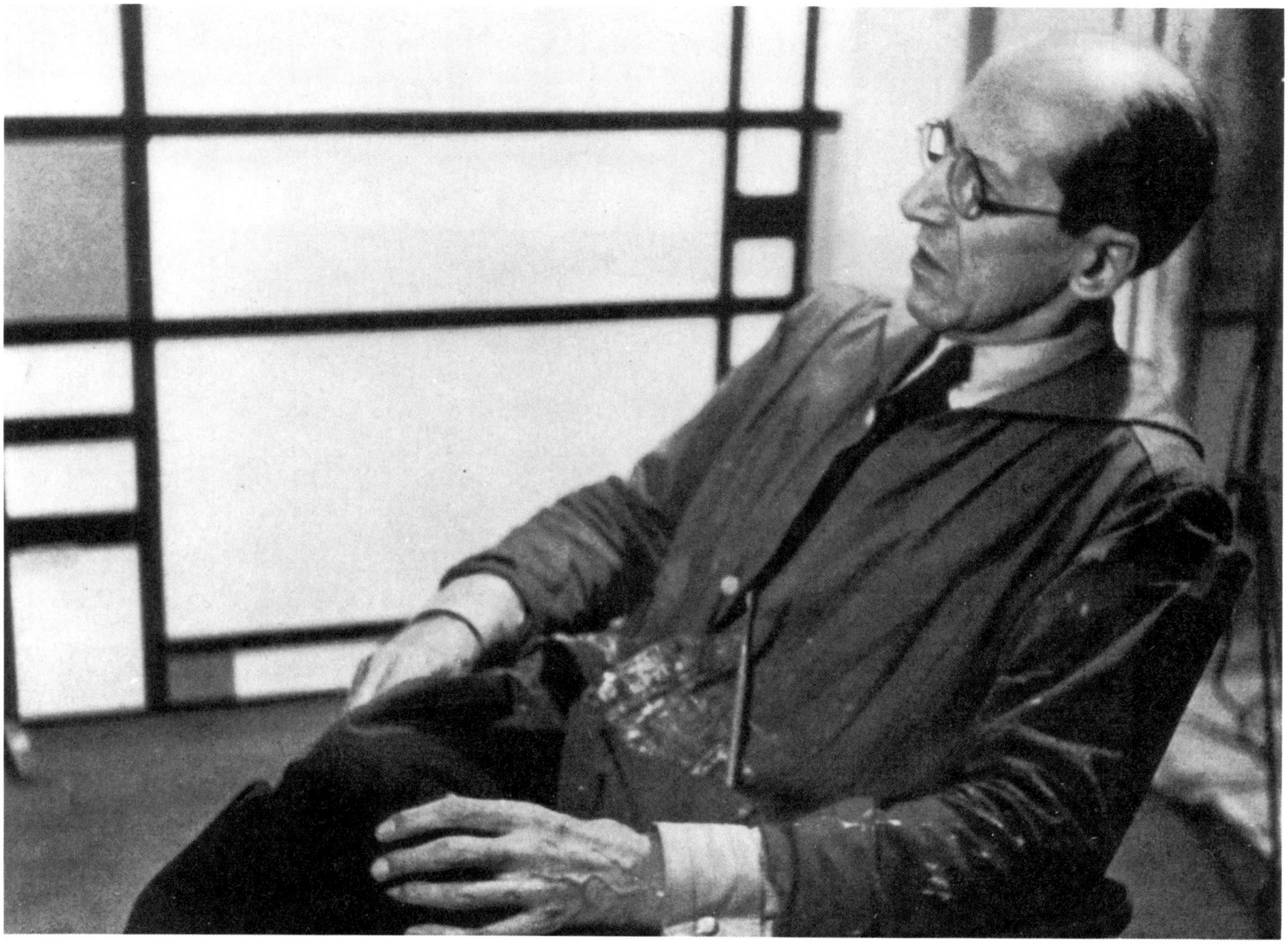

Three portraits of Mondrian in his studio, 1943.

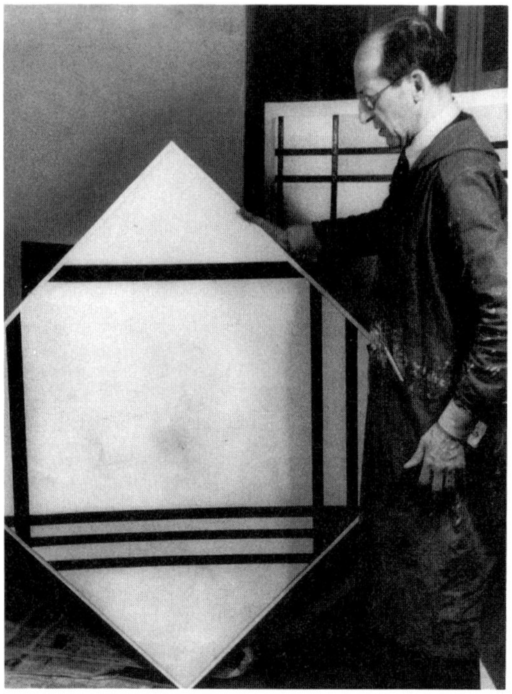

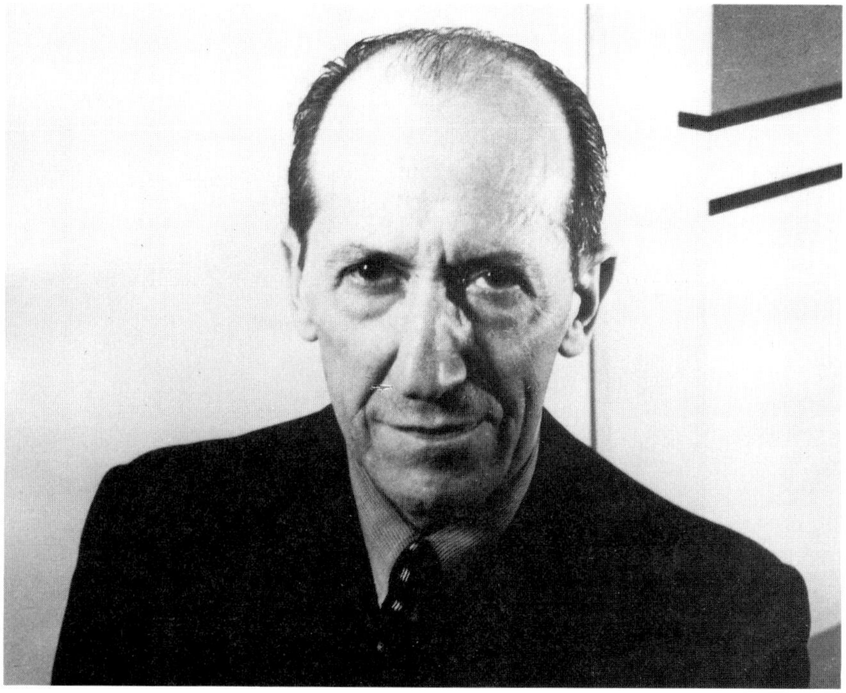

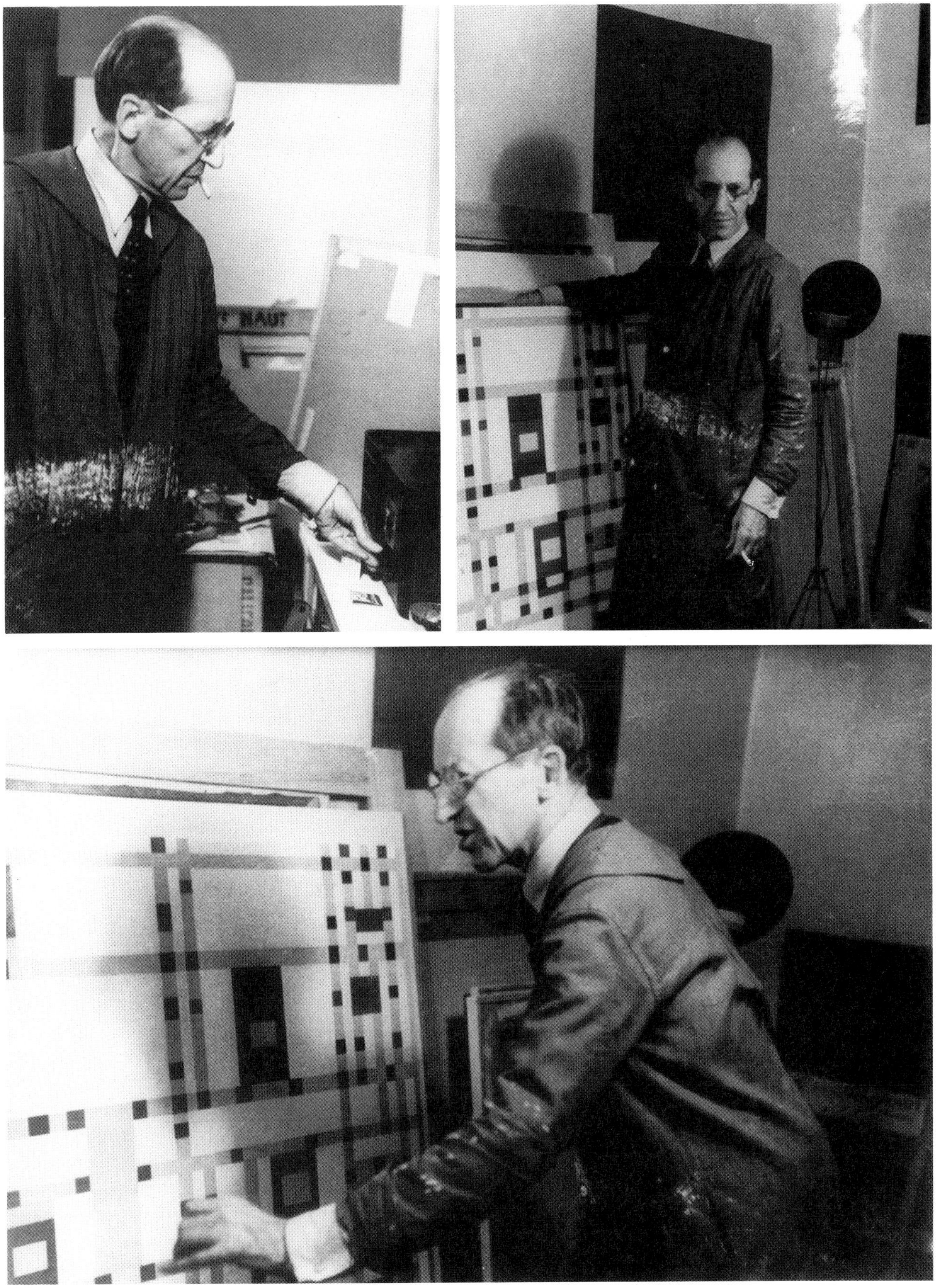

F. Glarner, Three portraits of Mondrian working on 'Broadway Boogie-Woogie', 1942/43.

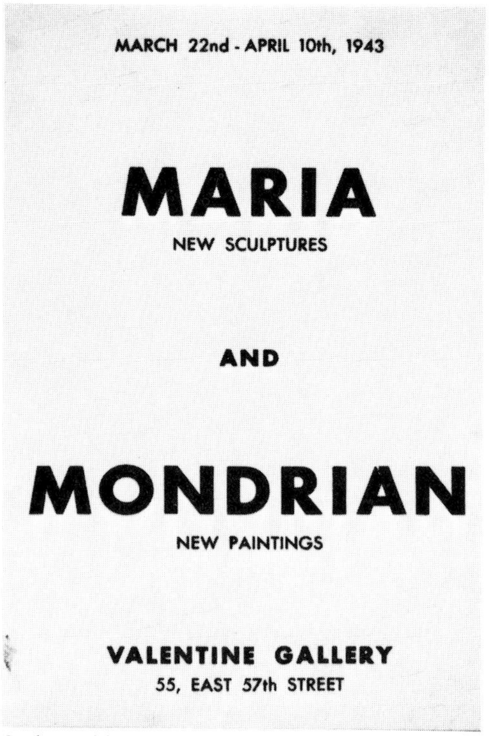
MARCH 22nd - APRIL 10th, 1943

MARIA

NEW SCULPTURES

AND

MONDRIAN

NEW PAINTINGS

VALENTINE GALLERY

55, EAST 57th STREET

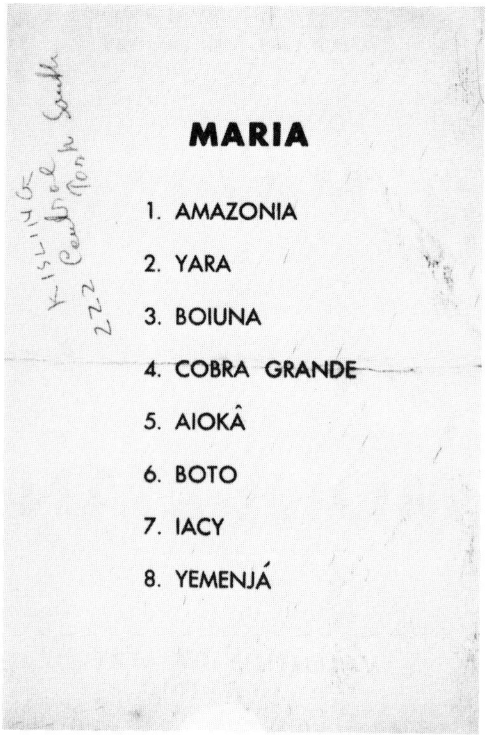
KISLING
222 Central Park South

MARIA

1. AMAZONIA
2. YARA
3. BOIUNA
4. COBRA GRANDE
5. AIOKÂ
6. BOTO
7. IACY
8. YEMENJÁ

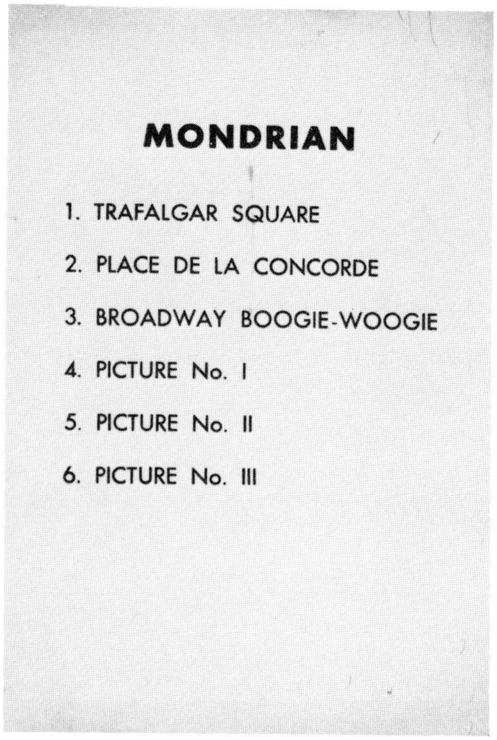
MONDRIAN

1. TRAFALGAR SQUARE
2. PLACE DE LA CONCORDE
3. BROADWAY BOOGIE-WOOGIE
4. PICTURE No. I
5. PICTURE No. II
6. PICTURE No. III

Catalogue of the second show of Mondrian in New York, 1943.

Detail of studio wall, 1943.

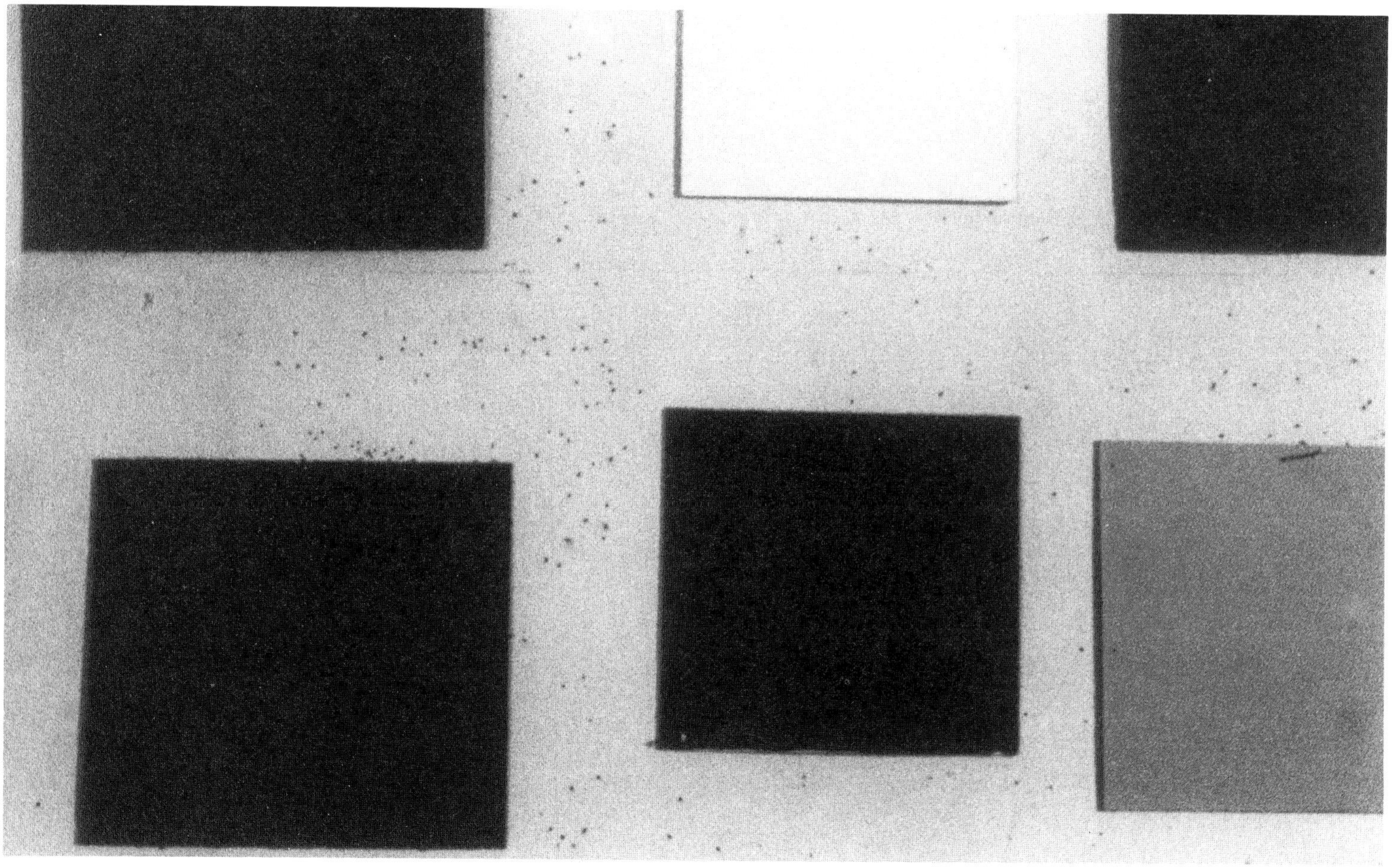

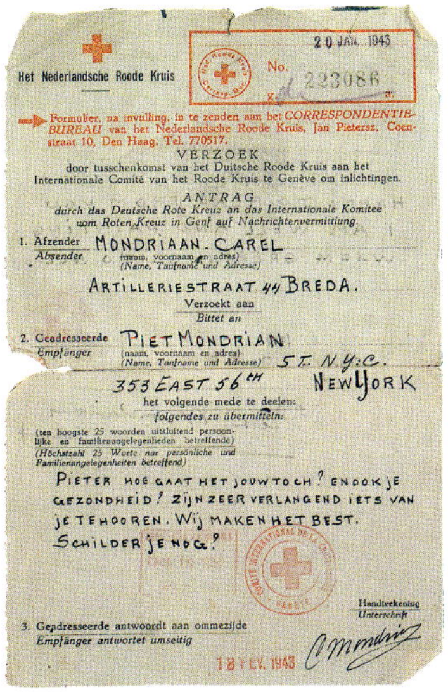

Het Nederlandsche Roode Kruis

20 JAN. 1943

No. 223086

Formulier, na invulling, in te zenden aan het CORRESPONDENTIE-BUREAU van het Nederlandsche Roode Kruis, Jan Pieterss. Coenstraat 10, Den Haag. Tel. 770517.

VERZOEK
door tusschenkomst van het Duitsche Roode Kruis aan het Internationale Comité van het Roode Kruis te Genève om inlichtingen.

ANTRAG
durch das Deutsche Rote Kreuz an das Internationale Komitee vom Roten Kreuz in Genf auf Nachrichtenvermittlung.

1. Afzender / Absender (naam, voornaam en adres) (Name, Taufname und Adresse): MONDRIAAN. CAREL
ARTILLERIESTRAAT 44 BREDA.

Verzoekt aan / Bittet an

2. Geadresseerde / Empfänger (naam, voornaam en adres) (Name, Taufname und Adresse): PIET MONDRIAN
353 EAST 56TH ST. N.Y.C. NEW YORK

het volgende mede te deelen: / folgendes zu übermitteln:
(ten hoogste 25 woorden uitsluitend persoonlijke en familieaangelegenheden betreffende) (Höchstzahl 25 Worte nur persönliche und Familienangelegenheiten betreffend)

PIETER HOE GAAT HET JOUW TOCH? EN OOK JE GEZONDHEID? ZIJN ZEER VERLANGEND IETS VAN JE TE HOOREN. WIJ MAKEN HET BEST. SCHILDER JE NOG?

Handteekening / Unterschrift: C. Mondriaan

3. Geadresseerde antwoordt aan ommezijde / Empfänger antwortet umseitig

18 FEV. 1943

Excerpt from a telegram from the Dutch Red Cross dated 20/1/1943:

REQUEST
conveyed by the German Red Cross to the International Red Cross Committee in Geneva, for information.

PIETER HOW ARE YOU? ARE YOU HEALTHY? LONGING TO HEAR FROM YOU. WE ARE WELL. ARE YOU STILL PAINTING?

C. Mondrian

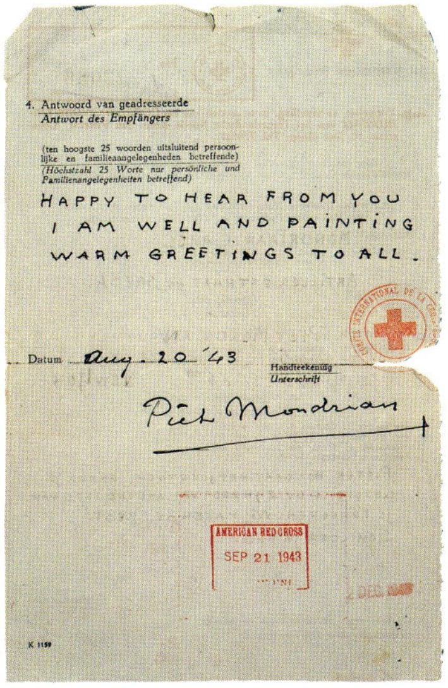

4. Antwoord van geadresseerde / Antwort des Empfängers

(ten hoogste 25 woorden uitsluitend persoonlijke en familieaangelegenheden betreffende) (Höchstzahl 25 Worte nur persönliche und Familienangelegenheiten betreffend)

HAPPY TO HEAR FROM YOU
I AM WELL AND PAINTING
WARM GREETINGS TO ALL.

Datum Aug. 20 '43

Handteekening / Unterschrift: Piet Mondrian

AMERICAN RED CROSS SEP 21 1943

Reply dated 20/8/1943:

HAPPY TO HEAR FROM YOU
I AM WELL AND PAINTING
WARM GREETINGS TO ALL

Piet Mondrian

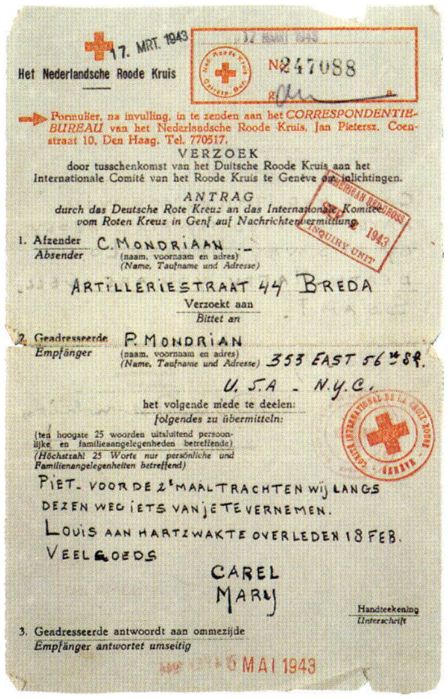

Het Nederlandsche Roode Kruis

17. MRT. 1943

Nº 247088

Formulier, na invulling, in te zenden aan het CORRESPONDENTIE-BUREAU van het Nederlandsche Roode Kruis, Jan Pieterss. Coenstraat 10, Den Haag. Tel. 770517.

VERZOEK
door tusschenkomst van het Duitsche Roode Kruis aan het Internationale Comité van het Roode Kruis te Genève om inlichtingen.

ANTRAG
durch das Deutsche Rote Kreuz an das Internationale Komitee vom Roten Kreuz in Genf auf Nachrichtenvermittlung.

1. Afzender / Absender (naam, voornaam en adres) (Name, Taufname und Adresse): C. MONDRIAAN
ARTILLERIESTRAAT 44 BREDA

Verzoekt aan / Bittet an

2. Geadresseerde / Empfänger (naam, voornaam en adres) (Name, Taufname und Adresse): P. MONDRIAN 353 EAST 56TH ST.
U.S.A. - N.Y.C.

het volgende mede te deelen: / folgendes zu übermitteln:
(ten hoogste 25 woorden uitsluitend persoonlijke en familieaangelegenheden betreffende) (Höchstzahl 25 Worte nur persönliche und Familienangelegenheiten betreffend)

PIET. VOOR DE 2E MAAL TRACHTEN WIJ LANGS DEZEN WEG IETS VAN JE TE VERNEMEN.
LOUIS AAN HARTZWAKTE OVERLEDEN 18 FEB.
VEEL GOEDS
CAREL
MARY

Handteekening / Unterschrift

3. Geadresseerde antwoordt aan ommezijde / Empfänger antwortet umseitig

6 MAI 1943

March 17th 1943

'PIET, TRYING TO HEAR FROM YOU FOR THE SECOND TIME THIS WAY. LOUIS DIED OF HEART ATTACK AT FEBR. 18TH.
ALL THE BEST
CAREL
MARY'

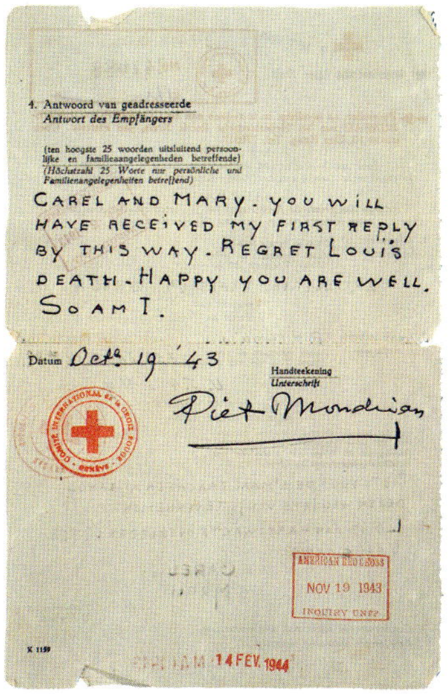

4. Antwoord van geadresseerde / Antwort des Empfängers

(ten hoogste 25 woorden uitsluitend persoonlijke en familieaangelegenheden betreffende) (Höchstzahl 25 Worte nur persönliche und Familienangelegenheiten betreffend)

CAREL AND MARY. YOU WILL HAVE RECEIVED MY FIRST REPLY BY THIS WAY. REGRET LOUIS' DEATH. HAPPY YOU ARE WELL. SO AM I.

Datum Oct. 19 '43

Handteekening / Unterschrift: Piet Mondrian

NOV 19 1943 INQUIRY UNIT

14 FEV. 1944

Mondrian answered:

'CAREL AND MARY. YOU WILL HAVE RECEIVED MY FIRST REPLY BY THIS WAY. REGRET LOUIS DEATH, HAPPY YOU ARE WELL.
SO AM I.
OCT. 19
PIET MONDRIAN'

Two Red Cross telegrams to and from his brother Carel Mondriaan.

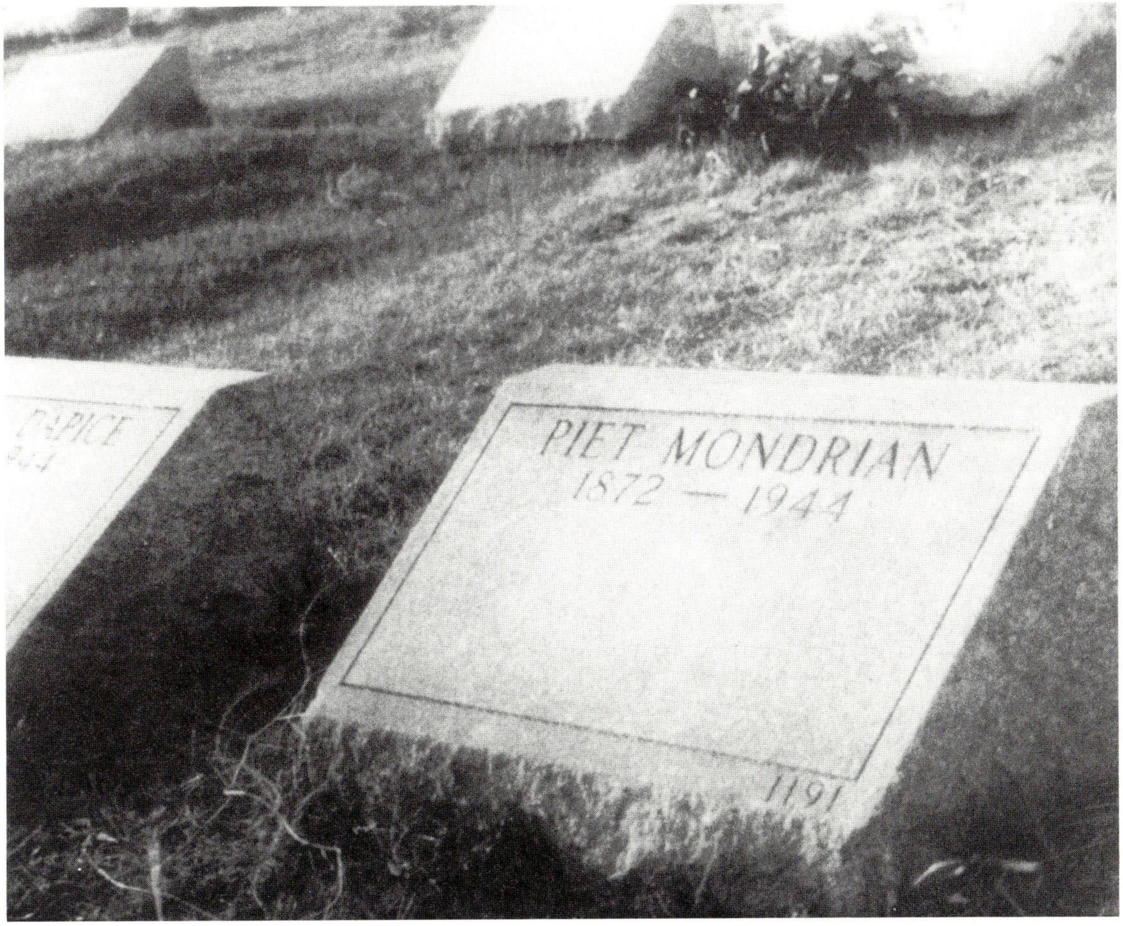

Mondrian's grave at Cypress Hills Cemetery, New York (photograph 1948).

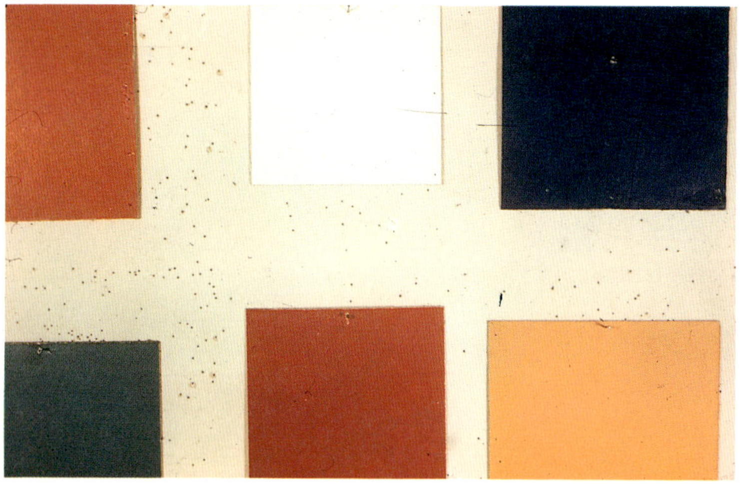
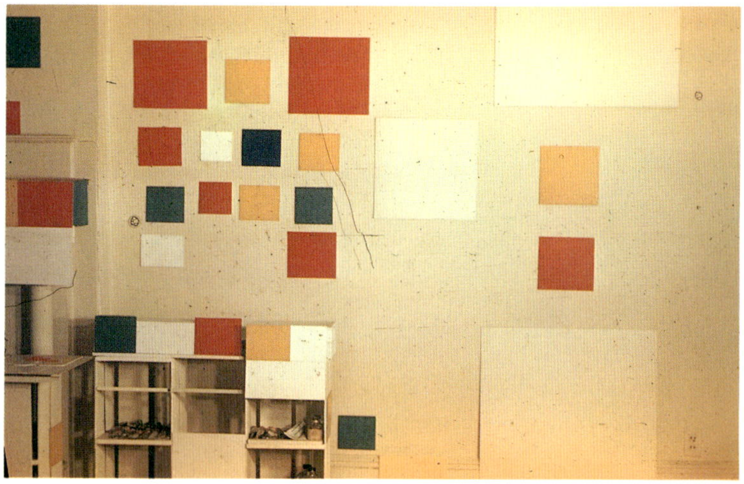
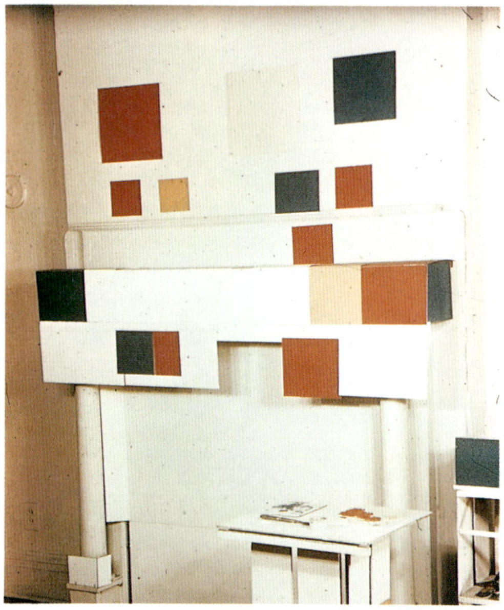
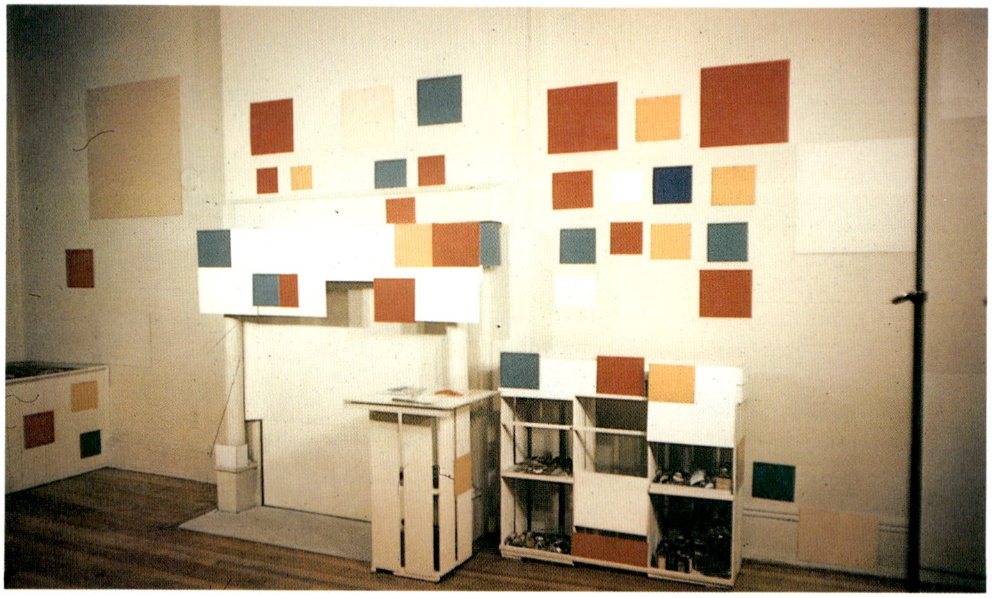

F. Glarner/H. Holtzman, Mondrian's studio—15 East 59th St. after his death.

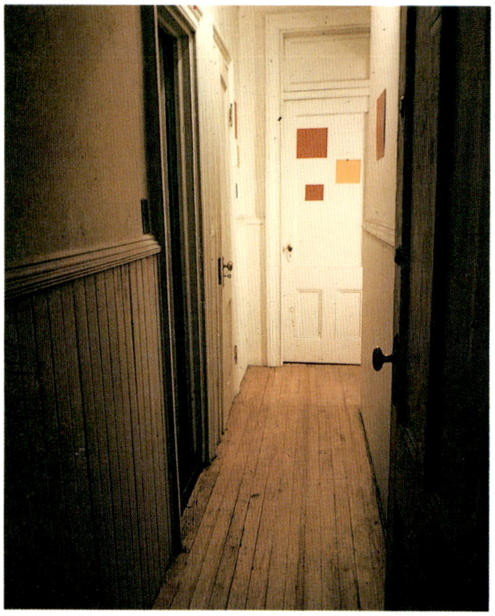
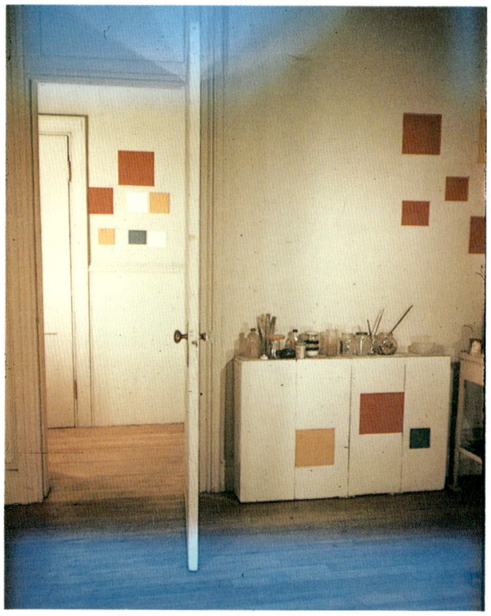
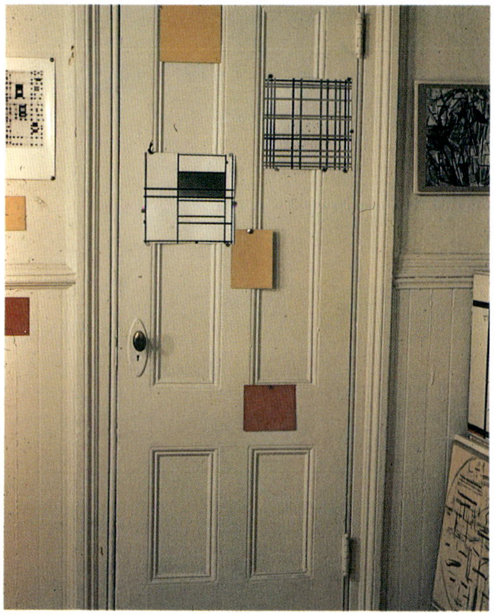

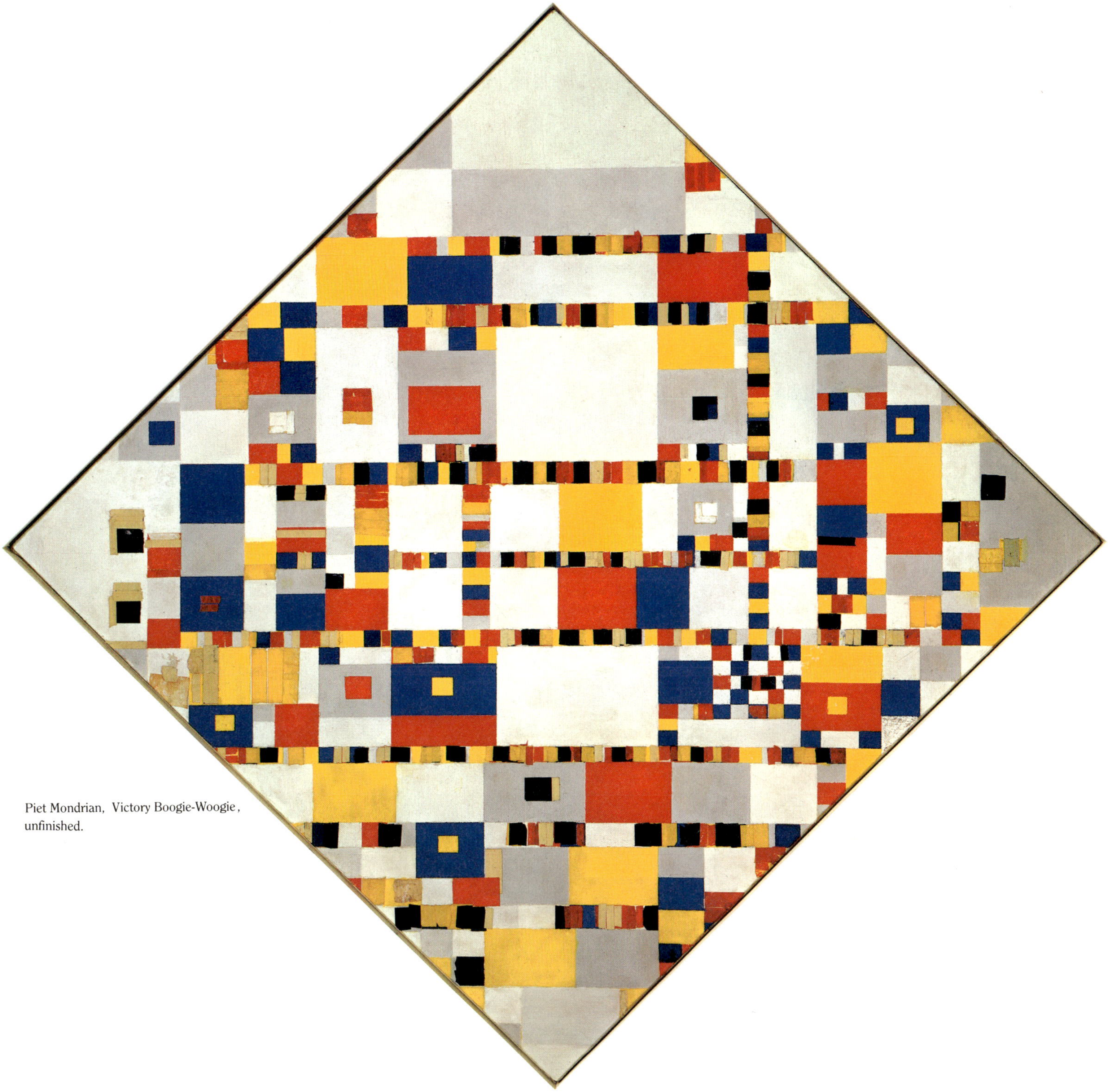

Piet Mondrian, Victory Boogie-Woogie, unfinished.

Bibliography

Monographs

M. Seuphor, *Piet Mondrian*, Paris 1987; reprint from the 1970 Flammarion edition; contains the most complete catalogue of his works.

C.L. Raggianti, *Mondrian e l'arte del XX secolo*, Milano 1962.

Kazuo Akane, *Piet Mondrian, life and work*, 1971; text in Japanese.

Cor Blok, *Piet Mondriaan, een catalogus van zijn werk in Nederlands Openbaar bezit*, Amsterdam 1974; a catalogue of Mondrian's work in Dutch public collections; the edition of 1967 contains an extensive bibliography.

M.G. Ottolenghi, *Mondrian*, Milano 1974.

Principal Monographic Exhibition Catalogues

1946—Amsterdam, Stedelijk Museum: *Piet Mondrian*; with contributions by Michel Seuphor, C. van Eesteren, J.J.P. Oud, T. Brugman.

1955—The Hague, Gemeentemuseum: *Piet Mondrian*; with contributions by L.J.F. Wijsenbeek and Michel Seuphor.

1966—Toronto, The Art Gallery of Toronto: *Piet Mondrian 1872-1944*; catalogue by R.P. Welsh, an essay by R. Rosenblum.

1969—Paris, Orangerie des Tuileries: *Mondrian*; catalogue and essay by Michel Seuphor.

1971—New York, The S. Guggenheim Museum; *Piet Mondrian, Centennial Exhibition*; contributions by L.J.F. Wijsenbeek (Introduction), R.P. Welsh (Mondrian and Theosophy), J. Joosten (Mondrian: Between Cubism and Abstraction), Nelly van Doesburg (Some Memoirs of Mondrian), Max Bill (Composition I with Blue and Yellow 1925), Margit Rowell (Interview with Charmion von Wiegand).

1980—Stuttgart, Staatsgalerie: *Mondrian: Drawings, Watercolors, New York Paintings*; with contributions by H. Holtzman (Mondrian and 'Liberation'), R.P. Welsh (Mondrian as Draftsman), J.Joosten (Mondrian's lost sketchbooks from the years 1911-1914), H. Henkels (Mondrian in his studio), K. von Maur (Mondrian and Music), catalogue by U. Gauss.

1985—St. Paul-de-Vence, Fondation Maeght: *Piet Mondrian: de la figuration à l'abstraction (œuvres du Gemeentemuseum à La Haye);* Piet Mondrian, L'Art plastique et l'art plastique pur, 1937; herbert henkels, Mondrian dans son atelier: portrait de l'artiste par lui-même.

Published Collections of Writings

1925—P. Mondrian, Neue Gestaltung, Bauhausbuch (reprint 1974).

1945—Plastic Art and Pure Plastic Art, 1937, and other essays 1941-1943, ed. by H. Holtzman, New York, Wittenborn.

1969—J. Joosten/R.P. Welsh, Two Mondrian Sketchbooks 1912-1914, Amsterdam 1969; complete facsimile edition with English translation and introduction by R.P. Welsh.

1975—Piet Mondrian: Tutti gli scritti, a cura di H. Holtzman, prefazione di Filiberto Menna, Milano.

1986—Piet Mondrian, gedurende een wandeling van buiten naar de stad: Dialoog en Trialoog over de Nieuwe Beelding, edited by herbert henkels, ed. Gravura/Haags Gemeentemuseum.

1986—Piet Mondrian, The New Art—the New Life, the collected writings of Piet Mondrian, edited and translated by H. Holtzman and Martin S. James, G.K. Hall, Boston.

Special Subjects

W. Scholtz, *Tweemaal Mondriaan en het Mondriaanhuis*, in: Jaarboek Achterhoek en Liemers, 1986, pag.101-116. (Two Mondriaan's and the Mondriaan house).

H. Henkels, *Mondrian and the Hague School of Painting*, in: exh. cat. The Hague School, London 1983, pp.147-154, 308-315.

Martin S. James *Mondrian and the Dutch Symbolists*, in: The Art Journal XXIII, no.2, winter 1963-64, pp.103-111.

H. Henkels, *La Vibration des Couleurs: Mondrian, Sluyters, Gestel*, Winterswijk 1985.

R.P. Welsh, *The Hortus Conclusus of Piet Mondrian*, in : The Connoisseur, 161, Febr. 1966, pp.33-39.

Y.A. Bois, *Mondrian et la Théorie de l'Architecture*, in: Revue de L'Art, 53, 1981, pp.39-52.

H. Henkels, *Must Architecture be inferior to Painting? Mondrian's Challenge to Architecture*, in: De Stijl—Neo-Plasticism in Architecture, Delft University Press 1983, pag.162-175.

Meyer Shapiro, *Mondrian: Order and Randomness in Abstract Painting*, in: Selected papers: Modern Art 19th and 20th Century, New York 1978.

E.A. Carmean jr., *Mondrian: the Diamond Compositions*, Washington, The National Gallery of Art 1979.

Nancy J. Troy, *Mondrian's Designs for the Salon de Madame B, à Dresden*, in: The Art Bulletin 62, no.4 (Dec. 1980), pp.640-647.

Nancy J. Troy, *Mondrian and Neo-Plasticism in America*, New Haven, Yale University Art Gallery 1979.

Y.A. Bois, *Mondrian's New York City*, in: Cahiers, Centre Pompidou, Paris 1985.

Context

G. Imanse e.a., *Van Gogh bis Cobra, Holländische Malerei 1880-1950*, Stuttgart 1981.

H.L.C. Jaffé, *De Stijl 1917-1931: the Dutch contribution to Modern Art*, New York 1986.

M. Friedman (ed.), *De Stijl 1917-1931: Visions of Utopia*, Minneapolis, Walker Art Center 1982.

Nancy J. Troy, *The De Stijl Environment*, Cambridge MIT Press 1983.

C. Boekraad, F. Bool, H. Henkels (ed.), *De Stijl: Neo-Plasticism in Architecture*, Delft University Press 1983.

Y.A. Bois, *De Stijl à Paris et l'Architecture en France*, Paris 1985

Towards a New Art, essays on the background to abstract art 1910-1920, The Tate Gallery, London 1980.

M.A. Prat, *Cercle et Carré, peinture et Avant-garde au seuil des années 30*, Paris 1984.

J. Lewison (ed.), *Circle: Constructive Art in Britain 1934-40*, Cambridge 1982.

R. Rosenblum, *Modern Painting and the Northern Tradition: Friedrich to Rothko*, New York 1975.

R. Nasgaard, *The Mystic North: Symbolist Landscape Painting in Northern Europe and North America 1890-1940*, University of Toronto Press 1984.

M. Tuchman (ed.), *The Spiritual in Art 1890-1980*, Los Angeles/New York 1986.